Serpent in the Bosom

Serpent in the Bosom

The Rise and Fall
of Slobodan Milošević

Revised Edition

LENARD J. COHEN

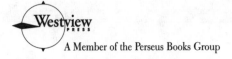

A Member of the Perseus Books Group

Copyright © 2002 by Westview Press, A Member of the Perseus Books Group

Published in 2002 in the United States of America by Westview Press, 5500 Central
Avenue, Boulder, Colorado 80301–2877, and in the United Kingdom by Westview
Press, 12 Hid's Copse Road, Cumnor Hill, Oxford OX2 9JJ

Find us on the World Wide Web at www.westviewpress.com

Library of Congress Cataloging-in-Publication Data
Cohen, Lenard J.
Serpent in the bosom : The rise and fall of Slobodan Milošević / Lenard J. Cohen.
    p.   cm.
Includes bibliographical references and index.
ISBN 0-8133-2902-7 (alk. paper); 0-8133-4023-3(pbk)
1. Yugoslavia—Politics and government—1980–1992.   2. Yugoslavia—Politics and
government—1992–1993.   Authoritarianism—Yugoslavia. 4. Milošević, Slobodan,
1941–.
Title.
DR1309.C644   2000
949.71'02—dc21 00–049965

Designed by Nighthawk Design

10   9   8   7   6   5   4   3   2   1

A strange destiny to be an unlucky people with a great spirit. A people who reckon their defeats as victories . . . A people who sing songs of their defeats. That is the Serbian Idea. A song of misfortune. How long must it be so?

—*Milovan Djilas*

Wretched is a state whose freedom depends on one man alone. Wretched is a state whose welfare depends on one man alone. Wretched is a state whose defense depends on one man alone. Wretched is a state which is hostage to one man alone.

—*Vojislav Koštunica*

To Terri

CONTENTS

TABLES AND ILLUSTRATIONS

PREFACE TO
THE REVISED EDITION

Authoritarian political systems—a closely related but less repressive and politically demanding subspecies of nondemocratic rule than totalitarianism—rarely seek or obtain political uniformity or the full engagement of a state's citizens. Rather, the authoritarian dictatorship, while usually enjoying considerable popular appeal at its point of origin, typically elicits a mixture of sentiments, a continuum ranging from fear through nominal acceptance to enthusiastic support. Disinclined to genuinely share power, or for that matter to leave power, authoritarian political leaders face a permanent crisis of legitimation.

Authoritarian regimes are the kind of dictatorships that seek popular consent but shun any real competitive pluralism; they try to avoid the role of an intrusive Leviathan engineering societal change, but do not shrink from "softer" forms of repression in order to maintain control. Such regimes are thus "mixed" political systems, ideologically diffuse, which blend aspects of contestation and coercion, authoritarian pluralism with restrictive monism. Political life in the authoritarian system exhibits facets that are free and unfree; they are systems poised between democracy and more radical dictatorship. Partly because of their nature as hybrid models, analysts and observers of political power have found that the dynamics of such systems—how they arise, the manner in which they are sustained, and the factors that contribute to their decay and collapse—are both complex and immensely interesting.

One of the most significant sets of factors when probing the illiberal, albeit sometimes semi-democratic, practices of authoritarian systems pertains to the outlook and actions of the top leaders who manipulate the political passions, ostensible beliefs, and governmental levers supporting dictatorial power. Indeed, as Franz Neumann pointed out during the middle of the twentieth century, more often than not, the quintessential psychological element underlying a highly personalized authoritarian dictatorship is the ability of the single leader to alternatively respond to, and activate, the anxieties and fears of a political class as well as other major segments of society. As a rule, that leader, or emergent dictator, having succeeded in becoming a "hero" of the masses, channels those activated anxieties into "aggressiveness and destruction."[1]

This book focuses on Slobodan Milošević's authoritarian governance of Serbia (and to a somewhat lesser extent Montenegro) from the late 1980s to the autumn of 2000. Milošević's personal history and traits, the frequent oscillations in his policies, and his evolution as a political figure are closely examined as important factors that are essential in explaining the authoritarian system he established. The study is not, however, a biography of one man, but rather an inquiry into a specific illiberal political system, during a particular period of time. The analysis is premised on the notion that Serbian political development from the late 1980s to the early twenty-first century can best be explained by the interaction between various socio-cultural features of Serbian society, situational developments, and the political personality and policies of Slobodan Milošević. The following discussion therefore endeavors to avoid both historical reductionism and an overly personalistic or leader-centered account of Serbian political life. As Zevedi Barbu pointed out in his very useful account of the conditions that give rise to dictatorship: "One is too often inclined to see historical forms related to actual personalities; one too often couples communism with Marxist messianic feelings, Nazism with Hitler's paranoia and even history with Cleopatra's nose."[2]

The traits and behavior of the top political personality exercising control are highly significant for understanding a dictatorial regime, but must be considered along with the cultural patterns in a society and political dynamics that allow the dictator to become a decisive and active factor in historical-political development. Thus, while fully recognizing the repressive and brutal side of Milošević's actions (e.g., in May 1999 he was formally indicted as a war criminal), it is also important to understand the changing characteristics and level of support for his regime. Indeed, one of the most interesting and tragic facets of the Milošević phenomenon is that he was able to convince a large segment of his ethnic brethren that he would successfully advance Serbian national interests in the Balkans, while in fact devoting primary attention to his most compelling interest, namely, the retention of political power at any cost.

The study also explores the structure and dynamics of nondemocratic, semi-democratic, or "pseudo-democratic" rule in Serbia during the period of the Milošević regime. Indeed, up to late 1999, many features of Milošević's regime would qualify it as a "soft dictatorship," at least with respect to the domestic political environment inside Serbia (i.e., leaving aside the havoc and suffering that the regime's foreign policy had wrought in other areas of the Balkans, which have been directly subject to the "wars of the Yugoslav succession"). For example, Dragoslav Avramović, onetime governor of the Yugoslav National Bank, who in the late 1990s became a major leader in Serbia's democratic opposition, rejected any comparison between Milošević and more repressive and violent authoritarian leaders: "I would not compare him to Saddam [Hussein]. Milošević's methods and strategies are wrong, but he did not rule by terror. People who thought differently were not thrown into prison. Ibrahim Rugova, the leader of the Kosovo Albanians, was able to travel throughout the world. A tyrant would have put him behind bars."[3] And while Milošević maintained tight control over the electronic media, and periodically waged crackdowns on opposition newspapers, he also permitted a remarkable extent of personal and artistic expression in Serbia, even allowing satiric performances that lampooned the ruling couple—Milošević and his wife, Mirjana Marković. "This has never been a police state like Iraq," commented the actor and theater director Svetozar Cvetković. "So long as we are not too influential with the masses, we don't have to worry about censorship. It's a smart way for Milošević to keep his opponents off balance. He can afford to be flexible so long as there is no serious threat to his authority."[4]

By late 1999, however, with his authority under increasing assault, it was an open question whether Milošević could continue to combine strong-arm executive-centered state intervention with the provision of limited space for free expression and low-level nonconformity, that is, the seemingly incompatible features that constitute the hallmark of a soft dictatorship.[5] There were already clear signs by mid-2000 that Milošević's dictatorship was acquiring a much harder edge, and it seemed increasingly doubtful that a debilitated and angst-ridden regime—which had long tolerated islands of autonomy, privacy, and free expression—could muster the fortitude and unified resources for long-term survival. Some of those seeking to replace him, like the leader of the opposition Democratic Party, Zoran Djindjić, even suggested that the authoritarian dictatorship had become a paper tiger: "Milošević's power lies in the illusion that he is strong. He is not strong. A dictator cannot be strong in a poor country. We are faced with a mentality problem in our country. People are afraid of his mental [psychological] power. But when people come to understand that Milošević has no influence in their lives, then he will lose."[6]

But other Serbian politicians feared that Milošević's increasing anxiety and narrowing space for political maneuver (as an indicted war criminal whose prospects for negotiated resignation from office and safe retirement abroad had become problematic) created a dangerous and potentially chaotic situation of escalating repression and resistance. Indeed, the introduction of various repressive measures, constitutional amendments, and laws in Yugoslavia during the summer of 2000 indicated that Milošević was preparing to employ harsher and more transparently nondemocratic measures in order to preserve his regime. German chancellor Gerhard Schroeder claimed that such steps by Milošević were reminiscent of methods employed by Adolph Hitler to impose his own dictatorship.[7] Schroeder's analogy between Milošević and the leader of the Third Reich may have been exaggerated, but by 2000 Milošević had clearly become more desperate about his regime's longevity and his personal survival.

The Belgrade historian Latinka Perović, a former reform communist, pointed to an interesting irony regarding the development of the Milošević regime: "One learned Serb in the nineteenth century . . . Dragiša Stanojević, wrote that if they are already inevitable, better harder than softer dictatorships. At least the former know their limits. If a regime calculates that the condition of its existence requires new restrictions it only invites resistance."[8] As the fall of 2000 approached, and Milošević manipulated Yugoslavia's constitutional structure and electoral laws to preserve his political control, it remained an open question whether the end of soft dictatorship would mark the prelude to his rapid demise or the prolongation of his rule as an authoritarian figure. By early October, Milošević had lost formal authority, but was still lingering in the shadows. Indeed, he would continue to have a political impact on Serbian political life many months after the collapse of his regime.

Though this book is primarily a case study of political development and a particular leader in one authoritarian polity, the analysis addresses a number of themes and issues drawn from the rich literature in the social sciences, and the field of comparative politics. For example, what factors are responsible for the emergence and the appeals of populist leaders who circumvent established political practices (in this case a stagnant and deteriorated communist regime), and seek to mobilize the passions of political masses as a basis for acquiring and consolidating power? How long can the mobilization of anxiety and fear as a basis for popular support be sustained, and what happens when such methods are supplanted by an institutionalized system of political rule that relies on more routine and repressive dictatorial practices? To what extent is politicized ethnicity, or virulent ethnic nationalism in a political system, the outcome of deeply embedded (primordial or perennial) antagonisms between different ethno-cultural communities or, in contrast, do such conflicts result primarily from policies adopted by ambitious and unscrupulous leaders who either manufacture interethnic animosities or revivify latent "prejudices" in order to garner political support? How and why do highly personalized dictatorships erode, and if such decomposing regimes attempt to perpetuate themselves after losing substantial popular support, what are the consequences and various alternative modes of regime transformation to post-dictatorial rule?

In an effort to address these and other questions, this second edition of *Serpent in the Bosom* consists of a new Introduction and major revision of Chapters 8, 9, and 10. The Introduction provides an update since the publication of the first edition and discusses the initial period of political development in Serbia and Montenegro following the collapse of the Milošević regime. In particular, the Introduction explores how Milošević continued to influence political development in Serbia even after he was jailed and put on trial abroad. Following the Introduction's focus on "Milošević after Milošević," subsequent sections of the book systematically explore the ascent, internal dynamics, and collapse of the Milošević regime. The first part of the book discusses the context for Slobodan Milošević's rise to power, and particularly the political situation in Kosovo and Serbia that provided the background for his utilization of Serbian nationalism—which he once described as a "serpent in the bosom" *(zmija u nedrima)* of the Serb people—and his emergence as a major political figure. The second part of the study explores the techniques and operation of the Milošević regime during the tumultuous course of Balkan politics over the last decade. In the third section, attention is directed towards the erosion of support for the authoritarian system established by Milošević, including several developments that challenged his regime: the student and civic protests of 1996–1997, which seriously destabilized Serbia; the surge of popularity for an extreme rightist alternative to Milošević's oligarchy during the fall of 1997; and the escalation of the Serb–Albanian conflict that finally resulted in the 1999 NATO bombing campaign against Yugoslavia. Consideration will also be given to the problems and prospects of political transition in Kosovo and Serbia during 1999–2000, as well as to the most likely scenarios of post-Milošević political development that were expected to accompany the end of his dictatorial regime. The last section of the book focuses on an examination of the factors associated with the last days of the Milošević regime and the nature of Balkan politics. This discussion includes an analysis of the dramatic electoral defeat of the old regime and the assumption of power by a new democratically oriented party coalition. Finally, the last chapter, in an attempt to draw together the threads of the preceding analysis, examines the consequences of efforts by some policy-makers to justify their Balkan policies through the often hasty and superficial use of historical studies, which purport to explain political development in Southeastern Europe.

All social science research depends on the cooperation and assistance of many generous people. Over nearly 35 years, this author has depended on the willingness of many hundreds of Yugoslav citizens and specialists to share their views regarding their country's political development. Because of such cooperation—prior to, during, and after the Milošević regime—the author was able to gather invaluable interviews, research studies, and other documentation that provide the basis for the analysis in this book.

Special appreciation is extended to Nicholas J. Miller, Duncan Perry, and Mihajlo Crnobrnja for reading a first draft of the manuscript and offering many constructive suggestions and corrections. Mile Bjelajac, Zvonko Novosel, Miroslav Ambruš-Kiš, Branka Vujčić Hrgović, Ivan Hrgović, Vuk Radmilović, Tim Came, Boris Subašić, Ratko Spasojević, Djordje Stefanović, Aleksandar Pavković, Peter Radan, Stojan Bulat, Sherry Lloyd, Julie Nixon, Dina Smeltz, and Obrad Kesić also provided very useful and generous assistance at various stages of the project. Gratitude is also due to Steve Catalano, Katharine Chandler, and Connie Oehring of Westview Press, as well as to Christine Marra, Carol Jones, and Rob Williams. Vladimir Goati, Ljiljana Bačević, Dragomir Pantić, Predrag Simić, and Slobodan Samardžić were also very helpful in providing research material and important insights. Many thanks are also extended to Andre Gerolymatos, Steve McBride, John Pierce, and Jack Blaney for their collegial assistance and support. Finally, very special thanks to my family for their love, patience, and encouragement throughout this project.

Lenard J. Cohen
Ten Mile Point, Victoria
British Columbia
March 2002

NOTES

1. Franz Neumann, "Notes on the Theory of Dictatorship," in *The Democratic and Authoritarian State* (New York: The Free Press, 1957), pp. 252–253.

2. Zevedi Barbu, *Democracy and Dictatorship: Their Psychology and Patterns of Life* (New York: Grove Press, 1956), p. 263.

3. *Der Spiegel*, October 4, 1999.

4. *International Herald Tribune*, November 3, 1999, p. 2.

5. For useful discussions of the variations in authoritarian states see Juan Linz, "Totalitarianism and Authoritarian Regimes," in Nelson Polsby and Fred Greenstein (eds.), *Handbook of Political Science, Vol. 3* (Reading, Mass.: Addison Wesley, 1975), pp. 175–411; "An Authoritarian Regime: Spain," in Erik Allardt and Yrjo Littunen (eds.), *Cleavages, Ideologies, and Party Systems* (Helsinki: Transactions of the Westermarck Society, 10, 1964), pp. 291–394; Stanley G. Payne, "Authoritarianism in Smaller States of Southern Europe," in H. E. Chehabi and Alfred Stepan (eds.), *Politics, Soci-*

ety, and Democracy: Comparative Studies (Essays in Honor of Juan Linz) (Boulder: Westview Press, 1995), pp. 183–196; Edwin A. Winkler, "Institutionalization and Participation on Taiwan: From Hard to Soft Authoritarianism?" *China Quarterly* (1984), pp. 482–497; and Barry Sautman, "The Devil to Pay: The 1989 Debate and the Intellectual Origins of Yeltsin's 'Soft Authoritarianism,'" *Communist and Post-Communist Studies*, Vol. 28, No. 1 (1995), pp. 131–151.

6. *Bucharest Evenimentul Zilei* in *Foreign Broadcast Information Service* (hereafter *FBIS*) EEU-1999-0914, September 9, 1999.

7. Free B-92 News, July 23, 2000.

8. *Danas*, June 24–25, 2000.

Former Yugoslavia

Introduction

Milošević's Shadow: Transition Politics in Serbia and Montenegro

Milošević is campaigning for his image . . . to present his trial before The Hague Tribunal as a trial of the Serb people. [But] nobody is looking for collective responsibility. He says "this is a trial of the Serb people." I think this is very selfish, purportedly political, very irresponsible. . . . Eventually, everything will come down to the personal, and personal responsibility. . . . When Milošević was in Belgrade, we had a problem, but now that he is in The Hague they have a problem.

—*Zoran Djindjić,*
Prime Minister of Serbia, February 15, 2002

In the initial proceedings of the trial of President Milošević there is not much law, but a lot of shallow digested, and often forged, quasi-history. There is a lot of politicking, hypocrisy and strange and illogical things. . . . The Hague Tribunal is writing our history for us . . . and we have to do everything as a state to influence the writing of history. . . . [One is] wrong to say that while Milošević was in Belgrade, he was our problem, and now that he is at The Hague, he is no longer our problem. Milošević remains our problem in the same way as the past remains our problem.

—*Vojislav Koštunica,*
President of Yugoslavia, February 20, 2002

On February 12, 2002, Slobodan Milošević—who had been forced to resign his post as president of Yugoslavia only sixteen months earlier—became the first former head of state to stand trial before an international tribunal for war crimes. Once again, as during his thirteen years of illiberal rule, and the dramatic "revolutionary" days associated with his fall from the pinnacle of the Yugoslav power pyramid, Milošević attracted world attention; this time as he sought to wage another self-proclaimed "heroic" struggle by

1

defending himself before the International Criminal Tribunal for the Former Yugoslavia (ICTY) at The Hague. Charged with 66 counts alleging that he had been responsible for crimes against humanity in Kosovo and Croatia, and for genocide in Bosnia–Herzegovina, Milošević—who refused to acknowledge the ICTY's legitimacy—acted as his own advocate in attempting both to refute the prosecution's case and also to indict segments of the international community for "genocide" and "illegal" intervention in the Balkans.

The first edition of this book, published in early 2001, explored how Milošević originally rose to power, how he maintained control over the reconfigured Yugoslav state (Serbia–Montenegro) throughout the 1990s, and the dramatic circumstances of his eventual political demise in the autumn of 2000. This new Introduction surveys the initial transition period that followed the collapse of the Milošević regime in October 2000, and explores the major factors that led to the former dictator's appearance before The Hague Tribunal. Although the trial at The Hague will likely be protracted, perhaps lasting as long as two years, the material in this revised and updated paperback edition will hopefully provide the background information and analysis necessary for understanding the ongoing saga of the Milošević phenomenon, and its continuing impact on Yugoslav political development.

Consolidating the "Velvet Revolution": Initial Problems of Transition

During the fall of 2000, Serbia had experienced—over only a three-month period—a profound political realignment and transfer of power from Slobodan Milošević to moderate and centrist opposition forces. A dictatorial leader and his political elite were replaced by a counter-elite committed to democratic development. In order to oust Milošević, Serbia's opposition parties had finally coalesced within the DOS coalition (the Democratic Opposition of Serbia), and advanced an attractive and fresh candidate for the presidency of Yugoslavia, who could, and did, successfully challenge the tottering and weakened dictator. This new candidate, Vojislav Koštunica, proved appealing to the majority of Serbian voters, not because he was a particularly telegenic or charismatic figure, but because of his basic modesty, honesty, and innate "grayness," not to mention his relative marginal position on the existing Yugoslav political stage. Indeed, Koštunica, who headed the small Democratic Party of Serbia (DSS), was considered a democratic nationalist. He also had the distinct advantage of never even having met, let alone brokered any deals, with Slobodan Milošević.

The decision to advance Koštunica, and thereby temporarily circumvent the two major established and long-standing opposition figures—Zoran Djindjić and Vuk Drašković—was a gamble that paid off. Koštunica quickly took the lead over Milošević in public opinion polls, and won the presidential election of September 24, 2001. In retrospect, it was clear that when Milošević had called the election in July, he had seriously underestimated the intensity and scale of popular antipathy towards his regime and his family. That fatal miscalculation was probably due to hubris, in this case an unfounded belief that the majority of Serbian citizens would remain politically obedient as they had during and immediately after the 1999 NATO attack against Yugoslavia. But despite having lost the September election, Milošević refused to acknowledge Koštunica's victory and tenaciously clung to power for ten days following the election. The fallen leader was finally ousted only as a result of a domestically coordinated, but largely externally funded, "spontaneous eruption" of post-election popular demonstrations, or what amounted to a relatively peaceful and nearly bloodless "democratic revolution" (see Chapter 9).[1]

Koštunica was sworn in as president of Yugoslavia on October 7, 2000. For his part, Milošević, in another example of his political unpredictability, chose neither to take his life, as a great many observers hoped or calculated, nor to flee to some safe haven (e.g., Belarus, Libya, Cuba, or China), as others expected. Instead, he decided to remain in Yugoslavia; this decision would have a profound impact on the country's political life well into 2002. The old regime had fallen. But with the former dictator remaining in the country and unwilling to retire from political life or voluntarily surrender to The Hague Tribunal in the Netherlands, the Milošević question remained high on the agenda of Serbia's new political leaders, a situation that would cast a long shadow over the country's political transition.

DOS had won an impressive electoral victory in September 2000, including winning a majority of seats allotted to Serbia in the federal legislature. In Montenegro, however, the anti-Milošević and reformist (though not completely uncorrupted) leadership, headed by Milo Djukanović, had boycotted the September 24 election, thereby allowing pro-Milošević forces to win the federal-level electoral contest in that republic. As a result of the Montenegrin boycott, Milošević's rump supporters in Serbia, together with his old allies from Montenegro, continued to exercise a substantial degree of influence on Yugoslav federal politics. But the collapse of support for the old regime in October 2000, and the extent of the DOS victory, was unquestionable. In September 24 municipal elections, for example, Milošević forces suffered an ignominious defeat as DOS swept to power in over 90 cities. In Belgrade, DOS took 96 of the Citizen Assembly's 110 seats. When, on December 23, 2000, republic-level elections were finally held in Serbia, the full extent of popular support for DOS and the post-Milošević regime became fully apparent, with the coalition winning 64 percent of the vote in Serbia, and 176 of the 250 seats in Serbia's legislature (Table I.1).

Table I.1   Voting Support and Distribution of Seats in the National Assembly of Serbia (December 23, 2000)

Party and Leader(s)	% of Votes	% of Seats
DOS, Democratic Opposition of Serbia, an 18-party coalition[a] (Zoran Djindjić/Vojislav Koštunica, etc.)	64.4	70.4 (176)
SPS, Socialist Party of Serbia (Slobodan Milošević)	13.5	14.8 (37)
SRS, Serbian Radical Party (Vojislav Šešelj)	8.5	9.2 (23)
SSU, Serbian Unity Party (Borislav Pelević)	5.3	5.6 (14)
SPO, Serbian Party of Renewal (Vuk Drašković)	3.7	—
DSP, Democratic Socialist Party (Milorad Vučelić)	0.85	—
SSDP, Serbian Social Democratic Party (Zoran Lilić)	0.78	—
JUL, Yugoslav Left (Mira Marković)	0.37	—
Total	**100.0** (3,745,623 or 57% of electorate; invalid votes, 2.39%)	**100.0 (250 seats)**

[a]Democratic Party, Democratic Party of Serbia, Civic Alliance of Serbia, Christian Democratic Party of Serbia, New Serbia, Democratic Alternative, Democratic Center, New Democracy, Social Democrat Union, Association of Free and Independent Trade Unions, Reform Democratic Party of Vojvodina, League of Social Democrats of Vojvodina, Coalition Sumadija, Party of Democratic Action, Alliance of Vojvodina Hungarians, Social-Democracy, Coalition Vojvodina, Movement for Democratic Serbia.

Vojislav Koštunica's popularity had undoubtedly helped DOS achieve an even more impressive victory in the December 2000 republic-level elections than it had in the September federal-level contest. But the DOS electoral campaign in Serbia had been led by Zoran Djindjić—an old archrival of Koštunica's from the democratic opposition ranks—and it was Djindjić who was installed in December as Serbia's new prime minister. Thus, alongside the important Milošević question, there was now new uncertainty in Yugoslavia's post-Milošević transition, namely, whether the seasoned, highly pragmatic, Western-oriented, and very ambitious Djindjić would be able to cooperate successfully with the incrementalist, legally oriented, and decidedly anti-American Vojislav Koštunica. More broadly, could the unwieldy 18-party DOS coalition transcend the Koštunica–Djindjić rivalry, and how would this duumvirate affect the new government's ability to deal with both the thorny Milošević question and the even more daunting economic and territorial problems faced by the country?

Throughout the period of Milošević's rule, Yugoslavia's opposition political leaders had debated about the various steps that would be necessary to
politically democratize and restructure post-dictatorial Yugoslavia. But the
opposition coalition that won federal power in September-October 2000, and
then took control over Serbia in December 2000, had no settled or detailed
program for transformation of the country. As a diverse coalition of 18 parties, DOS had successfully coordinated its electoral campaigns against
Milošević at the ballot box and in the streets. But it lacked strong organization or experience in governance. Moreover, in addition to the personal rivalries and jealousies that had long fragmented the opposition, the DOS coalition
was also bedeviled by a mixture of ideological and political views. Thus,
although having worked together to replace the previous dictatorship, the various parties and factions that constituted DOS had very diverse notions regarding how to reconstruct Serbia and Yugoslavia.

During the three-month interregnum between the meltdown of the
Milošević regime in October and the December 2000 legislative elections in
Serbia, Koštunica turned his attention to the important task of reestablishing
Yugoslavia's relationship with the international community and other states in
the Balkan region. Still lacking full political legitimation in Serbia, and with
Milošević working furtively behind the scenes to obstruct fundamental change,
Koštunica traveled extensively early on in his mandate seeking diplomatic and
economic support for his new regime. Back in Belgrade, a newly constituted
federal government was able to make some personnel and policy changes. But
much of Milošević's power structure, particularly the military, police, and economic apparatus, remained largely intact, and Milošević's party (the Socialist
Party of Serbia) continued to have political representation at the republic and
federal levels. Dislodging the remnants of this established apparatus, with its
leader still on the political scene, was no easy task. Koštunica—influenced by
his legal convictions and innate prudence—took on this challenge cautiously,
and resisted initiating a comprehensive political sweep of the previous regime's
elite personnel. Thus, during its first weeks in power, the post-Milošević federal
government functioned as an awkward, compromise-driven, power-sharing
body run by DOS and selected members of the former regime. It was only at
the end of 2000 and the beginning of 2001, particularly after DOS's consolidation of power in the Serbian elections, that the new regime slowly began to
take charge and turn to the difficult tasks that lay ahead. As the transition
process unfolded, it became clear that federal president Koštunica had a very
different perspective regarding the tempo and character of change than did Serbian prime minister Djindjić.

Several major aspects of transition preoccupied Serbia's newly elected
political leaders during the first stage of the post-Milošević period, including:

(1) the residual Milošević factor and issues relating to cooperation with the ICTY; (2) the difficulties of economic restructuring and economic transformation; (3) the reconfiguration of federal relations between Serbia and Montenegro; (4) the Kosovo question, and Serb–Albanian relations in southern Serbia; and (5) political democratization and establishment of the rule of law within Yugoslavia.

Bringing Milošević to Justice: The Politics of Extradition

Serbia's initial political and economic transition was complicated by Slobodan Milošević's determination to remain active in Serbian political life following the collapse of his authoritarian regime, and by disagreements within the DOS leadership regarding how to deal with the former dictator. Political support for Milošević plummeted after the October 2000 democratic revolution, and there were numerous defections from his Socialist Party of Serbia (SPS), not to mention the creation of rival socialist party formations by former SPS stalwarts. But Milošević nevertheless managed to be reelected president of the SPS near the end of November 2000, and initially remained politically active, if considerably less visible. Indeed, the enigmatic fallen dictator told an interviewer during the December 2000 election race in Serbia that he was able to "sleep peacefully" and that his conscience was "completely clear." In the republic-level December 2000 election, the SPS took only 13.5 percent of the vote in the contests for the Serbian Assembly, but the former ruling party still constituted the largest opposition party (37 seats) in the Serbian legislature.

Milošević had more to contend with, however, than simply his new opposition status in the Serbian legislature. Indicted for war crimes in May 1999 by the International Criminal Tribunal for the Former Yugoslavia, Milošević and the authorities in Belgrade fell under increasing pressure to consent to the growing international demands for the ex-president's extradition to The Hague. The former Yugoslav leader was outspoken in rejecting the legitimacy of the UN-sponsored organization. "That institution," Milošević maintained, "is a political institution which is one of the means for carrying out genocide against the Serb people—a people who dared to defend their country and to defend their national interest." In early 2001, Milošević could still take some comfort in the fact that President Koštunica, and quite a number of other DOS leaders, also held a highly negative view of The Hague Tribunal, if not necessarily disagreeing with all the particulars of the indictment against Milošević, or the former dictator's alleged record of criminal behavior with regard to other matters. For Koštunica, and many others in Serbia, The Hague Tribunal's request for Milošević's extradition did not constitute a priority concern for the new regime in Belgrade. Justice would better be served, it was agreed, if Milošević first faced trial in Yugoslavia for abuse of power charges (rather than for crimes in other Balkan countries, against members of other ethnic communities). Public opinion polling early in 2001 revealed that Serbs overwhelmingly agreed that Milošević should be tried within Yugoslavia "for things that have been done to the Serbian people."

Having rejected the idea of extraditing Milošević and other high-ranking former officials to The Hague, and realizing that considerable skepticism existed abroad regarding the ability of Yugoslavia's courts to mete out appropriate justice, the DOS leadership initially seemed to settle on a compromise: Yugoslavia would cooperate with The Hague Tribunal to facilitate the prosecution of Milošević by the ICTY on Yugoslav territory, and within the Yugoslav legal and judicial structure. As of mid-January 2001, however, the specific modalities of such proceedings had not been worked out, or even accepted by the ICTY. But the Yugoslav authorities eventually permitted the ICTY to open an office in Belgrade, and President Koštunica, after initially refusing, finally agreed to meet with the tribunal's chief prosecutor, Carla del Ponte.

Del Ponte's agenda for the meeting was to impress on President Koštunica the need to extradite Milošević to The Hague, as well as to allow the prosecution of Serbs for war crimes.[2] Koštunica was unyielding. He responded to del Ponte that his focus would continue to be the indictment of NATO officials for the bombing of Yugoslavia, as well as NATO's use of depleted uranium shells, and its alleged fabrication of the 1999 Račak massacre of Kosovo Albanians, which had contributed to precipitating NATO hostilities against Yugoslavia. But Koštunica's personal views aside, the Belgrade regime was under strong international pressure to cooperate with the ICTY and expeditiously embark on judicial proceedings against Milošević. Thus, Koštunica's obdurate refusal to cooperate with the demands of the ICTY clearly had the potential of costing Yugoslavia desperately needed foreign assistance and undermining the country's effort to obtain membership in international economic organizations.[3] It would not take long for Koštunica's strong feelings about the ICTY to precipitate a split in the DOS leadership.

Milošević, meanwhile, was desperately hoping that a more pragmatic viewpoint would prevail in Western policy. For example, many in the international community believed (and this was also Koštunica's view) that excessive pressure on countries that refuse to cooperate with the ICTY—for example, making economic assistance contingent on cooperation with the tribunal or employing economic sanctions against recalcitrant states—could actually impede democratic transition, exacerbate internal nationalist forces, and allow extremist leaders to resume power in the midst of further economic deterioration. Sensing that some legal action against him was imminent, Milošević requested, and was granted, a meeting with Koštunica on January 13, 2001, during which they reportedly discussed the rights of former state officials, among other matters. For his part, Serb prime minister designate Djindjić, who appeared to be more willing than Koštunica to cooperate with the ICTY on the Milošević matter, pointed out that the former leader was being treated fairly, and that his safety was not threatened. He enjoys "all the rights granted to him by law," Djindjić asserted, and "his son and wife walk about freely, leaving and reentering the country as they please." Indeed, in February 2001, four months after his fall from power, Milošević was still living in the presidential residence under 24-hour surveillance by the same special guard unit that had served him during his presidency.

Unfortunately for Milošević, it soon became apparent that foreign governments and international financial institutions were unwilling to provide assistance to Yugoslavia unless Belgrade complied with the ICTY's demands. Deputy Premier Miroljub Labus observed, for example, that foreign lending institutions had given the Koštunica leadership a deadline of March 31, 2001, "to solve the problem of Slobodan Milošević's accountability for the crimes imputed to him. From that date, voting in all the international financial organizations will directly depend on this decision. The world is not forcing us to let Milošević go on trial in The Hague, but we are expected to pose the question of his accountability."

Bowing to such international pressure, and seeking to differentiate himself from the more intransigent Koštunica, Serbia's prime minister, Zoran Djindjić, met the foreign deadline and ordered police operatives under his personal control to arrest Slobodan Milošević on March 31, 2001. "We should not be made hostages to Milošević," claimed Djindjić, who was assuming considerable political risk in taking action against the former dictator. But though a good portion of Serbian society was opposed to the extradition and incarceration of Milošević, a majority supported Djindjić's action and viewed the arrest as imperative if Serbia was to obtain the foreign assistance necessary to rebuild the country. Although some Milošević supporters mounted a "people's guard" around his residence, they proved too few in number to halt the dramatic police action against Milošević. For the next 89 days, Milošević would remain Prisoner No. 1121 in Belgrade's central prison.[4] President Koštunica, although disapproving of the Djindjić-led action, took no measures to prevent Milošević's imprisonment.

From April 1 to the end of June 2001, the central political drama in Yugoslavia crystallized around the question of whether Slobodan Milošević would be taken from his jail cell in Belgrade and extradited to The Hague in order to face war crimes charges. In a manner similar to the earlier debate regarding Milošević's arrest, the "Milošević question" again became a politi-

cal hot potato within the ruling DOS coalition, and particularly between Koštunica and Djindjić. Once again, an externally imposed deadline—this time the
planned International Donors' Conference to be held at the end of June, at
which millions of dollars were to be pledged to assist in Yugoslavia's reconstruction and development—turned the issue of Milošević's extradition into a
question of whether the DOS leadership would accommodate foreign pressure
in order to potentially improve the country's standard of living. With the economy in shambles, prices increasing, and wages at a very low level, many
Yugoslav citizens had begun to feel that whatever their personal beliefs about
foreign pressure tactics and "blackmail," it was time to get rid of Milošević,
or as some suggested, "sell him to the highest bidder." It was finally the pragmatic and ambitious Djindjić who cut the Gordian knot regarding the question of Milošević's future and arranged for police officials to turn Milošević
over to the ICTY, and permit his extradition to The Hague.

In deciding to extradite Milošević, Djindjić calculated that he could politically profit from the move by obtaining foreign funds for Yugoslavia and tap-
ping into the growing revulsion for Milošević on the part of many Serbs in the
wake of recent reports regarding crimes committed by Serbian forces in
Kosovo during 1999. For example, just before Milošević's extradition, the Serbian media reported the discovery of sunken freezer trucks and mass graves
containing bodies of Albanians that had been transported out of Kosovo by
Serbian forces in order to thwart potential war crimes investigations. Other
reports detailed criminal and self-serving activities by members of the
Milošević family. In a dramatic gesture, Djindjić approved the extradition of
Milošević to The Hague to occur on June 28, 2001, a Serbian religious holiday (St. Vitus Day), and perhaps the most famous day in Serbian history (i.e.,
the 1389 Battle of Kosovo and the assassination of Archduke Franz Ferdi-
nand). Making reference to Milošević's famous June 28, 1989 speech at Gazimestan, when the former dictator had outlined a program of national renaissance (see Chapter 3), Djindjić announced the extradition plan by remarking
that it was "exactly twelve years ago that Slobodan Milošević had promised
the ideal of a Heavenly Serbia. The government today has pledged to obtain
the ideal of an Earthly Serbia, not so much for us, as much as for our children."

Djindjić's move to facilitate Milošević's extradition came on the heels
of a ruling by Yugoslavia's constitutional court—made up of Milošević
appointees—that the Serbian government's decision authorizing the transfer of
Milošević to The Hague was unconstitutional. The court decision endangered
the survival of the country, Djindjić claimed, because noncompliance with The
Hague Tribunal meant that a number of countries would cancel their participation in the upcoming International Donors' Conference. The Serbian government session that addressed the potential extradition of Milošević was

attended by 15 of 23 ministers, and all but one—a member of Koštunica's DSS—voted in favor of his extradition. Thus—in a plan that Djindjić had worked out with the American ambassador in Belgrade, William Montgomery—Milošević was transported to the airport outside Belgrade on June 28, 2001, and was flown by a Serbian police helicopter to the Stabilization Force (SFOR) base in Tuzla, Bosnia (escorted by several U.S. Apache combat helicopters), where he was transferred to a NATO plane that flew him to the Netherlands. Another police helicopter then transported Milošević to the ICTY prison at Scheveningen. The head of the Yugoslav military establishment, army chief of staff General Nebojša Pavković, had earlier assured Djindjić that the army would not interfere with the extradition process. Milošević arrived at The Hague only hours before the International Donors' Conference for Yugoslavia opened in Brussels, Belgium.

Instinctively overoptimistic, Djindjić now called the Milošević question a "closed chapter" in Serbian political life. Though many Serbs bitterly opposed his move against Milošević, there were no significant public protests in the wake of the extradition. For his part, President Koštunica, who had kept his distance from the decision-making surrounding Milošević's extradition, attempted to gain some political advantage by rhetorically opposing Milošević's transfer out of the country. But having failed to take any meaningful steps to halt the extradition, Koštunica was unable to derive much advantage from the affair, and actually lost some support as a result of the episode.[5]

Meanwhile at The Hague, Milošević was summoned to a public hearing on July 13, 2001, in order to hear the charges against him and to enter a plea. Adopting a position he would maintain throughout the months ahead, Milošević assumed a defiant posture, which is exemplified in the following exchange with Judge May, who headed the ICTY Court.

Proceeding IT–99–37–1

Judge May: This is the initial appearance of the accused in this case upon his transfer to the Tribunal. Mr. Milošević, I see that you are not represented by counsel today. We understand this is of your own choice . . . these proceedings will be long and complex and you may wish to consider the position . . . now, do you want some time to consider now whether you wish to be represented?

The Accused (Slobodan Milošević): I consider this Tribunal a false Tribunal and the indictment a false indictment. It is illegal being not appointed by the UN General Assembly, so I have no need to appoint counsel [to] an illegal organ.

Judge May: Mr. Milošević, in due course you will have the chance to put in motions challenging the jurisdiction or any other preliminary matters

which you wish to. We take it that you wish to proceed without counsel
... this Initial Appearance is simply to deal with these matters; first of
all, the indictment itself and, secondly for you, if you wish, to enter your
plea of guilty or not guilty to it. Now do you want to have the indictment
read out or not?

The Accused: That's your problem. . . .

Judge May: Mr. Milošević, you are now before this Tribunal and you are
within the jurisdiction of it. You will be tried by the Tribunal. You will
be accorded the full rights of the accused according to international law
and the full protections of international law and the statute. . . . The trial
chamber will treat your response as a waiver of your right to have the
indictment read out . . . Now, do you want to enter pleas today or are
you asking for an adjournment to consider the matter further?

The Accused: This trial's aim is to produce false justification for the war
crimes of NATO committed in Yugoslavia.

Judge May: Mr. Milošević, I asked you a question. . . .

The Accused: I have given you my answer. Furthermore this so-called Tribunal . . .

[microphone switched off]

Judge May: The rules state that if the accused fails to enter a plea, then the
trial chamber shall enter a plea of not guilty on his behalf.

The Accused: As I have said, the aim of this Tribunal is to justify the crimes
committed in Yugoslavia. That is why I think this is a false Tribunal. . . .

Judge May: Mr. Milošević, this is not—

The Accused:—an illegitimate one.

The Interpreter: I'm sorry, the microphone is not on.

Judge May: Mr. Milošević, this is not the time for speeches. . . . The matter
is now adjourned.

Throughout 2001, Milošević used various opportunities and intermedi-
aries to speak out in a similar fashion against the UN tribunal. For example,
in a written submission filed on August 9, Milošević challenged the tribunal's
jurisdiction over him, a circumstance, he claimed, that resulted in the indictment against him being "non-existent." The tribunal's chief prosecutor, Carla
del Ponte—trained in the civil law tradition—sharply and inappropriately by
the standards of common law practice ridiculed Milošević in an interview with
a Swiss daily, claiming that the former Yugoslav leader was acting like a "stubborn, capricious, child who can't look me in the face because he is sulking."[6]
During his second appearance at The Hague on August 30, Milošević again
challenged the authority of the court, and complained bitterly of discrimination and his situation in prison. "Can I speak? Or are you going to turn off my

microphone like the first time?" asked Milošević in an opening gambit designed to obtain time to express his views. The judge demurred, and only agreed to accept Milošević's comments in written form.

On October 30, Milošević appeared before the tribunal for a third time since his transfer to the Netherlands. This time, he angrily refused to answer newly filed charges against him regarding atrocities in Kosovo and Croatia, and also twice prompted the judges to shut off his microphone. For example, on the second day of the hearing, Milošević once again described the war crimes proceeding against him as a "farce," and told the judges not to bother him with indictments that could have been written by a "retarded seven-year-old child." The Court then asked Milošević if there was anything he wished to say about the conditions of his detention. He replied that there was no need for the prison authorities to maintain a suicide watch over him as he had absolutely no intention of killing himself. "I would never commit suicide. I do not wish to do it for my family. I will struggle here to topple this farce of a Tribunal."

In November 2001, the list of indictments against Milošević was amended to include a charge of genocide during the 1992–1995 war in Bosnia. At his appearance to hear the charges against him, Milošević listened impassively for more than an hour as a lengthy list of criminal acts he allegedly committed was read out. Once again he questioned the legality of the UN court and refused to cooperate. "This miserable text is the ultimate absurdity," Milošević observed. "I should be given credit for peace in Bosnia, not war." Before Judge May could again cut him off, Milošević pointed out that the "responsibility for the war in Bosnia lies with the [Western] powers and their agents, not in Bosnia, and not with the Serbs, Serb people, or Serb policy."[7]

Although Milošević was no longer present in Yugoslavia after June 28, 2001, the issue of cooperation between Belgrade and the UN tribunal continued to divide the members of the DOS coalition, and became a controversial issue in the Koštunica–Djindjić power struggle to control Yugoslavia's political transition. The issue of extradition to The Hague also involved top-level associates of the former dictator who had been indicted with him in May 1999, including Bosnian Serb leaders (such as Ratko Mladić and Radovan Karadžić, who were reportedly hiding in Bosnia and Serbia) and various other Yugoslavian citizens who had been publicly or secretly indicted by the tribunal. In November 2001, for example, a Belgrade news magazine claimed that more than 360 Serb police officers were targets of an investigation by the International Criminal Tribunal for the Former Yugoslavia. Indeed, in early November, members of the "Red Berets," a Serbian elite secret police unit (technically the Special Operations Unit or JSO), were directed to arrest two police officers pending their extradition to the Netherlands. This provocative order sparked a police rebellion, with scores of Red Berets—whose members had operated in

Bosnia and Kosovo and who had a reputation for brutality—deploying armored personnel carriers to block the Belgrade–Budapest highway (from November 9 to November 16) and demanding a halt to all extraditions for war crimes until a Yugoslav law was passed on the issue. They also demanded the sacking of Serbia's minister of the interior. The JSO protest ended only after a compromise was reached involving the reorganization of the state security leadership, and an agreement by the government not to hold Red Beret commandos criminally responsible for their participation in earlier military operations. During the dispute, President Koštunica, who had been a vocal critic of extradition to The Hague, supported the demands of the JSO officers. For his part, Serbian prime minister Djindjić harshly criticized Koštunica's approach to the JSO rebellion as "inappropriate," and ordered the restructuring of the JSO into a nonsecret, anti-terror unit within the regular police chain of command.

The JSO rebellion once again served to illustrate the ongoing tug of war between Koštunica and Djindjić over control of the security services, and more broadly over the country itself. For example, in early August 2001, an incident known as the Gavrilović case led to a scandal that prompted ministers from Koštunica's DSS to leave the Serbian cabinet in protest. The August events occurred when Momir Gavrilović, a former secret service official, was killed just hours after a visit to President Koštunica's office, where he purportedly advised the Yugoslav president of serious corruption in Djindjić's government. Both the Gavrilović murder (whose perpetrators were never discovered) and the subsequent JSO episode widened the distance between Koštunica and Djindjić. Thus, long after Milošević was removed from active political life, the legacy of his repressive power apparatus and the issues of extradition and appropriate justice for members of the old regime continued to disrupt Yugoslav political life.

The continued grip of Slobodan Milošević on the collective consciousness and memory of Yugoslavia's citizens and other Serbs in and outside the Balkans was brought into sharp relief on February 12, 2002, as the initial stage of his trial began at the Hague.[8] Opening arguments by the prosecution and the defense made it immediately apparent that two very different, highly politicized, and equally partial and unsatisfying accounts of the Balkans' recent history would be offered during the court proceedings.

The prosecution used its opening statement to lay the groundwork for its theory that Milošević's "quest for power" had motivated the Serbian dictator and was responsible for the litany of crimes and atrocities detailed in the indictment against him. In order to meet the legal burden of proving Milošević's personal culpability for the crimes he was charged with, the prosecution argued that the mass violence in the Balkan region was not attributable to "the Balkan peoples," but rather was entirely the fault of unscrupulous leaders, chief among them Slobodan Milošević, who were the "true culprits" or "real culprits" behind the region's violence.[9] Focussed on proving Milošević's personal guilt, the prosecution sidestepped the cultural underpinnings of his rise to power, and also chose not to dwell on the complex interplay of historical grievances and leadership ambitions that is necessary for any complete understanding of Balkan political developments during the 1990s (see Chapter 10). For example, when presenting Milošević's rise to power, the prosecution predictably reviewed his June 1989 speech at Gazimestan in Kosovo—or what The Hague prosecutors called "a skillful speech of great power"—which he made on the occasion of the 600th anniversary of the Battle of Kosovo. But seeking to minimize any collective responsibility in Serbia for Milošević and his rule, the prosecutors failed to provide any details concerning the socio-political context of the speech, and how that context was associated with deeply felt facets of Serbian political culture and identity, the background of Serbian-Albanian relations, and the violent dissolution of Yugoslavia (see Chapter 2).

The Hague prosecutors also emphasized that Milošević "understood the power of the crowd," and how "developing sentiments of anti-communism" in Serbia influenced his view that "nationalism was a force." By fanning nationalism, the prosecution maintained, Milošević was able to mobilize Serb terror against non-Serbs in one region of the Balkans after another, including the ethnic cleansing of Albanians in the province of Kosovo during 1999. Indeed, the overall scheme of violence and ethnic cleansing, according the prosecutors, was purportedly part of a broader plan by Milošević and his regime to carve out a "Greater Serbia"—a notion that the prosecution alleged had been developed and justified prior to socialist Yugoslavia's disintegration in the infamous 1986 "Memorandum" of the Serbian Academy of Sciences and Arts (SANU).[10] But by attempting to explain re-emergent Serb nationalism almost entirely with reference to Milošević's personality and personal ambitions,[11] The Hague prosecutors, at least initially, provided a very incomplete portrait and biased analysis of Yugoslav political life during the late 1980s and 1990s.

Defendant Milošević exploited this tactical position during the first weeks of the trial. He offered a contrasting portrayal of events in the Balkans associated with his rule, and shifted the spotlight away from his personal culpability by directing attention to collective Serb and non-Serb responsibility for much that had occurred during the wars of the Yugoslav succession and their aftermath. Thus, Milošević—who faces life imprisonment if convicted of the charges against him—attributed most of the bloodshed in Kosovo not to the Serbian military or para-military elements operating in that province, but to NATO political operations, and the insurgent activities by Albanians who were members of the "terrorist" Kosovo Liberation Army (KLA, or UCK in Albanian).

Continuing a line of argument he had voiced during his pre-trial appearances, Milošević refused to acknowledge the legitimacy of The Hague Tribunal—categorically rejecting responsibility for criminal acts—and drew attention to what he called the prosecution's "blanket" condemnation of the Serb people. After all, Milošević claimed, he was no magician, and surely not omnipotent enough to have directly controlled all the operations attributed to him in the ICTY charges. Rather, he contended, he was simply the elected representative of the Serb people, whose interests and agenda he had attempted to advance. In remarks that resonated in many quarters of Serbian society, Milošević maintained that though the tribunal asserted it was only trying him personally for crimes, the ICTY was actually holding a "trial of the whole country . . . a country that stood up in defense against its attackers." Claiming that he was wrongly charged with offenses actually committed by others, primarily forces outside Yugoslavia who had hoped for Yugoslavia's dissolution and wanted to avoid responsibility for their own deeds (e.g., NATO leaders), Milošević emphatically suggested that he had "nothing" to defend himself from. "My name is Slobodan," he exhorted, "with a capital 'S', which means 'free' in my language." Thus, while the prosecution took the extreme position of focusing almost exclusively on Milošević's "personal responsibility" for the crimes he was charged with, his defense veered to the other extreme, that is, his complete innocence, as evidenced by the record of substantial "collective" support among Serbs for his actions in Kosovo, Croatia, and Bosnia.

At least in the initial weeks of his trial at The Hague, as Serbian citizens became increasingly riveted to the televised coverage of the proceedings, Milošević pugnaciously and even, some conceded, impressively defended himself against the well-staffed and well-financed prosecution's accusations regarding his alleged personal culpability for various savage crimes committed in Kosovo during 1998 and 1999. Interestingly, having combined the charges against Milošević in connection with the wars in Croatia, Bosnia, and Kosovo (Prosecutor del Ponte suggested this was done to facilitate the scheduling of witnesses, and to spare witnesses excessive psychological stress), The Hague prosecutors first took up the case of Kosovo, thereby reversing the actual chronological order of the conflicts. They may have adopted this sequence with the expectation that the eventual arrival at The Hague of top Serb actors in the Bosnian war would prove highly beneficial to the prosecution's case. So the trial and Milošević's rebuttal of the charges began with matters that were still fresh in the minds of most Yugoslav citizens, including the NATO bombing of Yugoslavia, which highlighted highly sensitive issues of Serbian national psyche and history, and which also still engendered considerable trauma for many Serbs (e.g., the continued, albeit episodic interethnic violence in Kosovo, the unresolved status of the UN protectorate, and the difficulties of thousands of Serbian refugees who were forced to flee the province in 1999). Therefore, it was not surprising that The Hague trial of Milošević both captivated and disgusted Yugoslav citizens.

Milošević's successor, Yugoslav president Koštunica, a long-time opponent of the ICTY, sympathized with his predecessor's view that The Hague proceedings were harming Serbia's image and interests: "[The] prosecutor has said that this is a trial not of the Serbs but of Slobodan Milošević; that there is no collective guilt, but a number of individual responsibilities also sounds thin. This [prosecutorial argument] is what is called in the Bosnian and Croatian indictments a joint criminal enterprise. . . . Milošević is not just an individual. He was the head of state, and not an insignificant number of voters voted for him on several occasions. We cannot wash our hands of this, and say that the Serbs did not know what was going on because of a media blockage." Concerned that The Hague was "writing history," Koštunica argued that Yugoslavia needed to do "everything as a state to influence the writing of history," strongly implying that his country should have official representation at Milošević's trial (a move that was denied by the ICTY), and even assist in his defense. As for "writing history," Koštunica indicated that he preferred the work of his own Truth and Reconciliation Commission—which, as of summer 2002, had barely got under way—because, he maintained, The Hague Tribunal contributed to neither truth nor reconciliation. "Media trials of this kind," he observed, "trials that are not guided by the truth, or not to a great extent, can re-ignite nationalism, exclusivity, and many other evils."[12] Koštunica's view was shared by many other Yugoslav and foreign observers of the initial phase of Milošević's trial, who sensed that the proceedings at The Hague had unleashed a "psychological Balkans war," and that the detailed rendition of savage crimes might actually intensify anti-Serb hatred among Albanian Muslims and Croats, while causing Serbs to feel that the ICTY was part of an anti-Serb witch-hunt.[13]

Revitalized by the opportunity to defend and mold his historical image before a global television audience, which included his ethnic brethren in Serbia, Milošević vigorously, and sometimes successfully, presented his own case and cross-examined prosecution witnesses. For example, Milošević scored an early victory by persuading the Court to reject the prosecution's motion to allow Kevin Curtis, the leader of a prosecution team that had investigated crimes in Kosovo, to testify. Speaking against the motion, Milošević demonstrated that Curtis could only provide unhelpful and secondhand hearsay evidence of events that had occurred in Kosovo, gratuitously adding that he had been "illegally" arrested by Curtis during his extradition on June 28, 2001. Milošević was clearly making the prosecution's case more difficult. By extensive and intensive cross-examination of witnesses, Milošević demonstrated that, notwithstanding his rhetoric challenging the Court's legitimacy, he was prepared to fully participate in his defense. For instance, in his cross-examination of certain Kosovo Albanians who were called by the prosecution to testify about Serb atrocities against civilians in Kosovo, Milošević was able to skillfully undermine the prosecution's leader-focussed or "personal ambition" theory of Balkan violence by successfully connecting the witnesses to the KLA. He pointed out that the KLA had been described by U.S. officials in 1998 as a terrorist organization (see Chapter 6).

Milošević was initially quite adept at demonstrating how prosecution evidence presented to help convict him could skillfully be utilized to assist his defense. For example, on February 18, 2002, the first prosecution witness, Mahmut Bakalli, a former Albanian communist politician from Kosovo, told the court that in a meeting in April 1998, Milošević had defended as a justified police action the March 1998 killing of KLA leader Adem Jashari and some two dozen members of the extended Jashari family in the central Drenica area of Kosovo (see Chapter 5). Bakalli claimed that Milošević showed no "emotion or guilt" when describing how the police gave Albanian civilians two hours to escape prior to authorizing violent force against them. Though the action by Serbian police against the Jashari family was an extremely brutal assault, which also killed many of their distant relatives and innocent civilian bystanders, the event demonstrated to the Court that the war in Kosovo originated as a struggle between armed Albanian insurgents in pursuit of independence and Serbian government forces who were trying to put down a separatist revolt.[14]

Indeed, a pamphlet distributed at the memorial site in Drenica in 2002, but not utilized by Milošević in his defense, is a tribute to Adem Jashari's so-called eight-year armed struggle against the Serbian police (1981–1989). "Feelings of patriotism had been cultivated remarkably well in each member of this family," the pamphlet points out. "The family had put all its economic and human potential in the service of a sole ideal: liberation from Serbia. . . . In 1991 Adem and his friends went to Albania to get prepared for the battles to come. . . . They frequently crossed the Kosova–Albania border beginning armed actions against the Serbian police. Numerous actions were undertaken . . . the Serb state was being hit in its most sensitive part: in its repressive apparatus."[15] Commenting on the police siege and the attack on the Jashari family, the pamphlet goes on to note: "The siege had been noticed by Adem, and all the others who had been staying awake. They did not try anything to get away although they were in [a] position to do so. On the contrary, they remembered their sworn *besa* [oath] . . . Adem told them: 'We'll have a war today. Let it be in good luck.'"

Cross-examining Bakalli on February 19, 2002, Milošević attempted to establish, with some success, that Serbian actions in Kosovo were simply a state response to insurgent violence perpetrated by "terrorists" who were hiding among their relatives. He asked Bakalli: "Do you consider that any other police force anywhere in the world would have fled when somebody was shooting at it from a barricaded house behind whose walls they were hiding? Is that your opinion?" Bakalli responded that he could not answer the question because he had nothing to do with police operations. He also claimed, however, that Milošević was behind the killing of civilians, although he was not able to provide proof to support his accusation. Milošević clinically continued his cross-examination, pointing out in passing that the Jashari family had killed many Serb and non-Serb policemen, not to mention Albanians.

Milošević's vigorous defense during the first weeks of his trial not only made the prosecution's case more difficult, but also made it more politically uncomfortable for Serbian leaders like Zoran Djindjić, who had facilitated Milošević's extradition, and who were cooperating with The Hague Tribunal to facilitate the extradition of other Serbs. Indeed, Djindjić complained that the tribunal was "enabling Milošević to give vent to his demagoguery, and control the court proceedings." Djindjić added:

> I am speechless over the amount of money that is being squandered after four years to enable such inconsequential witnesses to appear. This circus is posing a massive dilemma to myself and my reformist government . . . it is easy for Koštunica to play the patriot after the tribunal has lost all its vestiges of confidence among our public. Even Milošević's opponents are developing sympathy for him, and are asking me why did we hand him over? Many have been convinced that he has successfully portrayed NATO as the main criminal. What justification can I now have for handing over more individuals? . . . Milošević ruined this country, and every day I am struggling against the consequences of his rule. But no one can prove that he waged an imperialist war alone. He was just one of many rogues in a civil war, who sought to take power over the authoritarian state through ethnic cleansing.[16]

Djindjić also warned that should he try to arrest and extradite General Ratko Mladić, he would be risking "civil war," as Serbia was a haven for 200,000 Bosnian Serb refugees, "many of whom have weapons." Djindjić continued, "We expected a legal proceeding in which evidence of personal responsibility could be proved. What we do not need is a seminar on history and politics. . . . It's beginning to resemble a Spanish soap opera of 50 or 500 episodes in which even some ghosts of the past are being raised."

Even before the Milošević trial began, many Serbs were disturbed that the proceedings at The Hague amounted to what they viewed as "selective" or "victor's justice," that the ICTY was circumventing Serbia's own judicial procedures and desire for an accounting with Milošević, that pressure from the ICTY to extradite Serbs represented unfair Western "conditionality" or blackmail, and that the prosecutors for The Hague were exaggerating Serb responsibility for the Balkan wars of the 1990s, instead of properly apportioning blame among different ethnic groups. As a result of such factors, the tribunal's reputation among Serbs plummeted in the first days of the Milošević trial, and the former dictator's defense of his "heroic image" engendered considerable support. This surge of pro-Milošević sentiment occurred not only among those Serbs who had previously supported him, but also on the part of many Serbs who viewed his record with contempt.

The media audience that followed the tribunal's televised trial quickly grew to an estimated half of the adult population, and surveys indicated a groundswell of popular support for the former Yugoslav leader. According to pollsters, the former dictator left an excellent or good impression on some 60 percent of Serbian viewers.[17] Milošević's average rating on a scale from one to five in regular polls jumped from 1.5 to 2.7 during the first two weeks of the trial.[18] Although a large number of Serbs had no sympathy for Milošević, and even expressed extreme bitterness towards him, the trial, initially at least, captured the attention of his countrymen, most of whom share a deep sense of national pride, as well as sensitivity regarding their ethnic group's historical image.[19]

The controversy over the question of what is really under scrutiny at the trial of Slobodan Milošević—the "personal responsibility" of a loathsome leader versus the "collective" cultural mindset and historical behavior of one ethno-cultural group—resembled the contradictory paradigms that have often been employed to explain the Balkan political landscape, interpretations that have sometimes caused confusion among observers who are presented with the politically correct or expedient viewpoint of the moment (see Chapter 10). From this perspective, the proceedings at The Hague are likely—especially when taken out of context, or read as an account of the rise and fall of Slobodan Milošević—to prove highly unsatisfying. Indeed, while President Koštunica may be genuinely concerned that "history" is being written at The Hague, the passionate advocacy of the initially rather disorganized prosecution and the desperate, if disingenuous and spirited rebuttal of the defendant more clearly resemble a politicized public relations battle that skews or eschews the full record of evidence in order to achieve victory. On the one side, Milošević views the tribunal as a political court, and is using the trial as a political pulpit to redeem his record and historical image; meanwhile the prosecution—not entirely guided by common law notions informing a dispassionate quest for justice, and highly oriented to seeking retribution for the victims of injustice—has also demonstrated a tendency to mobilize public opinion and serve a political agenda.[20] But prosecutor Carla del Ponte remained confident that she had damning evidence of Milošević's guilt. "I never prosecute the innocent," del Ponte told one interviewer. Given such a political context, the trial—which was only in its first stage by mid-2002, and would undoubtedly still take many twists and turns—is likely to provide only parts of the truth, and very little reconciliation.

Economic Transformation

For Serbia's new democratic leaders, the difficult challenge of restructuring their country's deteriorated and corrupted economy was closely linked to the Milošević question. After thirteen years of economic mismanagement, as well as international sanctions and the direct and indirect costs associated with several armed struggles sponsored by the Milošević regime, the majority of Yugoslavia's citizens at the outset of the new millennium were experiencing widespread poverty, low wages, a badly deteriorated health system, and a failing economic infrastructure. Unemployment early in 2001 was estimated at roughly 50 percent, inflation at 70 percent annually, and some 40 percent of the people were living on less than $2 a day. Crop failures also endangered the supply of state-subsidized food to pensioners. An estimated one million people, or roughly 10 percent of the population, were dependent on some form of food aid. As Belgrade's political leaders squabbled over the allocation of ministerial portfolios in the new Serbian government during the winter of 2000–2001, the capital's citizens also faced lengthy and frequent power outages. Even the new Yugoslav foreign minister, Goran Svilanović, admitted feeling embarrassed at his fellow citizens watching him on TV shaking hands with foreign officials: "The people watching me are wondering what has happened, because for them nothing has changed."

Although Koštunica's initial campaign to restore Yugoslavia's relationship to the international community quickly led to promises of stepped-up foreign assistance to reverse the country's economic difficulties, very little in the way of economic stimulus had occurred by the onset of 2001. Granted, the problems of economic deterioration were too complex and deeply rooted to expect any quick fix. But there was also a delay in receiving foreign investment and aid, a difficulty that initially could be traced to the unconsolidated nature of the new regime, as well as the unresolved status of Slobodan Milošević. For example, the arrival of funds and assistance was hampered by problems with the unreformed and inefficient banking system and the continued presence of many Milošević cronies in the country. Indeed, U.S. economic and financial sanctions against Yugoslavia were lifted by President Clinton only on January 19, 2001, on the eve of his departure from office.

The Yugoslav deputy prime minister, Miroljub Labus, cautioned that the main tasks in 2001 would be "first to survive the winter and the energy crisis, and second to bring the economy out of recession." According to Labus, the economy would only pick up strength after March 2001, that is, when he expected an "auspicious climate for profitable investment in the domestic economy" (e.g., a reduction in taxes and customs fees, deregulation of the foreign trade regime, and the establishment of "legal security")(Table I.2). However, Yugoslavia's ability to adhere to the schedule elaborated by Labus appeared doubtful at the outset of 2001. By mid-January, for example, Zoran Djindjić had still not been able to form a new government in Serbia. Much of the delay was caused by a fierce struggle by different DOS parties and factions for various positions in the new government (competition for control of police and security was extremely contentious). Djindjić also attributed the delay to the activities of certain "interest groups" who were engaged in what he called "dirty business." He specifically charged the Serbian Radical Party of Vojislav Šešelj with obstructing the convocation of the Serbian Assembly and government (which was finally installed on January 22, 2001) by legally challenging the results of repeat elections carried out in nineteen constituencies of Serbia. Djindjić also condemned the activities of the incumbent minister of privatization (a Milošević appointee), who was allegedly "stamping out privatization committees night and day" to take control of enterprises, and also manipulating the evaluation of facilities to be privatized. Djindjić warned that the "DOS secretariat" had not given anyone the mandate to change the leadership in any enterprise and those engaging in any illegal privatization practices would be penalized.

By the fall of 2001, economic reforms had not moved very far ahead, and progress in the important privatization process was moving very slowly. For example, a year after Milošević had fallen from power, and months after his corrupt municipal team was purged, not one major industry or firm had been privatized or opened to competition. In early fall, a Privatization Act was finally passed and 500 companies were expected to undergo privatization in the spring of 2002 (300 via auctions and 200 via tenders), and by early 2002, companies had begun looking for "strategic partners" (i.e., potential investors). The risk-averse environment created by the terrorist events of September 11 also made it extremely difficult to find new investors, especially in an uncertain crisis region such as the Balkans. The banking and financial services sector demonstrated the best record of liberalization under the influence of the competent and technically proficient Ministry of Finance and the National Bank headed by Mladen Dinkić. Foreign currency reserves were climbing, taxes on financial services were about to be abolished, and by the end of 2001 the *dinar* had stabilized. But in view of a worldwide economic slump, the question at the end of 2001 was whether the development of a free market, privatization, and real free trade could emerge in Yugoslavia before the window of opportunity abroad shut entirely. The collapse of several large

Table I.2   Achievement of Promises by New DOS Regime After 100 Days/One Year (September 2000–September 2001)

Promise	Achievement
First 100 Days	
Package of economic reform laws (currency, budget, privatization, social security, foreign trade protection)	Yes
Anti-corruption law (in practice)	No (partially later)
Law on army and police	No
Law on courts and judges	No
Law on public prosecutor's office	No
Penal code and law on criminal procedure	No
Law on the media (in practice)	No (partially later)
Law on universities	No
Law on local self-government	No
Law on elections	No
First Year	
Inclusion in international organizations (financial and political)	Yes
Stability Pact and Donor's Conference	Yes
Resolution of succession issues (within Former Yugoslav states)	Yes
Talks on EU membership launched	Yes
Harmonization of laws with European standards	Partially
Balancing the state budget	Partially
Launching fiscal reform	Yes
State currency	Yes
Restoration of confidence in banks	Partially
Foreign financial support	Partially
Liberalization of prices	Yes
Debt rescheduling	Partially
Foreign trade liberalization	Yes
Privatization	Partially
New agrarian policy	Partially
Citizen's social security	Partially
Initiate major investments in infrastructure	Partially

SOURCE: Miroljub Labus, "Reform One Year After," G-17 Institute Economic Review, Vol. 2, Issue 9 (September 2001).

banks in 2002 also sent tremors through the economy and led to widespread layoffs in the financial sector.

Throughout 2001, international assistance for Yugoslav economic development remained minimal, despite promises made to Yugoslavia's leaders in exchange for the arrest and extradition of Slobodan Milošević. The $1.28 billion in pledges at the Brussels Donors' Conference in June 2001 constituted only a small step in transforming Yugoslavia's economy. Yugoslavia's foreign debt, for example, was $12 billion in July 2001, and payments were late on $9.6 billion of the sum. Moreover, foreign pledges of aid did not include sufficient amounts of cash to enable the government to pay pensions and provide other essential social services such as health care. Most of the pledges were also tied to specific projects in the fields of transportation and energy infrastructure, fertilizer and animal feed, customs and border management, legal services, and medical supplies. All of these areas are important to the economy, but they do not provide quick cash outlays for social benefits. In an interview in July 2001, Djindjić remarked that if Yugoslavia did not get an immediate injection of foreign capital, the country would face demonstrations and social unrest by the fall of 2001.

> We have been unable to fulfill our promises. Three hundred and thirty thousand families live on less than 40 marks a month, our budget is being weighed down by 600,000 refugees, and 100,000 people will lose their jobs because of the transformations to the economy demanded by Western creditors. No investments are being made, no work is being done, nothing is being built . . . if my government topples that will cost the international community 10 billion dollars. When I was in the opposition, the European Union promised us 3 billion marks in cash if we brought down Milošević. Where is that money?[21]

Djindjić was not far off the mark. Strikes at the Kolubara coal mine, and also a general strike in October 2001, demonstrated the potential for socioeconomic unrest in Yugoslavia. The plight of the coal miners became a political football, with Koštunica appearing to be sensitive to the miners' demands, and Djindjić refusing to budge on their demand for higher wages, or what he deemed politically motivated "blackmail," or a "political strike inspired by someone well-known to everyone."[22] Djindjić was also annoyed with the West for not delivering adequately on promises of support for economic development. In early December 2001, in a frank interview, he claimed that the reformist forces had been promised $1 billion in reconstruction aid if they took the gamble to topple Milošević. But after October 5, 2000, the outside countries "began pursuing certain tactics . . . and setting conditions . . . there hasn't been a single serious foreign investment this year." Djindjić also bluntly blamed Koštunica for working against Serbia's reformed government. According to Djindjić, the goal of economic transformation requires "blood, sweat and tears," while "Koštunica and his people think this goal can be achieved without paying a certain price."[23]

The economy was still in critical condition at the onset of 2002, although inflation was down to nearly 30 percent. At the end of 2001, the G-17 Institute (an independent reformist think tank) reported that the purchasing power of citizens had significantly increased when compared to a year before, that is, the amount of "consumer basket products that citizens are able to buy for their pay in real terms." It further stated that, "Taken as a whole the government has met the promise made earlier this year. The living standards have improved."[24] Yugoslavia's foreign trade balance had also become somewhat more balanced during 2001, primarily owing to the export of food and live-stock as well as some finished products. Of course, enormous problems in the economy remained, not least of which was the obsolescence of older enter-prises, widespread poverty, and corruption.[25] In a G-17 survey that asked whether there was corruption among public servants, as many as 72.7 percent of the respondents answered affirmatively, 9.2 percent negatively, and 20 percent cautiously made no comment.

Meanwhile, as of early 2002, the U.S. Congress continued to deny Yugoslavia financial aid unless Belgrade would fully accommodate the demands of The Hague Tribunal by March 2002 (as well as provisions in the Dayton accord, and the demand for the release of political prisoners). Most parties in the DOS coalition blamed federal president Koštunica for the con-tinued problems with The Hague. But for Koštunica, refusal to allow The Hague to "write history" for Yugoslavia was a way to defend the "national interest." Serb prime minister Djindjić, in contrast, believed the national inter-est could best be served by cooperation with the international community. Thus, Djindjić recommended that, regarding the matter of The Hague, there should be "less talk and polemics in public on the issue and more endeavor to protect national interests. In the eyes of the world we should be a government that honors its international commitments, makes progress in the democrati-zation process, and deserves support."[26] Milošević's early success during his trial at The Hague made Djindjić's position regarding cooperation with the ICTY more difficult, but the Serbian prime minister still claimed that it was important to cooperate with the international court.

Federalism Reconfigured

Beyond the country's daunting economic problems, Yugoslavia's new leaders also had to confront serious issues related to territorial unity and ethnic rela-tions. For example, by the fall of 2000, political relations between Serbia and Montenegro had deteriorated to the point that the latter republic had essen-tially become a quasi-independent state. The dispute between the two federal units could be traced to decisions made during 1996 and 1997 by Montenegrin political leader Milo Djukanović, and members of his party coalition, to break ranks with the dictatorial methods of the Milošević regime in Belgrade and reorient Montenegro in a more reformist direction (see Chapter 7). This pos-ture, which included Djukanović's cooperation with the international community, and his disavowal of strident nationalism, allowed Montenegro to avoid any substantial destruction during the NATO bombardment of Yugoslavia in the spring of 1999. Moreover, in the wake of NATO hostilities, Montenegro became the back door used by the international community for access to Yugoslavia, and for personal contacts with members of the Serbian opposition.

But despite his independent political posture, Djukanović initially hesitated to endorse the idea of full-blown sovereignty for his small Adriatic republic. Recognizing that public opinion in Montenegro was split rather evenly between those supporting independence for the republic and those favoring continued union with Serbia,[27] and also that the international community opposed Montenegrin separatism, Djukanović bided his time during the last months of the Milošević regime. Meanwhile, Milošević, who was already challenged on several fronts, had chosen not to risk a major military incursion into Montenegro, but rather to isolate and harass the Montenegrin authorities. When Milošević pushed through constitutional changes in July 2000 that essentially eliminated Montenegrin influence in Yugoslavia's political system, Djukanović announced that federalism had essentially ceased to exist, and then hunkered down to await Belgrade's next move.

The DOS electoral victory in September–October 2000 opened a new phase in Serbian–Montenegrin relations. Many observers expected that the post-Milošević regime and the Montenegrin reformists would quickly find common ground and negotiate a new federal arrangement. But dynamics between the two republics turned out to be more complex than had been anticipated. For one thing, the Djukanović forces in Montenegro, who had become accustomed to functioning as independent state authorities both internally and in international relations, began to conduct relations with the new DOS leadership in Belgrade as if they were members of a foreign state elite. For its part, the DOS leadership—still somewhat chagrined that Montenegro had boycotted the September 2000 election, and had taken no major part in Milošević's removal—expected that Djukanović and the Montenegrins would be willing to abandon the anti-Belgrade posture they had adopted in preceding years, and readily participate in the operation of a post-Milošević "democratic" federation.

In early 2001, the political authorities in Belgrade, headed by Koštunica but now also including Serbian prime minister designate Djindjić, engaged in negotiations with the Djukanović leadership in an attempt to find a way out of the impasse between the two republics. But by the end of January, the Montenegrin leadership still remained adamant that the departure point for negotiations was mutual recognition that two independent states, Montenegro and Serbia, were endeavoring to create a "voluntary alliance" of equal units, which would each have a seat in the United Nations, thereby avoiding a "disproportional federation." Montenegro's Djukanović claimed he would go on negotiating for a month or two but, if necessary, would eventually schedule a referendum on the matter of independence (probably after April parliamentary elections in Montenegro). The Montenegrin leader explained that though it might be difficult for the average Serbian citizen to understand, it was precisely because Montenegro has "17 or 18 times fewer people and less territory" than Serbia that the Montenegrins were seeking to be an "equal partner" in any union with Serbia. For the Montenegrin leadership, the joint functions of their proposed bi-state union or confederation would be limited to the army, foreign policy, and a common market and common currency. Djukanović also claimed that Montenegrin equality was a practical and strategic matter, not some kind of "romantic nationalism." Consequently, "any kind of integration between Serbia and Montenegro higher than an alliance between two independent and internationally recognized states . . . would be hard for Montenegro to accept."

Meanwhile, Koštunica and the DOS leadership in Belgrade advanced their proposal outlining a united Yugoslav federal state—premised on the existing position of Montenegro and Serbia in the 1992 Yugoslav constitutional system—in which the federation encompassing the two republics would only have jurisdiction over a small number of joint functions, including foreign policy, national defense, monetary and custom systems, transport and communications, and the protection of basic rights and freedoms (including minority and social rights). Such a "functional federation" would not recognize Montenegro as a separate sovereign state. "Serbia," Koštunica noted, "has no interest in living in some kind of alliance of sovereign states, in some quasi-state of two sovereign states, and pretending the two states are the same as one state."

Most of the DOS elite in Serbia regarded Montenegro's quest for state recognition as "irrational" and contrary to the "integrationist processes in Europe." One DOS leader remarked, for example, "we now have a paradoxical situation in that Djukanović has offered DOS worse conditions for redefining relations in the federation than he offered Milošević." A Serbian economist also claimed that Montenegro would lose more than it would gain from independence: "In the overall scope of the Yugoslav economy Montenegro carries the importance of a statistical error. The domestic product, expenditure, export, and import are all within five percent, except for tourism. . . . Montenegro used to get cheap food from Serbia, but I do not know what they delivered to us except for smuggled cigarettes."

But there was also real concern in Belgrade that Montenegro's secession from Yugoslavia would lead to the withdrawal of substantial promised Western economic assistance (e.g., the EU suggested that its aid was linked to the continuation of a federal system), and would intensify the sovereignty-seeking aspirations of Kosovo's Albanians. The latter development was particularly unacceptable to most Serbs, and had the real potential to foster instability throughout the Balkan region. A declaration of Montenegrin independence could also significantly influence Serbian domestic politics. Thus, the dissolution of the Yugoslav federal state would result in the elimination of the federal presidency—a position currently occupied by President Koštunica. This development would leave Serbia's prime minister, Zoran Djindjić, holding the strongest political position in the post-Milošević landscape, and could possibly motivate Koštunica to run for the presidency of Serbia (a potentially powerful political post at the time marginalized owing to the fact that its incumbent, Milan Milutinović, was a Milošević crony and indicted war criminal).

Hoping to eventually garner sufficient support for the sovereignty of his republic, Djukanović continued to threaten that a referendum on the question of independence would eventually be held. Meanwhile, DOS leaders continued to hope that they could dissuade Djukanović (who criticized "early pessimism" and talked about the need for "mutual compromise") from any unilateral drive towards secessionism, although happily the Belgrade regime also rejected the use of force to preserve the existing Yugoslav federation.

In April 2001, Djukanović suffered a major setback when, in legislative elections, his "Victory of Montenegro–Democratic Coalition" won only 42 percent of the vote (46.8 percent of the seats), against 40 percent for the anti-sovereigntists coalition "Together for Yugoslavia," which took 40.4 percent of the vote and 42.9 percent of the seats. Although Djukanović's coalition achieved considerable support from the republic's Albanians and other minorities, the election results significantly dampened the momentum towards Montenegrin independence. In the wake of the election, Djukanović observed that the polls indicated the existence of a "divided society" and the need for cautious and prudent rule.[28] Djukanović's position was also partially undermined by the decision of the strongly pro-independence Liberal Party—previously allied with Djukanović's Democratic Party of Socialists (DPS) and the Social-Democratic Party—to run alone in the election. With six seats in the Montenegrin parliament of 77, the Liberals could tip the scales in favor of Djukanović's coalition with 36 seats, or the pro-federation "Together for Yugoslavia" coalition with 33 seats. Accusations by the Croatian media that linked Djukanović to a cigarette-smuggling network also weakened his position.

Although throughout the summer and fall of 2001 Djukanović continued to assert his commitment to hold a referendum and create a "union of two independent and internationally recognized states," international pressure mounted against Montenegrin sovereignty. For example, according to French president Chirac in mid-December 2001: "The European Union opposes the idea of an independent Montenegro because it feels that Southeastern Europe has no need to go through a 'process of dissolution' while the process of integration is being strengthened elsewhere on the European continent." Moreover, the United States, which strongly supported a "democratic Montenegro within a democratic Yugoslavia," used considerable financial pressure on Djukanović to secure the preservation of the Yugoslav federation (e.g., not a cent of the $80 million U.S. aid package pledged in 2000 had arrived in Montenegro by early August 2001). At the same time, Djukanović was well aware that it was difficult for Washington to support the pro-Yugoslav forces in Yugoslavia who opposed the extradition of Milošević. This gave the Montenegrin president hope that he could still obtain sympathy in U.S. government circles for an eventual walkout from the Yugoslav federation. Realizing that holding a legitimate referendum would also require the cooperation of Montenegrin parties opposed to independence, Djukanović also focussed attention on cooperation with opposition elements within his own republic.

Meanwhile, the federal government's platform for revamping the federation called for a federal framework of joint states. In September, President Koštunica urged dialogue and compromise between Serbia and Montenegro to preserve Yugoslavia, but also noted that if the citizens of the two republics wished to live in two separate states he would encourage a "peaceful separation." Meanwhile, polls indicated that, as of early in 2002, the Montenegrin people were still divided over the status of their republic, but that when asked if Montenegro should continue to exist together with Serbia, 53.8 percent answered in the affirmative.

In December 2001, Serbian prime minister Djindjić remarked that "the chances of the joint state surviving are greater today than they were a month ago, and particularly six months ago." He attributed his optimism to the international community's inclusion in the negotiations regarding the federation, and he described "hypocritical" the Montenegrin proposal to form an alliance of two independent states.[29] Initially, Montenegrin authorities refused any negotiations with federal and Serbian authorities on the formation of a joint state. But near the end of December 2001, Montenegro and the federal authorities finally agreed that "expert teams" would conduct preliminary negotiations on constitutional and legal issues related to reconfiguring the confederation. The meetings of the experts, however, proved futile. For his part, Djukanović persisted in his pro-independence stance and confirmed his intention to hold a referendum, claiming that Serbia and Montenegro should not be "slaves of the exhausted Yugoslav idea."[30] Djukanović predicted that 2002 would "finally be the year of decision" for Yugoslavia, and also observed that no regime of the "federation type can secure equality in the case of two states whose sizes are completely different."[31]

The situation took another turn in early 2002, when the European Union

and its top foreign policy official, Javier Solana, became more active in negotiations on Montenegro's future. Discussions soon centered on a Solana proposal, which provided a new name, "The Union of Serbia–Montenegro," for
a state arrangement designed to preserve the two-unit federation, but allowing a good deal of devolution to the republican level. As the outline of the
Solana plan emerged—what one expert characterized as "a pragmatic federation with confederative elements"—Serbian and Montenegrin political forces
continued to reject it. But with strong international pressure to preserve the
Yugoslav federation, and with Djukanović facing an internal revolt in his own
party against the sovereigntist option, the time was ripe for a deal.

A tentative agreement was finally reached on March 14, 2002. According
to the plan, the new federal state—called simply "Serbia and Montenegro"—
was to have four federal ministries (foreign affairs, defense, international economic relations, and protection of human and minority rights). The federal
state would also have a one-chamber legislature and a constitutional-
administrative court. The president would be elected by the legislature. Each
of the two-member units in the union would have an opportunity in three years
to reconsider their respective decisions about whether to live in a joint state (if
Montenegro withdraws at that time, Serbia becomes the successor state at the
United Nations). Meanwhile, each unit of the federation will retain separate
customs, monetary, and financial systems. The deal—which still needed to be
confirmed by the assemblies of Montenegro, Serbia, and Yugoslavia—immediately engendered strong criticism from those forces wanting a much more
integrated and centralized federation on the one side, and proponents of Montenegrin independence or Serbian sovereignty on the other. Thus, although the
new arrangement anticipated a reconfiguration of Serb–Montenegrin relations
within a federal system, there was no certainty that the plan would have long-
term viability, or that it was little more than a postponement of Montenegro's
push towards independence.[32]

Kosovo and the New Albanian Insurgency

The collapse of the Milošević regime also opened a new but very difficult phase
with respect to Kosovo and Serb–Albanian relations. For Albanian political
forces in Kosovo, the emergence of a potentially "democratic" post-Milošević
Serbia was not entirely welcome. By the late 1990s, nearly all Albanian political elements in Kosovo—whether extreme or moderate—had come to support
various plans for Kosovo's complete independence (see Chapter 7). Thus, in a
political sense, Kosovars had found both the existence of the repressive
Milošević regime and the initial establishment of the UN–NATO international

protectorate in the province buffering Albanians from Serbian political control to be extremely useful. Because the idea of renewed participation with the Serbian political elite in a joint state was unacceptable to almost all Kosovar leaders, the DOS victory in Serbia and subsequent optimistic statements by international officials regarding the potential for Kosovar–Serbian reconciliation in a common state were not welcome developments.

Koštunica and other DOS leaders, in contrast, came to power firmly committed to Kosovo's reintegration into Serbia and Yugoslavia, although fully aware of the serious impediments to any such outcome. Having criticized Milošević's management of Kosovo, DOS leaders were challenged to provide some way to recover a semblance of sovereignty over Kosovo, and also protect the much reduced community of Serbs still remaining in the province (most of whom fled after the collapse of Serb control in June 1999, when a wave of Albanian revanchism followed the return of Kosovars who had voluntarily or involuntarily been forced out of Kosovo by Milošević's Serbian forces and by the NATO–Yugoslav hostilities). Under the agreement signed by the previous regime with the United Nations, Kosovo technically remains part of the Yugoslav state. But though DOS leaders such as Koštunica and Djindjić regarded Kosovo as an "integral and inalienable part of Serbia and Yugoslavia," they found themselves unable to do much but issue statements about their eventual hope to find a political solution to the Kosovo conundrum. Indeed, Yugoslav officials initially proposed postponing the issue of Kosovo's status until greater stability could be achieved in the Balkan region.

However, even after the OSCE-run (Organization for Security and Cooperation in Europe) local elections of October 2000 in Kosovo, when moderate forces loyal to the Kosovar leader, Ibrahim Rugova, made an impressive showing (58 percent of the vote), and political parties derived from the former KLA did poorly, the prospect of closer ties between Kosovo Albanians and Serbia seemed very remote. As Bernard Kouchner, the UN's highest official in Kosovo for its first eighteen months as an international protectorate, conceded as he departed his post at the end of 2000: "Kosovo remains a violent society in which guns are used to resolve arguments and exact revenge." And Kouchner added: "The Kosovo Albanians have already damaged their reputation in the eyes of the world and undercut international sympathy by the culture of impunity and tolerance for reverse ethnic cleansing and violence."

The existence of a guerilla war organized by extremist Kosovo forces within southern Serbia's five-kilometer-wide security zone along the border with Kosovo (the Ground Safety Zone established by the Kumanovo agreement ending NATO's campaign against Yugoslavia) seriously complicated the situation at the end of 2000 and early 2001. The Albanian militants, most of whom were from Kosovo and Albania proper and were associated with the extremist KLA, were able to infiltrate the buffer zone by circumventing NATO/Kosovo Force (KFOR) troops assigned to patrol the Kosovo border. The infiltrators were also recruiting and training local Albanians living in southern Serbia. Organized as the "Preševo, Medvedja, and Bujanovac Liberation Army" (the Albanian acronym is UCPMB), the Albanian insurgents, who attacked Yugoslav police patrols and kidnapped and killed local Serbs, quickly presented the new Belgrade regime with its first real security crisis.

The insurgency also became an issue in domestic Serbian politics, with President Koštunica advocating the stepped-up activity of KFOR troops to combat Albanian "terrorism" and a reduction in the size of the buffer zone, and Prime Minister Djindjić taking a more bellicose line in advocating the possible use of Yugoslav military personnel against the Albanian militants. Such a tough approach, Djindjić claimed, was "not belligerency, but self-defense." But his remarks were made in the heat of the DOS campaign during Serbian legislative elections, and contemplated measures that were not likely to be permitted by NATO forces in Kosovo. The Albanian insurgency in the Preševo Valley area of the security zone continued throughout early 2001 and was a serious threat to Balkan stability (the buffer zone also bordered politically fragile Macedonia), which threatened to undermine any chance of a peaceful solution to the Kosovo issue and a stable transition in Yugoslavia. Indeed, by February 2001, Albanian infiltrators from Kosovo and southern Serbia had begun an insurrection in Macedonia.

It was only in late May 2001 that a NATO-backed peace accord ended months of fighting between the Albanian rebels and Yugoslav government forces in southern Serbia, and the rebels in the area were finally disarmed. The Serbian deputy prime minister, Nebojša Čović, who also served as head of a newly formed Yugoslav coordinating center for Kosovo, was instrumental in developing the peace plan, which contemplated that Serbian military and police units would eventually be returned to the area in stages. In August, NATO and the Yugoslav army signed an accord allowing Belgrade security forces to control the entire Serbian buffer zone with Kosovo that had been established in 1999. A multi-ethnic police force would also be trained to patrol the area.[33]

During the first half of 2001, numerous international agencies and non-governmental organizations (NGOs) worked hard at transforming political life in the UN-administered former Serbian province of Kosovo. The experiment in state-building and democratization in the Kosovo protectorate was an uphill battle, as a document prepared by the OSCE's Department of Elections in mid-January 2001 suggested. For example, surveys indicated an unwillingness by the majority Albanian population of Kosovo to support a multi-ethnic community, with 72 percent of the Albanian respondents indicating an unwillingness to live in the same state as Serbs, 68 percent unwilling to live in the same city or town, and 80 percent considering a family member entering into marriage with a person of Serb ethnicity as unacceptable. Against this background, in May 2001 a proposal was made by Serbian deputy minister Čović to reorganize Kosovo into two entities. He characterized his proposal as a way to avoid the full partitioning of Kosovo by advancing a compromise that recognized two competing rights: the Serb historical right and the Albanian ethnic right. Needless to say, Čović's plan was completely antithetical to the international community's idea of establishing a multi-ethnic Kosovo, and consequently his remarks caused consternation in the ranks of the United Nations Interim Administration Mission in Kosovo (UNMIK), not to mention among top Kosovo Albanian and Serb leaders.

In May, UNMIK elaborated a Constitutional Framework for Provisional Self-Government in Kosovo, and by the summer the prospects of the upcoming November 2001 election for a central Kosovo legislature began to stir political emotions and episodic violence in Kosovo. The international community exerted considerable pressure on the Serbian regime in Belgrade to permit Kosovo Serb participation the November elections, and registration for the elections by Kosovo Serbs was managed by the OSCE. Yugoslav and Serbian political authorities continuously demanded guarantees for the personal security of Serbs participating in the Kosovo political process (it was estimated that 250,000 Serbs and other non-Albanians had fled Kosovo since June 1999). As Slobodan Samardžić, an advisor to Yugoslav president Koštunica, remarked: "Serbs and Albanians cannot live in Kosovo mixed with each other, but only one [community] alongside the other . . . one way to find a solution [is] to establish autonomy within autonomy."[34]

Initially, local Serb leaders were almost uniformly opposed to participation in the elections (they had already boycotted the municipal elections in October 2000), although most hoped to negotiate fuller autonomy for the Serb community. By September 2001, however, the registration of Serbs was stepped up owing in part to the support of the Serbian Orthodox Church for the electoral process. The only Serbian party to register for the election was the Coalition for Return, KP (Koalicija Povratak), headed by Gojko Savić. Meanwhile, three major Albanian parties emerged in Kosovo: Rugova's Democratic Alliance of Kosovo, LDK; former KLA leader Hashim Thaci's Democratic Party of Kosovo, PDK; and the Alliance for the Future of Kosovo, AAK, led by former KLA commander Ramush Haradinaj.

The results of the Kosovo election gave Rugova's LDK 47 seats in the 120-person Assembly, 26 seats to Thaci's PDK, 22 seats to the Serbian KP, and 8 seats to Haradinaj's AAK. Rugova retained his first-rank position among the Albanians, although his popularity had declined somewhat in comparison to the October 2000 local elections. After the election, Rugova enthusiastically claimed: "Kosovo is practically independent. We are free, under NATO forces." The overwhelming majority of Kosovars shared Rugova's commitment to the idea of Kosovo's eventual fully independent status, despite the unlikelihood of such a scenario being recognized by the international community. Meanwhile, the moderate Serb leaders of Kosovo were hoping to cooperate with the international community's representatives to gradually dampen Albanian attitudes regarding independence. But the Albanians of Kosovo were unlikely to give up their dreams of independence, and would never voluntarily accept reintegration into Serbia or Yugoslavia. In contrast, the citizens of Yugoslavia and most Serbian political leaders opposed Kosovo independence (see Chapter 7), though there was little expectation that the province could be reintegrated into Yugoslavia. Most Serbian politicians, preoccupied with other matters, were reluctant to press the Kosovo issue. Thus, in view of the international community's desire to maintain stability in the Balkans, Kosovo's status as a protectorate was very likely to remain frozen for many years. This situation intensified tension between international bureaucrats ruling Kosovo and the Albanian political leadership, and seemed likely to deepen the Serb–Albanian rift within Kosovo.

Meanwhile, the various Albanian parties in the new central legislature, none of whom enjoyed an absolute majority of seats, could not initially agree among themselves, nor with the Serbs in the legislature, on some form of coalition that would provide the necessary votes for the legislature's election of a new Kosovo president and government. Agreement was only reached at the end of February 2002, after a new UN administrator for Kosovo warned that "there is no functioning society without a stable functioning government . . . it is high time that the parties get their act together. . . . I can help but they have to make the decision."[35] Pushed to make a deal, the two major Albanian parties in the Kosovo legislature finally elected Ibrahim Rugova as president of Kosovo (still a UN protectorate), and an official from Thaci's Democratic Party of Kosovo (Bajram Rexhepi, a surgeon educated in Croatia who was originally a Rugova follower but broke off in 1998 to join the KLA) was awarded the premiership. In their inaugural addresses to their respective three-year terms, Rugova and Rexhepi stated that the independence and freedom of Kosovo would be their priority concerns.[36] For their part, Serb legislators abstained from voting on the new Kosovo executive officials. Indeed, the agreement between the major Albanian parties in the Kosovo Assembly created a substantial Albanian legislative majority or bloc that could effectively marginalize Kosovo's Serb parties. Moreover, the lukewarm commitment of Albanian politicians in Kosovo to the return of refugee Serbs, along with Albanian intentions to fully assert authority over Serb enclaves in the province, will certainly intensify Serb anxiety in the future.

Building Democracy: Difficulties and Trends

The continued salience of the Milošević question in Serbian political life during the first half of 2001, the three-month hiatus before the DOS victory on the federal level was followed by a similar vote in Serbia, and also the subsequent delay in convening a new legislative assembly and installing a Serbian government (finally confirmed on January 24, 2001) were all factors that severely limited the ability of Milošević's successors to quickly dismantle the illiberal structures of the former regime. Thus, it was only in the first few months of 2001 that serious planning began for the restructuring of the police and the judiciary on a nonauthoritarian basis. For example, an advisor to the federal police minister announced that the new government in Serbia would combat corruption and the local mafia by appointing special prosecutors along the lines of the Italian model. Former Milošević cronies that fled abroad would, he claimed, also be extradited to face criminal charges. The prospective Serbian justice minister maintained early in 2001 that after new laws were adopted there would be a "Caesarian section in the judicial system . . . because radical changes in terms of personnel are needed. We have had a situation of unprecedented corruption, unsolved criminal acts, and a marriage of power, capital and big crime. We used to be a Balkan banana republic. To put an end to this we need to create new political institutions."

Early on in the post-Milošević period, according to Serbian human rights activists, ongoing problems associated with the administration of justice in Yugoslavia appeared to result not only from the actions of officials from the old regime, but also from the illegal acts of nonaccountable "informal power centers" (in the judiciary, the prisons, the economy, and other sectors) that took advantage of the vacuum in political authority. Judicial reform thus proceeded at an excruciatingly slow pace during 2001. At the end of the year, for example, Prime Minister Djindjić indicated that it was in the judicial sector that "the least has been accomplished," and that the DSS, headed by Vojislav Koštunica, was on the whole responsible for that situation. "We have several problems," Djindjić remarked, "the laws have been drafted in such a way that there is no way of providing justice through the institutions. Also judges are a class of several thousand people whose replacement is not easy. The third problem is the indecisiveness in the DOS (coalition) . . . how will the courts be capable of judging failing enterprises without humiliating us by allowing local strongmen from influencing the judges in lawsuits where foreign companies and investors will also appear as parties."[37] Djindjić also announced a national program for curbing crime and corruption that would be launched in 2002.

One of the most successful facets of democratization in the country appeared to be in the state sector of the media, which quite quickly helped to create an improved climate for freedom of expression and enhanced pluralism of opinion. For example, an analysis of the print and electronic media conducted in the fall of 2000 claimed that the old division into regime and independent media no longer pertained, and that most media reflected a mainly "neutral tone." In President Koštunica's view, democratic media development in Serbia could rely on historical precedents that go back to the Serbian constitutions of 1888 and 1903. In fact, by distorting reality, according to Koštunica, Milošević's propaganda machine lost credibility and actually helped set the stage for the DOS victory. Near the end of January 2001, the area of electoral democratization was also addressed when legal proceedings were initiated against electoral officials who had attempted to manipulate the September 2000 elections on instructions from Milošević.

Another factor assisting democratic development in Serbia was the relatively substantial and growing number of nongovernmental associations in the republic, many of which were initially formed in the limited but not inconsequential space for pluralistic activity that existed under Milošević's soft dictatorship. Ironically, in the fourteen months after the fall of the Milošević regime, data indicated that the position of NGOs had not significantly improved with regard to their ability to influence government. But some changes did occur according to surveys conducted with NGO members: a better atmosphere existed for access in solving problems; more citizens wished to participate in nongovernmental organizations; there was no longer harassment of NGOs; the climate for communication and expression was much improved; NGOs received better treatment by the media; and the country was more open to the world.[38]

In the spring of 2002, the pressures of the post-Milošević transition on Serbia's new democratic leaders continued to be significant in essential areas: restructuring the economy, creating the rule-of-law and fighting corruption, and fostering democratic political change. An agreement for a renewed federation had finally been reached, but there still remained the serious difficulties of confirming and implementing that arrangement. Meanwhile, the Albanian insurgency in southern Serbia had substantially diminished, and the Kosovo question, though an ongoing concern for the Belgrade regime (e.g., the protection of Serb enclaves and the return of Serb refugees), was no longer a central issue in day-to-day Serbian political life. Thanks to his extradition to The Hague, the problem of what venue would be used to bring Milošević to "justice" no longer directly preoccupied Yugoslavia's leaders. But the politics of extradition with respect to other indicted Serb officials sought by the ICTY still polarized and troubled political forces in Belgrade. Moreover, the drama associated with Milošević's trial continued to excite political commentary and debate in Yugoslavia. Thus, Milošević continued to cast a shadow over

Yugoslav political life, and indirectly influenced clashes among different political forces and personalities.

But, notwithstanding these vexing issues, the most immediate political
problem in Yugoslavia during late 2001 and early 2002 was the coherence of
the DOS coalition. DOS remained a relatively inexperienced and fragile grouping of parties divided by political rivalries, while the unity of its top leadership
in particular remained highly problematic. The incessant struggle for power
within DOS between Koštunica and Djindjić replicated the kinds of political
battles within the former opposition ranks that had retarded Yugoslavia's
democratic political development under Milošević. The Koštunica–Djindjić
face-off also drained energy, time, and resources from other pressing issues,
and undermined foreign confidence in the Yugoslav transition process. On the
other hand, given the proclivities of Serbian political culture to monism, the
strong hand, and centralization, the existence of countervailing power and
competition was not all bad.

Thus, in early 2002, Koštunica remained Yugoslavia's most popular
politician, but his position at the top of the new political hierarchy had fallen
considerably relative to October 2000. Djindjić, meanwhile, was still
extremely unpopular, but his ratings were slowly improving. Of the parties
within DOS, Koštunica's DSS led the popularity race with 17 percent support,
and Djindjić's Democratic Party followed at 15 percent. The other sixteen DOS
parties made up a total of 5 percent. DOS had initially taken shape as a highly
diverse union of political elements united solely for the goal of bringing down
the old regime. It was therefore not surprising that it fragmented in the year
following its historic victory over Milošević. Remarkably, by early 2002, some
sixteen parties were still lined up behind Djindjić and his DS—which might be
called the "Djindjić-bloc"—while in the Serbian Assembly, Koštunica's DSS
had become a *de facto* opposition spearhead, often working with the party
organizations that had comprised the former ruling coalition. As of spring
2002, Koštunica's DSS was still not strong enough to emerge victorious if the
party ran alone against the Djindjić-bloc in a future election. Thus, Koštunica
and his politically conservative and religiously oriented democratic nationalists in the DSS appeared willing to seek constituents from the very societal segments and political forces that had previously been mobilized and exploited
by Slobodan Milošević.

Serbia still did not have a real party system in early 2002, that is, a crystallized governmental team from one party or parties facing an opposition
party or coalition on either the federal or republican levels. Indeed, it was suggested that even the inclusion of the word "opposition" signified by the letter
"O" in the acronym "DOS" confused matters on the political scene, and that
the ruling coalition should drop the "O" and rename itself "DS," that is,

Democratic Serbia (the problem was that the acronym "DS" was already used by Djindjić's party). Intra-DOS rivalry, and particularly the fractious relations between Koštunica's DSS and Djindjić's DS, seemed to reach a high boiling point at the beginning of March 2002, when a bomb was thrown into the head-quarters of the DSS in Belgrade. Koštunica claimed that the incident revealed that "an extremely serious moment had been reached," and that Serbian "society is in a deep crisis."[39] At the same time, Yugoslavia seemed to be slowly moving towards a more crystallized multi-party system. The next elections will probably see DOS—minus the DSS—facing the DSS and the other old ruling bloc parties. In other words, a kind of European, substantially left of center reformist democratic bloc may be competing with a democratic nationalist bloc that is supported by remnant parties from the pre-war regime. The pos-sibility that G-17—an independent network of intellectuals and professionals committed to reform—might constitute itself as a political party and become a "third force" in some future election is a factor that could also reshape the party system in Serbia.

In view of these circumstances, the Serbian transition to post-authoritarian rule is likely to prove protracted and characterized by intense political infight-ing. The first phase of the transition has not been all that positive, but the over-all trend has been forward. In early 2001, Yugoslav foreign minister Svilanović observed: "We have to be aware that from where we were—a kind of dictator-ship until very recently—to where we want to be—and this is a stable and open economy and stable political institutions—we might have to pass through a period of difficult, very corrupted society . . . it may be inevitable to go through it, but maybe it can last several months, not several years." In spite of these con-siderable obstacles, it can be said that during 2001 and early 2002, the process of democratic consolidation in Serbia had begun in earnest. The present trend of democratic consolidation is, however, by no means free of major difficulties. Thus, the absence of a true opposition and the lack of a balanced distribution of power among the three branches of the governmental system are disturbing facets of the initial transition period. Indeed, there does seem to be a very strong predominance of executive power in both federal and Serbian political life, at the expense of legislative and judicial influence. But it is fair to say that there also exists a much stronger civil society than in earlier years, and also, for all its flaws, a more pluralistic party system with at least two or three countervailing party blocs. Still, until privatization of the economy is more fully implemented, Serbia will lack the strong middle class that can become the bulwark of a stable demo-cratic order.[40]

The positive trends do not ensure that a reversion to the values and behav-ior patterns associated with the Milošević regime may not present a danger to Serbia's future political transition, or guarantee that a climate conducive to some form of authoritarianism may not re-emerge. Indeed, part of the reaction among the Serbian public to the initial phase of the Milošević trial at The Hague illustrates that the embryonic elements of renewed national populism are still present in Serbian society (the potential difficulties of implementing a new agreement between Serbia and Montenegro, and also the perennial hazards associated with Serb–Albanian relations, may also feed the same tendency).[41] This does not mean that in the foreseeable future the specious super-patriotism and discredited soft dictatorship of the Milošević variety are likely to hold great appeal. Thus, the more virulent xenophobic and radically authoritarian facets of Serbian political culture, though certainly still embedded in the value matrix of the society, have waned considerably following the fall of Milošević. But a strong yearning for order and even charismatic leadership will be present in Serbian political life in the years ahead.

The genetic structure of Serbian political culture, as shaped by Serbia's historical experience, which by and large is not associated with liberal democracy, cannot be easily altered. As the former Tito-era politician and historian Latinka Perović observed in July 2001: "It remains to be seen whether the removal of Milošević marked a clean break with the past policy, or the dislodgement of a dictator who embodied that policy [and] paved the way for a continuation of that very policy, but with other instruments. That in fact is a key question, and is currently under examination every day."[42] The former anti-Milošević dissident Vesna Pešić recently made a similar observation from her vantage point as Yugoslavia's ambassador to Mexico: "Milošević's departure has not eliminated from political life [an] anachronistic tendency which is keeping us away from the developed world. He is gone as a personality, but [his] mental makeup or world view has not disappeared. Not only has it not disappeared, it is, in fact, still very strong."[43] Milošević may be politically dead and presently locked up on the North Sea, but Serbia has yet to bury his legacy and the long-standing values that brought him to power.

NOTES

1. One of the best recent accounts of anti-regime nongovernmental organization (NGO) activities during the 1990s listed the following "key" factors that were most responsible for the fall of the Milošević regime: (1) the "creation of a firm coalition of various political parties, movements, trade unions and minority and national communities" committed to toppling the Milošević regime; (2) the withdrawal of Drašković's Serbian Party of Renewal (SPO) from the political scene; and (3) the decision by the coalition to back Vojislav Koštunica as a presidential candidate. Other "necessary political preconditions" for the fall of Milošević included NGO and independent and media activity; the activity of the Otpor (Resistance) movement; door-to-door campaigning to get out the vote for the September 2000 election; the work of the Center for Free Elec-

tions and Democracy; intensive work of think tanks of independent intellectuals working with the media; support of the civil sector by international organizations and donors; and the new political, economic, and social contexts created by the 1999 Kosovo war (particularly the Serb refugees from Kosovo who entered Serbia, and the regime's "vulgar propaganda that it had achieved a grand historical victory" in Kosovo). One of the most difficult aspects of the post-Milošević period, it is argued, has been to overcome the "unreal" and "dangerous" dreams that "everything may be solved by abolishing the role of one man, or rather one family. People tended to forget that this authoritarian personal rule was the consequence of much more complex relations and the historical and political contexts." Velimir Curgus Kazimir, "From Islands to the Mainland," in *The Last Decade: Serbian Citizens in the Struggle for Democracy and an Open Society 1991–2001* (Belgrade: Medija Center, 2001). See also Mladen Lazić, *Rački hod: Srbija u transformacijskim procesima* (Belgrade: Filip Višnjić, 2000); Ivana Spasić and Milan Subotić (eds.), *Revolucija i poredak: o dinamici promena u Srbiji* (Belgrade: Institut za filozofiju i društvenu teoriju, 2001); and Dragan Bujošević and Ivan Radovanović, *5. Oktobar: dvadeset četiri sata prevrata* (Belgrade: Medija Center, 2001).

2. The ICTY asked the Yugoslav authorities to discuss the arrest and transfer to The Hague of Milošević, four of his former ministers, and a number of other Serbs (including some from Bosnia such as Radovan Karadžić and Ratko Mladić) who have been indicted for war crimes.

3. President Bush was required to certify by April 1, 2001, whether Yugoslavia was cooperating with the ICTY, or Congress could withhold several hundred million dollars promised to Yugoslavia. Washington could also veto Yugoslavia's application to join the World Bank.

4. The Belgrade prison governor wrote a book about Milošević's captivity in Belgrade, in which he claims that the former ruler said he should have fled into exile while he still had a chance. According to the account, Milošević exhibited a good deal of relaxed defiance while in the Belgrade prison, blamed the Germans for the dissolution of Yugoslavia, and felt he was the "moral victor" in the 1999 confrontation with NATO. The book also emphasized Milošević's extremely close relationship with his wife, Mira Marković. Dragiša Blanuša, *Čuvao sam Miloševića: Dnevnik iz ćelije broj 1121* (Belgrade: Glas javnosti, 2001). Milošević's lawyers claimed that their imprisoned client dismissed the book as a "tissue of lies." Belgrade authorities eventually removed Blanuša from his post for violating Milošević's privacy. In the year after Milošević's fall from power, several more books appeared on the fallen leader. For example, Vojislav Lalić, *Pad* (Belgrade: Zavet, 2001); Djuro Zagorac, *Slobodan Milošević: lične i političke drame* (Belgrade: Archive Media, 2001); Borisav Jović, *Knjige o Miloševiću* (Belgrade: Nikola Pašić, 2001); Dragan Vukšić, *Pukovnikov otkaz krvavomu komandantu: Miloševićevo srljanje na mač NATO alijanse* (Belgrade: Nidda, 2001); and Dejan Lukić and Pero Simić, *Vatre i potop* (Belgrade: Filip Višnjić, 2001).

5. Surveys in spring 2001 indicated that Koštunica's initially high popularity ratings were slowly declining, and the substantially less popular Djindjić was slowly picking up support among the population.

6. Paris, *Agence-France Presse*, August 31, 2001.

7. *London Free Press*, December 12, 2001.

8. Transcripts for the Milošević trial at the International Criminal Tribunal for the Former Yugoslavia can be found on the ICTY website: Transcripts Milošević "Kosovo, Croatia, Bosnia Herzegovina" (IT–02–54) at http://www.un.org/icty/transe54/transe54.htm.

9. In this regard, the prosecution found justification in remarks made by the chairman of the International Commission that explored the causes of the Balkan wars in 1912–1913.

10. See Chapter 2. SANU member Vasilije Krestić claimed that The Hague prosecution was using the Memorandum because the prosecutors lacked proof and "are ready to manipulate history and historic documents . . . according to the needs and goals of the court. . . . [N]ot only Slobodan Milošević is sitting in the defendant's chair, but also the SANU and its members who dared—during the time of the one-party authorities—not to think in the same way as the communist party." *Večernje novosti*, February 23, 2002, p. 2. SANU also issued a statement signed by its president, Dejan Medaković, reaffirming the conclusions of the Memorandum, and attacking The Hague Tribunal for alleging the "greater Serbia character of the Memorandum." *BETA*, February 25, 2002. The prosecutor's office at The Hague Tribunal also commissioned, for use by the Tribunal's judges, an independent academic study concerning the development of Serbian nationalism during the twentieth century.

11. The tribunal's profile of Milošević's personality (compare Chapter 3) suggests he is a "clever and ambitious man . . . not a racist in the sense of someone determined to live only with fellow Serbs, not an idealist; someone concerned more, if not exclusively, with the maintenance of personal power . . . a complex man. A man who would leave no traces if he could avoid them or who indeed destroyed traces of his control. A man who in order to do that avoided large meetings . . . preferred one-to-one encounters, personal control. . . . A man who was prepared to use different objectives to stimulate different people; all Serbs in one state, anti-capitalism, or when dealing with the international community, the preservation of the integrity of the former Yugoslavia, as appropriate summaries of his position. A man who it may be thought counted on the short-term memories of observers and who was able to play the peacemaker. A man, it may be, who simply regards those as fools who cannot see how easy it is to say one thing and to do another." *ICTY Transcripts*, February 12, 2002, p. 44.

12. BBC, February 19, 2002. Timothy Garton Ash has persuasively argued that a truth and reconciliation commission that attempts to concentrate not on attributing blame primarily to what one's own people have done, but to everyone involved in a multi-sided interethnic struggle, is unlikely to provide a real catharsis for the ethnic community conducting the trial. Ash remarks that neither the "Slobo and Carla show from The Hague" or a Belgrade-directed Truth and Reconciliation Commission focussed on both Serb *and* non-Serb crimes will prove helpful at breaking through "the immensely strong psychological barrier of denial . . . when people feel themselves to be victims of history, as most Serbs do." The Serbs, Ash suggests, need a Serb-oriented "domestically produced reality show." *Guardian*, March 7, 2002, p. 19. The seeming surge of nationalism in Serbia during the early stage of the Milošević trial runs against

the notion that by individualizing guilt, or conducting a "narrow and well-focussed purge" of only the major perpetrators of war crime, a trial, such as the type being undertaken at The Hague, can lessen the danger of a "nationalist backlash." See Gary Jonathon Bass, *Stay the Hand of Vengeance: The Politics of War Crimes Tribunals* (Princeton: Princeton University Press, 2000), pp. 300–301.

13. See, for example, Louise Branson, "With Milošević on Trial, Reconciliation Becomes a Casualty in the Balkans," *Washington Post*, February 24, 2002, p. B1.

14. David Holly, "Ruin Marks Blood, Honor in Kosovo; Yugoslavia," *Los Angeles Times*, February 26, 2002, Part A, Part I, p. 4.

15. *The Jashari's, the Story of a Resistance* (Skenderaj, Kosova: Rilindja, 2001).

16. Belgrade, Radio B–92, February 24, 2002.

17. See *BETA*, February 20, 2002, and *The Independent*, February 26, 2002, p. 14.

18. *BETA*, March 2, 2002.

19. Teofil Pančić suggests that Milošević's behavior at The Hague "cannot tell us why and how Milošević lost power, but can indicate how he so easily rose to power and held on to power for such a long time. . . . [H]is demagogical populist rhetoric is based on exploitation of deeply embedded prejudices in the mob-mindset. . . . Milošević easily and naturally fitted into the majority 'ambiance,' into the dumb mindset of the majority, by slyly insisting in the stages of the consolidation of his power, on sending, through every gesture and word, conduct and appearance, a coded message to the 'people': I am one of you, you like me for my contrived grayness—both physically and spiritually—you recognize a somewhat more 'sophisticated' version of yourselves." "Sex in the City, Sloba and The Hague," *Helsinki Charter*, No. 49 (February 2002). A decision by Serbian authorities to end live broadcasts of the Milošević trial in Yugoslavia touched off small protests by Milošević supporters in Belgrade. The shutdown by Prime Minister Djindjić and Radio-Television Serbia was an indication of the concern over the political impact of The Hague proceedings.

20. The procedures for the ICTY are a hybrid of practice from common law tradition ("the adversarial mode") and the continental civil law system ("the inquisitional mode"). The various judges on the court and members of the prosecution do not share a common legal culture, and officers of the court tend to apply whatever norms "come naturally." For example, when it comes to criminal law, the common law practice includes detailed rules on the admissibility of evidence to the court, and also rules regarding what the actors in the court can expect from one another. In contrast, civil court judges tend to allow more evidence into a case than a common law trial would permit. Also, in the civil law tradition, the judge takes a more active role in the direction of the trial and questioning. The blend of two legal traditions sometimes creates tensions and certain awkward facets of ICTY trials, and also seems to account for the more politicized character of such trials than would be the case under a pure common law system. One former American judge, who served on the ICTY, described such mixed ingredients and called the prosecutor the "chief policy maker and political lightning rod of the tribunal." Moreover, the rules of the tribunal have been tilting away from the Anglo-American common law practice in recent years. Patricia Wald, "The International Criminal Tribunal for the Former Yugoslavia Comes of Age: Some Observations

on Day-to-Day Dilemmas of an International Court," *Washington University Journal of Law and Policy*, Vol. 87, No. 5 (2001).

21. *Der Spiegel*, July 16, 2001.

22. Tanjug, October 4, 2001.

23. *Suddeutsche Zeitung*, December 5, 2001.

24. *Večernje novosti*, December 27, 2001, p. 7.

25. See Boris Begović and Boško Mjiatović (eds.), *Corruption in Serbia* (Belgrade: Center for Liberal-Democratic Studies, 2001).

26. Tanjug, December 21, 2001.

27. On the development and intensity of different types of nationalism among various subgroups within the Montenegrin population, see Borislav Djukanović, Bora Kuzmanović, Mladen Lazić, and Miloš Bešić, *Nacija i država: istraživanje nacionalne svijesti i stanovišta o državi u Crnoj Gori* (Podgorica, Montenegro: CID and Socen, 2001).

28. *ARP*, April 25, 2001.

29. *BETA*, December 26, 2001.

30. Tanjug, December 16, 2001.

31. Tanjug, December 20, 2001.

32. The post-Milošević elite in Belgrade is also under constant challenge from forces in Vojvodina who have been pushing for greater political autonomy, although legislation adopted in 2001 by the Serbian Assembly was designed to accommodate such demands. Meanwhile, a new federal law adopted in late February 2002 was meant to establish fuller rights for ethnic minorities. The new law established a federal Minorities Council, consisting of representatives from minority communities.

33. In the summer of 2001, a new rebel group, the Albanian National Army (ANA), was reportedly set up in southern Serbia, but local Albanians denied its existence. The Albanians in southern Serbia also established a National Council to advance their concerns about Serbian policy in the region.

34. For a recent and very useful Albanian-oriented history of Serb–Albanian relations, see Petrit Imami, *Srbi i Albanci kroz vekove* (Belgrade: Samizdat, Free B–92, 2000).

35. Paris, *Agence-France Presse*, February 15, 2002.

36. Rexhepi appointed one of Kosovo's most renowned Albanian activists, Adem Demaci (see Chapter 4), as his advisor. At the roundtable "The Impact of the Milošević Trial on Serb–Albanian Relations," in March 2002, Demaci commented that Milošević's punishment at The Hague would not influence Serb–Albanian relations, or the future of Kosovo, and also that the worst punishment for Milošević would be the independence of Kosovo. KosovoLive, March 9, 2002.

37. December 26, 2001. The post-Milošević political elite also continues to face the problem of hundreds of unsolved crimes connected with the breakdown of law and order and state-sponsored murders during the last years of the Milošević regime. While in late 2000 the incoming DOS leadership promised to deal with such problems, prominent cases such as the murders of Slavko Ćuruvija and Ivan Stambolić still remain open. See, for example, Latinka Perović (ed.), *Case of Ivan Stambolić* (Belgrade: Helsinki Committee for Human Rights in Serbia, 2001). On the importance of corruption and

criminalization as major factors in Serbian political life, see *Challenges of Implementing the Reform Agenda: One Year After the Democratic Breakthrough* (Belgrade: United Nations Development Program, 2001), pp. 91–94.

38. Žarko Paunović, "Novi odnosi nevladinog sektora i vlasti," *Republika*, No. 272 (2001).

39. Radio-Television Serbia, March 1, 2002. In early March, Nenad Čanak, the head of the League of Social Democrats of Vojvodina, one of the smaller parties in the DOS coalition, tabled a proposal at the DOS presidency urging the expulsion of the DSS from DOS. A few days later, the DSS withdrew from the DOS presidency, although party spokesmen warned that the DSS was not leaving DOS itself, and that any move to strip the party of its seats in legislative bodies would touch off a major crisis. When Djindjić-led DOS forces in the Serbian Assembly expelled 35 delegates from the legislature, including 21 members of the DSS, on the pretext of their chronic absenteeism, the entire DSS 45-member contingent boycotted the body. In mid-July, against the background of such polarization, a presidential election was scheduled for September 29, 2002. It was initially unclear if Koštunica would decide to step away from his federal post and run for the Serbian presidency as a way to challenge Djindjić's control of Serbia. In any case, Koštunica remained the most popular political figure in Yugoslavia, and it seemed that his struggle with Djindjić would continue for some time.

40. Veljko Vujačić, "Godina dana kasnije: neki problemi konsolidacije demokratskog poretka u Srbiji," *Prizma*, December 2001, pp. 17–19.

41. On the continued appeal of nationalist values among Serbian young people, including those connected with resistance to the Milošević regime, see Vladimir Ilić, *Otpor—vise ili manje od politike* (Belgrade: Helsinki odbor, 2001), pp. 33–40.

42. Radio Free Europe, July 15, 2001. On the failure of the post-Milošević regime to come to terms with recent Serbian history, see Dubravka Stojanović, "DOS otvaranje traumatičnog kruga?" *Republika,* (2002) No. 286–287, and Olivera Milosavljevic, "New/Old Nationalism," in *The Balkans Rachomon: Historiography and Literature on the Dissolution of Yugoslavia* (Belgrade: Helsinki Committee for Human Rights, 2002), pp. 46–75.

43. *BETA*, December 13, 2001.

PART I

THE KOSOVO FACTOR AND THE RISE OF A SERB "HERO"

CHAPTER 1

Nationalism and Political Power in Kosovo: From the Sultanate to Slobodan Milošević (1912–1986)

> The Serb of today looks at [Kosovo] as part of his birthright, and of its recapture the young men see visions and the old men dream dreams. . . . Ineradicably fixed in the breast of the Albanian . . . is the belief that the land has been his for all time. The Serb conquered him, held him for a few passing centuries, was swept out and shall never return again. He has but done to the Serb as he was done by.
>
> —*Edith Durham*, High Albania *(1909)*

Kosovo (Kosova in Albanian),[1] a small and, up until the end of the second millennium, remote region of Southeastern Europe, is historically renowned as the area where a mainly Slavic army failed to defeat expansionist Ottoman Turk forces in June 1389. That legendary battle, which occurred on the so-called Field of Blackbirds at Kosovo Polje, marked the terminal phase of the Serbian medieval state. In military terms, the battle is now thought to have been a draw, and it would actually take another seventy years for the Turks to conquer Serbia.[2] For most of the roughly six centuries between the Ottoman conquest and present times, ethnic conflict between Kosovo's two principal ethnic communities, the Albanians and Serbs, has been deep and persistent. It would be inaccurate, however, to explain such conflict as a product of primordial or immutable "hatreds" that constitute the entire fabric of ethnic relations in the region. Thus, periods of nonviolent Serb–Albanian interaction, and even, at times, intergroup cooperation at both the mass and elite levels, also formed an integral part of the region's history. Indeed, the fact that episodic interethnic coexistence and also violent intergroup conflict have both been features of Kosovo's history is an important dimension of the complex

South Balkans that is frequently lost in the contemporary swirl of contending interests and propaganda about the region.

Both Albanians and Serbs alike regard Kosovo as part of their national patrimony, a critical zone in their early historical development as peoples, and also seminal in their respective nineteenth-century national awakenings. This dual claim to Kosovo has been at the core of conflict between the two ethnic communities. For most Albanians, the Serbs are relatively recent interlopers in the Balkan peninsula whose medieval control of Kosovo hardly serves as a basis for Serbian claims of permanent territorial ownership. Ismail Kadare, a leading Albanian writer and poet expresses the emotional character of Albanian–Serb differences over the "facts" regarding Kosovo.

> Any discussion on Kosovo today begins with the cliché: "sacred territory for the Serbs"; "the cradle of the Serb nation.". . . The core of the [Serb] mythology goes as follows: at the time of the Battle in 1389, the Serbs were in a majority in a region that was at the heart of their Kingdom; the Albanians only came into the territory after the Battle. This is a crude distortion and its effect in any public discussion on TV or elsewhere is to preempt any Albanian from putting across a different view or attempting some clarification of history. . . . The Battle of Kosovo was not a confrontation solely between Serbs and Turks. It was a battle fought by all the people of the Balkans united against an invader. All the histories list the names of the Balkan peoples who fought alongside one another against a common disaster: Serbs, Bosnians, Albanians, and Romanians. . . . The Battle, which should have been preserved in memory as a symbol of friendship between the Balkan peoples, was appropriated exclusively by criminal Serbs to serve their purposes.[3]

In contrast, most Serbs hold Kosovo in special regard because it is the site where their state was first created and flourished (from the twelfth to the fifteenth century), a development that occurred well before the Albanians—who had settled in the Balkan peninsula earlier than the Serbs—contemplated such a state-building goal. "Kosovo is the cradle of the medieval Serbian state," the Serbian writer Dobrica Ćosić points out, "with Christian relics which have a high artistic value. Kosovo is the source of major epic poetry and is the precious receptacle of the Serbs' spiritual identity. It is not a piece of land, it is the Serb identity. With the loss of Kosovo [near the end of the twentieth century], the Serb people has been spiritually mutilated."[4] Albanians not only came late to the process of state-building, but are also often viewed by Serb ultranationalists as a primitive people who accomplished little through their own energies, failed to appreciate the benefits of Serb "civilization," and who after, in large part, embracing the religion of the Ottoman conquerors,[5] ruthlessly collaborated in the subjugation of the area's non-Islamic population. Thus, throughout and beyond the apogee of Ottoman rule, many Serbs have regarded the period of Islamic control over the Balkans as a joint Turkish–Albanian enterprise, in which non-Muslims, although enjoying a measure of ecclesiastical autonomy, were—depending on the period and the region of imperial rule from Constantinople—subjected to various measures of cruelty, discrimination, and repression.[6] Indeed, in Serbian popular imagination, the Albanians are often substituted for the Ottoman Turks when assigning responsibility for the Serbs' 1389 military setback in Kosovo. For the Serbs, the battle of Kosovo was not just a defeat to be avenged, but also an event to celebrate the valor of the Serbs exhibited in defending Orthodox Christian and "Western" civilization. As such, the myth of Kosovo evolved into a "philosophy of suffering," a case of national victimization, the "Serbian Golgotha," sentiments that became central features of Serbian political culture. As one Serbian author has described it, the myth of Kosovo

> served as a political program in demands for freedom, unification and [an] independent state, as a patriotic motive when it was necessary to strengthen the confidence in one's own devices, as a war cry when it was necessary to show heroism. It was used in developing moral principles, judging good and evil. On the other hand, it nurtured irrational notions . . . it promoted reconciliation to one's fate, fatality and necessity of sacrifice by promising the "Kingdom of Heaven," it favored death over life . . . its role was fatal when it became [a] lifestyle or political program.[7]

In their most emotional and extreme versions, both Serb and Albanian perspectives on Kosovo are often exaggerated, and replete with inaccuracy. For example, relations between Albanians and Turks were not only characterized by frequent cooperation against the Serbs, but also by Albanian–Turk rivalry, and an ongoing pattern of Albanian rebellion against Ottoman power. Indeed, in 1908–1909, Serbs and Montenegrins would assist Albanians in an uprising against Turkish control, while a substantial number of non-Muslim Albanians were enlisted to assist the forces of Serbia–Montenegro in the Balkan wars.[8] Misrepresentations also characterize pro-Albanian interpretations of Kosovo history, which often downplay or glibly dismiss the discrimination and other injuries suffered by Serbs and other non-Muslims under Ottoman rule. Thus, compared to many other authoritarian and imperial regimes, the level of religious toleration and self-government by ethno-religious communities within the Ottoman empire was often impressive. But such relative benefits were hardly a compensation to its subject non-Muslim peoples such as the Serbs, who generally possessed only a second-class citizenship behind Turks, Bosnian Muslims, Albanians of the Muslim faith, and other Islamic communities, and could not erase the deeply engrained negative sentiments stimulated by the reality of such discriminatory rule. Self-confident about the primacy of their claim to Kosovo, Albanians often underestimate or ignore historically shaped Serbian anxieties about living as a political minority in Balkan state units. Moreover, exaggerated claims of intergroup coexistence and tolerance in the history of Kosovo and the Ottoman-controlled Balkans[9] have often led to a mistaken optimism in current policy-making expectations regarding the prospects for harmonious Serb–Albanian relations. That optimism, just as the policy consequences of the antipodal pessimism that assumes modern Balkan violence is the inexorable outcome of hatreds shaped in the Middle Ages or the early Ottoman period, is one of many issues discussed more fully in the conclusion of this study.

In any event, throughout the twentieth century reciprocal ethnic stereotypes, nationalist myths, and contending collective mindsets, such as those historically exhibited by both Albanians and Serbs, have remained enduring features of the Balkan landscape. More importantly, nationalist ideologues and political activists in the Balkans have typically exploited such perceptions and beliefs in order to mobilize support of their respective ethnic constituencies, and also to legitimate their quest or exercise of power. Such nationalistically rationalized patterns of rule have routinely crystallized into a system of ethno-political stratification, that is, the positioning of ethnic groups on a hierarchy of political power that itself, over time, influences perspectives between and among different ethnic, confessional, and cultural communities.

In the case of Kosovo, the alternating sequence of political domination between Albanians and Serbs, and the strong animosities dividing the two groups, generated in part by the experience that each ethnic community endured under the control of the other, is crucial to an understanding of contemporary conflict in the region. Moreover, the focus of this book—consideration of the emergence, evolution, and eventual demise of the Milošević regime—is closely connected to the alternation of ethnic elites in Kosovo, and particularly how successive nationalist authorities exercised brutal, discriminatory, or exclusivist policies towards members of ethnic groups who previously held power. In order to provide a historical context for the book's subsequent discussion of the Milošević regime's development, the present chapter surveys the changing dynamics of power and elite control in Kosovo from the collapse of Turkish rule during the Balkan Wars (1912–1913), to the twilight years of the Titoist regime in the mid-1980s.

Re-conquest and Internal Colonialism: 1912–1940

In the fall of 1912, during the First Balkan War, the newly independent Serbian state re-conquered the Kosovo region from Turkey, thereby achieving a goal that had long been at the core of the Serbian national mindset. Indeed, even before they had failed to stop the Ottoman incursion into the Balkans at the battle of Kosovo, the Serbs had established the first Patriarchate of their Orthodox Church in Kosovo at Peć in 1346. Soon after the battle, legends and religious iconography concerning the fourteenth-century conflict with the Turks became an important underpinning of Serb mythology. As a result, over the next five and a half centuries memories of Kosovo and latent Serbian ethno-nationalism became inextricably linked. It is, therefore, hardly accidental that during the first part of the nineteenth century, the recovery of Kosovo became a central feature in the awakening of Serb national consciousness, including Serb state-seeking aspirations.[10] Thus, only 34 years before the Balkan Wars, during negotiations at the 1878 Congress of Berlin—which recognized Serbia's *de jure* independence from Ottoman rule (technically achieved a few months earlier under the Treaty of St. Stefano)—Serbian politicians were anguished when they were forced to accept territorial borders that denied them control of Kosovo (only partially and temporarily occupied by Serb troops during the Russo–Ottoman War of 1877–1878). At the same time, however, Montenegro, already *de facto* an independent kingdom, and composed largely of Slavic inhabitants that constitute a branch of the Serbian ethnic family, was legally recognized as a sovereign state and allocated a small slice of Ottoman-controlled northwestern Kosovo, much to the chagrin of the Albanians. Still, at this point in time, the Serbs of Serbia and their ethnic kinsmen in Montenegro were not yet territorially connected in one state. The recapture of Kosovo in 1912 was the source of enormous jubilation to the Serbs, who were by now also linked to their Montenegrin brethren in a military alliance. Serbian and Montenegrin authorities also had some success in enlisting Kosovo Albanians—particularly of the Orthodox and Catholic faiths—to join in the anti-Ottoman alliance during the Balkan wars. Serbian troops not only sang "On to Gazimestan," referring to the site of the 1389 battle, but soldiers are said to have reverentially removed their peasant moccasins (*opanke*) when crossing the battleground, and sometimes to have taken bits of soil as a remembrance of the occasion. A journalist chronicling this history and travelling with the Serbian army wrote that: "Mass was held today at Kosovo, and a requiem for Lazar [the King who led the army against the Ottomans in 1389] in the place that he was killed . . . the first Christian Orthodox Mass at this site after more than 500 years."[11] As a result of its victories in the Balkan Wars of 1912 and 1913, Serbia doubled its territory from 48,300 to 87,300 square kilometers, and increased its population from 2.9 million to 4.4 million. But the socio-economic toll on the country was horrific, and together with subsequent losses in World War I, would have an important influence in strongly reinforcing the already deeply felt sense of victimization characterizing Serbian political culture. But by fulfilling their national dream and militarily seizing Kosovo at the end of 1912, Serbia had temporarily extinguished the hopes of Albanian state-seeking forces. Indeed, it was in Kosovo at Prizren in 1878 that the Albanians had established their first national movement, which aimed at achieving, if not full state independence, at least a unified Albanian zone within the Ottoman Empire (hopefully by linking four Turkish administrative units into one political entity). From 1908 to 1912, Albanian insurgents had successfully waged a rebellion against the Turks, and eventually were promised a quasi-independent status for their ethnic community in the Balkans. That Albanian entity, or virtual state, would have included the territory of Kosovo. In brief, during the late nineteenth century, and the first decade of the twentieth century, Kosovo had become the epicenter for efforts by Albanian intellectuals and political activists to reawaken "Albanianism" as a basis for state formation. Thus, while Serbia celebrated the conquest of Kosovo in 1912, and, together with Montenegro and Greece, also managed to temporarily seize parts of northern Albania, the disparate consequences for Serbs and Albanians associated with the end of Ottoman power in the Balkans opened a new chapter in interethnic antagonism. The Serbs' long-awaited revenge for their fourteenth-century national "defeat" by the Turks was accomplished, but at the expense of Albanian nationalist goals, and the traumatic territorial division of the area's ethnic Albanian population. Instead of becoming part of the independent Albanian state established in November 1912, Kosovo was reincorporated into the Serbian Kingdom.[12] This new reality seriously exacerbated the preexisting Serb–Albanian ethnic conflict, spawning episodes of intercommunal violence that would wax and wane throughout the entire twentieth century.

The ferocity of the Balkan Wars of 1912 and 1913 was a further stimulant to Serb–Albanian conflict. One of the most fascinating accounts of the actual course of military activity and civilian suffering during the wars was offered by the Russian revolutionary Leon Trotsky, who covered the war as a journalist for a Ukrainian newspaper. Trotsky, drawing on his own experience in the region, and also other eyewitness accounts, not only treats the war as a story of how "Turkish despotism" was overcome, but also how the various Balkan states—Serbia, Montenegro, Bulgaria, Romania and Greece—utilized "their own barbarous methods [in] destroying that despotism." Trotsky's revolutionary Marxist political agenda was to reveal how the large and small capitalist countries (Russia and the "Balkan dynasties"), who either supported or carried out the war against Turkey, were compromised by the atrocities committed during the struggle. But he also provides an important glimpse of the character and political context of the 1912–1913 wars. He concludes, for example, that the "Bulgars in Macedonia, and the Serbs in 'Old Serbia'

(Kosovo), in their national endeavor to correct data in the ethnographical statistics that are not quite favorable to them, are engaged quite simply in systematic extermination of the Muslim population in the villages, towns and districts." But Trotsky extensively quotes from the observations of a Serbian officer, who claimed that "responsibility for atrocities lies, however, only to a minor extent with the regular forces." Rather he blames irregular militia elements (chetniks), a mixture of "intellectuals, men of ideas, nationalist zealots," as well as "isolated individuals . . . thugs, robbers" and those "who had joined the army for the sake of loot. They sometimes came in handy because they held life cheap—not only the enemy's but their own as well."

Trotsky also relies upon the same officer's description of the Albanians. Thus, although the Serb officer acknowledges the Albanians' "courage," he adds that such "bravery of theirs is of a quite particular sort. . . . They throw themselves impetuously into an attack, reckless of the consequences, smashing everything they can, utterly ruthless in their onslaught and in slaughtering the vanquished." As for the atrocities against Muslims committed by the irregular militia, Trotsky points out that such undisciplined activity caused the Serbian Army command to "disband them [the militia] even before the end of hostilities, although the Bulgarian Army command did not do likewise."[13]

Serbia's long-awaited reintegration of Kosovo was soon interrupted by the destabilization and widespread destruction of Southeastern Europe during World War I. The young Serbs whose "tyrannicide" in Bosnia would precipitate the First World War in 1914 were in part motivated—as so many other Serbian activists in the decades of the preceding century—by the Kosovo myth's heroic notion of expelling the foreign enemy from Serbian soil. But in the course of battle, Serbia was once again forced to cede control of Kosovo to foreign powers, this time Austria–Hungary and Bulgaria. Many of the Albanians of Kosovo, who had been under Serbian rule for only a few years, viewed the new occupying forces as liberators. Serbian authorities had treated Albanians of the Muslim faith particularly harshly between 1912 and 1914, and many had been forcibly converted to Catholicism or Orthodoxy. Meanwhile, the heavy loss of human life among Serbian civilians fleeing from Kosovo, together with the brutality inflicted by the occupation armies and authorities of the Great Powers on the Serbs throughout the South Balkans, provided a fresh impetus to Serbian nationalism and revanchism. John Reed, the American journalist, later famous for his observation of and association with the Russian revolution, visited Serbia in 1915, and commented on the Serb view of Kosovo and Macedonia:

> The secret dream of every Serb is the uniting of all the Serbian people in one great
> Empire . . . every peasant soldier knows what he is fighting for. When he was a

baby his mother greeted him "hail, little avenger of Kossovo" . . . when he had done something wrong his mother reproved him thus: "not that way will you deliver Macedonia!". . . Now Kossovo is avenged and Macedonia delivered, within the lifetimes of these soldiers who listened to their mothers and never forgot their "brothers, numerous as grapes in the vineyard." An old officer that we met later said, with a sort of holy enthusiasm: "we thought that this dream of a great Serbia would come true—but many years in the future, many years. And here it is realized in our time! This is something to die for!"

Travelling and interviewing throughout Southeastern Europe, Reed observed that "the salient characteristic of Balkan peoples is bitter hatred of the nearest aliens." He also expressed concern about the future of the Serbs, with their ethnic pride that he had come to admire, and their recent struggle for independence (1804–1878): "While such a stock, with such a history, with the imperialistic impulse growing daily, hourly in the hearts of her peasant soldiers, into what tremendous conflicts will Serbia's ambition lead her!"[14]

The defeat of the Central Powers in World War I opened the way for politicians from victorious Serbia to spearhead the formation of a broader South Slav or "Yugoslav" state, in what was initially termed the "Kingdom of Serbs, Croats, and Slovenes" (and beginning in 1929 the "Kingdom of Yugoslavia"). Kosovo was re-liberated by Serbia, but not without a heavy loss of Albanian life at the hands of the returning Serbian army. Administratively, Kosovo became an integral part of the Serbian-controlled sphere within the new and highly centralized Kingdom. Revealingly, Kosovo, together with most of present-day Macedonia, comprised part of a single administrative unit termed "South Serbia" by the authorities in the new state. Meanwhile, Montenegro, whose royal dynasty had been deposed by its citizens (prompted and assisted by the regime in Belgrade), also joined the new South Slav Kingdom in 1918. Thus, for the first time since the medieval period, Montenegrins were politically and territorially united with other Balkan Serbs within a single independent state unit.

The ethnically Serbian royal dynasty and political oligarchy that would control interwar Yugoslavia eagerly welcomed the opportunity to begin systematically implementing Belgrade's control over "liberated" Kosovo for the first sustained period since the fourteenth century.[15] Kosovo, after all, had enormous historical significance for the Serbs, and also for the Montenegrin branch of the Serbian ethnic community, that went far beyond the region's small size and population (approximately 11,000 square kilometers, with a population of approximately 439,000 in 1921 and 552,000 in 1931). But at the beginning of the interwar period, approximately two-thirds of Kosovo's inhabitants were ethnic Albanians, nearly three-quarters of whom belonged to the Muslim faith. Only about one-quarter of the region's population were ethnic Slavs, overwhelmingly Serbs, who were adherents of the Orthodox faith. Regrettably, the suffering experienced by both the Serb and Albanian ethnic communities during the Balkan wars and World War I poisoned relations between the two groups at the very time they were beginning a period of mutual coexistence in a single post-Ottoman state framework. The attitude of the new Kingdom's authorities in Belgrade toward the future structure of power in Kosovo only exacerbated difficulties that were already quite evident.

Adopting an official strategy toward cultural diversity that accorded Serbs the paramount position in the area, Belgrade's central government set out to "Serbianize" Kosovo through demographic engineering and political manipulation. In the same way that the Ottoman authorities up to 1912 had encouraged the colonization of Kosovo by Albanian Muslims from elsewhere in the Balkans, the Yugoslav regime during the 1920s sponsored the migration of Serbs and Montenegrins into the region as a means "to correct the national composition of the area."[16] In 1928 the top administrator responsible for the colonization of South Serbia claimed that in some places the central government's policy had significantly changed the "ethnic composition of the entire region," noting that in 1913 there were areas in which "there had been not a single Serbian inhabitant."[17] By 1940 approximately 18,000 Slavic families had been settled in Kosovo, many relocated from impoverished areas of Bosnia–Herzegovina and Montenegro, as a reward for their service to Serbia in the World War.

Although labeled as a "national minority" in interwar Yugoslavia, the Albanian population of the country was denied any legitimate political symbols or channels for the expression of their corporate identity as a separate ethnic group. Albanians could risk voting for one or another of the Muslim political parties, as many did during the more liberal period of interwar rule (1918–1928). But any advocacy of union with neighboring Albania, or support for the political autonomy of the Kosovo region and the Albanian population within the Yugoslav state, was regarded by the authorities as outright subversion. The fact that Kosovo was of considerable significance to the history and goals of "greater Albanian nationalism" only made Serbian politicians more intransigent in their treatment of minority issues.[18] All leading positions of administrative authority in the region were in the hands of ethnic Serbs appointed by the central government. The intention of the regime in Belgrade was not to aggressively assimilate the overwhelmingly non-Slavic population, that is, by conversion to the Serbian nationality in a cultural or religious sense, but rather to maintain and expand the presence and political hegemony of the Serbs in Kosovo while suppressing any trace of non-Serb national consciousness. Faced with brutal and heavy-handed treatment, first from the Serbian and Montenegrin armies during the wartime liberation of Kosovo (during 1912 and 1917–1918),[19] and later from the local gendarmerie, many Albanians fled the country while others resorted to traditional forms of Balkan guerrilla resistance against governmental authority. One of the most popular anti-regime organizations among the Kosovars in the early postwar years was the Kachak movement, composed mainly of Albanian emigrants receiving support from Italy. Employing tactics that resembled a bandit organization as much as a national liberation movement, Kachak leaders launched attacks on Serb officials, and offered a refuge for young Albanians who refused to cooperate with the authorities.[20] Such Albanian rebel bands were not effectively suppressed by the regime until the mid-1920s, after the mass detention of family members who could only be ransomed by the surrender of their outlaw relatives. These measures, predictably, only increased anti-Serb sentiments. Thus, many discontented Albanians throughout the interwar years continued to join the various organizations advocating union with Albania. The majority of Kosovars, however, adopted a substantially passive role towards the Serb authorities, and waited for a future opportunity to express their opposition to, and secure some type of autonomy from, Belgrade's control.[21]

The structure of the Kosovo elite during this period reflected both the area's extreme backwardness, and also the pattern of political domination in the province. Indeed, it is difficult to even point to a very sizeable or truly indigenous elite in the region. The end of Ottoman power and wartime chaos witnessed the exodus of Turkish officials from Kosovo, along with many Albanian Muslims from urban areas who had either served in the region's civil administration or had been members of the small mercantile community (skilled artisans, small merchants, etc.). As a result of elite and mass out-migration during this period, the population of Kosovo actually decreased by about 60,000 between 1913 and 1920. This vacuum was soon filled by an influx of Serbian civil, military, and police officials, together with a contingent of skilled technicians to run the region's minuscule industrial structure.[22] Meanwhile, many of the largest and choicest tracts of agricultural land previously owned by Turkish and Albanian families were divided by the authorities among the new Serbian and Montenegrin colonists. For example, Nikola Pašić, one of the country's first prime ministers (formerly the prime minister of Serbia), appropriated 3,000 hectares of land for himself near one of the region's most historic sites.

The most striking characteristic of Kosovo's elite structure between the two world wars was not so much its small size, but its ethnic composition. A largely imported Serbian intelligentsia, itself undergoing the first stage of elite development, was ruling the region's population, composed largely of Albanian peasants and proletarians. This pattern of a regional ruling class drawn from one ethnic group, and a subordinated class from another ethnic background, closely resembles what has been described as a system of "internal colonialism," and is typically found in states with marked regional economic disparities. The most distinctive feature of internal colonialism is the attempt by a more modernized core group from one culture to establish a persistently discriminatory system of stratification upon less modernized groups from other cultures. In this way a system of objective cultural differences is super-imposed upon—or merged with—class divisions, thus creating what has been termed a "cultural division of labor."[23] Many dimensions of the internal colonialism model were exhibited in the elite structure and ethnic politics of the Kosovo region at this time. One might even say that a good deal of Albanian group consciousness and "reactive" political nationalism up to and beyond 1940 resulted from the prevailing cultural division of labor in Yugoslavia. Indeed, to extend the model further, the status of the Albanians in interwar Yugoslavia was not unlike the colonial position earlier accorded the Serbs by their Ottoman and Austro–Hungarian imperial rulers in different sections of the Balkans. Thus, the pre–1912 Serbian "national liberation movement" against foreign predominance in the cultural division of labor could also be considered an example of reactive ethnicity. The success of Serbian arms during 1912–1913, and again in 1918, had simply established a new pecking order in the South Balkan subregion.

The educational system, a key factor in political and economic development, both reflected and reinforced the colonial status of "South Serbia" and its predominantly Albanian population. The central authorities in Belgrade were primarily concerned with the political mission of Kosovo's school system, namely, cultivating loyalty to the new government in Belgrade, and not with expanding educational opportunities. The language of instruction was Serbian, and every effort was made to restrict the development of an Albanian national consciousness. But with only about 30 percent of eligible children actually receiving an education in the region, the school system did not actually play a significant a role in the political socialization process. Over 90 percent of the Albanian population was illiterate and only about two percent of the eligible Albanians were enrolled in secondary schools.[24] There were no higher education facilities in the region, and only a handful of Albanian students attended universities elsewhere in Yugoslavia or abroad. While the interwar regime had a better record than their Turkish predecessors regarding educational development, such progress still had little effect on modernization or elite formation in Kosovo.

Ethnic War and Power Inversion: 1941–1945

The invasion and dismemberment of the Yugoslav Kingdom in April 1941 was not an unwelcome event to the country's Albanian population. Most of

Kosovo was incorporated into Italian-controlled Albania, with smaller portions of the region parceled out to the new German-run Serbian puppet state (including the Trepča lead and zinc mine) and to Axis Bulgaria's enlarged province of Macedonia.

For most of Kosovo's Albanians, "liberation" from nearly three decades of Serbian "domination," and the opportunity to be reunited in a single territorial unit with Albanians outside Kosovo, initially offset the reality of subordination to Fascist control. Offering the inhabitants of the newly co-opted territory the vision of a "greater" and "ethnically pure" Albania allied to the Axis, the Fascist authorities found many enthusiastic collaborators among the Albanians of Kosovo. Shkelzen Maliqi, a leading present-day Kosovar analyst, has pointed out, for example, that: "Albanians chose to look upon the Italians and Germans as liberators and protectors from the Serbs, which explains the weakness of the resistance movement again Fascist occupation in Kosovo."[25] Reverting to the situation before 1912 and during a good part of World War I, the Serb and Montenegrin inhabitants of the region once again became second-class citizens, while Albanians assumed a position not without similarities to the status they had enjoyed under Ottoman rule. Indeed, some members of the former Turkish and Albanian economic elite were even allowed to reassert their earlier feudal control over agricultural production. The small Albanian intelligentsia was also recruited to work in the bureaucratic apparatus of the occupation authorities, and an Albania gendarmerie was established to police each local district. The new regime also provided Albanians with schools, media facilities, and other outlets for ethnic expression in their own language, opportunities that had been prohibited under the interwar Yugoslav regime. For their part, a large number of Serbian and Montenegrin colonists subjected to an official policy of discrimination, violent harassment, confiscation of their properties, and sometimes deportation, were forced to flee from Kosovo. Interethnic animosity reached a high pitch as the population chose up sides in an emerging civil war and resistance struggle.[26]

At the outbreak of the Second World War in Yugoslavia, the Communist Party barely maintained a foothold in Kosovo.[27] In April 1941, there were 260 members in the region, 240 of whom were Serbs and Montenegrins (many of them children of colonists). The communists' most serious activity in Kosovo between the wars had been concentrated in the area around the Trepča mine, where they had helped organize a strike in 1936.[28] The party could also claim to have aided in organizing a protest by Belgrade University students in 1938 against a government plan to expel some 200,000 Albanians from South Serbia to Turkey (that was never carried out because of the war). Thousands of Albanians were forced to emigrate during the interwar period.[29] The communists were proud, however, of their multinational program adopted in the mid-1930s, which offered equality to the Albanian population along with other ethnic groups in a new federalized Yugoslav state. By implication, Kosovo would receive separate status as a territorial unit in any new federation, although the precise details of the plan were not elaborated. Thus, the party resolution adopted in October 1940 simply promised a "struggle for the freedom and equality of the Arnaut [Albanian] minorities in Kosovo and Metohija, and the Sandžak (sic)" and "against the colonizing methods of the Serbian bourgeoisie in these regions."[30]

Despite its programmatic intentions, the Communist Party of Yugoslavia had considerable difficulty attracting Albanians to the Partisan resistance organization. In addition to the rather successful appeal of the occupation authorities to the Albanians, the communists also had to compete with a noncommunist resistance movement, Balli Kombetar ("National Front"), which advocated an ethnic Albania including Albania proper, as well as the population of Kosovo, Western Macedonia, and sections of Montenegro. Perhaps more significantly, and an early indicator of later difficulties, members of the communist resistance movement were themselves divided about the future status of Albanians in Kosovo. In a speech made at the end of 1943, Mehmet Hoxha, an Albanian communist leader from Kosovo working with the Yugoslav Partisans, suggested that Albanians must join with "the other nations of Yugoslavia and the [communist] National Liberation Army of Albania" to fight against the Fascist forces, though he did acknowledge that "we know that Kosovo and Metohija are inhabited mostly by Albanians who want to unite with Albania."[31] At the meeting that he addressed, it was resolved that "Kosovo and Metohija form a region in which Albanian inhabitants preponderate; they as always still wish to be united with Albania." It was only after a reprimand from the Central Committee of the Yugoslav Communist Party in March 1944 that the resolution was amended to remove the section that referred to the desired union of Kosovo's Albanians with their brethren in Albania.

The content of theoretical debates in the party leadership about Kosovo had no effect, however, on the general indifference or opposition to the Partisan movement by most Albanians. It was not until late 1943 (after the capitulation of Italy) and 1944 that the communists succeeded in organizing Albanian military detachments on a substantial scale. While late in the war Tito and his colleagues had at least some success in attracting Albanian recruits (most of whom were not party members) to the mass-based Partisan "National Liberation Movement," the Communist Party made very slow progress in either expanding the size or improving the ethnic composition of its organization in Kosovo. At the end of 1944, for example, the party only had 1,238 members in the region, less than 30 percent of whom were Albanians. Admittedly, this was a five-fold increase in the size of the party since 1941, but only a minuscule portion of Kosovo's population were party members. Controlling the regional party organization, and having played a major role in the Partisan movement of Kosovo (as well as the country as a whole), the Serbs and Montenegrins felt entitled to maintain control over political decision-making. But the rapid return to Kosovo (late 1944 to early 1945) of interwar Serbian and Montenegrin colonists, who had been dispossessed by the Italian and Albanian occupation authorities, soon brought Serb–Albanian tensions to a boiling point. The situation worsened when newly established "poverty committees," who were authorized to redistribute land to those in need, began working under the control of Serbian and Montenegrin party officials, who tended to favor members of their own nationality. The state of interethnic tensions was revealed in an internal Communist Party communication urging the Kosovo communist party organization to: (1) purge the party of all chauvinists; (2) secure the ideological improvement of the younger party members against the phenomenon of chauvinism; (3) enroll more Albanians in the party and raise their ideological level; (4) "implant the conviction among Serbian and Montenegrin communists that the Albanian masses can quickly achieve a higher cultural and political level having in mind the backwardness of nationalities in the USSR"; and (5) ensure that the Montenegrins stop emphasizing their contribution during the war.[32] The last injunction related to the existence of certain intra-ethnic rivalry between the Serbian and Montenegrin minorities in Kosovo, which existed alongside the more serious tension between the two Slavic groups and the non-Slav Albanians.

Having collaborated extensively with the Fascists, and once again having been dislodged from their superior position vis-à-vis the Slavic population in Kosovo, members of the Albanian community expected to be targeted for communist persecution and collective retribution. This situation provided the context for a "mass counter-revolutionary uprising" among the Albanians of Kosovo in December 1944, simultaneous with the final stage of the war in Yugoslavia. The rebellion was led by members of the Balli Kombetar anticommunist resistance forces, who, having failed to achieve their wartime goals in Kosovo or Albania, now saw a final opportunity to mobilize the Albanian population against the Partisan victors. The "Ballists" had opposed the Axis occupation authorities but had often fought the communists more vigorously than the Fascists. The magnitude of the uprising forced the newly installed communist regime to place Kosovo under military administration and to dispatch armed forces to the region from elsewhere in Yugoslavia, raising the troop strength of the communist-led forces in Kosovo to over 30,000. The rebelling Albanian forces, which were divided into numerous small units, initially numbered around 15,000, and were capable of attacking many of Kosovo's major towns. The military administration was lifted only after six months of fighting, and it was not until the end of 1945 that the communist forces were able to drive the principal Albanian Ballist units into Macedonia (a newly formed republic in the communist federation), and over the borders of Greece and Albania.[33] Years later, Milovan Djilas (a Montenegrin) commented that "[the Albanian rebellion] didn't disturb our top echelon. . . . For us this was a military problem. Our regime was as foreign to the Albanian peasant masses as that of the Serbian kings. . . . The public [outside Kosovo] knew hardly anything about this broad uprising."[34] But the significant popular support for the early postwar Albanian armed uprising, sharply revealed the very tenuous legitimacy and ethnically skewed basis of communist rule in Kosovo. Moreover, considered together with the Albanian guerrilla resistance of the early 1920, the Albanian rebellion of 1944–1945 enhanced the notion that an armed struggle was an avenue to Kosovo's freedom from Serbian power. Until the 1960s, however, Albanian nationalist opposition in the province would remain limited to a few weak anti-communist groups associated with émigré organizations.

Socialist Modernization and Ethnic Dominance: 1946–1966

By 1946, the "pacification" of Kosovo by the Tito regime had been accomplished, at least superficially, and in many respects the region settled into a routine pattern of postwar reconstruction and transformation. Kosovo was established as an Autonomous Region (Oblast) within the Republic of Serbia—a symbolic recognition of the region's separate position in the federal structure—and the Albanian population was theoretically granted the same rights and privileges as other "minorities" in the country. The creation of Albanian schools was accelerated, together with other cultural outlets, for the "free use" (mainly *de jure*) of the Albanian language. Constitutional and statutory laws provided for equal access of all citizens to public office and made ethnic "hatred and discord" a punishable offense. The regime also proclaimed a solemn commitment to the rapid economic modernization of the country's backward areas. "It is clear," remarked one top economic decision maker, "that we would not be able to speak of a full definite solution of the national question if inequality existed in the economic respect among the republics, or if, on the other hand, our Yugoslav economy were not to develop in the sense and in the direction of a united socialist economic whole."[35]

But while the Tito regime was willing to grant Kosovo many formal rights, and also promised the province a share in the country's planned modernization, the communist authorities also harbored a profound distrust regarding Kosovar political loyalty to Belgrade. When Albania took Stalin's side in the 1948 Soviet–Yugoslav rift, the Belgrade communist hierarchy began to view Kosovo as an area of subversive activity that might threaten the cohesion of the Yugoslav federation. For Serbian party hard-liners in the early 1950s, the best policy was to encourage Kosovo Albanians to reclassify themselves as Turkish nationals, and whenever possible, to emigrate to Turkey. Vaso Čubrilović, the former Serb nationalist turned communist official, who had promoted the idea of forced Albanian emigration during interwar Yugoslavia—and who many regard as the inspirer of later schemes for "ethnic cleansing" of Albanians from Kosovo—was responsible for such an emigration initiative in the early 1950s. It is estimated that approximately 100,000 Albanians (many coerced into declaring themselves as Turks) joined thousands more Muslim Slavs and Turks in the post–World War II emigration from Kosovo.[36]

However, during the first two decades of "socialist construction in Yugoslavia," Kosovo's citizens slowly began to share in the benefits of the country's overall transformation. By 1948 Kosovo had a population of 728,000 (compared to 439,000 in 1921), 68 percent of whom were Albanians, 24 percent Serbs, and about four percent Montenegrins. Although the Albanian population remained politically subordinated, and in a position of relative economic weakness, census data from 1948 and 1953 indicate interesting patterns of change and continuity. For example, information on the generational structure and field of specialization of Kosovo's inhabitants with a higher education in 1948 reveals a very small educated elite (449 persons or .06 percent of the population), over three-quarters of whom were under 50 years of age, and 27 percent under 35 years of age. Most individuals received training in traditional disciplines such as law and philosophy, although a more technically proficient elite group was emerging from the younger generation (i.e., with degrees in engineering, agronomy, etc.). Not surprisingly, in what was predominantly a patriarchal society, the majority of persons with a higher education were males; however, more women were beginning to appear among the younger age cohorts. Roughly 70 percent of the educated elite resided in Kosovo's four largest towns, 29 percent of whom lived in Priština, the new capital of the region. The first postwar census only captures the initial traces of modernization, but it offers a substantial picture of the intelligentsia that was already present during the pre-war period, together with those few members of the new communist administrative and political leadership who had completed a higher education.

An analysis of the ethnic composition of the workforce in Kosovo indicates remnants of the cultural division of labor so characteristic during the interwar years. For example, in 1948 and 1953, when Albanians constituted over two-thirds of the economically active population, they composed only about one-third of the active white-collar employees in the province (the fact that in 1948, 75 percent of all pensioners in the "employee" category were

Serbs and Montenegrins is also revealing).[37] By 1953, Serbs and Montenegrins, who together made up 31.5 percent of Kosovo's active population, still held 68 percent of the "administrative and leading" positions in the province. Albanians also made up only one-third of the personnel in the important "defense and security" area in 1953, though they composed about one-half of all industrial workers and two-thirds of the agricultural workers. Montenegrins were especially well placed, having approximately three times as many employees in administrative and security posts as their small, relative size in the active population (four percent) would seem to warrant. In 1953, only one-third of the 11,430 Montenegrins actively employed in Kosovo were actually born in the region, compared with 85 percent of the Serbian workforce, and 98 percent of both the Albanian and Turkish nationality groups. As far as most citizens in the latter two groups were concerned, the Montenegrins and Serbs represented a communist colonial elite reaping the fruits of wartime success.

In spite of these imbalances in the pattern of ethnic employment, and the intergroup tensions they generated, important changes were beginning to take place in postwar Kosovo. For example, Albanian children comprised 46 percent of students enrolled in elementary schools students during the 1945–1946 period, but 67 percent in 1962–1963. Albanian representation in secondary schools rose from 23 percent to 47 percent.[38] In 1962–1963, Albanians still made up only 40 percent of the approximately 1,400 students in Kosovo's few post-secondary education facilities (no regional university had yet been established), but this represented an enormous increase from the pre-war period. By 1961, 59 percent of the population over ten years of age was literate, compared with only 37 percent in 1948. Kosovo was slowly becoming more urbanized. Two decades after the communists had taken power, the province had gradually begun to develop a sizeable indigenous Albanian intelligentsia.[39] Between 1945 and 1960, Priština, the region's new capital, grew from about 16,000 to over 35,000 inhabitants and the share of the urban sector in the total population grew from 15 to 20 percent.

But the modernization process in Yugoslavia was not as successful or untroubled as statistical indicators of growth and change might at first suggest. For example, the annual growth rate of the country as a whole, and especially in its more developed regions, considerably outstripped such growth in Kosovo. By the 1960s, this trend led to a greater gap between the more advanced and less developed regions of the country than had existed just after the war. From 1946 to 1964, the per capita income of Slovenia, the most developed region of the country, rose from three to five times the level of that in Kosovo.[40] Growing resentment also existed in the more developed regions of the country, where it was thought that even greater economic strides could be made had not the federal government—dominated by personnel from the less developed southeastern part of the country—transferred resources to Kosovo and other backward regions. This argument was often supported by pointing to the many federally subsidized and generally inefficient show projects or so-called "political factories" in Yugoslavia's less developed regions.

Economic difficulties, including insufficient or delayed capital investment, capital allocation in the wrong industrial sectors, and poor productivity, undoubtedly contributed to Kosovo's persistent lag behind the rest of the country. Perhaps the most serious problem hampering modernization, however, was the rapid increase in the size of the region's total population. Between 1947 and 1966, Kosovo's population grew by 54 percent, or at twice the rate for the country as a whole (the equivalent figures were 15 percent for Croatia, 16 percent for Slovenia, and 17 percent for Vojvodina, that is, the country's three most prosperous regions). Kosovo's mortality rate dropped slowly in the decades after World War II, mainly as a result of improved hygiene, health care, and nutrition, whereas the region's overall birth rate remained rather constant and above levels in other parts of the country. Kosovo's unique demographic development is attributable, in part, to the exceptionally high birth rate of its Albanian population, which at the end of the 1960s was twice that of the Serbs and Montenegrins. Albanians comprised about 95 percent of the region's total population growth in the decade after 1961.[41]

Kosovo's ethnically skewed population expansion tended to dilute the benefits of economic progress, and helped set the stage for heightened Serb–Albanian tensions in the province. The rapid population growth, for example, outstripped even a growing economy's capacity to provide jobs, thereby leading to an increase in unemployment, especially among younger Albanians eager to enter the workforce.[42] The same problem also undercut other aspects of the modernization process. Thus, while there was a decline in the relative size of Kosovo's agricultural workforce, unlike in other regions of Yugoslavia, the absolute number of persons in farming actually increased.[43] The relative level of illiteracy in the province similarly declined in each succeeding postwar census. But because the construction of education facilities could not keep pace with the birth rate, the absolute number of illiterate persons remained almost constant. The negative impact of demographic factors on modernization in Kosovo seriously offset the overall pattern of advancement in the province, intensifying the frustration of both the Albanian and Serbian ethnic communities.

Kosovo's relative socio-economic deprivation in the Yugoslav federal system was not, however, the only problem experienced in the region in the two decades following World War II. Of even more potential danger was that while the rest of the country was enjoying at least limited political liberalization, Kosovo remained locked in a far more rigid pattern of "administrative socialism." Thus, while the province exhibited the more symbolic features of Titoist reform—workers' councils, communal self-government, etc.—political control remained tightly concentrated in the hands of state and party functionaries, especially those having links to the security services. The fact that "leading personnel" in the party and police were mainly Serbs and Montenegrins created a pattern of ethno-political stratification with disquieting similarities to the pre-war regime. By the mid-1960s about half of the party membership in Kosovo was ethnically Albanian, but the members of that group enjoyed very little real political influence in the province.

Given the general indifference or outright resistance of Kosovo's Albanian population to the Partisan movement and communists during and just after World War II, the more conservative Serbian and Montenegrin politicians had few qualms about retaining strict control over the province. The Tito–Stalin break in 1948, and the participation of communist Albania in the Cominform's (the Soviet-dominated Communist Information Bureau) pressure on the Yugoslav state,[44] only served to reinforce this policy. The infiltration of agents and irredentist propaganda into Kosovo from neighboring Albania, and the undoubted reservoir of support for such advances in Yugoslavia, encouraged the tendency of the authorities to collectively treat the Albanian population (both of Kosovo and other regions) as a basically subversive element, not yet entitled to the fruits of self-managed socialism.[45] In 1955 and 1956, the problem of political control in Kosovo prompted the authorities to forcibly collect firearms from the Albanian population under a "state of emergency." Political subversion and political repression remained a strong undercurrent in the province over the next decade, with frequent arrests and trials of Albanians for alleged espionage and conspiracy against the government.[46] In this atmosphere, a considerable number of Albanians chose to reclassify themselves as "Turks" and to take advantage of the opportunity for emigration to Turkey in the mid-1950s.[47] It was only in 1966, following the dismissal of Aleksandar Ranković, the Serbian vice president of the country, and head of the internal security service, that the full extent of repression against the Albanians and the nature of political tutelage in Kosovo became known. During the twenty years of impressive post–World War II socioeconomic transformation, Kosovo had functioned largely as a satrapy of the Serbian-dominated security forces (and their chief in Belgrade), rather than as an "Autonomous Region" in a truly federal system.

Ethnic Polarization and Elite Change: 1967–1979

The "democratization" of the party and security forces in the wake of the Ranković dismissal opened a new period for the development of the Albanian population in Kosovo and Yugoslavia. A first step in this regard was the implementation of nationality "rights" and the principles of provincial "autonomy," which had been in place since 1948 but had remained mainly decorative or symbolic features of the system. For example, Albanians were encouraged to study and use their national language freely, and criticism was leveled at the earlier *de facto* position of Serbo-Croatian as a "state language" in Kosovo.[48] Plans were developed for the expansion of local higher educational facilities that would enable Kosovars to receive instruction in their own language and province. Members of the Albanian intelligentsia began to re-examine the portrayal of Albanians in historical studies, and to offer a more balanced or multicultural picture of the region's ethnic heritage. Cultural exchanges were arranged between Yugoslavia and neighboring Albania, including visits to Kosovo by professors from the University in Tirana, and the importation of Albanian language books and materials printed in Albania. The term Šiptari was replaced by Albanci for Yugoslav Albanians, a change designed to avoid the derogatory connotations of the old usage and to eliminate any distinction in reference to Albanians within or outside Yugoslavia. Kosovars (Albanci who lived in Kosovo) were permitted to display the Albanian flag, not as a "state" symbol, but as a sign of "national" or ethnic expression.[49]

Though the constitutional status of Kosovo had already been changed from an "Autonomous Region" to an "Autonomous Province" in 1963 (thereby placing the area on an equal footing with Vojvodina in the Serbian Republic), it was only after 1966 that the indigenous Albanian ethnic majority of Kosovo (67 percent in 1961) was provided with a real opportunity to assert itself in cultural, economic, and political life. In March 1967, paying his first visit to Kosovo in 16 years, Tito drew attention to the earlier pattern of Serbian elite control and the need for a change in recruitment policy. One "cannot talk about equal rights," he remarked, "when Serbs are given preference in the factories, even when they are under-qualified, and Albanians are rejected although they have the same or better qualifications."[50] The new atmosphere encouraged some officials to urge even bolder steps in the new quest for equality. For example, Mehmet Hoxha, the prominent Albanian resistance leader from the Yugoslav Partisan movement (who was chastised during the war for suggesting that Kosovars desired to join Albania proper), was emboldened to ask: "Why do 370,000 Montenegrins have their own republic, while 1.2 million Albanians don't even have total autonomy?"[51]

As might be anticipated, the sudden improvement in the political climate for Kosovo Albanians, who had suffered years of police repression and discrimination, also unleashed officially unsanctioned expressions of "ethnic affirmation." The first signs of such politicized ethnic sentiment occurred between May and October 1968, and included minor incidents such as student celebrations of major anniversaries and personalities from Albanian history, disruption by Albanian young people of entertainment events performed in the Serbo-Croatian language, and street processions displaying Albanian flags. By the end of November 1968, full-scale organized Albanian demonstrations erupted, first at the Humanities Faculty of the university structure in Priština (still a branch of Belgrade University), and then spreading to other localities in Kosovo and western Macedonia. Some of the demonstrators—mainly university and secondary school students—called for the creation of Kosovo as a separate republic within Yugoslavia (i.e., outside Serbia), with its "own constitution" and the "right of self-determination." Other demonstrators, using the Albanian flag as their banner, took a more extreme stance, advocating the union of Kosovo with communist Albania. The latter protesters cheered the Albanian chief of state, Enver Hoxha, and denounced officials of Albanian origin, such as Veli Deva, the Chairman of the League of Communists' provincial committee. Widespread arrests were quickly made and order restored, but only after one demonstrator was shot to death and about forty others wounded.[52]

Though the authorities in Kosovo urged increased vigilance against Albanian "chauvinists" and "irredentists" following the demonstrations, the Titoist regime continued to move ahead with the program of Albanianization and local reforms. Thus, use of newly achieved rights by the Albanian demonstrators (i.e., language use and flag display, etc.) did not result in the withdrawal of these rights. Moreover, what was viewed as a misguided nationalistic orientation on the part of certain Albanian intellectuals did not diminish regime support for the overall advancement of Kosovo's growing Albanian intelligentsia. Kosovo party chief Veli Deva attributed participation of many Albanians and Albanian intellectuals in the demonstrations to their "one-sided structure," that is, the fact that they are "predominantly representatives of humanist, social and historical linguistics." He further suggested that among the intelligentsia "and not only the Albanian [intelligentsia] . . . national romanticism has increasingly gained ground, because there was formerly not an opportunity to live it out."[53] Communist officials also blamed the demonstrations on alleged irredentist propaganda, which was considered to have an "influence on events" in Kosovo, although, it was conceded, "internal movements" were mainly responsible for the uprisings.[54]

The most ominous consequence of the demonstrations was the growing sense of mistrust in Kosovo between Slavic and non-Slavic ethnic groups, which resulted in a sizeable exodus of Serbs and Montenegrins from the province after 1968. By the early 1970s the various reforms adopted by the regime, together with the outflow of many Serbian and Montenegrin families from Kosovo, noticeably affected the region's elite structure.[55] In brief, the data reveal the emergence of an Albanian leadership group that could begin to challenge the Slavic ethnic groups that had enjoyed predominance in Kosovo's elite structure since 1912. Highly qualified Albanians still found themselves, however, functioning in a political environment that continued to be heavily influenced by Serbs and Montenegrins, and also by older Albanians from the Partisan generation, who often lacked higher or modern educational credentials. While aggregate census data alone is not an indicator of elite cleavage or behavior, information concerning the changing number and nationality composition of elite actors by generation clearly illustrates the new context of elite and ethnic relations. For example, evidence of the marked decline in the relative position of Serbs and Montenegrins in Kosovo's elite structure undoubtedly contributed to the anxiety expressed by members of those groups about their influence and future role in the province. The Albanian intelligentsia had clearly become more active spectators and participants in both Kosovo's elite structure and in the Yugoslav political system.

The 1971 census data reveal that although the Albanian position in the overall elite structure had greatly improved over a relatively short period of time, significant inequities still existed with regard to the ethnic "representativeness" in most elite sectors. For example, the data regarding various occupational groups indicate that though Serbs and Montenegrins made up approximately 21 percent of the total population in Kosovo, they still composed over one-third of the functionaries working in the party and mass organizations, 45 percent of the legislative and government functionaries, and 52 percent of the province's managerial personnel. In 1971, the region's technical intelligentsia and scientific elite were also still overwhelming non-Albanian.

Leaving aside the ethnically more balanced recruitment for political positions after 1966, the increasing Albanian presence was most apparent among teachers and the literary-artistic intelligentsia, that is, the portion of the elite most self-conscious about "ethnic affirmation" and most susceptible to appeals of "national romanticism." In 1971, approximately 80 percent of the Albanians in Kosovo's elite were teachers. Such "one-sided" Albanian elite development hindered the contribution and influence that Kosovo's ethnic majority could have had on the province's economic growth and created an added basis for interethnic and interelite friction. Though in earlier years the cultural division of labor in Kosovo had been largely "hierarchical," with Slavs controlling the elite and Albanians making up the nonelite, the division of labor now was more "horizontally segmented," with members from all ethnic communities enjoying higher training and social rank, but with different ethnic groups predominating in different elite occupational sectors.[56]

The extent of ethnic domination and ethnic distance within various elite sectors, or between elite sectors, depends on the particular occupational areas involved. Thus, Slavs and non-Slavs in Kosovo appear to have enjoyed rather good relations in the technical and scientific intelligentsia, with members of both groups resenting the influence of all outside representation—whether by Albanian or non-Albanian officials—from the less educationally qualified political sector. On the other hand, cross-ethnic intraelite bonds were apparently less close-knit in the predominantly literary intelligentsia, and also the mainly Serbian managerial elite. In any case, throughout the 1970s, the principal meeting ground for Serbs and Albanian leaders within Kosovo's ethnically segmented and polarized elite was in the province's governmental institutions, in which all ethnic groups were proportionately represented.

During the 1970s, changes occurred in higher education, which would eventually have a major impact on Kosovo's elite structure and ethnic relations. The creation of a separate university in Priština in 1970, based upon a few core faculties formerly associated with the University of Belgrade, opened the way for a very rapid acceleration in the size and expectations of the Albanian intelligentsia.[57] By 1978, four times as many students were enrolled in universities in Kosovo than in 1966, and the percentage of Albanians among those who graduated had doubled from 27 to 54 percent. The ominous aspect of this educational explosion was the inability of Kosovo's economy to absorb the newly qualified graduates seeking to enter the workforce. Indeed, while Yugoslavia had embarked on an ambitious program of economic reform beginning in 1965, this program was actually followed by a period of declining growth rates, and also an increasing disparity between the more advanced and less developed parts of the country.[58] Another complication related to the fact that during the mid-1970s, approximately two-thirds of university enrollments and graduations in Kosovo were from nontechnical faculties, a situation which did little to overcome the already skewed elite educational structure discussed above.

The spectacular increase in the size of the province's population—an increase of 27 percent from 1971 to 1981, or three times the country-wide rate—further compounded the problem by exerting even more pressure on authorities to expand school facilities and enrollments, and by undermining the overall progress of the modernization program. It is doubtful, in fact, whether even a slightly more successful program of economic growth could have coped any better with the simultaneous pressures of rapid intellectual overproduction and agrarian overpopulation that afflicted Kosovo in the 1970s. Moreover, the concentration of a large number of upwardly mobile and ethnically mobilized Albanian students at Kosovo's urban university centers (mainly in Priština, which virtually became a university town), who were painfully aware of their dismal job prospects in a slow growth economy, and also the relative underdevelopment of their potentially rich and populous province, created a tinderbox for nationalist unrest. It was only at the beginning of the 1980s, that the authorities were to learn about the combustible properties of excessively rapid university growth under conditions of persistent economic backwardness and sharp ethnic rivalry.

The decade following the 1968 student demonstrations in Kosovo was also characterized by a process of Albanianization in the political sphere. Increasingly, Slavic and non-Slavic party professionals from the Partisan generation retired or were transferred to sinecure positions, while younger more highly educated Albanian personnel were recruited to top political positions. The replacement in 1971 of Kosovo party chief Veli Deva by Mahmut Bakalli, a younger Albanian apparatchik, symbolized the transformation taking place in the regional political elite. Bakalli, who was only thirty-five years old, had joined the party after the war, had completed some postgraduate university work, and even served for a time as a university professor. He had attracted special attention with respect to his work first as a youth leader and later as a Priština communist official struggling to cope with the student demonstrations. Deva not only had the misfortune of being regional party chief during the 1968 demonstrations, but had also angered Tito and others because of his strong-arm tactics and blunt criticism of Serbian nationalism in Kosovo.

Albanian membership in the Kosovo League of Communists also increased during this period, partially as a result of Serbian and Montenegrin emigration from the province, and to some extent because of the recruitment of larger numbers of Albanians. Albanians composed only eight percent of the communist membership in Kosovo in 1941, and 30 percent in 1945, but increased to comprise half the provincial organization in the 1950s, and nearly two-thirds of the membership by 1978. Although the political influence of Kosovo's Serb and Montenegrin inhabitants did not drop as precipitously in the population and party membership, it was apparent that a significant change was taking place. Despite the rapid Albanianization process underway in the province, and the clear threat to the hegemony of the previously ruling Slavic elite contingents, the political authorities in the 1970s expressed public confidence that ethnic relations would remain stable. Communist officials were particularly proud of the country's 1974 constitution, which formally designated Kosovo (and also Vojvodina), as provinces in Serbia, but in practical terms, accorded the two provinces similar political status as the six republics in Yugoslavia's federation. The 1974 constitution also gave Kosovo's Albanians broad cultural and linguistic rights, which were effectively utilized, especially in the media sector, during the second half of the 1970s. Looking back at the 1974 constitutional framework twenty years later, Mahmut Bakalli, the communist party chief at the time—who claims that he had assisted authorities in writing the document—has said that the objective was to find a way "both to loosen and to tighten the federation. Kosovo's development was fantastic. Things were constantly being built."[59] Bakalli and his colleagues in the

Kosovo League of Communists, in what might be described as a kind of regional national-communism, encouraged Albanian support for the one-party regime by focussing on practical economic results and a limited loosening of controls on Albanian cultural expression.

In view of Kosovo's history of ethnic divisions, such a policy was not without its dangers. Thus, regime spokesmen admitted there were serious problems in the province, and that "individuals and groups" from the Albanian ethnic community, whose "proletarian communist consciousness had been extinguished," existed within the Kosovo League of Communists. There also existed among these individuals and groups, it was officially claimed, some "false national leaders" who use "bureaucratic, demagogic and careerist methods" and affect to "protect" the national interests by turning towards the past rather than toward the future.[60] Ultra-nationalist groups and agents from Albania were also closely monitored by Yugoslav security forces (who, in Kosovo, it was claimed, were 75 percent Albanian by 1981), and numerous arrests were made, but the level of police vigilance and repression was greatly reduced from the pre-1966 levels.

Yugoslav politicians were well aware of persistent nationality difficulties in Kosovo, as well as sources of dissatisfaction within the Albanian population of the country, but most officials in the ruling party maintained that constitutional reforms and economic development would gradually resolve any remaining traces of the "national question."[61] For example, visiting the province in October 1979, Tito commented that Kosovo "is subjected to the increased activities of nationalists, irredentists, a hostile sector of the clergy and other ideological forces." But, he suggested, the fuller development of "self-managing relations" could resolve the threats from such "diverse Prophets." Speaking to a local audience, Tito claimed to see a "great difference" from his visit four years earlier, "not only in the construction of various projects, but also in the people." Thus, he reported that: "They [the Albanians] look different, more cheerful . . . on my way here in the car from Priština I watched to see how people bear themselves. All right, someone may come out because he was asked to do so, but in such a case he is really absent. On his face there would be no smile which is an expression of joy, pleasure. And this is what followed us along the whole route. All of this amounts to a belief in a better future. To me this is a good indication."[62]

Post-Tito Kosovo: The Early 1980s

In March and April 1981, roughly one year after Tito's death, violent Albanian protests once again erupted in Kosovo. As in 1968, such dissidence began with demonstrations by Albanian students at the university in Priština, and quickly mushroomed throughout the province, as well as among the Albanian population in neighboring regions. Demonstrating street crowds, sometimes numbering in the thousands, and composed largely of students and young people, advanced a wide array of nationalist and separatist demands (many similar to those articulated a dozen years before), including the establishment of Kosovo as a separate republic in the Yugoslav federation, and the union of Yugoslavia's predominantly Albanian regions with Enver Hoxha's communist regime in Albania. Violent clashes resulted in a high toll of dead and injured (officials estimated under a dozen; unofficial estimates were closer to a thousand), as well as a significant loss in property and economic output. Shocked by the scale of violence and resistance, Yugoslav authorities took strong measures to quash the demonstrations, which were officially characterized as a "counter-revolutionary uprising." Declaring a state of emergency, the regime transferred in armed internal security forces and military units from elsewhere in the country and, for a short term, virtually sealed off the province from all outside contact. By July, after carrying out widespread arrests and suppressing most overt opposition, the regime was sufficiently confident to lift the state of emergency, although officials admitted that the situation in Kosovo would remain exceptionally "complex" for some time to come, and only superficially "stable."[63]

Relations between Yugoslavia and Albania seriously deteriorated in the wake of the Kosovo demonstrations. The polemics emanating from Tiranë were particularly intense, charging Yugoslav authorities, and especially the Serbs, with exploitation and repression of the Kosovars. Albania also condemned Belgrade's handling of the Kosovo crisis. Meanwhile Yugoslav authorities accused Albania of actively encouraging the separatist and irredentist groups who, they charged, had spearheaded the demonstrations. The Yugoslav authorities abrogated a formal agreement for the exchange of instructors and cultural material with Albania. In addition, a propaganda campaign was launched in Belgrade and Priština to illustrate the difficulties of life in communist Albania, and the comparative advantages enjoyed by Albanians in Yugoslavia. Though Yugoslav leaders were eager to identify externally inspired nationalism as a central factor behind the 1981 violence in Kosovo (including allegations of Soviet meddling in the region), they were frank in admitting that much deeper internal socio-economic problems were also at work. As Stane Dolanc, a member of the top party leadership, told a press conference soon after the demonstrations, "we should be politically blind and deaf if we reduced all that [trouble] only to a foreign factor."[64]

Both Yugoslav commentators and foreign observers noted that Kosovo's difficulties could be largely traced to its relative economic backwardness. Thus, following the 1981 demonstrations, plans were developed to increase economic aid to Kosovo, and criticism was leveled against both the inefficiency of earlier economic investments, as well at the poor labor productivity in the province. According to Yugoslavia's medium-term development plan for the 1981–1985 period, approximately $2.5 billion was to be invested in Kosovo, two-thirds of which was to come from the federal fund for assisting the development of insufficiently advanced areas (Kosovo's share was about 42 percent of the total fund allocation). Two-thirds of the overall economic investment program was allotted to industry, with a priority on the development of processing industries. The overall development program envisaged an average annual growth rate of 8.4 percent for industrial production and 5.7 percent for agricultural production, both target rates notably higher than for the country as a whole.[65] Suggestions were even made that some of the region's surplus intellectual cadre could be employed elsewhere in Yugoslavia.[66] The sensitive matter of the very high Albanian birth rate in Yugoslavia and its impact on Kosovo's continued economic difficulties also was the subject of very candid discussion. Although some experts warned that demographic trends in Kosovo could result in Yugoslavia facing some kind of demographic "catastrophe" in the years ahead, it was also pointed out by the Croatian political sociologist and politician, Stipe Šuvar, that "any reproaches to Albanians that they are multiplying too rapidly in relation to members of other Yugoslav peoples would be akin to racism."[67]

Given the long range and complex nature of the economic and demographic issues, the immediate response of the post-Tito communist regime to the events in Kosovo focussed on the tractable areas of political control and educational policy. In addition to imposing severe sentences on those convicted of participating in the demonstrations, the regime chastised and removed officials and other party members whose policies or indifference allegedly permitted matters in the province to get out of hand. A detailed assessment of the internal counter-revolution, issued by the League of Communists at the end of November 1981, placed major blame for the crisis on Kosovo's political leadership, who had allowed or encouraged the province's isolation from the Republic of Serbia and the rest of the country, and who had failed to resolutely resist "enemy" forces and the Albanianization of the region. "In some cases," the report pointed out, "there was insistence that members of nations and nationalities in Kosovo must know Albanian if they want to obtain employment in specific places of work. . . . National affirmation is conceived of as being cultural and socio-psychological 'homogenization' of all Albanians at all costs."[68] The clear implication was that a pattern of elite cleavage and elite direction was behind the popular Albanian dissidence that had finally erupted.

Attention was also drawn to the difficulties created by the educational explosion that had occurred over the past decade: "It is no accident that the highest number of participants in the demonstrations and those who carried enemy slogans came from the ranks of the young university students and grade school pupils and from a selection of the intelligentsia, especially as hostile indoctrination has had a broad area opened to it and parts of the leadership itself were affected by nationalism."[69] In order to deal with the problem at hand, political organizations in Kosovo launched a process of "political differentiation" designed to purge those persons deemed responsible for the escalation of Albanian nationalism, or who were unable to support the new hard-line anti-nationalist strategy adopted by the authorities. As one provincial politician put it, "because something has been routed and taken off the streets, it has not necessarily been annihilated ideologically."[70] Between March 11 and November 6, 1981, over 1,000 members of the League of Communists (that is, roughly one percent of the regional party) were either formally fired, or simply struck off the membership rolls, and eleven basic party organizations were completely eliminated. Nearly 350 people were expelled from their jobs, approximately one-half of whom were working in the field of education.[71] The leading politicians in Kosovo were not immune to the regional political purge. One of the first steps taken was the removal of Mahmut Bakalli, Kosovo's Albanian party president, who had presided over a decade of *de facto* Albanianization in Kosovo. He was expelled from the League two years later. "I was a liberal," Bakalli later told a reporter. "They pushed me out of politics because I did not accept the proposition that those demonstrations in 1981 were counterrevolutionary."[72] Bakalli was initially succeeded by his own predecessor, Veli Deva, the popular Albanian apparatchik who had been pushed aside at the beginning of the 1970s reform period, and had been serving out his political retirement as director-general of the Trepča mining complex. A number of other experienced political leaders were also rotated back into political positions, replacing generally younger and more highly educated officials who had failed to "behave decisively and combatively" in opposing the growth of Albanian nationalism. Some younger political functionaries were also advanced in the personnel reshuffle, and it was made clear that future cadre policy would stress the "moral-political suitability" of appointees.[73] Among the new generation of Albanian leaders was 33-year-old Azem Vllasi, who had served from 1974 to 1978 as president of the country's major youth organization, and was regarded as a "Titoist communist," who could "ideologically combat irredentism" and promote the "broadest brotherhood and unity in the province."

Steps were also taken following the 1981 demonstrations to eliminate Albanian nationalist influences in the educational system and to ensure that the schools "coordinate better with the needs of the economy." Many Albanian instructors were fired, suspended, or reprimanded for taking a "nationalist-oriented" approach to their subjects, and a campaign was launched to purge chauvinistic and separatist perspectives from the curriculum and school materials. Importation of books from Albania was discontinued, and a more careful examination of educational materials was undertaken to prevent further "legalized indoctrination of the young" (or more accurately, to allow for correct indoctrination in the future). A limit was placed on the number of new university enrollments in the fall of 1981, in contrast to the open admission policy employed in earlier years, and greater care was taken to screen out potential trouble-makers. An effort was also made to reduce the previously excessive enrollments in the arts faculties and to recruit students for "vocations required by economic development." Despite all these measures, disruptive behavior (e.g., short demonstrations, nationalistic graffiti, etc.) continued at Kosovo University throughout the 1981–1982 academic year.[74] In addition to organizing an intense round of meetings at the university to correct such matters, the authorities responded by trying to mobilize public opinion against student protesters, and especially the type of student labeled as a "spoiled class opponent."

The intensification of ethnic tension between Slavs and Albanians as a result of the 1981 demonstrations led to a new exodus of Serbs and Montenegrins from Kosovo. It was estimated, for example, that between March and October approximately 10,000 people left the province, and although the authorities condemned this trend and its causes, reports of continued Serbian and Montenegrin emigration persisted throughout the 1980s.[75] Serbian communists were especially critical of commentaries that attributed such emigration to the poor economy, instead emphasizing the need for severe action against the harassment of Slavs by Albanian nationalists and local bullies. Ironically, as was the case after the 1968 demonstrations, the process of Albanianization in Kosovo was not as evident during the period when the momentum of Albanian nationalism and discontent was building, but rather directly after the violent climax of ethnic tensions, that is, when the regime belatedly reacted to the simmering tensions. Thus, it was only in the aftermath of the 1981 events, in an atmosphere hardly conducive to interethnic accommodation, that regime spokesmen began emphasizing the importance of bilingual education, and suggesting that the very delinquent efforts to ensure Albanian language rights after 1966 may have sometimes resulted in reverse discrimination against those speaking Slavic languages (e.g., Serbo-Croatian, Macedonian etc.). A public relations campaign was also launched to enhance the "togetherness," *zajedništvo*, of all nationalities residing in Kosovo and to denigrate the notion that the region could or should ever be made ethnically "pure."

The Yugoslav communist regime was less flexible or innovative regarding Kosovo's territorial status as an autonomous province within the Republic of Serbia. The official view was that nationalist agitation to make Kosovo

a "seventh republic" in the Yugoslav federation, or even more radical proposals that such a new governmental unit should include predominantly
Albanian areas of other republics adjacent to Kosovo (i.e., Montenegro and
Macedonia) were simply part of the "first stage" of a broader plot, hatched
in Tirana, for the eventual incorporation of Yugoslavia's Albanian population
into an enlarged Albanian state. Beyond their natural fear of ethnic secessionism, the Yugoslav authorities worried that any concessions to Kosovo's
demand for a republic might create a precedent for other territorially concentrated nationalities in Yugoslavia (e.g., the Hungarians in Vojvodina) who
might seek a similar political status and eventual association with a neighboring state. Such official anxiety in the period after the 1981 Kosovo crisis
encouraged an outpouring of commentary by political functionaries and constitutional specialists, all attempting to support the legal basis and continued
necessity for Kosovo's position as a province within Serbia.[76]

For their part, leading Serbian communist officials and "loyal" Albanians
in Yugoslavia went to great pains to demonstrate the inextricable link between
Kosovo and Serbia, and strongly criticized the tendency, especially after 1966,
to "isolate" the predominantly Albanian province from the rest of the predominantly Slavic republic. Even the habit of referring to Serbia "proper" in
order to distinguish that core territorial area from the two autonomous
provinces in the Republic of Serbia, was said to have encouraged "isolationism" and nationalist feeling in the provinces. Although the use of punitive measures against demonstrators and an extensive purge of the Albanian political
and cultural intelligentsia enabled the regime to stifle the most vocal manifestations of Albanian nationalism in Kosovo in the aftermath of the 1981 crisis,
no comprehensive strategy regarding Kosovo's ethnic problems was formulated. Regrettably—particularly in view of subsequent events—the yearning
for change on the part of the young and burgeoning Albanian population was
largely ignored, at the same time Serbs in the province were becoming increasingly anxious about their status, and fearful of their Albanian neighbors. The
Yugoslav communist regime was consequently forced to contend not only with
a continuation of Albanian political dissidence boiling beneath the surface of
the political landscape, but also with a serious upsurge of anti-Albanian
nationalism among the members of the Serbian intelligentsia. Police repression
and judicial action against members of so-called "Albanian irredentist
groups," including summary proceedings and harsh sentences, also stimulated
Albanian political activists to adopt a "syndrome of defensive homogenization."[77] Meanwhile, suggestions, such as those advanced by one top party official in 1983, that Kosovo's serious economic problems could be alleviated by
a "counter-migration" of non-Albanian specialists into the province, while
perhaps an efficacious idea from a modernization perspective, was naturally

viewed by many Albanians as simply a tactic to reintroduce Serbian colonial-type tutelage. In response to the idea, one influential Albanian official remarked that the time had passed when people could be sent "by decree" to settle somewhere else, an obvious allusion to the policies practiced in Kosovo by the Serbian and Yugoslav royalist regimes.[78] Meanwhile, as a result of demographic and migration patterns, Kosovo had acquired a more Albanian ethnic make-up. By 1981, Albanians made up 77.4 percent of Kosovo, Serbs 13.2 percent, and Montenegrins 1.7 percent. The same trend continued during the next several years, not entirely due to a high Albanian birthrate. For example, many Albanians migrated from Kosovo from other regions of Yugoslavia because of the opening of Priština University, while the porous border with socialist Albania also stimulated Albanians in that country to illegally enter Kosovo in order to escape political authoritarianism and economic impoverishment. At the same time, Serbs continued to leave Kosovo due to harassment, anxiety, and a perception of poor long-term prospects for their ethnic community.

In retrospect, the 1981 nationalist demonstrations clearly marked a new and more aggressive phase of Albanian nationalism, and the beginning of a major Kosovar secessionist struggle from Yugoslavia that would eventually have a profound impact on South Balkan stability. During the second half of the 1980s, Kosovo's Albanian dissident activists could be divided into two main groups, both of which had a communist ideological orientation. The Albanian analyst Shkelzen Maliqi refers to the first group as the "Enverists," because they supported a variant of Marxism-Leninism advanced by the leader of communist Albania, Enver Hoxha. The Enverists encompassed a variety of illegal underground groups advocating Kosovo's secession from Yugoslavia and its union with Albania. Kosovar Enverists evinced a kind of Marxist populism, and many of its adherents took part in the 1981 uprising. The second group identified by Maliqi were Titoists, that is, Albanian members of the League of Communists operating legally through intellectual associations, mass socio-political organizations, and the official political-governmental institutions of the country. Together, the Enverists and Titoists constituted a Kosovar intellectual counter-elite, hoping to transform their province's political status. Unorganized members of the Albanian intelligentsia, who exhibited allegiance to the regime but covertly supported Albanian nationalist goals, comprised a more amorphous third group that might be termed "crypto-nationalists" or "conformist patriots."[79] This last group mirrored the feelings of many members of Kosovo's Albanian population who kept their distance from political life, but held strong patriotic and nationalist sentiments. Until some new leader, program or opportunity would attract this group, it essentially remained a silent majority. But constrained by the regime's consolidation

of tight political and police controls over Kosovo in the wake of the 1981 crisis, the province's Albanian elite was unable to establish a broad membership
or effective organizational structure.

Moreover, as Marxism-Leninism, including its Yugoslav variant, lost
much of its attraction among citizens from all ethnic groups in the country during the 1980s, the appeal of the Titoist and Enverist groups in Kosovo also
gradually diminished. Thus, during the second half of the 1980s, post-Tito
Yugoslavia would be characterized by a mounting economic crisis, escalating
ethnic conflicts (within and outside Kosovo), and political drift, as Tito's heirs
attempted to grapple with a host of accumulated problems. In this atmosphere,
both Marxism and Titoist self-managing socialism were discredited, and most
citizens of Yugoslavia greeted any scheme by communist hard-liners or communist reformers for the reorganization of the country's federation with cynicism or indifference.

Meanwhile, within Kosovo, the heightened levels of mistrust and division
between Albanians and Serbs was palpable, if temporarily still a latent ethnic
conflict. For example, a 1990 study carried out by Belgrade's Institute of Social
Sciences, revealed that while comparative research demonstrated that, in most
countries, race was a more significant factor than other aspects of identity in
accounting for ethnic distance, surveys of young Serbs revealed a greater willingness on their part to choose Blacks and Japanese as marriage partners,
rather than Albanians and Muslims.[80] On the other side of Kosovo's ethnic
divide, most Albanians were biding their time, and privately harboring bitter
memories of the crushed 1981 demonstrations. "The prevailing feeling among
the Albanians was one of revenge," observed one of the province's keenest analysts. "They waited for a moment of maximum mobilization to start a massive
armed uprising."[81] In fact, that waiting period would stretch over a decade, or
considerably longer than most Albanians expected. For the moment, the communist regime in Serbia was proving strong enough to keep the lid on Kosovo.
But the festering "Albanian problem," and the equally virulent "Serbian question," were about to converge. The result would impel the emergence of new
elite personalities and perspectives, both among the Serbs and the Albanians,
which would drastically change the ethnic dynamics in the Balkans.

NOTES

1. The name "Kosovo" is used for convenience throughout this study, rather than
the formal designation of the area in each period of recent history: part of "South Serbia," 1912–1941; "Greater Albania," 1941–1944; the Autonomous Region (Oblast) of
Kosovo and Metohija (or sometimes Kosmet), 1945–1963; the Autonomous Province
of Kosovo–Metohija, 1962–1968; the Autonomous Province of Kosovo, 1968–1973;

the Socialist Autonomous Province of Kosovo, after 1974 (Metohija, a Serbian term was dropped from the title in deference to Albanian demands). Under the Serbian Constitution of 1990, the province was again termed the Autonomous Province of Kosovo and Metohija.

2. Thomas A. Emmert, *Serbian Golgotha: Kosovo, 1389* (New York: East European Monographs, 1990).

3. "Who Owns the Battlefield?" *Index*, April 30, 1999.

4. *Milan Corriere della Sera*, July 8, 1999, p. 11, as translated in FBIS-WEU–1999–0708, July 8, 1999. For the Serb view of Kosovo, see also Dušan Bataković, *The Kosovo Chronicles* (Belgrade: Plato, 1992), and Rade Mihaljčić, *The Battle of Kosovo in History and in Popular Tradition* (Belgrade, 1989).

5. In the 1953 census, Albanians (then labelled Šiptari), constituted 65 percent of Kosovo's population (roughly 525,000), of whom 2.3 percent claimed to be without any religious affiliation, 94 percent identified themselves as Islamic, and 3.9 percent as Catholics (just over 200 people). Approximately 17 percent of the Serbs claimed to be nonbelievers, while 82 percent identified themselves as Orthodox. *Popis Stanovništva 1953, Knjiga I, Vitalna i etnička obeležja* (Belgrade: Savezni zavod za statistiku, 1959), pp. 282–283. During the post–World War II period, the Albanian population was predominantly Sunni Muslim (roughly 70 percent), and the non-Muslim Albanians, who were either Catholic or Eastern Orthodox.

6. Branomir Anzulović has reminded readers that Ottoman rule was not based on terror alone, and that the Ottoman army was not "more cruel than other armies at the time." But he also points out that Turkish rule was brutal, involved "the devastation and depopulation that frequently preceded the conquest of new territories," included large-scale atrocities committed by unpaid Tatar horsemen and other Ottoman subjects, and that violence increased during the last two centuries of the Ottoman empire. *Heavenly Serbia: From Myth to Genocide* (New York: New York University Press, 1999), pp. 34–35. Serbian national sentiments were aroused in 1766 when a Sultan abolished the Peć Patriarchate (it had been restored in 1557, after being abolished in 1459), and subordinated the Serbian Church to the Greek Patriarchate of Constantinople. "The Serbian Church became even more of a people's Church, spreading national mythology that idealized memories of medieval Serbia through art, literature, and numerous saints." Davis MacKenzie, *Violent Solutions: Revolutions, Nationalism, and Secret Societies in Europe to 1918* (Lanham, Md.: University Press of America, 1996), p. 207. On the role of the Serbian Orthodox Church in creating an ethno-religious identity, see also John R. Lampe, *Yugoslavia as History: Twice There was a Country* (Cambridge: Cambridge University Press, 1996).

7. Ljubinka Trgovčević, *The Kosovo Myth in the First World War* (Belgrade: Association for Social History, 1999). See also Zoran Avramović in "Mitopoetsko mišljenje u Srpskoj političkoj kulturi," in Mirjana Vasović (ed.), *Fragmenti političke kulture* (Belgrade: Institut društvenih nauka, 1968), pp. 285–302. For the view that the Kosovo myth has reinforced national consciousness, but not served as an inducement for belligerence see G. N. W. Locke, "Myths About Myths: The Serbian Epics," *South Slav Journal*, Vol. 20, Nos. 3–4 (Autumn-Winter, 1999), pp. 77–78.

8. Albanian oral literature includes heroic songs of the war of the Albanians against the hated "enemy Turks," as well as songs of war against Montenegro and a general hatred of the Shkje, as Slavs are called by northern Albanian highlanders. Stavro Skendi (ed.), *Albania* (New York: Praeger, 1956), pp. 302–303.

9. For example, Noel Malcolm, *Kosovo: A Short History* (New York: Harper, 1999), and also his *Bosnia: A Short History* (London: Macmillan, 1994). A more balanced account of the Kosovo case, but one that appears to represent in part a compilation of unattributed views, is Miranda Vickers, *Between Serbs and Albanians: A History of Kosovo* (New York: Columbia University Press, 1998). See also Djordje Mikić,"The Albanians in Serbia During the Balkan Wars," in B. K. Kiraly and D. Djordjević (eds.), *East Central European Society During the Balkan Wars* (New York: East European Monographs, 1987), pp. 165–196. George W. Gawrych points out that during the last century of Ottoman rule that "there exists a danger of overemphasizing the harmonious relations between Albanians and other minorities. . . . An Albanian could have learned his neighbor's native tongue while still possessing an internal psychological state of sub-dued tensions, repressed hatreds, and harbored suspicions which sometimes found out-ward expression in intolerant actions of other minorities. . . . Furthermore, later nega-tive experiences, such as the murder of a relative or a social affront by a non-Albanian could nullify for an Albanian, either Moslem or Christian, any commitment to toler-ance." Moreover, as growing Albanian "cultural assertiveness" confronted the nation-alism of other Ottoman minorities "the Albanian cultural renewal reflected nascent, and sometimes intolerant nationalism." "Tolerant Dimension of Cultural Pluralism in the Ottoman Empire: The Albanian Community, 1800–1912," *International Journal of Middle East Studies*, Vol. 15 (1983), pp. 519–536.

10. Thomas A. Emmert, *Serbian Golgotha: Kosovo, 1389*, op. cit.

11. J. Tomić, *Rat na Kosovu i Staroj Srbiji 1912 godine* (Novi Sad, 1913), p. 120, cited in Krinka Vidaković Petrov, "Memory and Oral Tradition," in Thomas Butter-field, *Memory: History, Culture and the Mind* (Oxford: Basil Blackwell, 1989), p. 82.

12. Efforts by Serbia and Montenegro during 1912 and 1913 to organize a separate state consisting of territory controlled by Catholic Albanian clans in northern Albania and Kosovo—an idea supported by Russia in order to preclude the formation of a larger independent Albania—proved futile. Radoslav M. Raspopović, *Diplomatija Crne Gore 1711–1918* (Podgorica/Belgrade, 1996), pp. 552–584.

13. Leon Trotsky, *The Balkan Wars 1912–1913* (New York: Monad, 1980), pp. 119–120, 294, 303. For a rather selective and skewed use of Trotsky's discussion see Noel Malcolm, *Kosovo*, op. cit., p. 253.

14. *The War in Eastern Europe* (New York: Charles Scribner's Sons, 1916), pp. 54–56, 106, 332.

15. Portions of the following sections of this chapter draw upon the author's dis-cussion of Kosovo in *The Socialist Pyramid: Elites and Power in Yugoslavia* (Oakville, Ontario: Mosaic Press, 1989), pp. 335–394.

16. Ramadan Marmullaku, *Albania and the Albanians* (Hamden, Conn.: Archon, 1975), 138.

17. Ibid., p. 139.

18. In 1878 Albanian tribal leaders, merchants, and intelligentsia met at Prizren in Kosovo to form the League for the Defense of the Albanian nation, usually called the "League of Prizren." Designed initially to oppose the decision by the Congress of Berlin to allocate Turkish areas inhabited by Albanians to Montenegro, the League became the nucleus of the Albanian "national awakening." See Stavro Skendi, "Beginning of Albanian Nationalist and Autonomous Trends: The Albanian League 1878–1881," *American Slavic and East European Review*, Vol. XII (1953), pp. 219–232.

19. The Albanian population of Kosovo fought with the Turks against the Serbs in the Serbo–Turkish War of 1876–1877, and during the Balkan Wars.

20. Noel Malcolm, *Kosovo,* op. cit., pp. 273–278.

21. The anthropologist Vera St. Erlich, discussing family relationships in interwar Yugoslavia, comments on the repression of the Albanian population: "Yet, although they had dropped from a high position to a rather low one, the effects on family life were hardly noticeable. The subjective reactions to the objective measures were surprisingly weak. People in these areas did not appear pauperized or declassed; alcoholism and prostitution, squandering of property, and crime did not enter. The patriarchical dignity and responsibility remained, the concentrated pressure could not bend or break them." Vera St. Erlich, *Family in Transition: A Study of 300 Yugoslav Villages* (Princeton: Princeton University Press, 1968), p. 362.

22. Apart from the sizable British controlled Trepča-Mines Ltd. and some smaller mines, very few industrial plants existed in the area in 1939 (ten sawmills, two brickyards, five lumbermills, three icehouses, and three small electric plants).

23. Michael Hechter, *Internal Colonialism* (Berkeley and Los Angeles: University of California Press, 1975), and "Ethnicity and Industrialization: On the Proliferation of the Cultural Division of Labor," *Ethnicity*, Vol. III (1976), pp. 219–224.

24. During the 1940–1941 school year, which immediately preceded World War II in the Balkans, approximately 25,000 Serbian and Montenegrin children, and 12,000 Albanian students, were enrolled in Kosovo's secondary schools. Mark Krasnici, *Savremene društveno-geografske promene na Kosovu i Metohiji* (Priština: Muzej Kosova i Metohije, 1963), p. 265. A 1978 report prepared by the Ministry of Internal Affairs emphasized the link between educational development and political stability. Cited in Pavle Jovičević and Mita Miljković, "Odbrana Albanaca," *Nedeljne informativne novine* (hereafter *NIN*), September 17, 1978, p. 61.

25. Shkelzen Maliqi, "Demand for a New Status: The Albanian Movement in Kosovo," in Dušan Janjić (ed.), *Serbia Between Past and Future* (Belgrade: Institute of Social Sciences, and the Forum for Ethnic Relations, 1997), p. 269.

26. Ramadan Marmullaku, *Albania and the Albanians,* op. cit., pp. 139–145.

27. Milutin Folić, "Obnavljanje i konsolidacija KPJ, pojava frakcija na Kosovu i uticaj Titovog delovanja na njihovom prevazilaženju," *Osma konferncija Zagrebačkih Komunista i razvoj KPJ-SKJ kao moderne partije radničke klase* (Zagreb: Vjesnikova Press agencija, 1978), pp. 129–160.

28. After the strike at Trepča, membership picked up in the district party organization around the mine. From 1938 to 1941 the local party unit grew from 46 to 75, of whom 29 were Serbs, 25 Montenegrins, 9 Albanians, and 12 others. Ibid., p. 134.

29. See Noel Malcolm, *Kosovo*, op. cit., pp. 285–286.

30. See "Josip Broz Tito on the National Question," *Yugoslav Survey*, Vol. XVIIII (May 1978), pp. 3–24.

31. Ramadan Marmullaka, *Albania and the Albanians*, op. cit., p. 143.

32. Branko Petranović, *Politička i ekonomska osnova narodne vlasti u Jugoslaviji za vreme obnove* (Belgrade: Institut za savremenu istoriju, 1969), pp. 44–45.

33. Ibid., pp. 177–179.

34. Milovan Djilas, *Wartime* (New York: Harcourt Brace and World, 1977), p. 430. The uprising of 1944–1945 has received almost no attention from Western scholars of Yugoslav "minority problems."

35. Boris Kidrić, *On the Construction of Socialist Economy in the FNRJ* (Belgrade: Office of Information of FNRJ, 1948), p. 40.

36. Noel Malcolm, *Kosovo*, op. cit., pp. 322–323.

37. *Konačni rezultati Popiša Stanovništva od 15 marta 1948 knjiga IX stanovništvo narodnosti* (Belgrade: Savezni zavod za statistiku, 1954), *Popis Stanovništva 1953. Knjiga I. Vitalna i etnička obeležja* (Belgrade: Savezni zavod za statistiku, 1959).

38. Mark Krasnici, *Savremene društveno-geografske promene na Kosovu i Metohiji*, op. cit., p. 299.

39. Between 1947 and 1965, the average annual growth rate of the province's economy was about 6.1 percent (compared to a national rate of seven percent). During the same period, overall income in the region derived from industrial production rose from around 20 percent to 37 percent, and the percentage of the agricultural workforce dropped from approximately 85 percent in 1948 to 70 percent in 1961. Educational expansion was especially impressive. In 1939–1940 only 30 percent of eligible children were enrolled in elementary schools, while by 1958–1959 this percentage had doubled, and by 1963–1964 had reached 85 percent. Ilija Vakić (ed.), "Razvoj, položaj i perspektive Autonomne Pokrajine Kosova i Metohije," *Društveno-politička Zajednice, Tom 11. Socijalističke Republike i Autonomne Pokrajine, Nine Opačić* (Belgrade: Medjunarodna Štampa-Interpres, 1968), p. 555.

40. M. Bazler-Madžar, "Regional Development," in Branko Horvat (ed.), *The Yugoslav Economic System* (White Plains, N.Y.: International Arts and Science Press, 1976), p. 62.

41. H. Islami, "Osvrt na razvitak stanovništva Kosova," *Sociologija*, Vol. 1 (1977), pp. 153–73, and "Problemi društvenog razvitka Kosovskog sela," *Sociologija*, Vol. IV (1979), pp. 397–417.

42. One study reported a 25.6 percent level of unemployment in Kosovo in 1973. See Miroslav Rasević, T. Mulina, and M. Macura, *The Determinants of Labor Force Participation in Yugoslavia* (Geneva: International Labor Organization, 1978). See also H. Islami, "Osvrt na razvitak stanovništva Kosova," op. cit., p. 412.

43. The Albanian population of Kosovo and Yugoslavia in the 1970s lived primarily in rural areas and exhibit characteristics of a "traditional rural social life." In 1961, 16.7 percent of the Kosovo Albanian population lived in cities, and by 1971 this figure had only increased to 23.4 percent. Traditional practices such as a patriarchical authority structure in the family and blood feuds to settle disputes among family members

continued among Kosovo's Albanian rural inhabitants, although to a lesser extent than in the past. The extended family structure (*zadruga*) in rural Kosovo also persisted and often included members of more "modern" occupations such as employees, teachers, professors, and engineers. See H. Islami, "Problemi društvenog razvitka Kosovskog sela," op. cit., p. 415, M. Kavran, "Rugovska povelja-dokument samoupravnog suzbijanja krvne osvete u Kosovskom selu," *Sociologija Sela*, Vol. X11 (1974), pp. 28–36; Ruza First, "Struktura autoriteta u seoskim domaćinstvima," *Sociologija Sela*, Vol. VII, (1969); pp. 53–61, and M. Marković, "Relativno duže održavanje porodičnih zadruga u Albanaca na Kosovu," *Sociologija Sela*, Vol. XII (1974), pp. 95–100.

44. Vladimir Dedijer, *Jugoslovensko-Albanski Odnosi* (Belgrade: Borba, 1949).

45. Prior to 1966, the training handbook of the security form emphasized that "national feelings among national minorities are strong; because of this the minorities are very often ready to work for the intelligence agencies of their mother countries." Paul Shoup, *Communism and the National Question in Yugoslavia* (New York: Columbia University Press, 1968), p. 217.

46. Ibid., pp. 216–218.

47. Other data also illustrate the dissatisfaction of the Yugoslav Albanians and the vigilance of the regime in dealing with this group. Thus, when the number of convictions for "crimes against the state" between 1953 and 1961 is calculated as a percentage of total crimes recorded for various ethnic groups, Albanians generally manifest a political crime rate double or triple that of Serbs and Montenegrins. The relative political dissidence levels of the Albanians even exceed the rate for Croats during this period. Moreover, while the level of Serbian political criminality declines gradually, and remains rather constant in the case of the Montenegrins, the Albanian pattern is far more erratic, reflecting frequent outbursts, and a cycle of dissidence and repression.

48. Speaking to a closed meeting in Serbia shortly after the Ranković dismissal, one specialist on language rights observed: "In Trepča [the mining complex], for example, about 63 percent of those employed are Shiptars [Albanians]. For quite some time . . . skilled producers operated only in the Serbo-Croatian language, in the language of 37 percent of those employed. Is that a privilege in socio-economic relations? I think it is. Because a Serbian or Montenegrin worker can conduct his specialty much easier in his own language, and also have a general knowledge concerning the areas of social insurance, the political system, etc., and advance more quickly than a Shiptar who must master Serbo-Croat. But the Shiptars in Trepča contribute twice as much as do others to the general revenue for education." *Koca Jončić, Medjunacionalni odnosi i idejno političko delovanje Saveza Komunista-Jugoslavije* (Belgrade: Centar za političke studije i obrazovanje, 1967), p. 18. The traditional language of the Kosovo Albanians is the Gheg dialect of Northern Albania. The Albanian students and intelligentsia of the region, however, have supported the use of the literary language of Tirana (a mixture of Gheg and the Tosk dialect) under the slogan "one nation, one language." Stavro Skendi, *Balkan Cultural Studies* (Boulder, Colo.: East European Monographs, 1980), pp. 38–41.

49. At some point in the eighteenth century, Albanians began to call themselves "Shqiptare" ("Sons of the Eagle"). In Titoist Yugoslavia, the Albanians were designated

as a minority and initially labeled "Šiptari" (usually translated in English as "Shqiptars" or "Shiptar"). Because that latter designation was widely used in Yugoslavia (and especially in Serbia) in a derogatory and discriminatory manner, it was officially replaced in the 1960s by the term "Albanci."

50. *Vjesnik*, March 30, 1967, p. 4.

51. *Borba*, April 10, 1968, p. 5.

52. "The Problem of the Albanians in Yugoslavia," *Wissenschaftlicher Dienst Suedosteuropa*, Vol. XVIII (1969), pp. 1–9. Translated in *Joint Publication Research Service, Eastern Europe, Political, Sociological, and Military Affairs* (Belgrade: June 5, 1969), pp. 100–119.

53. Ibid., p. 17.

54. Veli Deva, "Medjunacionalni odnosi i politička situacija na Kosovu," in Ljubiša Stankov (ed.), *Politička situacija i medjunacionalni odnosi u savremenoj fazi socijalističkog razvitka i zadaci Saveza Komunista Srbije* (Belgrade: Institut za političke studije FPN, 1969), p. 142.

55. For example, censuses taken between 1961 and 1971 indicate considerable change occurred in the overall size and ethnic composition of the workforce. The number of actively employed persons with higher education had more than tripled in the intervening decade, and there was an eight-fold increase in the absolute number of Albanians in this category. By 1971 non-Slavs made up 50 percent of all highly specialized personnel compared to only 20 percent in 1961. The generational structure of persons with a formal higher education in 1971 (a smaller group than those included in the category "highly specialized") revealed the significant changes occurring in Kosovo, and previewed the potential difficulties that might unfold. Thus, while Albanians made up less than one-fifth of all individuals over 50 years of age with a higher education, and under one-third of those in the 35 to 49 year old age range, they composed nearly half of the educated elite under 35 years of age.

56. According to one Albanian sociologist at the university in Priština, a pattern of ecological stratification continued among different nationalities in Kosovo's urban centers: "In the so-called core of the cities and other urban settlements in Kosovo one finds those nationality groups who have the most favorable material and social positions (Serbs, Montenegrins, and even Turks) while the periphery of those settlements are occupied by the most underdeveloped strata in a socio-professional and cultural sense (Albanians, Gypsies, etc.). The Serbs and Montenegrins live in socially [state] owned apartments, while the Albanians live mainly in private homes which were constructed during the recent years of increasing urbanization." H. Islami, "Problemi društvenog razvitka Kosovskog sela," op. cit., p. 415. A 1986 study of Priština found that while Serbs and Montenegrins together made up 29 percent of the city's population, they occupied 49 percent of the state housing. The least developed district of Priština was 89 percent Albanian. The authors of the study suggest that such data "is a mirror in which we see social segregation according to national groups, and even 'ghettos.'" *FBIS*, February 13, 1986, p. 114.

57. The number of Albanian students increased from approximately 38 percent of total regional university enrollment in 1967–1968 to 72 percent by the end of the decade.

58. A. Sapir, "Economic Growth and Factor Substitution: What Ever Happened to the Yugoslav Economic Miracle?" *Economic Journal*, Vol. LXXXX, No. 358 (June 1980), pp. 294–313.

59. *Duga*, October 1–14, 1994, pp. 18–23.

60. *Jedinstvo*, February 14, 1974, p. 5.

61. In a 1977 secret speech to Kosovo party leaders (officially quoted only in part in 1981), Edward Kardelj warned against the serious danger of both continued Serbian and Albanian nationalism in the province, but added that "today the Albanians in Kosovo bear a particular responsibility because they are the people in the majority here in Kosovo." *FBIS*, November 27, 1981, p. 120. According to another top Slovenian official, Kardelj suggested that nationalism in Kosovo could erupt into "direct counter-revolution." *NIN*, June 7, 1981, p. 13. In May 1982, one of Kosovo's top political leaders claimed that during Tito's 1979 visit to the region he had secretly warned officials that Albanian nationalism was underestimated. *FBIS*, May 13, 1982, p. 16.

62. *FBIS*, October 17, 1979, pp. 114–115.

63. According to an official report, in the two months after the March–April demonstrations, "repressive and preventative measures were taken against 1,700 people of whom 506 were convicted: because of participation in the demonstrations 287, because of offering support to the demonstrators 38, because of attempts to organize demonstrations 31; 46 more were authors of enemy slogans and 104 because of public enemy secessionist acts. Stricter criminal procedures were begun against 154 of these persons, including 39 members of illegal organizations, 29 direct organizers of demonstrations and others involved in destructive behavior. Among the individuals against whom judicial measures were taken the largest number were intellectuals." *Skupština SFRJ, Stenografske beleške, Savezno veće*, June 9, 1981, p. 46.

64. *FBIS*, April 13, 1981, p. 17.

65. Ibid., November 2, 1981, p. 16.

66. Ibid., November 27, 1981, p. I26.

67. *NIN*, November 8, 1981, pp. 17–19, *FBIS*, September 4, 1981, p. 16. Kosovo had the highest annual birth rate in Europe at the time: 27 live births per thousand population. It has been officially estimated that the region's population (1.6 million in 1981) would reach 2.6 million by 2001 and 3.5 million by 2021. At this rate Yugoslavia's Albanian population may be greater than that of neighboring Albania by the middle of the twenty-first century. *Radio Free Europe Research*, August 7, 1987, p. 11.

68. *FBIS*, July 18, 1981, p. I16. Bakarič died in January 1983.

69. Ibid., pp. 3–4.

70. Ibid., p. I3.

71. Ibid., p. I32.

72. *Duga*, October 1–14, 1994, pp. 18–23.

73. By 1986, moral-political suitability was still a necessary, but not an entirely sufficient factor in Yugoslav elite recruitment. A new generation of younger leaders combining political reliability with higher educational specialization and a fresh perspective appeared to be gaining control in the Kosovo party organization. Louis Zanga, "The New Strong Men of Kosovo," *Radio Free Europe RAD Background Report*, No. 77

(May 31, 1986). It is also worth noting that in May 1986, the first party leader of Albanian origin became president of the nine-member collective state presidency. His election to this one-year post was a previously scheduled rotation among the republics and provinces, but it undoubtedly helped to assuage, at least symbolically, Albanian grievances about their previous positions.

74. About 1,000 Albanian students demonstrated in Priština and protests were repeated in other towns on the first anniversary of the 1981 "counter-revolution." Demonstrators were dispersed by special riot police. *Borba*, March 15, 1982, p. 3. Protests on a smaller scale marked the second anniversary. *FBIS*, March 14, 1983, pp. 110–111. A professor at the philosophy department of Priština University claimed that the center of the counter-revolution was at the university and that Kosovo's Albanian professors could be divided into three groups: (1) extremists who endorse Albanian irredentism; (2) those who support the League of Communists and work to implement its policies; and (3) "sympathizers," the largest of the three groups, including those who verbally support the League of Communists but privately support the ideas of Albanian nationalism and irredentism. *FBIS*, April 7, 1982, pp. 17–18.

75. *Politika*, October 27, 1981, p. 7. The Priština Communal Assembly reported that during the six months following the 1981 demonstrations, 4,000 Serbs and Montenegrins had emigrated from Priština. Ibid., October 5, 1981. This figure suggests that roughly eight percent of the Serbs and Montenegrins living in Priština emigrated directly after the 1981 crisis. Another report from Priština noted that "there is the phenomenon of the departure of highly trained and qualified cadres, cadres who are essential to the economy, and social activities in the municipality." Ibid., November 12,1981, p. 131. From 1981 to February 1987, 22,307 Serbs and Montenegrins were reported to have left Kosovo, lowering their proportion in the province's total population from 14.9 percent to 13.5 percent. Out of 1,445 communities in Kosovo, 650 had no Serbs and Montenegrins. *NIN*, No. 1904, June 28, 1987, p. 12.

76. *Borba*, June 19, 1981, p. 7; *NIN*, December 27, 1981, pp. 19–21; Ibid., January 3, 1982, pp. 24, 32.

77. Shkelzen Maliqi, "Demand for a New Status in the Albanian Movement in Kosovo," op. cit., p. 170.

78. Louis Zanga, "Rise of Tension in Kosovo Due to Migration," Radio Free Europe, June 28, 1983, p. 2.

79. Shkelzen Maliqi, "Demand for a New Status in the Albanian Movement in Kosovo," op. cit., pp. 269–270.

80. Ljiljana Bačević, "Nacionalna svest omladine," in *Djeca kriza; omladina Jugoslavije krajem osamdesetih* (Belgrade: Institut društvenih nauka, 1990), p. 160.

81. Shkelzen Maliqi, "Self-Understanding of the Albanians in Nonviolence," in Dušan Janjić and Shkelzen Maliqi (eds.), *Conflict or Dialogue: Serbian–Albanian Relations and Integration of the Balkans, Studies and Essays* (Subotica: Open University, European Civic Center for Conflict Resolution, 1994), p. 239.

CHAPTER 2

The Rise of Slobodan Milošević

Why did the Serbian people desire this great illusion named Slobodan Milošević . . . ? I emphasize the Serbian people wanted the illusion. And it has been living quite long under this illusion, as you can see, despite all that has happened to them, and is happening.

—*Ivan Stambolić (1995)*

Encouragement of "brotherhood and unity" among Yugoslavia's different ethnic groups was the quintessential feature of Titoist ideology. However, throughout Yugoslav communist history, some party leaders viewed expression of ethnic identity, and even ethnic tensions in the country, not as a danger, but as an opportunity. In the late 1960s and early 1970s, for example, several top Croatian communist officials seeking a popular base of support both tapped into, and helped stimulate, the mass ethno-nationalist sentiments sweeping their republic. As discussed in Chapter 1, a similar development occurred in Kosovo between 1968 and 1981, when the regime's strategy of tolerance for ethno-regional autonomy in that region impelled provincial Albanian communist leaders to mobilize the previously suppressed political aspirations of their ethnic constituents. But when the central leadership of the League of Communists perceived that local expressions of nationalism in both Croatia and Kosovo were being used to build up regional political machines at the expense of the fundamental authority of the broader regime, steps were quickly taken to halt the elite mobilization of ethnic identity and ethnic dissatisfaction.

Despite its aversion to any "anti-socialist" manifestations of nationalism, the Titoist regime's commitment (especially after the mid-1960s) to a pluralist brand of socialism fostered a considerable devolution of political authority to Yugoslavia's republics and provinces. The constitution of 1974 significantly enhanced such centrifugal tendencies in the Yugoslav federal system,

87

and—particularly after Tito's death in 1980—expanded the power of regional political elites. Indeed, although Tito's heirs opposed the development of a multi-party system, the hallmark of post-Tito Yugoslav political life was the ethnic and territorial "pluralism of elites." Such in-system pluralization, together with the gradual delegitimation of the incumbent communist party leaders who had succeeded Tito, dramatically expanded opportunities during the 1980s for the use of nationalism as a political resource both by politicians outside the League of Communists, and also by former Titoist stalwarts seeking a new formula to mobilize political support. Communist ideology had substantially lost its appeal. But in the Balkans nationalism remained a potent force available to ambitious political leaders.

The Upwardly Mobile Manager

Slobodan Milošević would prove to be the most successful Yugoslav communist functionary to exploit ethnic nationalism as a political tool. Paradoxically, Milošević was politically spawned and shaped by the very Yugoslav communist regime he would eventually help destroy. Indeed, consideration of Milošević's early life, his political socialization, and the profound political metamorphosis he underwent in middle age, reflect and illustrate the fascinating and traumatic transformation of Balkan and Serbian society during the twentieth century.

Slobodan Milošević was both a war baby and a child of the revolution. He was born on August 20, 1941 in the provincial Serbian town of Požarevac (about 70 kilometers southeast of Belgrade), only four months after Yugoslavia's dismemberment by Nazi Germany and its allies, and two months after Tito and the Yugoslav Communist Party initiated a guerrilla struggle against both the fascist occupation forces and various anticommunist nationalist groups. Milošević's mother and father were both of Montenegrin origin. His father, Svetozar—the son of an officer in the Montenegrin army—was born in Uvač, Montenegro in 1907, and completed his university education at the Theological Faculty in Belgrade. His mother, Stanislava, was also born in Montenegro. Her father, a Montenegrin army officer, was killed during the first Balkan War.[1]

During his early career, Svetozar Milošević worked as a Russian language teacher in Serbian Orthodox high schools, first in Kosovo, and then in Požarevac, where he had moved in 1941 with his wife and Slobodan's older brother, Borislav. When Slobodan was nine years old, Svetozar Milošević separated from his wife, leaving her and their two small children alone while he returned to Montenegro. His father's departure from the family in 1950 was one in a series of traumatic personal episodes for Milošević. Two years earlier, in 1948, a favorite uncle, Milislav Koljenšić, who was a communist strongly committed to the USSR, committed suicide, probably owing to his depression over the Tito–Stalin split.[2] Milošević's father, Svetozar, would also commit suicide in 1962, at a time when Slobodan was a 21-year-old university student on an excursion in the Soviet Union. Stanislava Milošević raised Slobodan and his older brother Borislav (who regards himself as a Montenegrin) in Požarevac, where she worked as a teacher. A neighbor remembers her as a tall, dark and exceptionally beautiful woman, who was highly intelligent, very strict, and honest.[3] Milošević's mother had joined the communist party at the end of the war, and later served as a member of the local party committee. In 1973, when Milošević was 32 years old and working as a young managerial official in Belgrade, his mother committed suicide.

The town of Požarevac, where Slobodan grew up during the 1940s and 1950s, had a population of about 15,000. It was, in some respects, a microcosm of communist Yugoslavia, but hardly a bastion of multicultural diversity. For example, ethnically, Serbs constituted about 95 percent of the Požarevac area (in 1948 central Serbia as a whole was about 92 percent ethnically Serb). Life in Požarevac, as much of post–World War II Yugoslavia, exhibited the features and problems of a developing society in transition. Like most Serbian provincial areas, the predominantly agrarian town was still going through the early stages of industrialization. A traditionally bustling market center, located in one of Serbia's moderately well-developed areas, Požarevac was designated as one of the republic's 62 "third order" regional centers in 1954 (that is, a town beginning to experience the impact of higher levels of economic development).[4] The town's main claim to historical fame—before attracting attention as the birthplace of Slobodan Milošević—was its role as the site of the Treaty of Požarevac in 1718, when the Ottoman Turks had been forced to relinquish various territories to the Hapsburg empire. Undistinguished architecturally, the town's two major landmarks are a famous prison in nearby Zabela, where many Serbian political figures have been incarcerated (a "university of revolutionaries"), and a well-known horse breeding stable. By the time Milošević was a young man, the main street of the town had dreary rows of long four-story apartment houses, a department store located in the middle of town, and a flea market. Požarevac was a rapidly developing town, but still on the political and economic periphery of a country undergoing dynamic change.

As a boy in Požarevac during the mid-1950s, Milošević attended the same local secondary school where his mother worked as a teacher. By most accounts, Milošević was an excellent student, and impressed everyone as a serious, industrious, and responsible young man. An acquaintance at the

Požarevac secondary school remembers Slobodan: "He looked handsome, his hair was black, well combed, his cheeks were also red. I remember that he was never messy or disobedient. He wasn't like the other boys."[5] Later after becoming a successful politician, an official biographical statement would mention his role as chief editor of his high school newspaper as an example of his early socio-political participation.

In December 1958, when he was seventeen, Slobodan met the 16-year-old Mirjana Marković (Mira to her friends), the woman who would eventually become his wife (in 1965), his best friend, and closest political confidant. Mirjana Marković came from a prominent communist family from Požarevac. Her parents were both communist members of the Partisans, who did not marry. During the war, Mirjana's mother, Vera Miletić, served as a leading official (secretary) of the Belgrade Communist Party's local committee organization. Her father was Moma Marković, a Partisan hero, who had organized the guerilla uprising in the Požarevac area. Her mother's relative, Davorjanka-Zdenka Paunović, was Tito's secretary and mistress during the war. "I was born on July 10, 1942 in the ranks of the Partisans," Mirjana has remarked. "This influenced significantly the formation of my personality: my mother and Zdenka [Paunović] are cousins, but might be sisters, they were so close. . . . Zdenka went with Tito, my mother went to the Partisan detachments. Neither of them returned home. My mother was executed at the age of 24 in the concentration camp at Banjica."[6] Some observers regard Mirjana's account of her mother's death at the hands of the Nazis as contrived and rather vague. According to a different view, Vera Miletić was executed by the Partisans at the conclusion of the war for betraying secrets to the Gestapo when under torture. Whichever version is true, Mirjana has had to bear a heavy political legacy since childhood. "From the moment I was born," Mirjana wrote in 1991, "the world was political. For me, it has more or less remained so."[7] Her father, who became a politically influential communist after the war, had little to do with Mirjana (he died in 1992). As a baby, Mirjana was sent to live with her mother's parents at Požarevac. She grew up as part of the communist elite, but felt marginal and emotionally driven to prove herself politically. She had goals and connections, but needed a devoted soul mate. He had insecurities and talent, but needed love and direction. At the time they met in 1958, Mirjana, although a year younger than Slobodan, had already joined the League of Communists, and had served as president of the communist youth group in their school. From the time they met, the two teenagers were inseparable, and in their circle of friends were known as "Romeo and Juliet." Beyond their close personal relationship, and obvious reliance on one another, close observers of the couple have suggested that Mirjana would become crucial to Slobodan's overall psychological stability. Considering his parents' separation during his youth, their eventual suicides, and Milošević's penchant for privacy during his adult years, Mirjana undoubtedly filled a void in his life, and not surprisingly would later be able to exert enormous influence on her husband.

During the period Milošević was attending secondary school (1953–1958), Yugoslav socialism was undergoing considerable political change. After a period of uncertainty and improvisation, which followed the 1948 Tito–Stalin rift, the country's model of communism evolved into a unique political amalgam comprised of a one-party oligarchy, a conservative police apparatus, a spurious federal system, and a novel structure of promising, but politically powerless, workers' councils. During the 1950s, young people such as Slobodan and Mirjana were expected to imbibe the values of the regime's distinct anti-statist ideology. At the heart of this system was the idea of "Yugoslav socialist patriotism," that is, the notion that the "national question" had been solved and that ideological bonds among "producers" would gradually transcend traditional ethno-regional forms of identity. Like thousands of other young Yugoslav citizens, especially those from politically active families, Slobodan and Mirjana voluntarily participated (first during 1958, but again in 1959 and 1963) in the construction of the so-called "Brotherhood and Unity" highway between Belgrade and Niš (the Belgrade–Zagreb portion had been completed in 1948). The participation of youth brigades from all Yugoslavia's republics was regarded by the regime, and also by early Yugoslav sociological studies, as an important factor strengthening bonds among the country's diverse ethnic groups, and creating an enhanced commitment to the political values of Tito's socialist regime.[8]

Most ambitious young people, particularly with good political connections, couldn't wait to leave Serbian provincial towns such as Požarevac for the excitement and opportunities offered by nearby Belgrade. A city with a population of about half a million in the mid-1950s, Belgrade, which had rapidly grown in the postwar period into a "core city," or "metropolitan complex," was the capital of both Serbia and the Yugoslav socialist federation. Members of the younger generation who flocked to Belgrade during the massive migration to urban centers in the 1950s and 1960s, typically kept in close touch with their provincial roots, retreating from the city on holidays and weekends to relax and visit their relatives, and replenish their cupboards with local staples. Moreover, whether the new city dwellers in Belgrade joined the ranks of the rapidly expanding urban intelligentsia and "red bourgeoisie," or were part of the capital's growing industrial proletariat, the migrants were in many respects "urban villagers" who usually retained their traditional "nationalist fervor and symbolic devotion to Serbian folkways."[9] Upwardly mobile young people such as Slobodan Milošević and Mirjana Marković might identify with the ideology and values of the new regime, and seek to migrate from the periphery to the center of society, but like many of their fellow citizens, their provincial backgrounds undoubtedly shaped many facets of their political outlook and behavior. As their careers advanced, Slobodan and Mirjana would enjoy weekends in their home town—staying at her family house, an old Serbian-style one-story structure, blocked from street view by a large walnut tree—removed from the pressure of power and glare of publicity. This was an easily arranged retreat since, as Milošević reminded an interviewer in December 1998, "Požarevac is only 40 minutes by car from Belgrade."[10] Milošević's associates have said that he likes to relax in the country. He is also apparently fond of animals—he doesn't hunt but loves guns (revolvers)—and enjoys occasionally feeding the chickens around the family's country home.

In January 1959, at the age of eighteen, Slobodan joined the League of Communists. The next year he entered law school at Belgrade University, the faculty renowned for preparing young people to serve as officials in the Serbian communist establishment. Mirjana moved to the capital a year later, and registered at the Philosophy Faculty. Milošević lived in one of the university's student dormitories during his law school days. Some observers suggest that during his years of study, he may have experienced some economic difficulties. Mirjana, far better-connected in Belgrade's top communist circles, lived with her aunt. While studying law in Belgrade during the first part of the 1960s, Milošević served as the law school's Secretary of the Faculty Committee of the League of Communists, and subsequently as secretary for ideological political work in the League's Belgrade University Committee, and president of that committee's Ideological Commission.[11] One of his former classmates claims Milošević was "incredibly disciplined, and took communism with deadly earnestness when everybody else thought it was a terrible bore."[12] It was at law school that Milošević forged a close friendship with another young communist, Ivan Stambolić. Stambolić, five years older than Milošević, was the nephew of Petar Stambolić, one of Serbia's leading communist officials. Elected President of the Serbian League of Communists in 1966, the older Stambolić was strategically placed to assist his nephew's friends. Close observers of Milošević say that he would genuinely come to "adore" Ivan Stambolić, and looked upon him as an elder brother. It was Ivan Stambolić who nominated Milošević for the post of Secretary of the League of Communists at the law school, a position which in many respects marked the first step in Milošević's career as a communist functionary.[13] For her part, however, Mirjana Marković appeared to be jealous of Stambolić, and often took issue with his political views, although she was careful not to be too critical for fear of upsetting Slobodan. During this period, the Milošević's were also raising a family. Their daughter, Marija, was born in 1965, and their son Marko in 1974. Beginning in 1974, Mirjana began teaching at Belgrade University. During this time she also finished her doctoral thesis, which she received from the University of Niš in 1979.

The post-secondary education of the young Milošević couple, and their early working life following their university education, coincided with a decade of steady Titoist reform including the adoption of a liberalized constitution (1962–1963); a bold, albeit limited, market reform of the economy (1965); a purge of the secret police (1966); the decentralization of the League of Communists (1967); the adoption of constitutional amendments creating a confederalized state framework (1968); and Tito's introduction of a rotating state leadership (1970–1971). It was also a phase when the regime officially recognized that the "national question" had reemerged as a major problem in Yugoslavia, and that social conflicts constituted a normal facet of a socialist society.

Milošević's friends from his law school days generally point out that the young Slobodan's commitment to Yugoslav Marxist ideology was rather superficial, and that he tended to view adherence to communist orthodoxy primarily as a vehicle for career advancement.[14] In this regard, Milošević was not atypical of pro-regime political activists from his particular generation and milieu. For example, Milošević and his counterparts avoided any association with individuals and episodes (such as the June 1968 demonstrations at Belgrade University), which might tarnish their "moral-political suitability" and could jeopardize their future career prospects. A Yugoslav opinion survey of the younger generation about the same time Milošević graduated from law school identified the use of "friendly connections and acquaintances" as the most successful method of occupational advancement used by the majority of people.[15] The young, ambitious, and politically conformist Milošević proved highly adept at exploiting such contacts or patron–client networks, which were a characteristic feature of Titoist Yugoslavia (and other one-party states), for his early career advancement. Milošević's major patron was Ivan Stambolić.

Throughout the two decades following Milošević's graduation from law school in 1964, Stambolić generously helped the younger Slobodan to obtain a succession of jobs, some of which had already been occupied by Stambolić. As Stambolić advanced up the economic and political ladder in communist Yugoslavia, the ambitious Milošević eagerly stepped into the posts offered to him by his successful comrade and friend. For example, from 1969 to 1973, after holding some minor posts in the Belgrade city administration, and also spending a year and a half completing his military service (1968–1969), Milošević became Assistant General Director under Stambolić at "Tehnogas," a major Yugoslav enterprise producing technical industrial gases. He then followed Stambolić (1973–1978) to become the firm's General Director. During these years, Stambolić's career progressed rapidly in the Serbian economic and political hierarchy. For example, he served as the president of the Belgrade City Chamber [*Komora*], and was a member of the Central Committee of the Serbian League of Communists (SKS). He eventually became the Secretary of the

Central Committee of the Serbian League of Communists, and then served as prime minister of Serbia, president of the City of the League of Communists of Belgrade, president of the Central Committee of the SKS and, until 1987, president of Serbia's collective state presidency. Milošević closely linked himself to his friend's steady advancement and network of contacts, and in 1978 moved into a new role as president of one of Yugoslavia's leading commercial banks, the United Belgrade Bank or UBB (Udružena beogradska banka), where he remained until 1984. While certainly a loyal Titoist, and a card-carrying member of the League of Communists, Milošević at this stage in his career was primarily a politically well-connected technocrat, and not a highly ideological party apparatchik.

During his years as a banking official, Milošević forged many of the key friendships and political relationships that would be crucial to his later success. One contact of particular importance was Borka Vučić, a professional banker, who was thirteen years older than Milošević. Some observers of the relationship between Vučić—a stern-looking and shrewd communist financial bureaucrat who had been a Partisan during World War II—and Milošević say that she was largely responsible for helping him become a successful banking official, and that his subsequent reliance on her as a mentor and loyal friend, was the key to his success in Serbia's financial circles (during the 1990s, Vučić would become his agent in managing Yugoslavia's off-shore financial operation on Cyprus, and in 1999 became a minister for "Cooperation with International Financial Organizations").

As a Yugoslav banker, Milošević came into contact with the higher echelons of the international financial community. During 1979, for example, Milošević attended the annual meeting of the World Bank and International Monetary Fund, held in Belgrade where he met David Rockefeller, of the Chase Manhattan Bank. It was during this period that he made several visits to the United States, where, with his solid command of English, he made many useful contacts and also developed a self-proclaimed understanding and affinity for various American perspectives. For example, in March 1980, Milošević visited New York, where UBB had established an office on Madison Avenue to promote joint ventures, where he met a number of leading American bankers, including David Rockefeller once again, Leland Prussia, Chairman of the Bank of America, and John F. McGillicuddy, Chairman of the Board of Manufacturers Hanover Trust. When McGillicuddy visited Yugoslavia the following year, Milošević was his host. Although still ensconced in the ruling circles of a one-party communist regime, Milošević was regarded as having "liberal" and reformist views. Those who worked closely with Milošević feel that he genuinely believed that Yugoslavia should become more integrated into the world economy, and also favored the development of some form of market socialism. He also developed a keen appreciation for American efficiency and organization. Interestingly, his wife has claimed that her husband's visits to the United States had a significant impact on his personality and work. According to Mirjana Marković, Slobodan admired the pragmatic and down-to-earth style of Americans, which he felt was similar to his personality, and which contrasted markedly with the "imaginary, the dark and metaphysical" aspects present in the "Slavic nature."[16]

Looking back on his years in banking and his visits to the United States, Milošević claims that he worked in an atmosphere unfettered by excessive state control, and that he had a preference for such arrangements. "Yugoslavia was never [a] communist country, never a member of the Eastern bloc . . . we were a free country. . . . As a banker in Tito's Yugoslavia I was free. And nobody was telling me from the government what to do . . . at that time the state was not involved in the banks." He also later claimed that as a banker he fought to establish a market economy, because "the only future for the economy can be [a] market economy, because what is the alternative?" In fact, Milošević has asserted that one of the reasons he became more involved in politics is because of his concern that the state was beginning to excessively meddle in banking affairs, and particularly to subsidize unprofitable banks.[17] When asked by an American interviewer in 1994 if he was a "communist philosophically," Milošević claimed that the "expression" had been "demonized in the American language." "We want to create a wealthy society," he explained, "on the basis of a market economy and we are a market economy . . . and also a just society."[18]

Entering the Political Fray: Serbian Politics and the Stambolić Line

In the early 1980s, after spending over a decade in the economic sector, Milošević followed his old friend Ivan Stambolić into the sharply factionalized and hardball world of Serbian politics. Stambolić was already an established member of the Titoist communist elite, and was responsible for managing a large and important republic. Having mastered the game of musical chairs routinely played by members of the Yugoslav elite (a process referred to in the Yugoslav communist lexicon as the "rotation of cadre"), who wanted to remain professional politicians despite official encouragement of "de-professionalized" politics, Stambolić smoothed the way for the ascent of a new postwar generation of Serbian communist politicians, who gradually sidelined the earlier Partisan cadre. Slobodan's political advancement was part of this Stambolić-led process of elite change. In 1982, while still serving as a bank president, Milošević became a member of the collective presidency of the SKS, a vantage point from which he could closely observe the dynamics of political power in his native republic. An even more important power base for Milošević, however, was his nonprofessional and unsalaried position as the president of the Municipal Committee of the League of Communists in Stari Grad, the largest of Belgrade's municipalities. And in the spring of 1984, Milošević assumed his first solo role as a major Serbian political functionary in Serbia, when he became President of the City Committee of the League of Communists in Belgrade (a post that had been held by Stambolić from 1982 to 1984). There was no evidence, as yet, that Milošević and his old friend of twenty years, Ivan Stambolić, were anything but a close-knit team. The younger and less visible Milošević was, however, still the junior partner.

Milošević joined Ivan Stambolić in the higher echelons of Serbian political hierarchy at a time when the republic's communist regime was faced with a number of serious challenges. Briefly, during the first half of the 1980s the Serbian communist leadership was preoccupied with three closely related negative legacies of the Tito era: (1) an economic crisis growing out of structural problems in the economy and economic mismanagement (that could be traced back to the mid-1970s); (2) an internationality crisis traceable to the persistence of the deep interethnic conflict in Kosovo, and; (3) a political crisis arising from the general delegitimation of the long-ruling League of Communists. The political and economic crises were interdependent, and both crises stimulated, and in turn were exacerbated, by the problem of ethnonationalism in the perennially fragile country. Throughout this period, the Serbian political scene and elite structure continued to be dominated by the same clique of passive, obedient, and uninspired political leaders whom Tito had foisted on the republic a decade earlier.[19] Tito's move had been connected with a purge of regional liberal leaders in Yugoslavia that began with the removal of independent-minded Croatian communists in late 1971, and later was extended to include the removal of other leading party officials in different republics. Thus, the political delegitimation of the Serbian communist leadership was well underway in 1981 when, as discussed in Chapter 1, only a year after Tito's death, the republic was hit by growing economic difficulties and a serious escalation of tensions between Albanians and Serbs in the province of Kosovo.

Lacking a coherent strategy to deal with its multiple crises, the republic's relatively weak communist establishment turned to its seasoned tactics of limited repression and drift in order to maintain power. Of particular future significance, Serbian leaders, both in the decade before and the years immediately after Tito's death, avoided taking any innovative steps with regard to the issue of politicized ethnicity. Thus, all nonsocialist forms of ethnic participation were officially prohibited, while extreme or vocal expressions of nationalism on the part of any ethnic group were strongly condemned and often harshly punished. The regime's policy for dealing with resurgent nationalism was rarely consistent, or able to remedy the serious problems that motivated ethnic conflict. For example, although the violent outburst of nationalism by Albanian nationalists and their sympathizers in Kosovo during 1968 had been quashed, Tito, together with the weak Serbian communist leadership, permitted Albanian communist leaders in Kosovo to gradually consolidate their hold on the province's political machine.

For most Serbs, Tito's policy in Kosovo amounted to a process of officially sanctioned "Albanianization" which, they believed, threatened the influence and survival of the local Serbian community in the province. When the prominent Serbian writer and longtime communist Dobrica Ćosić warned in 1968 of dangers connected with Albanian nationalism, he was politically chastised and placed under surveillance. He soon resigned from the League of Communists. Outside public view, intellectual concern regarding Serbian rights in Kosovo also intensified during the 1970s, along with popular dissatisfaction with the regime's policy toward Serbian interests generally. The republican leadership's political position was further weakened by crudely managed repression of neo-Marxist dissidents and other politically nonconformist Serbs in the mid and late 1970s, and also by the Belgrade regime's failure to adequately address the republic's looming economic problems. Thus, in the first years following Tito's death in mid-1980, the Serbian leadership faced a groundswell of dissatisfaction within both the general population and the ranks of the Serbian intelligentsia. That the Serbian elite had been purged of strong liberal leaders in the 1970s, and for the next 15 years would be guided by relatively weak officials who lacked substantial political legitimacy in their republic, are extremely important factors explaining both the failure of Serbia to creatively cope with the problems it faced, and also the eventual success of Slobodan Milošević and his illiberal political orientation.

Ivan Stambolić, who had already emerged as an important political force in the late Tito era, tended to regard creative constitutional engineering as the best strategy for deflecting anticommunist and anti-regime criticism in Serbia. Like Stambolić, many Serbs felt that the republic's major economic and ethnic difficulties were fundamentally related to flaws in the 1974 federal constitution that had essentially fragmented Serbia by granting the republic's two autonomous provinces, Kosovo and Vojvodina, near republican-level status. The devolutionary and divisive trends stimulated by the 1974 constitution were viewed by many Serbs as having encouraged Albanian nationalism in Kosovo, and stimulated a growing drive for political autonomy by leaders in Vojvodina. In Serbian public opinion, something like a "wounded lion psychology" gradually developed, namely, the feeling that Serbia had been gravely weakened by the constitutional power that had been accorded to the two provinces.[20] In order to rectify matters, and also to reverse the regime's debilitated image, many Serbian leaders argued for a full-scale revision of the 1974 constitution.

The 1981 round of Albanian nationalist demonstrations in Kosovo once again brought the issue of provincial powers and ethnic relations within Serbia to the top of the political agenda. Indeed, during the first part of the 1980s, Ivan Stambolić would be required to spend much of his time trying to assuage an upsurge of Serbian political dissatisfaction by dangling the promise of constitutional and economic reforms that would, he maintained, reassert Serbian paramountcy vis-à-vis its two provincial units, as well as improve the republic's alleged weakness within Yugoslavia. Through such change, Stambolić and his closest allies asserted, Serbia would cease to simply be one player in an eight-sided political structure (i.e., the six republics and Serbia's two provinces). Though Stambolić struggled to identify problems and develop solutions, his promises of future constitutional change did little to moderate immediate ethnic and economic discontent within Serbia. Thus, political resentment against the constitution and the communist regime steadily increased, while gratification continued to be postponed. For example, efforts by Stambolić and other communist officials to balance official condemnation of Albanian nationalism in Kosovo with a reciprocal indictment of Serbian nationalism only dissatisfied both sides in the growing Albanian–Serbian divide in the republic.

One expression of the latent support for officially condemned ethno-political sentiment within Serbia occurred in August 1983 when thousands of Serbs turned out for the funeral of Aleksandar Ranković. Ranković had been purged by Tito in July 1966, but his wartime record as a Partisan leader, his conservative political views, and his heavy-handed police repression against Albanians in Kosovo had made him a hero to the majority of Serbs.[21] Moreover, in Serbian public opinion there was considerable antipathy toward the members of the post-Ranković Serbian political oligarchy, who were perceived as having capitulated to Tito and to the non-Serb communist leaders in the country.[22] It does not seem too far-fetched to speculate that Slobodan Milošević, an ambitious official just beginning his political ascent in Belgrade's communist hierarchy, must have been impressed by the phenomenon of the popular outpouring of recognition and emotion for Ranković. The message seemed clear: whomever assumed Ranković's mantle as a hard-nosed communist leader devoted to Serbian national interests would likely enjoy the support of an important but still rather silent constituency in Serbian politics. At the time of Ranković's death, when Serbia's political elite met to discuss the funeral arrangements, Milošević appeared to show little concern, and remained a stalwart Titoist opposed to any manifestation of nationalism. But when he later calculated the utility of populist mobilization as a political method, Milošević may well have remembered the large number of people in 1983 who had spontaneously paid their respects to a Serbian "national" leader.

Throughout this period, Stambolić attempted to calm nationalist sentiments in Serbia, and also cooperate with communist leaders in the other Yugoslav republics. Although he downplayed the potential of danger from extreme Serb nationalists who favored radical measures toward Albanians and other minorities in Serbia, Stambolić was not reluctant to speak out against the growing chorus of strident Serbian nationalism that was being voiced both within and outside communist ranks. For example, in May 1985 at a meeting of the Serbian Central Committee dealing with ideology, Stambolić warned against any "reconciliation" between Yugoslav Marxist or "Partisan perspectives" on nationalism, and the officially discredited view of the anticommunist Chetniks. "Nationalist views and action," Stambolić insisted, "must be beaten everywhere and at all times. We have realistically grasped this danger and have tried to examine its roots and causes." Stambolić also cautioned that Serbian communists must take a "permanent militant attitude to nationalistic poisoning of the young."[23] The communist leader conceded that serious ideological and political divisions existed in the Serbian political elite concerning matters such as Kosovo, and relations among the various republics, but he urged a "patient" and "tolerant" approach to reconciling such differences. And he stressed that in Yugoslavia "the bad and the good are not distributed territorially."[24]

During the period from roughly 1981 through early 1986, Slobodan Milošević appeared to adhere quite closely to the Stambolić line and the general parameters of discourse among Serbia's communist political elite. Indeed, most public statements by Milošević at this time regarding political matters amounted to little more than ritualistic incantations of accepted Titoist orthodoxy, and uninspired variations of the latest views espoused by Stambolić. In retrospect, however, one statement by Milošević does indicate that an important new perspective was beginning to influence his thinking. Thus, in November 1984, at a meeting of the Serbian Central Committee, and only some seven months after becoming head of the Belgrade organization of the League of Communists, Milošević made an intriguing remark about the need for Serbian communists to liberate themselves from a sense of guilt about the historic nationalism of the Serbian bourgeoisie. On the contrary, he observed, Serbian communists should feel "untainted by a complex of unitarism," should not "cover their heads in shame, and have every reason to say what they think."[25] In a volume of Milošević's collected remarks, which would be published in 1989 and that included about sixty of his selected statements, the November 1984 speech was featured as one of his first major public statements. Moreover, his wife would later identify November 1984 as the beginning of the "just and beautiful struggle for the national affirmation of the Serbian people in Yugoslavia."[26] But though Milošević's November 1984 remarks are suggestive of his future tactics, and may have enhanced his popularity in some nationalist quarters, they did not yet represent a fundamental break with the prevailing views of the Yugoslav communist establishment, nor a coherent public program for mobilizing popular support. Thus, other Serbian communist politicians were also asserting that Yugoslavia should play a more active role in Yugoslav political life, endeavor to address the republic's special grievances (e.g., the excessive power given to Serbia's provinces under the 1974 constitution), and get over any "complex of hegemonism." Milošević was still far from endorsing a novel program of militant Serb nationalism mixed with communist rhetoric. Indeed, at the May 1985 Serbian Central Committee Meeting on Ideology, Milošević, who was the first speaker on the roster, was careful to attack efforts by the "old dogmatic opportunists" and new anticommunists to "question the fundamental values" of Yugoslav society, including the "reality of the concept of brotherhood and unity."

Meanwhile, Milošević ran the party apparatus in Belgrade so effectively that his closest associates referred to him as the "little Lenin."[27] Such organizational efficiency, along with his ostensible ideological orthodoxy and loyalty to Ivan Stambolić, were rewarded in early 1986 when Stambolić advanced Milošević as the sole candidate for the important post of President of the Central Committee of the Serbian League of Communists. In nominating Milošević, Stambolić, who was vacating his post to become state president of Serbia, faced strong opposition from the Serbian political leader, Dragoslav Marković. Though the uncle of Milošević's wife, Marković's long-time political feud with Ivan Stambolić had alienated him from both the latter's politically powerful uncle, Petar Stambolić, and the younger ally of the Stambolić family, Slobodan Milošević. Other members of the Serbian political establishment also shared certain reservations about Milošević, but Ivan Stambolić lobbied hard to help his younger friend win the post. Milošević also received the endorsement of a key figure in the Yugoslav military-police apparatus, the respected and feared Titoist general, Nikola Ljubičić. Ljubičić's evaluation of Milošević's credentials in early 1986 provide a revealing indication of how the old guard viewed the younger leader: "Slobodan engaged in a struggle against nationalism, against liberalism, and against all forms of counter-revolution in Belgrade. I think he has passed the test. I would hope he would take such activity farther, with even more persistence."[28] By the "struggle against nationalism," Ljubičić was referring to the "Albanian problem," which had become paramount in the concerns of hard-line Serbian communist officials.[29]

As for the more moderate Ivan Stambolić, he would later reflect on his own reasons for supporting Milošević at the time.

> After much discussion in the Serbian leadership, my wish was to create a homogeneous team of the middle generation, a dynamic team, who judged matters similarly, and who could finish the job they began. . . . And on basic questions of the

Constitution, Kosovo, the development of Serbia, Slobodan and I had the same outlook . . . for me he was a devoted friend.[30]

In later years, Stambolić would also accent his responsibility for this crucial step in Milošević's career:

[It] derived from the unwritten rule that the head of the party decides who his successor will be. . . . I myself thought that it would be easier for me to curb him. . . . Milošević was well received in Yugoslavia because of the sharp actions that he carried out in Belgrade. He was considered a real communist, even less in doubt than myself. I knew about his mistakes, but I was convinced that his virtues were more vital. . . . I also stated some misgivings, and he took that very hard. It was the first time that he was not able to conceal his reaction. . . . I saw that sometimes he was too abrupt, that he took shortcuts, that he took some steps too quickly, that he made superficial decisions, that he judged too harshly . . . and that he had other similar mistakes characteristic of a hardhearted man. . . . At that time Milošević seemed the most suitable to me. The problem is that I did not foresee that all of his traits could turn into ghastly mistakes if they developed to an extreme.[31]

Ivan Stambolić clearly hoped that Milošević could assist him in obtaining a measured resolution to Serbia's internal problems and divisions, and also improving the republic's relations with the other parts of the multinational federation. In April 1986, just one month before securing Milošević's promotion as leader of Serbia's communists, Stambolić had visited two communities in Kosovo Polje, the heart of Kosovo's Serbian ethnic community. During his visit, Stambolić had urged that "paranoia and 'ghosts'" be placated, and he pleaded for "disinformation which introduces confusion to be prevented." Stambolić also commented sympathetically about the serious threats to the security of Serbs in Kosovo, on the unfortunate emigration of Serbs and Montenegrins out of the province, and on the need to challenge Albanian "irredentists" and "separatists." But the Serbian leader also warned his listeners that they should not seek to resolve their local difficulties by a populist mobilization of Serbian nationalist solidarity, especially through rallies and demonstrations. "This is a great evil and is playing with fire," he warned.[32] Moreover, after returning from Belgrade, Stambolić cautioned his comrades that in order to curb Albanian nationalism in Kosovo, the Serbian leaders would have to give their full backing to the moderate pro-regime Albanian communist political leaders. "Every Serb," Stambolić emphasized, "who denies confidence to Albanian communists should be told that he is a Serbian nationalist."[33] Only one year after Stambolić's visit to Kosovo, the citizens of the province would receive another guest from the Belgrade communist leadership. However, the second visitor's response to Serbian concerns about Kosovo would depart significantly from the Stambolić line.

Milošević's Metamorphosis: "Power Above Ideas"

In late September 1986, the Belgrade newspaper *Večernje Novosti* published sections of a draft "Memorandum" which had been under preparation by members of the Serbian Academy of Sciences and Arts (SANU) since May 1985. Serbia's top political leaders were aware that the SANU document was being written, but had no idea about the controversial details that would soon engender a firestorm of critical comment throughout Yugoslavia. Among other things, the Memorandum asserted that since before World War II, when the Comintern directed the underground Communist Party of Yugoslavia, Yugoslav communist leaders had adopted policies contrary to Serbian interests; that a longtime anti-Serb coalition had existed between Croatian and Slovenian communists, which was responsible for Serbia's growing difficulties; that the anti-Serb coalition had deliberately weakened Serbia by strengthening the power of the republic's two provinces, and; that except for the period of the Independent State of Croatia during World War II, the position of the Serbian minority communities in Croatia and Bosnia–Herzegovina had never been worse.[34]

The events set out in the Memorandum were also alleged to have contributed to the communist regime's repression of the Serbian cultural intelligentsia in Yugoslavia, as well as the dire situation reputedly faced by the Serbs of Kosovo. In essence, the Memorandum characterized the Titoist approach to the "national question" as an elaborate deceit and failure that had seriously harmed Serbia and Serbian interests, and also had stimulated interethnic and interregional conflict throughout the country. Although the solutions recommended by the Memorandum's authors indicated their loyalty to Marxist political ideals, and to the potential reformability of socialist Yugoslavia, their attack sharply undercut the political and constitutional legitimacy of the Titoist regime.[35] As for Serbia itself, the Memorandum urged that after "four decades of Serbian passivity," it was time for the republic "to define and declare its own national interests." Only through "Social Democracy" and the assertion of Serbian equality in Yugoslavia, the Memorandum suggested, could Serbs overcome the legacy of an "historically worn out ideology."[36] The writer, Dobrica Ćosić, who has denied any part in drafting the Memorandum, argues that "the police seized the draft and had it published in the paper, together with their own comments in order to compromise democratic opposition to Titoism, in which the Academy was a very strong reference point. The draft Memorandum was markedly anti-Titoist and pro-Yugoslav, without one single chauvinistic sentence. . . . The communist leadership in Yugoslavia, and of the Croat and Slovene separatists . . . believed that any defense of Yugoslavia was to be seen as an expression of Serb nationalism."[37]

The publication of the Memorandum naturally added grist to the mill of those political forces in Yugoslavia, and also in Serbia, who believed that the Serbian communist leadership was committed to the goal of restoring Greater Serbian hegemony on both the republican and federal levels. Although the Memorandum was an unfinished document, leaked for political purposes, and representing only a section of SANU, it could hardly be ignored by Serbian political authorities. Thus, Stambolić and his leadership group were immediately forced to respond to the controversial contents of the Memorandum, and also to adopt an attitude toward the SANU intellectuals who had prepared the document. Interestingly, Milošević, who for years had passionately voiced his devotion to Titoist precepts regarding inter-nationality relations, adopted an unusually cautious and ambiguous approach to the Memorandum. For example, his remarks about the Memorandum at a February 1987 meeting of the Belgrade City Committee of the League of Communists amounted to a lukewarm and rather hesitant condemnation of the SANU members who, he suggested, must change their views and exercise "responsibility toward their communist consciences."[38] Although Milošević took a somewhat harsher view of the Memorandum behind closed doors, he left public condemnation of the document's contents to Stambolić and other Serbian party leaders.

Such tactics allowed Milošević maximum room for maneuver. For example, he took care not to publicly ridicule the prominent nationalist intellectuals who had crafted the Memorandum, and who played an enormous role in shaping Serbian elite and public opinion. However, temporarily, Milošević still avoided an open break with Ivan Stambolić. Thus, though Stambolić and others busily engaged in sharp polemics with intellectuals from the Serbian Academy, Milošević was able to position himself advantageously in the evolving political struggle taking place in the republic. In this regard Milošević was typical of most Serbian communists who were reevaluating or hedging their positions on the critical question of how best to advance Serbian national interests. Thus, as ethnopolitical sentiments became increasingly inflamed, and overshadowed "Yugoslav socialist patriotism" in the post-Titoist period (e.g., the Serb–Albanian conflict and growing nationalism in each of the six republics), members of the Serbian League of Communists were forced to confront the question of how they were going to respond to this issue. For example, did the vigorous protection of Serb national goals regarding issues raised in the Memorandum constitute a legitimate perspective within the regime's ideological boundaries, or, in contrast, did the Memorandum exemplify the aggressive and overt type of "unitarism" and "hegemonic" nationalism long condemned by Yugoslav communists?

For many Serbian communists there seemed to be a good deal of common ground between the concerns advanced by the authors of the Memorandum, and positions and policies that had been endorsed by leading Serb politicians, such as Ivan Stambolić.[39] Thus, for example, Memorandum intellectuals and party leaders in Serbia could agree on matters such as the dangers of Albanian nationalism, the need for Serbia to reduce the powers enjoyed by its provinces since 1974, the importance of centralizing state authority, as well as the unfairness of federal policies that had financially burdened Serbia. What divided the incumbent party leadership from the Academy intellectuals was the question of what methods to utilize in order to resolve Serbia's difficulties. The leaders of the SKS during the aegis of Ivan Stambolić were only willing to redress Serbia's concerns within the confines of the existing Titoist rules-of-the-game, which meant they would have to consider the interests and demands of non-Serbs, and also the other republics in the federation. This essential conclusion made it impossible for the Stambolić-led political leadership to officially embrace the views in the Memorandum, despite the fact that a large number of Serbian communists actually supported many of the Memorandum's ideas. Thus, a mood of national opposition became increasingly palpable not only among Serbs in intellectual circles and in the party membership, but also in the general population.

What had still not occurred on the Serbian political landscape, however, was for a major communist political leader to publicly defend and advance a broad-ranging Serbian nationalist program. For the moment, Milošević appeared not to have decided exactly how to exploit the national malaise among his fellow Serbs, and the yearning within the increasingly divided and moribund League of Communists to find some new legitimating formula to maintain their monopolistic control. But Milošević continued to send out signals to his comrades in Serbia that, in his opinion, deep concern over Serbian national interests was not anything to be ashamed about. For example, in October 1986, the top Serbian leadership was berated by leading officials from the League of Communists in Vojvodina for tolerating nationalist activities in SANU and other intellectual circles. The Vojvodina leadership had been chafing at the idea that imminent constitutional centralization in Serbia would weaken its province's autonomy. Milošević struck back and rejected such "grave" charges. He claimed that the accusation his policies were "tolerant toward Serbian nationalism at the same time that we advocate draconian measures against Albanian nationalism in Kosovo" was politically motivated. "The danger hanging over our head is that we may be accused of nationalism, and of a mass movement, and that we must constantly watch out what we do." The critique of a political "mass movement," was one of the first indications that some communists in the republic were concerned about signs hinting at Milošević's nascent populism, that is, the idea that the existing communist leadership could not resolve problems alone, and what was needed was a "mobilization of the entire League of Communists."

During 1986, Milošević was still proceeding cautiously with regard to the "national question." But his wife, Mirjana Marković, appeared to be laying the groundwork for the couple's foray into a debate on the national question in Serbian political life. In 1984, as her husband moved up the political ladder in Belgrade, Marković, who was already teaching at Belgrade University, was elected to the presidency of the University Committee of the League of Communists. Her political work was in the sphere of ideology and theory, but she was part of a small circle of party intellectuals who were preoccupied with changing the orientation of the SKS. Self-proclaimed as "reformers," their focus ranged from restructuring the economy to altering the cultural and educational spheres, and the "democratization" of party and political life. A central component of their program involved what she would later call "rehabilitation of the 'Serbian cause,'" including a refusal to let themselves be burdened by a "guilt complex" about historical episodes of Serbian nationalism in Balkan history. This latter view echoed a perspective that Slobodan Milošević, among others, had been advancing as early as the winter of 1984.

It was the question of Kosovo, Mirjana Marković recalls, that was the "trigger" or "catalyst" for greater "self-awareness" among the Serbian people regarding their situation as an ethnic group in the country.[40] "For a long time the Serbian population had suffered from a complex caused by anxiety that the nation's size jeopardized the interests and offended the sensibilities of other Yugoslavia peoples."[41] According to Mirjana, her small and slowly growing circle during the mid-1980s became aware of the "Serbian people's need to throw off their complex." The behind-the-scenes battle for the "Serb cause" that first engaged Mirjana Marković and her circle in the middle and early second half of the 1980s occurred parallel to the activities of the Belgrade intellectuals at the Serbian Academy, whose Memorandum had provided their own vision of Serbian nationalist "rehabilitation." Dissatisfaction with the leaders and policies of the incumbent Serbian and Yugoslav communist establishment was a major commonality and a basis for later cooperation between the SANU intellectuals and Mirjana's circle of comrades. But initially, the well-established and respected SANU intellectuals had little time for the second echelon academic wife of a relatively new political official, who was not yet perceived as having any special political influence of her own.

Meanwhile, Slobodan Milošević, who clearly, but still rather tentatively, had signaled his support for the "Serb cause," maintained lines of communication with all sides of the ruling party hierarchy, as well as with both the "reform" intellectuals associated with his wife and, the still unorthodox Memorandum intellectuals. Being strategically positioned in the capital city of the country and its largest republic, Milošević had at his disposal the resources necessary to manipulate political power and ideas at a critical moment in Serbian political history. Tito had been dead for seven years, but no new dominant political figure had emerged in Serbia, or elsewhere in the country for that matter. It was also a period during which the one-party regime and Tito's unimpressive "heirs" in each republic were rapidly losing their legitimacy. And, more importantly, in Serbia, where notions of a national renaissance were already bubbling through the intelligentsia, within and outside the League of Communists, no political leader had yet managed to harness the potential political energy at hand, and construct a new coalition of forces to fill the existing leadership and ideological vacuum.

The Epiphanal Moment

Polemics concerning the Memorandum continued to preoccupy Serbian politicians throughout the late fall of 1986. In early 1987, however, attention once again shifted to Kosovo as relations worsened between the province's Serbs and Albanians.[42] Near the end of April, Milošević—now head of the republic's party machine—was invited to make an official visit to Kosovo Polje. Ivan Stambolić had encouraged him to make the journey, although he was aware that the Serbian community in the province of Kosovo had become politically mobilized and was in a state of considerable agitation about growing displays of Albanian nationalism. Milošević first arrived in Kosovo Polje on April 20, and gave a brief speech to about 3,000 Serbs and Montenegrins in the playground of a primary school. Employing conventional party jargon, Milošević promised the crowd that the League of Communists planned to improve the situation of the Serbs in Kosovo by devoting more attention to policies designed to encourage "brotherhood and unity" among the different ethnic groups in the province. He stressed that "intolerance and hatred is not right and we shall do everything to prevent it."[43] Following his speech, it was agreed that Milošević would return with other party officials on April 24 to listen to citizen complaints and to continue the dialogue about Serbian–Albanian relations. In preparation for the next meeting, Milošević's supporters apparently worked hard to prepare the setting for his return visit, arranging media coverage, and assuring a large turnout.[44] But no one could have predicted the dynamics of what was about to take place.

On April 24, 1987, early in the evening, Slobodan Milošević and local Albanian communist leaders arrived at the hall of Kosovo Polje's cultural center (Dom kulture), where an unexpectedly large crowd of approximately 15,000 Serbs and Montenegrins had gathered to meet the visiting communist officials. The crowd surged forward, chanting slogans and trying to break through the police cordon in order to speak directly to Milošević. When Milošević and his delegation finally entered the hall, the crowd outside began shouting insults and throwing stones at the building and windows. The Albanian communist leader Azem Vllasi, who was a part of the political delegation, observed that in the middle of the fray, Milošević was trying to jot down some additional remarks on a prepared speech that he had brought with him. "I was hoping," Vllasi has claimed, "that he would disassociate himself from nationalistic incidents." For example, according to Vllasi:

> Some of the speakers said that the troubles for Serbs began when Albanians came to power [in Kosovo], that the Serbs had nothing against the illiterate Albanian peasants, but the ones that went to schools were to blame, that they could no longer put up with Albanian women wearing hats, Albanian women driving cars, etc. I swear they did mention the hats. There was a lot of talk like "I don't object to anything in particular, but I don't feel comfortable."[45]

But a more intense surge of collective emotions, and a desire to express grievances to the visiting Serbian communist leader, engulfed the crowd. When members of the throng outside the hall again tried to break through police lines and into the building, they were brutally clubbed and beaten back by the police (composed mainly of Albanian officers, but including some Serbs). Informed of what was taking place outside, Milošević exited the building and approached the still highly volatile crowd. According to eyewitness reports at the time, the Serbian leader was visibly upset, physically shaken, and trembling. When a dialogue ensued between the demonstrators and Milošević, they implored him to protect them from the police violence. Acting on a journalist's suggestion, Milošević re-entered the hall, and proceeded to a second-floor window. From that vantage point he nervously addressed the frenzied demonstrators, and uttered his soon-to-be legendary remarks: "No one will be allowed to beat you! No one will be allowed to beat you!" Milošević also invited the demonstrators to send a delegation into the hall to discuss their grievances. That meeting would last twelve hours, and would become a major benchmark in contemporary Serbian and world history.

As the crowd outside calmed down, Milošević listened to a litany of complaints by local Serbs and Montenegrins. It was one of those rare occasions in an Eastern European one-party communist regime when a leading political official was forced to come face to face with the views of the working class, in this case, the aggrieved members of the shrinking Serbian and Montenegrin ethnic group in Kosovo. Before leaving Kosovo Polje, Milošević reassured the members of his audience that they were entitled to reside safely in Kosovo, and to struggle for their rights. "We must not let the misfortunes of people to be exploited by nationalists," Milošević told those who remained. "We must preserve brotherhood and unity as the apple of our eye." But, he added: "We cannot and we do not want to divide people into Serbs and Albanians but we must draw the line that divides the honest and progressive people . . . from the counter-revolutionaries and nationalists on the other side" (author's emphasis). "This is your land," he told the audience,

> . . . your homes, your fields, your gardens, your memories are here. Surely you will not leave your land because it is difficult to live there and you are oppressed. . . . You should also stay here because of your ancestors and because of your descendants. Otherwise you would disgrace your ancestors, and disappoint your descendants. I do not propose, comrades, that in staying you should suffer, carry on and tolerate a situation with which you are not satisfied. On the contrary you should change it.[46]

At the conclusion of his remarks, Milošević reassured the Serbs and Montenegrins that "Yugoslavia does not exist without Kosovo. Yugoslavia disintegrates without Kosovo, Yugoslavia and Serbia will not give Kosovo away."[47] It was a remarkable exchange between members of an angst-ridden ethnic community and a communist official who was still by no means an avowed advocate of Serbian ethnic interests. It was also an astounding performance by a communist functionary whose early speeches and personal style had hardly been dramatic or exceptional.

The intensity of views advanced by the demonstrators at Kosovo Polje to Milošević undoubtedly had a major impact on his perception of the seriousness and depth of nationalist feeling in the province, and also his subsequent decision to exploit Serbian nationalism. Milošević certainly recognized, well before his arrival in Kosovo, the political benefits that might accrue from a skillful mobilization of Serbian nationalist grievances. Milošević's wife would later remember, for example, that prior to her husband's trip to Kosovo Polje, they had discussed "how he should speak and what he should say. I felt that he should speak constructively, offering the Serbs the support that belongs to them."[48] The particular dynamic of Milošević's experience at Kosovo Polje, and the results of his partially prepared and partially intuitive response to the demonstrators, precipitated a major turning point in his political life, and constituted a benchmark in Serbia's political development. Thus, Serbian analysts of the events of April in Kosovo Polje claim that the episode had a profound affect on Milošević's behavior as a politician. It was his epiphanal moment. When he arrived at Kosovo, he had been a cautious and reserved Titoist apparatchik offering the population vapid formulations from a lexicon of well-honed and officially condoned platitudes. But when he left Kosovo, Milošević had acquired a far more intimate appreciation of nationalist sentiments in Serbia—feelings that local Serbs regarded as legitimate defensive or reactive nationalism—and also the limitations of existing Serbian communist methods and policies to address those concerns. After Kosovo Polje, one observer noted, Milošević was "a different man."[49] Milošević was poised to make a major U-turn in his political career, from a Titoist apparatchik, known primarily for his espousal of liberal views regarding the marketization of the economy, to a post-Titoist populist, who would selectively use both nationalism and socialism to build a personalized authoritarian dictatorship. For the moment, however, he had still not determined just how to exploit his revelation and opportunity.

As word of Milošević's Kosovo meeting spread among Serbs within and outside Serbia, his popularity rapidly grew. The Serbian leader's instinctive decision to protect the demonstrators against the police was interpreted as a sign of bravery and Serbian patriotism. The nature and setting of his encounter in Kosovo Polje—a night-time meeting in an unimpressive hall located in a remote European province—hardly seemed the stuff of momentous historical change. But for the nationally downtrodden Serbian psyche, and for many members of the Serbian intelligentsia searching for an event to ignite national consciousness in the general population, Milošević's visit to Kosovo Polje began to take on certain idealized mythic and romantic overtones. Just as Serbia's victory in the Balkan Wars had liberated Serbs from the defeat at Kosovo Polje in 1389, a popular belief took hold that Milošević's ringing defense of Serbian interests could liberate Serbs from the powers that had gravitated to Kosovo's large Albanian population under the detested 1974 constitution. The stage was now set for the political use of the Serbs' most important cultural myth, the Battle of Kosovo.

Prior to April 1987, Milošević had been extremely careful not to strike out too independently from his comrades regarding the Kosovo issue, and Albanian nationalism, and had rarely commented officially on the situation in the Serbian province. Like other Serbian leaders during the mid-1980s, Milošević had supported the idea of amending the 1974 constitution in order to reassert Serbian control over its provinces. His 1984 remarks to the effect that Serbian communists need not suffer from a sense of guilt about the historic nationalism of the Serbian bourgeoisie, nor be ashamed about feeling a sense of Serbian national pride, were to be sure, provocative and revealed his political inclination. The populist overtones of his call for potential mobilization of Serbian communists had also drawn criticism. But such comments were not radically at odds with dominant Serbian communist thinking and the Stambolić line, and Stambolić, though having some serious reservations about his younger protégé, believed he could control Milošević. Informed observers believe that Milošević and Marković had been scheming in early 1986 about how to harness the political force of nationalism, and to unseat Stambolić, possibly on her initiative, but they moved very cautiously. However, following his April 1987 encounter in Kosovo Polje, the issue of Serbian–Albanian relations and Kosovo became frequently recurring themes in Milošević's speeches.[50] But though the Kosovo experience had changed Milošević's outlook in many respects, he still seemed unsure of how or when to openly sever his personal and political bonds to Ivan Stambolić, and fully profit from the growing attraction of nationalism in the Serbian body politic. As would become better known later on, Milošević's strength was in tactical maneuver, and not strategic planning. Although he was certainly on the verge of playing his own "national" card, he would only do so after having completely prepared the political ground. In May 1987, Milošević was able to bolster his credentials as a loyal Titoist and "Yugoslav" when the editors of the Belgrade paper, *Student*, the mouthpiece of Belgrade university students, was attacked for using the front page of two issues to demean the late President Tito and the achievements of the revolution. In the brouhaha over the publication of the issues, two ministers, both protégés of Ivan Stambolić, were forced to resign their posts. Indirectly, however, Stambolić and his close protégé, Dragiša Pavlović, the president of the City Committee of the Belgrade League of Communists (who had held the job since 1986 when he had replaced Milošević), were implicated as supporters of the offending "Student" editorial board. In fact, Stambolić and Pavlović had simply wanted to downplay the political incident, and not turn the accused editors and other officials into political victims. But in ensuring the affair would become a widely discussed scandal with political consequences, Milošević was indirectly able to paint Pavlović and Stambolić as unreliable and unpatriotic.[51] Looking back at the *Student* affair, it appears to have been the opening stage of a campaign to completely marginalize Stambolić within the Serbian political elite. But for the moment, Milošević was exceedingly careful not to ideologically deviate from the main principles of the Titoist legacy. Thus, shortly after the *Student* incident, Milošević took the occasion of a closed meeting with communists from the Federal Secretariat of Internal Affairs on June 4, 1987—just ten weeks after the episode in Kosovo Polje—to make an uncharacteristically impassioned attack on the infamous Memorandum.

> The appearance of the Memorandum of the Serbian Academy of Sciences and Arts represents nothing else but the darkest nationalism. It means the liquidation of the current socialist system in our country, that is, the disintegration after which there is no survival to any nation or nationality . . . any kind of flirting with nationalism or yielding to it, cannot contribute, but on the contrary can only halt, impede, slowdown and ruin a successful political development which the League of Communists has taken to be the goal. That is Tito's brotherhood and unity which is the only basis that can secure Yugoslavia's survival. [52]

Considering his remarks in light of the policies he would later espouse, and the impact of those policies on the disintegration and aftermath of the Second Yugoslavia, Milošević appears to have been a master of political guile who was willing to both attack and forecast his own course of action. Indeed, only a short time after making this speech, Milošević would begin appropriating and encouraging viewpoints that he had just condemned as examples of the "darkest nationalism." Within a year or two, he would also co-opt many of the Memorandum's authors and supporters as an intellectual brain trust. Meanwhile, Milošević bided his time while continuing his policy of quietly advancing his supporters and admirers into key positions throughout the Serbian party apparatus, and the state-controlled media; a process which he had initiated in Belgrade beginning in 1984, and which would make a critical difference in the republic's future political course.

During mid-1987, Ivan Stambolić's standing was significantly weakened by various factional struggles within both the higher ranks of the League of Communists and the military establishment. For many Serbian communists who were deeply concerned with growing Albanian nationalism in Kosovo, and also the defense of Serbian national interests against other ethnic communities in Yugoslavia, Stambolić had demonstrated an insufficient national orientation on behalf of Serbia. But at the same time, many political leaders on the federal level, and especially in the Yugoslav-oriented military elite, also believed that Stambolić had not exhibited sufficient resistance to Serbian nationalism. Indeed, for many in the military establishment, Milošević had a positive reputation as a solid "Yugoslav" and a reliable apparatchik loyal to Titoist and communist norms. Ironically, though many members of the political elite saw Stambolić as a Serbian leader, Milošević was viewed as a "Yugoslav" official, who claimed to be devoted to "protecting Yugoslavia," a mission that the still multi-ethnic military apparatus could readily identify with.[53] Moreover, some provincial party leaders in Serbia (that is, in Vojvodina and Kosovo) were worried that Stambolić intended to push through constitutional changes that would lead to a recentralization of authority within Serbia. Stambolić's political difficulties provided Milošević with the opportunity to step completely out of the shadow cast by his former mentor and friend.

Not surprisingly, in view of what had transpired at Kosovo Polje, the issue of Serbian–Albanian ethnic relations became the central vehicle in Milošević's bid for power. The pretext for Milošević's move was a controversial news conference held on September 11, 1987 by Dragiša Pavlović. Two years younger than Milošević, Pavlović was self-confident and well educated (he had completed the faculties of both machine engineering and economics, and had a doctorate in political science).[54] The party's City Committee in Belgrade was an important power base, and Milošević, who had begun to look to the future, had tried and failed to choose his own successor to head the Committee. But Stambolić had insisted that Pavlović be offered the position. Although he did not strongly object to Stambolić's initiative, Milošević clearly remained bitter about Pavlović's appointment.

Most of Pavlović's comments on September 11—made to a political group composed of chief editors from the media and local party secretaries—offered a relatively moderate and sensible assessment of how the League could best manage growing nationalism in Serbia, and particularly the grievances of Kosovo Serbs regarding Albanian nationalism. Pavlović warned that "the total situation in Kosovo, which is unnecessary and undesirable, cannot be improved by carelessly promised haste." A "dangerous atmosphere" had arisen in his opinion, in which any sober words uttered against ascendant Serbian nationalism were wrongly being construed as "yielding to Albanian nationalism." In preserving their rights, Pavlović cautioned, the Serbian people "must not be led astray through wrongly chosen methods of struggle. . . . Inflammatory words result in nothing but a conflagration."

> What has happened to make us realize that ill-considered words pronounced on the public scene, or a single line in the newspaper, can lead to the pulling of a trigger? How many Albanian shop windows must be broken to convince us that anti-Albanian feeling does not exist only in the warnings issued by the highest organs [of the League], but in our streets as well? . . . Serbian nationalism now feeds not only on the situation in Kosovo, but also on the various ill-considered statements concerning Kosovo that appear in some of our media, public speeches, and some of the institutions of our system. . . . We must criticize Serbian nationalism today because, among other things, Serbian nationalists imagine themselves as saviors of the Serbian cause in Kosovo, without in fact being able to solve a single social problem, and especially without being able to improve inter-nationality relations.[55]

Pavlović was clearly encouraging Serbian public leaders to exercise restraint when dealing with the highly incendiary "national question." His news conference took place only a week after a soldier of Albanian origin had gone berserk in Serbia and killed and wounded several fellow conscripts. Although the incident was not a political act, around 10,000 Serbs appeared at the cemetery when the single dead soldier of Serbian ethnic origin was laid to rest (the other three killed included two Muslims, and a Croat), and the funeral acquired the character of a mass political demonstration. Under these circumstances, Pavlović's remarks were intended to be calming and prudent. But in the atmosphere of growing interethnic polarization in Serbia, they had exactly the opposite effect on many Serbs. Moreover, his comments were also construed as a not too thinly veiled indictment of Milošević's emotional response to the demonstrators at Kosovo Polje the previous spring, not to mention the subsequent sensational and anti-Albanian celebration of that incident and Milošević's "heroism" in the Serbian media. Still riding the wave of his April experience in Kosovo, which had dramatically increased his popularity among Serbs and allowed him to temporarily at least forge an unusual plebiscitarian-type bond with aggrieved Serbs throughout Yugoslavia, Milošević was in no mood to accept criticism or advice from one of his junior colleagues in the Belgrade political establishment. Pavlović's habit of engaging in sharp debates with his fellow members in the Serbian political elite had earned him numerous political enemies, and made him a vulnerable target for Milošević to attack. Unwittingly, Pavlović was about to become the sacrificial lamb in a much larger domestic Serbian political coup orchestrated by Slobodan Milošević.

Milošević's initial maneuver occurred on September 18 and 19 at a closed meeting of the Presidium of the Serbian Central Committee. Stambolić's attempt to achieve a reconciliation between Milošević and Pavlović were to no avail. Instead, Milošević turned the meeting into an attack on both Pavlović and Stambolić. For his part, Pavlović was alleged to have resisted the implementation of party policy in the struggle for "ideological unity." At the conclusion of the meeting, it was decided to recommend to the Central Committee that Pavlović should be removed from his duties as a member of the Presidium of the Serbian League of Communists. Only 11 of the 20 voting participants supported Milošević (five opposed expulsion, and four others—including the Kosovo Albanian leader, Azem Vllasi—abstained). Milošević still needed a definitive victory over the Stambolić faction in the Serbian party.

Only a few days later, at the Eighth Session of the Central Committee of the Serbian League of Communists (held September 22–24, 1987), ostensibly called to discuss Serbia's economic situation, Milošević, together with a coalition of prominent Serbian political and military figures that he had been cultivating over the past several months, launched a sharp assault on both Dragiša Pavlović, and more importantly, the policies of the leading moderate and anti-nationalist in the Serbian political leadership, Ivan Stambolić. At Kosovo Polje in April, Milošević had cannily identified the instrument necessary for his political advancement; now, less than six months later, he began to openly wield that political tool. Milošević had apparently determined that the substance and style of his future approach to Serbian–Albanian relations, and more broadly toward the assertion of Serbian interests within Yugoslavia, could be modeled on the emotional, patriotic, and populist dynamics of Kosovo Polje. Such a fundamental political reorientation demanded that Milošević acquire total control over the Serbian communist opposition and political elite. Having committed himself to this new course of action, Milošević had also made the cold-blooded decision to terminate his past political alliance and friendship with Ivan Stambolić.

The Eighth Session turned into an intense and lengthy debate between Serbian party moderates and Milošević's adherents, many of whom had only recently migrated to the side of the rising Serbian politician. Most new members of Milošević's camp were motivated by the controversial issue of Serbian nationalism, but political repositioning at the Eighth Session derived from a variety of careerist and political motives. Faced with a torrent of criticism and a proposal for his dismissal, Pavlović attempted to explain his earlier remarks, claiming that he may have "exaggerated something," and that at his news conference he did not have Milošević or the Serbian party leadership in mind. Stambolić proved more pugnacious in standing up to the new Milošević line. Pavlović was being thrown out, Stambolić observed, because "in one of his [Pavlović's] sentences Slobodan Milošević or some others saw an allusion to themselves."[56] Stambolić chastised Milošević for always speaking about party "unity," but taking measures which actually encouraged dissent in the ranks of the League. He also urged his junior colleague to "manifest a greater degree of ability" and to avoid conflict. After all, Stambolić lectured Milošević, "nobody is right about everything and nobody is wrong about everything."[57] When Stambolić had completed his remarks, Milošević took the floor and denounced Stambolić's efforts to personally link him with the assault on Pavlović, claiming that such remarks were "insulting" to the Central Committee Presidium. Stambolić would later acknowledge that he had been set up by Milošević at the Eighth Session. As previously mentioned, he also had reservations about Milošević when he first advanced him for high office, and had received strong warnings about Milošević's hot-headed and domineering character from others. But as Stambolić would later recount, he chose to ignore such warnings, believing that he could control Milošević's "vices," or that such traits would simply "disappear."[58] Some speakers at the Eighth Session refused to wait for a later occasion to expose the deficiencies in Milošević's politics and character. Vaso Milinčević, a professor at the Philosophy Faculty and member of the Serbian Party Presidency, who supported Pavlović, presciently identified the main problem at hand as Milošević's autocratic style of control and his intolerance of genuine political pluralism.

> I have had experience with Comrade Milošević . . . and I certainly value Comrade Milošević and his ability and energy and so forth . . . Comrade Milošević shows an inclination towards, and indulges in the practice of, solving numerous important questions by himself. . . . The danger exists that the League of Communists may be transformed into a unique commissariat to create order. The President [of the League in Serbia, that is, Milošević] and those who think alike will have the right to determine the orthodox truth. In this way are we not heading towards a party of like-minded and obedient people?[59]

However, if Milošević had his personal and political deficits, he also had his appeals. Looking back at the period leading up to the Eighth Session, Ivan Stambolić has observed that Milošević was able to associate himself with both Serbian national goals, as well as the sentiments of the older, more dogmatic elements in the party. For example, during the mid-1980s, the growing political delegitimation and poor economic performance of post-Tito Yugoslavia had stimulated an obsession in Serbia with the Serbs' alleged historical uniqueness, their courage, and their martyrdom. Belgrade theaters featured performances such as *The Fall of the Serbian Empire, World War I Veterans Speak, The Battle of Kolubara, Prince Miloš Has Been Killed*, etc. The same revival of traditional national themes and heroes was also found in newspapers, exhibitions, lectures, and novels. But Milošević's appeal to the older generation of Partisan revolutionaries derived far more than just the appeals of tradition and nationalism. Stambolić has noted, for example: "They liked him for several reasons. He reminded them of themselves, when they were young, strong, decisive. They liked his vigor, acuteness, revolutionary style. Also he consulted them. He pleased them."[60] Consulting and courting the old guard, Milošević was slowly establishing his own network of power and support. Stambolić has admitted that prior to the Eighth Session he had noticed that Milošević was slowly beginning to circumvent established patterns of intra-elite consultation, "pushing" his own supporters for advancement and forming an "illegal nucleus" of power in the Serbian political elite. Stambolić concedes that he naively believed that following the party line was the "ticket to power," and that he failed to understand that in fact the most important consideration in the search for political advancement was "who stood with whom and who was behind whom in the worst clan-like manner. I underestimated envy, jealousy."[61]

As the Eighth Session came to an end, Milošević remained unapologetic about his orientation to the issues under debate, and was especially enigmatic in his commentary about Serbian nationalism. Removing Pavlović was not a "purge" or "squaring of accounts," Milošević claimed. He further observed that it was "politically unacceptable for the leaders of the Serbian League of Communists to be threatened with accusations of Serbian nationalism."

> Serbian nationalism today is not only intolerance and hatred of another nation or nations, but is itself a serpent deep in the bosom of the Serbian people. . . . Serbian nationalists would do the greatest harm to the Serbian people today by what they offer as being allegedly the best thing, namely isolating the Serbian people. . . . No one can label us Serbian nationalists because we want to, and really will, resolve the problem of Kosovo in the interests of all the people who live there.[62]

It was at the Eighth Session that Slobodan Milošević came into his own as

Serbia's top leader. At the same time, Milošević's former mentor, Ivan Stambolić, had committed political suicide by defending Dragiša Pavlović and
attacking Milošević. Thus, at the conclusion of the Eighth Session, Pavlović
was removed from his position on the Serbian Party Presidium (in October he
resigned his post as head of the Belgrade City Committee of the League). Stambolić was replaced as President of Serbia's collective state presidency in mid-
December 1987. Not long afterward he left political life to begin a new career
in international banking.[63]

For some observers, such as several Serbian opposition journalists from the
Belgrade weekly, *Vreme*, the SANU Memorandum is viewed as the intellectual
impetus and framework for the Eighth Session. Thus, it has been argued, the
authors and supporters of the Memorandum constituted a kind of "nationalistic pseudo-opposition" ready "at the signal" to endorse Milošević.[64] According to this perspective, members of the intelligentsia who only a few months
earlier had been accused by Milošević of endorsing "the darkest nationalism,"
actually engaged in a tacit or secret alliance with the Serbian leader in order to
ensure his political victory. What seems more likely, however, is that Milošević,
buoyed by his new-found popularity and seeking to expand his power through
the populist methods he had more or less improvised at Kosovo Polje, had
decided that the moment was right to push aside Stambolić and other moderate members of Serbia's communist elite. There is no evidence of any direct contacts that occurred between Milošević and the authors of the Memorandum
during the summer of 1987. And it does not appear that by the time of the
Eighth Session in September, Milošević had fully consolidated his ties with the
leading nationalist intellectuals; though he was undoubtedly counting on their
tacit support, and was preparing to unabashedly appropriate various components of their nationalist platform.[65] It would be fair to say that at this point,
the SANU intellectuals were advancing his agenda without the need for him to
orchestrate or direct their efforts.

For several years prior to the Memorandum becoming public, "loyal
nationalist intellectuals," particularly in the Serbian Academy of Sciences and
Arts and the Serbian Writers' Association, had been allowed to articulate
scholarly and aesthetic treatises relating to the Serbian national question. Serbia's political leadership had permitted publication of such work because it did
not directly or blatantly challenge the one-party regime and its policy of
"brotherhood and unity."[66] But the Memorandum departed from earlier treatises and represented a more direct challenge to the party leadership, exposing
the real split between nationalist and the anti-nationalist faction in the Serbian political elite. Milošević had been able to skillfully navigate between
the regime and SANU perspectives,[67] although it would eventually become
apparent that he was preparing to utilize and broaden the nationalist political

discourse, and exploit the intellectual purveyors of nationalism for his own political ends. For their part, by the time of the Eighth Session in September 1987, the nationalist intellectuals associated with the Memorandum had still not completely embraced Milošević and were not exactly sure of his intentions, and the full implication of his tactics. In this regard it is interesting to consider remarks made by Dobrica Ćosić shortly after the Eighth Session. While Ćosić's well-known views on Serbia's difficulties were utilized by the Special Commission of SANU, which had prepared the Memorandum, he had only participated indirectly in the process of writing the document. Ćosić saw the Stambolić–Milošević conflict, and other events at the Eighth Session, as essentially an intra-elite struggle characteristic of communist politics. But it is his remarks regarding the sources of that struggle, and Milošević's political prospects, which are most interesting.

> If one would consider this conflict from the national-anthropological perspective I would say that it illustrates the worst political traditions of the Serbian people— radical politics, power-seeking, nepotism, careerism, political vassalage from its general founder Miloš Obrenović [who ruled Serbia from 1815 to 1839, and from 1858 to 1860], up to the prince of the contemporary Serbian bureaucracy, Petar Stambolić, the longest Serbian ruler since King Milutin [1281–1321], Ivan Stambolić's nephew represents the domestic moral and power-seeking mentality of our middle generation. . . . But Milošević's intentions remain a big question. Is this present victor a democratic reformer or a new political chief who threatens to draw upon the conservative essence of the League of Communists and a deluded and desperate [Serbian] people? I'm not acquainted with him. We will see.[68]

Whatever the nationalist intellectuals may have thought about Milošević at the time of the Eighth Session, the rising Serbian leader appeared well aware of the significant appeal that the Memorandum's nationalist message had among Serbs, and members of the SKS. The Memorandum, as Ivan Stambolić would later observe, represented the "great divide" between two factions in the Serbian League of Communists: "the dogmatists (potentially nationalistic) and the reform currents."[69] For Stambolić, the "dogmatists" were conservatives who viewed nationalism as a new basis for legitimating communist rule, while reformers like himself were moderates who saw nationalism as a "negation of patriotism," and wanted to maintain the brotherhood and unity model that had sustained the Yugoslav community of nations and nationalities since World War II. Milošević twisted this nomenclature and claimed to cast his message to true "reform" elements in the party and intelligentsia, such as his wife, who continued to claim to be waging a "just and beautiful struggle for the national affirmation" of Serbia. He shrewdly had developed a platform that enabled him to reach out to those SKS members whose views, since at least 1984, regarding Serbia's "humiliation" and need of constitutional reform (e.g., eliminating the power of the autonomous provinces) dovetailed in most respects with the nationalism of Memorandum intellectuals. Keenly aware of the nationalistic mood in the Serbian intelligentsia and elements of the SKS, and sensing support for such perspectives in the general population, particularly after his long night at Kosovo Polje, the ambitious Milošević deftly took advantage of the split in party ranks, and enlisted the dogmatists, crypto-nationalists, and disgruntled nationally oriented "reformists" in the SKS in order to topple the principal reform political figure who stood in his way. Milošević's attack also appealed to many intellectuals who were dissatisfied with Serbian officialdom for one reason or another. Having forged a strong political coalition, and having vanquished Stambolić, Milošević turned to the task of purging his remaining elite-led opposition and solidifying a popular base of support.

Milošević's Mobilization Regime: Nationalist-Populist Authoritarianism

During the two years following the Eighth Session, Milošević focussed on consolidating his power in Serbia, using primarily extra-institutional methods. His initial action in this regard aimed at eliminating pockets of political resistance to his nationalist and socialist policies, and settling old scores. He first turned toward the republic's northern province of Vojvodina, where for several years he had faced strong opposition from the local political leadership. For example, during a party meeting in mid-1986, some Vojvodina officials had compared the alleged national activity in the Serbian communist regime to the nationalist mass movement that occurred in Croatia at the end of the 1960s and outset of the 1970s. At the time, Milošević and his allies had strongly denied such charges. With the ousting of Ivan Stambolić, Milošević was now free to take stronger measures against his Vojvodina detractors. Serbs were a majority of the population in Vojvodina (54.4 percent in 1981), and under the constitution of 1974, the province was granted considerable self-governing powers and rights. The political elite in Vojvodina recognized that Milošević's plan to reduce the power of Serbia's provinces as a means to deal with the Kosovo problem, also threatened Vojvodina's position and their own power, and they were not about to give in to these plans without a struggle.

In order to unseat Vojvodina's political establishment, Milošević employed a new tactic; namely, orchestrating mass protest meetings and demonstrations against his party opponents in the League of Communists. For example,

Milošević actively encouraged groups of Serbs and Montenegrins from Kosovo—who had provided the populist wave that had carried him to popularity in Serbia—to travel to Vojvodina and agitate in rallies and demonstrations for a change in the provincial leadership. By 1988, Serb leaders from Kosovo already had considerable experience in mobilizing groups of activists to lobby for their grievances, including the organization of media campaigns, public demonstrations, and sending delegations to Belgrade. Milošević had some political concerns about the emotional nature and loose organization of such a movement. But he soon realized that the Kosovo Serbs were determined to pursue an extra-institutional and nonconventional approach to fulfilling their goals, and that he might as well mobilize their energies for his own political purposes. Thus, Milošević essentially appropriated what had been an authentic and spontaneous Serb movement in Kosovo, and transformed it into a tool for advancing his own power within and outside Serbia. As Ivan Stambolić would later remark: "Milošević did not aggravate the Kosovo question just for the sake of the Serbs in Kosovo but rather because that was the way to Kosovize the Serbs on the other side of the Drina [e.g., in Croatia and Bosnia], as the most suitable element for the unitarization [centralized integration] of Yugoslavia, not Kosovo. At first he barely knew about the Serbs on the other side of the Drina, and then he suddenly realized that inducing them to revolt was the way to seize Yugoslavia."[70]

By circumventing the established party hierarchy and using "the people" to challenge his own party, Milošević would change the rules of the game in his own republic and Yugoslavia. As for those traditional communist leaders inside and outside Serbia who disapproved of his popular "mobilization" of the masses or the "street making decisions," Milošević accused them of trying to protect themselves by resorting to old dogmas and methods. His new methods were necessary, he claimed, because "the institutions are not functioning," and the people are "trying in many ways, even in the streets to activate the system." Problems of an economic nature, he maintained, require a change in political power. The workers react "angrily" when they are simply told they are really just "dissatisfied with their economic position. Of course they are dissatisfied with their economic position and this is the cause of their protests. But they cannot improve this position without those political changes in which they will have the power in society, and not the bureaucrats."[71] This was the essence of Milošević's "anti-bureaucratic revolution." During the late 1980s and early 1990s, Milošević offered Serbs a message and promise of economic hope and future prosperity, but always linked to the eventual solution of political and national problems—real, imagined, and manufactured—which he had discerned and which only he could allegedly resolve.

Indeed, the new style of political struggle sponsored by Milošević, which became known as the "happenings of the people," the "mass movement," or "street democracy," opened a new phase in Serbian political life. The first mass protests that took place in Vojvodina were held in the capital of Novi Sad on July 9, 1988. During the summer and autumn a wave of street demonstrations spread to over twenty-five communities in Vojvodina. Before they ended, it is estimated that over 575,000 people participated in demonstrations, or about 28 percent of Vojvodina's population.[72] The dominant slogans in the protests were "Kosovo is Serbia," and "Vojvodina is Serbia." The provincial leadership in Vojvodina was accused of being insensitive to the plight of Serbs in Kosovo, and obstructing constitutional changes that would reassert Serb "sovereignty" by restructuring power in Belgrade. In a meeting on July 15, Vojvodina leaders condemned the demonstrations as efforts to "destabilize" their province, and as a "crude" and "most undemocratic form of pressure." "Serbia," said one Vojvodina party leader, "will survive with or without Milošević." And another party official offered a prescient viewpoint: "If [Milošević] does not stop, and if we do not muster enough strength . . . who knows where we will end up and where all this will take us to. What would happen if everyone in Yugoslavia today, the communists and the leadership, were to start crying to one's nation that everything has been lost, and [it has] been deprived of its rights."[73]

A large role in the demonstrations was played by Serbs who had arrived in Vojvodina as colonists, particularly after World War II when many Serbs from Bosnia–Herzegovina, Croatia, South Serbia and Montenegro were given land in the province (some of it previously held by ethnic Germans), as a reward for their service in the Partisan struggle. Clergymen from the Ortho-dox Church also played an influential role in the mass meetings. Nearly half of the demonstrators were members of the League of Communists who were fed up with the provincial party leadership. The protesters also expressed a strong anti-Albanian sentiment, including chants to kill Azem Vllasi (the Albanian communist leader of Kosovo), and "down with the Siptars!" Demon-strators at the protests carried pictures and slogans in support of Slobodan Milošević and his allies in the Serbian elite. An emerging cult of personality was becoming more evident in Serbia, with Milošević as Serbia's paramount charismatic "national leader" (*narodni vodja*).

The culmination of the mass demonstrations occurred at a protest rally held on October 6, 1988 in Novi Sad. Angry citizens agitated by throwing yogurt packets at the building where the provincial communist leadership was in session. The ensuing demonstrations, which became known as the "Yogurt Revolution," were only ended by Milošević when Vojvodina officials agreed to resign. Before stepping aside, Vojvodina officials had asked for military intervention to curb what was gradually turning from demonstrations into a violent riot. But Milošević's supporters blocked any move by federal officials to deploy troops to the city.

The provincial leaders in Vojvodina eventually resigned in November, after being accused of opposing constitutional changes that would have centralized political authority in Serbia. Following the demonstrations, Milošević claimed that "cadre changes" in Vojvodina had reversed "one of the biggest obstacles to constitutional change" in Serbia, by which, of course, he meant his own power and policies. He admitted that his methodology of political change was unorthodox. But he blamed those in the provincial elite for having opposed him: "We could have done this in a civilized way, had we been lucky. . . . Instead we had a war, if I may say, between the citizens and the communists on the one hand, and certain leaders on the other hand. The war must be ended, of course, in the interests of the citizens . . . above all in the interests of those who are currently exposed to terror in Kosovo."[74] The mixture of regime-sponsored populism and nationalism in the Vojvodina mass meetings not only injected a novel methodology for Milošević's drive to control Serbian politics, but also established a new and broad basis of legitimacy for the rising Serbian leader. Only a day after the dramatic leadership changes in Vojvodina, Milošević began applying the same kind of pressure in order to topple the communist leadership in Montenegro (where he was finally successful in January 1989). In the meantime (November 1988), a number of key leaders in the Kosovo League of Communists were purged. Criticism of Milošević's tactics from the leaders of Yugoslavia's republics in the fall of 1988 had no effect on his nationalist and populist drive to consolidate power within all the country's Serbian communities.

It was Kosovo, however, that remained the symbolic "epicenter" of the political "war" that Milošević had instigated after the Eighth Session, ostensibly on behalf of Serbian national interests. But because of the huge and growing Albanian majority in Kosovo, Milošević actually had little chance of broadening his popular base in the province. Indeed, the wave of nationalist fervor and populist rallies that had been sweeping Serbia throughout the summer and early fall of 1988, together with Milošević's plan to curtail Kosovo's autonomy, finally provoked a reaction among the province's Albanian population. In November, Albanian miners from the pits at the Trepča mine marched 80 kilometers to Priština and joined students in peaceful meetings to protest the forced resignation of the province's political leaders. Security forces did not intervene and the miners went back to work, but tensions escalated in the republic. Thousands of Albanians joined the miners and students in their protests. The Serbian leadership characterized the Albanian demonstrations in Kosovo as separatist outbursts, similar to those that had occurred in the 1981 protests. Albanian commentators disagreed with this analysis, claiming that the rallies were in fact Kosovo's last pro-Yugoslav and pro-Titoist demonstrations: "The Albanian flags were tied into a knot with the Yugoslav flag. The Albanians carried Tito's pictures and cheered the constitution of 1974."[75] Azem Vllasi, whose removal from office had helped spark the demonstration, has said that it was impossible to determine who organized the events "in a direct sense. There was no illegal enterprise. The organizers were people from the nation, from the League of Communists, from working organizations, from the schools." In retrospect, Vllasi has emphasized that the Albanian people remained peaceful even after listening to anti-Albanian propaganda from Belgrade for the two-to three-year period prior to the autumn of 1988, and that they had only engaged in nonviolent protests, when things began to cross a certain line.[76]

In response to the events in Kosovo, a massive meeting was held in Belgrade on November 19, 1988 with close to a million citizens—the rally of "Brotherhood and Unity"—at which Milošević emphasized that Kosovo would remain in Serbia, although not at the expense of the Albanians. "It isn't a time for sadness, but for struggle," Milošević claimed. "Every nation has a love which eternally warms its heart. For Serbia it is Kosovo. Because of that Kosovo will remain in Serbia. . . . Kosovo is Serbia![77] Political leaders in the other republics found the volatile demonstrations in Serbia, and Milošević's emotional rallies, extremely alarming. For example, Vasil Tupurkovski, a Macedonian communist leader, warned that the League of Communists could not survive if it became divided on the basis of nationality. "Nationalism is introducing into our relations primitivism and base passions . . . pushing us to the margin of historical world trends."[78] And he lectured Serbian communists that they had a responsibility to eradicate Serbian nationalism "in the best tradition of great Serbian creators and humanists."

But such prudent advice fell on deaf ears. As Milošević prepared to alter the Serbian constitution at the provinces' expense, Kosovo's Trepča miners began (on February 20, 1989) a sit-in strike at their pits. Milošević was incensed, and against advice of party leaders from other republics, refused to back down on the question of constitutional change in Serbia. Although the miners went back to work after Milošević arranged for three of his handpicked Albanian communist leaders to resign, the crisis did not end. A rally in Slovenia in support of the Kosovars near the end of February created a firestorm of opposition in Serbia, which included a mass protest meeting in Belgrade choreographed by Milošević's henchmen. Waiting until the demonstrators had reached fever pitch, Milošević's supporters prompted protesters to yell: "Arrest Vllasi, arrest Vllasi!" Milošević put his hand to his ear and primed the crowd: "I can't hear you very well!" and asked what they wanted from him. Milošević finally spoke briefly, ordering the crowd to disperse, but ominously promising to arrest the Albanian leader, Azem Vllasi. The following day, circumventing any pretense of legal propriety, Vllasi and the manager of Kosovo's largest enterprise were arrested.[79] Vllasi, who was quite popular among Kosovo's Albanians, was one of the leading representatives of the post-Partisan generation of communist leaders who had tried hard to dampen interethnic conflict in the country. In fact, in earlier times, when Milošević had served as party leader in Belgrade, he and Vllasi had been very close friends.

But Vllasi, who in September 1987 had abstained during the removal of Ivan Stambolić, became another close friend who would experience the sharp sting of Milošević's ambition and revenge. More importantly, the move against Vllasi marked the end of any dialogue between the Serbian regime and moderate members of the Albanian intelligentsia within and outside the League of Communists. Earlier meetings between Serb and Albanian intellectuals had often had the character of a discussion "with no discussion," or a "dialogue of monologues."[80] Perhaps the last and best chance of reaching a negotiated settlement of the Kosovo issue had now been lost. In March 1989, only a month after Vllasi's arrest, and following tightened political and police control over Kosovo, the province's assembly rubber-stamped amendments to the Serbian constitution strengthening Belgrade's control over its two provinces. Kosovo's previous legislative and political autonomy effectively ended. The constitutional changes were formally proclaimed in the Serbian Assembly on March 28, 1989. "Serbia is again equal," proudly exclaimed Borislav Jović, one of Milošević's principal political allies in the "battle" against Kosovar autonomy, to the assembled political establishment (it was the aggressively anti-Albanian Jović, who had also helped to turn Milošević against Vllasi). In the riots in Kosovo that followed the adoption of the constitutional amendments, over two dozen Albanians were killed. Approximately a dozen years had passed since a faction of Serb politicians had first begun to press for an end to Kosovo's constitutional autonomy under the 1974 constitution. Slobodan Milošević had brilliantly used that issue, and the history of embittered Serb–Albanian relations, to snatch power from his political rivals. He could now claim, at least temporarily, to have fulfilled his promise and reinstated Serbian sovereignty throughout the republic's borders. Ivan Stambolić, who had been pushed aside on the pretext that Serbia needed a new approach to deal with Kosovo, would later provide his own view of what had transpired at the end of the 1980s, and the resulting impact: "We were trying to untie the Kosovo knot together with the Kosovo Albanians. Others cut it with a sword, thereby tying themselves and us into thousands of new knots—rolling from one defeat into another headlong. They were doing that on the wave of mass, force and speed, hot-headed and overcome with crazed nationalist hatred."[81]

Explaining Milošević's Appeal: Patriotism and Political Culture

Answering the question of why Milošević chose to play the nationalist card during the second half of the 1980s is easier than explaining why the Serbian people, at least initially, found his message so appealing. It is widely recognized that political leaders typically adopt nationalist programs in order to acquire and maintain power. What is more difficult to understand is why the message of such leaders so often proves successful.[82] In one sense, Milošević's rise to power can be viewed as a classic case of unbridled political ambition and brilliant political opportunism. In that regard, Aleksa Djilas has aptly described Milošević's exploitation of nationalism as an inspired "act of political cannibalism" by a communist seeking to develop a new legitimating formula for his politically bankrupt, but still power-hungry party machine. Thus, Djilas observed: "The opponent [of the communists], Serbian nationalism, was devoured and its spirit permeated the eater. Milošević reinvigorated the party by forcing it to embrace nationalism."[83] Serbian nationalism, which Milošević had called the "serpent in the bosom" (*zmija u nedrima*) of the Serb people, had become part of his political persona, and the leitmotiv of his regime.

But beyond the all too familiar drives and cynical methods of power-seeking politicians, Milošević also intuitively understood and effectively expressed the nationalist yearning of large numbers of Serbs on both the elite and popular levels. Indeed, Milošević's presumptuous decision to become the "voice" of the Serbian people, not to mention the strident tone of his statements on behalf of Serbian interests, and the populist mobilization of his ethnic constituency on behalf of national goals, exemplify the kind of pragmatic and plebiscitarian political style that has had a deep resonance in the Serbian and Balkan body politic. As the 1980s drew to a close, popular adulation of Milošević was at its peak. His picture had not only replaced Tito's in every Serbian office and enterprise, but could also be seen displayed in private dwellings and cars. Most of the Serb community celebrated the appearance of a strong and outspoken leader, and looked forward to even better times to come.

Collectivist Nationalism as a Cultural Dimension

Jettisoning the political constraints and exhausted platitudes of the Titoist apparatus, Milošević's political techniques and methods exhibited many aspects of the "heroic," patriarchal, and aggressively patriotic characteristics associated with Serbian political culture. While many "national-anthropological" features of Serbian political tradition are often deprecated by educated and urban Serbs, such attitudes remained deeply engrained facets of Serbian political life. Milošević not only clearly perceived what was troubling the majority of his ethnic brethren, he also very shrewdly anticipated how they would respond to his rhetoric and problematic remedies. Thus, during 1988 and 1989, the hundreds of thousands of Serbs who attended the rallies organized by the Milošević-controlled Serbian communist party machine, and who sympathized with the Serbs of Kosovo, did not feel they were exponents of radical, expansionist, or potentially violent nationalism, but rather were citizens democratically expressing heartfelt and long-suppressed support for their patriotic values.

While aspects of political repression, electoral chicanery, and media manipulation would later emerge as prominent components of Milošević's management style, his political ascendancy and initial consolidation of power depended primarily on factors having more to do with the cultural underpinnings, rather than the structural features, of the Serbian polity. Thus during the second part of the 1980s, Milošević's appeal to patriotic sentiments, which were deeply rooted in Serbian political culture, clearly enhanced his popularity within the Serbian working class, agricultural population, employees of the state apparatus, and segments of the intelligentsia. Milošević was aware that many urban and highly educated Serbs with liberal-democratic leanings might view his reliance on mass rallies and "street democracy" as expressions of authoritarian manipulation. However, he also recognized that most Serbs would regard such populist tactics as a legitimate means to achieve the requisite and traditional linkage between strong Serbian leaders and the Serbian people, a bond that had the added value of circumventing the established intermediacy of discredited communist bureaucrats and the largely powerless edifice of Titoist "self-managing" institutions.

Politically socialized in the oppositionless and bureaucratic environment of the Tito regime's restricted pluralism, and enmeshed in the network of patron–client communist recruitment, it is not surprising that Milošević's political techniques and message would ultimately draw upon the potentially illiberal facets of Serbian political culture. Such historically shaped factors included, for example, a strong penchant for centralized modes of political control, and particularly "heroic leaders" who can maintain political order and preserve the "unity" of the nation; a disinclination to accept rules-of-the-game that would allow Serbs to accept minority status within other multinational Balkan political units dominated by other ethnic groups; a predilection for statist collective unity in the face of a perceived external danger to the Serb nation (including identification of nonconformists as traitors or enemies, and a suspicion of democratic pluralism as a potential threat); and an exaggerated emphasis on sanguinity—"Serbian blood and origins"—territorial control, and national religious myths as defining features of collective identity.[84] The historical experience of the Serbs—especially under the long period of Turkish domination, and the nineteenth- and twentieth-century struggles with Austria–Hungary's and Germany's intervention in the Balkans—also created a deep sense of victimization in the Serbian political psyche and political culture. Taken to its extreme, this feeling of historical victimization is often expressed in delusions of persecution and also the rectitude of one's cause, or what has been comparatively termed a "paranoid style of politics" that results in modes of political expression that are "overheated, oversuspicious, overaggressive, grandiose, and apocalyptic expression."[85]

Although it is analytically difficult, and even dangerous, to extrapolate from the presence of such dimensions in the historically conditioned Serbian political mindset directly to contemporary and current political dynamics, the importance of cultural factors in understanding Serbian politics should not be ignored. Indeed, many analysts of Balkan historical development have pointed to the important role of patriarchal patterns stemming from tribal society, and especially the *zadruga* form of landholding and family organization, as major elements shaping contemporary Serbian political culture.[86] Thus although important elements of "democratic" participation—for example, the right of members of the community to openly express their individual ambitions and views—can be identified as dimensions of tribal society and the *zadruga* system, the overall collectivist nature of the patriarchal legacy gives the Balkan notion of "democracy" a "somewhat different meaning than in the Western world."[87]

Under the strong influence of the patriarchal tradition, it has been argued, the meaning of democracy in Serbian and other Balkan contexts came to include strong imperatives for politicians and policies to reach unanimity, to overcome minority nonconformism, and to assert the "sole truth." The influence of patriarchal and aggressively patriotic components of Serbian political culture appear to be particularly strong among Serbs living in, or originating from, the Dinaric areas of the Balkan region, which include most of Bosnia–Herzegovina, northwestern Serbia, western Croatia, and Montenegro.[88] Dinaric Serbs are characterized as extremely patriotic, and having a highly developed "consciousness of nationality." For example, according to the ethnographer Jovan Cvijić, who has provided a rich and detailed, if rather idealized, portrait of Dinaric Serbian characteristics, "Dinaric people feel themselves just as closely connected with their national heroes as with blood relatives."[89] According to Cvijić, Dinaric Serbs have a consuming and often violently expressed commitment to the "national mission." Moreover, he asserts: "They will stop at absolutely nothing. It does not matter in the least if they 'drown in blood' so long as they preserve the heroic traditions, their great name and their 'sacred freedom.'"[90]

Cultural explanations of Serbian politics cannot, of course, neglect the presence and influence of Western liberal values in Serbian society and intellectual circles, especially during the late nineteenth and early twentieth centuries. However, the illiberal facets in the Serbian political legacy were reinforced by the long period of Ottoman rule, and subsequently by the serious weaknesses of emergent parliamentary government before (1903–1914) and after (1918–1929) World War I.[91] As Dubravka Stojanović has remarked in her study of party elites in the Kingdom of Serbia during its most democratic phase of development: "Under-developed liberal traditions, weakly nurtured political culture, lack of tolerance and a surplus of 'party fanaticism and unscrupulous-ness' specific conceptions of the state and old models of political behavior pre-vented modern institutions from assuming modern contents. A political men-tality, customs, and a philosophy of politics formed through historical development assimilated the parliamentary system to the Serbian environment, and to some extent in practice alienated it from basic principles. Party elites, the main creators of political modernization, became its most visible barrier."[92] Indeed, while enthusiasm for "instinctive democracy," "self-determination," and "democratic" participation are often noted as major components of the Serbian "national character," historically Serbian political culture placed even more emphasis on the value of strong leaders and party elites who can pursue their community's national mission while still constraining tendencies toward "democratic chaos"[93] and "excessive individualism."[94] The provision of "structure" and "order" are highly valued leadership traits among Serbs, as in many Slavic and non-Slavic cultures. Four and a half decades of one-party com-munist rule emphasizing collectivist "class" values, accompanied by either cen-tralized charismatic (1945–1980) or oligarchical (1980–1990) forms of gov-ernment would also undermine embryonic liberal democracy in Serbia during the late 1980s and throughout the 1990s. As one Serbian analyst pointed out, opposition reformers who supported a liberal democratic orientation in Serbia at the end of the 1980s and early 1990s were advancing atypical ideas "of civic self-expression, stimulation of individual rights and freedoms, individual cre-ativity, basic economic reform according to the example of developed societies in the West, all of which were against the traditions and deeply rooted habits of a great part of the Serbian population."[95]

The Belgrade social psychologist Bora Kuzmanović has also argued that an "uncritical attitude toward authority," and "collectivism" in Serbian cul-ture, have created a certain intolerance and "rigidity in thinking."

> All are either patriots or traitors. People push themselves into one category or another. Naturally I don't think that only the Serbs are prone to a black-white view of the world. But there is something in the Balkans that conditions such an opinion. . . . There are social-historical roots tied to conflicts in those areas that have sharpened the people's perception of others as either friend or enemy. Con-ditions in the Balkans have been like this, people have clashed with each other, the principle of domination has been expressed, everything has been resolved by victory or defeat.[96]

Kuzmanović has also observed among Serbs that the legitimacy of Tito's regime after World War II was enhanced by the association between the promised goals of socialist doctrine and traditional Serb values:

It was tied to recognizable old values—solidarity, collectivism, justice. . . . Thus our peasants said of Tito that he was our ruler. He had a similar function for them as a king. To be sure he also behaved that way, so he "fit" well into that Serbian framework of mentality and those Serbian symbols of mentality. . . . It was logical for people to seek alternative values after the collapse of the socialist project. [Such values] were offered by ideologues, disgruntled intellectuals who supported a return to tradition and national roots. They proclaimed "we have lost our way, and we are returning where we came from."[97]

Deeply engrained facets of Serbian political culture clearly provided especially fertile soil for Milošević's populist leadership style and appeal to traditional patriotic values. Indeed, survey research during the late 1970s and early 1980s has also revealed that popular Serbian attitudes congruent with such cultural expectations and values remained highly salient dimensions of the prevailing political mood. Surveys conducted by the Belgrade Institute of Social Sciences, for example, pointed to an increasing disenchantment with, and abandonment of, regime-sponsored values connected with self-management socialism, and also a growing preference for a "traditional syndrome" of beliefs. Thus, survey results demonstrated an emerging or reemerging mentality in Serbian society that reflected a deep strain of authoritarianism. Such attitudes were highly support-ive of social conformism, egalitarianism, and a immoderate devotion to pre-ferred political leaders that bordered on "idolatry."[98] Aspects of what are char-acterized as an "authoritarian syndrome" were particularly apparent among the agricultural population in the rural and underdeveloped regions of Serbia, as well as among unskilled, semi-skilled, and highly skilled industrial workers. Milošević would rely on such aspects of Serbian political culture to help per-petuate his power well beyond the populist methods of authoritarian control associated with his early style of rule. Himself the embodiment of Serbian cul-tural patterns, and fully aware of their strength and latent appeal in his ethnic community, Milošević would also shrewdly exploit the more paranoid style associated with Serbian authoritarianism and politics. As Richard Hofstadter has pointed out, the clinical paranoiac believes he is living in a hostile and con-spiratorial world that is directed specifically against him, whereas the political spokesman of the paranoid style finds such perceived external pressures being directed "against a nation, a culture, a way of life whose fate affects not himself alone, but millions of others. Insofar as he does not usually see himself singled out as the individual victim of a personal conspiracy, he is somewhat more ratio-nal and much more disinterested. His sense that his political passions are unselfish and patriotic, in fact, goes far to intensify his feeling of righteousness and moral indignation."[99] As a political spokesman of nationalism, rather than a committed nationalist himself, Milošević was highly adept at appealing to national sentiment—including the paranoiac fringe of Serbian political life—while remaining an ethnically "disinterested" and prudent political tactician.

"Patriarchal Patriotism" in the Intelligentsia

Milošević's alliance with sections of the Serbian cultural intelligentsia during the late 1980s and early 1990s also represented a fascinating case where reemergent "patriotic" political values served mutual political interests. For the savvy Milošević, the creative intelligentsia, and particularly the SANU intellectuals, represented an established opposition bloc that could be, and from his perspective needed to be, co-opted and contained. They were also a group, Milošević calculated, that could provide an intellectual underpinning for his national-patriotic program. Meanwhile, many of the intellectuals who had broken with the communist regime, and who now espoused an eclectic blend of nationalist and communist views, saw Milošević as a unique opportunity to advance their own political and personal agendas. For example, Professor Kosta Mihailović, the economist and SANU member who became a Milošević adviser, explained that Serbia had been "politically and economically dominated in Yugoslavia. An anti-Serbia coalition existed for a long time. We occupied a vassal position in Yugoslavia for a long time. . . . Serbia's wartime leaders were chased from power. The Serbian intelligentsia was under terrible pressure. I was eliminated from public life for twenty years." According to Mihailović, all "this was totally changed by the appearance of Slobodan Milošević."[100] For many intellectuals, Milošević represented the first Serbian politician since Aleksandar Ranković (removed by Tito in 1966) who was willing to remain ideologically committed to socialism, but would still take a strong stand on behalf of Serbian national interests. Thus by the summer of 1988, Milošević was closely collaborating with the authors of the Memorandum, or the same intellectuals he had conveniently criticized during 1986 and 1987.

Badly disappointed by the failures and repression of the communist regime, many of the SANU intellectuals, and their peers, reverted to a framework of beliefs that has usefully been characterized as "patriarchal patriotism." Among other things, such views prescribe a "morality of simple but inflexible duties towards one's nation."[101] Thus, many of the intellectuals embracing such patriotic attitudes found it profitable to idealize Milošević as the personification of the best Serbian political principles and traditional values. For example, Antonije Isaković, the President of the SANU commission that had prepared the Memorandum, claimed that Milošević's mode of behavior and policies combined the positive features of the nineteenth-century Serbian politicians Karadjordje (Djordje Petrović, known as Kara or Black Djordje) and Miloš Obrenović; the first political figure allegedly exhibiting the principles of a well-meaning revolutionary nationalist, and the second leader typifying aspects of an "evolutionary" but essentially pragmatic, conspiratorial, and sometimes ruthless (Obrenović eventually murdered Karadjordje) administrator and politician. While most Serbs, including his own supporters, often characterize Milošević's aloofness and reclusiveness as rather "strange" behavior, Isaković's sycophantic and rather defensive description of the same traits illustrates how such idiosyncrasies may be perceived and recast as qualities that serve the interests of the nation. "I consider," Isaković claims, "that Slobodan Milošević embodies more of Karadjordje's principles, but I think he also has Miloš' principles."[102]

Viewing Milošević's alliance with the SANU intellectuals in retrospect, some Balkan and foreign analysts have incorrectly assumed that the Serbian leader sympathetically observed the preparation of the Memorandum during 1985 and 1986, and plotted from the very outset to exploit its general principles as part of his own pursuit of power. It would also be wrong to assume that the blueprint for the entire course of events connected with the disintegration of Yugoslavia, the subsequent wars in Croatia and Bosnia, and various policies such as "ethnic cleansing," were all part of some master plan or conspiracy hatched by Milošević and a coterie of Serbian intellectuals during the 1987–1988 period. What can be concluded, however, is that following Milošević's calculated alliance with the SANU academicians, his views acquired a patina of intellectual respectability and coherence. He also obtained an important vehicle for disseminating and defending his policies in the Serbian media and Serbian cultural circles. In his drive to obtain and maintain power, Milošević—who, during the mid-1980s had, together with his wife, begun to only tentatively explore the appeals of nationalism as a political platform—would selectively appropriate the views and energies of leading Serbian national ideologues.[103] However, Milošević appears not to have established a close working political relationship with the Memorandum authors until early 1988, that is, well after his April 1987 visit to Kosovo Polje, and some months after he played the nationalist card against Pavlović and Stambolić in the latter part of 1987. It would be Milošević's interests, instincts, and imperatives, not the Memorandum or its authors, that guided Serbian policy in the 1990s and ultimately accounted for the violent disintegration of the Yugoslav communist federation. Thus as the political situation evolved over the next decade, Milošević would frequently demonstrate his willingness to callously, and even ruthlessly sacrifice those Serbian nationalists who previously appeared to be his close friends and allies. Unlike most Balkan politicians in the 1980s and 1990s for whom power was a means to achieve their nationalist goals, for Milošević nationalism was simply the paramount instrument to achieve and solidify political power. Astutely understanding his cultural milieu, he knew precisely how to package and convey such nationalist appeals, and also when to adopt a new style of political discourse.

Milošević's political pragmatism and nonideological style also contributed to his appeal among segments of the intelligentsia that had previously remained more or less committed to the communist regime. For example, Milošević was able to co-opt a small subgroup of neo-Marxist dissidents who had conducted a protracted struggle with the political establishment throughout the 1970s and early 1980s. Thus, well-known and vocal Belgrade University intellectuals (e.g., Mihajlo Marković and several Serbian members belonging to the Praxis group of marxist philosophers)[104]—whose espousal of participatory forms of socialist democracy and ideological distance from the Tito regime had made them the darlings of the neo-Marxist community around the world—decided (like the SANU intellectuals who had broken completely with the League of Communists in the 1960s and 1970s) that Milošević's creatively mixed cocktail of skin-deep socialism and "Serbian patriotism" justified their return to the mainstream of what was still a one-party regime. Meanwhile, most members of Serbia's communist cultural intelligentsia, who had worked loyally for the regime, simply transferred their allegiance to Milošević as the new head of the political establishment.

To some extent, Milošević's appeal to the communist and neo-Marxist intelligentsia also was enhanced by the political role of his wife. Mirjana Marković's communist family background, and her orthodox Yugoslav communist views, provided a natural bridge to selected sections of the intelligentsia who had remained suspicious of Slobodan Milošević's break with Titoist policy on the national question, and uncomfortable with his unconventional populist tactics. During 1988, for example, Milošević's wife had played a key role behind the scenes at the important Eighth Session of the Central Committee of the Serbian League of Communists (drafting his speeches, communicating with his allies, etc.). For her part, Mirjana Marković would help coordinate a small so-called "hard Marxist-Leninist core" at Belgrade University, where she worked as a sociology professor. However, Mirjana Marković's most important political influence occurred behind the scenes, that is, in private discussions with her husband at home and within the inner circles of their few close friends and cronies. Moreover, to some extent the rigidity and orthodoxy of her communist beliefs, actually cost Milošević support among more moderate communists and neo-Marxists, who had nothing but disdain for Mirjana and her political circle of followers. Thus, it was only after Milošević had successfully consolidated his power base in Serbia and Montenegro that Mirjana began to play a more high profile role in Serbian political life. In October 1989, for example, she became more directly involved in the Belgrade City League of Communists. Following the advent of multi-party politics in 1990, she would become a top leader and chief ideologist of the "League of Communists–Movement for Yugoslavia," which served as an adjunct to Milošević's newly formed Socialist Party of Serbia (a reconfigured combination of the Serbian League of Communists and the

Serbian Socialist Alliance) in maintaining links to conservative communist politicians, military officers, and pro-regime intellectuals.

Mirjana Marković has frequently maintained that she was repelled by the explosion of nationalism and violence during the 1990s, not to mention extreme policies that contributed to "Serbian apartheid."[105] But revealingly, Marković carefully distinguishes between the allegedly positive national revival led by her husband in the late 1980s and the subsequent course of nationalist activity. For example, Marković has looked back nostalgically at the populist mass gatherings of support for the Serbs and Montenegrins of Kosovo, which were held throughout the summer and fall of 1988, but also expressed concern that the "people themselves were not always aware of the extent of their political action at such rallies." The million-strong Brotherhood and Unity rally in Belgrade on November 19, 1988, according to Marković, was supposed to bring the cycle of meetings to a close, and "see the end of the summer fever . . . everything went according to plan. Even better, in fact." But she observes "if only it had stopped there. At least regarding the demonstrators connected with nationalism."[106] As with many other communist and neo-Marxist intellectuals who initially endorsed Milošević's nationalism-populism, his wife has undoubtedly felt, or has needed to convey, that she felt she was participating in a patriotic (as opposed to a nationalistic) regime devoted to socialist principles that somehow got out of control. Of course, not all members of the Serbian intelligentsia joined the Milošević bandwagon. Although Milošević had been successful at co-opting the bulk of the patriotic dissidents from SANU, as well as most neo-Marxist and communist intellectuals, a sizeable portion of the intelligentsia, and especially the anticommunist nationalists and the small group of liberal-democrats, remained steadfastly opposed to his regime. Personal and political divisions within the ranks of the anti-Milošević intelligentsia, however, made it difficult for them to mount a viable opposition during the late 1980s, or even after the advent of pluralist politics in the early 1990s (see Chapter 3).[107] Meanwhile, in the climate of the 1980s and early 1990s, those few Serbian intellectuals who did advance a truly non-nationalist and liberal democratic program were largely marginalized and ostracized.[108]

Looking back at Milošević's race to power during the last phase of the Titoist regime, one is most impressed by his proficiency in utilizing specifically Serbian notions of patriotism and democracy as a means of sustaining a diverse coalition of seemingly incompatible constituencies. As incisive journalists from the Belgrade magazine *Vreme* have observed in this regard: "He succeeded in tricking both the communists and the nationalists; the communists believed he was only pretending to be a nationalist, and the nationalists that he was only pretending to be communist."[109] Caught up in their yearnings to overcome the perceived political subordination of the Serbs in Yugoslavia, few of Milošević's supporters during the second half of the 1980s fully considered where his still evolving and ostensibly patriotic program would eventually lead. Those that did speak out regarding the dangers of runaway Serbian nationalism, either within or outside the League of Communists, proved powerless to resist the culturally-based infatuation with Milošević on the part of so many of his ethnic brethren.

NOTES

1. Gojko Desnica, *Vodj* (Belgrade: Naučna književna zadruga, 1992), pp. 18–20. Both Desnica and a later biographer, Slavoljub Djukić, derived their information on this period of Milošević's life from Jovan Plamenac, "Djedovina Slobodana Miloševića," *Barske novine*, No. 139 (March 1990), p. 10.

2. Duško Doder and Louise Branson, *Milošević: Portrait of a Tyrant* (New York: The Free Press, 1999), p. 16.

3. *Vodj*, op. cit., p. 24. One source suggests that Milošević's mother was an "obsessive puritan" who "cut off her pupils' long hair and smashed their mirrors so they could not see themselves." Gavin Hewitt, "Inside the Mind of Milošević," *CBC National*, March 30, 1999. Laura Silber suggests that Milošević's mother hung herself hours after being turned away from her son's home by Mira Marković. "Milošević Family Values," *The New Republic*, Vol. 221, No. 9 (August 30, 1999), pp. 23–27.

4. Ian Hamilton, *Yugoslavia's Pattern of Economic Activity* (New York: Praeger, 1968), pp. 333–336.

5. BBC, *Correspondent Special*, April 24, 1999 (script from audio tape).

6. *Answer* (Kingston, Ontario: Quarry Press, 1995) (first published in Serbian, 1993).

7. Ibid., p. 106.

8. Rudi Supek, *Omladina na putu bratstva: psiho-sociologija radne akcije* (Zagreb: Mladost, 1963).

9. Andrei Simic, *The Peasant Urbanites: A Study of Rural Urban Mobility in Serbia* (New York: Seminar Press, 1973), p. 149.

10. *Newsweek*, December 21, 1998.

11. Milošević's early ideological dedication and political activism were illustrated in 1963 during a debate on proposed constitutional changes when he proposed that the word "socialist" precede "federal" in the country's new official name, rather than the other way around. His proposal was accepted and the amended name of the country became "The Socialist Federal Republic of Yugoslavia." Slavoljub Djukić, *Kraj Srpske bajke* (Belgrade: "K.V.S.", 1999), p. 17.

12. *Houston Chronicle*, December 27, 1992, p. 24.

13. *BETA*, August 30, 2000.

14. Stephen Engelberg, "Carving Out of Greater Serbia," *New York Times Magazine*, September 1, 1991, p. 23.

15. Miloslav Janićijević, *et al.*, *Jugoslovenski studenti: socializam* (Belgrade: IDN, 1966), pp. 74–75.

16. Ljiljana Habjanović-Djurović, *Srbija pred ogledalom* (Belgrade: BMG, 1994), p. 233.

134   *Serpent in the Bosom*

17. *Newsweek*, December 21, 1998.

18. Larry King: CNN Interview with President Milošević of Serbia, December 22, 1994.

19. Slavoljub Djukić, *Slom Srpskih liberala: tehnologia političkih obračuna Josipa Broza* (Belgrade: Filip Višnjić, 1996). See also, Mirko Tepavac, *Sećanja i komentari* (Belgrade: Radio B–92, 1998).

20. Dušan Janjić, "Serbia Between an Identity Crisis and the Challenge of Modernization (1987–1994)," in Dušan Janjić (ed.), *Serbia Between the Past and the Future* (Belgrade: Institute of Social Sciences, Forum for Ethnic Relations, 1997), p. 25.

21. Zoran Sekulić, *Pad i ćutnja Aleksandra Rankovića* (Belgrade Dositej, 1989).

22. Slavoljub Djukić, *Izmedju slave i anateme: politička biografija Slobodana Miloševića* (Belgrade: Filip Višnijić, 1994), p. 26.

23. *BBC Summary of World Broadcasts* (hereafter, *BBCSWB*), EE/7939/B/1, May 1, 1985.

24. *FBIS*, September 9, 1985, p. I4.

25. *Godine raspleta* (Belgrade: Beogradski izdavačko-grafički zavod, 1989), p. 34.

26. Mirjana Marković, *Night and Day: A Diary* (December 1992–July 1994) (Kingston, Ontario: Quarry Press, 1995) (first published in Serbian, 1994), p. 159.

27. Slavoljub Djukić, *Izmedju slave i anateme*, op. cit., p. 29.

28. Ibid., p. 35.

29. In an interview in December 1983, Ljubičić had spoken of the solution to the ethnic problem in Kosovo: "we must be far more effective in crushing and taking measures against those who engage in hostile behavior." He also warned against "the confusion of democracy with anti-socialist activity." *Vjesnik*, December 3, 1983.

30. Slavoljub Djukić, *Kako se dogodio vodja: borba za vlast u Srbiji posle Josipa Broza* (Belgrade: Filip Višnjić, 1992), p. 100.

31. *Mladina*, August 6, 1996, pp. 34–39.

32. *BBC Summary of World Broadcasts*, EE/8229/B/6, April 10, 1986.

33. *FBIS*, May 5, 1986, p. 58.

34. *Nacrt memoranduma Srpske akademije nauka u Beogradu* (Toronto: Srpske narodne odbrane, 1987). Audrey Budding believes that the Memorandum was not a coherent document, and offered no real prescription to the problems it identified. Audrey Helfant Budding, *Serb Intellectuals and the National Question*, Ph.D. Thesis, Department of History, Harvard University, January 1998, pp. 195–206.

35. Aleksandar Pavković, "The Serb National Idea: A Revival, 1986–1992," *Slavonic and East European Review*, Vol. 72, No. 3 (July 1994), pp. 440–455.

36. *Nacrt memoranduma Srpske Akademije Nauka u Beogradu*, op. cit., pp. 41–42.

37. *Milan corriere dela serra*, July 8, 1999, translated in *FBIS-WEU–1997–0708*, July 8, 1999.

38. Slavoljub Djukić, *Kako se dogodio vodja*, op. cit., p. 189.

39. See Audrey Helfant Budding, *Serb Intellectuals and the National Question*, op. cit., pp. 195–206.

40. Mirjana Marković, *Night and Day*, op. cit., p. 157.

41. Ibid.

42. The following two paragraphs draw heavily on Slavoljub Djukić, *Kako se dogo-dio vodja*, op. cit., pp. 122–130.

43. Tanjug, April 20, 1987 in *BBCSWB*: Part 2 Eastern Europe, B. Internal Affairs; Yugoslavia; EE/8549/B1, April 23, 1987.

44. Azem Vllasi, "Eighth Session in Kosovo," in Ivan Stambolić, *The Key Witness, Dossier* (Vreme News Digest, 1995), p. 23.

45. Ibid.

46. Belgrade Home Service, April 25, 1987 in *BBCSWB*: Part 2 Eastern Europe, B. Internal Affairs; Yugoslavia; EE/8553/B/I, April 28, 1987.

47. Ibid.

48. "Vreme" News Digest Agency [hereafter *VND*], No. 215 (November 13, 1995). Ivan Stambolić claims that prior to the trip to Kosovo, he had warned Milošević "not to yield to emotions," but that Milošević "succumbed to the atmosphere. He even fueled the fire." *Put u bespuće* (Belgrade: Radio B-92, 1995), p. 167.

49. Slavoljub Djukić, *Kako se dogodio vodja*, op. cit., p. 127. See also Slavko Ćuru-vija and Ivan Torov, "The March To War (1980–1990)," in Jasminka Udovicki and James Ridgeway (eds.), *Yugoslavia's Ethnic Nightmare* (New York: Lawrence Hill Books, 1995), pp. 81–83.

50. Slobodan Milošević, *Godine raspleta*, op. cit., p. 34.

51. Slavoljub Djukić, *On, ona, i mi* (Belgrade: Radio B-92, 1997), p. 64.

52. Internal Bulletin of the League of Communists in the Federal Secretariat of Inter-nal Affairs, "Naše aktuelnosti," (June 1987) cited in *VND*, No. 99 (August 16, 1993), p. 15.

53. See Mile Bjelajac, *Jugoslovenskas iskustva sa multietničkom armijom 1918–1991* (Belgrade: Udruženje za društvenu istoriju 1999).

54. Slavoljub Djukić, *Kako se dogodio vodja*, op. cit., pp. 108–109.

55. *FBIS*, October 8, 1987, pp. 49–51. Pavlović's remarks and his views on the polit-ical struggles that ensued can also be found in *Olako obećana brzina* (Zagreb: Globus, 1988).

56. *FBIS*, October 16, 1987, p. 62.

57. Ibid.

58. Ivan Stambolić, *Put u bespuće*, op. cit., pp. 135–136, 138–139, 141.

59. *FBIS*, October 16, 1987, p. 67.

60. Ivan Stambolić, *Put u bespuće*, op. cit., pp., 137, 143, 147, 156–159, 160.

61. Ibid., p. 111.

62. *NIN*, Vol. 30, No. 1918 (October 4, 1987), pp. 12–13.

63. His successor was retired General Petar Gračanin.

64. Miloš Vasić, Roksanda Ninčić, and Tanja Topić, "A Tired Serbia," *VND*, No. 52 (September 21, 1992), p. 5.

65. Audrey Helfant Budding, *Serb Intellectuals and the National Question*, op. cit., p. 206.

66. Nenad Dimitrijević, "Words and Death: Serbian Nationalist Intellectuals," in Andras Bozoki (ed.), *Intellectuals and Politics in Central Europe* (Budapest: Central European University Press, 1999), pp. 126–128.

67. Audrey Helfant Budding, *Serb Intellectuals and the National Question,* op. cit.

68. Slavoljub Djukić, *Čovek u svom vremenu: Razgovori sa Dobricom Ćosićem* (Belgrade: Filip Višnjić, 1989), p. 282. For some background on Ćosić's views see Vlasa D. Mihailovich, "Aspects of Nationalism in Dobrica Ćosić's Novel A Time of Death: Chauvinism or Sincere Patriotism?" *World Literature Today,* Vol. 60, No. 3 (Summer 1986), pp. 413–416.

69. Ivan Stambolić, *Put u bespuće,* op. cit., p. 131.

70. *Mladina,* August 6, 1996, pp. 34–39.

71. *BBCSWB,* February 2, 1989, EE/0374/C1.

72. Sava Kercov, Jovo Radoš, Aleksandar Raić, *Mitinzi u Vojvodini 1988.godine* (Novi Sad: Dnevnik, 1990), p. 36.

73. Tanjug, July 15, 1988 in *BBCSWB,* Part 2 Eastern Europe, B. International Affairs; Yugoslavia; EE/0207/B/I, July 19, 1988.

74. Belgrade Home Service, October 11, 1988 in *BBCSWB,* Part 2 Eastern Europe, B. Internal Affairs; Yugoslavia; EE/02811/B/I, October 13, 1988.

75. Shkelzen Maliqi, "Self-Understanding of the Albanian in Nonviolence," op. cit., p. 241.

76. Momčilo Petrović, *Pitao sam Albance šta žele a oni su rekli: republiku . . . ako može* (Belgrade: Radio B-92, 1996), p. 51.

77. Slavoljub Djukić, *Izmedju slave i anateme,* op. cit., p. 113.

78. Tanjug, November 21, 1988 in *BBCSWB,* Part 2 Eastern Europe, B. Internal Affairs; Yugoslavia; EE/0316/B/I, November 23, 1988.

79. Slavoljub Djukić, *Izmedju slave i anateme,* op. cit., p. 122.

80. For example, see the discussion of the April 1988 meeting of Serb and Albanian writers held in Belgrade. Drinka Gojković, "The Birth of Nationalism from the Spirit of Democracy: The Association of Writers of Serbia and the War," in Nebojša Popov (ed.), *The Road to War in Serbia: Trauma and Catharsis* (Budapest: Central European University Press, 1996), pp. 334–337.

81. Stambolić quoted in *BETA,* August 30, 2000.

82. See Gale Stokes, "Cognition, Consciousness, and Nationalism," *Ethnic Studies,* Vol. 10 (1993), pp. 27–42.

83. "A Profile of Slobodan Milošević," *Foreign Affairs,* Vol. 72, No. 3 (Summer 1993), p. 87.

84. For the impact of Serbian historical patterns on political culture see Dunja Melcic, "Communication and National Identity: Croatian and Serbian Patterns," *Praxis International,* Vol. 13, No. 4 (1993), pp. 360–363, and Paul Hehn, "Man and the State in Serbia, From the Fourteenth to the Mid-Nineteenth Century: A Study in Centralist and Anti-Centralist Conflict," *Balkan Studies,* Vol. 27, No. 1 (1986), pp. 3–27. See Srbobran Branković, *Serbia at War with Itself: Political Choice in Serbia 1990–1994* (Belgrade: Sociological Society of Serbia, 1995), pp. 43–53.

85. Richard Hofstadter, *The Paranoid Style in American Politics* (New York: Alfred Knopf, 1965), p. 4.

86. For important studies of this aspect of Serbian political culture as it relates to democracy and the mobilization of nationalist sentiments see Jovan Cvijić, *Iz društvenih nauka* (Belgrade: "Vuk Karadžić," 1965), 79–135; Vladimir Dvorniković,

Karakterologija Jugoslovena (Belgrade: Kosmos, 1939), pp. 193–250; Slobodan Jovanović, "Jedan prilog za proučavanje Srpskog nacionalnog karakteri," in *Sabrana dela Slobodana Jovanovića* (Belgrade: Beogradski izdavačko-grafički zavod, 1990), pp. 12, 543–582; Vera St. Erlich, *Family in Transition: A Study of Three Hundred Yugoslav Villages* (Princeton: Princeton University Press, 1966), pp. 373–393; Jozo Tomasevich, *Peasants, Politics and Economic Change in Yugoslavia* (Stanford: Stanford University Press, 1955), pp. 192–197 and 247–249; Olivera Buric, "The Zadruga and the Contemporary Family in Yugoslavia," in Robert F. Brynes (ed.), *Communal Families in the Balkans: The Zadruga* (Notre Dame: University of Notre Dame Press, 1976), pp. 117–138; and Ivan Lucev, "Socijalni karaktera i politička kultura," *Sociologija*, No. 1 (1974), pp. 23–41, and the studies in M. Vasović, *et al.*, *Fragmenti političke kulture* (Belgrade: Institut društvenih nauka, 1998).

87. St. Erlich, *Family in Transition: A Study of Three Hundred Yugoslav Villages,* op. cit., p. 393.

88. Milošević's Montenegrin family background places his roots squarely in the "Dinaric Zone."

89. "Studies in Jugoslav Psychology (I):" *The Slavonic Review*, Vol. 9, No. 26 (1930/31), p. 381.

90. Ibid., p. 383. It is important to note that aspects of the syndrome of Dinaric characteristics described by Cvijić and other analysts are also exhibited by members of several Balkan ethnic groups, and particularly by Croats and Moslems living in the "Dinaric zone."

91. Zagorka Golubović argues that the mentality and operation of Yugoslavia's communist state bureaucracy—including its monopoly over the agencies of political socialization—reinforced traditional habits and attitudes despite the self-management system. *Kriza identiteta savremenog Jugoslovenskog društva* (Belgrade: Filip Višnjić, 1988), pp. 285–391.

92. *Party Elites in Serbia 1903–1914: Their Role, Style of Ruling, Way of Thinking* (Association for Social History, 1999). See also, Olga Popović-Obradović, *Parlamentarizam u Srbiji (1903–1914)* (Belgrade: Službeni list, 1998), and Gale Stokes, *Politics as Development: The Emergence of Political Parties in Nineteenth-Century Serbia* (Durham: Duke University Press, 1990).

93. Cvijić, "Studies in Jugoslav Psychology (I)," op. cit., p. 383.

94. Nearly a half century ago, for example, such dual and seemingly contradictory features of Serbian political culture were noted by Cvijić in his incisive inventory of Serbian folkways. "The whole national tradition is democratic in trend. It is true that we have a long succession of famous emperors, heroes, and martyrs: but the Serbs regard this in a way of their own . . . one does find individual persons or families who seem to have a natural instinct towards leadership: and for this reason people consider that we have undemocratic tendencies. These are individual cases however, and do not occur often." Jovan Cvijić, "Studies in Jugoslav Psychology (II)," *The Slavonic Review*, Vol. 9, No. 27 (1930/31), pp. 676–678.

95. Zlatoje Martinov, *U podnožju demokratskih propileja: Izbori u Srbiji 1990–2000* (Belgrade: Republika, 2000).

96. *Duga*, October 28–November 10, 1995, pp. 23–25.

97. Ibid.

98. The discussion of survey results that follows is based on several studies by Dragomir Pantić, *Vrednosne orijentacije mladih u Srbiji* (Belgrade: SSO Srbije, 1981); "Odnos mladih prema (inter)nacionalnom, zatvorenost-otvorenost prema svetu," in *Omladina '86: Sondaža javnog mnenja* (Belgrade: Kultura, 1986), pp. 136–159; *Klasična i svetovna religioznost* (Belgrade: Institut društvenih nauka, 1988) and; *Promene vrednosnih orijentacija mladih u Srbiji* (Belgrade: Institut društvenih nauka, 1990). Some Serbian research conducted in the early 1970s with secondary school students in Serbia found that those individuals who declared themselves to be "Serbs" rather than "Yugoslav" in terms of their national designation had a slightly lower level of attachment to Yugoslavia as a state community. Those with a "Yugoslav attachment" had less preference for autocracy, religiosity, power, and dominance. Nikola Rot and Nenad Havelka, *Nacionalna vezanost i vrednosti kod srednjoškolske omladine* (Belgrade: Institut za psihologiju/Institut društvenih nauka, 1973), pp. 270, 280.

99. Hofstadter, *The Paranoid Style in American Politics*, op. cit., p. 4.

100. *New York Times*, August 6, 1989, Section 1, Part I, p. 12.

101. Aleksandar Pavković, "Intellectuals into Politicians: Serbia 1990–1992," *Meanjin*, Vol. 52, No. 1 (1993), pp. 107–116. Pavković argues that the Serbian cultural intelligentsia is strongly attached to patriotic values expressed in traditional Serbian folk epics, nineteenth-century Serbian literature, and historiography. In his opinion, both patriotically oriented intellectuals, and those who were more attracted by the European liberal tradition, rejected communist rule.

102. *NIN*, No. 2158 (May 8, 1993), pp. 18–21.

103. Nenad Dimitrijević, "Words and Death: Serbian Nationalist Intellectuals," op. cit., pp. 134–142. For the controversy among SANU members regarding the responsibility of the Serbian intellectual elite for the nationalist activities of the Milošević regime, see Olivera Milosavljević, "Od memorandoma do 'kolektivne odgovorost'," in *Srpska elita* (Belgrade: Helsinški odbor, 2001), pp. 7–38. See also, Slavoljub Djukić, *Lovljena vetra: politička ispovest Dobrice Ćosića* (Belgrade: B-92, 2001), pp. 155–160.

104. Laura Seccor, "Testament Betrayed: Yugoslav Intellectuals on the Road to War," *Lingua franca*, September 1999.

105. *Washington Post*, June 17, 1993, p. 5.

106. *Answer*, op. cit., pp. 9, 10.

107. For interesting discussions of problems faced by the democratic opposition see Srdja Trifković, "Illiberal Legacy in Former Yugoslavia as an Impediment to Market Reforms," *Serbian Studies*, Vol. 6, No. 4 (Fall 1992), pp. 5–20; Vladimir Gligorov, "The Discovery of Liberalism in Yugoslavia," *East European Politics and Societies*, Vol. 5, No. 1 (Winter 1991), pp. 5–21, and; Srdja Popović, "Political Opposition in Serbia," *New Politics*, Vol. 4, No. 4 (Winter 1993), pp. 91–97.

108. For the views of one of Serbia's leading non-nationalist intellectuals see Vesna Pešić, "The Cruel Face of Nationalism," *Journal of Democracy*, Vol. 4, No. 4 (October 1993), pp. 100–103.

109. Miloš Vasić, Roksanda Ninčić, and Tanja Topić, "A Tired Serbia," op. cit., p. 6. Some extremely self-critical Serb intellectuals, such as Mirjana Miočinović, traced

CHAPTER 3

Politics in a "Soft Dictatorship": The Methodology and Mechanisms of Control

Nationalism stands no chance unless it is backed by something really powerful, like the state.

—*Miroslav Šolević, Kosovo Serb Leader (1989)*

We live under a regime that is neither communist nor post-communist, nationalist or post-nationalist. Again we are between the East and the West; there is a little bit of freedom, and a little bit of tyranny, a little justice as well as anarchy. We can start off from here in any direction: forward or backward, left or right, providing we move at all.

—*Stojan Cerović, Independent Journalist (1995)*

Socialism with an Ethnic Face

In one of the most dramatic and carefully choreographed events in modern Serbian history, Slobodan Milošević, the president of Serbia, arrived by helicopter on June 28, 1989, at the austere Gazimestan shrine located on a plain near Kosovo's capital of Priština. The Gazimestan site, a concrete tower, memorializes the famous 1389 Battle of Kosovo, which had been a military setback for the Serbian empire, and had marked the onset of nearly 500 years of Ottoman political supremacy over the Balkan peninsula. Waiting to greet Milošević was a flag-waving crowd of hundreds of thousands of Serbs and Montenegrins, who had come from all over socialist Yugoslavia, and from around the world, to celebrate the 600th anniversary of the famous battle.

The elaborate ceremonies preceding Milošević's speech reflected the Serbian peoples' profound emotional and cultural attachment to the rich mythology surrounding the historical events that had unfolded in Kosovo. The preliminary festivities in 1989 included a presentation from the musical-poetry work, "The Passion of the Holy Prince Lazar," honoring the Serb leader who had been captured in the Battle of 1389 and then beheaded by the Turks, a memorial service at the medieval Gračanica Monastery led by the Patriarch of the Serbian Orthodox Church (attended by 300 priests, the religious service was broadcast by the state media for the first time in Yugoslav history), national dances, special exhibitions, as well as various television and radio programs. The living mythology surrounding the Battle of Kosovo reflected a deeply engrained facet of the Serb people's cultural mindset, a mentality historically communicated through a process of transgenerational value socialization, which included the recitation of oral ballads, storytelling at home and at school, epic poetry, and representational symbolism.

The throng gathered at Gazimestan held up pictures of Slobodan Milošević, which had been distributed earlier. There were, however, no pictures of Socialist Yugoslavia's founder, Josip Broz Tito, who had died in 1980. Milošević's arrival, and later his short walk to a platform high above the enormous crowd, was greeted by shouts "Slobo!" Slobo!" and "Kosovo is Serbia!" The guests of honor observing the spectacle included most of the leading communist officials from the country's other republics, and from the federal level of government. The meticulously stage-managed Gazimestan meeting contrasted with the unruly meetings that Milošević's lieutenants had organized as part of their populist "anti-bureaucratic revolution" over the previous two years. The Kosovo extravaganza, as one observer later put it, was "a peaceful national mega-celebration which was organized by a stable and consolidated Milošević administration."[1] Unlike Milošević's turbulent meeting with the Kosovo Serbs over two years earlier, the Serbian regime's authoritarian populism had now become routinized into a systematic formula of mass political mobilization that left very little to chance.

Janez Drnovšek, the Slovene leader who at that time was head of Yugoslavia's collective state presidency, has given an account of his qualms about attending the celebration, his impression of the event, and the general political atmosphere in the country at the time. Though worried "that the Serbs would try to use the manifestation of 'Serbianness' as an opportunity to put pressure on the Albanians" as part of Milošević's effort to limit Kosovo's autonomy, Drnovšek decided, after conversations with a number of other officials that he would travel to Gazimestan:

In the morning we traveled from Belgrade to Priština by plane. In the plane were General Kadijević [the Minister of Defense] and the President of the Federal Government, Ante Marković. My feeling was that they did not find the trip very enjoyable. Both viewed their attendance as an effort more at saving the federation and preventing any new conflict, than as support for the Serbian regime.... They regarded the whole project as a necessary evil, something to extract some benefit

Serb peasant women in ceremonial costumes on the eve of Kosovo's liberation by Serbia during the First Balkan War (November 1912). *Credit:* Rista Marjanović, War Museum, Belgrade.

Serb cavalry located in village of Dobrošane, Kosovo (October 1912). *Credit:* War Museum in Belgrade, R-701

Serb officers and soldiers with allied Catholic Albanian troops (and Catholic priest) in Southern Kosovo (April 1913). *Credit:* War Museum, Belgrade.

Slobodan Milošević (in center) as a young official in the Serbian League of Communists shaking hands with his mentor, Ivan Stambolić. Seated next to Milošević is Petar Stambolić, Ivan's uncle. *Credit:* Balkan Historical Archive.

Ivan Stambolić and Milošević, close friends and allies in mid-1980s. *Credit:* Balkan Historical Archive.

Milošević, the young communist manager, with briefcase on the way to his office in mid-1980s. On his right is his bodyguard. *Credit:* Balkan Historical Archive.

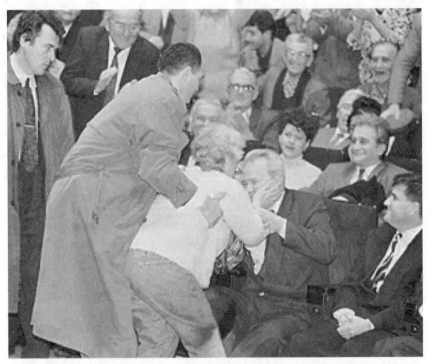

The best days of his political life: Milošević being hugged by devoted Kosovo Serb woman. She is being restrained by the leader's bodyguard. *Credit:* Balkan Historical Archive.

Milošević (in center) with (on his right) Yugoslav President, Janez Drnovšek at Gaz-imestan celebration (June 1989). *Credit:* Balkan Historical Archive.

Milošević speaking at Gazimestan. *Credit:* Balkan Historical Archive.

Serbian woman, wearing peasant hat (*šajkaca*) adorned with Milošević's picture, listening to him at Gazimestan. *Credit:* Balkan Historical Archive.

Corax's cartoon of Milošević in *Borba* (July 23, 1990) as a national communist, holding shield with coat of arms that uses hammers and sickles to portray the four Cyrillic "C's" (Latin "S's") from the Serbian nationalist slogan (*Samo Sloga Srbina Spasava,* or "Only Unity Saves the Serbs"). *Credit:* Predrag Korakšić.

the "collusion between communism and nationalism" that Milošević exploited to the fact that both Serbian nationalists and communists "share a strong Russophile sentiment and deep hostility to the West. There was and still remains a fatal bond between Orthodoxy and the revolutionary myth, 'the Comintern and Dostoievsky,' as [Danilo] Kiš himself defines this typically Serbian characteristic in 1986." "Terror of a Society Without Points of Reference," *Bosnia Report* (August–November 1999), New Series, No. 11/12.

PART II

POWER AND THE MANIPULATION OF TRADITION

Corax's cartoon of Mirjana Marković, with the trademark rose in her hair, enveloped by her ideological inspiration, Karl Marx. *Credit:* Predrag Korakšić.

Corax's cartoon in *Borba* (January 23, 1992) portraying the Serbian Orthodox Church's Patriarch on the sharp edge of a dilemma: the nation vs. support for Miloše-vić and state power. *Credit:* Predrag Korakšić.

Željko Ražnjatović (Arkan), the Serbian ultra-nationalist and underworld figure in Banja Luka, Bosnia, during the war in Bosnia. *Credit:* Balkan Historical Archive.

From left to right, Milošević's son Marko, Marko's girlfriend, and Marko's mother, Mirjana Marković. *Credit:* Balkan Historical Archive.

Milošević's daughter, Marija. *Credit:* Balkan Historical Archive.

Vuk Drašković and his wife Danica. *Credit:* Balkan Historical Archive.

Zoran Djindjić, President of the Democratic Party. *Credit:* Balkan Historical Archive.

Dobrica Ćosić (on left), famed Serbian writer and President of Yugoslavia in 1992 with Yugoslav Prime Minister Milan Panić (in Serbian Parliament). *Credit:* ICN Pharmaceuticals.

Milan Panić, on the occasion of his swearing-in as Yugoslav Prime Minister, July 14, 1992. Seated before him (from left to right) are Slobodan Milošević, Dobrica Ćosić and Montenegrin President, Momir Bulatović. *Credit:* ICN Pharmaceuticals.

Milan Panić (center) speaking to electoral rally in December 1992. On his left is Vuk Drašković, the President of the Serbian Party of Renewal (SPO); to his right is Vesna Pesić, head of the Citizen's Alliance of Serbia (GSS). *Credit:* ICN Pharmaceuticals.

Richard Holbrooke, American Balkan envoy, who eventually ended the Bosnian war through the Dayton peace accord, straining to hear a media query. *Credit:* Balkan Historical Archive.

Corax's cartoon of Richard Holbrooke psychoanalyzing Slobodan Milošević in uniform. *Credit:* Predrag Korakšić.

from while avoiding any potential damage. An honor guard awaited us in Priština. Milošević was in a euphoric mood. He escorted me into the tent set aside for honored guests. Other members of the presidency were gathered there with politicians and members of the diplomatic corps. . . . I remember the comments of some ambassadors that my participation was of great significance for resolving the Yugoslav crisis. The ambassadors from the European Union and the United States were not there. . . . During the short cultural program Milošević sat next to me. I remember that several times he looked around and tried to figure out how many people were present. Kadijević estimated around half a million, which Milošević said was an underestimate. He counted more, at least a million. After his emotional speech Milošević estimated that the crowd was one and a half million. That evening the Serbian media [controlled by Milošević] reported it was two million.[2]

Aside from representatives of the East European states and several neutral countries, the only ambassador of a major European country present at Gazimestan was the envoy of Serbia's historical nemesis, Turkey; a fact which provoked humorous commentaries on the part of observers. But important foreign ambassadors were not the only missing element in the audience. Many Albanians, fearful of the atmosphere surrounding the celebration, had decided to spend the day with their families in the countryside away from the Gazimestan festivities.

The highlight of the day's events was to be Milošević's speech to the excited crowd.[3] In carefully scripted remarks, Milošević observed that the current anniversary was being held at a time when Serbia had finally regained its "state, national, and spiritual integrity," and that the Serbian defeat of the fourteenth century, as well as later Serbian failures, including those during the Titoist period, had occurred owing to discord within the ranks of the Serb elite and political compromises by Serbia's leaders. "Six centuries ago," Milošević pointed out, Serbia had fought the Turks and served as a "bulwark defending European culture, civilization and religion." Alluding to a perennial theme in Serbian culture, Milošević observed that although some might claim the Serbian nation had been defeated at the Battle of Kosovo, the incident could also be regarded as "heroic" because of the Serbs' valiant performance, and the fact that the victorious Turkish Sultan had been stabbed to death—the first Ottoman ruler to be killed in war—by a Serbian commander. Milošević was well aware that although the 1389 battle had been a technical military defeat, that most Serbs regarded the event and its aftermath, as emblematic of how such a defeat can engender a stubbornness and fortitude to struggle against non-Serb control. He left it to his audience to ponder over the clear implication that perhaps the very traits that had allowed Serbs to overcome the tribulations of Ottoman rule might also assist them in dealing with their current concerns regarding Kosovo.

Tactfully, in view of his position as a high official in a multinational federation, Milošević urged toleration among the various nations and nationalities of socialist Yugoslavia, and also carefully avoided referring to the Albanians of Kosovo (who had boycotted the ceremony) or any other specific ethnic group by name. But near the end of his speech, he reminded the gathering that six centuries after the Battle of Kosovo, Serbs were "again today, engaged in battles and facing battles." Indeed, he observed ominously, although the struggles presently involving the Serbs were "not armed battles . . . such things cannot yet be excluded. But no matter what their character, battles can't be won without decisiveness, bravery, and a readiness to sacrifice." Milošević had put his fellow Serbs on notice regarding what measures he might take, and what might be expected from them. In the excitement of the historical celebration, his audience appeared wildly eager to follow their determined new leader. Milošević's remarks were made two years prior to socialist Yugoslavia's disintegration and the warfare that would soon follow in its wake.

The celebration in mid-1989 at Gazimestan presaged the climax of Milošević's rise to power through the use of extra-institutional political tactics, that is, popular rallies, or what became known as "happenings of the people," to attack the old communist establishment. Milošević and his supporters had now become the establishment, and any further expression of regime-sponsored populism would be far more controlled. Other forms of extra-institutional political behavior would continue in Serbia, such as the militant populism of the extreme ultra-nationalist groups (often allied to the regime), and political rallies by various anti-regime opposition forces,[4] but they would only be tolerated as marginal phenomena that could be exploited or quashed by a regime that was now confidently holding the reins of political power. During 1989 and early 1990, Milošević's authoritarian regime gradually moved out of its initial mobilizational and populist phase, and evolved toward a mixed form of personal and bureaucratic authoritarianism that would characterize it throughout the last decade of the twentieth century. Such institutionalized authoritarianism would alternate between "softer" and "harder" forms of repression and control depending on the circumstances and Milošević's immediate preferences. Mobilizational rhetoric was still employed after 1989, but rather than a prelude to demonstrations, it was used mainly as a threat that the "happenings of the people" could again be unleashed if necessary. As Milošević remarked in February 1990: "Serbs and Montenegrins in Kosovo have not been alone . . . every house in Serbia is with them and every house in Serbia is ready to go to Kosovo tomorrow if the methods of protection currently used is not sufficient. Everyone who knows the history of Serbia knows what Serbian citizens feel, knows what will happen . . . recently many more people have expressed a readiness to go to Kosovo with arms to defend children and women, land, and nation." But Milošević did call for a mobilization of Serbian volunteers to go and live in Kosovo, "to the south on a great mission of work, peace, and revival."[5] For the moment though, in the wake of the Gazimestan meeting, Kosovo was under control. But reference to the need for continued vigilance in the province, and the legend of his ostensible success in managing Serbian problems there, still served Milošević's consolidation of power.

Indeed by 1989–1990, the regime was also exhibiting a rather distinctive ideological underpinning; an admixture of notions consisting partially of warmed-over socialist phraseology from the old regime's political lexicon, but also, and more significantly, the appropriation of symbols and heroes from Serbian history, religion, and tradition. The "mega-celebration" of Gazimestan illustrated Milošević's full-blown utilization of the mythic power residing in the fourteenth-century Battle of Kosovo as a means for political mobilization. Central to the myth is the notion of heroism, both a heroic figure who although lonely and misunderstood on the eve of battle will single-handedly sacrifice his life against superior odds to achieve glory, and also the heroic existence of the Serbian army, which is willing to offer resistance to a superior force no matter what the cost.[6]

After his visit to Kosovo Polje, Milošević had cleverly nurtured the revival of the Kosovo myth, but in a revised version in which he was playing the leading role, with his supporters in the League of Communists and the military-security establishment serving as his supporting cast. In this role, Milošević could also pose as the "unifier and savior of the Serbs and Serbia, as the guarantor of Yugoslav unity, and as the strongman which Yugoslavia had been waiting for since Tito's death."[7] In only a few years following Milošević's legendary "long night" with the local Serbs at Kosovo Polje, almost every sphere of Serbian cultural expression—ranging from folkloric publications, comic strips, popular music, to historiography, school textbooks, poetry and literature—would reflect a new obsession with national history, religious heritage and the popularization of national heroes. For example, history textbooks were rewritten to emphasize the historical "righteousness" of the Serbian tradition, and to downplay any "dark spots" in the nation's past and recent experiences. The politicization of instructional materials was designed to "adjust history to current events," especially as the Titoist Yugoslav state violently disintegrated during 1991 and 1992. As one analysis of a textbook by a Belgrade historian put it: "brimming with xenophobia, contempt and hatred for neighboring countries the European and world community, such texts fit well into the propaganda system which has made the war psychologically possible."[8] Together with superficial strands of socialist thought, these views were offered as a "distinctive parallel ideology" to replace the principles of self-managed socialism, or the Titoist variant of Marxism.

Popular culture was also affected by the regime's preference for "assertive ethnicity." Thus, in the first part of the 1990s, older folk tunes that either explicitly or implicitly conveyed Serbian ethnic themes were rearranged with contemporary dance music into a new nationalistic form of culture called "Turbofolk." In a society "still heavily structured by patriarchical and the cult of force," observed one commentator, "Turbo" is an aggressive nationalist adaptation of pop culture used as a generator of a nationalist-consumerist mode of Serbness.[9] The highly publicized marriage of the acclaimed 22-year-old Turbofolk singer Ceca (Svetlana) Veličković to the 42-year-old military leader and notorious underworld businessman Arkan (Željko Ražnjatović) symbolized the linkage between the ultra-nationalistic popular music craze and the criminalized subculture which arose in Serbia during the early 1990s as a protest against the hyperinflation and sanction-busting activities linked to the nearby wars in Croatia and Bosnia. For many Serbs, the former Titoist values of interethnic coexistence and nonviolence seemed an impediment to fulfilling their national interests. As the Belgrade sociologist Vesna Korać remarked in May 1994, "what was once considered the subculture of violence became the dominant culture in which we all live."[10] Turbofolk's glorification of Serbian historical battles and myths, as well as current paramilitary commanders, helped to fuel and legitimize the prevailing ethno-nationalism that was encouraged by the Milošević regime during its first phase of political development.

The "cult of the past" or "cult of the ethno-nation"[11] effectively resulted in a state-sponsored re-socialization of the Serbian population with an ostensibly "new" value system. In essence this amounted to what has been termed the "ethnicization" of political life.[12] Historical facets of Serbian ethnic and religious nationalism, aspects of a latent collectivist outlook that had been more or less dormant, and indeed officially repressed, under the communist regime, were now substituted for the exhausted and discredited ideas of communist collectivism. Titoism had certainly constituted a more relaxed and novel form of communist organization than found elsewhere in Eastern Europe. But the notions of benign self-managing producers toiling in solidarity and interethnic harmony ("brotherhood and unity") were central to the goals of the Titoist regime. Milošević's eclectic concoction of perspectives, "a synthesis of state socialism and Serbianism,"[13] abandoned attempts by Yugoslav theorists and social scientists to understand and overcome ethnic conflicts (areas about which Yugoslav academics in the late 1960s and 1970s had been especially sensitive). Instead, a conception of the national enemy or enemies—that is, any ethnic group in Serbia or in any other republic viewed as opposing Serb interests—became the regime's central focus, and also served as a surrogate for the class enemy or retrograde economic and bureaucratic forces previously identified in communist doctrine. And once again, as so often in Serbian history, non-collectivist notions of individual freedom and a civic polity remained largely marginal in the official political culture.[14] Enthusiasm for liberal democracy and civic nationalism would be limited to the musings and periodic protests of urban intellectuals, and a portion of the younger generation, desperately searching for a wider base of support.

As early as the late 1980s, Milošević turned to the Serbian intelligentsia to help develop his regime's new post-Tito ideological outlook. Prior to the infamous Eighth Session of the Serbian League of Communists' Central Committee, where he had pushed aside Ivan Stambolić and other leaders associated with the moderate or anti-nationalist perspective in the party, Milošević had formed a more or less "tacit alliance"[15] with Serbia's nationalist intellectuals. But by late 1987 and early 1988, this nexus became more open and operational.[16] Nationalist intellectuals were now enlisted to assist Milošević's political supporters elaborate politically correct discourse, or the "symbolic universe" for the nationalist-oriented regime. As a rule, such intellectuals were not assigned positions directly in the apparatus of power, but typically were provided with generous access to the mass media, the educational system, and other means of expression. Ironically, many intellectuals whose independent thinking had made them nonconformists and dissidents during the Titoist authoritarian era now supported the eclectic body of nationalist images and ideas comprising the discourse of the Milošević regime's mass populism, and its ideological strivings.[17] By the fall of 1987 and winter of 1988, the ruling authorities and the Serbian Academy of Sciences and Arts (SANU) exchanged conciliatory messages in order to facilitate the new relationship between the regime and the intellectuals. A leading official of the League of Communists even publicly apologized for the campaign against the 1986 SANU Memorandum, and promised to put an end to unfounded accusations against SANU members. The same official signaled that the ruling party now intended to fully utilize the talents of the intelligentsia: "If the Party wants to gather the most creative intellectual forces, it ought to distance itself from quasi-fighters against nationalism."[18] Members of SANU reciprocated the invitation of the regime to become more politically engaged and nationally sensitive. For example, at the beginning of 1988, a discussion was held at SANU on the issue of constitutional changes in Serbia, which essentially summarized points made in the Memorandum that offered support to the regime's campaign to weaken Kosovo's political autonomy.

By the time of Milošević's arrival at Gazimestan in mid-1989 his attempted transformation of values in Serbia was well underway, though it would be accelerated in the early 1990s, particularly after the outbreak of the wars in Croatia and Bosnia. Thus, many members of the Serb intelligentsia, within and outside Serbia, became, what has been referred to, as "professional patriots" or "Serbs by profession."[19] In part, the emphasis on historical tradition was a natural consequence to the ideological void left by the atrophy and collapse of the communist regime. But the systematic appropriation of past and neo-nationalist notions, which could be melded together with a hodge-podge of residual socialist ideas, was also a calculated strategic maneuver in Milošević's consolidation of power. Thus in effect, Milošević was able to hijack an extant Serbian national renaissance for his own political purposes. Slavoljub Djukić has pointed out that the zealous support of the Serbian intelligentsia was "decisive" to Milošević's quest to obtain legitimacy as a national "leader." The intelligentsia, according to Djukić, "introduced him to history through an open door." Milošević in turn cleverly used the intelligentsia.

> In the struggle for acquiring power [1984–1987] he had no mercy towards opposition views endorsed by the current dissidents. That period was characterized by many prohibitions and cases of persecution. Indeed his severity towards noncon-formers served as a good recommendation for him in party circles. But after he took power and consolidated his position he changed course towards those whom he had persecuted earlier, giving them honors, including those who had for a decade craved such respect. They could publicly express their views, publish their books, and not have their opinions censored, particularly if those opinions favored the new regime, and they could find a place in the institutions of power.[20]

At the nerve-center of Milošević's power system was the press and electronic media, which served as the main vehicle for the dissemination of nationalist ideas. Indeed, as early as the mid-1980s, while serving as the party chief in Belgrade, Milošević had installed loyalists in the media (e.g., Dušan Mitević[21] and Živorad Minović[22]) to curtail any expressions of liberalism and expedite his control. By 1987, and particularly after his visit to Kosovo, Milošević utilized his domination of the media (e.g., the biggest media outlets, Politika, and Belgrade Television)[23] to challenge Dragiša Pavlović and Ivan Stambolić for control of Serbia.

After Milošević's victory over the moderates in 1987, nationalist discourse intensified significantly in the media. The pattern of "us" and "them" became the norm: "us" being Serbs and Serbian national interests, which were portrayed in a positive light, and "them," the "enemy nations" described in a negative and threatening manner. The "ethnicization" or "national homogenization" and politicization of the Serbian media by the ruling regime enhanced the political control of the authorities—even after the advent of pluralist politics in 1990—and helped whip up enthusiasm for military struggles against non-Serb ethnic groups such as the Croats, Slovenes, and Bosnian Muslims during and after the dissolution of the Titoist federation. In an attempt to forge unity behind his leadership, Milošević encouraged a "psychosis of general national threat," which only abated in 1994–1995 when he turned against the policies of the Bosnian Serb leadership[24] (a similar use of the media for war propaganda would resume in 1998–1999).

Following the establishment of "independent" media outlets in 1989–1990, the regime began taking steps to monopolize print and electronic communications. During the next decade, a constant struggle would take place by the independent media to provide alternative sources of information to the official line. Though the regime managed to dominate the media, and made it difficult for opposition parties to convey their messages to the public, the effort to completely marginalize the independent media would prove unsuccessful. Indeed, the regime's repressive measures actually stimulated resistance by independent journalists and media personnel, which led to the formation of various autonomous media organizations and associations throughout the 1990s. But while some independent journalists succeeded in presenting an impartial treatment of the regime and opposition parties, official media coverage during electoral campaigns typically involved "glorification" of the regime's "favorites," and the "Satanization" of the Serbian nation's opponents.[25]

The official media's politicization of myth and national history in the late 1980s and early 1990s, often in the most sensational, paranoid, and incredulous manner, appeared far-fetched and even comical to many in Serbia's urban intelligentsia and independent media circles. But significant segments of the intellectual elite also became "engineers" in the dissemination of nationalist ideology or the national identity sponsored by Milošević's mass media; a concocted "instrumental rationality" of perspectives ranging from paranoid ethnocentrism, xenophobia, and chauvinism to moderate forms of religious and national traditionalism.[26] The politicization of the media had a significant impact on many segments of society—the young, the elderly, the semi-skilled and less educated, the rural sector, and the uninformed—groups that together composed the bulk of Serbia's population. Alternative press and broadcast media did exist during the early 1990s, but they were often inaccessible due to cost, limited circulation, or in the case of the electronic media, range of transmission. State television in the service of the ruling party was particularly important in the regime's electoral successes, and also in the dissemination of official nationalism and war propaganda during the first half of the 1990s. For example, during 1993 the six major political dailies in Belgrade had a combined circulation of over 500,000, while news programs on the Central State television network alone, had a daily audience of approximately 3.5 million. In early 1994, some 4.9 million people over ten years of age (76 percent of the adult population) watched television on a daily basis, 62 percent listened to radio, and 13.7 percent read a newspaper.[27] Thus, overall media control proved to be a crucial tool in the mobilization of political nationalism by the early Milošević regime. The pattern of authoritarian domination required, however, far more than just a partial monopoly over communications, and limits on free expression. As a leading student of the Yugoslav media has pointed out "the concentration of communications and media power in the hands of the ruling party is the result of its political and economic domination, not the reverse."[28]

Institutionalizing Personal Power

The Ruling Personality and the Mystery of Power

Beginning in 1987, Slobodan Milošević became the political lynchpin of Serbia's personalistic authoritarian system. What kind of political skills did Milošević bring to the tasks of governance; in maintaining power? Why did his personality and style of political management engender political support, and how did those crucial aspects of his rule change with the evolution of his regime and alter political circumstances? How did the political rule of his wife, and her personality, influence politics in Serbia?

Most close observers have emphasized that Milošević is a very intelligent and capable man. Although deprecated as a "butcher" and "thug," whose prowess at political negotiation is essentially "Byzantine" and dishonest, he is also regarded as a formidable advocate of his views, who is very adept at facilitating and implementing a political deal. One former associate has observed that Milošević "decides first what is expedient for him to believe, and then he believes it."[29] This trait has often led to the suggestion that Milošević is "detached from reality," and that although he is a good tactician, he is a weak strategic thinker. For example, Dragoslav Avramović, the former governor of the National Bank in Belgrade, and recent opposition activist, who has described Milošević as a very clever and capable man, has commented: "I think that Milošević's fundamental problem is that he doesn't have a strategy. He is an excellent tactician, who knows how to survive until tomorrow. I call it the 'theory of the next eight hours'—if everything is okay until tomorrow morning somehow we will get by."[30] The Bosnian Serb politician Biljana Plavšić, who got to know Milošević quite well, and crossed swords with him on several occasions, has also observed: "he's certainly one of a kind, he's not an ordinary man. . . . On first contact with people he has charm, there's no doubt about it, he's smart, intelligent, eloquent, he knows how to handle an unpleasant situation quickly, but he's lacking in that he's not interested in the long-term future."[31] Close associates have described Milošević's style as dispassionate, cool and unrattled."[32] Diplomats who have observed his behavior emphasize Milošević's enigmatic manner, and considerable agility in pursuit of political goals. "He likes an argument," claims former British foreign secretary Douglas Hurd. "He's quick with reasons and explanations. I found it impossible to tell behind that equipment, what man was there. There was never any genuine expression of emotion or particular light or darkness in his face. A very competent, level performance."[33] Richard Holbrooke, the Western negotiator who has spent the most time with him, has noted that Milošević can "switch moods with astonishing speed, perhaps to keep others off balance. He could range from charm to brutality, from emotional outburst to calm discussions of legal minutiae. When he was angry, his face wrinkled up but he could regain control of himself instantly."[34] During the Bosnian peace negotiations at Dayton, U.S. Secretary of State Warren Christopher remarked that had Milošević been born in a democratic system he would very likely have also been a successful politician.[35]

Even as a young communist apparatchik in the 1980s, Milošević exhibited many of the traits that he would draw on in order to acquire and hold political power. Perhaps most importantly he had a likeable and nonthreatening personality that attracted friends and allowed him to influence others. "No doubt about it," Ivan Stambolić has recounted, years after Milošević cold-bloodedly pushed him aside, "he knows how to win people over when he needs them. At those times he was attentive and affectionate, amiable and 'well balanced,' gentle, even obedient." Stambolić has also pointed out that when he was an up and coming politician, Milošević would extend birthday greetings to the older generation of communist leaders; a gesture which helped Milošević develop a reputation as being a considerate and sensitive person.[36] But Milošević's reputation for congeniality was not only limited to raw political opportunism. He was well regarded for his loyalty to his relatively small circle of friends—most made during his days as communist banker—a bond which was contingent, however, on absolute loyalty to him. Milošević's sensitivity and loyalty apparently extend to his personal staff (secretaries, bodyguards, drivers, etc.), about whom he is very protective and caring, and who "tend to adore him." Milošević is also a devoted family man. Indeed, one of the most frequently mentioned facets of Milošević's personality is his extremely close emotional bonds to his wife. The only possible lapse in fidelity to his wife was an occasion that she publicly, but very obliquely, hinted at in her weekly column for the Belgrade magazine *Duga*. Milošević is also regarded as a caring father, who has tended to spoil his children. In fact, some observers say Milošević played a considerable role in the parenting of his children because of his wife's career as a university professor and political activist.

Two of Milošević's personal attributes seem to have contributed to his political success: a penchant for privacy, and, especially in his early political career, his modesty. While an outgoing man, Milošević appears to be more confident, comfortable and effective in smaller groups rather than in public ceremonies, particularly those which call for impromptu behavior. Outside his official functions, Milošević almost never appears in public, in contrast to most Serbian leaders who maintain highly visible public profiles and tend to frequent restaurants, sports events, hunting parties, etc. Milošević prefers to entertain at home, or to visit the homes of his small circle of close friends.[37] While craving political power, the Serbian leader has, both before and after acquiring high office, led a rather non-ostentatious lifestyle. As he made his way up the banking and political hierarchy, for example, Milošević and his family lived in a modest apartment and he drove an inexpensive car. Thus, he has not given the appearance of being an acquisitive leader who is hungry for wealth. His most frequently mentioned self-indulgences are a preference for Dutch cigarillos (he smoked cigarettes earlier in his career), good whisky and wine (although he is not an excessive drinker). The trappings of power—a villa in the posh Belgrade suburb of Dedinje, expensive cars, etc.—naturally came with his political success, but throughout the 1990s Milošević never developed a reputation for self-glorification or an insatiable taste for the perks and privileges of higher office. As one close confidant put it, he enjoys the "sheer power" of his position, and not so much the outward appointments of the role. In this respect, the flamboyant lifestyle of Milošević's son Marko—a race car driver, who used his family connections to become a tycoon (operating a nightclub and amusement park)—represents a sharp contrast to the lifestyle of his parents.[38]

Sensationalistic media accounts about his "legendary" behavior at Kosovo Polje and his devotion to Serbian national interests contributed to Milošević's growing support in the late 1980s. But during the early years of his populist and nationalist regime, the desire of Serbs to display his picture in their homes and at their rallies was quite spontaneous and authentic. An artificial and synthetic "cult of personality," though hardly on the scale of totalitarian dictatorships, came later, during the more institutionalized phase of his authoritarian regime. The decorations, monuments, and honors accorded to high office holders have had little appeal to Milošević, even when they were showered upon him during the first phase of his regime. His "exalted position of rule is his highest distinction," observes Slavoljub Djukić. And Milošević's relative isolation and distance from his countrymen, "magnifies his charisma."[39] For Djukić, Milošević's behavior exemplifies "a man of power, a lonely and self-confident bureaucrat who does not show a desire to please those around him nor to bother many of his compatriots." For the Yugoslav psychiatrist Žarko Trebješanin Milošević is the "cold narcissist," whose insensitivity to and exploitation of others "is a means for the satisfaction of his own interests, and is typical of a narcissistic person's need for idolizers, who offer them unreserved admiration."[40]

Milošević's instrumental use of nationalist appeals, along with his willingness to quickly change course, condemn nationalism, and to cold-bloodedly sacrifice national political goals and his ethnic kinsmen (e.g., in Croatia and Bosnia) when he perceived such a reorientation to be expedient, appears to reflect such a narcissistic and detached psychological make-up. As Harold Laswell first pointed out in the 1930s regarding some leaders of nationalist movements: "There are persons who act on the masses, but who are not psychologically acting with them. . . . I have the case history of one orator who could never understand why the masses always 'fell' for him. He described to his physician how one part of his personality, his real self, seemed to sit sardonically commenting on the rest of his self while it performed the curious laryngeal and gesticulatory operations that thrilled the masses."[41] Montenegrin president Milo Djukanović claims that Milošević has no firm beliefs at all; "his ideology is power. He has no nationalist or communist program."[42] Slavoljub Djukić has also emphasized Milošević's lack of chauvinistic intolerance toward other nationalities: "Milošević has carried the national standard, although that fire does not burn within him. . . . And when he agitated the Serbs, it was because he saw the possibility of strengthening his own ruling position. . . . While Franjo Tudjman and Alija Izetbegović toiled for their political convictions, he was a committed Yugoslav. He accepted nationalism and inhaled its lethal power, in order to consolidate his rule."[43]

A useful, if rather condescending portrait of Milošević's working environment and style of hospitality towards important foreign visitors has been provided by Hrvoje Šarinić, Croatian President Tudjman's long-time assistant, who negotiated secretly with Milošević during the 1990s.[44] At his first negotiating meeting in 1993, Šarinić met the Serbian President at his Andrić Street office in the heart of Belgrade. After being searched for listening devices, Šarinić was greeted by Senta, the head of Milošević's personal security, and then taken to meet Milošević. Mirjana Marković was seated outside her husband's office, and opened the first set of doors for Šarinić. "Please, the President expects you," exclaimed Mirjana. "Milošević was waiting for me with his characteristic smile. . . . Milošević's office was rectangular in form. Across from the dual doors at the end of the room, alongside a window looking over the street stood Milošević's desk decoratively carved from a massive tree. To the right of the entry door was a table at which we sat, and around it modern massive armchairs. A modest library was located in the office, merely of decorative significance. Everything was not very defined. The visitor did not get an impression of elegance nor tradition, history, or even art." In describing his ensuing meeting, Šarinić gives a glimpse of one of Milošević's few indulgences. "The whole time Milošević very attentively followed my remarks, enjoying himself with his usual glass of brandy [Viljamovka], and as usual takes no notes. I don't ever remember a meeting with him where he drank something other than Viljamovka. He praised the drink, recounting how Americans in the course of their visits admire its taste and qualities." Milošević's convivial style and preference for pear liqueur has often been recounted by observers. For example, he is alleged to have plied Richard Holbrooke with brandy at midmorning peace talks in 1995. Responding to light-hearted comments that he was getting Holbrooke drunk on plum brandy, Milošević clarified: "No I didn't get him drunk on plum brandy. I got him drunk on pear brandy."[45]

On a later visit to Yugoslavia in 1998, Šarinić met Milošević at his new office, in the residence of the President of Yugoslavia (a post which Milošević assumed in 1997) located in the elite Belgrade suburb of Dedinje. The presidential residence had once been Tito's official home, and Šarinić was moderately more impressed. "Far different from the building of the Presidency of Serbia on Andrić Street . . . this was a building of more modern design, with well laid out gardens. And a presidential atmosphere. At the entry soldiers dressed in military uniforms from the Kingdom of Yugoslavia continuously stood guard. A winding path led to the building of the Presidency . . . on the left side a beautiful wood house in the mountain style in which there was a fully equipped workshop where Tito tried to preserve his vocational skill [as a metal worker] and temporarily forget political problems. It went through two or three courtyards before getting to the door of the Presidential office. . . . By itself it was impressive, but only in terms of size: there was no refinement in the arrangement or choice of furniture that we were accustomed to." Šarinić's snobbish appraisal may be based on a comparative allusion to the more elaborate, if rather kitschy, presidential trappings favored by his boss in Zagreb, Croatian President Franjo Tudjman.[46]

Although Milošević can be personable and outgoing on occasion, an innate shyness and insecurity—perhaps derived from the personal tragedies in his life, reinforced by his tremendous dependence on his wife, and also his self-perceived inadequacies—have indirectly contributed to his charismatic appeal to many segments of Serbian society. Thus, his reputation for reclusiveness and aloofness have given him an air of mystery, and has contributed to observations that he is an "unusual" or "strange" person; traits sometimes associated in the Serbian public view with leadership qualities and "heroic" potential. Replying to a December 1994 question as to why he appeared so rarely in public Milošević replied: "It seems to me that I appear enough. Otherwise I think that politicians appear on TV too often, I would even say inappropriately— daily appearances in public are an effort to brainwash the people, to make them think a certain way."[47] Milošević has preferred to cultivate a more distant and mysterious image, corresponding to his own preference for privacy, and for pulling the strings of power outside of public view. As for brainwashing by the media, he has left that to others chosen to work for his regime.

It has been suggested by those close to Milošević that his public displays of authority and self-confidence are "not artificial," although his behavior on such occasions—for example, during the populist rallies of the late 1980s—usually requires that he is "primed" or "pumped-up" by his advisers and wife until he almost assumes an almost trance-like demeanor. A convincing and persuasive speaker when prepared, whose rhythm and style of speech—if not always the content of his message in recent years—resonate with the "average" Serb, Milošević has usually been able to "connect" with his audience. "He understands perfectly the mentality of the people," observes Veran Matić, the director of the independent Radio B-92, "what political culture demands here, what rhetoric sells."[48] Milošević's habit has been to speak in short and clipped sentences, in clear language—not the political jargon of the old communist bureaucrats—using phrases that appeal to the "national ear."[49] His phrasing also has enough ambiguity and double meaning to give him considerable flexibility in interpreting and carrying out what he promises. "Either Serbia will be a state, or it won't exist," he told his audiences, for example, in the late 1980's, promising some vague notion of enhanced sovereignty, or perhaps national suicide. Similarly at Gazimestan in mid-1989 he reminded his audience that they "were in battles and facing battles." But although their struggles were not yet "armed battles," he warned them that "such things cannot be excluded." Playing to the hopes and anxieties of his audience, Milošević told them very little of what would be required of them, or what they would experience as he charted the course of the Serbian national renaissance.

Brilliantly understanding Serbian political culture, the pragmatic and shrewd Milošević also used the egomania and opportunism of his political rivals to his maximum political advantage. Thus, throughout the 1990s he proved highly adept at splitting his opposition forces and using individual opposition leaders for his own political purposes. Milošević also understood how to exploit political ambition and loyalty in the ranks of his own party. "One aspect of Milošević's character," Lord David Owen has aptly observed, "is his readiness to regard individuals as disposable: to use them and discard them."[50] In fact, Milošević is constantly enlisting, discarding, and recycling officials in a rotating game of musical chairs. "During his life," Slavoljub Djukić has observed, Milošević "has had plenty of friends, allies, and political sympathizers, but except for his family, he was devoted to no one, and no one was allowed to get too close. He treated people as biological material, and divided them into subjects and enemies. Nothing in between. He used communists and anti-communists, nationalists and Yugoslavs, patriots, the Chetnik emigration, the intelligentsia, the church, and the Serbs outside Serbia. And he jettisoned everyone when they became unneeded."[51] Nebojša Čović, the former mayor of Belgrade who broke with Milošević in 1996, has observed that the Serbian leader "buys [you], places you in a role, and once he has done that it is very difficult to go back and free yourself from those claws." Aleksandr Tijanić, Milošević's former Minister of Information, claims the regime "chose about 10,000 people who were loyal to the regime. These people were allowed in a short time to accumulate great wealth. An extremely rich new economic class emerged . . . the [ruling] couple treated state industry and government concessions as a source of largesse for their followers."[52]

The influence of Mira Marković on her husband is one of the most frequently noted characteristics of power in the Milošević regime. For example, Nebojša Čović claims that Mira Marković molded Milošević "into a man who saw his destiny was to be a politician. . . . Their conversations are in baby talk. They always use pet names, like my little pussy cat, bunny, and so on. I found it very funny, especially when it always happens while we dealt with serious issues such as politics."[53] Slavko Ćuruvija, another former colleague and family friend (eventually murdered by the regime or its allies), noted that when Milošević telephoned Mira "he was never the one who was talking. She was talking, he was listening." At the Dayton peace conference in 1995 Ćuruvija claimed that Milošević called his wife "seven, eight, nine times a day."[54] The extremely close bond between Mira and Slobodan suggests that her role must be carefully considered when assessing the strengths and deficiencies of Milošević's political behavior. "There is one thing you must understand about Milošević," Belgrade Professor Svetozar Stojanović has pointed out, "unlike most men in the Balkans he has only slept with one woman."[55] Former friend and former director of Belgrade TV Dušan Mitević has observed that Milošević "is not just a sensitive husband, he's an over-sensitive husband. He can never be alright, if he knows that something is wrong with her. [This] sometimes influences his decisions."[56]

The close bond between Slobodan and his wife developed years earlier, in Požarevac (see Chapter 2). Mirjana has told a Serbian interviewer in 1999 that they first met in a library while she was reading the Greek tragedy *Antigone*. According to the interviewer it was Mirjana's "sorrow" that attracted Milošević to his future wife. He felt the need to "ease her pain," to "console and protect her."[57] Mirjana allegedly harbored political ambitions for her husband ever since he was a young law graduate completing his military service in Zadar, on the Croatian coast. Walking with her cousin in Zadar's marketplace, Mira noticed Tito's picture in a store window. "Someday," she told her cousin, "my husband's picture, just like Tito's, will stand in a shop window."[58] Even more averse to public appearances than Milošević, Mirjana Marković only began to acquire her own higher political profile in the late 1980s. Writing the weekly column for years in the Belgrade magazine *Duga*, Mirjana's commentaries could make or break political and private reputations, and also signaled changes in regime policy. Mirjana's influence grew considerably during the 1990s as Milošević's position was becoming more precarious, and as his inner circle of friends and loyal advisers gradually shrank. Typically wearing a trademark bow and plastic rose in her dyed ink-black hair (allegedly a style favored by her mother), Mirjana Marković has none of Slobodan's charm, and is widely regarded as a singularly unimpressive speaker. Observers of the Milošević regime have been struck by the fact that the ruling couple was comprised of one of the most popular men in Serbia's political life, and one of the most unpopular female political figures. Dedicated to the ideals of Marxism, Mirjana views herself as a sociologist and a leftist ideological "theoretician," who leaves what she considers to be mundane political organization and political decision making to her husband. "Ideology has never been for my husband what it has been for me," Mira remarked to an interviewer in 1993. "He would never say, 'I shall die for socialism' or 'I shall die for internationalism'—statements to which I am inclined. But we agree on important ethical values."[59] Despite her higher academic degrees and intellectual airs close observers say she is actually poorly educated and does not display a keen intelligence. Her friends from the days she worked in the communist youth organization at Belgrade University are also largely regarded as second- and third-rate professors. Mirjana Marković's political leverage has derived from the psychological hold she has over her husband. She is considered more emotional and ruthless than Milošević. "She draws into herself," remarks Dušan Mitrović, "becomes passive, but harbors great aggression."[60] Mira exhibits a black and white image of the world, viewing political figures as either friends or enemies, loyal sycophants of the ruling couple or "traitors" to the Serbian people. When in 1995, cryptic comments in her *Duga* column suggested that she suspected Milošević was having an extra-marital affair, Stojan Cerović, the acerbic journalist at the opposition journal, Vreme, had his doubts: "We would have known by now if he were the kind of person who is capable of looking around rather than straight ahead. We would not be in the state we are in. . . . Why Serbia is so much out of step with the rest of the world is partly of moral nature, and lies in the morality of the ruling couple. As if the virtue and purity of mutual devotion somehow locks them in and isolates them, creating a feeling of superiority in terms of their righteousness and benevolence which in advance clears them of any guilt irrespective of what they might do."[61]

Although she claims to abhor nationalism and "primitivism," Mirjana Marković was a key actor in the revival of national consciousness by Serb communists in the mid and late 1980s. Thus, she has argued that the "mass manifestation of national identity could be supported until autumn 1988 at the last," but has pointed out that subsequently strivings for "nationhood became nationalism."[62] When Milošević broke with the Bosnian Serb nationalists in 1993 Mira wrote a scathing *Duga* column in which she sharply differentiated between the Serbs inside and outside Serbia. Ridiculing the "self-styled saviors of the Serbian people" as frustrated, rumpled, semi-educated idle beer drinkers," Mirjana condemned "vulgar nationalism" as "ridiculous" and "ugly." Choosing to forget the mobilization of pan-Serbian nationalism the ruling couple had previously sponsored, she now claimed that "idle loud-mouths" are using my husband as an endorsement for what they say and do. Without ever having met him and without a chance of ever doing so."[63]

It was not surprising that when many Serbs turned against Milošević in the mid-1990s for having "betrayed" the national cause, they had a special contempt for his spouse. To her admirers she remains "a born leader," for her detractors she is a "fiercesome Lady Macbeth," intoxicated by the power that derives from her hold over her husband. "There is not a single woman in Serbian history who people have been so afraid of, and towards whom they have showed so much servile attention," Belgrade journalist Slavoljub Djukić has remarked.[64] The Serbian writer Stanko Cerović is equally critical and cognizant of Mirjana's complexity: "She has the voice and sensibility of a child, she has no sense of reality, but like Milošević, she possesses a keen instinct for danger and has mastered the art of deceit—symptoms not uncommon in certain forms of madness."[65] Drawn closely together by mutual need—hardly an unusual motive for pairing—and then bonded by the successful pursuit of power against considerable odds, Serbia's ruling couple seemed to have fused into almost a single complex personality that thrives on political domination as both a means and an end.

Shaped by the unique mix of his own drives and insecurities—and undoubtedly by the enormous influence of his ambitious, troubled, and mercurial wife—Milošević has also exhibited a politically cold-blooded and brutal side, as his record in Yugoslav political life after 1987 attests. Preferring to use propaganda rather than terror as a means of persuasion and political control, Milošević has not shied away from using tougher methods and even terror as a last resort. "He's the coldest person I've ever met," remarked Warren Zimmerman, who served as the U.S. Ambassador to Yugoslavia from 1989 to 1992. "I believe that this sinister coldness has made it easy for him to order or condone the mass killings that have earned him his place in history."[66] "He's, I would say a very complicated individual," observed Bosnian president Alija Izetbegović. "He's not an unpleasant person when you have personal contacts with him, but his policy is not only unpleasant it's very brutal, and is very criminal. This is the paradox connected to his personality."[67] "Unfortunately, I really know him well," claimed Croatia's Franjo Tudjman in April 1999. "Simultaneously I could say I do not know him because he is absolutely unpredictable not to use a more insulting word. . . . He is unpredictable, I even think he is sick."[68] As a man who can be described as both extremely charming and warm, and alternatively brutal, cold, and deranged, Milošević's complexity and self-contradictions certainly served to assist him in his political short-term successes. Ultimately, however, the same characteristics will probably ensure that his political demise will be troubled and turbulent.

Starting his political ascent in the mid-1980s by telling people what they wanted to hear, Milošević spent the next decade persuading and compelling the Serbian people to do what he wanted them to do. It is not surprising, therefore, as the Belgrade academic Kosta Čavoški has observed, that "mobilization" is one of Milošević's favorite words. He utilizes the word in dozens of different ways. For example "political mobilization," "mobilization of all progressive forces," "mobilization of the working class," "mobilization of all nations and nationalities," "historical mobilization," "mobilization and unity of Serbia," "urgent and democratic mobilization," "mobilization for war," "mobilization for development," etc.[69] A favorite aphorism—"in a fight one can't be too choosy about what kind of stick one selects"—that is frequently used by Milošević in debates also reveals that he is ready to justify the most brutal measures when necessary. Another favorite Milošević phrase—"to convert a disadvantage into an advantage, a fault into a virtue, a weakness into a strength"—illustrates the extreme pragmatism that has enabled him to obtain and hold power in the face of many obstacles and adversity. However, gradually, as a result of his ill-conceived policies, Milošević's disadvantages would significantly multiply, and together with his faults and weaknesses, become increasingly less convertible as political currency.

The "Routinization of Charisma"

During the first phase of consolidating power, Milošević had engaged in an intra-party factional struggle to eliminate his rivals. He next turned to populist methods (the "anti-bureaucratic revolution" and "the happenings of the people"), and a new nationalist oriented ideology disseminated by co-opted members of the Serbian intelligentsia to enhance the regime's legitimacy. The extravaganza at Gazimestan was a measure of Milošević's success at using such methods of mobilization to gain broad public support among Serbs throughout Yugoslavia. In attempting to secure his political power Milošević had deftly courted three very different and often antagonistic constituencies: (1) the Partisans, or the old ruling Serbian communist elite that was looking for a new "nationalist" leader; (2) the noncommunist nationalists, who were part of the mass movement directed against the crumbling communist regime, and; (3) modernizers and technocratic reformists, who were loyal to the regime, but who wanted economic changes (many of whom had worked closely with Ivan Stambolić but who had transferred their loyalty to Milošević during 1987). During the late 1980s, Milošević had been playing a risky game, telling each constituency what it wanted to hear, and hoping none of the groups would become unhappy about his courtship of the others.[70] But once comfortably ensconced in power, Milošević concluded that he needed a more reliable foundation for governance. The formal disintegration of the League of Communists in early 1990, and the advent of a new pluralist phase in Serbian political life, provided Milošević with the opportunity for a tactical reorientation.

Up to the end of 1989, Milošević had been operating as a top regional leader within a federal one-party system. When the communist system collapsed, he reconfigured the regime, and moved to systematize his political control. Thus, during the early fall of 1990, as multi-party electoral competition was getting underway in Serbia, Milošević consolidated his power through the adoption of a new constitutional structure that provided for his personal rule, and which would greatly limit the influence of emergent pluralist politics in Serbia–Montenegro for the next several years. For example, the Constitution of the Republic of Serbia, adopted in September 1990 (building upon the constitutional amendments of March 1989), gave the president wide power to take measures not requiring the ratification of the government or the parliament, and that could not be challenged by the constitutional court. The president also enjoyed wide powers to introduce a state of emergency, including the curtailment of basic rights and freedoms. Although directly elected, the president of Serbia under the 1990 constitutional arrangement was effectively unaccountable to any other constitutional body, and provisions for his recall through a referendum required far more votes than were necessary for his election. A majority of the eligible electorate was needed for recall, but only a majority of votes cast was required for the election of the president.[71]

The centralized presidential system of rule in Serbia was custom-made by Milošević's lieutenants to facilitate their leader's *de facto* authoritarian and personal control. The system essentially relegates the legislature and cabinet to the role of "mere transmission belts."[72] Indeed, it is very revealing that when the Milošević regime was eventually seriously challenged by popular protests, for example, in March 1991 and again in 1996–1997, far more attention was concentrated on providing police protection to Milošević, and the state monopoly over the electronic media, than with safeguarding the legislative and governmental institutions. Structural features aside, Milošević's personal style of rule gave the system a fundamentally illiberal cast. Thus, in practical terms, decision-making at the summit of Serbia's political hierarchy was monopolized by Milošević, with his personal views dictating how all important issues would be resolved, and his handpicked officials implementing those decisions. Milošević's methodology for ensuring loyalty and preventing any threat to his control was to constantly reshuffle subordinate personnel with little regard to a person's technical qualifications. Though Milošević confided closely in his wife and a few old friends, the exercise of power in the Serbian regime throughout the 1990s was essentially a one-man show. During the initial populist phase of Milošević's political ascent, he had circumvented established political rules and deposed any political challengers in the old hierarchy. But once having consolidated power, and entered into the post-populist stage of his control, he saw little reason to defer to the members of his new handpicked elite, or what really amounted to a coalition of loyal factions.

Milošević had personally created the regime's new governing elite, and he now saw fit to utilize it as he wished. The personalistic authoritarian model of rule under Milošević was hardly a replica of the Stalinist system, nor totalitarian in operation, but the reality of political decision-making on issues that crucially mattered for the country were highly centralized. Indeed, disinclined to delegate authority, Milošević's ambit of control extended to things both large and small. Zvonimir Trajković, who served as Milošević's personal adviser after he became Serbian president (and who would later work for the Bosnian Serb leader, Radovan Karadžić), claims that Milošević maintained a very small staff, instead of a team of assistants and advisers, Milošević, according to Trajković, "relied too much on his intellect and neglected the analytic approach. . . . He practically does not need advisers. . . . for in the end everything ends up as what he orders. For example, he makes a hundred telephone calls a day; instead of allowing his assistants in the office to do it. If a government has to be formed, he forms it. He should rather appoint a person in charge of forming a government, who would consequently be responsible for the work of the government."[73] The Belgrade journalist Slavoljub Djukić has usefully described Milošević's patron–client relationship with his subordinates:

> Tito never had as much control and influence over his supporters as Milošević does . . . there is an enormous division between the first man [of Serbia] and all others. While alongside Tito there arose many personalities of considerable capability, Milošević has gone in an entirely opposite direction. . . . Among [his] Socialists there doesn't exist a second and third personality as you found Kardelj, Ranković and Djilas next to Tito. . . . Between Milošević and his party comrades there exists an unbridgeable gap. . . . Between Milošević and his allies and enemies there is no hate, nor love or disappointment, and least of all any ideological burden. Only raw interest exists. People are [politically] secure, only if they are indebted. In general one does not deal with biographies.[74]

Dominating Pluralism: Milošević-Managed Multi-partyism

The Hegemonic Party System

With the collapse of communist power in most East European states during the autumn of 1989, which was followed not long after by the dissolution of the League of Communists in Yugoslavia (January 20–22, 1990) as a unified political organization having a federal level of party authority, the entire political climate and party system changed in each of the Yugoslav republics.[75] However, in Serbia, the character of political change over the previous two years had been significantly different than elsewhere in Yugoslavia. In essence, from 1987 to 1989, the one-party communist oligarchy in Serbia, an East European nomenclature-type system with certain Yugoslav peculiarities, had been transformed by Milošević not into a fledgling democracy, but rather into a one-party authoritarian and populist dictatorship. Indeed, although Milošević became party chief in Serbia in mid-1986, he was not popularly elected the state president of the Socialist Republic of Serbia until November 12, 1989, or just two and a half months prior to the end of one-party communist rule in Yugoslavia. Moreover, the electoral process for choosing Serbia's president could hardly be classified as a real competitive exercise. Less than two weeks before the "election," three relatively unknown communist officials were selected to "compete" with Milošević for the office of Serbian president. As planned, Milošević handily won 80 percent of the votes cast. In central Serbia he took 82 percent of the vote, and in Belgrade over 92 percent. Not surprisingly, Milošević's appeal was heavily concentrated among the two-thirds of the population who were ethnic Serbs. Thus, in multi-ethnic Vojvodina, Milošević was only able to attract just over 60 percent of the vote (Milošević's crony, Mihalj Kertes, an apparatchik of Hungarian ethnic origin received around 15 percent of the vote), and less than 25 percent of the vote in Kosovo (where Albanian voters, by and large, boycotted the election, and Serbs split their vote). Milošević, according to a leading regime-controlled Belgrade weekly, symbolically represented the "personalization of the Serbian renewal . . . the renewal of the Serbian political tradition," a tradition according to which a person reaches the political summit at a time of crisis who will struggle for "freedom, a democratic state and progress."[76] Milošević was 48 years old and at the height of his popularity. He could now claim to have legitimacy of a sort among his republic's Serbian voters, albeit only on the basis of limited pluralism, and without being tested by genuine multi-party competition.

As Milošević and his minions watched democratic tendencies sweep most of the other Yugoslav republics, they resisted adopting a similar course for Serbia (or for Montenegro, which was already under their strong influence). At first Milošević endorsed a vague notion of nonparty pluralism. That conception was designed to obstruct genuine political competition, and limit pluralism to "multi-group" political discussion within the Socialist Alliance of Working People, a mass socio-political organization with a broad multi-class framework that was part of the Titoist system. Milošević identified pressures to accommodate free political expression, and the political claims in Serbia by non-Serbs for greater autonomy, as two facets of the same general threat: "Appeals for political pluralism, and applause for the [Kosovo Albanian] movement whose motto is blood, come from the same rostrum," he observed in February 1990.[77] But by early 1990, with post-communist regimes already unfolding in Eastern Europe, and internal pressure for political competition building throughout socialist Yugoslavia, the formula of nonparty pluralism was superceded by the promise of introducing multi-party pluralism. Not long afterwards (July 1990) legislative provisions were adopted in Serbia permitting the formation of new political parties. In the meantime, as a means to ensure his unchallenged dominance in political life, Milošević pushed through the new custom-made 1990 Serbian constitution (in a referendum on June 1–2, 1990, in which 78 percent of 6.6 million voters cast ballots, 97 percent of those voting supported the move), which essentially institutionalized the continuity of authoritarian governance and a system of personal rule. Authoritarianism was given democratic legitimation, but in a plebiscitarian manner, in which citizens were presented with a "take it or leave it" choice, designed by a leader, albeit a quite popular figure, who had emerged during the pre-pluralist one-party system. Opposition leaders who strenuously argued that the election should precede constitution-making were overruled. But though the new constitution, and the legislation providing for a pluralist electoral system, were formally adopted the same day (September 28, 1990), the basic spirit of competitive party politics remained fundamentally alien to the Belgrade ruling elite. Moreover, Milošević had defined the new rules of the game—both the constitution and provisions for the competitive electoral process—without consulting the emerging opposition parties.[78]

By the time that the first multi-party elections were held near the end of 1990, the general outline of the Serbian party system had already become clear.[79] Thus, in July 1990, in order to ensure his unchallenged political control over the country, Milošević revamped and renamed his ruling party organization. The former League of Communists of Serbia (SKS) was formally dissolved. A "new" organization, the Socialist Party of Serbia (SPS), was established, and became Serbia's paramount political framework. By dissolving the formerly ruling SKS and forming the SPS Milošević could claim that he had broken with the negative aspects of communist past practice, and created a "modern" and "democratic" political organization. But in most respects, especially its strong grip on various associated centers of power such as the police, military, the economy, and the media, and the fact that its core leaders and a large portion of its members either came from the SKS or shared the mentality of a centralized or single party run by a strong leader, the SPS was decidedly a party of continuity.[80] In effect, a one-party system of control was replaced by the hegemonic control of one party in a fledgling multi-party system. Moreover, unlike other parties that were being established more or less from scratch, the SPS inherited the assets, real estate, and physical infrastructure of the previous ruling party organization. Thus, while the end of communist one-party rule permitted the formation of a spate of opposition parties rhetorically challenging the regime, throughout the next decade such rivals to the "new" SPS proved unable to unite and challenge Milošević's control in any sustained or effective manner. Outwardly, the SPS presented itself as a party oriented to a pluralist system, no longer connected with the idea of self-management, programmatically committed to the coexistence of state and private property, and unabashedly standing for Serbia's national interest (without having to defer to Titoist perspectives on the nationalist question). In practice, however, the SPS was a cosmetically retooled vehicle allowing Milošević to retain a monopoly of power in a manner resembling the old regime.

Technically, the SPS was created by the fusion of the League of Communists of Serbia (SKS) and the Socialist Alliance of Working People of Yugoslavia (SSRNJ), at a Unity Congress on July 16, 1990. The SPS membership was drawn substantially, although not entirely, from the ranks of the SKS and its associated political forces. In 1989, the SKS had around 820,000 members, but after the break up of the League of Communists as a federal organization in 1990 and the advent of the multi-party political system, many of those individuals decided to either terminate their affiliation with any party, join non-communist or anti-communist organizations, or find an-other communist vehicle for their views. It is estimated that roughly 150,000 of some 450,000 members of the SPS in the early 1990s were former members of the SKS.[81] A large number of the newly recruited SPS members came from rural areas.[82] By early 1996, the SPS would grow to approximately 500,000 members.

Milošević also enjoyed the support of another "new" party organization, the League of Communists–Movement for Yugoslavia (SK-PJ), which was formed in December 1990. Sometimes referred to as the "General's 'Party,'" the SK-PJ initially was composed largely of members of the League of Communists working in the military sector. A small group of intellectuals also were in the founding membership of the SK-PJ, the most prominent of whom was Milošević's wife, Mirjana Marković. The SK-PJ eventually became the core of the Yugoslav United Left (JUL), formed in July 1994, which would cooperate closely with the SPS throughout the remainder of the 1990s. Initially, JUL brought together 23 minor parties and groups of a so-called "leftist" and pro-Yugoslav orientation. By early 1997, JUL claimed a membership of approximately 200,000. In effect, Marković's JUL organization was a SPS satellite party, espousing a hodgepodge of neo-communist views, and serving as an auxiliary framework through which Milošević could attract assorted elite-level forces (mostly industrial managers, military officers, former communist apparatchiks, and some intellectuals), who preferred not to be directly associated with the SPS and the regime's nationalist orientation. JUL also provided some additional voter support for the regime. But its main purpose was to help give a patina of legitimacy to a regime characterized by the overwhelming dominance of one party, and the exclusion of any viable opposition (as well as provide Milošević's wife with her own boutique party organization). Thus, Serbia technically became a multiparty democracy in 1990. But in practice, Milošević's SPS, together with JUL and some other allied parties, which cooperated with the regime at different points in time over the next decade, managed to function as a hegemonic coalition effectively blocking any political transition to a fully pluralist and genuinely competitive system. As one leading Serbian social scientist has characterized the continuity from one-party communist control to SPS supremacy in the multi-party system: "The party which was in power for 50 years remained in power under the pluralistic regime, but didn't change itself, which is exceptionally rare in history."[83]

In terms of its political positioning within the Serbian party system, the SPS has viewed itself as a moderate, nationally oriented, left-wing political organization. By 1990, Milošević's nationalist credentials were already established (e.g., his 1987 visit to Kosovo Polje, his coup against the anti-nationalist wing of the SKS later the same year, his leadership of the mass movement for a Serbian national renaissance, and the constitutional changes he introduced in 1988–1989). Thus, by the time he formed the SPS, Milošević could afford to move towards the center, temporarily moderate his nationalism, and accuse the more extreme right-wing parties of reckless "national radicalism."[84] By this point in time, Milošević had been able to convince many of Serbia's leading intellectuals that they should give their allegiance to a regime that was advancing national interests, and also preserving socialism of a sort. For example, the former "humanist" and Praxis philosopher Mihailjo Marković became vice president of the SPS in 1991. "I got involved in politics to save the Serbs of Eastern Croatia [Krajina]," Marković would claim; "they will be slaughtered."[85] Following the break-up of Titoist Yugoslavia in 1991, and the onset of the "wars of the Yugoslav succession," Milošević would shift the SPS towards a more nationalistically oriented perspective. But subsequently, as the outcome of the warfare in Bosnia became more problematic for Serbia, and international pressure on Belgrade increased, Milošević would again shift in a relatively more moderate direction (1993–1997). As a rule, Milošević endeavored to avoid being tagged as an extremist;[86] a fringe position that he preferred to leave to his surrogates and sycophantic associates in other parties, who were invited into, and forced out of, coalitions with the SPS during the 1990s. Indeed, right from its inception, Milošević carefully portrayed his ruling party as a "barrier against the right."

The "right" elements, which Milošević tried to distance himself from, were essentially nationalist and ultra-nationalist party groups predominantly composed of noncommunists and anti-communist forces, that is, political elements either not formerly connected with the SKS, or who had broken with their communist past. Generally more extreme, and overtly rightist or ultra-nationalistic than the SPS, many leaders of such fringe parties were political actors who had initially become politically conscious during the anti-bureaucratic revolution and mass movement, that is, the rallies and "happenings of the people," which Milošević had stimulated in 1988 and 1989. For example, the Sava Association—a group founded in March 1989 and dedicated to protecting the Serbian language and the defense of Kosovo–Metohija—included among its founders Vuk Drašković, Vojislav Šešelj, Mirko Jović, and Veljko Guberina. All of those individuals later became leaders of their own parties. The Sava Association itself became the Serbian National Renewal party (SNO) in January 1990 under Mirko Jović. In June, the SNO formed a paramilitary organization, the Beli orlovi (the White Eagles), which later became infamous for its wartime atrocities outside Serbia. In March 1990, Drašković and Šešelj merged their own small political groups to form Serbia's biggest opposition party, the Serbian Renewal Movement (SPO). But by June, Šešelj had split off to found the Serbian Radical Party (SRS) in February 1991. Initially, Šešelj remained at the margin of the right-wing forces, but he would gradually become a more important figure in Serbian political life (see Chapter 4).

During the first few years of pluralist development, Drašković would borrow from Milošević's populist tactics to build up the SPO and become the most effective challenger to the regime from the nationalist or right-wing side of the political spectrum. For example, on March 9, 1991, Drašković and the SPO were at the center of a mass opposition rally in Belgrade protesting against the monopoly of the ruling party. Police fired on the demonstrators, and in the turmoil an 18-year-old demonstrator and a policeman were killed, while 80 people were wounded. Milošević claimed that the seeds of "chaos and violence" were being planted in Serbia. Tanks were called out, and Drašković and others were arrested. The next day thousands of student demonstrators turned out to protest the arrests and demand changes in the management of the media and police. The protests also spread to other towns. Eventually the regime backed down, released Drašković, and ordered the requested personnel resignations. But on March 11, the regime also arranged its own rally of support in which the demonstrating students were portrayed as traitors. The March 9, 1991 student protests became a "cult date" in opposition circles that was remembered each year. But as a noninstitutionalized and rather amorphous protest with no directing leadership, and only loose ties to the opposition parties, such anti-regime demonstrations could not effectively alter the basic structure of power in Serbia. Subsequent student organized rallies, such as those held in June and July 1992, were more focussed on specific issues such as opposition to the war, but again were extra-institutional episodes, rather than electoral successes, that did not present a serious threat to the regime.[87] Trying to diffuse the protests, Milošević met with a selected delegation of students and professors in mid-June. His remarks to the meeting reveal a fundamentally anti-pluralist and populist outlook that restricted the regime's ostensible multi-party façade.

> You said that one should bear in mind different views. This is correct . . . different views and opinions should be respected. This is correct. However, they first of all should be borne in mind, but it is only the will of the people that should be respected when it comes to running the state, and not the will of various individuals, groups, parties, party factions, or other factors of political life, which as you know is very diverse in our country with some 70 different parties and various other groups.[88]

The most important political force in 1990 to the left of Milošević, that is, in the center and center-left of the new pluralist spectrum, was the Democratic Party (DS). Organized by Belgrade intellectuals who began discussion of the project in fall 1989, the party was formally established in February 1990. Its thirteen founding leaders included Dragoljub Mićunović, Kosta Čavoški, Vojislav Koštunica, Zoran Djindjić, and a number of other prominent members of the Belgrade intelligentsia. Only three of the original founding members were still in the party in 1999. Most of the founders were intellectuals of a liberal-democratic orientation, who had been anti-regime dissidents during the 1970s and 1980s. But in a pattern similar to development on the nationalist right wing of the political spectrum, personality and political-ideological clashes would soon weaken the Democratic Party, stimulating individuals such as Mićunović, Čavoški, and Koštunica to break with the party and found or join new political organizations. Indeed, even before the December 1990 elections, a clash occurred between Mićunović and Čavoški regarding strategy about the "national question." Čavoški, who wanted the DS to take a more assertive national orientation, lost when the party members voted on the disagreement in December 1990, and he eventually left the DS (and helped form the Serbian Liberal Party). Similar differences and Mićunović 's decision to keep the DS out of the larger opposition political bloc formed before the 1992 election would motivate Koštunica to leave the DS that year in order to form his own Democratic Party of Serbia (DSS). But Mićunović's moderation on the question of nationalism would eventually lead to his demise in the DS during 1993 and 1994 when the party moved to the right as a result of initiatives taken by his former student and long-standing ally, Zoran Djindjić. In January 1994, Djindjić ousted

Mićunović as DS party president, and in late 1995 he was expelled from the party. Mićunović later ascribed the constant defection of intellectual leaders from the Democratic Party to their dissident orientation and "moral narcissism": "Each of them considered themselves called upon to be a moral judge . . . rigidity and intolerance already began at the founding meeting . . . a party in which moral notions are so deeply established has to have different factions."[89] In 1994, Mićunović and some two dozen friends from the DS established a nongovernmental organization, the Democratic Center Fund, to promote their views (in 1996, this became the Democratic Center Party).

The fragmentation within and among the fledgling opposition parties due to various political, ideological, and personal disagreements proved crucial to Milošević's maintenance of a dominant position during the first stage of multiparty competition. Moreover, as an incumbent political decision maker, Milošević had already demonstrated his strong commitment and his initial effectiveness on behalf of Serbian national interests, and was continuing to do so in debates with leaders from other republics and provinces. In this context, and given their disunity, it was very difficult for Milošević's opponents from the Serbian intelligentsia on either the right or the left to attract substantial popular support for their respective programs. The extreme nationalists appeared to be unstable, dangerous, or ineffective. At the other extreme, the ostensible "liberal" intelligentsia were trying desperately to reconcile democratic norms and Serbian national interests in formulating their programs, and indeed often found it difficult to avoid making their own ethnically charged appeals to the country's voters. The constant dilemma for the avowedly centrist and liberal parties was how steal Milošević's nationalist thunder, while still claiming they offered citizens a genuinely democratic and civic-oriented alternative. Meanwhile, those few Serbian intellectuals who in the climate of the late 1980s and early 1990s did advance a genuinely non-nationalist and liberal-democratic program—such as Vesna Pešić and her Citizens' Alliance for Serbia (which grew out of elements from Ante Marković's League of Reform Forces and the Association for a Yugoslav Democratic Initiative)—were largely marginalized or ostracized as "traitors."

In the first half of the 1990s, Milošević won two competitive, albeit not fully democratic, elections to become president of Serbia (December 1990 and December 1992), and he also led the SPS to victory in four legislative elections (December 1990, May 1992, December 1992, and December 1993). Each election had, of course, its unique features, occurring in different political climates and situational settings, and also involving different party organizations, personalities, issues, and types of campaigns. Serbia's emergent party system was in constant flux, with some parties fragmenting, others completely collapsing, and new parties emerging.[90] But the fundamental stumbling block to democ-

Table 3.1   Distribution of Seats in the Serbian Assembly, 1990–1997

	December 1990	*December 1992*	*December 1993*	*September 1997*
Socialist Party of Serbia (SPS)	194	101	123	
Yugoslav United Left (JUL)	—	—	—	110[a]
New Democracy (ND)	—	—	6[b]	
Serbian Radical Party (SRS)	—	73	39	82[c]
Serbian Unity Party (SSJ)	—	5	—	—
Serbian Movement for Renewal (SPO)	19	49	37[b]	45
Democratic Party (DS)		79[d]	29	—[e]
Democratic Party of Serbia (DSS)	—	—	7	—[e]
Civic Alliance of Serbia (GSS)	—	—	2[b]	—[e]
Various minority & regional parties & others	30	13	7	13
Total	250	250	250	250
Electoral turnout	71.5%	69.7%	61.3%	57.0%[f]

[a]A three-party coalition (Socialist Party of Serbia, Yugoslav United Left, and New Democracy).
[b]During the election, New Democracy and the Civic Alliance were part of the DEPOS coalition (Democratic Movement for Serbia), but later New Democracy joined with SPS and enabled Milosevic to form a majority in the legislature.
[c]In early 1998, the Serbian Radical Party joined the SPS and JUL to make a new ruling party coalition. New Democracy had left the coalition earlier.
[d]Includes two members from the coalition between the Democratic Party and the Reformists.
[e]Boycotted the 1997 election.
[f]The parties that boycotted the September 1997 election claimed that the regime inflated the voter turnout in order to secure a valid parliamentary election.

ratic post-communist transition was traceable to the fact that Milošević's SPS were able to maintain its basic unity and dominance, while the opposition parties continued to be fractious, weak, and susceptible to Milošević's manipulation. The most constant feature in each election was the persistent political success of Slobodan Milošević and the SPS, although by declining margins of victory over time (see Table 3.1).

There are several major factors that account for Milošević's ability to retain power after the advent of a pluralist electoral system in 1990, but three broad reasons are most significant: (1) the strong tendency towards political conformism and conservatism in Serbian political culture, which in the 1990s was reinforced by the population's lack of experience with democratic competition following a long period of authoritarian rule; (2) the weakness of those forces attempting to replace Milošević, and; (3) his considerable abilities as a politician, especially regarding the effective use of the advantages at his disposal.

As pointed out in Chapter 2, throughout his career Milošević has been able to shrewdly mobilize support within a political culture that exhibited a proclivity towards authoritarian values, a willingness to support strong heroic leaders, and an established preference for collectivist nationalism.[91] A deep fear of radical and disorderly political change is also characteristic of Serbian political culture. Indeed, throughout Serbian electoral history, the most successful political party has generally been the one that dominated the incumbent regime and organized the elections. For example, in 1990, Milošević used this political conservatism to his advantage and his monopoly over the media apparatus to nurture a fear of change that was already very prevalent in the Serbian electorate. The slogan employed by the SPS that year, "With Us There Is No Uncertainty," appealed to worried voters who had experienced the political turbulence and economic deterioration in Yugoslavia during the period preceding the election. An emphasis on stability was also an appealing notion to the thousands of state employees and their families in Serbia who were concerned that the defeat of the previously ruling socialist authorities might spell the beginning of general societal disruption. Anxious that they might become the scapegoats for earlier mismanagement, or that overly rapid economic change in the direction of a market economy would result in their unemployment, members of Serbia's "parastate stratum"—including thousands of "socialist pensioners" and members of the military forces—gave their support at the ballot box to Milošević. Moreover, by 1990, Milošević had already established a strong and popular record of standing up for Serbia's national interests, thereby allowing him to appear as the candidate who could best combine patriotism with stability and the promise of renewed prosperity. Even after Milošević would fail miserably to fulfill the promises he made in 1990, the fear of change in a sizeable segment of the electorate would provide him with an important reservoir of political support from election to election.

The political deficits of the opposition parties in Serbia have also proved highly beneficial to Milošević. For example, because of their constant personal squabbling and political differences among the nonruling party rulers and elites, the opposition parties proved unable to maintain a coherent electoral alliance for any sustained period of time. Thus, successive opposition coalitions between the fall of 1990 and 1996–97 all failed to maintain cohesion or achieve their goals: the United Opposition, the United Serbian Opposition, the United Opposition of Serbia, DEPOS, the Democratic Alliance, the Parallel Parliament, and the Together (*Zajedno*) coalition. Divisions among the opposition forces, and especially among the most prominent figures in the Serbian intelligentsia, made it far easier for the SPS to dominate political life. More often than not, the divided nature of the opposition was often due to personal jealousies among party leaders, each wanting to control the interparty alliances, and to ensure a future position for themselves in an eventual government. The highly personalized control of leadership within most of the opposition parties tended to reinforce such power seeking and power struggles. Moreover, a large number of the opposition parties' leaders were intellectuals and former members of the Serbian League of Communists, who had already spent years debating and reflecting on ways to improve Serbia. As a result, each party leader believed that he or she deserved support, and had the correct answer to the problems at hand. Opposition leaders were also obsessed with holding power, even if they only controlled a minor nonruling party organization, and maintained the hope of acquiring more power once the incumbent ruler was unseated. Compromise and cooperation were of secondary value to power maintenance. Indeed, the word "compromise" was considered as highly negative, both in communist jargon and in traditional Serbia political discourse. Such unbridled ambition to become "the leader" is also captured by the Serbian term *liderstvo*, which denotes both blind ambition to get to the top of the greasy pole, and also a willingness to engage in a broad array of political machinations necessary to remain there. Rampant *liderstvo* resulted in a situation where typically the divisions between opposition parties, and between internal factions within opposition parties, were often deeper than the cleavage between any one of those parties or factions on the one side, and the ruling party on the other.[92]

The fact that hundreds of thousands of educated Serbs emigrated during the 1990s also weakened the pool of talent for opposition leadership, and the potential voting base of anti-regime parties. The constantly changing political orientation of the main opposition parties further made it difficult to sustain alliances, and confused voters about what policies Milošević's rivals would adopt if they were ever able to form a government. Moreover, the decision by certain opposition parties to boycott elections in order to demonstrate their contempt for Milošević's transparent manipulation of the electoral process may at times have diminished the regime's overall legitimacy, but it also had the effect of allowing Milošević to maintain his political control. Indeed, the electoral boycott strategy of Kosovo's "anti-system" Albanian parties throughout the 1990s, also significantly benefited the regime. For example, with only non-Albanian citizens of Kosovo voting, almost all the seats allocated to the province went to the SPS and other right of center Serbian parties. The boycott of Albanian parties in Kosovo also made it easier for the SPS to manipulate the number of registered voters in the province's constituencies, and therefore inflate the number of safe seats garnered by the regime. Largely as a result of such measures, Serbia's leading student of electoral politics, Vladimir Goati, has concluded that from 1990 onward, not one election was really free or democratic.[93]

But Milošević's advantages were not limited to the weakness of his rivals. For example, he inherited and controlled the organizational structure and resources of the former League of Communists in Serbia, as well as the state apparatus and economic infrastructure of the republic. He also dominated the most powerful media outlets, and was able to fashion the electoral system in a manner favorable to the ruling party. In almost every electoral campaign, the opposition naturally demanded that the regime establish fair conditions for competition, particularly an accessible and free media. However, little was accomplished in achieving this goal. Beyond the opposition's serious weakness and the regime's political advantages, Milošević must be given personal credit as an extremely shrewd and pragmatic political figure. As the Belgrade political analyst and activist, Ognjen Pribičević has remarked, Milošević's record in dealing with his political opponents is incomparable to any politician in Europe. Various opposition politicians or activists have been bribed, co-opted, manipulated, publicly embarrassed, jailed, harassed, and even in some cases probably murdered on Milošević's orders (or that of his wife), in order to preserve his power and maintain his regime. The most egregious tactics against opposition leaders and dissidents have typically followed their direct personal attack on Milošević and his wife. More conventional forms of manipulation and enticement were also used to constantly split up the opposition forces and prevent any serious alternatives to the regime that might excite voter support. Milošević also cleverly thwarted any move within his own ruling party that might constitute a political threat to his control. Belgrade sociologist Vladimir Goati has discussed several factors for Milošević's success at preventing significant internal dissent within the SPS in the early and mid-1990s. First, by the time of the party's establishment in 1990, Milošević had already gathered broad support for his personal leadership. Indeed, at least initially, Milošević enjoyed tremendous prestige as leader of the post-communist SPS. Second, as former members of a communist-style organization, many SPS followers were already disposed to view factionalism as inappropriate and politically dangerous, recognizing the repercussions that nonconformism could have for their political careers. Third, the liberal faction among Serbian communists had already been extensively purged in previous years (by Tito in 1972–1974, and by Milošević in 1987–1989). A rare case of internal dissent in the SPS occurred in June 1992, when ten SPS deputies in the Serbian legislature (out of 194 in a body having 250 members) broke off from the party to form their own political group, but they quickly split into two groups and proved little threat to Milošević.

Milošević has also had an excellent sense of which members of his inner circle might stand in his way as he made abrupt shifts in policy. For example, in 1995, after he helped negotiate the Dayton agreement, and effectively left the Bosnian Serbs with an agreement they strongly opposed, Milošević removed several outspoken stalwarts from the SPS elite circle (e.g., Borisav Jović, Mihajlo Marković, and others). Slobodan Antonić's description of the procedure for their removal is quite revealing of the way the regime has operated: "Milošević came to the Main Board meeting over which he was to preside, simply read out a list of those to be removed and appointed to duty; and, without asking whether anyone present had anything to say, and after only 12 minutes in session, closed the meeting! Meanwhile, not one member of the Main Board, the only body that has the right to appoint or replace functionaries by party statute, dared utter a single word, let alone ask for a vote!?"[94] In an open letter on November 28, 1996, Marković responded, pointing his finger at the board members who had helped to demote him and describing how their actions would strengthen authoritarianism: "You silently pushed through something that is completely counter to any democracy. How do you want to work from now on? Will you ever manage to stand up and tell the president that you are the highest party body between Congresses which defines policy and takes the most important decision, and that he has to listen to you, not the other way around?"[95] Mihajlo Marković, who had become one of Milošević's chief ideologists, but who had allowed himself to become embroiled in a heated debate with Mirjana Marković, finally claimed to have discovered the true character of the leader and regime he was serving.

The "Technology of Domination": State Control of the Economy, Police, and Justice

Milošević's domination over the SPS ruling party elite, and his more indirect, but operational control over the top ranks of his wife's JUL party hierarchy, served as the nucleus of a broader, although still relatively small, ruling political establishment in Serbia, which also included those in the top ranks of the state bureaucracy and the incumbents of the top economic and financial posts in Serbia. That broader political-economic oligarchy consisted of three elite subgroups: (1) individuals at the summit of both governmental-state authority and leading officials in the ruling party or interparty coalition; (2) a somewhat smaller number of directors and managers in state enterprises and banks, and; (3) the owners of individual private firms working closely with, or essentially linked to, the regime, thereby comprising a "parastate" economic elite. Throughout the 1990s, Milošević permitted these three elite sub-groups to enjoy a privileged and powerful position, subject to their complete loyalty to his political control.

The economic elite within the state and parastate subsectors of the ruling establishment was composed of individuals who had accumulated their wealth because of their legal, quasi-legal or illegal activities within the state apparatus, or by utilizing their connections with state officials. Most individuals in the regime's elite structure were originally members of the former ruling communist elite (either managers or political professionals) who had been incorporated into Milošević's ruling circles during the late 1980s. Initially, while he was still governing a single republic in the Yugoslav Socialist Federation, Milošević exhibited support for economic reform, including preference for a "mixed economy," and a "pluralism of property ownership." In fact, the members of Serbia's so-called "Milošević Commission" that was assembled in early 1988, premised their broad outline for Yugoslavia's economic recovery on the notion of developing "socialism as a wealthy society." This strategy envisioned market-oriented reforms in which the "world market and world competition represents the strongest generator of economic operation." The way out of the country's economic crisis was to be achieved by the stimulation of investments and production in enterprises, introduction of new programs and techniques, stepped-up development of the small-scale economy, and increased foreign investments. Milošević also urged Yugoslavs to overcome their "unfounded, irrational and . . . primitive fear of exploitation" by foreign capital. Indeed, Milošević's political opponents in the communist elites of Yugoslavia's other republics, although highly critical of his nationalist rhetoric and his populist style of mobilization, were nonetheless willing to acknowledge his credentials as an economic reformer. "The views of Mr. Milošević, with whom I disagree on political issues, do not differ from mine on economic matters," commented Slovenia's state president, Janez Stanovnik. And, Stanovnik added, "he is just as liberal as I am when it comes to economic matters."[96] Foreign officials during this period took Milošević's economic liberalism on face value, and welcomed him, more or less, as kind of a "Yugoslav Gorbachev." Thus initially, Milošević, like many other leaders with an authoritarian bent, who come to power during a time of societal crisis or trauma, not only played on a theme of the threat to his nation or ethnic group, but also on the promise that he would advance the nation's bread and butter interests. Building a new "socialism as a wealthy society," and nationalistic populism focussed initially on addressing the Kosovo problem, were the twin components of Milošević's early program designed to establish a linkage or transactional partnership with the Serbs of Yugoslavia in the troubled context of post-Titoist uncertainty.

But though Milošević endorsed a "reform program," he clearly favored the "social ownership sector" or "public means of production," over the private sector. Indeed, the establishment of any real equality between social and private ownership was viewed as a mistake by Milošević. Thus, one of the main features of the Milošević regime, which allowed it to perpetuate the monolithic political and economic control system of the previous Titoist regime, has been the monopolization of Yugoslavia's privatization process. While a substantial number of firms in Serbia were privatized in the early 1990s as a result of a federal law adopted before the collapse of socialist Yugoslavia in 1991, the

Milošević regime was able to slow this aspect of economic change, and thereby maintain state control over the economy by means of legislation applying to Serbia. After Yugoslavia disintegrated, the privatization process was further stalled, or fine-tuned to favor supporters of the regime. By the summer of 1994, the Milošević authorities would be able to push through a law—ostensibly designed to correct the injustices of the privatization process (and introduced into parliament by the opposition Democratic Party)—that allowed the state to re-socialize or re-nationalize property that had previously been transferred to private owners (many of whom in any case were managers connected to both the old and new regimes). A process of "statisation" or "re-nationalization" then ensued that returned the bulk of the economy to state control.[97] For example, some large enterprises were turned into "public firms" (e.g., railways, airlines, oil, forestry, water supply, radio and television, etc.). Others such as steel, the metal industry, and electronics became mixed property firms, in which the state is effectively the sole proprietor. One important result of this re-nationalization was the process of re-stratification in society, or essentially the ability of individuals connected with the state, that is, controlled by the ruling party elite, to convert their political power into economic control, property, and personal wealth. By blocking the transformation of ownership in Serbia after 1994, the Milošević regime also prevented the formation of a sufficiently "broad social bloc" to support a reformist platform. "Present day Serbia," a Belgrade sociologist would observe in 1999, "is in fact caught in circular causality; the ruling political elite passed decisions which hindered privatization and a change of the interest structure of society, and subsequently, thanks to a fossilized interest structure, managed to preserve its dominant position."[98] By way of contrast, in Montenegro, a change in the laws on ownership pushed through by more moderate elites slowly opened the way toward a general reformist process in that republic (see Chapter 7).

Stalled privatization and re-nationalization permitted many members of both the state and parastate economic sub-elites to grow enormously wealthy during the 1990s. This was not so much due to their entrepreneurial talents, but to their politically backed monopoly control over different segments of the economy, such as the issuing and distribution of money, imports and trade, production of goods, and the right to control financial transactions. The private or parastate elite grew substantially larger after the imposition of United Nations sanctions against Yugoslav (from May 1992 to December 1995) as a result of the war in Bosnia, when goods became extremely scarce. Owners and managers of enterprises importing oil, strategic raw materials, spare parts, etc., or exporting goods that could raise foreign currency, were able to make huge profits. Extra-legal wartime trade in arms, war materials, and stolen humanitarian aid also proved enormously lucrative.[99] The Serbian state and parastate economic and managerial stratum did not constitute a modernizing elite devoted to economic innovation and development, but rather a politically obedient oligarchy benefiting from the status quo.[100]

By the time of socialist Yugoslavia's dissolution in 1991, the Milošević regime not only had firm control over the party system, the media, and the economy in Serbia and Montenegro, but also firmly dominated the police apparatus and the administration of justice. Inheriting political management of Serbia's police operations in the late 1980s, Milošević quickly built up a strong and politically loyal internal security service. By 1993, 50,000 people were employed by the Ministry of Internal Affairs, and there were at least another 20,000 police reservists. By 1995, the police force was estimated to be around 100,000 strong, or larger than the combined military forces. Disciplined, generously financed, well-trained and equipped, including units with anti-aircraft cannons, heavy mortars and heavy artillery, the police also received better salaries than most other sectors of the state apparatus, including the military. The conspicuous differences between the police and military apparatuses in Milošević's Yugoslavia became strikingly apparent in the early 1990s as the Belgrade regime strove to maintain indirect control over the Serbian communities in Croatia and Bosnia, along with ensuring the political stability of Serbia and Montenegro.

Early on in his rise to power, Milošević also developed a close relationship with the military elite of the Yugoslav People's Army (JNA). In fact, he seemed to genuinely like the military, and leading members of the military appeared to like him. But Milošević quickly became disenchanted with the JNA high command when it refused to extend the army's whole-hearted political support during the disintegration of Yugoslavia. For example, in March 1991, when Milošević tried to engineer a power shift in the Yugoslav presidency in order to obtain authorization for federal-sponsored military action against a military buildup by republican authorities in Slovenia and Croatia, General Kadijević and other members of the JNA military elite—including some officers of Serbian background—maintained an impartial and apolitical stance. Moreover, the military failed to perform as effectively as expected in the short war in Slovenia in July 1991, and later in the war between the JNA and Croatian forces (1991–1992).[101] But if he was increasingly distrustful of the independent professional or corporate interests of the JNA elite—a leadership group that had been shaped during the Tito regime—Milošević was equally suspicious after 1991 regarding the successor and predominantly ethnic Serb "Army of Yugoslavia" (VJ). The VJ was formed as a result of the disintegration of the JNA during the break up of socialist Yugoslavia. But initially at least, Milošević felt he could not rely on the political loyalty of the VJ command structure. In response, he built up a powerful and well-armed police force as a politically loyal "para-army." For its part, the army command remained balanced between

Serb nationalists favored by Milošević, professionals who remained more or less politically neutral, and a smaller more or less "third force" of more liberal officers, who sympathized with the liberal democratic opposition parties. Thus, in 1992 and 1993, Milošević sacked dozens of generals and admirals, in an effort to establish greater control over the military. Denied the generous budget allocations of the Tito era, and faced with a deteriorating economy and a loss of status, the military became increasingly demoralized during the 1990s. In July 1993, a leading military commentator for Belgrade's daily *Politika* thus remarked that "the reputation of the army has collapsed, the renown of the military profession has hit rock bottom, and the army has touched the threshold of poverty."[102] By mid-1995, it was estimated that more than 300 officers had been purged from the military.[103] Passive resistance, or a defensive attitude, continued in some quarters of the military establishment, but no longer constituted a serious political threat to the regime.

The professional and political weakening of the army, and the militarization of the police apparatus allowed Milošević to guide the course of events in the Croatian and Bosnian Serb communities in a more surreptitious, personalized, and extra-constitutional manner. During and after the wars in Croatia and Bosnia, the Serbian police-state nexus would also function as an internal shield, a praetorian guard, protecting the authoritarian regime and its elite from its own citizens. In 1993, the "Police Academy of Serbia" was founded with a substantial budgetary allocation. The school's curriculum included courses on military doctrine, and the use of heavy armor and artillery. While the media may have served as the primary vehicle used by the Milošević regime for promoting the officially acceptable ideological and political line, including a steady diet of nationalist themes, the existence of a strong police apparatus that could be used selectively against nonconforming segments of the Yugoslav population constituted a central pillar of the outwardly "soft" authoritarian system.

The politicization of the judicial system was also a part of Milošević's "technology of domination." Judicial appointments were firmly in the hands of the regime as pro-regime judges headed all judicial election committees. The poor material position of judges, and cutbacks in the number of judicial appointees, also increased the insecurity of judges, and enhanced political control over the courts. As in the previous communist regime, "moral-political suitability," as interpreted by the ruling party, was critical in deciding eligibility for the bench. Thus, a former eminent judge observed in early 1993 that "the monster of the suitability criterion rides again around the courts, and the regime is still obviously trying to treat the courts of law as simple yes-man activity, and to regard them as an instrument of its daily political interests. The courts and the judges are pushed aside, and spend most of their time in chasing the people whose checks bounced or failing to pay their TV subscription, while the big crime and the flagrant violations of the law generally remain untouched."[104] Legislative oversight of judicial appointments was negligible because of the powerless position of the opposition parties in the Serbian assembly, and the overall impotence of parliamentary institutions in the structure of power. Political intervention in judicial decision-making also became the norm during the early 1990s.[105] The arbitrary and politicized nature of the prosecutorial and judicial sectors allowed the regime to protect its supporters and punish its opponents. With the growing criminalization of the economy, and growth in quasi-legal practices by the state's economic sector and state-linked private companies during the early 1990s, the politicization of justice was especially valuable to managerial sub-elites within the ruling establishment. "Financially insecure judges can be bribed very easily and it often looks as if they are," claimed one Serbian lawyer specializing in criminal law. "The first thing my clients want to know is how much money is needed for the judge. . . . Without hard currency or influential friends you have to wait a long time for justice, and the results are unpredictable."[106] Thus, by the early 1990s the ruling establishment in Serbia had a well-developed security network and pliant justice system to protect to both their legal and illegal operations, not to mention their privileges, perks, and positions.

In the atmosphere of political justice nurtured by the regime, it is not surprising that the members of Serbia's future legal elite exhibited little adherence to the rule of law and the protection of human rights. For example, a survey conducted among law students in Novi Sad in 1993 revealed that roughly one-third of the respondents felt that a leader whom the people can trust was more important than various laws. Moreover, 60 percent of the respondents felt that the state security service should be allowed to search homes without a warrant, and 51 percent felt the police should be able to independently open letters. Only 45 percent of the future lawyers believed judges should be chosen through local democratic elections. Indeed, 41 percent of the respondents believed that Serbs should have greater constitutional rights than other nationalities, "because they live in their own state."[107]

The impact of the wars of the Yugoslav secession on Serbia, and particularly the breakdown of routine economic activity under the pressure of United Nations sanctions, contributed to the growing criminalization of society in Serbia and Montenegro during the first half of the 1990s. The most representative example of this trend was the rise of Željko Ražnjatović, better known as Arkan, from a minor figure in Belgrade's underworld to a high-profile actor in Serbian political life. Wanted by Interpol and a dozen European countries in connection with bank robberies during the 1970s and 1980s, Arkan emerged as a prominent figure on the Belgrade scene when, with the help of the Serbian Ministry of the Interior, he organized paramilitary units to fight for Serb interests in Croatia and Bosnia. Arkan's Serbian National Guard, popularly known as the "Tigers," became notorious for their brutal "ethnic cleansing" campaigns in Croatia and Bosnia. But the Milošević-controlled media turned Arkan into a "hero of the Serbian nation." As most normal business activity was curtailed or disappeared due to international sanctions, Arkan's companies and his Obilić football club were allowed to flourish. In exchange, Arkan expressed admiration for Milošević. "Milošević woke up the Serbs," he remarked in one interview. "He woke me up as a Serb too."[108] When a Croatian diplomat conducting secret negotiations with Milošević asked about Arkan in 1993, the Serbian president only laughed and said "I too must have someone to do certain kinds of work for me."[109]

Wrapping himself in the Serb struggle of epic tradition—including the myth of the Battle of Kosovo, and the history of Serb brigandage against Turkish occupation (the *hajduk* tradition)—Arkan claimed that his activities demonstrated a commitment to the "defense of Serbs" throughout the former Yugoslavia.[110] The "heroization" of mafia activity in Serbia made a mockery of the regime's claim to be upholding the rule of law, and transformed the climate in Milošević's soft dictatorship into a disorderly and dangerous environment where wild and arbitrary justice became increasingly routine. Gradually, as one of Belgrade's journalists has observed, "the celebration of criminals as nationalist war heroes, or populist primitivism," would transform Serbia "into an isolated fortress of 'patriotic-national' uniformly-thinking people."[111]

At the beginning of his rise to power, most Serbs believed that not only would Milošević restore Serbian national pride and reassert Serbian control over the provinces, but that he would also preserve Yugoslavia within its Titoist borders, and provide enhanced influence for their republic in such a multinational federation. As hope faded for maintaining the cohesion of Titoist Yugoslavia during 1990–1991, Milošević continued to be perceived by most Serbs as a leader who could peacefully obtain a territorial adjustment of the country, and thereby allow most members of their ethnic group—including the large Serb communities in Croatia and Bosnia—to live in a single state controlled from Belgrade. The course and outcome of the wars in Croatia and Bosnia, however, would dash that expectation. When hostilities came to an end in Croatia during early 1992—leaving a cold peace between government forces and rebellious Krajina Serbs in that newly independent state—many of Milošević's ethnic brethren still believed he could achieve the goal of Serb unity in the Balkans, although now at considerably greater cost then they imagined in the late 1980s, or even at the outset of the 1990s, when the Serbian president still enjoyed enormous popularity. However, the length and intensity of the even more savage conflict in Bosnia (1992–1995), a struggle that in large measure the Belgrade regime had instigated, would seriously deplete

Milošević's remaining political support, and compel him to improvise new policies to obtain domestic and international backing.

NOTES

1. *NIN*, No. 2544 (September 30, 1999).

2. *Moja istina* (Ljubljana: Mladinska knjiga, 1996), as reported in *NIN*, No. 2544 (September 30, 1999).

3. Belgrade Home Service, June 28, 1989 in *BBCSWB*, Part 2, Eastern Europe; B. Internal Affairs; Yugoslavia, EE/0496/B1, June 30, 1989.

4. Nebojša Popov, "Srpski populizam: od marginalne do dominantne pojave," *VND*, No. 135 (May 24, 1993).

5. Belgrade Home Service in *BBCSWB*, February 7, 1990, Eastern Europe: B. Internal Affairs, EE/O682/B/1.

6. Srbobran Branković, *Serbia at War With Itself* (Belgrade: Sociological Society of Serbia, 1995), pp. 46–47.

7. Dušan Janjić, "Od etniciteta ka nacionalizmu," in Mirjana Prosić-Dvornić (ed.), *Kulture u tranziciji* (Belgrade: Plato, 1994), p. 29.

8. Dubravka Stojanović, *The Balkans, Wars and Textbooks: The Case of Serbia* (Belgrade Association for Social History, 1999). See also, Marko Živković "Stories Serbs tell Themselves: Discourses on Identify and Destiny in Serbia Since the Mid-1980s," *Problems of Communism* (July–August), Vol. 44, No. 4, pp. 22–29.

9. Alexei Monroe, "Pop Culture and Paramilitarism," *Central European Review*, June 19, 2000.

10. *Inter Press Service*, May 9, 1994.

11. Ivan Čolović, *Politika simbola: ogledi o političkoj antropologiji* (Belgrade: Radio B-92, 1997, pp. 41–48.

12. Claus Offe, *Varieties of Transition* (Cambridge: MIT Press, 1996), pp. 51–53.

13. Latinka Perović, "Istorijske uslovljenosti dezintegracije Jugoslavije: slučaj Srbije," in Velimir Tomanović, *et al.* (eds.), *Integrativni i dezintegrativni procesi u zemljama tranzicije* (Belgrade: Institut društvenih nauka, 1998), pp. 148–149.

14. Zoran Avramović, "Mitopoetska mišljenja u Srpskoj političkoj Kulturi," in Mirjana Vasović (ed.), *Fragmenti političke kulture* (Belgrade; Institut društvenih nauka, 1998), pp. 285–302. On the "retraditionalization" of values in Serbian society during the 1990s see also, Dragomir Pantić, "Dominantne vrednosne orijentacije u Srbiji i mogućnosti nastanka civilnog društva," in V. Pavlović (ed.), *Potisnuto civilno društvo* (Belgrade: Eko-Centar, 1995), pp. 71–103.

15. Audrey Helfant Budding, *Serb Intellectuals and the National Question*, op. cit., p. 206.

16. See Olivera Milosavljević, "The Abuse of the Authority of Science," in Nebojša Popov (ed.), *The Road to War in Serbia: Trauma and Catharsis* (Budapest: Central European University Press, 2000); first published in Serbian in Belgrade 1996.

17. See, for example, Nicholas Miller, "The Nonconformists: Dobrica Ćosić and Mića Popović Envision Serbia," *Slavic Review*, Vol. 58, No. 3 (Fall 1999), pp. 515–536.

18. *Politika*, February 5, 1988, cited and translated in Nenad Dimitrijević, "Words and Death: Serbian Nationalist Intellectuals," in Andras Bozoki, *Intellectuals and Politics in Central Europe*, op. cit., p. 145, note 19.

19. Ivan Čolović, *Politika simbola*, op. cit., p. 186.

20. *NIN*, October 11, 1994, pp. 30.

21. Deputy General Director of Radio-TV Belgrade (RTV), 1982–1989; General Director, 1989–1991.

22. Chief Editor of *Politika*, 1985–1991; Director and President of *Politika*, 1986–1995.

23. Slavoljub Djukić, *Kako se dogodio vodja*, op. cit., p. 186.

24. Srbobran Branković, "The Media in Serbia," *Southeast Europe Review*, Vol. 1, No. 3 (September 1998), pp. 135–142.

25. Borisav Dzuverović, Srećko Mihailović, and Slobodan Vuković, *Izborna upotreba medija* (Belgrade: Institut društvenih nauka, 1994).

26. Nenad Dimitrijević, "Words and Death: Serbian Nationalist Intellectuals," in Andras Bozoki, *Intellectuals and Politics in Central Europe*, op. cit., pp. 136–142.

27. Jovanka Matić, "The Role of the Media: Media Portraits of Government and Opposition," in Vladimir Goati (ed.), *Elections to the Federal and Republican Parliaments of Yugoslavia (Serbia and Montenegro), 1990–1996* (Berlin: Sigma, 1998), p. 109.

28. Ljiljana J. Bačević, "The Media and Elections," in Vladimir Goati (ed.), *Challenges of Parliamentarism: The Case of Serbia in the Early Nineties* (Belgrade: Institut društvenih nauka, 1995), p. 199.

29. *Houston Chronicle*, December 27, 1992, p. 24.

30. *Danas*, December 31, 1999.

31. *Free B-92*, November 1999.

32. *New York Times*, December 22, 1992, Section A, p. 16.

33. CBC *National*, "Inside the Mind of Slobodan Milošević," March 30, 1999.

34. Richard Holbrooke, *To End a War* (New York: Random House, 1998), p. 14.

35. Ibid., p. 35. On Milošević's ability to charm negotiators see also Carl Bildt, *Peace Journey: The Struggle for Peace in Bosnia* (Weidenfeld, 1999), pp. 363–364.

36. *Put u bespuće*, op. cit., p. 147.

37. Dr. Radmilla Milentijević, who served as Serbia's Minister for Information during 1997–1998, claims: "Milošević is a very warm person. Whether you meet with him one-to-one, which I had [on] many occasions, or whether you meet with him in larger groups, as we sometimes do at meetings or at some receptions, he's a very charming man. He talks, he laughs. He's a good singer. Likes a drink occasionally. I found him very pleasant, charming. But in my dealings with him in my official capacity I find also a very strong man." CBC *National*, "Inside the Mind of Slobodan Milošević," March 30, 1999.

38. Milošević's daughter Marija, a journalist who operated a local television and radio station and nightclub has had a lower public profile than her brother, although Laura Silber reports that she also "made the most of her family's power," and "remains a bit wild." "Milošević Family Values," *The New Republic*, op. cit.

39. Slavoljub Djukić, *On, ona i mi*, op. cit., p. 38.

40. *NIN*, No. 2449 (December 4, 1997).

41. *World Politics and Personal Insecurity* (New York: The Free Press, 1965), p. 76.

42. *Guardian*, April 24, 1999, p. 3.

43. Slavoljub Djukić, *Kraj Srpske bajke*, op. cit., p. 276.

44. Hrvoje Sarinić, *Svi moji tajni pregovori sa Slobodanom Miloševićem: Izmedju rata i diplomacije 1993–1995 (1998)* (Zagreb: Globus International, 1999), p. 40.

45. Roger Cohen, "Taming the Bullies of Bosnia," *New York Times Magazine*, December, 17, 1995, p. 58.

46. Hrvoje Sarinić, *Svi moji tajni pregovori sa Slobodanom Miloševićem: Izmedju rata i diplomacije 1993–1995 (1998)*, op. cit., pp. 38–40, 317–318.

47. *Danas*, December 16, 1999.

48. *NIN*, March 29, 1999.

49. Mile Stojić "Historija od nule," *Dani*, No. 88 (November 9, 1998).

50. *Balkan Odyssey* (New York: Harcourt Brace & Co., 1995), pp. 128–129.

51. Slavoljub Djukić, *Kraj Srpske bajke*, op. cit., p. 276.

52. *BBC Correspondents Show*, October 22, 1999.

53. *BBC Correspondent Special: Slobo and Mira*, April 24, 1999.

54. Ibid.

55. BBC, April 26, 1999.

56. *BBC Correspondent Special: Slobo and Mira*, April 24, 1999.

57. Ljiljana Habjanović-Djurović, *Srbija pred ogledalom*, op. cit., p. 223.

58. Slavoljub Djukić, *On, ona, i mi*, op. cit., p. 12.

59. *Answer*, op. cit., p. 194.

60. BBC, April 26, 1999.

61. *VND*, July 17, 1995.

62. *Answer*, op. cit., p. 162.

63. *Night and Day*, op. cit., pp. 197–199.

64. *Los Angeles Times*, December 26, 1996, p. 17.

65. *The Independent*, May 7, 1999, p. 4.

66. *Newsweek*, April 19, 1999, p. 31.

67. *Larry King Live*, April 9, 1999.

68. Sofia Trud, April 27, 1999, p. 9 in *FBIS*-EEU–1999–0427, April 27, 1999.

69. *Slobodan protiv slobode* (Belgrade: Prosveta, 1991), pp. 20–21.

70. Slobodan Antonić, "Vlada Slobodana Miloševića: pokušaj tipološkog odredjenja," *Srpska politička misao*, No. 1 (1995), pp. 91–127.

71. Ibid.

72. Ibid.

73. *Vreme*, September 11, 1999, pp. 2–3.

74. *NIN*, No. 2285 (October 14, 1994), p. 29.

75. Lenard J. Cohen, *Broken Bonds: Yugoslavia's Disintegration and Balkan Politics in Transition*, 2nd Edition (Boulder, Colorado: Westview Press, 1995), Chapters 3–5.

76. *NIN*, No. 2029 (November 19, 1985), p. 7.

77. Belgrade Home Service in *BBCSWB*, Eastern Europe: B. Internal Affairs. EE/0682/B/1, February 7, 1990.

78. Slobodan Antonić, "Vlada Slobodana Miloševića," op. cit.

79. Dijana Vukmanović, "Nastavak političkih partija," in Vladimir Goati (ed.), *Partijski mozaik Srbije 1990–1996* (Belgrade: Akapit, 1997), pp. 27–48.

80. Zoran Dj. Slavujević, "Election Campaigns," in Vladimir Goati (ed.), *Challenges of Parliamentarism: The Case of Serbia in the Early Nineties*, op. cit., p. 175.

81. Vladimir Goati, *Stabilzacija demokratije ili povratak monizim u: treća Jugoslavija sredinom devedesetih* (Podgorica Unireks, 1996), p. 104.

82. Milan Milošević, "Closed Circle," in Velimir Kazimir (ed.), *Political Guide to Yugoslavia* (Belgrade: Media Center, 1997), p. 11.

83. Vladimir Goati in *NIN*, No. 2437 (September 12, 1997).

84. Slobodan Antonić, "Promene stranačkog raspoloženja gradjena, Srbije 1990–1993," in Slobodan Antonić, Milan Jovanović, and Darko Marinković (eds.), *Srbija izmedju populizma i demokratije* (Belgrade: Institut za političke studije, 1993).

85. Laura Seccor, "Testament Betrayed: Yugoslav Intellectuals on the Road to War," *Lingua Franca*, September 1999.

86. Zoran Dj. Slavujević, "Election Campaigns," in Vladimir Goati (ed.), *Challenges of Parliamentarism: The Case of Serbia in the Early Ninties*, op. cit., p. 161.

87. See Mirjana Prošić-Dvornić, "Enough! Student Protest '92: The Youth of Belgrade in Quest of Another Serbia," in *Anthropology of East Europe Review*, Vol. 11, No. 1–2 (Autumn 1993).

88. Belgrade RTB Television, *FBIS-EEU–92–118*, June 18, 1992.

89. *NIN*, November 11, 1999.

90. Vladimir Goati, *Partijski mozaik Srbije 1990–1996* (Belgrade: Beogradski krug i AKAPIT, 1997); Vladimir Goati, *Izbori u SRJ od 1990 do 1998* (Belgrade: Centar za slobodne izbore i demokratiju, 1999), and "Stepen i činioci autoritarnosti," in S. Mihajlović (ed.), *Izmedju osporavanja i podrške* (Belgrade: Institut društvenih nauka, 1997), pp. 229–245.

91. See, for example, Zagorka Golubović, Bora Kuzmanović, and Mirjana Vasović (eds.), *Društveni karakter i društvene promene u svetlu nacionalnih sukoba* (Belgrade: Institut za filozofiju i društvenu teoriju, 1995), pp. 61–170, and Bora Kuzmanović, "Authoritarianism," in M. Lazić, *et al.*, (eds.), *Society in Crisis: Yugoslavia in the Early 1990s* (Belgrade: Filip Višnjić, 1996), pp. 161–187.

92. Vladimir Goati, "Serbian Parties and the Party System," in Dušan Janjić, op. cit. p. 168.

93. *Danas*, July 7, 2000.

94. Slobodan Antonić, "Slobodan Milošević's Rule: An Attempt of Typological Definition," (Belgrade: Institute for Political Studies, June 21, 1996).

95. *VND*, March 24, 1996.

96. *FBIS-EEU*, November 15, 1988, p. 65.

97. Mladen Lazić, "Otpori strukturalnim promenama u Jugoslovenskom društvu: Postsocijalistička transformacija i društvene grupe," in Slobodan Samardžić, Radmila Nakarada, and Djuro Kovačević (eds.), *Lavirinti krize: preduslovi demokratske transformacije SR Jugoslavije* (Belgrade: Institut za Europske studije, 1998), pp. 349–367.

98. Vladimir Goati, *Izbori u SRJ*, op. cit., p. 231.

99. Mladen Lazić and Laslo Sekelj, "Privatization in Yugoslavia/Serbia and Montenegro," *Europe-Asia Studies*, Vol. 49, No. 6 (1997), pp. 1057–1070.

100. Mladen Dinkić, *Ekonomija destrukcije: Velika pljačka naroda* (Belgrade: Stubovi kulture, 1996), p. 241.

101. Lenard J. Cohen, *Broken Bonds,* op. cit., pp. 203–207.

102. *Guardian*, July 16, 1993, p. 12.

103. *FBIS-EEU–95–124*, June 28, 1995, pp. 57–58.

104. Nenad Stefanović, "Judicial System in Serbia: The Notorious Footprints," *VND*, No. 20 (February 10, 1992), p. 8.

105. Zorica Mršević, *Izazovi sudske nezavisnosti* (Belgrade: Uprava za zajedničke poslove republičkih organa, 1998).

106. *Inter Press Service*, December 9, 1993.

107. Mikloš Biro, "Znanje i stavovi studenata prava o ustavnim rešenjima," *Glasnik advokatske komore Vojvodina*, No. 6 (1996), pp. 219–225.

108. *The Independent*, January 17, 2000, p. 10.

109. Hrvoje Sarinić, *Svi moji tajni pregovori sa Slobodanom Miloševićem: Izmedju rata i diplomacije 1993–1995* (1998), op. cit., p. 46.

110. Ivan Čolović, "Kriminalci kao ratni junaci," *Danas*, February 1–2, 2000.

111. *Danas*, January 29–30, 2000.

CHAPTER 4

Governing a Garrison State: The Early 1990s

Time has shown that the policies of Milošević's socialists were consistently authoritarian, and only hypocritically national, and by their essence and results anational or anti-national.

—*Vojislav Koštunica (February 1996)*

[We] have a confrontation of the political concepts of the ruling Serbian elite and the political elite of a segment of Kosovo Albanians. Part of this political elite of the Kosovo Albanians is building the concept of nationally clean territory as well . . . Guilt is a separate category. I'm talking about political concepts. . . . The political elites of both sides were manipulating their peoples. They were anything but tolerant of the people of other nations.

—*Milan Kučan (April 1999)*

Serbia and the Wars of the Yugoslav Succession

Coordinating a Camouflaged Conflict

During his first years in power (1987–1990), Slobodan Milošević focussed his attention on consolidating his position in Serbia and Montenegro, and also attempting to broaden his influence over affairs in the post-Tito Yugoslav federation. It has frequently been observed that Milošević was the first Yugoslav politician to realize that "Tito was dead," and that the principal ideological components of the Titoist system—"brotherhood and unity" among various ethnic communities and self-managed socialist institutions in a one-party framework—had become obsolete. Recognizing the vacuum that existed, and the opportunity it afforded him, Milošević undoubtedly came to regard himself as a potential successor to Tito, albeit within a re-modeled and Serb-dominated Yugoslav federation. But faced with strident opposition to his

187

methods and goals from non-Serb leaders and ethnic groups in most of Yugoslavia's republics, Milošević never really had much hope of becoming the dominant force on the federal level of the Yugoslav political system. His popularity among Serbs in Croatia and Bosnia–Herzegovina gave him considerable scope to meddle in the politics of those two republics, but Milošević could not aspire to anything like the pan-ethnic and cross-republic popularity once enjoyed by Tito. As the imminent dissolution of the Yugoslav socialist federation came more clearly into view during 1990 and 1991, Milošević turned his attention to efforts aimed at ensuring that Serbia obtain as much territory as possible for any new Serbian state. Although commentators were quick to point out that the Yugoslav president's plans were similar to historical goals advanced by earlier Serbian politicians of creating an expansive "Greater Serbia," Milošević's political calculations appeared to have little basis in any particular historical scheme. Rather, it appeared that he simply wished to acquire as much territory as possible, and to inflate his own "greatness," amidst an emerging landscape of relatively small Yugoslav successor states.

How Milošević came to believe that he could pursue his political goals in Southeastern Europe without external interference, and what accounted for his ability to actually do so with considerable success throughout at least the first half of the 1990s, are intriguing questions in considering his early achievement and impact as a political leader. Prior to the fall of 1989, when Milošević was preoccupied with consolidating power in Serbia, there is little evidence that he devoted much time to regional and international affairs, or had acquired a coherent world view. For example, although he had traveled and worked in the West, he apparently gave very little systematic thought to foreign policy and strategic relations. Having risen to power on the basis of populism and anti-Albanian sentiments he had helped ignite in Kosovo, Milošević appeared to assess states and individuals fundamentally on the basis of their receptiveness towards his nationalist methods and goals. Throughout 1989, for instance, Milošević, in contrast to party leaders in the other Yugoslav republics, refused to receive the new U.S. Ambassador, Warren Zimmerman, who had arrived in Belgrade early that year. Milošević—who was undoubtedly upset at some of Zimmerman's remarks concerning human rights violations in Kosovo—finally agreed to meet with the American official in January 1990. Milošević continued to focus primarily on domestic concerns, and accorded the same treatment to other foreign officials, claiming that bilateral relations were handled at the federal level by the Yugoslav Ministry of Foreign Affairs, or that he was too busy to receive diplomats.[1] But Milošević's horizons began to broaden considerably in the wake of the fall of the Berlin wall, the collapse of communist regimes elsewhere in Eastern Europe, and the breakup of the Yugoslav League of Communists as a federal organization. The end of the 1980s and the outset of the 1990s, was also a period when Milošević acquired more interest and more of a role in matters relating to the future of Titoist Yugoslavia, and to the future of Serbian ethnic communities in neighboring republics.

There is evidence that Milošević's perception regarding the concerns of the major world powers in Balkan affairs was shaped in large part by an internal strategic intelligence report prepared in the spring of 1990 by the Yugoslav military establishment. The report suggested, among other things, that following the end of the Cold War, Yugoslavia—whose status was that of a "gray zone," "strategic buffer," or self-proclaimed "nonaligned nation" between the NATO alliance and the Warsaw Treaty Organization—had lost much of its value to the West. However, according to the intelligence analysis, the United States and its allies felt strongly that the dissolution of Yugoslavia, and also the USSR, would be de-stabilizing events that should be avoided. But no longer involved in a two-way face off with a militant USSR, the United States was now allegedly fully prepared to permit European powers and particularly Germany to play a larger strategic role in European foreign and security policy. In brief, the report concluded that the United States would stand back should internal forces in Yugoslavia attempt to preserve the country's unity. Milošević may also have believed that he had been given an informal green light from various Washington diplomats who had previously served in Yugoslavia—most prominently, Larry Eagleburger, who served as U.S. Ambassador to Belgrade from 1977 to 1981, and was viewed as a member of the so-called "Yugoslav lobby" in the American foreign policy elite—to take an assertive role in preserving the unity of the Titoist state. As U.S. Secretary of State, James Baker III, made clear in Belgrade prior to the secession of Croatia and Slovenia from Yugoslavia in June 1991: "We will neither encourage or reward secession."[2] Throughout 1990–1991, this perception contributed to an over-confidence on Milošević's part that he could ignore with impunity criticism of his meddling in the affairs of the Yugoslav federation and its various republics. And though he may have essentially been correct regarding the hesitant attitude of the Bush administration about intervening in the Balkans, Milošević's assessment that Washington would prefer to avoid assertive Balkan engagement, ultimately led him to overplay his hand. Thus, Milošević was shocked when the Hague Conference on Yugoslavia recognized Yugoslavia's disintegration, and acknowledged the right of its republics to secede.[3] Indeed, he was even more astounded when, after the break up of the USSR, U.S. diplomacy gradually acquiesced in the German-led international recognition of the Yugoslav successor states, including Bosnia by the spring of 1992, and also acquired a more anti-Serbian tone. As a result, Milošević and members of the Yugoslav military elite soon came to regard Western policy in a far less benign light than they had only a few years earlier.[4] One indication of Milošević's changed perspective is revealed in his attempt to explain the reasons for the dissolution of Yugoslavia to a Russian reporter in a February 1993 interview. "I will tell you bluntly: It is German policy which lies behind all these events. It is the German-Catholic alliance's interest to destroy not just our country but yours too. . . . It all began with the unification of Germany. As soon as that happened Germany began punishing the victors in the Second World War. The press with German pedantry divided the world up into good and bad. . . . Yugoslavia was the first casualty of revanchism."[5]

At the Gazimestan anniversary mass celebration in mid-1989, Milošević had warned that violence among the republics and ethnic communities in Yugoslavia could not be ruled out as a future possibility. By February 1990, believing that the leaders of Croatia and Slovenia, for their own purposes, were encouraging Albanian separatism in Kosovo, Milošević predicted to his closest associates "really, there will be war."[6] Initially he focussed his attention on areas of Croatia and Bosnia–Herzegovina populated by substantial numbers of ethnic Serbs.[7] Working closely with sympathetic elements in the JNA, and clandestinely using his own security forces from Serbia—especially after his election as Serbia's president in the December 1990 multi-party elections— Milošević mobilized support among Croatian Serb and Bosnian Serb activists, and provided them with arms for their local constituents. The use of paramilitary forces led by Serb nationalists and ultra-nationalists such as Vuk Drašković (who would later moderate his views), Arkan and Vojislav Šešelj also constituted a key element of Milošević's strategy to maintain control over Croatia and Bosnia. Thus, by the time Croatian national leaders moved towards Croatia's unilateral secession from Yugoslavia in mid-1991, Croatian Serb militants directed from Belgrade and assisted by "volunteers" from Serbia, were deeply involved in an ongoing insurrection against the regime in Zagreb. Meanwhile, in Slovenia, which also took steps to break away from the Yugoslav federation, Milošević was frustrated by the inability of the JNA to militarily quash Slovene secessionism during a short ten-day war in that republic. Slovenia was not, however, of central importance for Milošević primarily because the republic did not have a substantial Serb minority. But Croatia with a Serb population of approximately 12 percent was an entirely different matter. Faced with the failure of joint JNA and Serb paramilitary efforts to rapidly stamp out Croat secessionism, Milošević welcomed an international proposal—the Vance peace plan—which in early 1992 inserted UN peace-keeping troops between Croat forces and the insurgent Serbs of Croatia located in the so-called "Republika Srpska Krajina" (RSK).

In many respects, however, the activities of the Krajina Serbs and the acquisition of territory in Croatia were a relative sideshow for Milošević. Even before the war in Croatia, Milošević had been involved in much more important negotiations with Croatian President Tudjman about the possibility of dividing Bosnia–Herzegovina between Serbia and Croatia. Both Milošević and his close associate, Borisav Jović, had suggested that Serbia wanted about two-thirds of Bosnia–Herzegovina in such a partition. Indeed, during the initial phase of the war in Bosnia (1992–1993), it appeared that Belgrade-backed Serb forces would take an even larger share. Coordination with the Croatian nationalist regime in Zagreb was a central element in Milošević's Bosnian policy. Years later, Stipe Mesić, who was one of President Tudjman's closest associates at the beginning of the war in Bosnia (in 1991 Mesić served as the last president of Titoist Yugoslavia, later broke with Tudjman, and in early 2000 was elected as his successor), observed that "Tudjman was impressed by Yugoslav President Slobodan Milošević's first success [in Bosnia], and he thought Croatia could also expand, and that he could be the one who created a Greater Croatia."[8]

Mesić has also aptly emphasized another key factor that proved crucial to Milošević's decision during 1990–1992 to pursue his military goals first in Croatia and then in Bosnia, namely, the support of the Yugoslav military establishment:

> It was completely clear that [Titoist] Yugoslavia no longer had integrative factors. In the course of its existence its three basic integrative factors were Tito's charisma, the multinational communist party organization, and the army which followed the orders of Tito and the party. But when Tito left the scene [1980], and there only remained the old structure of power, when the party broke up along republic lines [1989–1990], there remained only one integrative factor in search of a new sponsor. Unfortunately the army saw Milošević as a sponsor, they submitted themselves to Milošević. The military high command debated this for a long time, but then the generals conceived that Milošević was the only way out, because he offered the largest territory which could feed and pay a big army, necessary to an inert mechanism spending enormous sums.[9]

Admiral Branko Mamula, who had served as chief of the JNA general staff and Federal Secretary for National Defense, would later claim that in April 1991, as Yugoslavia was on the brink of disintegration, some members of the military who were disenchanted with the JNA's drift towards "Greater Serbian nationalism"—and particularly the fact that the Federal Defense Minister, General Veljko Kadijević, was allegedly "bewitched" with Milošević's nationalism—had planned to stage a coup against the country's political leadership in order to preserve Yugoslavia's unity. But plans for the coup went awry.[10] In any case, when the non-Serb elements of the military high command fled from the Yugoslav army during 1990 and 1991, joining new military establishments in Serbia's neighboring republics, or going into retirement, Milošević shaped a new military force in rump Yugoslavia, the Army of Yugoslavia (Vojska Jugoslavije, VJ) to do his bidding. Although Milošević did not fully trust or respect the military arm of his newly reconfigured state that was formed in 1992, the VJ became another facet of his technology of control which, together with the police and para-military forces, gave his regime many features of a garrison state during the early and mid-1990s.

Milošević's initial military success in Bosnia proved to be short-lived. By 1993, the international economic sanctions on Serbia and Montenegro were taking a heavy toll on Milošević's constituents.[11] Moreover, the savagery of the Bosnian war, and particularly the scale of "ethnic cleansing" operations carried out by some Bosnian Serbs, engendered world-wide outrage. Concluding that his designs on Bosnia might best be accomplished through a politically finessed deal, Milošević began looking for a negotiated end to the war in Bosnia–Herzegovina. Meanwhile, Bosnian Serb politicians, under the leadership of Radovan Karadžić, had become more intransigent and less amenable to Milošević's control. Milošević's patience with his allies in Bosnia came to an end when the Bosnian Serb leadership rejected his personal appeal to their legislature to ratify the Vance–Owen peace plan. Humiliated by the Bosnian Serbs' defiance, Milošević began to work more closely with the international community to bring an end to the conflict in Bosnia.[12] The stiffening military resistance of the previously divided Muslim and Croat forces in Bosnia—once again allied following the adoption of a Muslim–Croat federal alliance in early 1994 that was engineered by the United States—and the more active involvement of Washington in Bosnian affairs, also influenced Milošević's decision to change his tactics in Bosnia.

By mid-1994, Milošević had become convinced that his future success in maintaining power depended on extricating the Yugoslav state from sanctions, and also on severing his links with Serb-controlled Bosnia and Croatia. In mid-July, a peace plan developed by the Contact Group (the United States, Russia, Britain, France and Germany) was rejected by the Bosnian Serbs. That plan had already been accepted by two sides of the Bosnian triangle: the predominant Muslim Bosnian government in Sarajevo and the Bosnian Croats. However, once again, the obstreperous Bosnian Serbs, who controlled roughly seventy percent of Bosnia, and were organized into the Republika Srpska (Serb Republic) parastate, refused to go along with the plan. The various members of the Contact Group, who long had dithered regarding the Bosnian war, were now adamant that more decisive action should be taken. At the Naples summit of July 1994, members of the G-7 countries and Russia appeared to be closing ranks on a new and more robust policy toward the war in Bosnia. It was at this point that Milošević, under strong international pressure, decided to distance himself more completely from the Bosnian war he had helped initiate over two years earlier. To demonstrate his new policy, Milošević terminated Yugoslavia's sponsorship of, and material support for, the Republika Srpska and its military forces, including the imposition of a blockade on trade from Serbia–Montenegro to the Bosnian Serbs across the river Drina.

In late fall 1994, pressures directed against the Bosnian Serbs had begun to have a noticeable impact on changing the balance of power in Bosnia. But the Bosnian Serb leadership still defiantly refused to make peace on the terms of the Contact Group plan. Washington's ability to force Serbian compliance with the Contact Group plan was quite limited in view of its promise not to become directly involved in the Bosnian war through the intervention of ground troops. But the Clinton administration did undertake to its allies that it would send troops to Bosnia if and when a peace plan was accepted by the belligerents, and would also provide assistance should United Nations protection forces (UNPROFOR) be forced to withdraw from the Balkans. As long as the war continued, however, the Clinton administration insisted that American military activity would be limited to U.S. air power. Washington favored a more robust use of air power, but U.S. allies such as Britain, France and Canada who had troops on the ground in Bosnia, opposed the broadened use of such capability. Meanwhile, efforts by the United Nations to deal with the Bosnian war were restricted by the terms of its limited peace-keeping mandate. Near the end of 1994, faced with the prospect of ongoing and uncontrolled warfare in Bosnia, Washington decided (in violation of UN Security Council resolutions) to open a dialogue with the Bosnian Serbs. The change in U.S. policy seemed to offer a window of opportunity for peace in Bosnia, particularly following former President Carter's pre-Christmas trip to the region at the invitation of Republika Srpska president, Radovan Karadžić. Carter, whose mission benefited from the winter lull in Bosnian fighting, was able to arrange a four-month ceasefire between the protagonists. Unfortunately, the intransigent mood of the warring parties limited the long-term potential of his peace mission.

Efforts by U.S. diplomats to follow up on the Carter initiative and secure Bosnian Serb acceptance of the Contact Group plan proved fruitless. The main stumbling block was the territorial division of Bosnia. Washington was unwilling to make major concessions in the peace plan, which called for the Serbs to reduce their zone of control from roughly 70 to 49 percent of Bosnia, and for the Croat–Muslim federation to enlarge its area of control from approximately 30 to 51 percent of the country. For their part, Bosnian Serb leaders—emboldened by having convinced Carter to see their point of view, and sensing the impotence of the international community's peace-seeking efforts—mistakenly took advantage of their new dialogue with the U.S. and demanded extensive revisions to the peace plan. Exasperated, the United States closed down negotiations with the Bosnian Serbs in February and instead decided to intensify pressure against them. Assistant Secretary of State Richard Holbrooke, who had met with the Bosnian Serb president at his headquarters, bluntly declared "that there was no point in shuttling up the hill from Sarajevo to Pale to listen to the kind of crap which was dished out by Karadžić."[13]

During the next six months, the Clinton administration significantly increased pressure against the Bosnian Serbs. Considerable credit in the execution of the American plan must go to Richard Holbrooke, the aggressive and determined diplomat entrusted by President Clinton to induce a Bosnian peace settlement.[14] Holbrooke's outrage with Bosnian Serb leader Karadžić was more than just a question of explosively bad personal chemistry between the two men. It also reflected the tremendous frustration of the Clinton team with the seemingly intractable Bosnian crisis; a foreign policy conundrum that had bedevilled them since the Democrat victory in 1992. As the 1996 presidential election approached, and as Republican attacks on the president's foreign policy mounted, the administration's desire to resolve the Bosnian situation intensified.

Clinton was not the only Western political leader to become more focussed on Bosnian affairs. The new activist French president, Jacques Chirac, elected in May 1995, also supported a more robust approach to dealing with the Bosnian crisis. When Bosnian Serbs took some 350 UNPROFOR peace keepers hostage at the end of May, Chirac became even more resolute about taking strong action against the Serbian side. The hostage-taking incident was a response by Bosnian Serbs to NATO air strikes in retaliation for continuing Serb bombardment of Sarajevo. The crisis only ended after Milošević dispatched one of his top security officials, Jovica Stanišić, to Bosnian Serb headquarters. Stanišić allegedly threatened President Karadžić with severe repercussions if the matter was not peacefully resolved. The hostages were quickly released through Belgrade, providing a minor public relations victory for Milošević.

By the spring of 1995, as the Carter inspired ceasefire began to seriously unravel (the Bosnian army launched an offensive against the Serbs at the end of March), it seemed that pressure brought to bear on the Bosnian Serbs by the international community, and particularly Washington, was beginning to pay off. Most apparent in this regard was the battlefield victory of the Croatian military against Krajina Serb forces in western Slavonia during May. Zagreb's forces only were able to take back a relatively small chunk of its former territory in Slavonia, but the success boosted Croatian confidence, and was the first practical result of the closer informal and formal ties between Croatia and the United States. Croatia's victory in May also unnerved Serbian leaders in Croatia and Bosnia, already hard-pressed in the face of Milošević's blockade and their general isolation. As Croatia's military strength became apparent, and cooperation grew between Croat and Muslim forces in Bosnia, internal conflicts among Bosnian Serb political and military leaders also intensified regarding whether or not to accept some sort of peace agreement.

While a number of key events and dates might be identified as milestones in the Bosnian story during 1994 and 1995, the circumstances connected with the seizure by the Bosnian Serbs of the predominantly Muslim town of Srebrenica on July 11, 1995—previously designated as a "safe area" by the UN—undoubtedly qualifies as a major turning point. The seizure itself was seen as an outrage by the international community, not to mention a sign of the UN's failure to keep the peace and protect civilians. But reports of the mass killing of several thousand Muslim civilians seized at Srebrenica by Serb forces, allegedly at the direction of General Ratko Mladić, turned the incident into a "defining moment" (the safe area of Žepa fell to the Serbs two weeks later). Reports of events at Srebrenica galvanized the resolve of the international community to intensify the pressure on the Bosnian Serbs and bring the war to an end. The Srebrenica outrage also marked a significant blow to the UN's credibility, and raised the possibility of an emergency evacuation of UNPROFOR troops.

Members of the Clinton administration were quick to sense the opportunities created by the Srebrenica affair and the overall isolation of the Bosnian Serbs. At a London conference in July, the United States and its NATO partners agreed to new rules of engagement for NATO forces, including the launching of air strikes if any of the remaining safe areas were attacked, and the establishment of a Western rapid reaction force. Secretary Holbrooke would later claim that the new NATO rules of engagement had been "forced down the throats of some of our allies after the rape of Srebrenica." Holbrooke was untroubled by the fact that some of the allies had troops on the ground and had already suffered many casualties, not to mention the indignities of the hostage-taking incident. The American Assistant Secretary of State and the Clinton administration were determined to press forward with an entirely new approach to Bosnia, come what may.

This new approach had been worked out by Clinton's principal national security advisers in a series of meetings which took place between early June and early August 1995. A number of his more hawkish advisers on the question of Bosnia cautioned the president that he was in danger of becoming a "soldier of fortune" to Balkan developments. For example, in a memorandum to Clinton, U.S. Ambassador to the UN Madeleine Albright, recommended among other things, that a failure to end the war would "rob" the president of any chance to get credit for his foreign policy successes. She also advised the president that since American troops would have to go to Bosnia sooner or later, why not send them on Washington's timetable.[15] After the fall of Srebrenica, the Clinton administration's major paradigm shift on Bosnia had accelerated. A region that had once been considered a hellish "quagmire" of intractable problems had become amenable, almost overnight, to American-led military and diplomatic activism. The situation was still not quite opportune for reaching peace in Bosnia, but unfolding events, combined with Holbrooke's unique brand of "bulldozer diplomacy" would soon prevail.

Early in August 1995, the seeds of success sown by Washington finally bore fruit. In a lightning and carefully planned attack, assisted by U.S. consultants, Croatian forces retook almost all the Krajina region in a matter of days. Eastern Slavonia remained the only part of Croatia still under Serb control. Zagreb's military strike led to a massive exodus of Serbs from Croatia, and was followed by widespread human rights violations against the remaining Serbian population. Publicly, Washington had cautioned the Croats about using military action in the Krajina, but it was apparent that behind the scenes Zagreb had received unofficial American support and encouragement. With the capitulation of Serbian forces in the Krajina, and the ability of seasoned Croatian troops to link up with the Muslims in Bosnia, the already overextended and strained military forces of the Republika Srpska were in a very precarious position. Some of the Serb forces from the Krajina entered Bosnia, but the tide had definitely turned against the Serb side. Indeed, a subsequent Muslim–Croat offensive in north-western Bosnia captured roughly 1500 square miles of territory, and forced tens of thousands more Serbs to flee. For the Muslims and Croats such developments seemed a just retribution for Serbian onslaughts earlier in the war.

Slobodan Milošević passively watched the first stage in the Croatian reintegration of the Krajina in May 1995, and then the second more comprehensive stage (after making one of his own military commanders the head of the Serb Krajina army) in August. The Serbian president adopted the same inert posture later on as the Bosnian Serbs retreated in the face of a Muslim–Croat offensive. Milošević's blockade of the Bosnian Serbs continued. In 1991 and 1992, he had sponsored and manipulated the nationalistic drive of the Serbian diasporic communities in Bosnia and Croatia. But now, bent on lifting the sanctions against Yugoslavia, for his own political purposes, Milošević coldbloodedly sacrificed his aggressive and tainted clients. If the national interest of Serbs in Croatia and Bosnia had to be sacrificed, so be it, Milošević calculated. Moreover, Milošević had always counted on Croatian President Tudjman's anti-Muslim orientation and desire to partition Bosnia as a way for Belgrade to make a deal on Bosnia, and ultimately extract itself from entanglement in a savage war, while still allowing Serbia to make substantial gains on behalf of Serb national goals. For example, in several secret meetings held in Belgrade with Tudjman's emissary, Milošević indicated that he had "solved the Serb national question" by obtaining the formation and maintenance of a Bosnian Serb republic, and that he had no intention of uniting Bosnian Serb territory with Croatian Serb territory. In fact, Milošević conceded, he was fully willing to let the Tudjman regime in Zagreb resume political control of the Serbs in Croatia's Krajina region. Thus, in December 1994, Milošević informed the Croatian envoy: "the Bosnia–Herzegovina Serbs possess no more than 60 percent of Bosnia–Herzegovina. This has met my aims and now I must turn to peace." Milošević made it clear that he was even ready to recognize Croatia as a sovereign state in return for Croatian concessions in Bosnia. Indeed by 1995, Milošević was only looking for what Tudjman's representative called a "small Greater Serbia" that included about half of the Bosnian territory. Faced with Serbia's severe economic deterioration due to international sanctions, effectively now losing on the battlefield in Bosnia, and having lost his earlier control over Serbs in both Croatia and Bosnia, Milošević— in a cold-blooded tactical move—had decided to simply stand by and watch Croatia's military obliteration of the Krajina Serb enclave in August 1995.[16]

In practice, Serbian nationalism per se meant very little to Milošević. Although he desperately wanted to fulfill his promises regarding the need for "all Serbs to live in one state," he also wished to mask the public lie that he had kept Serbia out of war. The population of Serbia and Montenegro, however, was fully aware of both the human and material cost resulting from the wars in Croatia and Bosnia–Herzegovina. For example, the recruitment of young Serbs to fight in Croatia during 1991 and early 1992 had angered and demoralized many young people and families in Serbia. Draft dodging and desertion had occurred on a significant scale during 1991, not to mention widespread emigration from the country on the part of the younger generation. Indeed, the "mobilization crisis" of 1991, in which thousands of young men in Serbia sought to evade military service, would have long-term negative consequences on the overall legitimacy of the Milošević regime.[17] Fortunately for Milošević, although public disenchantment with the wars in Croatia and Bosnia significantly increased in Serbia during the mid-1990s, there were also political forces that helped bolster confidence in Serbian nationalism, and the desire of many Serbs to live in a single national state. One such force was the Serbian Orthodox Church (SPC). Indeed, together with the fact that a large segment of the political opposition supported the same nationalist goals advanced by Milošević (see this chapter below), the SPC's backing for Serbian nationalism proved to an important advantage to Milošević's initial polices within and outside Serbia.

The Serbian Orthodox Church: Nationalism and War

Milošević's ethno-populist mobilization during the late 1980s and 1990s benefited from the activities and indirect support of the SPC. Indeed, by the end of the 1980s, the Serbian Orthodox Church had already assumed an active role throughout Yugoslavia with regard to the Serbian nationalist cause. Guardianship of Serbian national interests had historically been viewed by the SPC clergy as one of their central tasks in relation to secular matters,[18] although Orthodoxy's Byzantine traditions also cast the church in a loyal and subordinate role vis-à-vis state authorities. But by the end of the Tito era, having endured a long period of manipulation and suppression by the communist one-party state,[19] the strongly anticommunist SPC began to seek greater influence with respect to the position of Serbs in Yugoslav society. The alleged grievances of the Serbian community in Kosovo (where Serbs and Montenegrins constituted roughly 15 percent of the province's population in 1981), as well as the position of Serbs in Croatia and Bosnia, were particularly important to the younger and more militant faction that emerged within the SPC clerical hierarchy.[20]

During the last years of control by Patriarch German—who headed the SPC from 1958–1990—the younger group of Orthodox leaders represented a sort of "clerical-political underground"[21] working to enhance the influence of the church in Yugoslav society, and also to advance the interests of the Serbian nation. Strongly conservative on religious and political matters, the younger clique of SPC leaders welcomed the nationalist renaissance taking place within Yugoslavia's Serbian community. The SPC and especially its younger zealots also viewed the growing delegitimation of the self-managing Titoist state, and the emergence of a more nationalist course by the Milošević regime in Serbia, as opportunities for advancing their various positions. Granted Milošević, though the son of an Orthodox priest, was an atheist, who disdained the church as an institution. His wife was even more unaccepting of the role of the church in Serbian life. But while naturally suspicious of Milošević—an attitude reciprocated by the rising new Serbian political leader—the Orthodox hierarchs were nevertheless very willing to take advantage of the new and more accommodating policies of Serbia's state authorities (e.g., support for the long-awaited completion of the massive Serbian Orthodox Cathedral of St. Sava in Belgrade that had been halted by the communist regime). Most importantly, the SPC leadership and Milošević shared a good deal of common ground regarding the grievances of the Serbian diaspora in Kosovo, Croatia and Bosnia.

Indeed, at the 600th anniversary of the Battle of Kosovo, at the shrine of Gazimestan (see Chapter 3), Patriarch German, together with his more aggressively nationalistic fellow clerics, joined with Milošević and Serbia's political and cultural elite in an emotional celebration of Serbian history and national feeling. On the eve of the celebration, Patriarch German commented that "the present changes in the attitude of the Serbian [political] leadership toward the Serbian Church and its people . . . is the beginning of good cooperation, that will benefit everybody."[22] Milošević's incendiary rhetoric at the celebration, however, was in no way uniformly endorsed by the SPC as an institution. In fact, the mainstream leadership of the SPC took a moderate, albeit sympathetic position regarding the growth of nationalist militancy in Yugoslavia. Thus in November

1991, Patriarch Pavle, who succeeded Patriarch German at the end of 1990 (German died in August 1991), suggested that if the nationalities which had formed the Yugoslav state in 1918 decided they must separate, they should do so "as reasonable people, calmly and in agreement with each other."[23] But the Patriarch also expressed his strong support for the idea of Serb solidarity and self-determination, that is, Milošević's idea that all Serbs should be allowed to live together in a single state if they so wished. Thus, overall, Milošević's state-sponsored nationalism and the general pattern of religious revival in Serbia, appeared to be a reciprocal process. The regime's legitimation of Serbian nationalism led Serbs to become more involved with their community's traditional religious practices. In turn, the increasing religiosity of the citizenry served the interests of the regime's policy, that is, the national "homogenization" of the people.[24]

To a large extent, SPC support for Serbian national interests was a reaction to developments in Croatia that had occurred at the end of the 1980s. The year following the Gazimestan celebration in Kosovo coincided, for example, with the rise of a strong Croatian nationalist movement headed by Franjo Tudjman. After Tudjman achieved electoral victory in Croatia in May 1990 and, among other inflammatory nationalist remarks, suggested that Bosnia was naturally in the Croatian sphere of interest—the SPC became more vigorously concerned with the grievances of the diasporic Serbs. Albanian nationalism in Kosovo had concerned the SPC hierarchy since the early 1980s; the new threat appeared to be Croatian nationalism.

For the most nationalistic Orthodox clerics, Tudjman's political movement (the Croatian Democratic Union) represented the rebirth of the World War II ultra-nationalist Ustasha organization that had massacred thousands of Serbs in Croatia and Bosnia–Herzegovina. Such SPC concerns seemed to be confirmed by the Tudjman government's support for the rehabilitation and honoring of Croatian Cardinal Alojzije Stepinac, Croatia's leading cleric at the time of the World War II Ustasha-inspired ethnic cleansing in Croatia and Bosnia (in which more than a few Franciscan and other Catholics clerics had participated).[25] After the war, Stepinac was subjected to a grotesque communist show trial, and based upon unfounded charges that were designed to discredit the Catholic church, he was jailed for ten years. In fact, Stepinac had never approved of the Ustasha killing, and as time passed his sympathy for the Ustasha state had declined. But the Croatian cleric had also not openly and directly condemned the Ustasha's activities. In any case, by the 1980s, Stepinac's ordeal at the hands of the communists had turned him into a eminent national and religious figure among Croats. For Serbs and the SPC, meanwhile, praise for the Cardinal by Tudjman and the HDZ symbolized a revival of "Serbophobia," and threatened the very existence of the Serbian ethno-religious community.[26]

The SPC association with the Serbian national renaissance was also apparent in Bosnia, where Orthodox prelates became closely associated with the Serbian Democratic Party (SDS), which was founded in 1990 in order to advance the interests of the Bosnian Serbs.[27] In the Bosnian context, Serb leaders were politically mobilizing and appealing to a population in which religious belief per se was far less salient than a general ethno-cultural form of identity (which included religious affiliation). Nevertheless, the Orthodox church enjoyed tremendous respect among the Bosnian Serbs as a cultural institution that had historically labored for the protection and preservation of Serbian interests, and that also served as a major link among Serbian communities throughout Yugoslavia. Moreover, by 1990, most SDS leaders, including its head, Radovan Karadžić, were noncommunist or anti-communist in outlook. Karadžić (who was a religious believer during the Titoist period) and other leaders of the Bosnian SDS, regarded a close link with the SPC as a useful tool in their effort to mobilize political support. Although dependent on support from Milošević, the Bosnian Serb political elite was also fundamentally suspicious of the Serbian president. Thus, by associating themselves with the Serbian Orthodox church, Bosnian Serb leaders also saw a way to enhance their position as political-cultural representatives of their people, while also gaining a certain amount of leverage in dealing with Milošević. This posture was reciprocated by the Serbian Orthodox hierarchy, and especially its more militant nationalist and noncommunist faction, who viewed Milošević as a necessary evil, and who regarded vigorous backing for the Serbian diaspora as a core facet of their clerical-political mission. During the second half of the 1980s and early half of the 1990s, the Orthodox church, as one Serbian author has observed:

... fostered national continuity, a cult of the national and religious grandeur, and also national history, national literature and traditional customs and values. ... It rejected every reproach concerning the politicization of the church, but early on part of the clergy and bishopric, together with part of the intelligentsia, set in motion the problems and offered solutions to the Serbian national question, the organization of the state, the position of the church in the state, relations toward the West and the East, etc. In that way an ideology was formed which deepened the crisis and opened new fronts. ... The fact is that the political actors would not have been able to carry out their successful homogenization of the Serbian ethnos, were it not for the support of the church.[28]

Prior to the breakup of socialist Yugoslavia, the SPC also maintained a good working relationship with the nationalistically oriented Milošević regime. But although Orthodox church leaders were pleased by various accommodations to the SPC proffered by Milošević, they were fundamentally hostile to the socialist orientation of his regime. Moreover, after witnessing the bitter warfare in Croatia during the second half of 1991, the onset of the war in Bosnia during the spring of 1992, and the imposition of painful international sanctions against Serbia and Montenegro, the SPC decided to adopt a more critical stance toward Milošević. Thus in May–June 1992, the Orthodox leadership publicly attacked Milošević's policies and demanded that he relinquish his leadership. Patriarch Pavle accused Serbia's leaders of "closing their eyes to crimes," an allusion to atrocities committed by Serbian paramilitary forces in Bosnia.[29] Joining with members of the opposition parties, and the anti-Milošević segments of the middle class and intelligentsia, some SPC leaders hoped to unseat Milošević and find a more internationally acceptable and moderate noncommunist leader to advance Serbian interests (such as Prince Alexandar Karadjordjević, who visited in Belgrade in June 1992). But the church's efforts at displacing Milošević proved fruitless, and the Serbian leader went on to handily triumph in the fall 1992 Serbian election.

While most Orthodox religious leaders were rather distrustful or skeptical about Milošević and his policies, the younger and more militant faction of SPC theologians also believed that official state support for the interests of the Serbs across the Drina in Bosnia was essential, and indeed should be intensified. For example, during Christmas 1992, the highly nationalistic and controversial Bishop Amfilohija Radović, the Metropolitan of Montenegro, met with and allegedly blessed Arkan, the Serbian paramilitary chief whose forces had taken part in attacks on Muslim civilians in Bosnia during April 1992. In any event, failing at their effort to influence the distribution of power in Serbia during 1992, SPC leaders turned their attention to assisting the struggle of the *prečani*, that is, Serbs outside Serbia. Indeed, over the next three years, the SPC, particularly its most militant clerics, would maintain close and supportive ties to Bosnian Serb president Radovan Karadžić and the leadership of the Republika Srpska headquartered at Pale.

The SPC was particularly sympathetic to the noncommunist orientation of the Bosnian Serb regime, and also its willingness to support traditional church goals. In the Republika Srpska, for example, the national anthem was entitled "God of Justice," religious instruction in the schools was mandatory, the history of the World War II Chetnik movement was treated respectfully, there was strong support for the Serbian monarchy, and the church hierarchy enjoyed high esteem.[30] The partial political benefits for the Bosnian Serb leadership in maintaining such a pro-Orthodox posture became evident during 1994 and 1995 when Slobodan Milošević decided to throw his full support behind the international community's Contact Group peace plan for Bosnia and, more importantly, to severely restrict his previous tangible backing for the Karadžić regime and the Bosnian Serb army. Friction between Karadžić and Milošević had been evident for years (e.g., a last-minute decision by the Bosn-

ian Serbs not to support the Vance–Owen plan in 1993 had greatly embarrassed Milošević), but in taking stiff measures to isolate the Bosnian Serbs in
1994 and 1995, the Belgrade regime precipitated a major intra-Serb conflict.

Disturbed by the breakdown in Serbian solidarity at a time when the international image of the Serbian ethnic community was already at an all-time low,
Orthodox church leaders attempted to repair the Milošević–Karadžić rupture.
The increasingly isolated Karadžić, who has described himself as the defender
of the Serb "tribe and our church,"[31] was effusive in his gratitude for the SPC's
mediation effort.

> We think the Serbian Orthodox Church is the most important connecting tissue
> that has preserved the unity of the Serbian people through centuries. . . . It is an
> honor for us that they are with us, that they assess the steps we take and support
> us . . . I have profited very much from my firm connections with the church. I
> have heard many useful pieces of advice, and received support for my deci
> sions. . . . Only those who are intolerant and are not interested in the opinion of
> the whole nation can fear the church.[32]

But once again, as in its effort to support opposition elements in Serbia during
1992, the SPC hierarchy failed to have any appreciable impact on Milošević.
Indeed, in August 1995, after facing Croatian and Bosnian Muslim military
successes, as well as intense NATO bombing, Karadžić and the Bosnian Serb
leadership would be forced to sign over authority for diplomatic negotiations
on Bosnia to Milošević.[33]

The End of the Bosnian War

On August 28, a shell exploded in Sarajevo's main market, killing 38 people
and wounding 85 others. It was the worst attack on the city in more than a
year, and occurred only yards from where a similar blast had killed 68 people
in February 1994. The question of who fired the shell was disputed by some
observers. But in view of the extensive shelling of Sarajevo by Serbian forces
since 1994, the burden of proof was quite low. Functioning under its new rules
of engagement, NATO launched a carefully targeted bombing campaign
against Bosnian Serb installations. The damaging attack, which included
destruction of the Serbs' air defense and communications network, was
designed to force compliance with the UN's demand that the Serbs pull back
their artillery from Sarajevo. NATO's broader purpose, however, was to force
the Serbs to begin serious negotiations on a peace settlement along the lines
specified by the international community. Though already reeling from the
Croat–Muslim military successes earlier in the month, the Bosnian Serbs were
initially defiant. Holbrooke, who had been tirelessly shuttling throughout the

region in order to jump-start the peace talks, used the bombing campaign to maximum diplomatic effect. His resolve to press the Serbs and end the war had been fortified by the overall change in the strategic equilibrium in Bosnia and also, on a more personal level, by the August 19 accidental deaths of three American diplomats accompanying him on a shuttle visit to Sarajevo.

On September 3, during a pause in NATO bombing designed to test Bosnian Serb assurances that the long siege of Sarajevo would finally be lifted, Holbrooke commented that the bombing had been carried out because "an outrageous, and unacceptable act had occurred." He added that the NATO action should have taken place back in 1991 or 1992. But as one of the chief architects of a more coercive approach, the imperious U.S. envoy could not resist pointing out that "there is an ancient theoretical debate about the interaction of the use of force and [diplomatic] negotiations . . . [the bombing] was done not entirely coincidentally just as the negotiations were reaching an intense phase. The response by the Serbs speaks for itself."

But Holbrooke would need to tighten the vise on the Serbs a bit more. On September 5, after Bosnian Serb General Mladić had failed to meet UN terms to pull back his weapons from Sarajevo, NATO bombing, including the use of Tomahawk cruise missiles, was resumed. While the bombing campaign continued in Bosnia, the foreign ministers of Yugoslavia, Croatia and Bosnia met with Holbrooke in Geneva. All sides agreed to attend U.S.-sponsored peace talks on Bosnia. Moreover, the Bosnian government agreed for the first time that its state would include two entities, a Muslim–Croat unit and the Republika Srpska. The agreement also provided that both entities would be allowed "to establish parallel special relationships with neighboring countries, consistent with the sovereignty and territorial integrity of Bosnia."

Although the agreement clearly gave the Bosnian Serbs a semi-autonomous status and a hope of some federative tie with Belgrade, it fell short of the international recognition which they sought. Milošević was only able to obtain reluctant Bosnian Serb acquiescence to the Geneva agreement because of a recent bargain—contained in a letter referred to as the "Patriarch Paper"—he had struck on August 29 with the hard-pressed Republika Srpska leaders. Thus, just prior to the bombing of the Bosnian Serbs by NATO, Milošević had received written authorization from Karadžić, Mladić and other Bosnian Serb leaders to head a joint Serbian negotiating team on Bosnian matters. The letter, which had also been delivered to Holbrooke in Belgrade, had been given contractual sanctity by Serbian Orthodox Patriarch Pavle. In retrospect it seems clear that the NATO bombing of the Bosnian Serbs had proceeded despite the fact that Washington and Holbrooke had known since August 29 that Mladić and Karadžić were ready to hand over control of the peace negotiations to Milošević.

NATO bombing, Holbrooke's aggressive brand of diplomacy, and Milošević's gifts at Balkan persuasion now converged to forge a breakthrough. It came on September 13 at a bizarre meeting near Belgrade between Milošević and Holbrooke. Believing, correctly, that Holbrooke could influence the course of the NATO bombing campaign against the Bosnian Serbs, Milošević pressed the American negotiator to cut a deal. In a surprise move during the meeting, Milošević produced Bosnian Serb President Karadžić and General Mladić, who had been waiting at a nearby villa. After eleven hours of difficult discussions between the American side and the Serbs, in which Holbrooke sanctimoniously refused to directly participate because of Karadžić's and Mladić's status as indicted war criminals, a deal was struck. In essence, the Bosnian Serbs agreed to pull back from Sarajevo, and the Americans undertook that NATO would stop its bombing. Having succeeded in Belgrade, Holbrooke went on to Zagreb and pressured Croatia's Tudjman and Bosnia's President Izetbegović to halt their joint offensive in northern Bosnia. General exhaustion, and a failure by all sides to achieve their respective goals, also added momentum for ending the war. On October 5, President Clinton was able to announce that a ceasefire had been agreed to by all sides in Bosnia. Hostilities were finally halted on October 12. Two and a half weeks later, a peace conference on Bosnia was convened at Wright-Patterson Air Force Base in Dayton, Ohio. Present, along with delegations from the Contact Group countries, the EU and the UN, were the presidents of Serbia, Croatia and Bosnia. The Serbian delegation included representatives of the Republika Srpska (but not Karadžić and Mladić), while the Bosnian Croats worked alongside the representatives from Croatia and the Bosnian government. The conference, which lasted 21 days, and utilized a variety of carrots and sticks to cajole the parties into agreement, was a tour de force of American diplomacy.

The negotiations were marked by three distinct phases. During the first phase of eight days, the focus was on strengthening the ties between the Bosnian Croats and Muslim side in order to present the Serbs with a unified front. Building on considerable groundwork, the initial stage went rather smoothly. An agreement was reached for a remodelled Muslim–Croat federation, including an annex reuniting the divided city of Mostar. Three days were then devoted to resolving the Croato–Serb dispute over eastern Slavonia. This resulted in an agreement between Milošević and Tudjman (which was not announced until after the conclusion of the Dayton negotiations) that Belgian and Russian troops would patrol eastern Slavonia for a one-year "transitional phase" under the direction of a civilian authority. The last period of negotiations dealt with the vexing territorial and political issues which had prevented a peace settlement over the previous three and a half years. This stage was also focussed on bringing pressure to bear on the Muslim side, which had been steadily improving its position on the battlefield, to accept peace.

The full agreement initialled on November 21, and signed in Paris on December 14, is a detailed document that included eleven annexes and maps. Its major elements consist of arrangements for: (1) establishing military security and separating the warring sides; (2) distribution of territory between the Croat–Muslim federation and the Bosnian Serbs; (3) the constitutional structure of Bosnia–Herzegovina; (4) the civilian transformation and policing of the country, and; (5) dealing with human rights, refugees, minorities, and war crimes.

In essence, the agreement reached at Dayton codified a series of compromises among the adversaries which left each of the parties partially dissatisfied. Serbia's Milošević appeared to be the most willing to provide concessions. Of course, he was not trading his own territory, but that of the Bosnian Serbs. Concentrated solely on having the economic sanctions against Serbia–Montenegro lifted, Milošević served as an invaluable partner to Holbrooke in overcoming stumbling blocks. Thus, it was Milošević who broke the deadlock over a number of problems, such as the question of who would exercise control over Sarajevo (the predominantly Serb districts will be placed under the control of the Muslim–Croat side); the link between Sarajevo and mainly Muslim Goražde (a road was being built in a wide corridor to the town through Serb-held territory); and the dispute, which nearly scuttled the talks, over Serb-held Brčko and the important Serbian corridor in northern Bosnia (the dispute will be subject to an arbitration panel after one year). Such concessions, particularly the loss of sections of Sarajevo, infuriated the Bosnian Serbs who were technically part of Milošević's delegation, and they initially refused to accept the agreement.

Croatian President Tudjman also proved helpful in developing compromises at crucial points in the negotiations. Tudjman's flexibility probably can be explained by the fact that he arrived in Dayton still flushed from battlefield success in the Krajina, and also his expectation of an imminent electoral victory back home. Thus, when it appeared that the talks might fail on the issue of territorial adjustments, Tudjman—after receiving a telephone call from President Clinton—agreed to give up land that Croatian forces had recently seized in northern Bosnia. He also agreed to Serb control of some Croatian population areas along the Sava river, a concession which was strongly protested by Bosnian Croat leaders and Zagreb political activists. For the moment, at least, the agreement's emphasis on building up the Muslim–Croat federation in Bosnia represented a setback for Tudjman's long-held aspirations of dividing Bosnia between Croatia and Serbia. Indeed, under the terms of the accord the expanded authority of the Muslim–Croat federation would lead to the replacement of the Croatian-run Herceg–Bosna parastate established in 1991. But politically dependent on his burgeoning U.S. alliance, Tudjman was willing to go along with territorial adjustments in Bosnia, and also a delay in the reintegration of eastern Slavonia. Tudjman's remarks at the signing ceremony on

December 14 revealed, however, that his jaundiced feelings about Bosnia's Muslims were unchanged: "Although Bosnia–Herzegovina was positioned in the middle of Yugoslavia, it could not become its mainstay because it was largely afflicted by civilizational differences. Communist ideas which tried to neutralize the Serbo–Croat national contrasts by declaring a specific Muslim religious population as a specific nationality have produced results that were opposite to the desired effect."

The Bosnian government gained considerably from its strong American backing at Dayton, and also from the willingness of Milošević and Tudjman to compromise. Bosnia–Herzegovina remained a united country with a relatively strong central governmental structure, and Sarajevo was to be reunited as the country's capital. The Serbs would lose some of their territorial gains, a link with Goražde would be established, refugees and the displaced would be allowed free movement, and also the right to return to their towns and villages. However, for many Muslim political leaders it was a hollow political victory. Nothing could undo what their people had suffered during the war, and after all was said and done, the country was sharply divided into two entities. Moreover, traditional Muslim areas, such as Srebrenica and Žepa, were to remain under Serb control.

The principal victory for the Muslims and the Bosnian government was having survived a battle with more powerful adversaries. Thus, at the initialling ceremony in Dayton, President Izetbegović bitterly observed that the agreement reached was an "unjust peace, but more just than a continuation of war," leaving the strong impression that he had been badgered into accepting the Dayton accords. Milošević, the self-styled peace broker, chose to give the Dayton settlement a different spin: "In a civil war like this one in Bosnia there are no winners and losers," he remarked. Later at the Belgrade airport, he added that "a just peace for all the nations living in this region had been reached."

Having manipulated Bosnian Serb interests for a half decade to serve his own political purposes, Milošević had proceeded to trade away their major interests during the Dayton peace negotiations. In return, Milošević had received the international community's promise to partially lift sanctions on Serbia–Montenegro. Meanwhile, Milošević was unrepentant regarding criticism by Serbs, within and outside Yugoslavia, that in 1995 he had betrayed the interests of the Bosnian and Croatian Serbs. For example, at a holy synod of the SPC held on December 22, 1995, militant Orthodox bishops condemned the Dayton agreement, and declared that the church's earlier endorsement for Milošević to represent the Bosnian Serbs at the peace conference was null and void.[34] The synod also argued that Milošević had "taken advantage" of Patriarch Pavle, and that the church leader should resign for not having opposed an "unjust" peace. However, after years of having cooperated with the pursuit of Serbian nationalist goals, the Serbian religious elite found itself politically marginalized. Devoted to preserving his power at almost any price, Milošević was unmoved by the plight of the Bosnian and Croatian Serbs whom he had once encouraged, and even less willing to accommodate the demands of a Serbian Orthodox hierarchy that had called for his removal, and derided his rule of a "godless regime." Even more than his counterparts in other ethnic communities—in the political leadership of the Croats in Zagreb and Bosnia, and in the Bosnian Muslim elite—who also took an inscrutably pragmatic approach regarding the role of religion in nationalist politics, Milošević was exclusively focussed on the imperatives of temporal power.

Coping with the Costs of War

A major facet of Milošević's technology of domination throughout the mid-1990s was the economic enrichment of the regime's political and economic elites (see Chapter 3). That process, which one critic has called "the great robbery of the people,"[35] occurred during a period when Serbian society as a whole was undergoing serious economic deterioration as a result of socialist Yugoslavia's disintegration, the wars of the Yugoslav succession, and internal economic mismanagement (including the manipulation of the privatization process). Thus, at the end of May 1992, Milošević claimed that Yugoslavia was a "medium-sized country with great possibilities for development." But he was forced to concede that he did "not believe there is a single citizen of Serbia who is not worried today." Milošević blamed this on the "civil war raging around" Yugoslavia and the enormous external pressures on the country, and also suggested that despite "reasons for concern" there was no cause for fear.[36] But the Yugoslav president was putting a brave face on a badly eroding economic situation that would soon become even worse.

During the first part of the 1990s, Serbia and Montenegro experienced an acute economic crisis, which led to the substantial economic pauperization of the population. That crisis reached its climax in January 1994, with the collapse of the monetary and fiscal system because of hyper-inflation. The economic crisis was primarily the result of two factors: first, the shock caused by the former Yugoslavia's disintegration—in which Serbia and Montenegro lost 60 percent of the former domestic market—and the imposition of international sanctions, and second, various internal factors stemming from inherited economic weaknesses of the old regime, and a maladjusted and unreformed economy. By the end of 1993 and beginning of 1994, Yugoslavia's inflation was running at 60 percent per day, or higher than the hyper-inflation in Weimar Germany in the early 1920s. Such hyper-inflation was the result of several factors: a sharp increase of governmental deficit spending due to war conditions, including the need to support hundreds of thousands of Serbian refugees who arrived from Croatia and Bosnia (by 1995, 460,000 officially registered and 120,000 unregistered, or about 4.2 percent of the country's population),[37] and worker unemployment; a massive increase in lending at interest rates below the rate of inflation supported by an expansion in the money supply; a deterioration in the terms of trade, capital flight, and a sharp increase in foreign exchange; and an economy prone to inflation owing to inefficiencies and huge costs for the administrative apparatus.[38]

In only four years, Yugoslavia's gross domestic product (GDP) slid by 60 percent (GDP in 1989 was about $3,300US, by 1993 it was $1,250US). Net real wages in 1993 were worth roughly 38 percent of their 1989 level. Industrial output also fell precipitously, while open and hidden unemployment rose sharply. Relative macro-economic stability and an end to hyper-inflation only came after January 1994, when a program of monetary reconstruction and economic recovery was adopted (developed by Dr. Dragoslav Avramović, who was governor of the National Bank from January 1994 to May 1996). That program and the post–Dayton accord lifting of some UN economic sanctions at the end of 1995 (the "outer wall" of international financial sanctions remained in place) spurred some recovery, but throughout the remainder of the decade the overall economy of Serbia and Montenegro continued to function at well below the 1989 level. In 1996, for example, the real average net wage remained 58.4 percent lower than in 1989, and the same year, 26 out of 35 branches of industry had an output that was less than 50 percent of the 1989 level.

Serbia's economic deterioration not only caused widespread poverty, it also stimulated the emigration of several hundred thousand Serbian citizens, particularly highly educated young people, and led to a severe weakening in the material position of Serbia's middle class. Many people survived the difficulties, particularly in smaller towns, because of their access to food supplies from the rural sector (indeed, the relative position of farmers improved during the economic crisis of the early 1990s), and also their activities in the parallel economy (the "gray market," "black market," "street trade," "unofficial" trade, etc.). Thus, the middle class did not disappear in Serbia, it just slid downward on the social hierarchy together with most other groups. This intensified the polarization between the "new rich" associated with Milošević's ruling establishment, and the embittered urban professionals whose social and material opportunities had significantly eroded.[39] Indeed, in the mid- and late 1990s, the greatest internal challenges to Milošević would come from the dissatisfaction of the urban professional sectors, and the student population of would-be professionals. It should be emphasized, however, that although the material status of the professional segment within the middle class—a group often seen as the essential bulwark of democratic political reform—declined, the overall social position of that group remained quite significant. Thus, in large part, professionals retained their educational status, former positions, and prestige, as well as some of their established material advantages such as above average quality housing and personal savings.

Wartime State-Building and Elite Co-optation

Near the end of April 1992, hoping to weather the political and economic crisis linked to the wars of the Yugoslav succession, which he had done so much to facilitate, Milošević established a new state, the Federal Republic of Yugoslavia (FRY)—sometimes termed the "Third Yugoslavia." The FRY was composed of two federal units, Serbia, and the much smaller Republic of Montenegro.[40] Titoist Yugoslavia had disintegrated. The new state was custom designed to consolidate Milošević's control over a new and predominantly Serbian federal entity that was erected upon the rubble of the old regime. When plans for the new state were first made public in February 1992, it was announced that a revised constitutional structure would allow for the unbroken continuity of "Yugoslavia," because it would enable Serbia and Montenegro to inherit, so to speak, the international recognition enjoyed by the former (Titoist) Yugoslavia. Endeavoring to quickly achieve that goal, which ultimately proved unsuccessful, the regime's constitutional experts cobbled together a new constitution for the federal unit of Serbia and Montenegro in only five days. The text of the preliminary draft of the constitution publicly appeared on April 15, and no official public debates on the document were announced. Despite many opposition complaints that, among other things, the constitution was only designed by one party (Milošević's ruling SPS), and that not enough time had been provided to discuss the document, the new FRY constitution—known as the "Žabljak Constitution" because of the mountain resort where it had been compiled—was formally proclaimed on April 27, 1992.[41]

Legitimation of Montenegro's accession to the new federal union was obtained through a referendum held in that republic on March 1. According to official reports, 66 percent of the roughly 418,000 people eligible to vote turned out for the referendum, and 96 percent supported the proposition that Montenegro "as a sovereign republic continue to live in a joint state of Yugoslavia, equally with other republics." However, most Albanians in Montenegro opposed the referendum's proposition, and considered the process illegitimate and nonbinding.[42] Indeed, within only a few years serious tension would arise between Montenegrin and Serbian politicians over the operation of the federation, and the entire direction of politics in FRY (see Chapter 7).

Much of the new constitution's language was a far cry from the reality of Serbian political life that Milošević had established over the past five years. For example, Article 14 stipulated that "political pluralism should be the prerequisite and guarantor of the democratic political order of Yugoslavia." But real power throughout the new Yugoslavia was concentrated in the hands of Milošević, who continued to govern from his post as president of Serbia. Under the Serbian constitution adopted in 1990, Milošević already enjoyed broad powers of presidential control.[43] In contrast, the Yugoslav constitution of 1992 only provided for a weak federal president (who could only serve one four-year term), elected by the Federal Assembly and possessing essentially formal power. Seeking to legitimate the new state, Milošević cleverly invited one of Serbia's most prominent writers, Dobrica Ćosić, to become president of the new federation. Ćosić, who had become a Serbian anti-Titoist and nationalist after breaking with the communist regime (albeit not with communism in his view) in the late 1960s, had at first been standoffish about Milošević. But like many of the intellectuals at the Serbian Academy of Science and Arts, Ćosić had joined Milošević's broad coalition during the nationalist-populist wave that swept the country in 1988, and which had restored Belgrade's control over Kosovo. Indeed, Ćosić quickly became enamored with Milošević's devotion to the Serbian cause. As the writer observed in a 1991 interview: "I consider that since Nikola Pašić during the First World War no one has had more difficult conditions and a greater burden. . . . Compared to all Serbian politicians over the last five decades I am confident that Slobodan Milošević has done the most for the Serbian people. His general national policy, strategy and tactics, I consider realistic and courageous."[44]

Ćosić would soon regret those words. With Milošević's approval, Ćosić and others convinced Milan Panić—the millionaire owner of an American pharmaceutical company who had emigrated from Serbia to the United States—to return to Belgrade and serve as the first prime minister of the rump Yugoslav federation. According to Slavoljub Djukić, when Panić asked Milošević why he had decided to "only" occupy the post of President of Serbia while allowing Ćosić to assume the role of President of Yugoslavia, Milošević answered: "Milan, it isn't important where I'm at. For Serbia I'm a kind of Khomeni."[45] But though in Milošević's shadow, Panić was brimming with enthusiasm for his new job; determined to enhance both Yugoslavia's international position and democratic development, and not to become Milošević's "marionette." Initially, Panić focussed on foreign policy, launching a peace offensive that was designed to get the international sanctions (enacted in May) against Yugoslavia lifted. For example, in his inaugural speech to the Federal Assembly in July 1992 Panić called for peace in Bosnia and the lifting of international economic sanctions against Yugoslavia. He also urged the complete removal of all regular and irregular Yugoslav military units from Bosnia, the recognition of all socialist Yugoslavia's successor states, and the establishment of economic ties between those states and the new Yugoslavia.

Panić's effort to fashion his own role in Yugoslav politics soon made him a rallying point for Serbia's chronically fragmented democratic opposition. In May 1992, when the regime had hastily arranged elections for the Chamber of Citizens in the federal assembly, the major parties in the opposition decided to boycott the process. As a result of the opposition boycott, two allied parties represented Serbia in the federal parliament: Milošević's SPS, with 69 percent of the seats, and the Serbian Radical Party, with 28 percent of the seats (two seats were won by a majority party from Vojvodina, and another seat went to an independent). However, in mid-May 1992, several opposition parties began to forge a united front through the coalition "Democratic Movement of Serbia" (DEPOS). Initially the DEPOS coalition consisted of fourteen parties and a couple of thousand Serbian intellectuals (of varied ideological views within or outside the many competing parties). Vuk Drašković's SPO was the most important party in DEPOS, but an effort at broad anti-regime unity was weakened by the refusal of the Democratic Party to join the coalition. DEPOS gained strength, and supported spontaneous student demonstrations in June and July 1992, which called for the resignation of Milošević, and for fair elections to be held for all political posts in the new federal state. Thus, the emergence of DEPOS as a force on the Serbian political landscape coincided with Panić's efforts to assert his independence from Milošević and take Yugoslavia in a new political direction. Moreover, both Panić and the opposition shared the conviction that Yugoslavia could not make progress toward democratic change until Milošević left power. During July, in personal discussions with Milošević, Panić even raised the issue of the latter's self-imposed exile, with the guarantee of a "comfortable position and income." Milošević listened politely, but rejected the offer.[46]

In August 1992, Panić enraged Milošević by firing Mihalj Kertes from his post as Deputy Head of the Federal Ministry of the Interior. Kertes, who had also been head of the Serbian Secret Police, was one of Milošević's key allies, and had coordinated the armed militia units that had helped arm the Bosnian Serbs before 1992, and eventually provoked hostilities with the Muslims and Croats (he would later serve as a Minister without Portfolio in the Serbian government and beginning in 1994, would head the federal customs administration). Not surprisingly, Milošević resisted any effort to expand the power of the federal level of governmental authority at the expense of his own power base in Serbia. Thus, it did not take long before Milošević would break with the Ćosić–Panić team. At one point, Milošević even threatened to arrest Panić, but Ćosić intervened. Meanwhile, Ćosić had become increasingly critical of the regime. He was especially annoyed by Milošević's tight grip on the state media, as well as the Serbian president's creation of a huge police apparatus in Serbia (around 70,000 strong at the time) as an armed counterweight to the country's military forces. But when the Serbian Minister of Internal Affairs seized the building and files of the Federal Ministry of the Interior in October 1992, it

was quite clear that Milošević intended to retain the upper hand in police matters.[47] Milošević made the move just as the UN launched an investigation into
alleged war crimes in the six-month old Bosnian civil war. The Ministry's
seizure also came after a Belgrade court had awarded ownership of the building to Serbia. Ćosić and Milošević also came into sharp disagreement over the
organization of the diplomatic service, as well as how to best extricate
Yugoslavia from the UN sanctions imposed in May 1992, and responsibility
for the war in Bosnia.[48] Milošević ultimately prevailed in all these disputes.
Thus, Svetozar Stojanović, who served as Ćosić's personal adviser, would aptly
describe the federal president's role as a case of "authority without power."[49]

As his power struggle with the Ćosić–Panić team deepened, Milošević began
to take a harder line regarding both internal and foreign policy. In October, the
Serbian president was able to side-step opposition pressure for immediate early
elections by engineering a snap referendum on the issue of such a vote. As
Milošević expected, the nearly unpublicized referendum, which was also boycotted by several opposition parties, failed to obtain the 50 percent majority
turnout necessary to pass a constitutional amendment on early elections
(although there was 95 percent support for holding such elections by those who
actually voted). Zoran Djindjić and the Democratic Party blamed Serbian
authorities for the failure of the referendum because they did "everything to
attach as little importance as possible to it."[50] Milošević would eventually hold
early presidential and parliamentary elections, but only in late December when
he was ready to proceed.[51] In October, Milošević also decided to boycott reconciliation talks with Croatia that had been promoted by Panić. For the moment,
Milošević chose to again play the nationalist card and support Serb militants in
Bosnia and Croatia. In order to undermine Panić, Milošević also arranged for
the resignation of several ministers in the Yugoslav cabinet. For example, at the
end of November, minister without portfolio Radmila Milentijević resigned, followed shortly by Nikola Šainović, the minister of the economy. In his letter of
resignation, Šainović accused Panić of letting "foreign powers dominate the government's policy," and thereby questioning "the very survival of the Serbian people." The Belgrade journalist, Miloš Vasic, aptly described such resignations as
examples of how Slobodan Milošević—from his vantage point in the Serbian
government—could activate his "moles" in the Panić government.

In the fall, Ćosić made his own attempt to negotiate Milošević's resignation as president of Serbia. "I advised Milošević to withdraw from active politics," Ćosić later remarked, "convinced that his political choices and normal
practices in the affairs of state would have damaged the national interest. Panić
also insisted that he resign [but] in vain. Unfortunately for Serbia and for him
personally, he did not heed us."[52] Panić then decided to challenge Milošević in
the December 1992 Serbian presidential election. Panić's candidacy gained

considerable support in opposition circles, and enlisted an enthusiastic coterie of followers to run a modern political campaign. But Milošević's hold on the media and other levers of power (which provided him with a small but useful segment of votes due to electoral chicanery), together with strong voter support outside the urban sector and the abstention of the Albanian population in Kosovo, would prove decisive. Panić was forced to defend himself against charges he was a traitor working for Washington (his chief adviser was the former American Ambassador to Belgrade, John Scanlon, and the New York polling firm Pen and Schoen managed his campaign), and also waste time in court proceedings to prove his eligibility to run. His candidacy was finally upheld by the Supreme Court of Serbia nine days before the election.[53]

Panić won roughly 32 percent of the vote in the election, while Milošević garnered 53 percent (down from 65 percent in 1990). Another five candidates split up seven percent of the vote. In the Serbian legislative election, Milošević's SPS received 32 percent of the vote, while the pro-Panić DEPOS coalition received 17 percent. Remarkably, Vojislav Šešelj's Serbian Radical Party (SRS) received 23 percent of the vote. The SRS had already acquired a high profile among nationalistically oriented voters in the May 1992 federal election, and the surge of popularity for that party in December probably was due to a certain feeling on the part of many voters that Milošević was not carrying through quickly enough on his promise of achieving a Serbian national renaissance. Yugoslav research revealed that both the SPS and SRS drew their support from the same pool of voters, and that a large segment of either party found it easy to transfer its support to the other.[54] Needing to demonstrate that their newly designed political system was pluralistic, and also desiring that an allied party absorb the boycotting votes of the SPO and the Democratic Party, Milošević's SPS was willing to temporarily build up the SRS as a parallel force in Serbian politics. Under the electoral law, the SPS and SRS together were able to control over 70 percent of the seats in the legislature. Compared to the first multiparty election in 1990, the SPS had lost considerable ground. But Milošević employed his *de facto* alliance with the SRS to obstruct any serious threat from the opposition. Šešelj's fortunes—and the regime's mobilization of nationalist fervor—would rise and fall again during the remainder of the decade depending largely on Milošević's attitudes and needs (see Chapter 4).

For the moment, Panić remained prime minister of Yugoslavia, and Milošević remained ensconced in the Serbian presidency. But by February 1993, Milošević significantly increased the level of political repression in the country, and forced Panić to resign. Panić returned to the United States claiming that the election had been stolen from him, and he continued to actively work and provide resources to strengthen Serbia's democratic opposition. At the end of May, Milošević collaborated with his ultra-nationalist ally, Vojislav Šešelj, to force Ćosić out of his position as president of Yugoslavia and replace him with a loyal SPS henchman. By this time Milošević, who worried about rumors of an internationally backed coup by the army, had become particularly suspicious of Ćosić's close contacts with the military leadership. Ćosić had served as president for only 350 days (June 15, 1992 to May 31, 1993).

In retrospect, the Ćosić–Panić interlude was largely a sideshow that Milošević had sponsored in order to gain legitimacy for his own new federal state structure, and to a certain extent also help dampen American and international criticism of Belgrade's role in the Bosnian war. However, once Panić and Ćosić had become assertive and politically threatening, Milošević brought the ostensible power-sharing arrangement to an end. Milošević simply decided "to take complete control of the levers of authority and power, even those more virtual than real."[55] After his short, unhappy experience as president of Yugoslavia, Ćosić—who had at first been skeptical of Milošević's intentions, but then had wholeheartedly decided to embrace him—concluded that the Serbian president was a man who, though intelligent, was of "modest general knowledge and a simple education . . . unscrupulous towards enemies and sentimental towards followers. Deceitful as Tito, arrogant, self-confidently uttering untruths and fiction, because he feels that the ends justify the means, and his position gives him that right. . . . He remains an arbitrary despot without original or great ideas, a real technician of power. He is ideologically ambivalent, since he didn't break with Titoism nor I believe, with the spirit of communism. . . . He wishes to create a unified Serbian state, stubbornly, passionately, by any method with everyone sacrificing—except himself." But Ćosić also conceded that "Milošević was a most successful politician when in combat, on the defense, in direct struggle." [56]

Serbian Regime and Opposition Elites: Socio-Political Characteristics

Though Milošević succeeded in shrewdly dominating the Serbian political landscape throughout the late 1980s and the 1990s, he did not do so alone. Who governed Serbia along with its top leader? And how did that elite group compare to the opposition activists wishing to take power? In order to help answer those questions, this section of the chapter analyzes biographical information on the social and political characteristics of Serbian elites provided in *Who is Who in Serbia* published in Belgrade in 1996, as well as from an earlier edition published in 1991. Less comprehensive, but nonetheless useful biographical details concerning government elite and leading members of the ruling party were also gleaned from the websites of the Federal Republic of Yugoslavia and the Republic of Serbia. Full or partial data on gender, ethnicity, age, social origins, education, and political experience under the old regime was obtained for a total of 388 members of Serbia's ruling and opposition political elites in 1997.

For purposes of discussion in this chapter, three major elite sectors can be identified (the number of persons actually considered in the sample for each elite sector or subsector is provided in parenthesis):

1. **Regime Elites** (236), comprised of two subsectors:
   A. *Ruling Party and Parliamentary Elites* (100): leading political officials and legislators of the SPS and its "left wing" coalition allies, the United Yugoslav Left (JUL) and (from 1994 to 1998) the New Democracy (ND).
   B. *Higher State Administrators* (136): top ranking members of the federal and republican state administration.
2. **Centrist Elites** (78), consisting of three elite subsectors:
   A. *The Liberal Elite* (49): leaders of the major moderate opposition parties, who have most consistently been associated with, or who have supported liberal principles. For example, the Democratic Party, and its later offshoot, the Democratic Party of Serbia, the Civic Alliance of Serbia, the Democratic Center, the Serbian Liberal Party, the Green Party, the People's Peasant Party, the Social Democratic Party, the League of Social Democrats of Vojvodina, the Reformist Democratic Party of Vojvodina.
   B. *The NGO Elite* (16): leaders of selected Serbian nongovernmental organizations.
   C. *The Minority Party Elites* (13): selected leaders of smaller minority parties including the Democratic Community of Vojvodina Hungarians, the League of Vojvodina Hungarians, the Democratic League of Croats in Vojvodina, the Democratic Party of Turks, the Democratic Community of Gypsies of Yugoslavia, the Democratic Party of Albanians, the [Muslim] Party of Democratic Action, the Democratic League of Kosovo.
3. **Rightist Elites** (74), divided into two subsectors:
   A. *The Moderate Right Elite* (29): leaders of the Serbian Movement for Renewal (SPO).
   B. *The Radical Right Elite* (45): predominantly made up of leaders from Vojislav Šešelj's Serbian Radical Party, but also including other parties, including the Serbian Unity Party, the Serbian Royalist Movement, the

Serbian Radical Party–Nikola Pašić, the Serbian Democratic Party of the Serbian Lands, the Democratic Homeland Party, the Saborna Narodna Stranka, etc.

The preceding classification is offered mainly as a general framework to differentiate among the major components of the Serbian elite structure, and not as a systematic alignment of each subelite or elite member on a left–right ideological continuum. Thus, though the party personnel included in the "regime elite" generally portray themselves as part of a "left-wing" governing elite coalition, the policy orientation of its members on many issues (and certainly Serbian nationalism) can be classified as moderate or radical rightist, depending on the particular point in time. The same could be said regarding the political mindset of many leaders classified as liberals, while members of what is identified here as the "moderate right" elite group, and indeed extreme right leaders, often perceive themselves as being centrist. Moreover, though elite subsectors can be differentiated in terms of their general attitudinal perspectives, there appeared to be very little cohesiveness on values and policy issues within any particular subelite. For example, in the early 1990s, the Serbian political analyst Slobodan Antonić usefully differentiated the general outlook of three subsectors in the Serbian political elite (the "statist elite;" the "liberal elite;" and the "national-populist elite") in a manner corresponding roughly to the classification used in this study.[57] Antonić determined that most members of the Serbian political elite—from the ruling party and opposition parties—were not strongly committed to, or familiar with, democratic values. However, in his view, "most of the electorate" was "hardly more democratic." In Antonić's opinion the ruling elite had established a "parasitic symbiosis" with the most undemocratic mass elements in Serbian society. In a later study, he concluded that the elite was rather "democratically oriented" and that support for authoritarian views and also xenophobic attitudes were actually more strongly felt by the general population than in the ranks of the various sectors of the Serbian political elite.[58] Moreover, members of the liberal opposition exhibited more democratic attitudes than the rightist and ruling parties, but a significant number of the entire elite, in Antonić's view, tended to view politics as a "war where the enemy must be destroyed by any means (including weakening or destroying the existing political order)."

Belgrade sociologist Mladen Lazić found that the ruling political elite in Serbia exhibited very little cohesion: "The ruling group is not systematically organized as it was in socialism. It is based on a consensus which, from one case to another, combines force and interest."[59] Lazić also found that there was an overall lack of acceptance within the elite as a whole (including segments of the opposition) regarding ideas such as privatization and political pluralism. More than one-third of the elite held anti-reformist views; regressive notions were also supported by a majority of the general population.[60] Anti-reformism is most pronounced in the ruling establishment and constitutes the attitudinal dimension most typical of that elite subsector: "Our political elite manages the economy and assures itself material privileges. By managing the economy it also maintains its political position . . . our elite does not permit one key reform—dividing the state from the party. By holding the state as the property of the ruling party it makes really free elections impossible or a democratic procedure of decision making. And that is the way it is possible to survive in power."[61]

Viewed as a group in 1997, the members of the Serbian elite analyzed here exhibit a good deal of homogeneity in terms of their general social characteristics. For example, many members of the elite in Serbia are middle-aged males who have completed higher educational studies, come from nonmanual social backgrounds (based on the occupations of their fathers), and are ethnically Serbian. Closer examination of the differences within and among elite sectors (Table 4.1), however, also reveals an interesting pattern of contrast in elite background features of different sectors. The most vivid and significant areas of contrast within and among elite sectors relate to age, social origin, education, and political experience under the old regime. In comparative terms, the most similarities are found in the areas of gender and ethnicity.

Gender and Elite Couples

All Serbia's elite sectors were heavily dominated by men. For example, only 6.8 percent of the total regime elite is female, a percentage that is only slightly greater in the regime higher administrative ranks than its party/parliamentary subelite. But the "liberal" elite and radical rightist leadership subsectors exhibit even less female representation (under 5 percent). The relative presence of women in the moderate right-wing SPO and the liberal NGO sample is somewhat higher, but women still comprised less than one-fifth of both those leadership groups.

The influence of women on Serbia's top political leaders is not, of course, fully or adequately captured in a comparative analysis of elite aggregates. Thus, Slobodan Milošević's wife, Mirjana Marković, was one of the most important factors influencing the political orientation of her husband and the ruling party coalition. As discussed earlier, Mirjana and Slobodan had been high school sweethearts, were married in 1965, and have almost been continuously together since they first met. At a minimum, Mirjana Marković was one-half of the governing partnership, which appears to be a system of co-equal rule, essentially a "ruling couple" who occupied the summit of Yugoslavia's political hierarchy.[62] Other women also have had an important influence near the apex of Milošević's power structure; for example, the banker

Borka Vučić, who mentored Milošević early in his career (see Chapter 2), and Gorica Gajević, the Secretary-General of the SPS after early 1996. The significant political role of Vuk Drašković's wife, Danica, in the Serbian Movement of Renewal (SPO), represented a counterpart to the Slobodan (SPS)–Mirjana (JUL) partnership.[63] While Mirjana Marković used a regular column in the magazine *Duga* to express her views, Danica Drašković served as director of *Srpska Reč,* the outlet of the SPO. At times during the 1990s, the two women engaged in vitriolic exchanges. For example, Mrs. Drašković, whose father was a leading Chetnik killed by the communists, has described Mirjana Marković (whose parents never married but were communist heroes in World War II), as the "bastard product of wild Partisan orgies in the woods." Marković responded by characterizing Drašković as an "unfulfilled woman who has the habits of cattle herders and highwaymen who steal baggage and kidnap children."[64]

Another influential woman in Serbian political life is Vesna Pešić,a who throughout most of the 1990s served as the head of the Civic Alliance of Serbia (GSS). Internationally recognized for her work as an anti-nationalist opposition figure, Pešić assumed a higher domestic profile when she became one of the three top leaders in the *Zajedno* coalition of opposition parties that guided the 1996–1997 civic protest movement. Pešić has linked her early socialization to her civic outlook, and her lack of enthusiasm for collectivism and a sense of victimization:

> My advantage or defect is that I didn't know national stories. The past didn't
> interest me much. Probably because Belgrade was so wonderful. At home Serbian suffering was never discussed, neither as the story of fellow victims nor as
> a major topic. I didn't know we are a "tragic people." ... I thought we were a
> well-disposed people. Others always lamented and sniveled, but we appeared
> secure in ourselves. I liked my society. We weren't dissatisfied. ... When I say
> "we" I am thinking of the people with whom I was friends. Yes, we were Serbs
> although that wasn't important. We weren't Serbs in the present Serbian manner.
> We were not tragic or victims (of others).[65]

Many other women have been active in Serbia's political life[66]—especially in the anti-war movement, although the overall data suggests the serious obstacles to female opportunity and influence at the top elite level. Indeed, the study "Women in Serbia 1991–95," completed by Belgrade sociologists claims that Serbian women have been the biggest losers from the breakup of the former Yugoslavia and the wars that followed. This situation appears to stem in part from what one of the study's authors refers to as "growing conservatism in society billed as a return to 'traditional values.'"[67]

Table 4.1 Serbian Political Elites: Party Leaders by Socio-Political Characteristics

	Regime Elites			Centrist Elites				Rightist Elites			Total Serbian Elite Sample
	Party/Parliamentary (SPS, JUL, ND)	Higher Administrators	Total Regime Elite	Liberal Opposition (DS, DSS, GSS, etc.)	NGOs	Minority Parties	Total Centrist Elites	Moderate Right (SPO)	Radical Right (SRS, etc.)	Total Rightist Elite	
Gender											
Men	94.0	92.6	93.2	95.9	81.3	100.0	93.8	82.8	95.6	90.5	92.8
Women	6.0	7.4	6.8	4.1	18.7	—	6.4	17.2	4.4	9.5	7.2
Total	100.0	100.0	100.0	100.0	100.0	100.0	100.0	100.0	100.0	100.0	100.0
(number)	(100)	(136)	(236)	(49)	(16)	(13)	(78)	(29)	(45)	(74)	(388)
Ethnicity											
Serb/Montenegrin	93.8	95.9	95.0	92.7	62.5	—	76.8	100.0	97.6	98.5	92.7
Other	6.2	4.1	5.0	7.3	37.5	100.0	23.2	—	2.4	1.5	7.3
Total	100.0	100.0	100.0	100.0	100.0	100.0	100.0	100.0	100.0	100.0	100.0
(number)	(96)	(122)	(218)	(49)	(8)	(8)	(56)	(25)	(42)	(67)	(341)
Age											
–34	7.0	—	3.0	10.2	—	7.7	7.7	10.3	8.9	9.5	5.2
35–44	28.0	8.8	16.9	16.3	—	23.1	14.1	20.7	35.6	29.7	18.8
45–54	37.0	30.9	33.5	40.8	50.0	30.8	41.0	37.9	33.3	35.1	35.8
55–64	27.0	49.3	39.8	24.5	31.3	15.4	24.4	27.6	17.8	21.6	32.7
65+	1.0	11.0	6.8	8.2	18.8	23.1	12.1	3.4	4.4	4.1	7.5
Total	100.0	100.0	100.0	100.0	100.0	100.0	100.0	100.0	100.0	100.0	100.0
(number)	(100)	(136)	(236)	(49)	(16)	(13)	(78)	(29)	(45)	(74)	(388)

Table 4.1 continued on next page

Table 4.1 (continued)

	Regime Elites			Centrist Elites				Rightist Elites			Total Serbian Elite Sample
	Party/ Parliamentary (SPS, JUL, ND)	Higher Administrators	Total Regime Elite	Liberal Opposition (DS, DSS, GSS, etc.)	NGOs	Minority Parties	Total Centrist Elites	Moderate Right (SPO)	Radical Right (SRS, etc.)	Total Rightist Elite	
Social Origin											
Peasant	21.3	27.5	24.1	10.0	—	25.0	10.0	18.2	16.1	17.0	19.5
Industrial worker	19.7	11.8	16.1	13.3	33.3	—	15.0	4.5	29.0	18.9	16.6
Non-manual	59.0	60.8	59.8	76.7	66.7	75.0	75.0	77.3	54.8	64.1	63.9
Total	100.0	100.0	100.0	100.0	100.0	100.0	100.0	100.0	100.0	100.0	100.0
(number)	(61)	(51)	(112)	(30)	(6)	(4)	(40)	(22)	(31)	(53)	(205)
Education											
Secondary or less	10.0	1.5	5.1	8.2	18.8	15.4	12.0	13.7	22.2	18.9	9.1
Higher diploma	71.0	56.6	62.7	46.9	43.8	38.5	44.9	75.9	62.2	67.6	60.8
Graduate degrees	18.0	41.2	31.4	42.8	37.5	30.8	39.8	10.3	15.5	13.5	30.1
Total	100.0	100.0	100.0	100.0	100.0	100.0	100.0	100.0	100.0	100.0	100.0
(number)	(99)	(135)	(234)	(48)	(16)	(11)	(75)	(29)	(45)	(74)	(383)
Political Experience in Old Regime											
Yes	58.1	82.2	71.0	15.2	12.5	30.0	16.7	18.5	13.3	15.3	48.0
No	41.9	17.8	29.0	84.8	87.5	70.0	83.3	81.5	86.7	84.7	52.0
Total	100.0	100.0	100.0	100.0	100.0	100.0	100.0	100.0	100.0	100.0	100.0
(number)	(93)	(107)	(200)	(46)	(16)	(10)	(72)	(27)	(45)	(72)	(344)

Ethnic Representation and the "National Card"

Although 33 percent of Serbia's population during the 1990s was neither Serb nor Montenegrin (32 percent of Yugoslavia as a whole), very few non-Serbs could be found in Serbia's corridors of power or in its established political organizations. Indeed, the rightist party elites were almost entirely ethnically Serb. The fact that Albanians—who constituted 17.1 percent of Serbia's population (and 16.5 percent of Yugoslavia's population)—decided to boycott political life in the republic beginning in 1989 contributed to the almost complete absence of that ethnic group in Serbia's elite structure. For example, in the Serbian parliamentary election of September 1997, the joint left-wing list did not include a single Albanian. One of the SPS leaders claimed that his party did have some Albanian members, but if they were listed as candidates "they will perhaps be killed immediately" by other Albanians.[68] Only a few Albanians, from smaller parties outside the mainstream of Albanian underground political life in Serbia, were represented in the Yugoslav and Serbian assemblies. Hungarian representation in the nonregime elite sectors was somewhat higher owing to the active role of Hungarian party organizations and NGOs, but only a mere handful of Hungarians are found in the regime's high-ranking administrative and political positions. The most prominent Hungarian in Milošević's regime was Mihalj Kertes, the Director of the Federal Customs Administration. Kertes previously served as Assistant Federal Minister of Internal Affairs, and was deeply involved in Belgrade's activity in Bosnia. Overall, however, minority representation has been quite negligible in the Serbian elite structure.

The findings on the elite's ethnic composition in part reflect the fact that centrist and moderate political forces have largely proved unable to fully embrace the idea of a genuinely multicultural or civic approach to political life, and to abandon the political expediency of flirting with Serbian ethnic nationalism. For example, though Vuk Drašković, who founded the SPO (together with the extreme right-wing leader Vojislav Šešelj, who later left the organization) moved to a more moderate and pacific political orientation during the war in Bosnia–Herzegovina, he and his party initially adopted decidedly nationalist policies. Thus, during the early 1990s, Drašković sponsored the formation of special paramilitary units to fight for Serbian interests in Croatia and Bosnia, and also supported the notion that territories held by both Macedonia and the Bosnian Muslims should be joined to a Serbian state. Drašković later disavowed such ideas, but endorsed an eclectic program of moderation, monarchism, and devotion to traditional Serbian mores. In June 1993, Drašković was arrested at this party headquarters, together with his wife Danica, and savagely beaten by the police. Hospitalized while under custody, he was later released after foreign leaders intervened on his behalf. Always a mercurial figure, Drašković would play an active role in opposition politics during the 1990s. However, he would lose some of his credibility as an anti-Milošević figure when he joined a coalition dominated by the ruling party in 1999 (see Chapter 5). Beginning in September 1997, Drašković also put forward the rather unorthodox idea of transforming Serbia into a multiethnic "Balkan America."

Zoran Djindjić and the Democratic Party (DS) generally offered a pragmatic approach to the national question. For example, in 1994, believing that opposition forces could not achieve success without playing the nationalist card, the Bosnian-born Djindjić decided to express support for Radovan Karadžić and his Bosnian Serb supporters. Djindjić took this position after Milošević backed away from supporting the Bosnian Serbs. "We did not want to let Milošević monopolize national organizing," Djindjić claimed, "and we did not want to let him manipulate it whenever he liked. We had to show national solidarity in order to be taken seriously."[69] Meanwhile, Vojislav Koštunica and the Democratic Party of Serbia (DSS) leadership in 1992 had broken with Djindjić and the DS for being too soft on the national question, and adopted a more explicitly nationalist orientation than most of the other political actors in the liberal elite. Koštunica maintained that he favored a "moderate" approach to the "Serbian national question," which would unify Serbian communities in the Balkans through the formation of a federation of Serb regions. Koštunica saw himself and his party as the only opposition component that could successfully blend liberalism with Serbian nationalism. As for the national views of his centrist and moderate colleagues, Koštunica claimed: "One attitude is fickle and calculating. It belongs to the Democratic Party [Djindjić]. Another attitude is anational, in many respects anti-national. This is the view of the Civic Alliance of Serbia [Pešić]. That attitude is also apparent in the Serbian Movement of Renewal [Drašković], only accompanied by an interest in nationalism in its archaic and caricatured form."[70] In the first half of 1997, a faction of the DSS led by Vladen Batić was expelled, and formed the Democratic Christian Party of Serbia. Batić claimed he remained loyal to "original concepts, convictions, principles, and ideas of the DSS, primarily to a balance between the democratic and the national"[71] (in 1998, Batić would become the second "coordinator" of a new multiparty opposition coalition, the "Alliance for Change"). Koštunica's opportunity to lead the democratic opposition and attract a broad audience for his program of moderate or soft nationalism would have to wait until the presidential election of 2000 (see Chapters 8 and 10).

Within the liberal opposition only Vesna Pešić and her small Civic Alliance of Serbia (GSS) maintained, by and large, a nonnational political orientation. For their part, Serbia's ethnic minorities, concerned by the nationalist rhetoric of most centrist political parties, either abstained from involvement in the formal political system or gave their allegiance to minority parties. The Kosovar elaboration of so-called "parallel" political, governmental, and societal institutions was the most striking example of this trend. Most of Serbia's Albanian "minority" have lived in the province of Kosovo, where they constituted a large majority of the population throughout the 1980s and 1990s. A 1997 study of Serbs and Albanians in Kosovo, "The Anatomy of the Kosovo Crisis," by the Belgrade-based Forum for Ethnic Relations, found that "the two communities are totally closed, limited and turned into their own ethnicity." Interestingly, 98 percent of the Albanians surveyed in 1997 thought independence was an appropriate option, a view shared by only 2 percent of the Serbs. Almost all Albanians intended to boycott Serbia's political process, while 93 percent of the local Serbs said they would be voting (43 percent for the ruling SPS, and 38 percent for Vojislav Šešelj's ultra-nationalist Serbian Radical Party).[72] Such data help explain the absence of Albanians in Serbia's elite structure, although after mid-June 1999, this situation would largely become an historical aside (see Chapters 6 and 7).

Age: Milošević's "Mature" Opposition

Unlike the findings on gender and ethnicity, there have been quite noticeable differences within and among Serbia's elite sectors when it comes to their generational structure. On the whole, regime elites have been considerably older than the centrists and rightist elites, a division that is even more pronounced if the regime's high-ranking bureaucrats and technocrats are considered separately (all ages were calculated as of 1997). Approximately 60 percent of the regime's higher administrators were over 54 years of age in 1997. In contrast, party activists and legislators from the SPS and JUL—politicians handpicked by Milošević or his wife—exhibited a much younger profile (roughly 28 percent are over 54, and 35 percent are under 45 years of age). Only the radical right elite subgroup (which was not in the ruling coalition until 1998) had a more "youthful" generational composition than politicians of the ruling left coalition.

The centrist and moderate right subelites exhibited a more balanced generational composition, with elite subjects from those leadership groups represented fairly evenly in each age cohort. Many members of these elite sectors are generationally mature leaders who first became active in politics during the late 1960s, the 1970s and 1980s, when they began working within, or more typically against, the communist regime. Thus, by the time they assumed major leadership positions in the new multiparty system during the 1990s, most centrist and moderate leaders had already been politically socialized in rather seasoned segments of Serbia's political class. For example, Dragolub Mićunović, who was born in 1930, and was arrested as a high school student in 1948 for his political nonconformism, was one of the oldest members of the centrist liberal opposition. Mićunović later took part in the 1968 student demonstrations at Belgrade University, as well as engaging in later dissident activity. In the fall of 1999, after a decade of involvement in pluralist politics, Mićunović was still active in the opposition, and assumed a major role in efforts to unite the divided anti-Milošević forces. Vesna Pešić, the head of the Civic Alliance of Serbia, was born in 1940 and became active as a dissident in the mid-1970s. She was a founding member of UJDI (the Association for Yugoslav Democratic Initiative) in 1989, which helped to launch competitive political life in the former Yugoslavia (in April 1999, the 59-year-old Pešić turned over leadership of the GSS to the 36-year-old Goran Svilanović). Vojislav Koštunica, the President of the Democratic Party of Serbia, was born in 1944, and became a human rights activist and dissident during the 1980s. The moderate right leader, Vuk Drašković, who heads the Serbian Renewal Movement, was born in 1946. In his official biography, Drašković stresses his role as one of the leaders of the 1968 student protests. But Drašković also worked as a journalist and writer until the mid-1980s, including a stint as a press counselor for a communist apparatchik. Danica Drašković (born in 1945) claims that one of the "dark stains" on her political biography is that she "fell in love with a communist." "Things became easier," she says, when he abandoned his communist views.[73] Zoran Djindjić, born in 1952, is one of the relatively younger leaders in the Serbian liberal elite pantheon, but still part of the core middle-aged (45–54) age cohort in the elite. Djindjić began his career as an anti-regime political activist during the first part of the 1970s, when he tried to form a student union not controlled by the League of Communists. Djindjić has explained the political context when he first began his dissident activity:

> My first conflict was at my first class in the Philosophy Faculty. Already at that time one of my very distinct traits had become apparent, that I am terribly irritated by something being called authoritative if it is not backed up by strong arguments. During that first class we were told that Marx was the greatest philosopher, but I said not only that he wasn't the greatest, but that in general he isn't a philosopher. That was the beginning of the dispute which marked my future life. It was the period of the post-1960s atmosphere during which we as a generation had the luck to be generationally liberated from the illusions which the preceding generation had. For us Tito was dead, communism was dead, Marx wasn't an authority figure; although we lived in a society that was Titoist, communist, and Marxist. You know, we didn't have the illusions of the 1968 [student demonstrators], but we had politically explosive energy they had. . . . I never was a member of the League of Communists. For many that is strange, because that was a time when everyone accepted the red carnation [party membership] . . . but not us in the Philosophy Faculty.[74]

On average, the leaders of the centrist NGOs and ethnic minority parties tend to be a rather older elite group, perhaps reflecting the special role of various spirited, independent, and politically experienced individuals who have long advocated nonconformist and minority causes in Serbian politics. However, the most "mature" member of the Serbian opposition in the late 1990s was Dragoslav Avramović, the former governor of the National Bank of Yugoslavia, and author of the Yugoslav government's temporarily successful 1994 policy "Program of Economic Stabilization." But Avramović, who was born in 1919, and graduated from Belgrade Law School in 1941, would be ousted from his post in Milošević's regime in May 1996, and his program discarded. After that, he became a key actor in the opposition, and was often referred to as "Grandpa Avram."

Social Origins: The Roots of Political Resistance and Radicalism

The extent and sources of social mobility into elite positions are important indicators that can help explain the beneficiaries and tempo of socio-political change. For example, the communist takeover of Yugoslavia at the end of World War II was a rapid and extensive exercise in social mobility and elite change with the arrival in power of an entirely new group of political decision makers. That new "revolutionary elite" was composed largely of political activists who were first generation intellectuals from peasant and working class families, a group who would have a profound impact on the course of the country over the next 45 years. Moreover, in the course of a relatively short period of time, the members of that new Titoist or Partisan elite evolved into a "new class," or ruling political establishment, which not only monopolized power, but also provided their offspring with privileges and special opportunities for advancement in the ranks of the elite structure. As Milovan Djilas would write in 1954, "a sense of caste solidarity," manifests itself in the communist elite, "a product of political power and the way power had been arrived at."[75] By the 1990s, the Yugoslav communist system had collapsed, and in Serbia, Tito's heirs—most notably Slobodan Milošević—together with their new political and intellectual allies, had established a new subspecies of authoritarian rule; a "soft dictatorship" that included aspects of hegemonic control by a powerful party, but also a multiparty system and elections, which were competitive to a limited extent. However, unlike the first decade after World War II, Serbian society was no longer overwhelmingly agrarian and economically underdeveloped. Viewed in that context, it is interesting to explore the social origins of the Serbian political elite in the mid-1990s; a group composed both of many individuals who began their political careers in the communist period, and others who entered politics on the eve, or just after, the disintegration of socialist Yugoslavia and the collapse of communist rule.

A request for information on social origin was included in the question-naire sent to members of the Serbian elite by the editors of the 1996 *Who's Who in Serbia*. Regrettably, many individuals chose not to include such information in their response, and such data is very difficult to come by from other sources. There is enough available information, however, to glean some valuable insights into this important dimension of elite background. Interestingly, the data indicates that the centrist and moderate right elites, that is, the core of the established opposition parties, come from families where their fathers worked (about three-quarters) in nonmanual occupations. In contrast, the social origins of the regime elites are more modest and more mixed. Thus, although roughly 60 percent of the fathers of the regime elite worked in nonmanual professions, about one-quarter of the fathers were peasants, and 16 percent held occupations in the industrial working class. The most proletarian and modest social origin profile among the elite sectors was displayed by the radical right elite, nearly 50 percent of whom had fathers who were peasants (16.1 percent) or industrial workers (29 percent). Meanwhile, the large contingent of professionals, specialists, and directors of industrial enterprises co-opted into the regime elite—many of whom are individuals who come from families that have previously been concentrated in urban areas and finished university—may partially account for the high nonmanual background of this group. For example, the Belgrade sociologist Mladen Lazić found that the children of the former communist political and economic elite are more interested in seeking elite positions in the new "private entrepreneurial [economic elite] substratum than in politics." Lazić also observed that the new economic elite is often involved in "para-legal and illegal forms of operation," and therefore constitutes a leadership group that is a "conservative rather than transforming political force" unlikely to initiate economic development. The new economic elite's substantial social origin in the old communist elite, and its close linkage to the SPS–JUL regime elite, are factors helping to preserve an "authoritarian political and command economic role" in Serbia.[76]

The high representation of peasant and working-class family backgrounds in the ranks of the more partisan subgroup of the "left-wing" ruling regime elite, and also in the radical right elite, is very suggestive when one considers the frequent alliance of those two subgroups during the last decade. Thus, superficially at least, and based on the partial data offered here, it appears that there is a general correspondence between the social origins of the elite subsectors which have supported the most illiberal positions in Yugoslav political life during Slobodan Milošević's rule, and have expounded the most anti-pluralist and nationalistic views. Lacking attitudinal data for the elite sample under discussion, the present analysis is rather limited, but it does indicate that both many members of the ruling political "left" (who at least initially supported Milošević's aggressively nationalist program) and also opposition extreme right, who often have advanced the most xenophobic perspectives, have come from families in which the father had a manual occupation.[77] In contrast, the social origins of centrist and moderate right elites—who generally express views that are more liberal and less xenophobic—are more closely associated with the urban and nonmanual sectors of Yugoslav society. Such social origins and attitudes may also help explain the relatively weak support, up until recently, of the centrist and moderate opposition parties in both rural and working class areas. For example, Yugoslav research shows that supporters of Drašković's SPO were more educated than SPS supporters, and are drawn typically from the upper-middle class.[78]

Educational Attainment: Intellectual Amateurs vs.
the School of Political Life

Social origin is typically closely associated with an individual's level of educational achievement. The findings on the members of the Serbian elite tend to reflect that linkage. Although the entire Yugoslav elite is rather well educated (60 percent hold bachelor's degrees, and 30 percent of the total hold graduate degrees), there are also very striking differences among the various elite sectors.

For example, the rightist elite exhibits the most modest level of educational attainment. This is particularly apparent in the case of the extreme right, roughly one-fifth of whom have no higher education, and only 15 percent of whom have graduate degrees. In sharp contrast, 43 percent of the liberal elite subsector have graduate degrees, and indeed 37 percent of that subgroup hold doctorates. The regime elite is also well educated, although there are notable differences between the very well educated higher administrators, 41 percent of whom have graduate degrees, and the more conventional higher educational achievement of the party and parliamentary politicians in the ruling left-wing coalition. The impressive educational qualifications of the centrist elites have frequently led observers to castigate them as a "club of writers," an "association of philosophers," or the "dissident circle," and to suggest that the political failure of the liberal and moderate opposition parties results from their leaders' lack of political savvy and professionalism. Vojislav Šešelj, although holding a doctorate himself, has expressed the anti-intellectual views of many of his more modestly educated radical right compatriots and followers: "They [the liberal intellectuals] are top specialists in their fields, but not in politics. They themselves hate to do the boring tasks that make up 90 percent of party work. They want to give political advice in the afternoon, when they don't know what else to do. Party policies can only be created by those who are involved in everyday party affairs."[79]

If the centrist elites have a surfeit of philosophically inclined intellectuals, the Milošević regime elite was distinguished by its specialization in political management and the technology of power. The educational qualifications of the regime's higher administrators in particular, identifies that group as a technocratic, pragmatic, and perhaps even more politically moderate sector of the ruling elite. Potentially those political technocrats seemed likely to support nonnationalist and nonstatist reform solutions (for example, following the departure of Milošević), which could eventually assist Serbia's transition toward a more democratic polity and privatized economy.[80]

Political Experience in the Old Regime: Outsiders vs.
the Renovated Nomenklatura

Participation or nonparticipation in the previous (pre-1990) communist elite distinguishes the regime elites most clearly from the nonruling elite sectors. Roughly 71 percent of the individuals in the regime elite sample for whom this information was available had been politically active (as a League of Communist party member, or party official) during the Titoist regime. That proportion rose to 82 percent when the higher administrators were taken alone. Highly educated, and perhaps pragmatic in outlook, the regime's administrative elite subsector, nonetheless, exhibits the highest continuity between the communist political system and Milošević's reconfigured "socialist" regime. Moreover, while Milošević has continuously jettisoned members of the regime elite as part of his abrupt policy shifts, that process of purging or rotation has been most extensive (and has most frequently led to complete exclusion from political life) in the SPS higher echelon (members of the party and parliamentary regime subelite), and not among higher administrators. Thus, it appears that this latter group, which served in the communist regime, had managed to survive, or be recycled back into new elite positions (changing either level of government activity or portfolios), throughout the 1990s. In sharp contrast, less than 20 percent of the sampled nonruling centrist and rightist elite actors were politically involved in the operation of the old regime, a feature that is even more marked in the case of the liberal NGO members (only 12.5 percent), and the stridently anticommunist radical right elite group (only 13.3 percent).[81]

But the radical right does stand out with respect to one particular form of socio-political engagement, which was reported by only a handful of individuals in other elite groups, namely, serving in armed formations during the recent wars associated with the former Yugoslavia's disintegration. Thus, 14 of the 45 members of the sampled radical right-wing elite contingent proudly provided information to the editors of the "Who's Who" regarding their participation in the "Yu-rat" (i.e., Yugoslav wars) in Croatia or Bosnia. For members of the extreme rightist elites, such service is a badge of honor, apparently comparable to the kind of meaning that was attached to participation in the World War II Partisan struggle by members of the Titoist elite. Thus, within the extreme right elite, the Yu-rat participants see themselves as a special elite corps.

Most members of Serbia's radical right elite have typically emphasized their antipathy to the communist regime, but during the first half of the 1990s, they collaborated closely with Milošević and his elite comrades. Thus, as Milošević fanned Serbian nationalism, and militarily sponsored Serbian territorial goals in Croatia and Bosnia, he also cleverly exploited the nationalist ardor and power aspirations of the extreme right elite, and particularly top leaders such as Vojislav Šešelj (born in Bosnia in 1954, who was from 1988 a self-proclaimed "Chetnik duke," founder and president of the Serbian Radical Party, and a "participant in the Yu-rat from 1991"), and Arkan Željko Ražnjatović, born in Slovenia in 1952, (his father was an Army officer) who was President of the Serbian Unity Party in 1993, and a "participant in the Yu-rat from 1990"). Šešelj, who at the age of 25 had received a doctorate at the University of Sarajevo, became an anti-communist dissident in the early 1980s, and served 22 months of an eight-year prison sentence for his political writings during 1984–1986[82] (i.e., the same period when Milošević was beginning his political ascent in the League of Communists).

Orchestrating successive coalitions between his regime elite and the radical right leadership, Milošević endeavored to portray himself as the only figure able to successfully defend Serbian nationalist interests, and also to politically marginalize (partially by depriving them of the ability to play the "national card") the already weak and squabbling opposition parties whose leaders belong to the centrist and moderate right elite sectors.[83] It was only when Milošević—politically weakened by Serbia's economic deterioration—decided to end his support for the military struggle of Serbian client regimes in Krajina and Bosnia that he began to publicly distance himself from close association with high profile, ultra-nationalist figures such as Vojislav Šešelj. For example, in November 1995, Gorica Gajević, the SPS Secretary-General, described her party's view of Šešelj's Serbian Radical Party: "At one time we found ourselves in similar positions. However he quickly showed that the ideas of the Serbian Radical Party are in large part pro-fascist, and that he isn't fighting for the national elements of the Serbs in a real sense. The Socialist Party of Serbia doesn't feel that everybody, except Serbs, needs to be second-class citizens."[84] Little more than two years later, Gajević would find the SPS back in an alliance with Šešelj (see below). But even after endorsing a more moderate policy, Milošević would continue to maintain alliances with less influential radical right figures, such as Arkan, and also to keep his lines of communication open with both the moderate and radical right elite sectors.

*Elite Change in Kosovo: The Passive and Proactive in
the Parallel Society (1990–1995)*

As illustrated by the preceding elite analysis, ethnic homogeneity and strong support for national interests have been hallmark features of Serbia's elite structure during the 1990s and 2000. Indeed few Serbian politicians and parties proved able to embrace policies that could be regarded as "multiethnic" or "civic-oriented." The most striking aspect of Serbian elite nationalism was reflected in the outlook of both regime officials, and the leaders of the non-ruling parties on the issue of Kosovo, and the political position of the Albanian population in that province. Thus, almost the entire spectrum of the Serbian party system viewed the 1981 Albanian insurrection in Kosovo, and subsequent resistance of the Kosovars against the curtailment of their constitutional rights, as highly subversive endeavors carried out by the leaders of a terroristic and secessionist underground movement. Such sentiments regarding the "Albanian question" significantly constrained pluralistic development with Serbia. Ethnic conflict in the province motivated the Kosovar Albanians to boycott the electoral process in Kosovo, and thereby allowed Milošević in each successive election to capture a relative majority of the votes cast, and the seats won, in the province. Indeed as Milošević's legitimacy eroded over time he became increasingly dependent on the safe seats his party was able to garner in Kosovo constituencies owing to absent Albanian voters. The conflict also motivated Serbian politicians of all stripes to avoid appearing "soft" on the national question, and thereby undermined the ability of the democratic opposition to adequately articulate a liberal and tolerant program for Serbia's future.

By the end of the 1980s, the escalation of tensions in Kosovo had polarized Serb–Albanian relations, and almost all dialogue between the leaders of those two communities regarding a more productive and peaceful form of coexistence had ceased. By early 1990, after the suppression of Albanian protests against Serbia's new constitutional amendments, and the purge of hundreds of Kosovar Albanians regarded as unreliable, it appeared that Kosovo was on the verge of an explosion. Early in 1990, claiming that "Albanian specialists were better organized than in the past," Milošević said that the Serbian people must be prepared for continuing the theme of struggle he had advanced as Gazimestan. But ironically, in one of those unexpected turns in history, just as the Milošević regime chose to step-up the harsh crackdown and long-term militarization of the Kosovo question (e.g., Belgrade's takeover of the Kosovo police, dissolution of local parliamentary and governmental institutions, abolition of local autonomy, seizure of the province's media outlets, etc.),[85] the leadership of the Kosovar Albanians opted to endorse a strategy of nonviolent resistance. How and why this situation came about is perhaps best explained by the significant changes in the Kosovo elite structure.

During 1988 and 1989, while Milošević was in the first phase of consolidating his power, the Belgrade regime effectively decapitated the top Albanian leadership in Kosovo's League of Communists, and also any Albanian activists advocating the province's unity with Albania (i.e., both the "Titoist" and "Enverist" elite segments of the 1980s). Roughly at the same time, however, a new group of Albanian intellectuals and political leaders began to emerge within the Association of Writers of Kosovo and the Association of Philosophers and Sociologists. The most prominent figure in this intellectual group was the writer Ibrahim Rugova. Rugova and his intellectual associates soon found themselves in a new and potentially promising political environment. Thus, many of the same external and internal factors that accounted for the unfolding of a pluralist party system in Serbia following the collapse of the League of Communists and the old federal system, permitted the formation of new Albanian opposition groups in Kosovo during late 1989 and early 1990. For example, it is during this period that the Kosovo branch of the Association for the Yugoslav Democratic Initiative (UJDI), which became entirely Albanian in its ethnic composition after the departure of its Serb members, would help various parties and movements to get organized in the province. But although political forces within Yugoslavia's republics and provinces were beginning to take advantage of the opportunities for multiparty development, Kosovo remained under police occupation. For Albanian Kosovars, active anti-regime nonconformity and protest in the ostensible pluralist climate still remained a high-risk enterprise. Thus, Rugova and his followers, who were operating in a repressive political environment, believed that a Gandhian strategy of passive resistance had certain appeals. Avoidance of aggressive tactics and violence was also seen as a rational necessity, and also a method of opposition that would attract international sympathy. The advent of party pluralism in Kosovo occurred during a period in which there was also a significant expansion in the size of Kosovo's Albanian nontechnical intelligentsia (see Table 4.2), largely because of the expansion in the province's educational system during the 1970s and 1980s (see also Chapter 1). The Serbs still maintained a disproportionately large number of jobs in the political system in managerial ranks, but there were now larger numbers of trained Albanians than ever before who were dissatisfied with such domination.

In December 1989, Rugova, along with like-minded Albanian leaders, took advantage of the somewhat broadened pluralist parameters in the province to establish the Democratic Alliance of Kosovo (LDK). The LDK rapidly increased its membership to approximately half a million members, and established an effective organizational network throughout Kosovo's Albanian community, and also among the large Albanian diasporic communities in

Europe and North America. By the time the regime in Belgrade had pushed through a new Serbian constitution and dissolved Kosovo's parliament, the LDK had become the major political force supported by Albanians. The principal goal of the LDK at this point was the creation of an autonomous "Kosovo Republic" within a reconfigured federal Yugoslav system.

But even as the Belgrade regime tightened its security over Kosovo, political development within the province's Albanian community moved forward rapidly. For example, on July 2, 1990, ethnic Albanian legislative deputies (most of whom were members of the LDK)—who effectively had been locked out of the technically dissolved Kosovo Assembly—met on the street outside their legislature and adopted a "Declaration" proclaiming Kosovo an independent unit within Yugoslavia. A few days later, the Belgrade regime suspended the legislature's operation and also the Kosovo government. In September 1990, deputies from the now dissolved Assembly met secretly at Kačanik and proclaimed a 140-article constitution of the "Sovereign Republic of Kosovo." They also adopted a law permitting citizens to organize themselves into political parties.

Meanwhile, a number of different Albanian party organizations and movements had sprung up in the province, including the Socialist Democratic Party, the Peasant Party, the Youth Parliament (which evolved into the Parliamentary Party of Kosovo), the Greens of Kosovo, and the Independent Trade Unions of Kosovo. Other parties would also emerge over the next several years. Noticeably absent from the new Albanian political landscape in Kosovo, however, were members of the former League of Communists, such as Azem Vllasi and Mahmut Bakali. While the spate of new parties differed in their specific programs and tactics, all of them, including the popular LDK, endorsed the idea that Kosovo should become politically independent. In September 1991, the politicians who had conceived the Kačanik Constitution a year earlier, adopted a new resolution on Kosovo's independence, and also organized a semi-clandestine plebiscite in the province. In the vote, held under the difficult conditions of Serbian police control, it was claimed that 87 percent of the eligible voters took part, and that over 99 percent of the Kosovar Albanians voting supported independence.[86] On October 18 independence was formally proclaimed, and Dr. Bujar Bukosi, a 43-year-old urologist living in Germany, was named prime minister. Believing itself to be the legitimate representative of the Albanian national movement in Kosovo, and faced with the strong-armed tactics of the regime in Belgrade, the LDK insisted that priority be placed on the question of the province's political status, rather than on democratization within Yugoslavia as a whole. Thus, most members of the new Albanian party elites saw little difference between the views of Slobodan Milošević on the Kosovo issue and the perspectives expressed by Serbian opposition parties on the same matter.

Table 4.2   The Ethnic Composition of Selected Intelligentsia Elites in Kosovo, 1981 (in percent)

			Elite Group			
	Governmental & Political	*Managerial*	*Technical Intelligentsia*	*Non-Technical Intelligentsia*	*Total Selected Intelligentsia*	*Total Population of Kosovo*
Ethnic Group						
Serbs	21.9	30.0	32.2	17.1	22.2	13.2
Montenegrins	6.5	7.3	5.5	5.3	5.6	1.7
Albanians	65.7	55.8	55.6	74.2	67.6	77.4
Other groups	5.9	6.9	6.7	3.4	4.6	7.7
Total (%)	100.0	100.0	100.0	100.0	100.0	100.0
(*n*)	(1022)	(3203)	(7292)	(19,266)	(30,783)	(1,584,440)

SOURCE: *Popis stanovništva, domaćinstava i stanova u 1981. Godini* (Belgrade: Savezni zavod za statistiku, 1984).

On the critical question of what political tactics needed to be employed in order to obtain independence, two broad and divergent approaches characterized the Albanian elite outlook during the first half of the 1990s. The first perspective was that of passive resistance, and the second, proactive mobilization. As president of the largest Kosovo party espousing what has been called a "radically peaceful option,"[87] Ibrahim Rugova became most closely associated with the idea of passive resistance as the path towards independence. His moderate and pragmatic approach gradually evolved into support for the creation of a UN protectorate over Kosovo, which would function as a transitional entity prior to independence. Rugova would ultimately see his proposal come to fruition, but only after excruciating twists and turns in the province's political development.

Rugova's background predisposed him to be both a passionate Albanian nationalist, and also an advocate of nonviolence. Rugova was born on December 2, 1944 in Crnce, a town in northwestern Kosovo. His family were Muslims, or as he puts it "symbolically Islamic," they were not practicing Muslims and did not attend a mosque. "The region I grew up in was always somewhere between Christianity . . . and paganism. Albanian culture was primarily Christian and European." His grandfather and father, who had worked with the nationalistic Albanian resistance, were arrested and executed by the security service of the communist regime immediately after World War II ended in the Balkans (his father was 27 years old at the time). Ibrahim was an only son raised by his mother in relative poverty. He did not begin elementary school until he was age nine. Rugova claims he was then a "Momma's boy." "My mother told me about my father (about his wisdom, gentleness, common sense,

nationalism), and in that way I remember him." The family's closeknit structure and traditional moral principles, Rugova claims, prevented them from
becoming "opportunistic communists." Certain "Albanian memories" from
this family setting would later influence his "national loyalty." For example,
he remembers his uncle singing and reciting stories to him from Albanian history, almost as school lessons. Rugova maintains that his family's nationalist
leanings would give him a "kind of legitimacy" among Kosovo Albanians,
although it was not the decisive factor in his future.

After graduating from secondary school in 1967, Rugova attended the
University of Priština. He graduated in 1971, and following his military service in Slovenia, taught Albanian studies in a village outside Priština.[88]
Although he was not one of the organizers of the 1968 student demonstrations
in the province, he took part in them. During the 1970s he drew his friends
from literary circles; groups he claimed that were "not nationalistic." Rather,
they were open towards the world and also towards Serbs, that is, "modern,
with a national orientation." During the period of 1976–1977 Rugova stud-
ied in France and after attending some lectures at the Sorbonne, claimed to
have become "contaminated with democracy." In 1986 he completed his doctoral thesis on Albanian Literary Criticism (1504–1983). After holding a number of jobs in journalism and literature Rugova became a literature professor.
At the time of the 1981 demonstrations he admits to have chosen books over
"action." It was only gradually through his literally work that Rugova claims
to have "invested his intellectual capacity in politics . . . in order to create better conditions for the people, and not as a political career." Indeed, Rugova's
image and demeanor even after he helped found the LDK in 1989 resembled
a West European intellectual dabbling in public affairs rather than a power-
seeking Balkan politician. A not particularly friendly, but very observant Belgrade interviewer, described Rugova in 1994 as wearing "a black suit and the
ever-present Bordeaux scarf whose ends are tucked into his red pullover
sweater. On his wrist . . . a gold watch à la Cartier, whose glamour is offset by
the ugly horned rimmed-glasses. He combs what little hair he has over the
crown of this head, he has a deep tan and his lips are broad and dark. His teeth
have not been cared for, which does not stop him from smiling frequently."[89]

For Rugova and his moderate intellectual followers the repressive political environment in which they found themselves during 1989 and 1990 neces-
sitated the adoption of a strategy that would gain international sympathy for
the Kosovars, but not invite an escalation of Serbian police pressure or an open
civil war. For those already disposed to this kind of thinking the restraint
shown by the Trepča miners in their February 1989 nonviolent protest made
a very strong impression. This was the background for the Kosovo variant of
a Gandhian strategy of passive resistance. Shkelzen Maliqi claims that Rugova

really did not initiate the Gandhian strategy, but rather accepted it as a sensible approach after it was more or less "spontaneously formulated" in Kosovo, and adopted by a new generation of intellectual leaders. In the "winter and spring of 1990," Maliqi points out, "there was a sudden and radical change. Warriors went out of fashion overnight . . . here were no major theoretical disputes, nor organized campaigns propagating nonviolence . . . [it] was somehow self imposed as the best, most pragmatic and most efficient response to Serbian aggressive plans." The new strategy, Maliqi also emphasizes, was antithetical to the Albanian tradition and political culture. "Albanian Gandhism came as a surprise not only to the Serbian military top ranks, but also to Albanians who could have hardly imagined themselves in that patriotic role. . . . The Albanians have never upheld values as nonviolence, patience, nonresponse to strikes and insults, sacrificing of national pride to economize with national forces etc."[90] Under the circumstances of Serbian occupation and repression, Maliqi explains, a time when Albanians had little space for political maneuver in any case, they wanted to show the world that they were better and more moral than the Serbs who oppressed them. In the spring of 1990 there was even a campaign to eradicate the infamous Albanian "blood feud" tradition in Kosovo. In a period of only several months about 2,000 Albanian families reached a reconciliation, thereby allowing some 20,000 people to escape earlier self-confinement in their homes in order to avoid being killed as the subject in a blood feud. Facing possible extermination by their Serbian occupiers, Maliqi suggests that the Kosovo reaction was "let's stop killing ourselves," and also accept taking a step towards adopting "Western civilization."[91]

Not all Kosovo's activists were enamored with passive resistance, nor for that matter with Ibrahim Rugova in the role of the Kosovo Gandhi. Not only did other moderate Albanian political organizations emerge during 1990–1991 as part of the new environment permitting party pluralism, but some individuals and groups favored a more activist brand of political engagement including armed political activity. The traditional "warrior" orientation of the Albanians may have temporarily gone out of fashion, but it certainly had not disappeared. The insurrectionist tradition was kept alive, if still only in a dormant posture, for example, by small unorganized underground groups in rural localities. A good portion of these Enverists were Marxist-Leninists (whose views at the time no longer had much appeal) who had been imprisoned during the 1980s and remained unsympathetic to Gandhi. But there were also other and newer constituencies supporting a more proactive orientation, including some elements who had substantial resources at their disposal. For example, many Albanians who lived abroad, and many of those who had emigrated during this period, harbored a desire for a more active method to confront the Serbian authorities. Most of the young Albanian men who had on their own initiative left Kosovo to fight against the Serbs in Croatia (1990–1991) and in Bosnia (1992–1995)—a group that would eventually number several thousand—also yearned to return to Kosovo to employ their newly honed combat skills. Many Albanians serving as officers in the Yugoslav military, often outside Kosovo, also shared that view (thereby becoming a special concern to Yugoslav military counter-intelligence). In fact, while an orientation of passive resistance prevailed within Kosovo, politically engaged Kosovar Albanians outside their native province—including intellectuals who had led the demonstrations during 1981 and had later escaped abroad—tended to express a far more proactive outlook.

During the second half of the 1990s, many of those supporting such a proactive stance would become the military nucleus of the Kosovo Liberation Army (KLA) or in Albanian, the *"Ushtria Clirimtare e Kosoves"* (UCK).[92] The UCK was first organized in 1993.[93] But it would be another half dozen years before the UCK, with NATO's assistance, would become the dominant polit-ical force in Kosovo (see Chapter 6). The full-blown emergence of the UCK would be the byproduct of growing dissatisfaction among Kosovar Albanians, and also new situational factors that influenced politics in the province during the late 1990s. Perhaps the most respected leader associated with the proac-tive wing in the Kosovo intelligentsia was Adem Demaci. Demaci had spent over 28 years in Yugoslav prisons for his nationalist activities, and became widely known as the "Kosovo Mandela." A writer, who was born in 1936, Demaci was first arrested in 1958 and served three years in jail. Released in 1961 he was re-arrested in 1964. Although out of jail for five months in 1974, he was soon once again incarcerated, this time until April 1990. Despite his long imprisonment, Demaci took a quite conciliatory tone following his release, and became head of the Kosovo Committee for the Protection of Human Rights and Freedom, formed in 1989. But Demaci expressed serious reservations regarding the Gandhian strategy supported by the popular LDK. In an interesting 1995 interview with an Albanian newspaper, Demaci describes a June 1991 conversation with Rugova and other Albanian leaders that took place during a car ride to Belgrade where they were to meet with U.S. Secretary of State James Baker. After telling his fellow intellectuals that, in his opinion the LDK and other parties would not achieve their goals unless they obtained control over the means of communication and schools in Kosovo, Demaci was asked by one fellow passenger how he was going to obtain that control without suffering a thousand causalities. "I don't know how you can make some political struggles without deprivations and sacrificing I told him . . . I think that 10,000 can die, and perhaps 20,000. Serbia is thinking seriously, while we are not showing and proving to Serbia and the world that we are thinking seriously . . . and the world will not take our concerns seri-ously and won't mediate or intervene to stop this wild Serbian enterprise [in

Kosovo]. I don't know how without sacrificing I can achieve the declaration [of independence] and the Kačanik Constitution."[94]

Demaci participated in demonstrations in June 1992, waged a 10-day hunger strike in May–June 1993, and another strike regarding schools in October 1993. All his activity was conducted, he has maintained, to demonstrate to the Serbian regime that Albanians were "thinking seriously." But he felt strongly that his own protests, and the entire potential of Albanian nationalism in the first half of the 1990's, were undermined by the LDK, and especially leaders he described as "careerists and mediocrities." As early as 1995 Demaci's main criticism was directed against Ibrahim Rugova, who in May 1992 had been elected president of the parallel state that established by the Albanians in Kosovo. In that election, Rugova, who ran unchallenged, won 99.7 percent of the votes cast. The 1992 election also included a legislative contest in which the LDK won 76 percent of the votes cast and a large majority of the seats.[95] In Demaci's opinion, the very features that helped prevent Rugova from becoming an authoritarian figure, also prevented him from being an effective leader. Rugova, claimed Demaci, had neither "the look, nor the appearance, nor the heart, nor the spirit of a dictator. He is a very docile and soft man, softer than cotton; no matter what's happened he hasn't raised his voice at anyone! He is so meek that he has allowed every responsibility to be lifted from his shoulders, just as Jesus Christ."[96] In Demaci's opinion, Rugova and his allies spent too much time "defending 'the legitimacy of the parallel system,'" and not enough energy confronting Serbian control of the province. The independent academic Rexhep Qosja would become another harsh critic of Rugova for his nonaction and failure to mobilize the Albanian resistance. According to Qosja, the spirit of the "national movement which has existed from the spring of 1990 [has become] closed up in offices . . . [what has been substituted] is party information, statements, press conferences, and other forms of verbalism!"[97]

Despite such criticisms of Rugova and the LDK, during the first half of the 1990s there was little support in Kosovo for a mass mobilization of Kosovar Albanians against Serbian power. The proactive stream in the Kosovo leadership was overshadowed by the strategy of passive resistance. At the same time Serbian police control prevented the Albanians from convening the parliament which they had elected in 1992. What political life there was among the Albanian population was dominated by Rugova's LDK. As one independent Albanian analyst noted "there is only a slight and quite unstable opposition," most of which came from intellectuals outside the larger Kosovo parties who had very little support.[98] Other political groups in Kosovo found it difficult to form a coherent organization with a broad appeal in the province. For example, Albanian activists were also divided regarding questions of ideology and tactics, not to mention segmentation along tribal and clan lines. Moreover, organizationally, the nascent UCK did not have a central command structure, although for such a subversive movement that situation might have constituted a definite advantage. However, the Albanian's parallel system led by Rugova, a formation which Demaci and others continued to rail against, did serve as an impressive demonstration of Albanian determination to peacefully delegitimize the Serbian administration of Kosovo. In effect a "segregated" or "apartheid" system was becoming institutionalized in the province. On the one side was the Serbian administration of the province that Albanians regarded as a classic example of "colonial" control or "annexation," and on the other side were subjugated Albanians. Thus, not only was the Kosovo governmental structure dissolved and replaced with Serbian organs of authority, but over 100,000 Albanians working in Kosovo's state sector—from managerial staff to office employees and blue collar workers—were discharged from their jobs.

By boycotting Serbian institutions, the Albanians established an elaborate network of governmental, economic, and social institutions. Self-organization, and self-financing in the areas of health care and education, were equally impressive in view of the large and rapidly growing Albanian population in the province. According to 1995 data, Albanian teachers, lecturers, professors and administrative and maintenance personnel were operating a parallel educational system that encompassed 185 preschool classes for over 5,000 pupils, 418 elementary school classes for over 300,000 students, 65 secondary schools for roughly 57,000 students, and 20 faculties and colleges for some 14,000 students. There were even two schools for handicapped children operating as part of this nonofficial network. In order to finance these activities Albanian workers within Kosovo, and in the diaspora, paid a monthly contribution from their wages.

But in both the educational and health areas the Kosovars faced tremendous economic difficulties and shortages that seriously detracted from the quality of the services provided.[99] As a result of such problems, and also the general political and economic situation, thousands of Kosovars emigrated from the province during the 1990s. An Albanian analyst of demographic changes in Kosovo during this period estimates that by 1994 there were approximately one million Albanians living in western countries, and that about one half had left Kosovo during the previous two decades (1974–1994).[100] Such immigration increased after 1991 when many younger Albanian men not wishing to fight in Croatia and Bosnia fled Yugoslavia. While the immediate goal of the younger generation was to obtain asylum, they also swelled the ranks of those supporting a more radical solution to the Kosovo "problem." Meanwhile, within Kosovo, communication between Albanians and Serbs had completely broken down. After 1988, Serbian republican authorities and the state media had fanned a "psychosis of threats," reinforcing Serb attitudes that perceived the Albanians as a "demographic time bomb," and center of terrorist resistance that needed to be contained through harsher measures. For their part, Albanians drifted into their parallel society, or fled abroad where they waited for a better moment and international assistance, to realize their goals. The climate in Kosovo at this point in time has aptly been characterized as a "sort of status quo based on the balance of fear."[101] For the moment, the Milošević regime in Serbia feared opening up another conflict, such as those occurring in Croatia and Bosnia, while the Kosovar Albanians feared embarking on a war strategy while they still remained militarily and organizationally inferior to the Serbs. Meanwhile a plethora of foreign proposals were floated concerning the best way to transcend such fear and nurture interethnic coexistence in the province. Unfortunately, most of the major political leaders on both sides of the ethnic divide were ill-disposed or ill-suited to break the stalemate.

NOTES

1. Predrag Simić, "Put u Rambuje," *NIN*, No. 2577 (May 18, 2000), and Warren Zimmerman, *Origins of a Catastrophe* (New York: Random House, 1996), pp. 16–20.

2. *Washington Post*, June 27, 1991. A U.S. State Department statement on May 24, 1991, issued on the instigation of the Secretary of State, had stipulated that "the U.S. will not encourage or reward secession."

3. See Milan St. Protić, *Causes of the Yugoslav Dissolution* (Belgrade: Center for Serbian Studies, no date).

4. Veljko Kadijević, *Moje vidjenje raspada* (Belgrade: Politika, 1993), pp. 9–22.

5. *Pravda*, February 20, 1993 in *BBCSWB*, East Europe, EE/1622/CI, February 25, 1993.

6. Borisav Jović, *Poslednji dani SFRJ* (Belgrade: Politika, 1995), p. 108.

7. In 1991, Serbs constituted approximately 12.2 percent of Croatia's population, and 31.4 percent of Bosnia.

8. *ONASA News Agency*, February 8, 2000. After Tudjman's death, it was reported that his successors had discovered a secret telephone link between his office in Zagreb and Miloševića's office in Belgrade. For an excellent account of the Bosnian war, see Stephen L. Burg and Paul Shoup, *The War in Bosnia–Herzegovina: Ethnic Conflict and International Intervention* (Armonk, New York: M.E. Sharpe, 1999). See also Branka Magaš and Ivo Žanić, *Rat u Hrvatskoj i Bosni i Hercegovini, 1991–1995* (London: The Bosnian Institute, 1999).

9. *Danas*, June 24 and 25, 2000.

10. *Slučaj Jugoslavije* (Podgorica, 2000). For rebuttal to Mamula's views on Serbian nationalism, see Boško Todorović and Dušan Vilić, *Slučaj Mamula* (Belgrade: Grafomark, 2001).

11. For example, by 1993, industrial production had dropped to 25 percent of the 1989 level. The level of unemployment was around 40 percent of the active workforce, and per capita income was some 40 percent of the level in 1989. Laslo Sekelj, "Učinak

sankcija saveta bezbednosti," in Miroslav Prokopijević and Jovan Teokarević (eds.), *Ekonomske sankcije UN: uporedna analiza i slučaj Jugoslavije* (Belgrade: Institut za Europske studije, 1998), p. 159.

12. See Obrad Kesić, "Defeating 'Greater Serbia,' Building Greater Milošević," in Constatine P. Danopoulos and Kostas G. Messas (eds.), *Crisis in the Balkans: Viewpoints from the Participants* (Boulder, Co.: Westview Press, 1997), pp. 60–65.

13. *Independent*, February 8, 1995, p. 12.

14. On the Holbrooke factor in the Bosnian crisis, see Michael Kelly, "The Negotiator," *New Yorker*, November 6, 1995, pp. 81–92, and Roger Cohen, "Taming the Bullies of Bosnia," *New York Times Magazine*, December 17, 1995, pp. 58–63, 76–78, 90–95.

15. Elaine Sciolino, "Clinton's Bosnia Stand: Political Risks Remain," *New York Times*, November 29, 1995, p. A12, and Thomas W. Lippman and Ann Devroy, "How Clinton Decided That U.S. Had to Lead in Balkans," *International Herald Tribune*, September 12, 1995, p. 1. The most detailed account of evolving U.S. views with respect to the Balkans during 1995 is David Halberstam, *War in a Time of Peace* (New York: Scribner, 2001).

16. Hrvoje Šarinić, *Svi moji tajni pregovori sa Slobodanom Miloševićem: Izmedju rata i diplomacije 1993–1995 (1998)* op. cit., passim.

17. Ofelija Backović, Miloš Vasić, and Aleksandar Vasović, "Mobilizacijska kriza, analitički pregled medijskog izveštavanja," *Republika*, No. 198–99 (October 1–31, 1998), pp. 11–22.

18. Branomir Anzulović, *Heavenly Serbia: From Myth to Genocide*, op. cit., pp. 23–31.

19. Radmila Radić, *Verom protiv vere: država i verske zajednice u Srbiji 1945–1953* (Belgrade: Institut za noviju istoriju Srbije, 1995).

20. Radmila Radić, "Srpska pravoslavna crkva u poratnim i ratnim godinama 1980–1985," *Republika*, Vol. 7, No. 121–122 (August 31, 1995), pp. 1–24. See also Sergej Flere, "Rasprostranjenost i prihvatanje pravoslavlja danas," in *Religija i društvo* (Zagreb: Centar za idejno-teorijski rad GKSKH, 1987), pp. 112–121.

21. Marinko Čulić, "Pastir svih Srba," *Danas*, No. 386 (July 11, 1989), p. 25.

22. Patriarch German interviewed in Milo Gligorijević, "Kosovo lekcije iz istorije," *NIN*, No. 2008 (Special Supplement), June 25, 1989, p. 5.

23. Patriarch Pavle interviewed in Milorad Vučelić (ed.), *Conversations with the Epoch* (Belgrade: Ministry of Information of the Republic of Serbia, 1991), p. 13.

24. Radio-Most, "Koliko je crkva doprinijela širenju nacionalizma?" November 22, 1998.

25. Yeshayahu Jelinik, "Clergy and Fascism: The Hlinka Party in Slovakia and the Croatian Ustasha Movement," in Stein Ugelvik Larson, *et al.* (eds.), *Who Were the Fascists: Social Roots of European Fascism* (Oslo: Universitetforlaget, 1980), pp. 369–372.

26. The Stepinac issue tended to overshadow the fact that the Catholic church hierarchy in Croatia had been positively influenced by the modernizing religious trends of the Second Vatican Council in the mid-1960s, generally expressed moderate perspectives on inter-religious matters, and also resisted establishing a close linkage with Croatia's noncommunist nationalist politicians.

27. There was also a strong SDS branch in Croatia.

28. Radmila Radić, "Srpska pravoslavna crkva u poratnim i ratnim godinama 1980–1985," op. cit., p. 24. See also, Milorad Tomanić, *Srpska crkva u ratu i ratovi u njoj* (Belgrade: Medijska knjižara krug, 2001).

29. *Independent*, June 15, 1992, p. 9.

30. *FBIS-EEU–94–178*, September 14, 1994, p. 57.

31. Karadžić interview with Paul Mojzes, "Confessions of a Serb Leader," *The Christian Century*, August 16, 1995.

32. *FBIS-EEU–95–009*, January 13, 1995, p. 43.

33. On August 7, 1995, after Croatian troops recaptured the Krajina area, Patriarch Pavle and the Holy Synod of Bishops of the Serbian Orthodox Church condemned the Milošević regime: "With its power-hungry actions and self-serving attitude, this same leadership trampled on all promises and guarantees it gave to the Serbian Krajina, and led the nation into a blind alley."

34. *Agence France-Presse*, December 23, 1995.

35. Mladen Dinkić, *Ekonomija destrukcije*, op. cit.

36. *Belgrade TV*, May 28, 1992 in *BBCSWB*: Part 2 Eastern Europe, B. Internal Affairs; Yugoslavia; EE/1395/C1, June 1, 1992.

37. Svetlana Adamović, "Efforts Towards Economic Recovery and Monetary Stabilisation in FR Yugoslavia," *Communist Economies and Economic Transformation*, Vol. 7, No. 4 (1995), pp. 529, 532.

38. Dragoslav Avramović, *Pobeda nad inflacijom 1994* (Belgrade: Institut društvenih nauka, 1998), and *Situation Analysis of Women and Children in the Federal Republic of Yugoslavia* (Belgrade: UNICEF, March 1998).

39. Mladen Lazić, "Resistance to Structural Changes in Yugoslav Society: Post-Socialist Transformation and Social Groups," Unpublished paper, 1999.

40. The new Federal Republic of Yugoslavia had a land surface of 102,173 square kilometers and 10,524,000 inhabitants, 44,000 of whom lived in Montenegro, and 9,880,000 in Serbia (including 2,103,889 in Vojvodina and 1,956,196 in Kosovo). Ethnically, Serbs comprised 63.3 percent of the total population, Montenegrins 5 percent, Albanians 16.6 percent, Muslims 3.3 percent, Hungarians 3.1 percent, Croats 1.1 percent, and Romanies 1.3 percent. All other national groups accounted for 6.3 percent of the population. The urban population was roughly 47 percent, and 76.1 percent of the population worked outside agriculture.

41. Stevan Lilić, *The Unbearable Lightness of Constitutional Being* (Belgrade: Yugoslav Association of Constitutional Law), 1995.

42. *BBCSWB*: Part 2 Eastern Europe, B. Internal Affairs; Yugoslavia, EE/1337/C1, March 24, 1992.

43. Milošević had expanded the already considerable semi-presidential powers he enjoyed by means of a 1991 law expanding the reasons for which a state of emergency could be introduced. Kosta Čavoški, *Half a Century of Distorted Constitutionality in Yugoslavia* (Belgrade: Center for Serbian Studies, 1997).

44. Dobrica Ćosić, "Istorijska prekretnica za srpski narod," in Milorad Vučelić (ed.), *Razgovori sa epohom* (Novi Sad: Politika, 1992), p. 48.

45. *Danas*, January 6–9, 2000.

46. *Washington Post*, June 20, 2000, p. A23.

47. Milan Nikolić, *Šta je stvarno rekao Dobrica Ćosić* (Belgrade: Draganić, 1995), p. 236.

48. Dragislav Rančić, *Dobrica Ćosić ili predsednik bez vlasti* (Belgrade: Art studio 'Crno na belo,' 1994).

49. Svetozar Stojanović, *Autoritet bez vlasti: Dobrica Ćosić kao šef države* (Belgrade: Filip Višnjić, 1993).

50. *Yugoslav News Agency*, October 13, 1992.

51. On Milošević's political machinations to get around constitutional restrictions limiting his ability to personally organize and set the date of the election see Kosta Čavoški, "Overstepping the Limits," in Mijat Damjanović, Stevan Vračar, and Ljubomir Madjar (eds.), *Democracy to Come* (Belgrade: Magna, 1997), pp. 106–107.

52. *Milan Corriere della Sera*, July 8, 1999, p. 11 as translated in *FBIS*, West Europe, East Europe, July 8, 1999.

53. Douglas E. Schoen, "How Milošević Stole the Election," *New York Times Magazine*, February 14, 1993. When U.S. Secretary of State Lawrence Eagleburger referred to Milošević as a war criminal, it allowed the Serbian president to portray himself as a victim of Western aggression (it would be another six years before Milošević was charged formally with such crimes).

54. Vladimir Goati, *Izbori u SRJ od 1990 do 1998*, op. cit., pp. 55–56 and 115–117.

55. Svetozar Stojanović, *Autoritet bez vlasti: Dobrica Ćosić kao šef države*, op. cit., p. 56.

56. Milan Nikolić, *Šta je stvarno rekao Dobrica Ćosić*, op. cit., p. 240.

57. "Demokratija u Srbiji-stvarno i moguće," in S. Antonić, *et al.* (eds.) *Srbija izmedju populizma i demokratije* (Belgrade: Institut za političke studije, 1993), pp. 153–211.

58. "Demokratija i političke elite u Srbiji" (1994), unpublished manuscript, and "Research on the Serbian Elite," *VND*, No. 251 (July 29, 1996), pp. 7–16.

59. *VND*, No. 232 (March 18, 1996), p. 69.

60. "The Anti-Reformist Elite," *VND*, No. 373 (November 30, 1998), pp. 22–25.

61. "Nule u eliti," *Naša Svetlost*, 1998, p. 120.

62. See Slavoljub Djukić, *On, ona, i mi*, op. cit.

63. *Washington Post*, January 15, 1997, p. D1.

64. The joint left-wing coalition—SPS–JUL–ND—listed only 13 women candidates, about 5 percent for the September 1997 Serbian parliamentary election).

65. *Razrešnica* (Belgrade: Res publica, 1999).

66. See, for example, Ljiljana Habjanović-Djurović, *Srbija pred ogledalom*, op. cit.

67. *Inter Press Service*, May 20, 1997.

68. *Naša Borba*, September 8, 1997. *Inter Press Service*, September 4, 1997.

69. *Globus*, November 1, 1996, p. 1.

70. *NIN*, March 21, 1997.

71. *BETA*, July 22, 1999, *FBIS-EEU–1999–0722*.

72. *Inter Press Service*, May 20, 1997.

73. Ljiljana Habjanović-Djurović, *Srbija pred ogledalom*, op. cit., p. 81.

74. *Intervju*, No. 409 (June 6, 1997).

75. Milovan Djilas, *Fall of the New Class: A History of Communism's Self-Destruction* (New York: Alfred A. Knopf, 1998), pp. 151–152.

76. "Old and New Elites in Serbia," in Dušan Janjić (ed.), *Serbia Between the Past and the Future* (Belgrade: Institute of Social Sciences, Forum on Ethnic Relations, 1995), pp. 45–50, and "Preobražaj ekonomske elite," in M. Lazić, *et al.* (eds.), *Razaranje društva* (Belgrade: Filip Višnjić, 1994), pp. 119–149.

77. Research indicates that within regime local elites, modest social origins are far more prevalent than among higher level officials working for the SPS and Milošević regime. For example, of 29 local SPS leaders for which this data was available, 51 percent of the fathers were peasants, 17 percent workers, and only 31 percent were in non-manual occupations. This finding may reflect the Milošević regime's traditional strength in agrarian areas, and also suggests the possibility that modest background may somehow be an impediment to advancement to the highest levels of the SPS.

78. Srećko Mihailović, cited in Vladimir Goati, "Socijalni sastav partija u 'Trećoj Jugoslaviji,'"in *Ciljevi i putevi društva u tranziciji* (Belgrade: Institut društvenih nauka, 1996), p. 260.

79. *NIN*, No. 2264 (May 20, 1994), p. 14.

80. Vladimir Milanović has argued that there is no real differentiation or competition within Yugoslavia's regime or power elite because all of those recruited into that elite are "absorbed by it," and become part of a closed circle whose members are rotated from one position to another. The same person can reappear "with high military rank, as a diplomat, as a business manager, as an administrator of all kinds of institutions, as a member of the government, or even a member of the Academy of Sciences. The position and the reputation of such a person do not depend on his personal abilities and his success in public matters. . . . Members of the power elite, except for rare cases, do not cling to one profession. . . . Scientists who are used by the power elite either leave their professions or stay in their power positions for a very short time. The members of the power elite are getting de-professionalized and de-intellectualized." "The Power Elite in Yugoslav Society," *Sociološke Studije, III, Društvene Promene i Postsocijalizam, Zbornik Radova* (1993), pp. 213–219.

81. It is possible that the proportion of opposition leaders who were politically active in the old regime may have dropped over the last few years, and also that some opposition leaders chose not to report such associations. Thus, Slobodan Antonić has established that out of 122 deputies from opposition parties in the 1993 Serbian Assembly, 97 had been members of the League of Communists before 1990, and about one-third of those individuals had been in leading positions in the League. "Demokratija i političke elite u Srbiji," (1994), unpublished manuscript, p. 5.

82. Šešelj admits that for a short time he was an "honest and convinced communist, but very sensitive when it came to Moslem fundamentalists." *BETA*, July 23, 1997.

83. A useful discussion detailing the reasons for the political weakness of the opposition in Serbia is Ognjen Pribičević, *Vlast i opozicija* (Belgrade: Radio B–92, 1997), pp. 34–51.

84. *Naša Borba*, August 3, 1997. Šešelj claims that his Radicals are not fascists but rather are "chauvinists and hated the Croats." *BETA*, September 8, 1997. The leader of a breakaway faction of the Radical Party, who formed the "Radical Party–Nikola Pašić," has recently attacked his former compatriots in a book entitled "How the Communists Milošević and Šešelj Defeated the Serbs." Jovan Glamočanin, *Kako su komunisti Milošević i Šešelj porazili Srbe* (Pančevo: Banjac-Print, 1997).

85. Shkelzen Maliqi, "Self-Understanding of the Albanian in Non-Violence," op. cit., p. 271.

86. Miranda Vickers, *Between Serbs and Albanians: A History of Kosovo*, op. cit., p. 251

87. Interview with Shkelzen Maliqi in *Globus*, April 19, 1999, pp. 17–18 in *FBIS-EEU–1999–0420*, April 9, 1999.

88. This paragraph is mainly drawn from the interview materials in "Ibrahim Rugova," in Momčilo Petrović, *Pitao sam*, op. cit., pp. 247–258 and *BETA*, May 12, 1999.

89. *Duga*, October 1–14, 1994, pp. 18–23.

90. Shkelzen Maliqi, "Self-Understanding of the Albanian in Non-Violence," op. cit., pp. 238–241.

91. Ibid., p. 242.

92. OVK in Serbian.

93. Interview with Sabri Kicmari, foreign representative of the Kosovo Liberation Army in *Berlin Tageszeitung*, March 1999 in *FBIS-WEU–1999–0304*, March 4, 1999 and interview with Shkelzen Maliqi in *Globus*, April 19, 1999, pp. 17–18 in *FBIS-EEU–1999–0420*, April 9, 1999. Some claim that the final UCK cells were formed in 1992. For example, Fehim Redzepi in *Monitor*, July 3, 1994, pp. 25–27 in *FBIS-EEU–98–209* and interview with UCK leader "Skender" in *Slobodna Bosna*, July 15, 1998 in *FBIS-EEU–98–023*.

94. "Adem Demaci," in Momčilo Petrović, *Pitao sam*, op. cit., p. 271

95. In the legislative election, 511 candidates from 22 parties took part. The LDK won 96 seats, the Parliamentary Party of Kosovo 13 seats, the Farmers' Party of Kosovo 7, the Albanian Christian Democratic Party 7, and independent candidates took 2 seats. Three seats were also awarded to 2 Muslims, but 14 such assigned seats—for Serbs and Montenegrins remained vacant. Zoran Lutovac, "The Participation of Minorities in Political Life," in Vladimir Goati (ed.), *Elections to the Federal and Republican Parliaments of Yugoslavia (Serbia and Montenegro) 1990–1996* (Berlin: Sigma, 1998), p. 128.

96. Momčilo Petrović, *Pitao sam*, op. cit., pp. 272–273.

97. "Redzep Cosja," in Ibid., p. 108.

98. Shkelzen Maliqi, *AIM*, Priština, January 3, 1996.

99. The healthcare system in Kosovo's parallel society was particularly hard hit. Miranda Vickers, *Between Serbs and Albanians: A History of Kosovo*, op. cit., p. 262.

100. Hivzi Islami, "Demographic Realities of Kosovo," in Dušan Janjić and Shkelzen Maliqi, *Conflict or Dialogue*, op. cit., p. 51.

101. Shkelzen Maliqi, *AIM*, Priština, October 7, 1996.

PART III
TWILIGHT OF THE MILOŠEVIĆ REGIME

CHAPTER 5

The Politics of Hope and Despair:
1995–1998

The leaders of our political parties, perhaps with the exception of two or three people, are individuals without experience, people without biographies, people who come down from the trees and jumped into the saddle. They don't know how to behave, they don't care about a program, they don't wish to learn because they all more or less feel like messiahs, but only those who are unwell declare themselves to be messiahs.

—Desimir Tošić,
President of the Serbian European Movement

The reason we participate and support these [1996–1997] demonstrations is not our support of the opposition leaders. It is not only that they are nationalistic, but they are also ignorant, without experience, greedy, authoritarian, craving for power. . . . We support each other. . . . We support the people who are liberating themselves from fear.

—Bojan Aleksov, self-proclaimed
"anti-authoritarian" demonstrator

By the onset of 1996, Slobodan Milošević had already been in power for almost a decade and his checkered record of performance was being more clearly perceived by his countrymen. Milošević's initial program of unrepentant nationalism and reworked state socialism, which had successfully resonated with the Serbian public during the late 1980s and even the early 1990s, no longer held its strong appeal. It had become apparent to most Serbs—and especially young people whose adolescent years paralleled Milošević's tenure—that in stoking the fire of Serbian nationalism, and thereby encouraging the reactive nationalism of non-Serb ethnic groups, Milošević had helped to precipitate communist Yugoslavia's disintegration, and also the bloodshed and economic deterioration that followed in its wake. For most Serbs the results were disastrous.

Not only had Milošević failed to unify the Serbs of Serbia, Croatia, and Bosnia into an enlarged state (though he did manage to form a rump Yugoslav state from Serbia and Montenegro), but adverse international reaction had forced Milošević's Serbia into the position of an isolated pariah entity; a country shunned by most other states and subjected to debilitating UN economic sanctions (1992–1995).[1] Over time, the living standard of the two republics in the "new Yugoslavia" declined to levels experienced decades earlier, but now within an economy affected by cycles of hyper-inflation, mass unemployment and underemployment (by fall 1996, well over 50 percent), widespread corruption, Mafia-like gangs, and a slide into poverty for roughly one-third of its nearly eleven million inhabitants. This economic disaster, which seriously eroded the position of Serbia's middle class, was further complicated by an influx of thousands of destitute Serb refugees from Bosnia and Croatia, and also the outflow of thousands of young Serbian professionals. Meanwhile, in Kosovo, which technically remained part of Serbia, the Serb ethnic community, including members of the large security apparatus in the province, lived in virtual segregation from the Albanian majority. The enormous cost of Serbian police control over the politically troubled province was an additional drain on the republic's already deteriorated economy. At the same time, the socio-economic and political activity of Kosovo's Albanians, who were closely tied to the more prosperous diasporic Albanian communities, occurred largely within the province's "parallel" state and societal structure.

As early as late 1992 and the beginning of 1993, Milošević had begun to tone down his nationalist program in an effort to recast himself as an icon of peace and reconciliation. The atrocities committed by Serb paramilitary forces in Bosnia, which he had previously armed and coordinated, had become a major embarrassment to Milošević. Bosnian Serb political and military leaders had also been growing more self-confident, and less responsive to routine direction from Belgrade. Moreover, Milošević also badly needed the lifting of international sanctions if he was to have any chance of reversing the deterioration of the Yugoslav economy. Granted the imposition of sanctions provided Milošević with a scapegoat for the existing economic problems (many of which were due to non-sanction related factors such as the loss of previous markets deriving from the collapse of Titoist Yugoslavia, spillover costs from the nearby wars, etc.). But the potential lifting of the sanctions would allow Milošević to portray himself as a successful statesman, who could proceed with the building of the "wealthy" society he had promised the Serbs. Fortunately for Milošević, by 1995 American officials, desperate not to let the war in Bosnia derail President Clinton's 1996 presidential campaign, viewed him (and his counterpart in Croatia, Franjo Tudjman) as crucial to the adoption of a Bosnian peace agreement.

As early as the 1992 Panić–Milošević electoral contest for president of Serbia, U.S. Secretary of State Eagleburger had described Milošević as a "war criminal." But though many international officials already recognized Milošević's substantial direct and indirect responsibility for the violent disintegration of Yugoslavia, and the atrocities that occurred in Croatia and Bosnia, and also agreed that Serbia–Montenegro should continue to be pressed by some form of sanctions, it was also well accepted conventional wisdom during 1993 and 1994 that the Yugoslav leader's cooperation would be an essential ingredient in reaching a Bosnian peace agreement. As a candidate for president in 1992, Clinton had mildly criticized the handling of Balkan affairs by the Bush administration, and termed Milošević the head of a "renegade regime."[2] But once elected to office, Clinton moved cautiously in the area of foreign affairs, and regarded Milošević as part of a solution to Balkan unrest. Thus, throughout most of the mid-1990s, Milošević was considered by the United States, and the bulk of the international community, as a potential partner for peace in the Balkans, and not as an intractable foe of democracy and stability. For example, writing later about his initial meeting with Milošević in August 1995, Richard Holbrooke described him as the "key actor in this stage of the drama . . . this would be my first meeting with a man who, in our view, bore the heaviest responsibility for the war. . . . Our most important point concerned whom we would negotiate with. The United States . . . would never again deal with the Bosnian Serbs." Holbrooke implored Milošević to serve as a broker: "you must speak for Pale [the Bosnian Serb capital] . . . we won't deal with them ever again."[3] As discussed in the last chapter, Holbrooke's plan to utilize Milošević had worked very effectively. At Dayton, in November 1995, Milošević's concessions and cooperation in brokering a peace deal won him a partial end to the sanctions against Serbia–Montenegro (an "outer wall" blocking ties to international financial institutions remained). As a result, in the momentary exultation celebrating the end of the war, Milošević obtained a short period to catch his breath, and appear as an internationally respected statesman. Even opposition leader Vuk Drašković was impressed: "Milošević is good with the Americans. He uses one point: 'maybe I'm not good, but compared to other nationalists in Serbia, I'm a real Thomas Jefferson.'"[4]

However, behind the outward appearance of cooperation between the international community and Milošević, the attitude toward the Serbian president was beginning to change. The Dayton agreement, for example, called for a thorough investigation into the issue of war crimes committed in Bosnia. And while only Bosnian Serb leaders Radovan Karadžić and Ratko Mladić were charged in July 1996 by the UN's War Crimes Tribunal for genocide and other crimes connected with their roles in the Bosnian war, the tribunal had already reputedly been secretly gathering evidence against Milošević for some time.[5]

For example, it was reported that in October 1995, prior to the Dayton conference, U.S. intelligence agencies had taped several telephone conversations between top commanders of the Yugoslav military and the Bosnian Serb forces that involved planning for the Bosnian Serb assault against Srebrenica, an operation which ultimately led to the disappearance of probable death of thousands of Bosnian Muslim civilians.[6] Moreover, at the same time it indicted Bosnian Serb leaders for war crimes, the UN tribunal called publicly for an investigation to determine whether Milošević shared responsibility for war crimes committed in Bosnia. In fact, Milošević's name was not publicly used by the tribunal's officials to describe the efforts of the Bosnian Serbs to establish a state through the use of violence. But it was implied that the highest level of the political and military command structure in Serbia, namely Milošević, was responsible for directing Bosnian Serb policy. Thus, although it would be another three years before he would be indicted for charges of war criminality, Milošević's room for maneuver with the members of the international community was becoming increasingly narrower.[7]

The attention and warm praise for Milošević from foreign diplomats during the negotiation of the Dayton peace accords for Bosnia allowed the Serbian leader to temporarily appear as a constructive actor on the international stage. His image as a peace-maker and world statesman also gave him some help in garnering domestic support among certain segments of the Serbian population during 1996. But Milošević's moment of triumph at Dayton was a false high at most. He could no longer ask the citizens of Serbia to patiently and patriotically accept the dismal economic and social situation in Serbia caused by warfare in a neighboring region. Moreover for many Serbs, Milošević had become at best a failed hero, and at worst a scoundrel responsible for betraying national goals, and causing economic misery.[8] Anticipating federal and local elections in the fall, the opposition forces tried yet again to coalesce, this time forming the so-called *Zajedno* coalition. By the beginning of September, three major opposition parties had joined *Zajedno*: Vuk Drašković's SPO, Zoran Djindjić's Democratic Party, and Vesna Pešić's GSS (and eventually the more nationally oriented DSS of Vojislav Koštunica). But Milošević's unmatched skill at electoral chicanery (that included an electoral system favoring the ruling party), his reservoir of hard-core support (particularly in rural and southern Serbia), and the regime's claim that it had substantially ended international sanctions did allow the SPS to handily win the early November 1996 elections for the Yugoslav Federal Assembly. In the November 1996 election, 108 of the 138 seats in the Chamber of Citizens of the Federal Assembly were elected within Serbia. The left coalition (SPS–JUL–ND) received 64 seats (59.3 percent), based on 45 percent of the vote in Serbia; the *Zajedno* coalition received 22 seats (20.4 percent) based on 23.8 percent of the vote. Šešelj's Radicals got 16 seats (15 percent) and 19 percent of the votes.[9]

But the outcome of the federal elections masked the extent of popular dissatisfaction in Serbia, and the dangerous polarization that had emerged between the regime and much of the public, particularly in urban areas. In the first round of balloting in the local elections—also held on November 3—no majority party emerged in 188 municipalities, thereby triggering another round of voting in those places two weeks later. The real political climate in the country became more apparent on November 17, when Serbs voted in the second round of the local elections. Thus, although many citizens of Serbia may have been reconciled, or saw little alternative, to Milošević's control of federal or "high politics," a substantial portion of the voting population used the local elections as an opportunity to vent their grievances against the more routine tribulations of daily existence, and also the abuses of Socialist Party leaders who did not have Milošević's political stature. Moreover, the *Zajedno* coalition proved to be far more effective in electoral contests on the local level than in the contest for the federal legislature. It was this background that provided the basis for impressive opposition victories at the second round of local elections. Out of 188 municipalities in Serbia, the SPS won 144, but astonishingly the parties in the *Zajedno* opposition coalition won control of 41 municipalities (21 percent of the municipalities in the republic), including Belgrade and over a dozen Serbian cities (Šešelj's SRS won control in the municipality of Zemun). The municipalities won by *Zajedno* accounted for 35.4 percent of Serbia's population, 50 percent of the employed workforce, and 63 percent of the employees with a higher education.[10]

Serbia's Civic Rebellion (1996–1997): The Failed
Rise of a Counter-elite

For Milošević, the political loss of Yugoslavia's capital city and other important localities constituted a serious challenge to his power, threatening the potential loss of his control over local media outlets, not to mention a possible investigation into SPS rule on the local level. Seriously concerned that the electoral outcome was the first stage of a groundswell that could drive him from power, Milošević arranged for local courts to annul most of the electoral results. His action quickly provoked large demonstrations by disaffected citizens in Belgrade and elsewhere. In Belgrade, protesters hurled eggs at the building of the Belgrade City Assembly and Serbian Radio and Television. Student protests also began in Belgrade and Niš. By the beginning of December, the daily mass protests concerning the annulment of the electoral results had burgeoned into a full-blown civic rebellion against the regime. As foreign media attention to the demonstrations grew, protest leaders became more self-confident, and willing to experiment with new tactics. The demonstrations acquired a carnival-like atmosphere with sound and visual effects, flags, and street theatre presentations. The protests extended into the first months of 1997 (the broader Civic Protest ended on February 15, and the student demonstrations on March 20, after 119 days), and Milošević was eventually pressured into recognizing the local electoral victories of the opposition coalition. Thus, on February 11, 1997, the Serbian assembly adopted a "special law" (*Lex Specialis*), which recognized the results of the November 17, 1996 election. But the broader goals of the protest movement—the resignation of Milošević and the end of political control by his left wing coalition—would not be fulfilled.

Etiology of a Protest

Although the protests that politically convulsed Serbia from November 1996 to the spring of 1997 ended in mixed results, the episode raised a number of important questions concerning Serbian politics. Who were the participants in the protests, and who were their leaders? What was the relationship between the civic rebellion and the "established" centrist and moderate opposition elite sectors? What impact, if any, did the protest have on Serbian political culture and Serbian political development?

As noted above, the 1996–1997 protests in Serbia began as part of the general reaction to Milošević's annulment of the local electoral results. The top leaders of the centrist and moderate opposition parties in the *Zajedno* coalition—and particularly Vesna Pešić, Zoran Djindjić, and Vuk Drašković—became the initial leaders of what was soon termed the "egg revolution," or the "civic rebellion." But as the protests acquired momentum, and the mass rallies grew in size, two other protesting groups, namely, students and university professors, also acquired significance in what was assuming the character of a general anti-regime movement. During the demonstrations, the three parallel components of the protest movement—opposition parties, students, and professors—worked relatively closely together. However, the protests by the students and professors spawned a new and younger anti-regime leadership subgroup, or counter-elite, which clearly wished to bring about the collapse of the existing regime, and a fundamental shift in the direction of Serbian political life. Many leaders and participants in the student protests were also dissatisfied with the established centrist and moderate opposition parties, most of which were headed by political figures who had first achieved prominence during the 1970s and 1980s, and had gone on to play major political roles in the multiparty system of the 1990s. The student protesters had a largely nonparty orientation and composition, and together with the professors (who organized the Initiative Board for the Defense of Democracy at Belgrade University), and the thousands of other citizens of Serbia who joined the daily demonstrations—including poverty-stricken pensioners, teachers, other former members of the impoverished middle class, and a small contingent of industrial workers—constituted a new and broad socio-political movement.

Generally speaking, the counter-elite of student leaders and activist professors sought to achieve goals that went well beyond the aim of the *Zajedno* opposition leadership. The pragmatic concern of the *Zajedno* party leaders was to consolidate their electoral gains, and to wrest control of Belgrade and other cities from the regime. In order to achieve the goal of taking local power, *Zajedno's* leaders appeared, at least initially, somewhat willing to cooperate with the regime elite in order to facilitate the kind of political transition in Yugoslavia that would involve real power sharing between the ruling party and the established opposition party organizations. For example, in December 1996, Djindjić told an interviewer that "it would be easier to restore the economy together with Milošević because you would not have to overthrow the regime, you could reform it from within. But he has been deaf to all our offers on our side and now it is too late for him."[11] In contrast to the opposition party elites, the student leaders and their professorial allies not only wanted their specific grievances within the educational sector to be addressed, but also sought a much deeper and rather incoherently formulated "transformation" of Serbian society. The student leadership generally ridiculed Milošević and his ruling party comrades, and seemed to have little interest in conducting business as usual with the regime elites. The notion of democratic transition as a "pact" resulting from a process of prolonged negotiation and even coalition formation between the reform segments of an authoritarian regime, and a pragmatic opposition leadership, appeared completely foreign to the student leaders and their followers. For the student demonstrators, political change in Serbia was viewed, more or less, as a zero-sum game (a view reciprocated by the hard-liners or "stand-patters" within the regime elite)[12] but not shared by the more seasoned opposition party leaders at the head of *Zajedno*.

One of the most interesting subgroups in the 1996–1997 protest movement was composed of thousands of young people, both within Serbia and abroad, who used the Internet, not only to disseminate accurate news about the unfolding events, which proved exceptionally important when Milošević attempted to shut down the opposition media, but also to encourage the protesters on the streets in Belgrade to continue with their demonstrations, and to directly participate in the discussions of the movement's objectives and potential. Constituting a kind of "wired" or "digital" elite, the Internet users broadened the scope and impact of the protest movement, and encouraged external actors (both NGOs and governments) to keep up pressure on Milošević. It has been estimated that around 10,000 out of roughly ten million people in Yugoslavia had personal computers in 1997, and an even smaller number utilized the Internet.[13] One of the most active segments of the digital elite were diasporic Serbs, most of whom were part of the exodus or brain drain of talent that left Serbia during the 1990s (an estimated 300,000 to 400,000 people, aged 25 to 40, have left since 1991, 35,000 holding university degrees).[14] For example, one report claims that in 1992 alone—the first year of the war in Bosnia—approximately 1,000 members of the Belgrade University staff left Serbia, and that in 1992 and first six months of 1993, 420 researchers from Belgrade's Institute of Electronics emigrated).[15]

The core of the protest movement was not, however, found in cyberspace, but was located on the streets of Belgrade. By January 1997, studies reported that approximately 700,000 adults had taken part in the protest movement, and that between 80,000 and 120,000 people were attending protests every day. Research on the social profile and attitudes of the demonstrators carried out by analysts at the Institute for Sociological Research at Belgrade's Faculty of Philosophy revealed that approximately 30 percent of those participating in the demonstrations were in the 20–29 age group, 23 percent were in their 40s, 14.5 percent were in their 50s, and 13.4 percent were in their 60s. Roughly 48 percent of the demonstrators had a secondary school background, and 46 percent had a higher education. Although city dwellers made up 92 percent of the protesters, only about 8 percent were industrial workers.[16] The fear by most workers that should they participate in demonstrations they might lose the meager salaries which they still enjoyed, along with the weakness of the trade union movement, and the regime's effort to portray itself as representing the working class, were all important reasons for the low participation of blue-collar laborers in the demonstrations. The proportion of men and women in the overall protest movement was about the same. However, research on the student portion of the movement reveals that there was only one woman out of 11 members serving on the Initiative Council of the Student Protest. But 30 percent of the members of the Main Council, representing students from all faculties were women.[17] In many respects, the 1996–1997 civic rebellion was an urban, middle-class revolt; that is, students joined by their parents and grandparents who were often unemployed or retired from their non-manual jobs (70 percent in the cities). But while an urban phenomenon, the protests were not limited to Belgrade. Thus by early January 1997, the demonstrations had spread to another 46 towns in Serbia. Many localities which were the site of opposition demonstrations, such as Niš, Kragujevac, Kraljevo and Pirot, had traditionally been "red cities" won by the SPS, and southern Serbian strongholds crucial to Milošević's power base. The municipalities won by

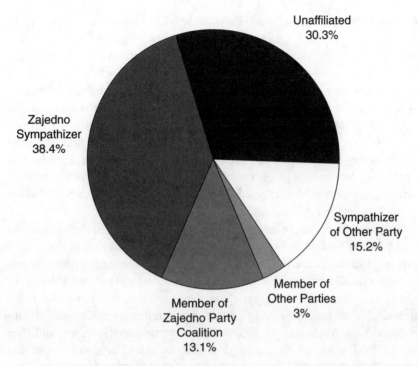

Unaffiliated
30.3%

Zajedno
Sympathizer
38.4%

Sympathizer
of Other Party
15.2%

Member of
Other Parties
3%

Member of
Zajedno Party
Coalition
13.1%

Figure 5.1   Political Orientation of Demonstrators in 1996–1997 Protests

Zajedno were localities containing 35.4 percent of Serbia's population, four university centers, a majority of industries and banks in the republic, and were centers conducting nearly all of Yugoslavia's foreign trade.[18]

Research on the political views of the protesters is equally interesting. Only 13 percent of the demonstrators claimed to be members of the centrist and moderate parties in the *Zajedno* coalition (12 percent of the men, 4.6 percent of the women), although 38 percent said they were sympathetic to those parties. Approximately 30 percent were neither members nor sympathizers of any party, and nearly 20 percent had never before protested in the streets. In the main, the protesters had an anti-regime orientation, but were not closely tied to the established opposition parties (see Figure 5.1).

Approximately 17 percent of the protesters claimed to be former supporters of Milošević, but 89 percent of the demonstrators surveyed claimed that he had done nothing useful in his career, and only 6.7 percent believed he had made a positive contribution by awakening national awareness. Still, only 40 percent said that one of their main goals was to remove Milošević from power, and just 3.9 percent said they had shouted slogans supporting the leaders of *Zajedno*. Overall, the findings suggest that the bulk of the demonstrators were simply fed up with the regime, and that Milošević's annulment of the local elections provided a pretext for their decision to protest. Clearly it was not a leaderless protest movement, but the demonstrators were not deeply committed to the established opposition party leaders, nor did they yet have strong attachments to the younger student activists who emerged on the scene in order to assist in coordinating the daily marches. Much of the anti-regime population in urban Serbia was voting with its feet, but beyond a general notion of "freedom," a desire for fundamental change in the societal situation (i.e., a "more secure future," a "better standard of living," "career advancement"), and recognition of the annulled electoral results, few of the demonstrators endorsed a particular political program or a team of leaders that might replace Milošević's left-wing coalition.

The research findings also indicate that only 8.3 percent of the participants in the protests held explicitly nationalist orientations, and that those respondents were mainly men. But interestingly, while 89 percent of the students among the protesters surveyed declared an "openness towards the world," 42 percent accepted the notion that "one needs to be cautious toward other nations," and 36 percent were against granting autonomy to Kosovo's Albanian population. Moreover, 47 percent of the participants surveyed said they placed a "high value" on the authority of a leader, and 43 percent believed that the most important consideration for the success of a group is "an energetic and righteous leader." Such attitudes may have reflected the diminishing residue of traditional patriarchal impulses often observed in Serbian political culture (see Chapter 2); a mindset that had routinely provided fertile soil for strong, demagogic, and authoritarian political leaders. There remained a danger, however, that in the future such views regarding leadership, and a suspicion toward non-Serbs, would continue to be manipulated by emergent elites or some new leader to again divert Serbia from a democratic course of development.

Leaders of the student protests, and others who sympathized with the civic rebellion, claimed that the young demonstrators of 1996–1997 did not suffer from any traditional Serbian type of "leadership syndrome" (*liderstvo*), which might lead to support for a strong heroic leader. For example, student protest spokesman, Dušan Vasiljević, a 23-year-old Belgrade political science student, claimed (in a long interview given to the Slovenian youth journal *Mladina* while the demonstrations were still in progress), that dissatisfied with years of poverty and dictatorship, the student demonstrators were simply fighting against the authorities in their own way, and avoiding dependence on the opposition coalition.[19] "Ours is a humanistic revolution," Vasiljević maintained, "we are fighting not for power, but for democracy." Thus, student leaders reacted angrily when *Zajedno* leader Vuk Drašković publicly rebuked a leader of the student movement (Čedomir Antić) as an "idiot" when he challenged Drašković's claim that the student protest movement was not self-motivated. According to Vasiljević:

> this movement was not started by [the opposition party leaders]. People think that they started it. . . . The student movement was started by a group of enthusiasts from the Philosophy and Language School. . . . I could not imagine in my wildest dreams that so many people in Belgrade thought the same as we do. . . . We all came to the first protest meeting, and we were, well, astounded by the number of people attending. It all started with a couple of jingles on Radio Indeks and B-92, and the help of flyers that appeared in the schools. . . . Afterward everything literally exploded.[20]

Top leaders of the student movement claimed that only a small proportion of its members belonged to the established opposition parties, though they do not dispute that they closely coordinated the organization of the demonstrations with *Zajedno's* leadership. Student spokesman Vasiljević maintained that student leaders who belonged to an opposition party were in a minority "which reflects the overall picture of the student population," and that the situation was an advantage to the students in achieving their aims: "The people in question are young individuals who are aware that the differences, which are not big, must be cast aside, and that we must concentrate on important issues." Along with most other optimists during the protests, Vasiljević hoped that bickering between anti-regime leaders would soon come to an end.

Vasiljević, along with most members of the protest movement, also suggested that the students were motivated primarily by patriotic rather than nationalistic views. "All this nationalism broke out in Serbia suddenly, and by the same token it now seems to be dead all of a sudden. I think it's a phase that all the citizens of this country would sooner forget, a phase that has no good memories for anyone." Protest leaders rejected reports that surfaced in the American press claiming that segments of the student movement exhibited "virulent Serbian nationalism."[21] One of the professors leading the protest of his colleagues at Belgrade University dismissed such media reports, observing that though "varying political convictions" existed among the students, "not a single extremist act" had occurred, and that the Belgrade students did not typically have a "racist orientation." There was more consensus among observers, however, regarding the willingness of established opposition leaders to periodically flirt with nationalist positions. But most protest sympathizers dismissed such tendencies as minor or excusable after years of nationalist propaganda. "You can't expect people to be good liberals in this toxic environment," observed Stojan Cerović from the Belgrade independent journal *Vreme*.[22]

On the whole, the student protesters were 20 to 25 years younger than the opposition party leaders and professors they associated with in the protest movement. But initially a spontaneous phenomenon, the student movement soon generated its own group of activists, or a new elite subgroup within the anti-regime sector. Indeed, research on the student protest indicates very interesting differences between the activist core, or leading "protagonists" of the student protest, and the broader group of "walkers" who made up the mass of student demonstrators. The group of activists/protagonists mainly had parents who were both professionals (roughly 70 percent) that is, came from families who belonged to the upper middle class that might be termed a social and cultural subelite of society. Roughly half the fathers of the student activists had formerly been members of the League of Communists, a proportion higher than the "walkers," but lower than among students who did not participate in the protests. Interestingly, the activist/protagonist group of students exhibited an extremely high level of earlier participation in protest activity: three quarters of that group had participated in one or more post–1991 successive student demonstrations or protests (e.g., the March 1991 protest in Belgrade, the May–June 1992 protests, a strike of secondary school graduates, peace action and protests during 1992–1993, protests against recruitment for the army). Moreover, 38 percent of the fathers and 36 percent of the mothers of the activist students had participated in the 1968 student revolt in the former Yugoslavia. Only 20 percent of the walkers' parents and 12–14 percent of the non-participant students had this parental background.[23]

Not surprisingly, the behavior of some student activists during the protests suggested traces of embryonic elite development within the young political generation currently committed to an anti-regime "mission." For example, during the demonstrations, Čedomir Jovanović, a 25-year-old student at the Academy of Dramatic Arts, known to the demonstrators by his nickname, Čedo, would roam the city addressing crowds from the back of his jeep. As a rule his arrival was greeted by welcoming cries and whistles from his fellow students, after which Jovanović would set out the daily strategy for the student protest. Jovanović eventually became so popular that students would pay a few dinars to have their picture taken with him.[24] Proceeds went into the coffers of the student protest, but such adulation suggested that a new elite was emerging from the ostensibly anti-elitist protest movement. Jovanović illustrated the generational gap between the student demonstrators and the political establishment—both the regime elites and the established opposition parties—when he described his own background:

> Whenever the police check on my identity papers, they find out that I was born in 1971, that I am a student, and that I am a resident of New Belgrade . . . they

could see that I have engaged in many things before I started to study. I worked as a beach guard . . . as a scuba diver. I was a reporter *on Television Politika* and *NIN* for four years, and I have also worked occasionally for other newspapers. There is nothing else they can find in my files. They would probably find something to discredit me if they could, but except for their unintelligent remarks such as 'the student gangster with earrings,' there is nothing else they can find out about me.[25]

"Fear Is Forever Behind Us": Political Development After the "Revolution"

Throughout most of the 1996–1997 protest, the leadership of the student movement maintained at least a lose sense of political solidarity with the leading opposition party leaders in *Zajedno*. Beyond a concern with the annulment of the local elections, all sectors of the protest movement could agree on one general goal: the imperative of political change in Serbia. However, the generational gap between the established opposition party figures and the student leaders, the nonpartisan character of most student activists, and the different priorities of those two anti-regime subelites, naturally led to internal political divisions and tensions between the subelites of the protest movement. Not surprisingly, the Milošević regime drew attention to such problems whenever possible, and also worked hard to exploit and exacerbate these tensions.

When in February 1997 the regime finally capitulated on the matter of the election results, the established opposition leaders, already perceiving that the demonstrations might be running out of steam, decided to call an end to the protest marches. Dissatisfied with such a partial victory—after all, the old regime was still intact and demands for reform at the University had still not been granted—student leaders called for the continuation of the student demonstrations. Student protests were thus only halted in March, following the resignation of an unpopular university rector. Protest participants then waited to see what changes would take place in Serbia. But the public disagreement over when to halt the demonstrations was only a symptom of deeper divisions among the leaders of the protest movement. Such difficulties would soon be compounded by other critical changes taking place in Serbian political life.

Three aspects of Serbian political development during the period from February–March 1997 to the late fall of 1997 proved highly significant for the future. First, Milošević launched a major program of damage control. This strategy included a purge of SPS leaders blamed for causing the regime's debacle in the local elections, and a "recycling" of other personnel back into the ruling elite. It was not the first time that Milošević had pragmatically moved back and forth between factions in the ruling party, and also made abrupt shifts in policy. For example, immediately following the signing of the Dayton peace accord, one of the most well-known SPS leaders, Milorad Vučelić, generally regarded as being in the SPS "nationalist faction," was dropped along with other prominent leaders of the subgroup. But in April 1997, the 49-year-old Vučelić was brought back into the inner circle. In an interview, Vučelić described the origin of his political convictions: "I remember when I was 22, I met Mihiz [a Serbian writer]. I was a leftist and a Yugoslav, and he asked me: 'How old are you?' I said 22, and Mihiz replied, 'There is still time . . . all smart Serbs become nationalists at 40.'" But on another occasion, Vučelić added: "I have always been against what is called the militant left, against chauvinism."[26] Vučelić's return to the SPS higher echelons did not necessarily mean that Milošević was adopting a "harder national line," but only that the regime was maneuvering for more support. As Vučelić told an electoral meeting in central Serbia: "The SPS has endorsed different forms of patriotism over the past seven years [1990–1997]. We adapt our patriotism to suit the challenges of the times."[27]

Having reached the end of his term as president of Serbia, Milošević also engineered a formal shift of his power base from the republican to the federal level of government. Thus, in July 1997 when Milošević was elected President of the Federal Republic of Yugoslavia (Serbia–Montenegro), he began the transfer of substantial powers and loyal personnel to the federal level of the political system. Other aspects of the regime's re-consolidation in the post-demonstration period included political attacks on his "reformist" opponents in Montenegro's political elite, the tightening of the SPS grip on the news media, shoring up support in the police, nurturing divisions within the ranks of the opposition party elite, and preparing the groundwork for winning the September 1997 Serbian parliamentary and presidential elections (the latter contest was to elect a replacement for Milošević). For example, in April, Vlajko Stojiljković, known mainly for his police experience in Milošević's home town of Požarevac, was appointed Serbia's Minister for the Interior. In July, the loyal Zoran Sokolović, previously the Serbian Police Minister, was appointed as federal Minister of Internal Affairs.

A second major dimension of "post-revolutionary" Serbian political development was the disintegration of the *Zajedno* coalition. By the summer of 1997, an acrimonious political and personal struggle between Vuk Drašković and Zoran Djindjić ended in the break up of the liberal and moderate right elite sectors that together had constituted *Zajedno*. One of the major causes of the split derives from long-standing jealousies and political differences between the two leaders. The more immediate problem arose from their differences about how best to exploit the wave of support garnered during the protests. Disagreement also quickly erupted between Drašković and Djindjić supporters in the various localities now governed by the opposition parties. Moreover, Djindjić, who had already been elected Mayor of Belgrade, showed little enthusiasm to support Drašković's planned candidacy for the vacant post of Serbian president. At the conclusion of the civic protests, Djindjić indicated that only a strong candidate could lead the movement forward and defeat Milošević in the coming September 1997 Serbian presidential and parliamentary elections. He was obviously thinking of someone like himself, not Vuk Drašković: "We don't need melancholic intellectuals in power," Djindjić remarked. "We need someone to tell the world what our interests are. We need a Benjamin Netanyahu. A man who will be tough and unpleasant, but with integrity."[28] Djindjić would later admit that he played an indirect role in causing *Zajedno's* demise by advocating expansion of the interparty coalition to include students, union activists, businessmen, specialists, and many others from the non-political sectors of society.[29] The parties in *Zajedno* continued to cooperate together loosely in most localities, but the rift in the coalition impeded the governance of cities where the opposition had won the elections. However, Djindjić and the liberal elite decided that with the former opposition coalition in disarray and Milošević unwilling to adopt an acceptable electoral system, or provide for a truly competitive political environment for the presidential and parliamentary elections (equal media access, etc.), a complete boycott of the electoral process would inflict the most harm on the legitimacy of the regime.

But spurned by his fellow leaders in *Zajedno*, Drašković struck back and pressed his own agenda. He sharply condemned Djindjić for having secretly met with Milošević during the protest marches, and in a bizarre twist for a political figure who had once been physically assaulted at the hands of the regime, Drašković tried to out-maneuver Djindjić by holding his own meeting with Milošević to discuss the possibility of SPO participation in the September 1997 elections, and possibly in a future government. The gambit did Drašković little good. He would come in third in the Serbian presidential race, and the SPO won only 45 seats in Serbia's 250-member Assembly (the SPO garnered about one-fifth of the overall vote in both contests). However, Drašković quickly took his revenge when the SPO joined in the Belgrade city council with Milošević's Socialists and Šešelj's Radicals to oust Djindjić from his post as Mayor of Belgrade (the vote was 68 to 1, with Djindjić and his Democratic Party supporters absent). The move immediately sparked street demonstrations by Djindjić adherents and provoked a heavy-handed response by riot police. It seemed that the regime was determined not to allow the outbreak of a new cycle of daily protests similar to the 1996–1997 events. Djindjić was bitter: "What we fought for last winter was thrown away."[30] One of Drašković's main goals was to marginalize competing opposition parties and leaders so that his SPO could dominate the anti-regime forces. This was a highly unrealistic goal, because Drašković's populist, traditionalist, and monarchist program had little appeal to the urban professional elite leading the major liberal opposition parties and groups.[31] Meanwhile the chasm between Drašković and the ultra-right populists and nationalists, such as Vojislav Šešelj, made it impossible for the SPO to garner any additional support from the nondemocratic opposition to Milošević. In fact, the Drašković-Djindjić feud, and also the Drašković-Šešelj schism, proved of inestimable political value to Milošević over the next three years, and would seriously impede the prospects of Yugoslavia's opposition forces into the next millennium.

Djindjić would later express regret at having ended the civic protests in early 1997, and having failed to request elections in May, that is, at a time when Milošević was in a weakened position and might have agreed to sharing power to some extent. "My mistake," Djindjić remarked, "was that I did not better analyze the situation at the time, nor [Milošević's] loss of contact with reality. I had it in front of my eyes and in the palm of my hand. . . . That is perhaps the biggest mistake in my entire career."[32] Vesna Pešić also claims that the broader problem of the opposition in 1997 was that it did not institutionalize the protest movement into an organized force that would take part in the electoral process. She blames competition and jealousy in the opposition ranks, and "underground maneuvers by the regime." But she ascribes even more blame to problems of a more personal nature: "We are in this situation because there are no solid people. . . . Djindjić grew, he became a more convincing democrat, than Drašković. Even in the coalition [Drašković] was very unstable. Drašković comes from the more traditional area, with dominance aspirations and I do not like to talk to someone who is always banging on the table. He does not accept any situation where he is not dominating, even in a normal conversation. It is not just a matter of political aspirations, but also personal aspects."[33]

A third facet of the Serbian political scene during 1997 that would have a major impact on future political development was the changing character of the student movement, and its relatively new leadership structure. Anxious not to loose the solidarity and politicization of the student population that developed during the 1996–1997 protests, student leaders moved quickly to establish new vehicles for student representation and mobilization. For example, almost immediately following the conclusion of the student marches, elections were held for the newly formed 70-member student parliament at Belgrade University. Approximately 11,000 of some 65,000 students took part in the elections, but most major elements in the leadership of the earlier demonstrations obtained seats in the new body. The first chairman of the Student Parliament, Slobodan Homen, had been at the head of the student leadership team during the protests (a broader organization, "the Movement of the Students of Serbia," was also established to coordinate with student parliaments in other cities). In May and April various segments of the student body in Serbia also formed a number of new student organizations such as the Student Initiative, the Student Political Club, and the Democratic Youth For a Kingdom.[34] These new organizations reflected the growing political concerns of university youth in Yugoslavia, which had been stimulated by the 1996–1997 demonstrations (there was a corresponding loss of student interest in organizations such as the Student Union, the Student Federation, and the SPS-controlled League of Students).

Ironically, growing divisions within the new student elite sector soon began to mirror the type of infighting that had proved politically suicidal to the leaders of the established centrist and moderate parties. But the leaders of the Student Political Club—who constituted the core of the emergent counter-elite during the student protest movement—still hoped to change the regime and the country through political pressure (and even the formation of a political party if necessary). Thus, the Student Political Club supported a plan by the liberal parties to boycott the 1997 election, though the members of the Club still saw themselves as acting separately from the established opposition elites, and wanted to eventually transform their student support into a distinct constituency for political mobilization. But some of the Club's leadership had begun to cross swords with the less politicized leaders of the Student Initiative, who perceived their organization as functioning more like an NGO, and hoped to focus primarily on improving conditions in Serbia's universities. Whether such tactical differences between the student organizations would further fracture the anti-regime forces, or would provide a rallying point for a broader democratic movement, remained to be seen.

On the whole, the 1996–1997 protest movement constituted a significant episode in Serbian political life that to some extent enhanced the fabric of civil society, and also strengthened the democratic impulses in Serbian political culture. Perhaps most importantly, the demonstrations expanded the political self-confidence of a new generation of political activists, and their student followers. As the General Secretary of the Student Political Club, Čedomir Antić, audaciously remarked in September 1997, after he and two female members of the Student Parliament were briefly detained by authorities for demonstrating in favor of an electoral boycott: "I believe that after the events which followed the November [1996] theft [of the local elections], fear is forever behind us, and I believe in our nonviolent struggle and a final victory over the regime which destroyed and enslaved our people."[35] But the future of Serbian democracy was still a very open question.

To some extent, the 1996–1997 civic protests did accelerate the process of political awareness in Serbia, and thereby enhanced the potential for future democratization. The Milošević regime remained intact, but its legitimacy had been considerably weakened. Moreover, new and potentially significant organizations had been established outside the control of the regime (i.e., the development of an association linking independent media outlets, a "League" for cooperation of the municipalities that were under the control of the opposition parties, a council coordinating all nongovernmental organizations, student representative and political organizations, etc.). These newer components of Serbia's civil society joined existing organizations for anti-war activity, human rights, the women's movement, and other types of independent intellectual and cultural activity, which were established during the decade prior to the 1996–1997 protests.[36] For example, during the period from 1970 to 1980 only six alternative groups were founded in Serbia. But during the next decade, 52 such organizations were established, and the figure rose to 116 founded from 1991 to 1994. The formal legalization of party and group pluralism in 1990 clearly was a take-off point in NGO development. By December 1996, Serbia had a total of 519 organizations and groups in the so-called "third sector," of which 377 were in "Serbia proper," 125 in Vojvodina, and 17 in Kosovo. Another 39 organizations were functioning in Montenegro. By 1997, approximately 700 NGOs were operating in Yugoslavia.

Most NGOs operated in Belgrade, but many were found in larger cities in the interior of Serbia, for example, Niš, Kragujevac, Novi Sad, Leskovac, etc. (that is, many of the locations where the opposition came to power in the 1996 election). A breakdown of the NGOs in Yugoslavia in late 1996, by type and location, reveals that most were established to achieve environmental goals, as well as human rights and support for peace and the women's movement (see Table 5.1). Serbian studies of NGO development reveal that most were marginal organizations, rather weak, with an insecure financial base, inadequate resources, poorly trained personnel, an inability to secure recognition by the regime (on certain legal regulations); and suffered from lack of fiscal incentives, episodic harassment, etc.

But though most NGOs were rather small in terms of their membership, they often were comprised of a highly educated and a highly committed activist core that was focussed on democratization and regime change. Moreover, the NGOs not only survived the three months of civic and student protests, there was actually an expansion in the number of such organizations.[37] Thus, despite the difficulties imposed by a fundamentally anti-pluralist regime, and also the problems of fragmentation which have bedeviled the liberal and moderate opposition forces, the organizational components of Serbian civil society preserved a good deal of their autonomy and potential energy following the 1996–1997 protests.

Table 5.1   Serbian Nongovernmental Organizations, 1998, Type and Location (in percent)

Major Type of Organizational Activity	Belgrade	Provincial Centers & Montenegro[a]	Other Towns	Unknown	Total
Humanitarian	52	34	38	1	125
Environmental	28	16	86	—	130
Youth	29	14	7	—	50
Community Action	33	8	33	9	83
Peace, Human Rights & Women	21	9	17	1	48
Educational	17	4	10	—	31
Professional	33	15	18	1	67
Other alternative groups	7	2	12	3	24
Total	220	102	221	15	558

[a]Novi Sad, Priština, Podgorica, Cetinje

SOURCE: Based on information listed in Branka Petrović, Žarko Paunović, Aco Diva, Tea Gorjanc, and Vesna Nenadić, *Directory of Nongovernmental Non-profit Organizations in the Federal Republic of Yugoslavia* (Belgrade: Centar za razvoj neprofitnog sektora, 1998).

The emergence of a young reformist leader in Montenegro, Milo Djukanović, the leader of the moderate reformist faction in that small republic's ruling Democratic Party of Socialists (DPS), was also an indirect by product of the 1996–1997 protests. During the demonstrations, Djukanović, whose quarrel with the regime had been building for some time (see Chapter 7), sharply attacked Milošević's record of political management. After the Montenegrin leader won his republic's presidential election in October 1997—garnering most of the minority Muslim and non-boycotting Albanian voters in the republic—he was able to present himself as a liberal alternative to the regime in Belgrade. Perhaps most importantly, however, as a lesson to all those hoping for political change in Yugoslavia, was the way the first stage of political change took place in Montenegro. Thus, Djukanović's success did not result from a clash between demonstrating citizens and a powerful regime, but rather from an internal factional split between pro-Serb hardliners and locally oriented reformers within Montenegro's ruling power structure, or an elite-level schism that was reminiscent of the meltdown in many other communist regimes in Eastern Europe during 1989.

Djukanović's political defection from the ruling circle underlined the growing erosion of support for the Belgrade regime. But in the fall of 1997, Milošević continued to maintain control of the major levers of power in Serbia: the police, the media, the judiciary, and his still politically powerful party machine. Moreover, the inability of liberal and moderate opposition parties to forge a stable coalition, and also the failure of any one of those parties or their leaders to break out of the pack and attract a broad following with a new program or counter-ideology that was reformist and nonnationalistic, remained vexing problems in Serbian political life. Citizen apathy also remained a serious problem for the opposition parties and NGOs, particularly in the context of *Zajedno's* collapse during 1997, and the Milošević regime's political reconsolidation. In fact it would not be an overstatement to conclude that there was deep popular disillusionment and an enormous negative public backlash regarding the failure of the established opposition party leaders to maintain a unified front. Svetozar Stojanović has observed that in Serbian political culture "there exists an unconscious democratic elitism. . . . Citizens accept that only elites, that is, parties, are involved in politics. But when a political elite doesn't fulfill their expectations, then they very quickly become disappointed, resigned, and passive."[38] Moreover, Serbia was still deeply polarized: on the one side there was a large bloc of voters who alternatively extended most of their support to either Milošević and his regime elite, or to the more radical right-wing leaders that often cooperated with Milošević; and on the other side, a growing, but still divided centrist-moderate bloc. Research on Serbia also revealed that from a quarter to a third of the population still held markedly anti-democratic attitudes supportive of an authoritarian political culture, and that an even larger segment of society held attitudes that, though not as extreme, were hardly conducive to democratic change.[39] Until a stronger center would develop, an eventuality which seemed entirely dependent on the emergence of capable centrist leaders, it appeared that the existing pattern of polarization would remain a serious impediment to further democratization.

The Šešelj Phenomenon: Mobilizing Despair in a Delegitimated Regime

During 1997, obstacles to democratization in Serbia directly related to the chronic crisis of the democratic center were compounded by a striking upsurge of radical nationalism. Ironically, many Serbs had grown disillusioned with nationalist politics. Indeed, survey research in Yugoslavia during the 1990s indicated that there had been a noticeable decrease in the magnitude of xenophobic and authoritarian sentiments in Serbia.[40] But the failure of the Serbs in

Bosnia and Croatia to achieve their maximalist goals, and the economic deterioration of Serbia as a result of Belgrade's support for those ventures, had left a large component of Yugoslavia's population both resentful of their leader and politically frustrated. Thus, though overt expressions of ultra-nationalism and illiberalism on the part of Serbs may have diminished somewhat, the level of popular frustration, cynicism, and bitterness regarding Serbia's internal problems, and pariah status in the world had actually substantially increased. By the fall of 1997, dissatisfaction with both the regime and the established opposition parties was at an all-time high. Milošević and the SPS were condemned by many Serbs for having "betrayed" Serbian national interests and allowed Yugoslavia to become an isolated state with a Third World economy. Moreover, most democratic opposition politicians were also discredited, owing largely to their constant squabbling and highly visible failure to maintain a politically united organizational structure, both before and after the 1996–1997 protests.

The main political beneficiary of such citizen anger and despair was Vojislav Šešelj, the controversial and charismatic leader of the Serbian Radical Party (SRS). In early 1990, Šešelj's small "Serbian Freethinkers Movement" had joined with Vuk Drašković to form the Serbian Movement of Renewal (SPO). But Šešelj soon broke with Drašković (who was the godfather of Šešelj's eldest child), and in June 1990 launched the Serbian Chetnik Movement (SCP). Šešelj then ran as an independent candidate in the 1990 presidential election, but received only 1.9 percent of the vote. In early 1991, Šešelj established the SRS, drawing together several disparate ultra-nationalist groups. Like other opposition parties, the SRS suffered from internal factionalism. For example, in early 1994, part of the leadership and membership left the SRS and formed the Radical Party of Serbia, a pattern repeated in mid-1994, with the formation of the Serbian Radical Party "Nikola Pašić."[41]

A former communist, who had first gained attention in the 1980s as a vocal anti-Titoist dissident, Šešelj was a rather enigmatic figure in Serbian political life. He was born in Sarajevo in 1954 to a family that had immigrated to that city from Herzegovina. His mother was illiterate and his father was a railway worker. As a boy, Šešelj was an activist in Titoist youth organizations and became a member of the League of Communists in 1971. In 1976, he graduated from university, and only three years later defended his doctoral thesis at Sarajevo's law school entitled "The Political Essence of Militarism and Fascism: A Contribution to the Marxian Critique of Political Forms of Civic Democracy." At that time, he was the youngest person in Yugoslavia who had received a doctorate in the legal sciences. From 1981 to 1984, Šešelj was one of the youngest docents at Sarajevo University. After becoming involved in dissident activity he lost his university job and moved to Belgrade, where he made many friends in dissident circles (including the nonconformist intellectual Dobrica Ćosić). His anti-regime views would eventually land him in jail for 22 months (1984–1986). Following his imprisonment, Šešelj returned to Belgrade as a prominent "victim" of communist oppression, and resumed his dissident publishing activity. On a visit to North America in 1989, Šešelj was awarded the title of Chetnik Vojvoda (Duke) by one of the oldest living Chetnik leaders. The title was later rescinded, but Šešelj kept using the honorary rank, and often was referred to as the "Red Duke." Embittered by the treatment he received from the communist regime, Šešelj was determined to reshape Serbia in accordance with his radical agenda. Indeed, he has remarked that "every one of his political attitudes, political perspectives, depends on his personal experience, his personal destiny, from one of his personal ordeals."[42]

Throughout his career, Šešelj has employed various brutish, belligerent, and often clownish maneuvers to gain publicity. In 1990, for example, he assaulted one of his comrades in the Serbian Chetnik Movement with a base-ball bat, and the same year he was involved in the forcible expulsion of Croatian families in a number of Vojvodina villages. During the wars in Croatia and Bosnia, Šešelj led paramilitary volunteer units against "anti-Serb" forces, and promised to use "rusty spoons" to mutilate his Muslim enemies. An ardent Serb nationalist and anticommunist who opposes monarchism, Šešelj's right-wing populist program is an eclectic admixture of themes from traditional European Fascism and newer ideas borrowed from Western Europe's current radical right. Tall and distinctive in appearance, Šešelj has been a highly visible fixture in Serbian politics over the last decade. A prolific writer, the SRS leader enjoyed appearing at public events surrounded by his entourage of lieutenants, where he generally stationed himself at the center of the room and proceeded to hold court. In order to obtain maximum effect, Šešelj earned a reputation for very carefully choreographing the content and style of his public appearances. Though considered a dull orator (who has problems with the Serbian pronunciation of the letter "r") when giving set speeches, Šešelj is very effective at debating, often fascinating his audience by crudely and provocatively "unmasking" his political adversaries. Not surprisingly, some of his very immoderate remarks and aggressive activities infuriated and frightened his domestic opponents, and also shaped his unsavory international image as a "Balkan Nazi extremist."

But for many of his countrymen, Šešelj represented a fearless and consistent advocate of their deepest concerns. Moreover, off the political stage, Šešelj developed a reputation among many Serbs as a rather intelligent and congenial figure. He was also a respected family man, with friends throughout Serbia's social and political circles. Indeed, Šešelj's political longevity and recent success in Serbian politics is a complex phenomenon, which results from more than superficial enthusiasm for his public antics, demagogic style, or the proto-Fascist details of his program. Additionally Šešelj, although personally abhorrent to most moderate Yugoslavs and most observers in the West, had his attractions and personal appeal as a political figure in Serbia. Many Serbs regarded him as a courageous, consistent and uncorrupted anti-communist and patriot. Even Vesna Pešić, who is certainly no friend of the Serbian Radicals, has commented that Šešelj is "always talking. He is a different kind of Serb, very decisive, knows the national interest. He is an anti-liberal, but supports the private sector, and nationalists go to him when they are fed up with Milošević."[43] For example, the populist message of Šešelj's SRS has resonated with those Serbian citizens who were most seriously affected by the country's severe economic collapse, namely, members of the former middle and lower middle class. This group includes a large pool of white-collar workers, lower ranking technicians, professionals and management personnel, private craftsmen and small-scale entrepreneurs, skilled and semi-skilled workers, pensioners, disgruntled students, and segments of the rural sector. Members of these groups have expressed extreme bitterness about their painful slide into poverty during the period of tough economic sanctions against Yugoslavia that began in 1992, measures that were only partially relaxed at the end of 1995. Though many members of that impoverished constituency had initially supported Milošević, during the second part of the 1990s, they gradually became more vulnerable to political appeals that blamed Serbia's plight on the regime in power, the international community, and non-Serbs. Šešelj's growing support in the late 1990s was particularly apparent in areas around the periphery of major cities, in medium-sized towns, and also among the elderly, low-paid workers, and younger unemployed people.[44]

But economic despair was not solely the source of Šešelj's success. He was also able to tap the deep sense of national humiliation that has been associated with Serbia's failure to either maintain the cohesion of the former Yugoslavia, or to realize the maximalist "Greater Serbia" national program that attracted widespread support during the late 1980s. The loss of the hegemonic position once enjoyed by Serbs in Croatia and Bosnia–Herzegovina, together with the disintegration of Socialist Yugoslavia, the partitioning of the Serb ethnic corpus among the former Yugoslavia's successor states, and the military defeats suffered by Serb forces, are developments that have collectively constituted a traumatic blow to the pride of the Serbian people. While the importance of "wounded pride and sense of humiliation" has been recognized as a significant factor in the development of most nationalist sentiments and movements,[45] the traditionally deep sense of victimization in Serbian political culture makes such attitudes particularly significant.

Understanding and exploiting the political climate in Serbia, Šešelj and the

SRS promised voters a way out of the economic desperation and ethnic humiliation they experienced under the Milošević regime. But unlike the moderate
democratic opposition parties, who suggested that Serbia must accommodate
itself to internationally accepted modes of economic development and "civilized" norms of interethnic relations, Šešelj focussed blame on the international community for Serbia's difficulties and, even while politically cooperating with Milošević, endeavored to present himself as an unashamed
spokesman for Serb nationalism and revanchist goals. On the economic front,
for example, Šešelj espoused a neo-liberal program relying primarily on Serbia's internal resources and traditional international friends, rather than on
connections to the global economy. His program called for an end to the statist policies employed by the ruling socialists, and other measures such as the
rapid expansion of the private sector, the development of tariff-free economic
zones, the renewal of "economic integration" among Serbian communities
throughout the Balkans, the intensification of economic links with Russia and
China (Japan and South Korea were also mentioned in 1992), and the reduction of economic dependence on the European Community. "Economically we
are liberals," Šešelj told an interviewer in 1996. "We support liberal capitalism and the complete privatization of everything that can be privatized and not
endanger the functioning of the state. Almost Thatcherism. We differ from others because we insist on a method of privatization which excludes stealing."[46]

   With regard to the national question, Šešelj emphasized his commitment
to Serbia's ethno-national aspirations, including "the unity of all Serbs," and
the "Greater Serbia" many Serbs feel Milošević had betrayed. Advocacy of
restored Serb control over Croatian and Bosnian territory not only appealed
to the roughly 600,000 refugees from these areas living in Serbia by the second half of the 1990s (who were not citizens of FRY and therefore could not
vote), but also to the large segment of Serbia's population who are deeply
angered by the refugee tragedy (and often are directly connected with the
refugees by family ties), and the loss of traditional Serb influence in other
regions. The events in Kosovo at the end of the 1990s (see below, and Chapters 6 and 7) would substantially increase the size of the refugee population in
Serbia, under even more difficult economic conditions. Šešelj also directed his
nationalist message against specific ethnic groups, such as Albanians and
Croats. His message resonated with many segments of the population. For
example, Serbian intolerance and prejudice was a long-standing feature of ethnic relations in the region, and had been growing during the 1990s.[47] Indeed,
the Belgrade sociologist Ognjen Pribičević has noted that "the Serbs do not
treat the Albanians as equal, they treat them as uncivilized, very primitive, dirty
. . . as humans of a lower profile. Of course Milošević who opened the bottle
and let the devil out, but these feelings are much older than Milošević."[48] In

the 1990s, Šešelj's anti-Albanian rhetoric successfully tapped such sentiments among many Serbian voters. Šešelj's pronouncements were also anti-Croat, and by 1997, surveys showed that anti-Croat feeling had actually surpassed anti-Albanian feeling in Serbia. Šešelj also called on Serbs still living in Croatia after 1995 to leave that country, and suggested that the Krajina would never be Croatian. If Serbs cannot return to the Krajina peacefully, he claimed, "there are other possibilities" for arranging their return. Šešelj's extreme nationalist message was also anti-foreign, especially anti-American and anti-German, and both USIA and Yugoslav surveys revealed the strong intensity of such feelings in Serbia during the late 1990s; a view which would grow during and following the 1999 hostilities in Kosovo.

During the 1990s, some Serbian intellectuals and opposition leaders urged members of their ethnic community to recognize the Serbian regime's responsibility for the warfare and atrocities in the Balkans following the disintegration of socialist Yugoslavia. They further suggested that, when appropriate, individuals should be required to personally assume responsibility for their actions. Šešelj has, in contrast, rationalized and exploited Serb resentment against failures, foreigners, and ethnic foes (see Table 5.2a). Indeed, even members of the younger generation who viewed themselves as democrats, and have actively demonstrated against the regime, expressed a strong sense of national identity (see Table 5.2b). Most of Šešelj's nationalist themes resembled repackaged ideas first advanced by Milošević at the end of the 1980s, but which the Socialist Party leader was perceived to have betrayed. Moreover, in the second half of the 1990s, Milošević could no longer convincingly portray himself as a heroic Serbian patriot to his embittered and deeply cynical countrymen. This situation provided a window of political opportunity for Šešelj, which seemed to reach its crescendo between the 1996–1997 civic protests and the escalation of violence in Kosovo during the spring of 1998.

Throughout his tenure, Milošević's shrewd strategy of power maintenance included abrupt tactical changes toward Šešelj.[49] Recognizing that the Radical Party leader appealed to an important pool of voters, Milošević alternatively praised, ignored, jailed, electorally cheated, or politically embraced Šešelj, depending on the prevailing domestic and international political situation. For example, at times (1992–1993), when the democratic opposition threatened regime control, an alliance between the ruling SPS and Šešelj's SRS appeared expedient, and Milošević encouraged the "controlled growth" of Šešelj's party. But when trying to project a more moderate and democratic image internationally (after mid-1993), Milošević chose to marginalize or neutralize Šešelj. In May 1994, for example, Mirjana Marković attacked Šešelj for his "red-necked brand of nationalism," which she claimed was a brutal and cruel extremism not typical of the Serbian people. Šešelj in her opinion was "not a

Table 5.2a   Distribution of Favorable and Unfavorable Opinions Towards Various National Groups Held by Citizens in Serbia, May 1998 (in percent)

	National Groups						
	Albanians	*Americans*	*Jews*	*Germans*	*Serbs*	*Muslims*	*Croats*
Very Favorable	4	6	8	5	40	7	4
Generally favorable	11	17	26	14	36	12	11
Neutral	36	36	51	34	17	30	27
Chiefly unfavorable	22	19	8	22	5	18	17
Very unfavorable	28	22	6	26	2	34	41
Total	100	100	100	100	100	100	100

SOURCE: Adapted from S. Mihailović (ed.), *Izmedju osporavanja i podrške: Javno mnenje o legitimitetu treće Jugoslavije* (Belgrade: Institut društvenih nauka, 1997), p. 23.

Table 5.2b   Importance of National Identity for Student Protesters (in percent)

	1996/97 Protests	*1992 Protest*	*General Population 1993*
Very important	27	12	31
Important	31	27	30
Medium importance	21	27	21
Little importance	11	16	10
Not important at all	11	18	8

SOURCE: Marija Babović *et al.* (eds.), *'Ajmo, 'ajde, svi u šetnju!: Gradjanski i studentski protest 96/97* (Belgrade: Medija Centar, 1997), p. 60.

son of the Serbian nation spiritually . . . he is an alien, a primitive and aggressive alien." In fact, she added a couple of months later, "Šešelj is not a Serb. He is a Turk in the most primitive, historical edition. Or perhaps he's just not a man. . . . Neither a Serb nor a man."[50] Even sidelined, however, Šešelj proved useful to Milošević. Thus, members of the international community could be convinced that if they did not deal with the Belgrade regime, the far worse specter of radical ultra-nationalism might fill the vacuum. But because the potential voting base of the Radicals and the SPS overlapped considerably, Milošević was always careful not to allow Šešelj to grow too strong. However, during mid-1997, the steep fall in Milošević's support, and *Zajedno*'s collapse (which created a fluid bloc of frustrated voters) created a difficult situation for the regime. It was this new political context that stimulated a surge of popular support for Šešelj and the Radical Party, and compelled Milošević to employ some of his most blatant and transparent techniques of electoral manipulation.

At the outset of the Serbian parliamentary and presidential election in September 1997, Šešelj demonstrated that he had become a formidable force. For example, in the legislative contest, the SRS won the second-largest contingent of seats in the Serbian National Assembly, capturing 82 seats (32.8 percent) and winning 29.3 percent of the vote. Milošević's SPS and left coalition took 35.7 percent of the votes and got 110 seats (44 percent). But Šešelj's effort to win the republic's presidential post presented an even more serious challenge to the regime. Milošević was not directly competing in the election, having relocated himself to the federal level of authority in July 1997 (he had arranged for the Federal Assembly to elect him to the post of president of Yugoslavia in a late night sparsely attended session). Milošević was therefore able to let others in the ruling party directly face Šešelj and other contenders in the Serbian presidential contest. Still, in view of Šešelj's growing political strength and self-confidence, Milošević could not afford to let the Radical leader take control of Serbia.

Sensing the political opportunity at hand in Serbia, Šešelj tried to present a more moderate "presidential" image. He stressed his effectiveness at managing the town of Zemun, near Belgrade—the sole municipality won by the Radical Party in the 1996 local elections—and offered voters a smorgasbord of social, economic, and nationalist promises. Šešelj also sought to position himself as a honest nationalist, the "law and order" candidate, who would be able to bring an end to the rampant corruption, violence, and "moral collapse" that had become endemic in Serbian society. By 1997, however, Šešelj's ultra-nationalist policies regarding minorities were well known to Serbian voters. For example, after the Radicals won control of the municipality of Zemun in 1996, Šešelj quickly offended the city's small Jewish community by turning the town's 147-year-old synagogue—that was no longer operative and had been sold to the communists in 1961—into a nightclub. About the same time, headstones in the Jewish cemetery were desecrated. But Šešelj enjoyed considerable support among the general population. As one citizen of Zemun remarked: "Šešelj also has his good side. The streets are cleaner, the garbage is collected more often, and the city administration runs more smoothly."[51] Far more politically important than Šešelj's anti-Semitism in Zemun, was the Radical leader's rabid anti-Albanian views. Indeed, many Serbian citizens believed that Šešelj was just the man to deal with the rebellious Albanians of Kosovo. Conscious of his image as an intolerant Fascist, Šešelj had tried to recast his political persona. For example, in 1996, Šešelj tried to improve his image by removing the explicitly discriminatory anti-Albanian aspects of his earlier party programs. But the 1994 program of the SRS had already made the perspectives of Šešelj and his Radical activists quite clear, and called for the expulsion of all Albanian immigrants and their descendants, termination of every state-financed subsidy received by the Albanian minority, disbanding of all institutions that operate in the Albanian language and are financed by the state budget, dismissal from employment of all "Šiptars" who are not citizens, abolition of all social assistance to "Šiptars," particularly those who have "too high a birth rate," etc.[52]

Šešelj's old appeals and cosmetic changes proved highly successful in the elections. With most of the democratic opposition boycotting Serbia's presidential election campaign, Šešelj came second in a field of 17 candidates (taking 27.2 percent of the vote in the initial round of voting), and on September 21 was able to force the front-runner-Milošević's hand-picked candidate, former Yugoslav president Zoran Lilić (who took 37.7 percent), into a runoff. Vuk Drašković came in third, receiving only 20.6 percent of the vote. Elated with his electoral success, Šešelj again insisted that he was not an extreme rightist or a centrist, but rather the leader of the moderate right: "The extreme right are those who use violence and threaten violence. We are a party which has a clearly expressed liberal economic program, an articulated social policy, we are against mixing the church and politics . . . we support a republican form of government. The extreme right is for monarchy and dictatorship. . . . In an ideological sense the political scene is without a center, but in a political sense it is represented by those who are weakest, who can only tip the scales. That is the SPO [Vuk Drašković]." Šešelj further suggested that Drašković had made a mistake in earlier supporting *Zajedno*, and liberals like Vesna Pešić, who "as a political force have nothing," and that at least working outside of *Zajedno* in the September 1997 election, Drašković had shown his real, albeit limited, strength.[53] On October 5, 1997, Šešelj defeated Lilić (49.1 percent to 47.9 percent), but since the overall voter turnout (48.97 percent) fell below 50 percent, the election was declared legally invalid. Widespread electoral fraud by the ruling party was in evidence (e.g., hundreds of thousands of absentee Albanian votes were awarded to the SPS candidate),[54] but Šešelj had nevertheless received over 1.7 million votes, and came within 1 percent of becoming Serbia's president.

Who were the individuals who comprised the Radical Party's activists in 1997, and who supported Šešelj at the ballot box? Examination of the Radical candidates running in the fall 1997 parliamentary election indicated that Šešelj's activists were predominantly lower-middle-class males from the smaller cities of Serbia, and from Serbia's rural areas, who had very little formal education. In fact, the comparison between the 250 SRS candidates and the 250 candidates of the Socialist Party running in the 1997 Serbian legislative election revealed that, compared to Milošević's Socialist activists, Šešelj's Radicals were younger, less educated, rural in origin, and had more humble social backgrounds. Indeed, while there has been an overlap in the sources of Radical Party and Socialist Party candidate recruitment, there have also been differences. The Radical activists appeared to be an aspiring, aggressive, and angry counter-elite with strong grassroots support in small towns and rural areas. According to Tomislav Nikolić, Šešelj's second-in-command, SRS party membership doubled from 70,000 in September 1997 to 140,000 in December 1997, after Šešelj's impressive electoral performance in the Serbian presidential race.

Yugoslav research on the attitudes of those supporting different political parties indicated that Radical Party followers were overwhelming hyper-patriotic, xenophobic, and quite authoritarian in their views, compared to the followers of parties from the "democratic opposition." The Radical voters (many of whom were former communists) revealed a nostalgia for the old pre-pluralist system of rule, a preference for nationalism, and little tolerance for minorities.[55] The Belgrade sociologist Srećko Mihajlović has argued that a substantial portion of Šešelj's voting support comes from the less educated segments of Serbia's population, that is, the roughly 60 percent of the republic's population that in 1991 had only partial or completed elementary education, or no education at all. A considerable number of the people in those categories

... if they vote at all, vote as told by the head of the family. If they decide for themselves they follow the authority of the local community leaders or what they hear on television. They don't think with their heads, but in politics are "followers" ... the SRS in its pre-election promises about making quick changes in voters' social positions succeed in establishing a link to the less educated voters. Decades of emphasizing national goals is a great deceit because the nation as the main lynchpin of political life becomes a new religion ... the goal is to put the nation at the center of attention, because it easier to deal with than with economic problems.[56]

The SRS itself was divided into different factions, and in terms of its own membership structure represented a red-brown extremist coalition. For example, many were ex-communists, while others were ex-members of the currently more moderate nationalist party, the SPO of Vuk Drašković. This reflected the Radical Party's original eclectic admixture of right-wing nationalism and left-wing social radicalism. In 1997, however, the SRS tried to tone down its ultra-nationalist rhetoric, and offered voters a neo-liberal economic program. Thus,

Šešelj's campaign rhetoric resembled a kind of social populism, fighting for payments for pensioners that were already several months in arrears, and were likely to fall further behind.

Though the Milošević regime had managed to stop Šešelj's drive to power, it could not compensate for the striking anti-regime mood of the voters, and the lukewarm enthusiasm generated by SPS candidate Lilić (who had formally presided over FRY for Milošević during Serbia's economic downslide). Some of Šešelj's support came from hardcore ultra-nationalist followers, but many others voted for him because of economic and ethnic grievances, and also a desire to get rid of Milošević "by any means and at any price."[57] Neutralized by SPS electoral manipulation, and shunned by most of the opposition parties, Šešelj, who had now recast himself as a law abiding main-line political actor, could do little more than forward his complaints about the electoral process to the appropriate authorities. Šešelj was also well aware that Milošević still enjoyed the tacit support of the international community, and could therefore take whatever measures were necessary to prevent an alleged "Fascist" takeover of Serbia. True to form, the politically anxious Milošević quickly dumped Lilić, and ran a new candidate for the Serbian presidency, foreign minister Milan Milutinović. For Milošević, who needed a trusted henchman to run Serbia, the stakes had become quite serious.

In a new round of voting in December, the SPS machine operated more effectively. Milutinović defeated Šešelj 43.7 percent to 32.1 percent in the next balloting, and emerged victorious at the run off (59.2 percent to 37.5 percent). One of the other big losers in the 1997 presidential election was the SPO's Vuk Drašković, who was in the forefront of the 1996–1997 demonstrations. Drašković's popularity had begun to fall soon after his split with the other parties in *Zajedno* in mid-1997. The SPO also suffered from severe internal factionalism, and Drašković lost further support when he began openly negotiating with Milošević for a place in his government. After four elections during a four-month period, Milošević's party machine had finally consolidated its grip on Serbia. But the number of voters who were willing to support Milošević and his lieutenants in Serbia had dropped sharply (Figure 5.2) compared to the early 1990s.

During the 1997 elections, Šešelj perversely used the slogan "We are coming." The surge of support for the Radicals during the fall, and the energy expended by the regime to block Šešelj, prompted renewed discussion within Serbia and abroad about the residual strength of Serbian nationalism, and also the potential for a "Fascist" victory in Serbia. Viewed from the perspective of conventional theories regarding Fascism, Šešelj's inability to make a breakthrough and take power can be explained rather easily. Thus, most analysts consider Fascist ascendancy as an outcome associated with the breakdown of

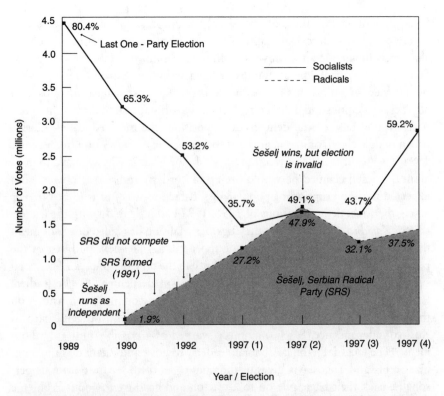

Figure 5.2   Presidential Elections in Serbia, 1989–1997, Socialist Party of Serbia and the Serbian Radical Party

relatively new liberal democracies that are governed by moderate and centrist parties, namely, a stage of political development that Serbia had not yet reached. Moreover, Milošević's ability to contain Šešelj corresponded to a pattern observed in other illiberal states (semi-democracies and soft dictatorships) with hegemonic party systems, that is, an authoritarian ruler who uses a dominant party and other levers of power to prevent radical nationalists or populist extremists from taking control. Such a pattern, for example, was apparent in Romania and Hungary between the world wars, and also in Royal Yugoslavia during the 1930s, where extreme ultra-nationalist movements were kept at bay, or partially absorbed, by conservative authoritarian regimes. In such cases, it was only after the authoritarian power structure collapsed, under conditions of internal civil strife and a breakdown of law and order, that the extreme right temporarily assumed control.[58] But with Šešelj still on the political stage, and support for the Milošević regime gradually declining, such a scenario could not be ruled out as a future possibility.

Following the December 1997 election, many observers wondered whether

Šešelj's popularity would continue to grow and create the preconditions that would allow the Radicals to capture power, either during a period of general chaos accompanying a meltdown of Milošević's authority, or after a period of failed post-Milošević liberal pluralism? Such scenarios seemed unlikely at the time in view of Milošević's impressive record of survival against the odds, and also Šešelj's demonstrated difficulty in expanding his appeal to attract the traditional voting base of the democratic opposition (the more educated, liberal, urban middle class), or in reaching out to non-Serbs. As Šešelj admitted in early 1998, "we want to take power, but with whom? That is why we have to go it alone."[59] Šešelj claimed he would prefer an "orderly transfer of power," but expected that an eruption of popular dissatisfaction was not too far off. For Šešelj, the street demonstrations of 1996–1997 had little to do with the leadership of *Zajedno*. "The fact that the *Together* coalition has failed does not mean that the people's dissatisfaction has disappeared. . . . The next outburst of the people's dissatisfaction will be much fiercer than the previous one. . . . The social situation is deteriorating . . . the economic crisis is deepening."[60] The Radical leader also continued his anti-Albanian rhetoric. For example, commenting on the activities of moderate Kosovar leaders who endorsed a peaceful path to Kosovo independence, Šešelj ominously warned of a possible future development: "The fact that [ethnic Albanian leaders] Rugova and Agani do not recognize Serbia and Yugoslavia gives us the right to let them separate from us personally, pack their bags, pile on to a tractor, and head over Mount Prokletije [into Albania]." One of Šešelj's fiercest critics, *Vreme*'s Stojan Cerović, cautioned that the SRS leader "sees his chance in complete dissolution and chaos. He is a hyena, which waits for an exhausted organism to cease putting up any resistance."[61] University of Belgrade psychologist Jelena Vlajković, worried about feelings associated with "the brutalization of everyday life, powerlessness and anger which have become embedded in people, because that can lead to an intense experience, an explosion of anger which results in a civil war in Serbia. The [1996–1997] civic protest was a civilized, whimsical, cathartic and coordinated protest, and I don't know if it can be repeated. But the possibility exists that the next outburst of anger will be far more brutal."[62] What Šešelj and most analysts could not foresee in 1997 was that Milošević would make a major change of policy in Kosovo, and thereby present the Radical leadership with an entirely new political opportunity. For the moment, Milošević had contained the Šešelj phenomenon, but the interesting and mutually exploitative love-hate relationship between the Radical leader and the Yugoslav president would continue. Indeed, the considerable similarity in the perceptions of supporters of the ruling party and the SRS, led many observers to view Šešelj's party organization as the government's "spare party" or a "constructive" opposition effectively working with the SPS.

The Emergence of the UCK: Radicalization of the Kosovo Issue

Kosovar Albanian political leaders were generally skeptical that a change in Yugoslav political leadership would result in a new policy toward Kosovo. Thus the small group of Kosovars who were following events in Belgrade closely tended to harbor equal distrust of the Milošević regime and the Serbian opposition. Fehmi Agani, a Kosovar moderate and vice chairman of Rugova's DSK, maintained, for example, that the Serbian democratic opposition had a "huge blind spot—the problem of Kosovo."[63] In fact, some Albanians believed it was better for the Kosovars "to opt for a weakened Milošević, than for a cacophonic nationalist opposition."[64] In the meantime, however, leading Kosovar Albanian politicians such as Agani and Rugova were willing to carry on negotiations with the Milošević regime. Indeed, on September 1, 1996—well before the outbreak of protest against Milošević in Belgrade—agreement was reached between the Serbian regime and Rugova concerning the "normalization" of education in Kosovo. The bilateral agreement that, if implemented, would have allowed the reopening of regular Kosovo schools to Albanians was mediated by a Catholic organization, the "Saint Egidio Community" associated with the Vatican.

Once the 1996–1997 demonstrations began in Belgrade, there was some optimism among Albanian moderates that the collapse of the Milošević regime might at least break the stalemate in Serb–Albanian relations regarding the province. Even Adem Demaci, who had spent 25 years in Yugoslav jails for his political activities, sent an open letter of support to the protesters in Belgrade: "Do not give up, Serb people," urged the bitter Demaci. "Although some of your wild sons still enforce violence against us [Albanians] we look at you with hope, give our hand of martyr to you . . . we are glad to see that the broad, free and European spirit is rising in Serbia."[65] Other Kosovar Albanians warned, however, that should the Milošević regime falter, or be weakened by the protests, the Serbian president might try to distract attention by provoking a Serb–Albanian war. Thus, when the protests ended in early 1997 with Milošević agreeing to recognize the opposition victories in the local elections, but with the regime's legitimacy severely depleted, most Kosovars expected the worst from Belgrade. The surge of support for Vojislav Šešelj in Serbia's fall parliamentary and presidential elections only strengthened this expectation. The majority of the Albanian community continued, however, to ignore events in Serbia, believing that their community should focus on maintaining passive resistance against the Belgrade authorities, and rely on international guarantees of support (especially from the United States). But by the fall of 1997 many Kosovar Albanian political activists had become convinced that passive resistance was futile, and that they should develop new and more assertive modes of political protest. Increasing disenchantment with the non-violent and gradualist strategy of the LDK was signaled in late October by Albanian student demonstrations "against the non-implementation of the 1996 Milošević–Rugova education agreements." Even more significant, however, was the onset of an armed Albanian insurgency in Kosovo, including attacks on Serbian police and Albanian officials working with the regime. The attacks were launched by a still shadowy underground organization, practically unknown in the Balkans or abroad, using the name "Kosovo Liberation Army," and soon to be better known by its Albanian acronym "UCK." The first substantial armed guerilla activity by the UCK occurred in April 1996, and escalated considerably during the summer and fall of 1997. Meanwhile, Rugova continued to advocate a policy of passive resistance although he was clearly aware of the changing mood in Kosovo: "Frustration exists among some young people and some leaders, but the vast majority of people know that a conflict would have tragic consequences for Kosovo. Serbia is still very strong. In order to avert a bloodbath and ethnic cleansing, there is no other solution than to continue the policy pursued for the past five years. The great student demonstrations of the fall were the first street demonstrations for years. Nobody was hurt because they did not leave the outgoing neighborhood from the city for the center and thus averted provocations."[66]

But a new force had arisen in Kosovo that was not concerned about provoking Serbia. As discussed in Chapter 4, the origins of the UCK have been a matter of some dispute. The most informed Kosovar commentators have traced the beginnings of the UCK as a guerilla movement to the summer of 1993, a time when several independent underground groups began cooperating with one another. An important impetus for the coordination of these groups was the failure of the international community to address the Kosovo problem at the August 1992 London conference convened to discuss the Yugoslav crisis associated with the country's disintegration. Not long after some members of the Kosovo People's Movement (LPK), a political party operating in Switzerland and Germany, began to discuss the idea of an armed struggle and, together with independent activists, decided to found the UCK. It has even been suggested, for example, that the first "cells" of UCK fighters were formed as early as 1991 and 1992. Shkelzen Maliqi, for example, claims that during the first part of the 1990s, the founding members of the UCK were former Marxist-Leninists-Enverists, who were already active in the 1970s and 1980s. The precise date of its origins remains contentious. However, what is clear, is that the UCK was a marginalized and passive organization until the Kosovo issue was once again ignored by the international community during the Bosnian peace negotiations in Dayton during November 1995. Although prior to Dayton, international officials dealing with the Balkans tried to link the situation in Kosovo to an overall Balkan peace settlement, Milošević was intransigent regarding any outside effort to resolve problems in the province. David Owen, the European envoy for the Yugoslav crisis from 1992–1995, has described the situation: "Well, I would always speak about Kosovo practically every time I met [Milošević] and I met him hundreds of times. Kosovo was on the agenda. And he didn't like it. In fact we used to discuss amongst ourselves when to raise it. Was it best to get it over and done with early on, raise it over a meal, or do it when you're just leaving? Because he would turn nasty."[67] With their hopes for international backing dashed, Kosovar Albanians in the émigré community, former JNA officers, and various other individuals and groups who had fought against the Serbs in Croatia and Bosnia and "spontaneously" formed armed units, decided to join the UCK's core Enverist group. What initially seemed to unite these desperate UCK recruits was adherence to a radical-left ideology and Albanian nationalism. As the journalist Veton Surroi would latter say, the UCK was clearly a "movement of many different flavors," from peasants to "organized political thinking" and, as such, had the potential for becoming a major agent of change in Kosovo.

Organizationally the UCK initially consisted of a rudimentary military organization, but gradually developed over a six-year period into a regular army and command structure. By 1998–1999, the military structure was divided into operational zones, and coordinated by a general staff, headed by a top commander—in 1999, Sulejman Selimi, a metallurgy student and former soccer player, who was also known as "the Sultan"—based in the Drenić area. The UCK structure also grew to include a number of sub-organizations or directorates (i.e., a political directorate, and directorates for information, a secret service, common health, common education, etc.). October 1997 marked the first recorded incident of a UCK member who was killed wearing the movement's official uniform. It was not until the winter of 1997–1998, however, that the organization began claiming control over "liberated territories" in Kosovo. Near the end of 1997 and in early 1998 the UCK carried out several guerilla attacks on Serbian police stations and patrols. In late November 1997, a representative of the UCK spoke openly at a funeral for a teacher (Halit Gecaj in the village Lausa, near Srbica) who had been killed in a clash between the UCK and Serbian police. The UCK representative, who was accompanied by fellow UCK members who wore masks on their faces in order to hide their identities, advocated an armed struggle for liberation during his speech at the funeral. In January 1998, the Serbian police instigated attacks against the Jashari family, one of which, Adem Jashari, was a 42-year-old farmer, and founding member of the UCK. These attacks culminated in the March 5, 1998 massacre by Serb police of some 51 people, including 29 members of the extended Jashari family group in the central Drenica area.[68]

The brutal assault on the Jashari civilians promoted an influx of new recruits into the UCK and helped the movement to mobilize various sympathizers, independent groups, and defense committees. Adem Jashari became a hero for Albanian Kosovars, and a legend which helped to legitimate the UCK. In the summer of 1998, "over-taxed organizationally," the UCK was reorganized into a "Peoples' Army." As the UCK expanded, many former activists and members of the Rugova's LDK transferred their allegiance to the new insurgent organization. But, generally speaking, most new UCK converts were skeptical of all political groups and political personalities. They were simply frustrated with passive resistance and were ready to more actively oppose Serb rule. Within a short time, up to 20,000 Albanians were estimated to have joined the UCK.

In early 1998, the Belgrade regime launched a major campaign to eradicate the UCK. That effort included indiscriminate assaults against Kosovo's civilian population in areas considered to be UCK strongholds. Whether the UCK can be blamed for provoking the Serbian action, with its inevitable collateral civilian impact, or the Serbs used the emergence and increasing activity of the UCK as a pretext for commencing "ethnic cleansing" in Kosovo, is a matter of one's political perspective. "The KLA [UCK] political objective," Skhelzen Maliqi later observed, was to provoke Milošević, obstruct his rule in Kosovo, and incite the international community to react, possibly through NATO intervention. . . . Rugova and the Democratic League of Kosovo lost all their influence at that time [in the first part of 1998]. . . . They should have taken the initiative, but they only waited passively for some one else to do the job." Rugova had been using Gandhian tactics against the Serbs for a decade. Those moderate tactics, both against the Serbs and his own Albanian political foes, would now cost him dearly in Kosovo politics.

In any case, Serbs forces clearly escalated their attacks on the UCK, and widened their targets to include civilians. Thus in March 1998, Serbian police began major "ground-clearing operations," which included the forced resettlement of Albanians in zones of known UCK activity (first in the Drenica area, and later in other border areas). The cycle of violence intensified as Serbian massacres of civilians and shelling of villages drove many Albanians into the UCK. The "Lebanonization" of Kosovo was gaining momentum. By the summer of 1998, the killing of civilians, along with UCK fighters, and also the widespread destruction of villages, had forced somewhere between 200,000 and 300,000 Albanians to flee their homes. But areas of UCK control grew, from the west to the east of Kosovo.

Milošević's decision to adopt tougher measures in Kosovo can be traced to a number of factors: (1) strong pressure from the hard-line faction within the SPS and Serbian police to come to grips with the UCK insurrection; (2) a calculation that he could whip up civilian support behind a renewed patriotic-nationalist policy; (3) a belief that once the international community pushed the Serbs and Albanians into negotiations (that he assumed would be premised on Kosovo remaining in Serbia), he could pose as the architect of peace and reconciliation; and (4) ambiguous signals from the United States and the international community that his elimination of a separatist or alleged "terrorist" guerillas would not be strongly condemned (i.e., if not accompanied by brutality, and included a willingness to engage in diplomatic discussions concerning the future of Kosovo). For example, after visiting the province near the end of February, U.S. envoy Robert Gelbard made it clear that he deplored the escalation of violence that was occurring. But he also praised Milošević for his "important role" in helping to negotiate and implement the Dayton accord, and urged "dialogue" to resolve the situation in Kosovo. Although by this time, both the United States and the members of the European Union were already well aware that Milošević's influence on the Bosnian Serbs had significantly decreased, in that his political position was considerably weaker than at Dayton—as evidenced by the partially successful 1996–1997 protests against his regime—he was still regarded as an important factor in achieving regional stability. Moreover, though Gelbard claimed that mounting violence was mainly the fault of the Serbian police, the U.S. envoy balanced his comments by referring to the UCK as "terrorists." He emphasized that the United States condemned the "unacceptable violence" carried out by such groups in Kosovo. "This is without question a terrorist group. . . . Having worked for years on counter-terrorist activity I know very well what it is to look at a terrorist group; to define it you strip away the rhetoric and just look at actions."[69] Determined to deal with Kosovo in its own way, the Milošević regime ignored Gelbard's plea for "dialogue," but concluded that Belgrade and Washington were in basic agreement on the character of the Albanian guerilla struggle. Inadvertently perhaps, Gelbard had provided Milošević with a green light to launch his March 1998 offensive in Kosovo. Indeed, Serbian action in Kosovo escalated only four days after Gelbard's remarks. SPS moderates, such as former Yugoslav President Zoran Lilić, cautioned that Belgrade adopt a strategy of limited and controlled struggle against "Albanian terrorists" that would limit collateral damage against civilians, and thus lessen the possibility of intervention by the international community. But Milošević rebuffed such proposals throughout 1998 and early 1999, and opted for the views of hard-liners, such as Deputy Premier Nikola Šainović and others, who pressed for a full-blown assault against Albanian "separation" in Kosovo.

Meanwhile, Milošević had carefully been shoring up his domestic political support for the escalation of police measures in Kosovo. For example, in early 1998, Milošević, having perceived Šešelj's growing strength, and well aware of the regime's declining legitimacy, decided to co-opt Šešelj into the nationalist left-wing alliance running the Serbian government. Milošević was undoubtedly preparing for his assault on the UCK and wanted Šešelj under the regime's umbrella. On March 24, 1998, a new Serbian government was formed. Milošević's Socialist Party of Serbia continued to hold the key posts. But Šešelj's Serbian Radical Party received 16 of 36 portfolios. Šešelj, and the second-in-command in the SRS, Tomislav Nikolić were appointed as two of the five deputy prime ministers. The Yugoslav Left (JUL), headed by Milošević's wife, also received several ministerial posts. Thus, at one of the most crucial moments in Serbia's political history, Milošević had decided that his republic would be guided by a SPS/JUL/SRS alliance or what might be considered as a "red-brown coalition." The new coalition changed Šešelj's position and role in Serbian politics to some extent; strengthening him in certain respects and weakening him in others. For example, the Radicals now had real access to power, and genuine, albeit formal, authority. They wasted no time in placing their supporters into administrative posts, and taking policy initiatives, such as re-politicizing the universities. Some insiders have suggested that Šešelj's Radicals quietly began gathering evidence of corruption and abuse of power by Milošević and his cronies in the ruling coalition in order to use such material for their political advantage at the right moment. Many SRS members were also upset by their party's direct involvement with the Milošević regime, and would have preferred that Šešelj remain a "pure" anti-leftist, anti-communist, and anti-establishment figure. Thus, for many Serbs, Šešelj was now in bed with the arch-traitor to Serbian nationalist goals. Šešelj, meanwhile, was entirely pragmatic about his new alliance with Milošević. As he recalled some two years later, "when we formed the coalition with the SPS and JUL they knew we were Chetniks, and we knew they were communists . . . no one can encroach on our ideology, nor do we have any intention on encroaching on the ideology of the JUL and SPS."[70]

As the fighting in Kosovo intensified early in 1998, political differences among the province's Albanian politicians regarding tactics for securing Kosovo's future once again publicly surfaced. Ibrahim Rugova, although an advocate of passive resistance, could no longer ignore the existence of a new major political force in Kosovo that had rejected his tactics in favor of armed struggle. As surprised as most Serbs by the rapid growth of the UCK, Rugova could only hope that the guerilla leaders would defer to his authority as Kosovo's elected Albanian political leader. "There is a growing will to rebel," Rugova lamented. "These armed [Kosovo Albanian] groups or individuals will only give the Serbs a good excuse to carry out more bloodbaths with impunity." But despite criticism of his nonviolent approach, Rugova ran unchallenged in the March 22, 1998 election for "President" of the underground Kosovo state. Ten political parties participated in the election. However, several Albanian politicians, as well as student leaders and representatives of the UCK, demanded that the voting not take place because of the Serbian "police siege" in Kosovo. During the campaign, handbills appeared throughout the province attacking "passivism," and, by implication, Rugova: "For eight years the pacifists have been trying to convince you that the Albanians will have a state. Where is your state? Where is your government?" The handbills were signed by a group called the National Movement for the Liberation of Kosovo (LMCK)—an Albanian immigrant organization based in Switzerland since 1981)—and encouraged Albanians not to vote.[71]

Undeterred by his elected position or stature among many segments of the Albanian population, Rugova's rivals in Kosovo's political life called for the formation of a "national council," in which all parties in the province would have equal representation. Rugova's most outspoken opponent was Adem Demaci. Demaci had consistently advocated a more proactive strategy than Rugova, but his vague proposal, known as "Balkania," for an independent Kosovo that would have federal links with Serbia and Montenegro, enjoyed little support among Kosovars.[72] Demaci's offer in early 1998 to serve as the UCK political spokesman was initially rejected by the guerilla organization, but in mid-August he assumed that role. Rugova was also attacked by Rexhep Qosja, who had established the Albanian Democrat Movement, along with Rugova's former deputy, Hidjaid Hisini, and others advocating a armed struggle for independence. Another leading political actor among the Albanians was Germany-based Bujari Bukosi, prime minister of the "government-in-exile" of Kosovo. In June, Bukosi, along with other leading activists in Tirana, attempted to assume control of the UCK. Earlier, Bukosi had also established a government-backed armed force, Armed Forces of the Republic of Kosovo (FARK), which was sent into Kosovo. After Milošević began his offensive in 1998, FARK troops claimed to be operating under the UCK umbrella. But an uneasy relationship existed between the two Albanian insurgent organizations during early 1998. For example, a week after the Serbian offenses began Bukosi indicated that a new stage in the struggle against Belgrade had been reached: "The peaceful option in which we invested very much, which only signaled to Milošević to gather more strength and continue the occupation, has come to an end!.... The UCK has launched an unstoppable process." But at the end of 1998, Hashim Thaci, head of the UCK political directorate, who was known by the nom de guerre "the Snake," and who was emerging as one of the most important figures in Kosovo politics, accused Bukosi "of trying to provoke fratricide among the Albanians by creating FARK."[73] The divisions among Kosovo's Albanian leaders weakened their overall and individual political influence in Kosovo, at a time when the power of the UCK as a military insurgent organization was rapidly growing. Despite defeats on the battlefield, an emerging majority of the Kosovar Albanians, and especially the younger generation, took satisfaction in both the UCK resistance against the Serbs and its disdain for the current Albanian political leaders in the province. Meanwhile, the UCK expressed little tolerance for different political views, and its spokesman publicly admitted that "political pluralism is a luxury for Albanians."[74]

Kosovo's Internationalization and the "Brink of War"

In April 1998, clearly anticipating more outside pressure concerning his handling of the Kosovo problem, Milošević had orchestrated a referendum in Serbia to demonstrate domestic support for the regime's Kosovo policy. An overwhelming majority of Serbia's voters rejected foreign mediation in the resolution of the province's future status.[75] Confronted with the brutality of Milošević's ongoing campaign against Albanian insurgents and civilians in Kosovo, the United States, however, began devoting increased attention to Serb–Albanian relations. Robert Gelbard's February remark that the UCK were "terrorists" was now viewed as a major gaffe, and Washington had begun to reconsider its approach to dealing with Milošević. By June 1998, the United States and NATO were employing a two-track approach to the Kosovo issue: intensified diplomatic efforts to resolve the situation; and the threat of military operations if the first track failed (as General Wesley Clark would later admit). The latter strategy took the form of secret planning for a possible ground invasion of Kosovo, "Operation Bravo," which would involve up to 200,000 troops.

The diplomatic track was public, intense, and highly frustrating. As in the past, Richard Holbrooke, who had been widely praised for his ability to bring Milošević around through the combined use of diplomacy and force, assumed the major role. But in a May visit by Holbrooke and Clark to Belgrade, they failed to make a diplomatic breakthrough in the Kosovo stalemate. Milošević did agree, however, to begin talking to Rugova about the province's difficulties, and to work with Christopher Hill, the U.S. Ambassador to Macedonia, on a general peace settlement for Kosovo. Although a May 22 Milošević–Rugova meeting failed to achieve any essential progress, Milošević agreed to future discussions. One challenge for Hill through the late spring and summer was to create a unified negotiating team on the Kosovo Albanian side. The problem was that the UCK itself was internally fragmented, while the UCK forces and Rugova's LDK were also at political loggerheads regarding who would represent the Albanians and what tactics should be employed. Other Kosovar Albanian political elements also sought representation in the talks. To complicate matters further, by this time Rugova had become increasingly unpopular with most of his rival Albanian political factions. The United States, however, still viewed Rugova as an essential element in any settlement, particularly because of his opposition to violence, and also the fact that he had been "elected" by the Kosovo Albanian people.

During the summer of 1998, Hill made some progress on the issue of reconciling Kosovar Albanian political divisions. For example, he obtained general political agreement among the Albanians on a potential prime ministerial candidate, Mehmet Hajrizi, a person close to some of Rugova's non-LDK rivals. Hill even took Hajrizi to a meeting with the UCK, at which the potential candidate stressed his intention to take an independent position within Kosovo politics. But within Albanian circles, a struggle for power continued between the UCK and those wishing to uphold the authority of the LDK-run parallel institutions. That struggle continued to take place against the backdrop of the UCK's intense armed conflicts with Serb forces. Albanian political fragmentation would bedevil Hill's efforts to obtain a peace settlement in Kosovo over the next eight months, and added to the American envoy's challenge of trying to close the enormous gap between Milošević and the overall Kosovar side.

In June 1998, the Contact Group issued an ultimatum instructing Milošević to end the repression of Albanians in Kosovo, or face further sanctions and possible military action by NATO. On June 15, NATO carried out a show of force, Operation Determined Falcon, by means of a military overfly in nearby Albania and Macedonia. The next day, Milošević, who was in Moscow, rejected calls for the withdrawal of Serbian troops from Kosovo, but agreed to talk with Kosovar Albanian representatives. Meanwhile, Richard Holbrooke returned to Yugoslavia near the end of June in an attempt to push the diplomatic option forward, and also forge a coherent Kosovo Albanian team. Holbrooke's meeting with Albanian leaders included a meeting with a group of UCK fighters outside Serb-controlled territory in Kosovo. Lum Haxhiu, one of the UCK leaders who met with Holbrooke and Christopher Hill, later told an interviewer later that Holbrooke came to "impose a peace settlement. . . . I told him that I personally admired his effort, but unfortunately that he came too late. I said to him 'Mister Holbrooke, Kosovo does not need peace, but freedom. What we have is a regime close to slavery.'"[76] Haxhiu did not offer any comments concerning whether or not he had earlier ties with Washington, or what ties developed following Holbrooke's visit to Kosovo. But the UCK leader claimed that he had made it clear to Holbrooke that the passive resistance tactics employed by Rugova over the past decade had gone no where, and that the UCK had no intention of a future status for Kosovo inside Serbia or Yugoslavia. That position was directly contrary to the stated policy of the United States and the Contact Group, namely that Kosovo should enjoy some form of "enhanced autonomy" within the rump Yugoslav state. But Holbrooke's visit with the UCK leaders gave the insurgent movement international legitimation as a political actor in Kosovo political life; a development that was highly irritating to the "elected" president of Kosovo, Ibrahim Rugova.

From the summer of 1998 until early October diplomatic efforts led by Ambassador Hill moved slowly ahead, as the fighting on the ground in Kosovo continued unabated. A Kosovar negotiation team was formed by Rugova. But instead of direct bilateral talks between the Serbian regime and the Albanians, Hill operated as mediator for an indirect exchange of ideas between Belgrade and the Kosovar political leaders. By the end of August, the UCK conceded that because of serious setbacks resulting from the recent Serb offensives, its members had decided to resort to "hit and run operations," typical of classical guerilla warfare. The continued fighting in Kosovo throughout September resulted in the massive displacement of the civilian Albanian population (roughly 250,000 people), and the extensive destruction of Albanian villages. Members of a UN diplomatic observer mission deployed in Kosovo noted that atrocities against civilians had been committed by Serbian police and paramilitary units in several areas. The victims of the conflict, according to one United Nations report issued in October 1998, were "overwhelming ethnic Albanians." But the report further noted that "Kosovo Serbs are suffering as well," and were the subject of "kidnapping and killing" by "Kosovo Albanian paramilitary units."[77] In late August, U.S. diplomat David Schiffers had commented that "ethnic cleansing," that is, "the forced removal of an ethnic population from a region and replacing it with a different ethnic population . . . would not appear yet to be occurring" in Kosovo.[78]

Meanwhile, the fundamental stumbling block in the diplomatic track was concisely summed up by Ambassador Hill: "the Serbs want it very clear that Kosovo is a part of Serbia, the Albanians want it clear that it is not."[79] The fundamental Serb objection was that any sort of agreement other than Kosovo self government—Hill avoided the use of the ambiguous term autonomy—amounted to a "count-down to independence." For the UCK, an organization that was still not represented on the Kosovar negotiating team, although obviously in contact with U.S. representatives, that countdown had already begun. By mid-September, Hill had formulated a full draft agreement on Kosovo. He strongly denounced both Serbs and Albanians for not agreeing to sit down and talk face-to-face about a settlement, though both sides maintained serious objections to what he as proposing. Under the plan, Kosovo would function as a territory for a period of three years, with its own legislature, executive, judiciary and local police, but would continue to be represented in the Serb government and the Yugoslav government. Implementation of the plan would require the presence of an international peace-keeping force in Kosovo to prevent armed conflict. Serbian resistance to a diplomatic settlement along the lines suggested by the international community led to a ratcheting up of economic and transportation sanctions against Yugoslavia, and renewed threats of potential NATO intervention in the province.

But in early October, after Belgrade had ignored a UN resolution (calling for a ceasefire, a withdrawal of Serb and Yugoslav troops from Kosovo, access to the province by humanitarian groups, and also that Albanian leaders reject terrorism and violence), and had continued its police and military operations in Kosovo, the U.S. stepped up pressure on the Milošević regime. Belgrade was threatened with a NATO attack unless Milošević agreed to a NATO-monitored peace agreement along the lines outlined by Ambassador Hill. Faced with possible international intervention, Milošević had begun publicly withdrawing some military and police forces from Kosovo in September 1998, but evidence indicated there had been no substantial reduction in Serbian strength. Heavy shelling of Albanian villages also continued to occur, as did the displacement of thousands of Albanian families. But if there was broad agreement within NATO that Milošević's tactics in Kosovo were outrageous, there was also little enthusiasm for using force against him, or for militarily assisting the Kosovar Albanian insurgents in pursuing the goal of independence.[80] Adem Demaci, the political representative of the UCK, indicated that his organization was uncompromising on the goals of the armed struggle: "the Albanians cannot give up their rights of freedom, [just] because Kosovo has turned into a tragedy in the middle of Europe."[81] The unwillingness of the UCK to modify its radical tactics, including selective violence against Serb civilians—either as revenge, or provocation to keep the pot boiling and attract international attention—severely undercut efforts by Ambassador Hill to negotiate a Kosovo peace accord. The UCK tactics also served as a pretext for continued Serbian repression in Kosovo.

In early October, Richard Holbrooke was once again dispatched to Belgrade in an effort to defuse the crisis. Holbrooke and Milošević held nearly nine days of meetings in Belgrade. During the period from October 5 to 15, against the backdrop of NATO negotiations to bomb Yugoslavia (the activation order had already been issued), the two well-acquainted negotiators finally reached an agreement. Holbrooke would later describe the talks as "heated and emotional," and commented that he had made Milošević very aware that NATO bombing would result if the Belgrade regime failed to respect the terms presented.[82] "We came to the brink of war," Holbrooke reminisced.[83] In the end, Milošević agreed to substantially withdraw security forces from Kosovo (including anti-aircraft defense units), to permit NATO air surveillance over Kosovo, to allow for the stationing of an OSCE contingent of 2,000 observers in the province (the Kosovo Verification Mission or KVM), and to engage in serious negotiations on Kosovo's self-rule. Additionally, Belgrade was required to allow humanitarian aid to the displaced population, to repatriate refugees, and begin cooperating with the International Tribunal on War Crimes.

At a press conference on October 28, at which he introduced some of the personnel who would be carrying out the implementation of the agreement, Holbrooke proudly characterized his achievements with Milošević as part of the Clinton administration's "decision to make the United States a resurgent presence in Europe . . . working in close partnership with our NATO allies in enlarging NATO, in the Bosnia events, the bombing [in Bosnia], IFOR, SFOR, and now Kosovo."[84] Holbrooke also observed that neither the United States nor its allies supported Kosovo's independence, although he conceded that such a goal was the "core stated objective of the Albanian political leaders in Kosovo." "We are going to have to sort this out as we go along," Holbrooke added. "Everyone is aware of the dilemma and the problem. . . . We are not supporting independence. But I am not going to stand up and tell people who dream about it that they shouldn't dream that dream."[85]

Almost as soon as Holbrooke had left Belgrade, commentators began wondering about the durability of the accord Milošević had signed, and the real prospects for reaching a comprehensive peace agreement for Kosovo. One of the major problems in the implementation of the agreement that soon became apparent was the shortfall in the "number of compliance verifiers" that the OSCE could put in the field, not to mention the potential difficulty in how such an unarmed force, or what Holbrooke called a "civilian army," would deal with an armed conflict. The overall safety for the verifiers was to be supplied by a NATO "extraction force" that was shortly to be deployed in Macedonia. But security aside, the routine work of the OSCE was almost immediately impeded by the ongoing fighting in the province, in the form of "low-intensity" raids and reprisals.[86] Meanwhile, Albanian leaders and the Serbian regime remained diametrically opposed on what self-government for Kosovo actually meant. Indeed, faced with the growing popularity of the UCK, Rugova and his LDK colleagues had actually become more adamant about the importance of Kosovo moving to independence as quickly as possible. Once again it was unclear to what extent Milošević would actually withdraw police units from Kosovo as required under the agreement (that permitted only 10,000 Serbian security and border personnel in the province). NATO's activation order for bombing remained operational, but with the insertion of OSCE verifiers and the return of refugees to Kosovo, the reality on the ground was becoming more complex.

At the beginning of November 1998 the balance of military power, and also the political advantage, had shifted significantly in Kosovo. The UCK, which had nearly been eliminated in the summer and early fall, had an opportunity to regroup, recruit, and relocate to various areas abandoned by Serbian forces. Although its leaders were not completely unsatisfied with Holbrooke's accord, they now had some breathing space to "dream that dream" of independence. Moreover, the "internationalization" of the Albanian problem owing to NATO and OSCE involvement in Kosovo's affairs meant that Serbian control over the province had also been weakened somewhat. Thus, after the Holbrooke–Milošević agreement, Serbian–Albanian relations were no longer strictly an internal Serbian matter. Such setbacks only intensified anxiety and aggressiveness in Belgrade's ruling circles. Thus, still smarting from the concessions they were forced to make, and bitter over NATO's meddling in their country's affairs, Serbian leaders in Belgrade still hoped to strike out both against the Kosovar political class, and its civilian supporters, which many Serbs perceived as a monolithic subversive terroristic force. As the Albanian journalist Veton Surroi has suggested: "The KLA [UCK] has not been included in this [Holbrooke–Milošević] process so the Serbs can rightfully say that if they withdraw the KLA will come down from the hills into the towns. Of course they will."[87] Indeed, the UCK had no real incentive to live up to the Holbrooke–Milošević agreement, and soon moved to obstruct its implementation. From the UCK perspective, the more they harassed Serbian forces, the more those forces would be provoked into slowing their withdrawal and retaliating, thereby triggering a negative reaction against Belgrade from Washington and the international community. And though Holbrooke issued some relatively soft reprimands concerning such UCK provocations, Washington increasingly saw Milošević as the fundamental problem, and the Albanians as the underdog. Thus, slowly but surely, the Clinton administration tilted towards the Albanian side, and became the *de facto* protector, if not yet the full ally of the UCK.

Overall, the deal brokered by Holbrooke had left the future of Kosovo ambiguous, and thus had only really served to postpone matters. Critics would later blame Holbrooke for reaching an agreement that depended on Milošević to keep his word, and which allowed the Serbs to, in effect, make a tactical retreat.[88] For his part, Holbrooke eventually admitted that his agreement with Milošević really "didn't have teeth" because he was unable to get the Serb leader to accept the introduction of an international armed security presence in Kosovo. Moreover, Holbrooke has claimed that he expected all along the October 1998 agreement would only last until about March 1999. But he rationalized that at least he had bought some time for negotiations on a political framework, and had made it possible for about 150,000 displaced Kosovars to return before winter.[89]

Representing an administration that was highly distracted by the Monica Lewinsky affair in Washington, and a divided NATO alliance that was unprepared to follow up bombing with the commitment of ground troops, Holbrooke had actually achieved a good deal. Moreover, there was still hope, although rather a slim one, that the UCK might join the peace negotiations led by Ambassador Hill and that the diplomatic tract could still bear fruit. Looking back at the Holbrooke–Milošević agreement, and considering the dynamics of the spring 1999 NATO–Yugoslav war, it seems that more decisive "coercive diplomacy" in October 1998 may have averted the eventual tragedy experienced by the citizens of both Kosovo and Serbia. But it was the political circumstances in the autumn of 1998 that shaped Holbrooke's narrow instructions from the Clinton administration, as well as Milošević's calculations, and the UCK's persistence, factors that would result in events inexorably drifting forward to their tragic conclusion.

NOTES

1. Miroslav Prokopijević and Jovan Teokarević, *Ekonomske sankcije UN*, op. cit.
2. *Los Angeles Times*, July 28, 1992, p. 14.
3. Richard Holbrooke, *To End a War*, op. cit., pp. 4–5.
4. *International Herald Tribune*, January 24, 1996.
5. *New York Times*, July 12, 1996, Section A, p. 10.
6. *Deutsche Presse-Agentur*, December 14, 1995.
7. Two U.S. researchers prepared a detailed study to prove a chain of command between Slobodan Milošević and forces that were guilty of atrocities in Croatia and Bosnia. Paul Williams and Norman Cigar, *War Crimes and Individual Responsibility: A Prima Facie Case Against Slobodan Milošević* (Washington, D.C.: The Balkan Institute, 1996).
8. On the responsibility of Milošević and other segments of the "political-financial elite" for Serbia's economic difficulties, see Mladan Dinkić, *Ekonomija destrukcije: velika pljačka naroda* (Belgrade: 'Stubovi Kulture,' 1996), 4th edition. The importance that the regime attached to its association with Serbia's managerial elite was revealed at the 3rd Congress of the SPS in March 1996. From the 185 members elected to the main board of the party, 111 held a variety of political positions (deputies, ministers, presidents of municipalities, etc.), and 63 were enterprise directors. *NIN*, March 8, 1996, p. 15.
9. The Montenegrin portion of seats and votes is excluded from these calculations. In Serbia, six other seats were shared by parties from Vojvodina and Sandžak.
10. Sreten Vujović, "Protest as an Urban Phenomenon," in Mladen Lazić (ed.), *Protest in Belgrade Winter of Discontent* (Budapest: Central European University Press, 1999), p. 206, footnote 1.
11. *Die Welt* in German Newspaper News Service.
12. On the variety of elite groups involved in the transition process, see Samuel

Huntington, *The Third Wave: Democratization in the Late Twentieth Century* (Norman: University of Oklahoma Press, 1991), pp. 121–124.

13. On this aspect of the student movement see David S. Bennahum, "The Internet Revolution," *Wired*, No. 5.04 (April 1997).

14. Based on the study by Vladimir Grečić, "Migration of Highly Educated Cadres and Scientists of FR Yugoslavia," *Inter Press Service*, June 10, 1997.

15. Božidar Jakšić, "Young People Between War and Peace in the Former Yugoslavia," in James Riordan, *et al.* (eds.), *Young People in Post-Communist Russia and Eastern Europe* (Dartmouth: Aldershot, 1995), p. 133.

16. Zagorka Golubović, "Istraživanje o karakteru gradjanskog i studenskog protesta 96/97," *Naša Borba*, January 30, 1997; Slobodanka Ast, "Ajmo, ajde, svi u-šetnju," *Vreme*, December 28, 1996, pp. 22–23; and Vesna Bjekić, "Who are the Demonstrators," *AIM*, December 27, 1996. Detailed analytical research on the protests is offered in Marija Babović, "Maratonici šetaju (po)časni krug," in *Ajmo, ajde, svi u šetnju: Gradjanski i studentski protest 96/97* (Belgrade: Medija centar, 1997), pp. 19–30, and Mladen Lazić (ed.), *Protest in Belgrade: Winter of Discontent* (Budapest: Central European University Press, 1999).

17. Marina Blagojević, "Demokratija se radja iz jajeta, a žene?: žene u protestima 96/97," *Košava*, February-May 1997, pp. 32–33.

18. Sreten Vujović, "Protest as an Urban Phenomenon," in Mladen Lazić (ed.), *Protest in Belgrade*, op. cit., pp. 193–210.

19. *Mladina*, January 28, 1997, pp. 39–42.

20. Ibid.

21. *New York Times*, December 10, 1996, p. 1, and the response by Mladen Lazić, *New York Times*, December 15, 1996, p. 12.

22. *The Guardian*, December 17, 1996, p. 13.

23. See Andjelka Milić, Ljiljana Čičkarić, and Mihajlo Jojić, "A Generation in Protest," in Mladen Lazić, *Protest in Belgrade*, op. cit., pp. 168–193.

24. *Moscow News*, January 16, 1997.

25. *Naša Borba*, January 30, 1997, p. 14. For the view that the 1996–1997 protests constituted a cultural break in values, and the emergence of new forms of "generational politics," see also Andjelka Milić and Ljilijana Čičkarić, *Generacija u protestu: Sociološki portret učesnika studentskog protesta 96/97 na Beogradskom univerzitetetu* (Belgrade: Institut za sociološka istraživanja, 1998).

26. *Naša Borba*, June 14–15, 1997, p. 11.

27. Tanjug, August 21, 1997.

28. *VND*, No. 281 (February 22, 1997).

29. *Los Angeles Times*, August 3, 1997, p. 3.

30. *Associated Press*, September 30, 1997.

31. Mladen Lazić, *Protest in Belgrade*, op. cit., p. 24.

32. *VND*, No. 363 (September 21, 1998).

33. *Lisbon Publico*, May 25, 1999.

34. "Ko je ko na univerzitetu," *Naša Borba*, May 11, 1997.

35. *Naša Borba*, September 17, 1997.

36. On the changes in Serbian civil society, see Branka Petrović and Žarko Paunović, *Nevladine organizacije u SR Jugoslaviji* (Subotica: Otvoreni univerzitet, 1994); Djordje Pavićević, "Privikavanje na nemoć: Gradjanske inicijative u Srbiji," *Republika*, Vol. 9, No. 172 (1997); and V. Pavlović (ed.), *Potisnuto civilno društvo*, op. cit.

37. By 1999, it was estimated that there was approximately 1,200 NGOs in Serbia directly oriented toward the development of civil society. Olivija Rusovac, "Non-governmental Organizations in Serbia: In Search of Identity," *AIM*, September 25, 1999.

38. *Naša Borba*, July 20, 1997.

39. Mikloš Biro, "Koliko je Protest 96/97 promenio političku svest gradjana Srbije," *Košava*, No. 32–33 (February-March 1997).

40. Bora Kuzmanović, "Stepen i činioci autoritarnosti," and Mirjana Vasović, "Karakteristike grupnih indentifikacija i odnos prema drugim etničkim grupama," in S. Mihajlović (ed.)., *Izmedju osporavanja i podrške: Javno mnenje o legitimitetu treće Jugoslavije* (Belgrade: Institut društvenih nauka, 1997), pp. 229–245, 246–266.

41. See Vladimir Goati, *Stabilizacija demokratije ili povratak monizmu: treća Jugoslavija sredinom devedesetih* (Podgorica, 1996), p. 114.

42. *Intervju*, No. 410 (June 1997).

43. *The Weekly Standard*, July 27, 1998, p. 24.

44. Zoran Marković, "Revanšistički nacionalizam," *Republika*, September 1997.

45. See, for example, Isaiah Berlin, "Nationalism: Past Neglect and Present Power," in his *Against the Current: Essays in the History of Ideas* (Oxford: Clarendon Press, 1989), pp. 333–355.

46. *VND*, February 3, 1996, pp. 16–18.

47. Zagorka Golubović, et al. (eds.), *Društveni karakteri i društvene promene u svetlu nacionalnih sukoba* (Belgrade: "Filip Višnjić" 1995), pp. 225–244.

48. *Chicago Tribune*, March 22, 1998, p. 6. Albanian sociologist Fehmi Agani, who was a close associate of Ibrahim Rugova and an official of the LDK, remarked that negative Serbian stereotypes about Albanians perpetuated ethnic tension in Kosovo. "[The Albanians] were the ones that chopped the wood for heating, cleaned the streets and generally did all the dirtiest kind of work. And since this was associated with the name Shiptar [derogative Serbian slang for Albanians] today's propaganda . . . can convey a negative meaning. It has negative connotations that you cannot achieve by using the word Albanian . . . which is why one part of the media and Šešelj keep using it. As far as I'm concerned the use of the word Shiptar to denote a Kosovo Albanian is used as a form of chauvinist identification." *Naša Borba*, May 13, 1998, p. 9.

49. For an overview of some of Milošević's tactics toward Šešelj before 1997 see Ogjen Pribičević, "Changing Fortunes of the Serbian Radical Right," in S. P. Ramet (ed.), *The Radical Right in Central and Eastern Europe* (University Park Pennsylvania: Pennsylvania State University Press, 1999), pp. 192–211.

50. *Day and Night*, op. cit., pp. 216–217, 242.

51. *Jerusalem Post*, September 19, 1997, p. 10. In 1993, Siniša Vučinić, another self-proclaimed Chetnik leader (and future leader of the Serbian Radical Party–"Nikola Pašić") accused Jews of responsibility for the bankruptcy of pyramid schemes in Serbia.

A 1997 study concluded that anti-Semitism is a "marginal phenomenon" in Serbia, but that "there is a latent danger of anti-Semitism. The South Slav brothers hate each other sufficiently, they do not need Jews for their hatred." Laslo Sekelj, "Anti-Semitism and Jewish Identity in Serbia After the Collapse of the Yugoslav State," (Belgrade: unpublished manuscript, 1997), pp. 25–30. In 1997, Yugoslavia's Jewish community had approximately 3,350 members.

52. Vladimir Goati, *Partijski mozaik Srbije 1990–1996* (Belgrade: Beogradski Krug, 1997), p. 33, and *Politički program Srpske radikalne stranke* (Belgrade, 1992).

53. *Nedeljni telegraf*, No. 74 (September 24, 1997).

54. Roksanda Ninčić, "Radikalna kradja," *VND*, January 3, 1998, pp. 8–12.

55. Dijana Vukmanović, "Nastanak političkih partija," in Vladimir Goati (ed.), *Partijski mozaik Srbije 1990–1996*, op. cit., pp. 30–31.

56. *Blic*, December 18, 1998.

57. Stevan Nikšić, "Milošević on the Down Slope," *The New Leader*, December 1, 1997.

58. See, for example, Peter Sugar (ed.), *Native Fascism in the Successor States, 1918–1945* (Santa Barbara, California: ABC-CLIO, 1971) and Juan J. Linz, "Political Space and Fascism as a Late Comer," in Ugelvik Larsen, *et al.* (eds.), *Who Were the Fascists* (Bergen Universitetsforlaget, 1980), pp. 153–192.

59. *Demokratija*, January 19, 1998.

60. *NIN*, December 18, 1997.

61. *VND*, July 26, 1997, pp. 18–22.

62. *Naša Borba*, March 22, 1997.

63. *VND*, December 7, 1996, p. 24 in FBIS-EEU–96–244, December 7, 1996.

64. Shkelzen Maliqi, *AIM*, Priština, December 3, 1996. In a non-official survey of Kosovo Albanians conducted by an independent Belgrade polling organization, only 20.5 percent of those questioned said they would view Serbian opposition parties as possible coalition partners for Albanian parties.

65. *Inter Press Service*, December 9, 1996.

66. *Liberation*, November 22, 1997, p. 8. See also, Shkelzen Maliqi, "Why Peaceful Resistance Movement in Kosova Failed," in *New States, Old Problems, Innovative Solutions: The Case of Successor States of the Former Yugoslavia* (New York: UNDP/MDGD, 2001).

67. CBC *National*, "Inside the Mind of Slobodan Milošević," March 30, 1999. Holbrooke bristles at the accusation that he failed to resolve the Kosovo issue at Dayton, and therefore was responsible for later problems in the province. "[B]efore, during and after Dayton we repeatedly discussed it with Milošević . . . we were able to keep things under control for a while . . . but then they exploded, not because they weren't dealt with at Dayton. That is in my view reconstructive history. They exploded because Milošević played directly into the hands of the most extreme elements in Kosovo. . . . We told Milošević quite bluntly that he was going to be the KLA's greatest recruiting poster." *Federal News Service*, November 2, 1999.

68. *Washington Post*, March 9, 1998, p. A13.

69. Special representative Robert Gelbard, briefing (Belgrade, Hyatt Regency Hotel,

February 3, 1998). Gelbard added, however, that the "possibility of a police and or military crackdown must be avoided at all costs."

70. *Nedeljni telegraf*, July 12, 2000, p. 7.

71. *Los Angeles Times*, March 22, 1998, Part A, p. 8.

72. *Kosovo Daily Report*, 1997 (in English), No. 1, p. 184, in *FBIS*-EEU–97–196, July 15, 1997.

73. BBC, January 4, 1999.

74. *Inter Press Service*, July 13, 1998.

75. It was claimed that turnout was approximately 75 percent, and that 95 percent of those voting rejected foreign mediation. Serbian Radio, April 24, 1998, *BBCSWB*: Part 2, Central Europe, The Balkans; Federal Republic of Yugoslavia; EE/D3210/A, April 25, 1998.

76. *BBCSWB*: Part 2, Central Europe, The Balkans; Federal Republic of Yugoslavia; Kosovo Fighting; EE/D3289/A, 'ABC' Web Site, Madrid, July 24, 1998.

77. Report of the Secretary-General prepared pursuant to Resolution 1160 (1998) and 1199 (1998) of the UN Security Council, S/1998/912 (October 3, 1998).

78. Tihomir Loza, "A Milošević For All Seasons," *Central Europe Online*, November 5, 1998.

79. *Federal News Service*, September 4, 1998. Remarks of Ambassador Christopher Hill, State Department Special Envoy to Kosovo, to the Woodrow Wilson International Center for Scholars.

80. *New York Times*, November 8, 1998.

81. *BETA*, October 6, 1998.

82. *The NewsHour with Jim Lehrer*, October 4, 1998, Transcript #6276.

83. CNN, *Early Edition*, Transcript 98101404V08.

84. *Federal News Service*, October 28, 1998.

85. Ibid.

86. Russian Foreign Minister Ivanov later claimed that Russia was responsible for getting the OSCE mission deployed in October 1998, thereby averting military action, "although by that time," he claimed, "about everything was ready for the start of the military action." *FBIS*-SOV–1999–1215, December 16, 1999. *Federal News Service*, Official Kremlin International News Broadcast, December 16, 1999.

87. *Daily Telegraph*, October 21, 1998 p. 18.

88. Ivo Daalder, *The Weekly Standard*, June 30, 1999, p. 17.

89. ABC *Good Morning Show*, January 22 1999, #99012204-jO1. Holbrooke would later be taken to task, rather unfairly, for the October deal with Belgrade. Ivo Daalder, *The Weekly Standard*, June 30, 1999, p. 17.

CHAPTER 6

"War Against the Whole World": Serbian Nationalism vs. NATO

We are invincible. . . . The NATO soldiers will come at firing distance. This is where we're going to get them, when they will lose a large number of people. As soon as they come here, we will defend ourselves actively, and we'll be killing them.

—Slobodan Milošević (April 20, 1999)

Did we win? In one sense, of course, the answer is clearly "yes": as a result of NATO's political cohesion and military effectiveness, Slobodan Milošević capitulated to the terms that the leaders of the Alliance established . . . [but] asking whether the Alliance's first major military action in half a century was a success and a victory calls to mind Zhou Enlai's famous answer to the question of how he assessed the French Revolution: "It's too early to tell," he replied.

—Strobe Talbott (October 7, 1999)

Political Consolidation in Yugoslavia: Milošević Prepares for Battle

General Momčilo Perišić was one of the few members of the Serbian regime who had enthusiastically supported the October 1998 agreement bringing NATO and Serbia back from the "brink of war." The 54-year-old Perišić had been the chief of staff of the Yugoslav Army (VJ) since 1993. During the marathon October negotiations in Belgrade, U.S. envoy Richard Holbrooke and U.S. General Wesley Clark had met with Perišić and his staff in order to help cement the agreement, and open a more direct channel to the Yugoslav military. Milošević had agreed to the meeting when it was requested by Holbrooke, but he certainly could not have been very happy about it.

In a remarkable speech in Eastern Serbia on October 25, 1998, General Perišić undoubtedly heightened Milošević's anxiety about sentiments in the

Yugoslav military high command. Perišić praised the political leadership of Yugoslavia for making the correct decision in signing the October agreement. He also cautioned, however, that the Serbs had been waging war since the early 1990s and now "had no allies, not even the Russian Federation." "Never have we been so isolated," claimed Perišić, "and never have we been without an ally."

> We advised the state leadership that conflict should be avoided because our general situation and socio-economic conditions would not permit a long exhausting war at any costs, nor would it be a wise thing to do, militarily or politically. In that sense we proposed to the state leadership that a way must be found to avoid conflict with NATO. This was accepted, and there was nothing else we could do, given the situation. It is a different question altogether whether the situation should have arisen, whether we needed to get there [in the crisis], and if we did, how we should have gone about it.[1]

Perišić also suggested that without the agreement, NATO would probably have inflicted losses on the "army, police, economy, and infrastructure, and of course made the population suffer." And NATO couldn't have been stopped, he warned. "They would continue with the strikes, which would not have been limited to Kosovo, or the area around Kosovo, but which would extend throughout Yugoslavia. The question is: Why do we have to suffer the first strike, to have casualties, when we can accept the conditions before the strike?"

In the same remarks, Perišić went on to predict, extremely accurately as later events were to demonstrate, that the consequences of a NATO aerial war against Yugoslavia would lead to Serbs taking revenge against the country's Albanian population. "If we were unable to take revenge on those who are hitting us from the Ionian Sea or from the airspace of neighboring countries, then we would take vengeance on those who are the reason why NATO has come, and that would be the Albanian separatists. Instead of bringing peace the West would cause the conflict to escalate." Perišić was also critical of politicians who "beat their breasts," but "are the last to prove themselves in action." "Few politicians," he remarked, are prepared to say: "we can't handle this problem, let someone else come and do it." "I want you to realize," he also told his audience, "the army does not create politics: it is an instrument of the state and steps onto the scene when there is no alternative. But it will do everything to avoid the use of arms. That is why we advised, and still advise, against going to war against the whole world."

Much to Milošević's chagrin, Perišić's incisive and blunt remarks hardly put a positive spin on developments in Yugoslavia over the prior decade, not to mention over the preceding several months. Perišić had correctly suggested, in a manner that could only serve to embarrass Milošević, that the regime's leaders had made a deal with Holbrooke out of weakness, not strength. Indeed, Perišić raised important doubts about Serbian state policy—Milošević's policy—leading up to the October 1998 crisis. Moreover, he had presciently identified, and possibly even indirectly influenced, the NATO strategy of attack that it would eventually employ. He had also openly suggested the need for resignation by the individuals who had been directing state policy, and hinted at a possible scenario where the army might have to politically act in the interests of the country. Remarkably, only hours after presenting these remarks, NATO Supreme Commander General Clark and the U.S mediator for Kosovo Christopher Hill, held an extensive meeting with Milošević and Perišić regarding the details of Serbian police and army withdrawals from Kosovo.

Milošević, who had nurtured a strong police force as a key pillar of the regime's power, and had simultaneously weakened the military establishment and armed forces, had actually been having problems with Perišić for some time. For example, in the spring of 1997, Perišić, in a jibe at Milošević and the ruling elite, had given the VJ credit for having averted the kind of sociopolitical chaos that Albania was undergoing, adding that in Yugoslavia "less than one percent of the people who head institutions" are really working for their good.[2] During the civic protests of 1996–1997, Perišić had cautioned Milošević against using excessive force to break up the demonstrations, and the General had also promised a delegation of student protesters that he would not use the army to intervene in the political struggle. Even more distressing for Milošević was Perišić's opposition to employing the army in order to prevent the inauguration in January 1998 of the new reformist President of Montenegro, Milo Djukanović. Djukanović, who had won the presidency of his republic in November 1997, faced efforts by supporters of the defeated President Momir Bulatović, a Milošević loyalist, to disrupt the republic and trigger Yugoslav military intervention in the republic. In January, at a session of the Yugoslav Defense Council, General Perišić had refrained from supporting any involvement by the army in Montenegrin politics. In May 1998, Djukanović would go on to lead a multi-party coalition ("For a Better Life") to victory in the legislative elections, and thereby become a magnet for those challenging Milošević's rule. Western countries were quickly attracted to Djukanović as a potential ally who could appeal to those dissatisfied with Milošević, and become a partner in maintaining Balkan stability (see Chapter 7).

It is interesting to speculate about why, in view of his strong feelings about the course of Yugoslavia's policies, Perišić did not take more overt action against the Milošević regime. He would later suggest that he had long thought about launching a military coup, and that many people had encouraged him to take such action and become a Yugoslav "Jaruzelski." He claims, however, that he eventually decided against a coup owing to four principal reasons. First, he did not believe he had sufficient political forces to back such action. Second, he did not have international support. Third, he considered that before initiating a coup he needed to be sure both that civilians would come to power and that the military would be able to survive in a material sense. He had not been convinced in his deliberations that this would happen. Finally, Perišić rejected the coup option as, he believed, Serbian history had already been challenged by too much blood and struggle for power. Perišić's remarks regarding a potential coup were made a little over a year after the October 1998 agreement, and after a NATO–Serb war had made matters in the country even more complicated. But his reflections reveal that he had been giving the matter systematic thought for some time, and the factors that may have restrained the interventionist-prone military elite.[3]

Perišić's perspectives on both the handling of anti-regime protests during 1996–1997, and political change in Montenegro, had been supported by Jovica Stanišić, the head of the Serbian State Security Service (whom in 1999 Perišić had described as a "wise man and great patriot"). Stanišić had worked for Milošević for several years, and by the mid-1990s many people regarded him as the second or third most important decision maker in the Milošević regime. Stanišić, a Montenegrin born in Vojvodina, had worked his way up the police hierarchy, and by 1992 had become Deputy Minister of the Interior in Serbia and head of the State Security Police. Stanišić, like his boyhood friend and neighbor, Mihalj Kertes, had helped Milošević organize the Serbian insurrections in Croatia and Bosnia during 1991–1992. In 1995, as Milošević's Special Envoy, Stanišić negotiated the release of 220 UN soldiers held hostage by the Bosnian Serbs. At the time, Stanišić warned the Bosnian Serb leader, Radovan Karadžić, that his refusal to immediately release the hostages through Belgrade, as directed by Milošević, could prove personally fatal for the Bosnian president. During the second half of the 1990s, keenly aware of the regime's severely depleted legitimacy, Stanišić appears to have decided that realism and moderation should guide the regime's decision making. The pragmatic nationalism of Perišić and Stanišić—who both allegedly also opposed the Serbian offensive in Kosovo that began in early March 1998—was deeply resented by Milošević's wife and the top echelon of her influential JUL party organization, as well as by Vojislav Šešelj and his Serbian Radical Party (who, after March 1998, were part of the red–brown coalition governing Serbia).

By the time of the October 1998 Kosovo crisis, Milošević also had to contend with new efforts by Serbia's democratic opposition forces to form a coalition, the Alliance for Change (SZP). The SZP was spearheaded by Zoran Djindjić's Democratic Party (DP) and Vesna Pešić's Civic Alliance, but also initially included over fifteen opposition parties and associations, as well as several key opposition personalities. Milošević's nightmare was that regime moderates such as Perišić and Stanišić would lead other dissatisfied members of the ruling SPS to link up with Djukanović and his Montenegrin coalition members, and even potentially with the opposition SZP, to unseat—either at elections, or through street demonstrations—the ruling party coalition and his regime. Such a political "pact" between regime moderates and oppositionists had been the model leading to the collapse of other communist party regimes throughout much of Eastern Europe at the end of the 1980s and early 1990s, and represented a threat Milošević could not afford to ignore.

During the fall 1998 Kosovo crisis, Milošević had moved to tighten his hold on power. Having mobilized the Serbian people in an April referendum to reject foreign mediation on Kosovo's status, one of Milošević's top priorities was to ensure that as little attention as possible would be directed at his willingness to bargain with the international community over the province, and ultimately to make concessions to foreign negotiators. Thus, in the course of just several months the state-run and pro-regime media was employed to whip up nationalistic and xenophobic sentiments against foreign pressure. And then, once an agreement was reached with Holbrooke media conformity was employed to portray Milošević's policy in the best possible light. Integral to this media policy was the stifling of the independent media. Within days of the agreement with Holbrooke a government decree provided for the closure of three independent daily newspapers (*Danas, Dnevni telegraf,* and *Naša Borba*), and a new information law was passed giving the state the ability to restrict "anti-patriotic" and "anti-government" stories from the media. The new law also banned relays of broadcasts by foreign radio and television stations. In an attempt to continue publishing, some of the banned media set up operations in Montenegro, but the shipment of print media to Serbia was often stopped at the Serbian/Montenegrin border by the authorities. The Independent Association of Journalists of Serbia (NUNS) protested the new law, concluding that it "closes the circle of ten years of an 'information blackout' in Serbia."[4]

Beginning in the spring of 1998, Milošević had also used Vojislav Šešelj, now a part of the ruling coalition in Serbia, to intimidate opposition forces, and particularly the university intelligentsia. For example a Draconian law dealing with universities passed in May had forced many leading intellectuals out of their jobs, and made open dissent against the regime a far more costly activity. The law effectively eliminated university autonomy, gave the government control of administrative and faculty appointments, and abolished tenure and existing contracts. The university law stipulated that all professors sign new employment contracts with their institutions, in effect creating a "loyalty oath." As a result of the existing political climate and dire economic conditions in Serbia at the time, the overwhelming majority of professors decided to sign the new contracts. But an estimated 130 out of 3,500 professors in Belgrade did not sign the contracts, and many students participated in boycotts of classes and strikes to protest the law. A new student movement, called "Resistance" (*Otpor*), was also formed. But the regime pressed ahead with the implementation of the law without much difficulty, and only a couple of thousand out of some 60,000 students attending university participated in the protest (roughly half of that number came from areas outside of the capital). Student apathy was also apparent in the various student organizations and the Student Parliament that had been formed in 1997. The regime's success in turning most of the university community into "officials of the state" confirmed one dissenting academic's remark that "the intellectual elite cannot be differentiated much from the mentality of the 'common' citizens."[5] The regime's fear that protests against the law in certain faculties—Philology, Electro-Technology, Political Science and Law—might trigger a new explosion of civic unrest led the government to propose some compromises to the law in December, which would have reinstated some of the suspended professors, and restored some authority to the university faculties. But unwilling to cooperate, a number of professors filed lawsuits contesting their dismissals, while others organized an independent program of classes (the Alternative Academic Education Network, AAOL).

During 1998, Vojislav Šešelj appeared to be assuming increased influence in Serbia. For his part, Milošević fully realized that Šešelj's radical nationalism and extremism constituted a razor with two edges. Thus, Šešelj was useful in harassing the liberal opposition, and serving as a lightning rod for unsavory policies. But, as an advocate of hard-line measures in Kosovo, who also articulated an authoritarian sentiment in Serbian public opinion, Šešelj also limited Milošević's ability to rapidly change direction and accommodate foreign proposals regarding the treatment of the country's Albanian community. In order to give himself more room for political maneuver, Milošević had been carefully building bridges to the more nationalist leader, Vuk Drašković, who despised both the extremist Šešelj, and the Democratic Party's Zoran Djindjić. In 1997, for example, Milošević had convinced the ambitious Drašković, who had already broken with the *Zajedno* opposition alliance, that he should allow his party, the Serbian Movement for Renewal (SPO) to take part in Serbia's presidential and parliamentary election, even though Djindjić's Democratic Party and most other opposition forces had decided to boycott the election. By essentially co-opting the center-right SPO and Drašković (who assisted in forcing Djindjić from the post of Mayor of Belgrade) Milošević had brilliantly created a barrier against the growth of the liberal opposition, while also ensuring that the right-wing nationalists who were outside the ruling coalition would remain divided. But he was no longer able, as he was before the 1996–1997 protests, to wield absolute power through one omnipotent party. As he maneuvered to avoid the political consequences of his failed political and economic policies, Milošević was finding it necessary to constantly build and reshuffle coalitions, counting upon the ambitions and animosities of men such as Šešelj and Drašković. Milošević remained the dominant political actor in Yugoslavia, but he was less powerful than he had been earlier, and rather more anxious about the future of his regime.

In late October and early November Milošević, who had been rumored to be preparing the move for months, struck out against the moderates in the regime elite. Perhaps feeling vulnerable after NATO pressure and his capitulation on the Kosovo matter, Milošević did not want to take any chances of allowing divisions within his power structure. The first to go in October were Jovica Stanišić and Milorad Vučelić. The last straw for Milošević may have been Stanišić's connivance in the publication of an open letter severely critical of the regime. The letter, which appeared in the bi-monthly *Evropljanin*, was written by two prominent journalists, Slavko Ćuruvija and Aleksandar Tijanić, who had formerly been very close to the regime and ruling family. The letter called on Milošević to jettison radical elements in the ruling coalition, who were accused of carrying out a "state coup." Milošević did exactly the opposite of what Ćuruvija and Tijanić suggested, and he never forgave the authors of the letter or those who had permitted its publication. Stanišić's removal, which occurred just as some Yugoslav police units were being removed from Kosovo in compliance with the October agreement, was followed by the purge of his close associates throughout the security service.

Milorad Vučelić, who was associated with the pragmatic national swing in the SPS also was purged. Vučelić had been recycled back into the SPS in 1997 to shore up support for Milošević following the student and civic protests. During those demonstrations Vučelić had arranged a meeting between Stanišić and Djindjić to calm things down, and had also subsequently arranged a meeting between Djindjić and Milošević. Later Milošević asked Vučelić to use his personal associations in order to politically dampen the reformist policies of Montenegro's Milo Djukanović. However, Vučelić 's failure to perform that task, and his close association with Stanišić (both men were born in Bačka Palanka from families of Montenegrin origin who had settled in Vojvodina), now made Vučelić a liability to Milošević. Like Stanišić and Perišić, Vučelić was anathema to both the left-oriented JUL, and the ultra-right Serbian radicals who were now partners in Serbia's ruling coalition.

The removal of Stanišić and Vučelić was followed in mid-November by the dismissal—technically carried out by the Supreme Defense Council—of

General Perišić. Milo Djukanović, the Montenegrin representative on the Council, opposed the removal of Perišić. In addition to his policy differences with Milošević on the role of the army in important matters such as Kosovo, Montenegro, and managing political dissent, Perišić also was strongly opposed to the 1999 budget which gave the VJ far less material support than the Chief of Staff thought appropriate. "I was replaced without consultation," Perišić claimed, "in an inadequate and illegal way. This establishment does not like officials with high personal integrity who use their own heads. I am still at the disposal of the army, the people, and the state."[6]

Earlier on October 30, Milošević had also removed General Ljubiša Veličković, Commander of the Air Force and Air Defense, who had protested Milošević's approval for NATO surveillance flights over Kosovo. Veličković was transferred to the office of Federal Deputy Minister of Defense. According to one report, Veličković simply gathered his belongings, and walked out of his office in the Air Force Command Center, rather than share the building with six NATO officers who had arrived to supervise them.[7] Following the purge, Milošević appointed new officials who had the political support of his wife's JUL organization and the hard-line circles in the ruling coalition. Most importantly for the moment, the replacements were completely loyal to the Yugoslav president. Milošević's consolidation of control over the army in 1998 was particularly important because it was the only component of the power structure that he never had been able to totally rely upon. Perišić would later contend that prior to his removal, the army had been a "non-party, extra-party, supra-party" organization, but that with his departure the interests of the ruling party coalition became the guiding principle for the military establishment.[8]

All the so-called "moderates" removed in the fall of 1998 had, of course, taken an active part in assisting Milošević to carry out his policies. For example Vučelić was often referred to by Serbian commentators as "morally flexible," and someone who would cut his nationalism to suit his leader's wishes. For his part, Perišić had commanded Serb forces in Bosnia, and was sometimes called the "Knight of Mostar." Stanišić had directed much of the most ruthless cloak and dagger work for Milošević, as well as more well-known infamous deeds crucial to Milošević's maintenance of power (e.g., the arrest of Azem Vllasi and coordinating the activities of paramilitary formations during the war in Croatia, just to mention two). Indeed, Stanišić stood out as a man steeped in the authoritarian methods of a semi-police regime.[9] But by 1998, the three regime "moderates" represented saner voices in the Belgrade power structure, and their removal reflected a discernibly hard-line, anxious, and potentially dangerous turn in the course of the Milošević regime.

As Milošević proceeded to expel his more moderate associates from

Belgrade's ruling elites and tighten political control over the media and intelligentsia, the Clinton administration finally abandoned any hope that Yugoslavia's president might assist in the political stabilization of the Balkan region. Purging his ranks as a way to ensure unchallenged power Milošević inadvertently also had conveyed an image of a desperate authoritarian leader who was losing control and the ability to influence events. Meanwhile, negotiations concerning Kosovo were more or less bogged down, although Ambassador Hill continued his tireless shuttle diplomacy between the Albanian political leaders and the Serbian regime into November 1998. The fighting in Kosovo was not as intense as during the March–October period, but violence was increasing and intelligence was mounting that the Serb side was preparing another offensive against the UCK. There was also a concern that with the removal of Stanišić and Perišić, Milošević might at any time seek to take military measures against the reformist coalition in Montenegro.

By late November there was clear evidence that Washington's attitude towards Milošević had shifted. On December 1, Jamie Rubin, the spokesman for U.S. Secretary of State Albright, observed that "Milošević has been at the center of every crisis in the former Yugoslavia over the last decade. He is not simply part of the problem—Milošević is the problem." But Rubin, reflecting the State Department's continued dilemma concerning whom they should deal with in Yugoslavia, also added that while Milošević is "the source of the problem and the original sinner" in the Yugoslav "catastrophe," it was still necessary to talk to both the Serbian president and the Serbian opposition: "That's how you balance principle and pragmatism in a very complicated situation like Serbia," Rubin observed.[10] But Washington's position on Milošević had become more assertive. In a turnabout from established U.S. policy the Serb leader was no longer viewed as being interested or even strong enough to assist in stabilizing Eastern Europe. After all, Milošević had ceased to provide effective cooperation in the implementation of the Dayton agreement, seemed unwilling to find a diplomatic settlement of the Kosovo issue, and though he had survived the explosion of popular protest during 1996–1997, he appeared highly vulnerable on the domestic front.[11] Moreover, during the October 1998 crisis the NATO alliance—that was preparing for its fiftieth anniversary meeting in the spring of 1999, which would include a bold statement on its strategic role in the world—had been primed for military action in the Balkans. The Holbrooke–Milošević agreement had taken the Kosovo crisis off the front burner at a time when President Clinton was preoccupied with scandal-obsessed Washington politics. For the moment, the thorny issue of Serb-Albanian issues was postponed. But recognizing the significant issues at stake and the threat of future problems, top Clinton administration foreign policymakers, and especially Secretary of State Madeleine Albright, felt it was a good time to place maximum pressure on Belgrade. Unfortunately, the shriller rhetoric emanating from Washington came at a time when the American administration appeared completely immersed in the Lewinsky affair. This undoubtedly led Milošević to conclude that Washington's harsher tone did not amount to a serious change in policy.

By mid-December 1998 the temporary calm that had been achieved in Kosovo immediately after the Milošević–Holbrooke accord was coming to an end, and hopes for a negotiated settlement of the province's future were faltering. The level of violence between Serb forces and the UCK had decreased, but both sides were regrouping for bigger operations. For the moment the fighting was still at the level of small skirmishes initiated from the Serb side, and also hit and run attacks and assassinations organized by the UCK. Meanwhile, both the Kosovar Albanian negotiating teams—an internally divided grouping of political forces headed by Rugova and the rival UCK organization—had rejected the latest American proposal for peace fashioned by Christopher Hill. The main sticking points for the Albanians were provisions in the proposal that left Kosovo under Serbian rule, and denied the province the same level of autonomy enjoyed by the two republics in the Yugoslav federation (Serbia and Montenegro). Kosovar negotiators were offended that while the American administration had condemned Milošević's regime as illiberal and authoritarian, Washington was still willing to ask the Albanians to place themselves under Serbian control.[12] Thus for the moment, Albanian intransigence on the political aspects of the negotiations allowed Milošević to appear conciliatory.

But Milošević still had serious cause for concern. Thus, neither the Albanian side nor the international community was prepared to yield regarding their fundamental demands that the Kosovars eventually be granted broad powers of self-government. Moreover, the UCK was growing stronger each day, international verifiers were arriving in Kosovo (although because of various "bureaucratic delays" only a quarter of the total contingent were on the ground by mid-December) and, even closer to home, the Serbian opposition was showing some signs of resurgence. At the same time Milošević, after having decided to dismiss a number of key associates—who had helped him weather earlier crises, and perhaps had moderated his views to some extent—was increasingly coming under the influence of hard-line elements from within his inner circle and the red–brown ruling party coalition. The militant politicians and security personnel around Milošević were eager to break the ceasefire in Kosovo, and to carry out a full-scale campaign against the UCK. Indeed extremist views were fanned when Albanians killed six young Serbian men at a bar in Kosovo on December 20, 1998. William Walker, the head of the Kosovo monitoring mission (KVM)—who had been selected by Secretary of

State Albright—condemned the killing at the bar, but claimed that it was impossible to verify Belgrade government claims about what had actually happened. As Walker was later to admit, "both sides were doing things that were wrong," but it was generally "easier to point at the [Belgrade] government."[13] Serious fighting erupted on Christmas Eve when Milošević sent new police units and troops into Kosovo to dislodge UCK units that had threatened to block a major road, and the UCK subsequently announced it was breaking the ceasefire that had been loosely in effect since October. Belgrade and Washington were increasingly on a collision course. In the United States, various political forces both inside and outside the administration, who either sought a showdown with the Milošević regime, or supported the UCK's goals and had little sympathy for Serbian concerns, now believed that it was time for the international community to stand up to Milošević. To do otherwise, many argued, could badly tarnish NATO's credibility and President Clinton's image as a foreign policy leader. The stage was being set for a military confrontation between NATO and Yugoslavia the coming year.

The Failure of Diplomacy: Račak and Rambouillet

In early January 1999 violence in Kosovo rapidly escalated. On January 9, after the UCK had seized eight Yugoslav soldiers, Serbian forces began pounding Kosovar Albanian strongholds. The OSCE Verification Mission (KVM) eventually arranged for the release of the Yugoslav soldiers, but the fighting continued to escalate. On January 15, the bodies of 45 Albanian civilians were found by OSCE monitors and journalists in Račak, a town about 18 miles south of Priština. The killing at Račak had been carried out by members of the Serbian Special Anti-Terrorist unit (SAJ) and Ministry of the Interior police working with members of a local paramilitary unit. The operation had been a savage act of revenge for a UCK ambush about a week earlier, which had left four Serbian policemen dead. William Walker, the head of the KVM, was led to the massacre site by UCK insurgents who had retaken the village following the departure of Serb forces.[14] Walker accused Serbian security forces of having carried out the atrocities, and requested that international officials from the War Crimes Tribunal at the Hague be sent to Kosovo to investigate. Yugoslavia refused, and also declared Walker *persona non grata*. Only after international pressure was applied did Walker receive permission to remain in Kosovo. After discovering the Albanian bodies at Račak, Walker also called Richard Holbrooke and Wesley Clark to report on the matter.[15] For American officials, and particularly Secretary of State Albright, the Račak incident served as the green light to finally detach Kosovo from the control of the Milošević regime, and at the same time, potentially eliminate Milošević. "My first reaction," Albright later observed, "was that [the Serbs] had actually started their campaign of mowing down the Kosovars. . . . It was a galvanizing event . . . it energized all of us to say that this requires a larger plan, and a steady application of military planning for an air campaign."[16]

High-profile media reports and photos of the Račak massacre focussed international public and elite attention on the Kosovo issue in much the same manner that the 1995 events at Srebrenica had served as a turning point in the Bosnian war. The situation in Kosovo was deteriorating faster than most observers had expected only months earlier. Holbrooke's deal with Milošević in October had merely postponed a situation that now had to be faced head on. On January 19, Clinton's top foreign policy-makers met without the president in the Situation Room at the White House, and decided to use the threat of air strikes in Yugoslavia in order to force Belgrade to sign a peace agreement with the Kosovar Albanians. Urged on by Secretary of State Albright, who had been promoting tough action against Milošević throughout the prior year, it was agreed that the Albanians and Belgrade would be summoned to a speedily convened peace conference, and offered the basic principles of a non-negotiable settlement proposal. Should agreement be reached, the U.S. would participate in the international force that would enter Kosovo to monitor the implementation of the peace plan.

But with President Clinton still mired in the Lewinsky-related impeachment process, the administration ultimately decided to give the diplomatic track one more try. The plan outlined by his foreign policy team was forwarded to Clinton on January 19, 1999, and president discussed it with British Prime Minister Tony Blair on January 21. It was agreed by the leaders that no military action would be taken against Milošević until a diplomatic effort to obtain a political solution was attempted, and also that the Albanian side must be seen as agreeing to a nonmilitary outcome. Albright's task following these discussions was to convince the rest of the allies, as well as Russia, to go along with the plan. The proposal was premised on resolving the crisis diplomatically, but a credible threat of force was considered essential to drive negotiations.

At the same time these key meetings were taking place in Washington, NATO's top commander, General Wesley Clark, and the head of NATO's military council, General Klaus Naumann, were meeting in Belgrade with Milošević. Even after being shown the photographic evidence from Račak, and warned of air strikes if similar Serbian operations in Kosovo did not cease, Milošević continued to adamantly resist any new agreement. General Clark would later recount that on January 20, he warned Milošević (in a meeting where NATO General Klaus Naumann was also present), that NATO would order the bombing if he failed to keep the promise he had made to Holbrooke in October 1998. "That made him very angry and he looked quite worried. Of course he didn't want to be targeted from the air but he told me that Kosovo was more important to him than his own head."[17] Clark would later remark that he and Naumann "listened to that. But we didn't know what it meant."[18] In the light of what would occur in Kosovo several months later in 1999, Clark came to believe that Milošević proved to be a prototypical pragmatic decision maker, who would ultimately give up Kosovo "to save his regime, to save his army, and to save his head." But in retrospect, it appears that Milošević was signaling Clark that the Belgrade regime would not give up control of Kosovo easily or quickly, even if attacked by NATO.

General Naumann later remarked that, in contrast to his visit with General Clark to pressure Milošević in October 1998, "when we were sent to Belgrade with a clear stick in our hip pocket, the ultimatum . . . the second time in January [1999], this stick had been transformed into a rubber baton. . . . We had threatened too often and hadn't done anything. So it was no surprise that Milošević on this very day, was not in the mood to make concessions at all."[19] The same message that had been carried by the NATO generals was conveyed to Milošević the next day by two State Department officials, James Pardew and Christopher Hill. They had no more success than Clark. The will and credibility of the Clinton administration was now ominously pitted against Milošević's seemingly unbending commitment to not lose his control over Kosovo simply in response to NATO military threats. When President Clinton met his foreign policy team on February 1, 1999, he told them that he now realized, based on intelligence reports, that Kosovo was of more importance to Milošević than Bosnia had been, and that the Serbian president might therefore be tempted to withstand the first rounds of bombing strikes against his forces.[20] Clinton and his NATO allies also knew that sometime in the fall of 1998, Milošević had decided to resolve the Kosovo problem by using force in the first part of 1999. Though few believed that a Dayton-like peace conference could still stop Milošević in Kosovo, the Clinton administration, distracted by the drama of impeachment politics, and pressured by its major allies to find a non-military solution, decided to opt for one final diplomatic push. For the moment, the policy of continuing negotiations would have precedence over the views of those members of the U.S. administration who believed that Milošević would quickly acquiesce to NATO demands if exposed to the use of coercion by the alliance.

The United States' major European NATO allies wanted peace talks on Kosovo to be held on their continent, as a sort of European equivalent to the Dayton conference on Bosnia. It was eventually decided that the peace negotiations would be held in Rambouillet, France, under the auspices of the Contact Group and chaired jointly by British Foreign Minister Robin Cook and

French Foreign Minister Hubert Vedrine. There was, however, to be no direct negotiations between the Serbian and Albanian delegations. Mediation would instead be carried out by a "troika" of envoys: Christopher Hill for the United States, the Russian Boris Mayorsky, and Wolfgang Petritsch for the European Union. The initial absence of Madeleine Albright at Rambouillet seemed to indicate that Washington did not hold out much hope that the conference would succeed.

The peace plan offered by the Contact Group at Rambouillet was based on the proposal developed by Christopher Hill during the previous months of shuttle diplomacy. Its core elements, as the final version emerged at Rambouillet, provided for an interim three-year period of Kosovo "self-government," during which the province could *de jure* be part of Yugoslavia and Serbia, but the Kosovar Albanians would enjoy substantial political autonomy. The province would have its own separate legislative, executive and judicial institutions, as well as representation in the Yugoslav and Serbian assemblies. Under the plan, the UCK was to be demilitarized over a four-month period, Serb security and military personnel would substantially leave Kosovo (the army, over six months leaving 2,500 troops for border duty; the police over two years), and a NATO-led international armed force authorized by the United Nations (of about 28,000 troops) would enter the province to provide security. An interim administration run by the OSCE would be put in place and would eventually conduct free elections. At the end of three years an international conference would be held on Kosovo's future. There was also a statement that the conference would act (Chapter 8, article 1, section 3) "on the basis of the will of the people." This provision strongly suggested that a referendum could eventually permit the large Albanian majority in Kosovo to determine its own fate. According to the EU special envoy to the talks, Wolfgang Petritsch, "80 percent of the plan was nonnegotiable, just 20 percent subject to possible debate and adjustment. The calendar was set. It was a tight schedule. . . . Experience from the negotiations in Dayton on Bosnia showed that unless there was a rigid framework of reference, the talks risked charging off in all directions, of getting bogged down in every detail."[21] U.S. General Wesley Clark was not at Rambouillet, but later argued that the conference was not some kind of "lethal trap for the Serbs to assure the bombing would start. On the contrary—it was presented as the most artful way of dodging the question on what the eventual status would be, and trying to reach reconciliation between two, on the surface, irreconcilable positions."[22] The problem, however, was that Milošević was not yet prepared to accept an artful dodge on the matter of Kosovo. "Rambouillet was not a negotiation," Milošević later observed. "It was a Clinton administration diktat. It wasn't take it or leave it. Just take it or else. . . . Rambouillet was a recipe for the independence of

Kosovo, which clearly, we could not accept."[23] Adem Demaci, who for a time had been the UCK's political representative, also opposed the Rambouillet negotiation:

> I believed it was wrong to begin negotiations while the Serbian regime was doing what it was doing. Secondly, the preparations for Rambouillet were poor. The project of Ambassadors Hill and Petritsch was incomplete. You cannot draft an important accord in a few days, and then negotiate twenty days without meeting with the other side at all. . . . The Albanians spoke with Hill, and he went to the Serbs, and then again to the Albanians, and then back and forth. . . . Of course it was necessary to have someone to guarantee the agreement, but it was not good to have them negotiating on our behalf. If we are incapable of negotiating, how are we going to live together? . . . The Albanians should have insisted on direct negotiations . . . it is true that it could have lasted perhaps a year but I am sure that this bloodshed and everything else would have been avoided.[24]

As a result of such differing perceptions, the Rambouillet talks, which began on February 6, turned into a diplomatic debacle, a sideshow to unfolding events that only deepened mistrust between the Kosovar Albanians and the Serbs and ultimately failed to avert the drift towards war. Milošević, who refused to attend the talks in person (perhaps fearing a secret war crimes indictment against him), sent a second-string delegation to France. The activities of the Serbian negotiating team were coordinated by a nondelegate to the talks, Milan Milutinović, the President of Serbia, and one of Milošević's closest cronies. As usual, Milošević's strategy was to stretch out the negotiations as long as possible in order to obtain as many concessions as he could. While he wished to retain sovereignty over Kosovo and avoid the stationing of international troops on Yugoslav soil, his paramount goal was to retain power in Belgrade. To that end, his real agenda for discussion with the international community was probably less focussed on Kosovo than on receiving various other concessions for his regime. He was especially interested in matters such as the lifting of all international sanctions against Yugoslavia, obtaining financial support for economic development, the return of his country to international organizations, and personal assurances that he could avoid future prosecution for war crimes. But Milošević clearly was unprepared to pursue that agenda in the context of the Rambouillet meeting. As in earlier crises, his preference was that emissaries from the international community come to Belgrade to meet with him. Accordingly, Milošević basically let the Serbian delegation in France mark time. He was confident, as usual, that divisions among leading powers and their reluctance to use military force, and their inability to enforce a diplomatic agreement without his consent, would ultimately allow him to get his way. Though Milošević may have overestimated the extent of cleavage among the foreign powers, he was not far off the mark, at least as the Rambouillet discussions got under way. For example, EU envoy Petritsch has suggested that the Americans were the least willing to offer any incentives in order to get Milošević to sign an agreement, the Russians were most willing because they opposed the use of force, and the Europeans aiming at "the best possible compromise between these two positions."[25] Veton Surroi, an astute journalist (who also is the publisher of the Priština daily *Koha Doitre*), and member of the Albanian team, has offered his side's colorful perception of the atmosphere at the conference. "The Serbs were aware that they were not deciding about anything and that their boss was [back] in Belgrade. Therefore every evening they shouted, got drunk, and sang loudly until early morning hours. On the other hand, we and the Albanian delegation hardly ever slept. Not because we persistently analyzed the Contact Group proposals, but because of the noise made by the Serbian delegation lodged on the floor above ours."[26] Another Kosovo Albanian negotiator, Dugi Gorani, observed that his colleagues "became used to rare wines. We became used to delicious and I suspect tremendously expensive French specialties. We became used to luxury which the main aim was to see us taking up a pencil and signing a piece of paper."[27]

At the end of the first weeks of talks, Secretary of State Albright briefly joined the negotiations to advise both sides that they must make rapid progress. On February 14, she also met with Serb President Milutinović in Paris and bluntly demanded that the Serb side "engage seriously" in the discussions. The Contact Group extended the negotiating deadline to noon on February 20. Returning to Washington, Albright telephoned Milošević twice to explain the consequences of his continued refusal to sign a peace agreement. Albright also asked Ambassador Hill to leave Rambouillet—much to the chagrin of the other negotiators—and to meet with Milošević in Belgrade in order to reinforce Washington's view.[28]

For his part, Milošević hoped and expected the Albanians would reject the Contact Group proposal, and thereby essentially take Belgrade off the hook. Indeed the Albanian side was a deeply divided group of political activists, all committed to Kosovo's independence, but disagreeing on the best way to obtain that goal. Thus, most Kosovar Albanian delegates wanted to ensure that the Albanian population of Kosovo would no longer be subject to Belgrade's political control at the conclusion of the three-year interim arrangements provided for in the Contact Group's peace proposal, and that until then, the Kosovars would receive protection from NATO. The major problem for the Albanians was that they did not represent a recognized elected government controlling a state. Ibrahim Rugova was technically president of Kosovo's parallel state, but by the time the talks had begun, he had been completely marginalized by the UCK, whose successes had captured the imagination of most Kosovars, especially among the younger generation. Rugova's strategy of passive resistance simply no longer appeared to be a profitable avenue for Albanian political energies in Kosovo.

Persistent squabbling among the Albanian delegates at Rambouillet was a constant source of frustration to the international mediators and nearly scuttled the talks entirely. Moreover, as Rugova's political influence eroded, leadership on the Albanian side gradually shifted to the young chief of the UCK's political directorate, Hashim Thaci. Thaci actually represented the more pragmatic wing of the guerilla organization, but at first he was unwilling to sign any kind of agreement that it did not explicitly include provisions for a future referendum concerning the province's independence. Indeed, he would use blunt and even threatening language to intimidate his fellow delegates.[29] After all, on the ground in Kosovo the Albanian insurgents of the UCK had become a strong and united political force. Meanwhile, the more outspoken and veteran political activist, Adem Demaci, who was the civilian representative of the UCK, did not even come to the Rambouillet talks. Throughout the negotiations Kosovar Albanian delegates, such as Surroi, worked closely with the American representatives to forge a consensus among the various factions on the Albanian side. But when Secretary Albright joined the talks during the last three days (February 20–23), she still found the Albanians divided and resistant to the peace plan. Desperate for a breakthrough by this time (the talks had already been extended twice) Albright turned to the Albanian foreign minister, Pascal Milo, who was in close contact with the Kosovar Albanians and on his way to Paris. According to Milo he was telephoned by Mrs. Albright twice before going to Paris, and once in France he met with the American delegation on two occasions. Milo was asked to exert his influence on the Kosovo delegation to accept the agreement based on American guarantees. The United States, Milo claims, guaranteed a NATO presence in Kosovo, direct aid, including funding for democratic institutions during a transitional period, and also that the UCK would be assisted in its professionalization and becoming part of Kosovo's new military forces.[30]

Even after providing such guarantees to the Albanians, Albright was only able to convince them to endorse agreement to the peace plan in principle, pending further consultations in Kosovo. Albright's intervention may have helped to get the Albanians on board, but it only served to foster Serb suspicions and intransigence. Once Albright had promised that NATO would protect the agreement, she could only change the character of the international force at the risk of losing the Kosovar Albanian's approval for the plan. Veton Surroi has summarized what Albright told the Albanian side: "She was saying, you sign, the Serbs don't sign, we bomb. You sign, the Serbs sign, you have NATO in. So its up to you to say. [If] you don't sign, the Serbs don't sign, we forget about the subject. [It] was very explicit."[31] Ambassador Hill put Albright's role in the best possible light, but his remarks also revealed a general concern expressed by many observers, particularly the Europeans, that the United States was solidly positioned on the Albanian side during the negotiating process (a charge Milošević would also later make).

> [Madeleine Albright] played a really substantial role in making it clear to both parties what we were seeking. And I think her role, especially with the Albanians to show them what the U.S. can do for them and why they need to work with us on this, was absolutely critical in getting the Albanians to say "yes." I think with the Serbs . . . [she was important] especially to make it clear to them what their continued intransigence is going to mean.[32]

On February 23, the talks were postponed so that the Kosovar Albanian delegation could return home for consultations. Divisions among the Albanians, and their unwillingness to sign the peace plan, prompted the Serbs to believe they had bought some valuable time. But in fact the final countdown to war had begun. The Kosovar Albanians now had confidence that the Americans and NATO would not cave in to Milošević's tactics. But as Veton Surroi has suggested, the true test of American conviction would come after the bombing began:

> A good part of the Contact Group, particularly the Americans and British, has also developed the conviction that bombing can help in finding a solution, but that means that Milošević must see the consequences of his behavior, and must change that behavior. In a good part of the international community the question has arisen: "Good, we'll bomb, and what afterward, what will happen the day after that?" . . . they must bomb as much as necessary until Milošević is convinced that his rule, what he is ruling, has gone to ruin and that he could possibly save himself by changing his course.[33]

Indeed, by this time the Serbs were less inclined to sign a peace settlement than they had been when they first arrived at Rambouillet. Particularly galling to Belgrade was Appendix B of the proposed accord, which provided, among other things, that NATO troops would not be under Yugoslav legal jurisdiction, international troops could go anywhere in Yugoslavia in order to perform their duties, and had complete access to all forms of transportation and communication in Yugoslavia. Such provisions would in effect allow NATO to function as a parallel authority throughout Yugoslavia. From Milošević's perspective this would mean that NATO would be in a position not only to oppose a peace agreement, but also to potentially meddle in Yugoslav internal affairs, and possibly even assist political opposition elements challenging his rule. The Russians had rejected the Appendix B provisions as soon as they learned about such an addition to the agreement. Serbian delegates rejected the military clauses in the Appendix on February 22, on the grounds that they had not been approved by the entire Contact Group. For their part, NATO spokesmen interpreted the Appendix material in a far narrower manner, that is, as simply permission for logistical movement to facilitate peace-keeping forces in Kosovo. An intriguing open question is whether or not Appendix B was a "poison pill" deliberately added to the draft agreement in order to elicit certain Serbian rejection, and thus allow NATO bombing of Kosovo and Serbia to begin? For example, Russian foreign minister Igor Ivanov would later claim that the Appendix documents covering the role of the NATO-led force, and another item dealing with the deployment of Yugoslav army and police in Kosovo, were added to the Rambouillet accord by Christopher Hill during the very last stage of negotiations, and "behind Russia's back."[34]

Many in the international community, and certainly most Serbs, would later feel that Rambouillet did not provide a real opportunity for negotiations, and that the controversial Appendix items were an "excuse for war." Other observers, and particularly most members of the NATO alliance—which would soon take harsh military action against Serbia—felt that frustrating diplomatic discussions with the Milošević regime had been conducted in good faith for a period well beyond that which would normally be expected, and that it was the regime in Belgrade that had torpedoed the sensible peace proposal offered at Rambouillet. Interestingly, Richard Holbrooke, who at Dayton had negotiated the end of the war in Bosnia, and also the October 1998 agreement on Kosovo that Milošević had ultimately broken, was extremely critical in private of Mrs. Albright's management of the Rambouillet summit. Holbrooke let it be known that he favored a more traditional diplomatic approach, which did not involve negotiating only with the weaker Kosovar Albanian side. Holbrooke and Albright shared a belief that only a marriage of force and diplomacy could work with leaders such as Milošević. But Holbrooke would have preferred more latitude to negotiate directly deal with Milošević. In fact (at President Clinton's urging), Albright would give Holbrooke another opportunity to meet with the Yugoslav president, but with very narrow instructions regarding what could be discussed. For Mrs. Albright, who claimed to have a mindset shaped by the memory of great power failure at Munich before World War II (that had resulted in the dissection of her native Czechoslovakia), non-appeasement of an authoritarian leader such as Milošević was a matter of principle. Moreover, gripped by remorse over having only recently blocked the type of substantial international intervention in Rwanda which might have averted the genocide that ultimately took place in that country, Mrs. Albright was undoubtedly determined to avoid any suggestion that she had once again failed to prevent an ethnic massacre. Indeed, Albright was apparently ready to use force against Milošević even before Rambouillet. However, she felt that Washington needed to give the Europeans one more crack at diplomacy and, perhaps that the experience at those final negotiations might help to prepare the non-American members of NATO to ultimately employ military measures against Belgrade.[35]

On March 18, three weeks after the Albanians had requested a pause in peace negotiations, the conference reconvened at the Rue Kleber Conference Center in Paris. A few days later, four ethnic Albanian delegates signed the peace plan. While the agreement did not specify that a referendum on the province's future would definitely take place at the end of three years, American representatives were widely rumored to have given confidential assurances to Kosovo representatives that NATO's imminent leverage in Kosovo's affairs would guarantee that such a vote would eventually be held. Angered by the entire course of the negotiations, and the special consideration given to Albanian concerns, the Serbs rejected the proposal, including the embellished political components. Milošević's removal on March 22 of his military intelligence chief, Aleksandar Dimitrijević, who had warned against Yugoslavia calling NATO's bluff, was a strong signal that the Belgrade regime had decided to forgo a peaceful resolution of the Kosovo crisis.[36] Indeed, on March 16, the CIA warned senior American decision makers that a Serb offensive against Albanian fighters and civilians—modeled on the infamous plan Operation Horseshoe (*Potkovica*) that supposedly had been detected by Austrian and German intelligence in the fall of 1998—was about to begin in Kosovo. Based on such reports and also their own firsthand reconnaissance in Kosovo, the OSCE began pulling out its approximately 1,380 verification monitors (well short of the 2,000-person contingent planned the previous October) from the province. The departure of the KVM personnel immediately after the collapse of the Rambouillet talks eliminated the existence of any international buffer between Serbian forces and the Albanian population, and helped create a dangerous vacuum. Increasing numbers of Albanian civilians began to flee their homes as the OSCE monitors began their departure from the province. Several days before the NATO bombing campaign began, and before international emissaries would fly to Belgrade to attempt to reason with Milošević once again, a high-ranking OSCE official claimed he had received a ominous warning: "We've got indications that they're [Serbian forces] absolutely going to wreak havoc. Its going to be a really ugly scene."[37] Already accustomed to Serbian police onslaughts, the Albanian civilian population also knew that neither the UCK, nor allied bombers, could help them on the ground. Local Albanians, including those working for the OSCE, could take cold comfort from OSCE mission chief William Walker's observation when he left Kosovo that the international community would be watching developments.[38] The unarmed monitors would clearly be in danger if bombing were to commence, but their withdrawal could only exacerbate conflict on the ground, further undermine any final effort to resolve the crisis, and leave the civilian population to its own fate. As momentum spiraled toward war, one might legitimately ask whether NATO planners and politicians had really thought through the full implications of the Kosovo strategy they were about to employ?

Suggestions by some European foreign ministers that they fly to Belgrade and appeal to Milošević one last time were deflected by Mrs. Albright. Instead, she persuaded the U.S. allies to send the seasoned Richard Holbrooke to Belgrade, together with the Rambouillet mediators, to convey a final, essentially sign-up-or-be-bombed, ultimatum. But there were to be no marathon sessions devoted to deal-making and creative initiatives. This would deny Milošević the opportunity, which he had shrewdly exploited on so many previous occasions, to bargain for concessions. In the preceding weeks, several hundred thousand Kosovars had already been displaced from their homes by the Serbian assault on the UCK strongholds and the surrounding civilian population. Albright and the Clinton administration were aware of what was unfolding on the ground in Kosovo, and that a policy of no concessions would very likely make bombing inevitable, including its potentially uncertain consequences for the local population of Kosovo. But their policy remained steadfast. Either Belgrade would accept NATO-led forces and the Rambouillet peace plan, or the bombing would begin. The general expectation by most officials in Washington and NATO capitals—a point Albright strongly emphasized—was that once bombing began Milošević would quickly come to accept the urgency of a negotiated settlement, as he had done after allied bombing of the Bosnian Serbs in 1995. Emboldened by that conviction, and by the realization that Milošević had already subjected the Kosovar Albanians to considerable repression, and was planning more, little consideration was devoted to the possibility that a more terrible fate might await the Albanians in the province should bombing begin.

The assumption that only a short bombing campaign would be necessary is somewhat understandable in view of Milošević's earlier acquiescence to international demands once force was used. After all, Milošević had been willing to leave the Serbs in Bosnia, and also the Serbs in Croatia, to their fate. But if Albright and others were wrong, if Milošević withstood the bombing for any substantial period of time, and if allied ground troops were not deployed, Kosovar civilians would be left terribly exposed and in a very dangerous position. Milošević had warned foreign officials that he regarded Kosovo as a matter of crucial significance to the Serbs, and to his political future. NATO politicians also knew the kind of brutality Milošević was capable of setting in motion, and were well aware he had the forces and a plan of action at the ready to obtain his goals in Kosovo. But lacking a consensus, eager to avoid a ground war, and also needing to assert the alliance's credibility, bombing seemed the only viable option to NATO leaders. General Henry Shelton, Chairman of the U.S. Joint Chiefs of Staff, would later explain the thinking at the time: "And so when it came down to the end, there were only two options left. One was either to move forward with the air campaign or to not do anything. And none of us felt like that doing nothing was the right answer. And we looked at the air campaign, we felt that the air campaign would succeed and that it could be carried out with an acceptable risk. And so."[39] U.S. Secretary of Defense William Cohen has retrospectively advanced the same view. "We knew from the beginning that no air campaign—and certainly there was no ability at that time to conduct a ground operation or even threaten one at that moment—could have prevented him [Milošević] from carrying out this campaign of cleansing Kosovo of the ethnic Albanians."[40] This air campaign strategy hinged on the belief—premised on the rather thin reed of a CIA psychological profile of Milošević based on his compliant behavior after the Bosnian Serbs had been bombed four years earlier[41]—that the whole exercise could probably be concluded in just a few days. By that time, NATO leaders presumed the Kosovar Albanians would be out of the woods both figuratively and literally. Most observers and decision makers believed that there was little possibility that a rather lengthy conflagration might unfold. They were aware, however, that their miscalculation could result in enormous personal costs to both Albanians and Serbs should Milošević not quickly capitulate, and a situation arise where the civilians of the region would find themselves caught between the ruthlessness of an authoritarian regime and the fearsome bombing capability of a superpower. But Washington and NATO had decided to roll the dice, and finally deal with the Milošević problem. U.S. National Security Adviser Sandy Berger has commented on how much NATO know about Milošević's plans for "ethnic cleansing." "First of all we certainly knew. We had Bosnia as a graphical historical precedent. . . . Did we know he was amassing, getting ready to move into Kosovo? Yes. Did we hope we could stop it by acting? Yes. Did we realize we would not be able to stop it by acting? Yes to that, as well."[42]

Diplomacy by ultimatum, backed by bombing, had another risk. Thus, should Milošević not cave in immediately, it was also reasonable to expect that NATO would become the unofficial ally of the UCK, not to mention the guardian of the Kosovar Albanians for the foreseeable future. The United States and its allies had already become closely linked to the Kosovo Albanians during the Rambouillet conference. Once the Albanians agreed to those accords, an attack on Yugoslavia to obtain Milošević's signature appeared to constitute, as EU envoy Petritsch aptly put it on March 21, "support for the side which had signed the agreement." Moreover, he also observed, that "if a military strike becomes unavoidable then—following the logic of things—the North Atlantic Alliance would automatically help the UCK."[43]

When Milošević met with Holbrooke and others on March 22, he seemed fatalistic about what was unfolding: "You are a superpower," Ambassador Hill remembers Milošević saying. "You can do what you want. If you say Sunday is Wednesday, you can. It is all up to you." When Hill explained that without a peace agreement NATO would start bombing Yugoslavia, Milošević angrily retorted: "Anyone who does that—bomb—is going to spend the rest of his life on a psychiatric couch."[44] Holbrooke has described his last meeting with Milošević on March 23: "I said to him 'when I leave this room if you have not accepted the position that our NATO and Contact Group allies and friends including the Russians put forward at Rambouillet, is it clear to you that NATO bombing of the country will start and it will be,'—and I used these three words deliberately and after consultations with the Pentagon—'swift, severe, and sustained?' . . . Milošević said 'I understand this. You will bomb us. There is nothing I can do to prevent it' and I left the room."[45] Holbrooke and the delegation then left for Brussels to brief NATO leaders. President Clinton would later claim that he "had two models in mind on what would happen with the bombing campaign. I thought it would either be over within a couple of days because Milošević would see we were unified, or if he decided to sustain the damage to his country, that it would take a while longer for the damage to actually reach the point when it was unsustainable." What was unacceptable according to Clinton was to offer Milošević a UN force instead of a NATO force to monitor the peace agreement: "I think you have to see this through the lens of Bosnia . . . in Bosnia we had the UN in there first in a peacekeeping mission. Then we tried for four years, 50 different diplomatic solutions, all those different maps, all that different argument. And the end of it all, from 1991 to 1995, we still have Srebrenica . . . we had a quarter of a million people dead and two and a half million refugees . . . we saw [Kosovo] through the lens of Bosnia. And we said [in 1999] we are not going to wait a day, not a day if we can stop it [in Kosovo]."[46]

NATO vs. Serbia: The Politics of the Eleven-Week War

Mutual Miscalculations

The war between NATO and Yugoslavia that began on March 24, 1999, as most wars, largely resulted from mutual miscalculations and sharply divergent interests. Milošević never anticipated that a *sustained* bombing campaign against his country could be conducted by NATO, primarily because of the traditional political divisions among alliance members, and also because he believed that the Russians would bring pressure to bear on Yugoslavia's behalf. He further calculated that his domestic hold on political power—which had been severely undercut by the spring of 1999 in comparison to earlier years— would actually be enhanced by rejecting a foreign ultimatum on the matter of Kosovo's status. Kosovo, after all, was a subject that had traditionally been central to the Serb political psyche, and for over a decade Milošević had been successfully able to exploit the strong Serbian urge to maintain territorial control of the province. Indeed, he made the reasonable assumption that the majority of Yugoslav citizens would be more forgiving of his tough stand against NATO—even if such a policy would result in bombing of their country—than they would be of his acquiescence to NATO demands that effectively would establish a foreign or parallel authority in Kosovo and throughout Yugoslavia.

For their part, the majority of NATO leaders tended to view Milošević, and Serbian activity in Kosovo, through "the lens of Bosnia." Such a perspective rested on the expectation that when faced with a bombing campaign the Belgrade regime would rapidly capitulate. After all, it was argued anyone knowing Milošević's priorities and political history could reasonably conclude that faced with a threat to his hold on power, he would relinquish territory. But in the case of Kosovo, it was highly unlikely that he would give up territory without a tough fight. "Kosovo," as Milošević had pointed out, and repeated many times, "is not just a simple territory of Yugoslavia. Kosovo is the very heart of Serbia. Our entire history is tied to Kosovo. Only the people who do not know anything about Serbia or the Serbian people, nor about their culture and history, can assume that we could give Kosovo to somebody. This is out of the question."[47] Moreover, although Milošević had quickly acquiesced to international demands after the bombing of the Bosnian Serbs in 1995, he made that decision, in part, because of related ground advances by Bosnian and Croatian troops. But in Kosovo, the UCK—although growing more popular and militarily adept—had not yet become a cohesive organization maintaining control over numerous towns and extensive territory, and the insurgent movement at this point was still not closely allied with NATO. However, in March 1999 most NATO countries felt that something had to be urgently done to end Milošević's brutality in Kosovo, and to compel his acceptance of the Rambouillet accords. And as Washington and its allies lacked a consensus on the use of ground forces to deal with Belgrade's policy in Kosovo, air power seemed the only reasonable way to deal with the issue, and also to demonstrate NATO's credibility. Indeed, for most NATO members, severely wounding the Serbian military structure, or even eliminating Milošević—who was now regarded as a major impediment to the stabilization of Southern Europe—had considerable merit in its own right. Indeed, Madeleine Albright's spokesman, Jamie Rubin, would later suggest that privately, the members of Clinton's inner foreign policy elite did not entirely believe that prolonged hostilities could be avoided, and suspected that a ground war might become necessary. But administration officials could not be totally candid about their suspicions for fear of alienating members of Congress and coalition allies who opposed a long-term operation.[48] In any case those publicly subscribing to the Kosovo-will-be-Bosnia-again scenario posited a "relatively" quick end to both any NATO action, and also the humanitarian disaster that was beginning to unfold on the ground in Kosovo. Within the context of such politically expedient but inaccurate assumptions and calculations, further diplomatic negotiation made little sense, and also helped explain why the Rambouillet conference ended in failure. For his part, Milošević had never taken Rambouillet seriously, hoping instead to eventually wrest concessions from envoys sent to Belgrade to elicit his cooperation before NATO took any action. Washington, and particularly U.S. Secretary of State Albright, in contrast, had treated the conference in France as a place where the Albanian and Serbian sides would be compelled to accept what U.S. Ambassador Hill had already sketched out, or face the consequences.

Plans for the military resolution of the Kosovo crisis through a "phased air operation" had already been elaborated by NATO between June and October 1998, and agreed to at the White House in January. As General Clark later testified to the U.S. Congress, the activation order for NATO action that had been ready in October 1998 remained in place, and "it was subsequently incorporated as a threat into the Rambouillet process . . . we made these plans increasingly robust, we looked at the targeting processes and we had many other things underway as we moved to the final days up to the conclusion of Rambouillet. . . . The Serbs recognized this also by the way, and they immediately began deploying . . . their forces and preparing defenses to block an anticipated NATO invasion of Kosovo. No matter how many times we told them we had no intention of invading Kosovo in the period during the Rambouillet talks, in February they still assumed that we were going to invade."[49]

Once the NATO air attack began, and the humanitarian catastrophe on the ground in Kosovo became apparent, NATO leaders claimed that it was not their bombing, but the actions of Milošević's forces in the notorious Operation Horseshoe, which began as early as March 19, 1999 (after the Albanians signed the Rambouillet accords), that was the cause of the massive Albanian refugee migration out of Kosovo. Indeed, evidence indicates that for a time the Yugoslav side had been building up strength for just such an onslaught in

Kosovo. In fact Serbian police action against civilians in areas considered to be centers of UCK activity had accelerated. But Clark's comments, months after the war, reveal that, from his vantage point at least, the Serb military buildup was just as much a reaction to NATO military plans, albeit under the mistaken impression that NATO would actually use ground troops to invade the province, as it was part of preparation for an enlarged police and para-military assault against the UCK and Albanian civilians. Thus, though there is no proof that a plan called Operation Horseshoe even existed, sources gener-ally confirm that Yugoslav political and military planners believed that the only way to successfully counter an expected NATO ground assault in Kosovo would be to force thousands of Albanian civilians onto the main roads lead-ing in and out of the province. For Milošević and his cold-blooded inner cir-cle in Belgrade, it could not be helped if such tactics reduced the size of the Albanian population in Kosovo and generated a humanitarian crisis. Indeed, die-hard Serb ultra-nationalists explicitly hoped such methods would result in an improved ethnic balance in Kosovo's population. Later, during the war, Milošević would emphasize that his force build up on the eve of the NATO attack was carried out in order to deal with the Kosovo Liberation Army. "We reinforced our forces after Rambouillet for a major offensive against KLA [UCK] terrorists, not to ethnically cleanse Kosovo."[50] In any case, when the bombing campaign was launched, NATO believed that the military phase would conclude very quickly. As Clark additionally pointed out: "It was hoped that President Milošević wouldn't really require the full force of NATO, the full destruction of his country in order to comply with the reasonable demands put forth at Rambouillet. This accounts for the incremental approach of the air campaign."

An "Acceptable Risk"

On Christmas Eve 1992, during the last days of the Bush administration, Sec-retary of State Lawrence Eagleburger had sent a short classified cable to Bel-grade with instructions that the acting U.S. ambassador in Yugoslavia person-ally read it to Milošević. The text said: "In the event of conflict at Kosovo caused by Serbian action, the United States will be prepared to employ mili-tary force against Serbians in Kosovo and in Serbia proper." The same general warning had been reiterated to Milošević twice by the Clinton administration: first in February and again in July 1993.[51]

On March 24, 1999, over six years after their initial warning to Milošević, the United States and its allies began an air war against Yugoslavia. NATO listed five specific objectives it intended to achieve: (1) obtain a ceasefire in Kosovo; (2) force Serbian military, police and paramilitary forces out of the province; (3) allow the displaced and refugee Albanian population to return to

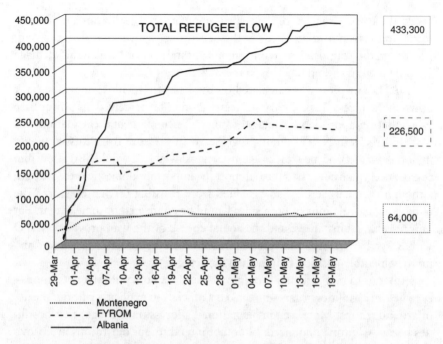

Figure 6.1   Refugee Outflow from Kosovo to Albania, FYROM, and Montenegro, March 29–May 19, 1999

their homes and a secure environment; (4) allow a NATO-led international peace keeping force into Kosovo, and; (5) allow Kosovars to begin practicing self-government as outlined in the Rambouillet agreement. Some two and a half months later those objectives were achieved, but only after thousands of deaths, the displacement of hundreds of thousands of civilians, and an air campaign that caused widespread destruction to the economic infrastructure of Kosovo and Serbia. Milošević did not capitulate in two or three days as expected. It took eleven weeks of punishing attacks against his country before he would finally capitulate to NATO's demands.

In effect two parallel military campaigns took place on the soil of the Federal Republic of Yugoslavia during the spring of 1999: the first involved the brutal attack of Serbian police and irregular forces against the initially weaker forces of the UCK and the completely unprotected civilian Albanian population of Kosovo; the second was a highly sophisticated air campaign carried out by nineteen NATO countries against the much smaller and weaker Yugoslav state. And though Milošević was eventually forced to accept NATO's terms for cessation of the bombing campaign, both facets of the overall war directly caused or precipitated humanitarian disasters: for Kosovo's Albanians, as a result of the first struggle; for the civilian population of Serbia, and, more indirectly and less immediately, the Serbs of Kosovo, as a result of the second. Moreover, the war also resulted in significant indirect or "collateral" damage for other countries and civilians in the Balkan region.

NATO's mission was calculated on the basis that Milošević would back down in the face of the military strikes as soon as he perceived his power base was suffering appreciable damage. Milošević's fundamental calculation was that the cracks in NATO's unity, together with pressure from Russia, would limit the intensity of the attacks against Yugoslavia, and would also allow him to extract enough concessions to support the important domestic pretense that, although crippled, Serbia had benefited from resisting foreign pressure. The underlying calculations of both sides would be confirmed to some extent. But unforeseen circumstances, and the actual course of the war, provided NATO with a Pyrrhic victory; and resulted in Milošević being left in a weaker and more vulnerable position than he had expected.

Anxious to mobilize public opinion behind his policy, President Clinton—even before hostilities began—directed his officials to explicitly rule out the use of ground troops. Moreover, in his national address on the night that hostilities began, Clinton announced: "I do not intend to put our troops in Kosovo to fight a war." But, he added, inaction was unacceptable: "there would be many massacres, tens of thousands of refugees, victims crying for revenge."[52] The sentence in Clinton's speech indicating that no ground troops would be sent to Kosovo allegedly was inserted at the last minute by National Security Adviser Sandy Berger without consulting Secretary of State Albright.[53] Milošević already knew, of course, that the allies had not prepared for a ground invasion. But statements by Clinton and members of his administration stipulating there would be an exclusive use of air operations in the struggle undoubtedly encouraged the Yugoslav president to try and withstand the bombing for as long as he could. If a central component of crisis resolution through the use of linked diplomatic and military power is to "preserve uncertainty" in the opponent's mind concerning the consequences of rejecting peaceful options, then the Clinton administration certainly made a crucial mistake in ruling out the possibility of a ground invasion of Kosovo at the beginning of the war. That mistake, as General Klaus Naumann would remark following the NATO-Yugoslav war (and his own retirement), "became most obvious when NATO began to prepare for military options . . . some NATO nations began to rule out simultaneously options such as the use of ground forces and said so without any need in public. This allowed Milošević to calculate his risk and speculate there might be a chance for him to ride the threat out, and to hope that NATO would either be unable to act at all, or that the cohesion of the alliance would melt away."[54] Ultimately the unity of the alliance did not crumble, but Milošević withstood the attack—or at least allowed his country-men to do so—much longer than had been expected. But the resulting human-itarian tragedy, as a consequence of the Serbian president's ruthlessness, and also as a consequence of the bombing, was also much worse than NATO plan-ners and leaders had anticipated. In the end, NATO pilots would have to launch over 38,000 sorties (over 10,000 of which were strike sorties) during a 78-day period before the alliance would fulfill its objectives. But luckily for Clinton, in the "fog of war," the anarchy on the ground in Kosovo, and the intense propaganda war between NATO and Yugoslavia, few commentators emphasized that the original bombing campaign was intended to *prevent*, not just *reverse* the savage attack launched by the Serb forces against the Alban-ian population of Kosovo. That assault focussed public attention on the humanitarian catastrophe that had been unleashed, and almost completely diverted attention away from the initial failure of the air war to secure Milošević's capitulation. The original intention of the bombing, that is, to secure compliance with the Rambouillet peace plan, also faded from memory, as the focus turned toward what British Defense Secretary George Robertson called "humanitarian intervention" against a "genocidal" power.[55]

Western intelligence sources had already predicted that Belgrade's Opera-tion Horseshoe, or some Yugoslav coercive move against Albanian Kosovars designed to disrupt the province's roads and arteries, would also likely have disastrous humanitarian consequences. But few observers could anticipate how quickly the plan would be executed, the magnitude of its consequences, or the length of time it would take to force the Serbian regime to fully accept international demands. "We were conscious," Britain's Lord Robertson would later write after the war, "that military action might be seized upon by Milošević as an excuse to accelerate the offensive already underway. But while we had anticipated that the offensive could involve operations against the KLA, and violent repression of the civilian population, we could not have pre-dicted the full horror and extent of the brutality, which was to include scenes reminiscent of the 1930s and 1940s."[56] But Robertson claims not to have known about intelligence concerning Operation Horseshoe until April 9, or two weeks after the war began (other reports indicated NATO awareness at least one week before the war, if not longer). Intensifying a campaign that had begun as soon as the Albanian side had signed the Rambouillet accords, Serb police and paramilitary forces, generally with the help of the army, secured control of the overall terrain and systematically moved through the villages of Kosovo killing and expelling defenseless Albanian civilians. Surviving civilians fled towards the borders of Kosovo on foot or using whatever transportation was readily at hand. One Serb unit commander from the Yugoslav army later recounted to an American reporter the activities he had seen carried out by police units and paramilitary forces in the village of Zegra: "About 260 of them [ethnically] cleansed Zegra in 12 hours, 6,000–7,000 people. They took about a minute a house. They were shooting. Volunteers go to the center of town and started to shoot the first people to come to them. The whole village heard this and the people started to run away on their own, and there were police to guide them to Macedonia . . . it was ugly, but it happened and everyone you saw felt like an enemy. Its the worst kind of war."[57]

The orgy of killing, deportation, and massacres along with the looting and destruction of property—approximately 68,000 homes were destroyed—created a situation of anarchy in Kosovo, as hundreds of thousands of people caught between the Serbian onslaught and the NATO bombing fled their villages. It is fair to say, as NATO leaders repeated incessantly and defensively during and after the war, that major responsibility for the humanitarian catastrophe and ethnic cleansing in Kosovo should be attributed to Milošević's long-standing policy, and not to the Alliance's campaign. But Alliance leaders also knew that bombing alone could not stop Milošević from acting against the Albanians. Moreover, it was reasonable to assume, although there is no evidence that the point was actually discussed, that if Milošević did not capitulate quickly, the Serb attacks on the Kosovar Albanians would escalate—and, as a response to Serb suffering at the hands of NATO, would possibly become quite savage (after the bombing, Alliance leaders acknowledged that Albanians were taking revenge on the Serbs in response to their earlier suffering at the hands of the Yugoslav police and military). Many Serbs who committed atrocities against Albanians during the NATO bombing also rationalized their activities under the circumstances of NATO's attacks. After the military struggle in Kosovo, NATO General Klaus Naumann would observe that "the ethnic cleansing and the explosion was not triggered by NATO. It may have been accelerated by NATO. And definitely, some of the atrocities which happened I think was caused by NATO bombs. And this was simply the vendetta feeling which is pervading the Balkans anyway. And they [the Serbs] saw that their compatriots were bombed. They saw that Belgrade was bombed. So they took revenge with these people who could not defend themselves."[58] NATO's principal press spokesman during the campaign would later put the reasoning and the dilemma of Alliance leaders into perspective:

[T]o be successful force has to create disorder in order to cure disorder. . . . All military interventions are based on the premise that you have to exacerbate a crisis in order to solve it. . . . But it proved difficult for us to make the case that NATO's action had not made an already bad situation far worse than it might otherwise have been. . . . Not to do anything would not to have saved the lives of Kosovar Albanians, but rather to abandon them to perhaps a slower, but at the same time equally relentless campaign of prosecution, persecution and denial of basic human rights. . . . Ultimately NATO's greatest embarrassment also proved to be its salvation. In expelling hundreds of thousands of Kosovar Albanians, Milošević cruelly exposed NATO's strategy to prevent a humanitarian disaster, but he also highlighted the barbaric nature of his regime and solidified Western media and public opinion pressure against him.[59]

There is no question that Milošević's assault against Albanian insurgents and civilians alike, which began after Rambouillet, and which was intensified after the NATO attack began, helped NATO to make points in the battle for public opinion. NATO's "embarrassment" is that in its effort to force Milošević to sign a peace agreement, and also to politically weaken if not eliminate him, the Alliance had greatly underestimated the Yugoslav leader's stubbornness and staying power, and also underestimated the potential scale of the humanitarian disaster that might unfold if the negotiating process was brought to an end. In that sense, the bombing campaign constituted an enormous gamble. Moreover, it was a gamble that NATO took primarily with Albanian lives. The Albanian activist Shkelzen Maliqi has pointed out that up to the last minute, no one from the UCK on the ground in Kosovo really knew what was going to happen. "We underestimated the effect of the NATO attack. We believed it would be a campaign of no more than ten days after which the Serbs would surrender. That was an illusion. The UCK was mistaken. And those people in Priština and staffs across the mountains sent messages that the UCK will defend the population, who should remain in their homes. Simply, no one had a plan for an extraordinary situation."[60]

Leaders of the Alliance were also well aware that an air campaign alone could not assist the Albanians in the short run. And there was no way of knowing how long Milošević was actually prepared to withstand a bombing campaign that inflicted enormous suffering on his own people. "We hoped," National Security Adviser Sandy Berger remarked after the war, "that initiating military action would stop them [the Serb forces]. But we knew it was equally possible that it would not and that a sustained campaign might be necessary. We were determined to do the best we could and if necessary, reverse a massive ethnic cleansing."[61] Berger rejects the notion that failure to send troops to Kosovo "undermined America's moral position. Morality in a military conflict, I would submit derives fundamentally from the justice of the cause and care taken to minimize civilian casualties. . . . We gain no moral elevation from needless loss of lives."[62] But Berger was speaking about the loss of American lives. He completely begs the question of whether further diplomatic efforts, not ultimatums, at or immediately after the Rambouillet conference, or even concessions to Milošević (regarding matters that ultimately would help end the war, such as giving the United Nations overall authority in a Kosovo peace operation, dropping Appendix B on NATO's unimpeded access throughout Yugoslavia, etc.), might have resolved the crisis and saved civilian Albanian and Serbian lives (not to mention sparing civilians from the trauma associated with the postwar anti-Serb cycle of revenge in Kosovo that followed Milošević's capitulation). An end to negotiations, and strict adherence to the Rambouillet framework, also excluded discussion of other options such as partition or cantonization of the province.[63] After the NATO bombing campaign, those commentators who maintained that continued negotiations with Milošević were warranted, and that more adept diplomacy may have averted a humanitarian catastrophe were sometimes ridiculed as "naïve critics." However, the view that NATO military intervention in Kosovo was the correct remedy, or inevitable, and indeed should have probably been more intensely pursued from the onset of hostilities with respect to bombing Serbia's infrastructure, is generally put forth by analysts who regard Kosovo's political separation from the Yugoslav state as a desirable goal, oppose any partition of the province along ethnic lines, and who have expressed few qualms about the disruption in the province during its first year as an international protectorate.[64]

The precise death toll from the NATO–Yugoslav hostilities over Kosovo remains uncertain and controversial. But many thousands of military personnel and civilians were killed and injured. As many as 11,000 Kosovar Albanians may have been killed in over 100 massacres (some estimates range from 5,000 to 10,000). Serbian civilian dead have been estimated at between 1,500 and 2,000,[65] and perhaps another 5,000 people were wounded by the bombing. Human Rights Watch documented 500 civilian deaths in Serbia in 90 separate incidents.[66] Serbian military losses have been estimated by NATO at nearly 5,000 dead and another 10,000 wounded, but by the Belgrade authorities at 524 dead[67] and perhaps three times that number wounded. By the time the conflict ended it was estimated that there may have been as many as 500,000 displaced persons in Kosovo (some NATO officials now put that figure at fewer than 100,000)[68] and some 990,000 Kosovo Albanians had fled the province (the majority, about 780,000 left after the start of NATO air strikes on March 24). A large portion of the population of both Kosovo and Serbia were also emotionally traumatized by the hostilities, not to mention politically radicalized and unwilling to coexist with their neighbors from other ethnic groups. Indeed, in the first two months following the war, approximately 174,000 Serbs, Gypsies, and other members of minority groups in Kosovo would flee the province, while revenge killing of those groups by Albanians rose dramatically. There were no U.S. or allied combat deaths, but two American army aviators were killed when an Apache helicopter crashed in Albania on a training mission.

The war-related humanitarian disaster in Kosovo encouraged strong and justifiable criticism of the failed diplomacy preceding the war, and also Clinton's error in definitively ruling out the ground invasion option. However, the human costs of the war also helped to galvanize allied solidarity for the necessity of defeating Milošević and his military in a decisive manner. Despite a determination by most members of the alliance to defeat Milošević and promote NATO credibility, serious tension arose within NATO between military and political leaders over the execution of the air war. According to NATO plans the bombing campaign was to be a multiphased operation that would gradually eliminate the effectiveness of the Serbian military force and place the Belgrade regime under increasing stress. During phase one, NATO would attack Yugoslavia's anti-aircraft defenses and command bunkers. Phase two would involve attacks on Yugoslavia's infrastructure in Kosovo and southern Serbia. Phase three would escalate the attacks to include strategic bombing of Belgrade, and the northern part of the country. At the outset of the campaign, when it was hoped that Milošević would back down in a matter of a few hours or days, there was no attempt to extensively damage the Yugoslav economy or military. A decision was also made to proceed cautiously by using smaller bombs that were likely to inflict less collateral damage, and primarily fly missions above 15,000 feet in order to protect aircraft and pilots from Serbian air defense. From the start of the war there was opposition to the multiphased bombing strategy, which only provided for the gradual intensification of pressure against the Milošević regime. Lt. General Short, who was NATO's principal commander in the operation, believed that a "philosophy of incrementalism" was inappropriate to the task at hand, and that Milošević and the Serbs should immediately experience the bite of maximalist air attack by NATO. As General Short would later explain:

> I'd have gone for the head of the snake on the first night. I'd have turned the lights out the first night. I'd have dropped the bridges across the Danube. I'd have hit five or six political-military headquarters in downtown Belgrade. Milošević and his cronies would have waked up the first morning and asked what the hell was going on. . . . Questioning would have started right away: "If this is what the first night is like what's the rest of it going to be like?" But you remember—there were rock concerts in downtown Belgrade ten days into the war—I'd have done this differently.[69]

General Short was particularly perturbed by Alliance officials who were convinced that a little light bombing for just a few days would be enough to persuade Milošević to capitulate: "There was a reluctance to really grab him by the throat and shake him."[70]

Throughout the war General Clark attempted to convince Washington to escalate the bombing; a policy that some NATO leaders such as British Prime Minister Tony Blair were pressing Clark to adopt. Indeed Clark would later complain that the alliance had been "hamstrung" during the war by competing political and military interests that may have prolonged the conflict.[71] Clark also claimed that the imperative of maintaining the political cohesion of the Alliance had forced him to compromise the military conduct of the war. A desire by NATO political leaders to avoid civilian casualties and allied pilot losses, and also their unwillingness to consider a ground invasion, according to Clark, imposed constraints that frustrated military planners. In Clark's opinion "once the barrier to using military forces is crossed, the natural desire among military commanders is to succeed by rapid intensification of warfare in order to achieve a state of objectives. The lesson is we should do as much as we possibly can as rapidly as we can do it."[72]

Clark was in fact echoing remarks made by German General Klaus Naumann during the air campaign on May 4: "Quite frankly and honestly," Naumann said, as he prepared for retirement, "we did not succeed in our initial attempt to coerce Milošević through air strikes to accept our demands, nor did we succeed in preventing [Yugoslavia from] pursuing a campaign of ethnic separation [in Kosovo] . . . we need to find a way to reconcile the conditions of a coalition war with the principal of military operation such as surprise and the use of overwhelming force."[73] The comments by Clark and Naumann are particularly interesting, not only as they reflect on the way the spring 1999 war was conducted, but in view of the well-known earlier controversy between Secretary of State Albright and General Colin Powell over the use of American military power. Thus, early in the Clinton administration, Powell, who at that time was head of the Joint Chiefs of Staff, had voiced serious reservations about using American military force unless certain very specific goals were stipulated, and there was general agreement on how they would be achieved. Albright, in contrast (at a meeting with Powell and others), had exclaimed: "What's the point of having this superb military, that you're always talking about, if we can't use it."[74] Indeed, as the savage war in Bosnia progressed, Albright became increasingly an advocate of strong measures to deal with aggression. It was largely on Albright's advice, for example, that Clinton adopted a more proactive position on Bosnia in 1995[75] and decided in 1999 to use military force against Milošević. In this context, Clark's remarks might be viewed as a corollary to the Powell doctrine, namely, if you think you may not be able to "do as much as you can" to win, don't get into the fight. As the air campaign dragged on into April and May 1999, and Albanian civilian suffering increased, concerns about whether the conflict should have been avoided, and also how much force should be used to win the struggle—a venture that some commentators had begun to call "Madeleine's war"—were increasingly debated.

The prolongation of the war, in contrast to earlier forecasts, placed Clark under increasing pressure from NATO leaders to obtain results. Tension also rose between the American general and certain NATO allies about the way the war was being run. For example, British leaders were pressing for more robust action, and preparation for a ground struggle. Clark, who had started talking about a ground option on the second day of the war was very sympathetic to the British view. "I've got to get the maximum violence out of this campaign— now!" he told an interviewer in late May 1999.[76] Clark often tried to improvise in order to get his way: "On any individual target I sort of worked it around through governments. I found which ones wanted to push harder, which ones were nervous, and I tried to pick out the targets in such a way that I might maintain support and cohesion and didn't always defer to those who always wanted targets withheld."[77] But French officials were uncomfortable with Clark's aggressiveness and management of the air campaign. French officials later described the "trial of strength" that emerged between Clark's headquarters and the French president's office over planned bombing sites. Owing to an informal arrangement among the major NATO states, the Alliance's principal political leaders, including France's President Jacques Chirac, were personally allowed to review "contentious targets." The French were particularly opposed to hitting any targets in Montenegro, a move which they felt might destabilize that republic's fledgling reformist government. Meanwhile, Clark worried that the Yugoslav military would be able to use Montenegro as a location to shield their fighters (who had been sent to the airport at Podgorica for protection), and also prevent NATO from bombing Yugoslavia's navy and coastal defenses. Paris also vetoed bombing attacks against Belgrade's bridges, which Clark allegedly wished to target for political and psychological reasons.[78] But the French were not the only obstacle to Clark's pressure for a more robust war. The Clinton administration refused to allow General Clark to employ Apache helicopters that had been brought to Albania in April in order to assist the war effort (although they served as a signal to Milošević that ground operations might eventually be employed).

At the end of March, at Clark's urging, it was decided to significantly intensify the bombing campaign. Instead of concentrating mainly on command bunkers and disrupting Yugoslav military communications, the air campaign turned to bridges, factories, the electrical system, and other "strategic targets" in Kosovo and Serbia that were deemed critical to both the military and civilian sectors. The earlier political restrictions on the air war—phase one and phase two type of targets—together with bad weather, had allowed Milošević to buy some time. Clark and other NATO hawks now wanted to turn up the pressure on Belgrade. NATO Secretary General Solana claimed that he was sure the bombing would be over before April 23, the date of NATO's 50th Anniversary Summit meeting to be held in Washington D.C.[79] It would, however, take considerably longer.

But by April NATO was concerned with more than just changes in targeting and the helicopters in Albania. The entire military strategy underlying the war had become extremely contentious. For example, strong doubts had been raised in the Alliance about whether overwhelming air power alone would be able to achieve NATO's objectives. NATO was also coming under increased media pressure because of collateral damage caused by the bombing. In what was increasingly a tacit psychological war, and also a propaganda war between the two sides in the struggle, NATO leaders came to believe that, at a minimum, they now needed to convince Milošević and his ruling circle that the Alliance was fully prepared to launch a ground campaign, should that option become necessary to achieve victory. In fact, hypothetical planning for such ground action had occurred even before the war. Such plans were also secretly reviewed during the air campaign, largely at General Clark's instigation. But NATO leaders remained deeply divided on the question of ground action. The German and Italian leaders were most opposed to that option, while the Greeks, who been against a military solution from the onset, were extremely reluctant to allow their territory to be used as a corridor for supply of a ground invasion. At the Washington summit in late April, there was a decision not to launch a ground war, but at the same time to send signals to the contrary. Thus, publicly NATO leaders remained steadfast in their original public position that ground troops would only be sent into a "permissive environment," that is, after Serbian forces were sufficiently "degraded." However, Alliance officials now hurried to add that NATO Secretary-General Solana was updating "the planning and assessment about ground forces under a variety of environments."[80] The urgency of bringing maximum pressure to bear on the Belgrade regime derived from a concern by some NATO leaders, and especially Madeleine Albright, that other actors such as UN Secretary-General Kofi Annan might step in and try to negotiate an end to hostilities directly with Milošević. For Albright and others, such a scenario would both give Milošević an easy way out, and also damage U.S. and NATO credibility.[81]

NATO's decision to accelerate the planning for potential ground action was in large part prompted by Milošević's unwillingness to capitulate, and also his apparent success at rallying the support of his countrymen. Thus, the first stage of the war generated a strong wave of patriotic fever in Serbia, as well as an intensification of xenophobia against NATO countries. Though such Serb attitudes were mainly an expression of resentment against the foreign attack on their country, and the need to patriotically defend Serb territory (including

Kosovo), the general mood of national solidarity—a situation which Milošević had counted on when he refused to sign the Rambouillet agreement—also temporarily benefited the Belgrade regime. The Serbian psychotherapist Zoran Milivojević has described the notion of resistance to strong external force that is rooted in the Serbian mindset.

In our country generally it is difficult to tolerate differences. Let's say differences in opinion even among good friends can be the source of insults, that arise in such a case because one side must be sensible and the other stupid.

For Serbs another characteristic is a feeling of spite [*inat*] or defiance [*prkos*]. We are really masters in that. Defiance always appears when someone important or stronger is regarded as having a negative image of us. By means of spite we convey a practical demonstration of our identity, thereby conveying that we are "someone." When you look at our national history we see that it is full of "no"— from "no" to the Turkish empire, to "no" to Austria-Hungary, "no" to Hitler and Stalin, to Europe, to the NATO pact. . . . Probably this is not the last such "no." But foreigners don't understand this. They seek rationality. . . . *inat* always derives from a position of inferiority. When someone is superior, he is mad. Let's say NATO is superior, and so in relation to us he is mad. And we can only spite him.[82]

For much of the Serbian public, the differences between the nation, the regime, and the leader became blurred under the relentless bombing by a foreign alliance. In fact, while Milošević's propaganda machine did everything it could to induce patriotic unity, it did not have to try very hard in the initial stage of the war. For example, both the state media and the independent media presented a patriotic message during the bombing campaign, although the former had a nationalist and jingoistic tone, while the latter focussed on resistance to aggression. After the end of hostilities, members of the international community, and particularly foreign NGOs, sharply criticized the Serbian independent media for not taking a more critical stance against the regime's treatment of Albanians, and not supporting NATO's action. But except for a few Serbian human rights activists, most members of the Serbian opposition felt that accusations they had gone easy on Milošević were naïve and misplaced. Even Slavko Ćuruvija, who was shot and killed after being denounced on state television for his independent views, and was widely mourned by the foreign NGO establishment, had described NATO intervention against his country as "illegal, illegitimate, and immoral."[83] As for the attitude of the general population, one leading opposition journalist expressed the attitude among most Serbs: "My friends in the West keep asking me why there is no rebellion. Where are the people who poured into the streets every day for three months in 1996 [and 1997] to demand democracy and human rights? . . .

Most of these people feel betrayed by the countries which were their model. . . . These people are now compelled to take up arms and join their sons already serving in the army. With the bombs falling all around them nobody can persuade them—though some have tried—that this is only an attack on their government and not their country."[84] The normally unemotional Belgrade survey research analyst, Srbobran Branković described Serbian public opinion a month before the end of the hostilities:

> We have always had in Serbia a high level of anti-Western feeling, especially after the sanctions between 1992 and 1995 . . . the anti-West feeling was more widespread than the anti-Milošević [feeling]. Because it was not just Milošević supporters who were affected by the sanctions, but everybody. . . . There are [now] no words strong enough to express the anger among the Serbians . . . the pro-reformists who are in the youth, the better educated people, urban dwellers, entrepreneurs, and private sector workers, intellectuals and students. These people now face a disaster, because those who support the West and see what the West is doing to us are facing a great personal dilemma. . . . Both sides—the pro-regime and the pro-reform—they really have a common enemy called NATO.[85]

Despite the relatively unified mood of resistance in Serbia, Milošević was also mindful of his regime's severely depleted legitimacy on the eve of the war, and certainly recognized that the wave of patriotism after March 24 would only be a transitory phenomenon. The mood in the country was not really pro-Milošević, but rather anti-NATO.[86] Thus, in terms of his internal system of controls, Milošević took no chances. Special legislation tightened police restrictions and thereby prevented any open display of opposition. Individual acts of nonconformism became high-risk enterprises. The April 11 murder of Slavko Ćuruvija, the owner/editor of *Dnevni telegraf*, who had become a thorn in the side of the regime, was certainly meant to be a lesson to opposition leaders that it had now become dangerous to openly criticize the regime. On April 28, Milošević also dismissed SPO leader Vuk Drašković from his post as one of Yugoslavia's federal deputy prime ministers (all of the SPO ministers in the federal government then tendered their resignations). Drašković and his colleagues had originally been co-opted into the federal government in January to shore up national unity in the face of NATO pressure. But, Drašković's offense had been to break ranks with Milošević and the ruling party coalition by publicly calling for compromises with the West to end the war in view of Yugoslavia's isolation, and particularly the disinclination of Russia to assist the Belgrade regime. "Let's tell the people the truth," Drašković had demanded. "There will be no third world war because of us . . . we are alone."[87] He also called for an end to policies which suggested that Serbs could "defeat the entire world." Drašković's wartime statements infuriated the Yugoslav president, who wished to convey the image of determined and unified resistance to the NATO bombing.[88]

Milošević certainly brooked no high-profile nonconformism directed against the regime's power structure. But NATO's decision to target him personally—he escaped the bombing at his official residence on April 22, but other missiles hit the headquarters of his Socialist Party of Serbia—had undoubtedly concentrated his attention on the need to look for some kind of negotiated deal with NATO. During April it was also becoming abundantly clear to the Yugoslav president that the Russians were not about to pull his chestnuts out of the fire. Thus, Washington had been spending as much time attempting to ensure that the Russian government not become more actively committed to the Serbian side as it was in maintaining the unity of the NATO alliance. Fortunately for the Clinton administration the unstable Yeltsin regime, vexed by continued internal problems, was more interested in obtaining economic assistance from the United States than in propping up Milošević. Although Yeltsin's government loudly opposed the use of force by NATO to resolve the Kosovo crisis, Moscow had little affection for Milošević (who had supported the anti-reform Soviet coup leaders in August 1991) and neither trusted in his promises (the previous year the Yugoslav leader had broken his word to Yeltsin regarding the withdrawal of Serbian troops from Kosovo), nor had a desire to become directly associated with the Belgrade regime's repressive "ethnic cleansing" tactics in Kosovo. Yeltsin's preference was to gain international stature for Russia by mediating the Kosovo conflict, a role that Washington endorsed and nurtured in order to keep a line of communication open with Belgrade, and to set the stage for ending the war. For example, in early May, Vice President Gore met with Yeltsin's special envoy for Kosovo, former Prime Minister Viktor Chernomyrdin, and informally convinced the Russian representative that an international military force rather than a monitoring mission would be needed in Kosovo once the bombing ended.[89] Chernomyrdin also advanced a suggestion that if he were to make any future peace overtures to Milošević he needed to be joined by someone who was agreeable to both the Yugoslav president and NATO. Mrs. Albright immediately suggested the experienced Finnish diplomat Martti Ahtissari. Chernomyrdin agreed, and thereby laid the groundwork for a peace settlement that was still, however, over a month away.

By mid-May NATO leaders faced a major dilemma regarding the war. Milošević remained intransigent—especially after the Alliance's controversial and possibly accidental bombing of the Chinese Embassy in Belgrade, which killed three Chinese and wounded at least twenty others[90]—and it appeared that possibly one million plus Albanians who had fled their homes would have to face winter in refugee camps or, for the even less fortunate, exposure to the elements somewhere in Kosovo. Moreover, any delay in assembling troops for an invasion of Kosovo, even in the "semi-permissive" or "semi-degraded" environment that the NATO bombing apparently had created in Kosovo through the alleged destruction of Serbian military assets, would mean fighting a winter ground war. With these considerations in mind, the most hawkish leader of the Alliance, British Prime Minister Blair, lobbied strongly to convince Clinton of the need to quickly and actively plan for a ground invasion of Kosovo. Clinton resisted, fully aware of a lack of NATO unity on the matter, and also growing public frustration about the collateral damage and the civilian suffering (both Albanian and Serb) caused by the war. Anxiety over possible casualties involved in a ground invasion—a so-called "body-bag" problem among Clinton's aides, especially National Security Adviser Sandy Berger and Secretary of Defense William Cohen, also influenced the American perspective. But Blair won a partial victory near the end of May when Clinton backed the plan to nearly double the KFOR "peacekeeping" force assembling on Kosovo's borders, from 28,000 to 48,000 troops. The British Prime Minister's principal ally on the issue of ground troops was U.S. General Wesley Clark, who reportedly argued that though nine weeks of bombing had seriously weakened the army, there was still no guarantee that the prevailing strategy could overcome Milošević's stubbornness.[91]

After the war, it was conceded by NATO officials that the enhanced KFOR contingent represented the core elements of a force for a ground invasion, should that option have been considered necessary. In the meantime, the announced build up of troops sent a strong signal to Milošević that NATO was finally prepared to use ground troops in order to win the war. British Air Marshall Sir John Day would later call the KFOR planning "a form of heavy breathing on Milošević . . . whilst keeping the coalition together."[92] Indeed, by early May, intensive planning was underway by NATO for a massive ground assault in Kosovo, "Operation Bravo Minus," that would take place before the end of September 1999. This was really an upgraded version of similar plans that had been on the NATO drawing board since at least mid-1998. Top NATO leaders were fully aware that Milošević had excellent intelligence sources regarding Alliance decision making, and hoped (indeed, perhaps even facilitated by means of "leaks") Belgrade's recognition that a ground invasion of Kosovo had become a real possibility. General Clark would later point out that Milošević had "ample evidence to conclude that had he not conceded when he did, the next step would have been the long-awaited and much talked about NATO ground effort. And so I think that evidence was available to President Milošević."[93] Near the end of May, Clark also received a green light to begin constructing a road in northern Albania for eventually transporting heavy military equipment into Kosovo, a corridor that could be used either for peacekeeping troops or a ground invasion force. After the war Sandy Berger also observed that "NATO did develop and update the ground force option. And if necessary the President was prepared to seek allied and congressional support for a ground option, because he was determined that NATO prevail."[94]

By the middle of May there were growing signs that Milošević could no longer rely on Serbian internal solidarity. On May 18, anti-war demonstrations took place in a number of towns in southern Serbia, and less than a week later between two and three thousand Yugoslav reserve troops refused to return to Kosovo at the end of their home leave. Serbian public morale was also under severe strain due to stepped-up NATO bombing around Belgrade. For example, on May 24, bombing with heavy ordnance completely knocked out the Yugoslav power grid, temporarily eliminating power to Belgrade civilians and the military infrastructure. The pressure on Milošević also increased on May 27, when the UN war crimes tribunal indicted him and other Yugoslav officials for crimes against humanity.[95] Faced with such mounting problems, the reality of sustained NATO unity, lack of substantial Russian support, and also knowing that the alliance was making plans for a ground invasion, Milošević was undoubtedly more inclined to make the best deal he could while a good portion of his military forces and infrastructure still remained intact. Moreover, Milošević knew what NATO would only learn about after the war, namely, that much of Serbia's heavy military and police equipment in Kosovo had escaped destruction from the bombing campaign (partially through the use of decoys). Of course, it could reasonably be argued that in some respects, Milošević actually relished a ground war with NATO, and that he also believed that the likelihood of extensive allied casualties in such a struggle would motivate NATO, and particularly the United States, to seek a diplomatic settlement quite favorable to Belgrade. However, he was also aware that the Alliance, or at least most of its members, were unprepared to accept defeat on their major goals. Milošević very likely did not wish to risk the possibility that he would be in a highly vulnerable position at the end of such a scenario, if he survived at all. The Yugoslav president, who had always focussed on power maintenance as his chief goal, could not help but conclude that it might be prudent to cash in his chips and still walk away from the war without having lost power, or suffered an ignominious defeat.

By this point in the war Serbian forces in Kosovo were also beginning to face a serious challenge from a strengthened and reorganized UCK. Initially forced to retreat by the Serbian ground campaign in March and April, UCK forces had subsequently grown in strength, partially protected in their temporary sanctuaries in northern Albania, where they also received considerable assistance from NATO. Should they be forced to deal with UCK attacks on the ground, Serbian forces that were hiding from NATO planes would find themselves in an exposed position. Prior to the war, American leaders such as Secretary Cohen had explicitly emphasized that the United States had no intention of becoming the UCK's airforce. But once the war began, NATO and the UCK quickly became *de facto* allies. "We are fighting the same enemy," UCK spokesman Jakub Krasniqi observed in 1999. "Let's say that NATO and the KLA [UCK] are unofficial allies, there is a mutual understanding."[96] According to top NATO military officials, UCK guerillas were constantly in communication with NATO regarding Serb targets, and NATO itself instigated the UCK's biggest offensive of the war in May 1999.[97]

By the end of May, the moment was right for a brokered end to the war. Thus, the Clinton administration, though still hopeful it could avoid using ground troops, was ready to use all means necessary in order to defeat Yugoslavia. As for Milošević, although still on his feet, he was isolated, fearful of serious internal political discontent, and aware that further resistance and the eventual ground invasion of Kosovo might spell his doom. On May 28, Milošević informed Chernomyrdin that Yugoslavia was ready to accept the Contact Group's principles for ending hostilities that had been laid out three weeks earlier by the group of eight. Interestingly, the Contact Group's provisions did not specifically mention NATO. The terms were: an immediate end to violence in Kosovo; the withdrawal of Serb military, police and paramilitary forces from Kosovo; an international security and civilian force in Kosovo mandated by the UN; the safe and free return of all refugees and displaced persons; and a temporary framework agreement giving Kosovo self-rule, taking into consideration the Rambouillet agreement.

Since early May, Russia's Chernomyrdin and Finland's Ahtissari, who officially served as an envoy for the European Union, and American Assistant Secretary of State Strobe Talbott—the so-called "Kosovo troika"—had been meeting to discuss the outline of a possible peace settlement. On June 2, the troika agreed to a two-page peace plan that included a provision that the Russians had previously objected to, namely, NATO command and control of the KFOR peacekeeping troops. Chernomyrdin also agreed to allow Ahtissari to present his plan to Milošević in Belgrade as a take-it-or-leave-it offer. There would be no negotiations with Milošević on the details of the plan. Ahtissari and Chernomyrdin flew to Belgrade on the same afternoon. Ahtissari later explained why he was ultimately successful: "First by not going to Belgrade too soon as Chernomyrdin did on two occasions without success. And then by not showing ourselves divided. No more bilateral meeting, only a triangular table. . . . I drew up the initial draft, then, at the cost of a major effort, we achieved a final communiqué signed both by the Russians and the Americans. At that point Milošević was in a corner. He was no longer able to play one off against the other. And when he asked me if the draft could be further toyed with, I said: 'No, this is the best that Viktor [Chernomyrdin] and I have managed to do, you have to agree to it in every part.'"[98] But Ahtissari cautioned Milošević that "all options remained open" for NATO, a signal that ground invasion was still possible if no settlement was reached.[99] Milošević, in a first indication that he might agree to the plan, said he would send the plan to a special session of the Serbian Legislature on June 3 (in a thinly veiled attempt to avoid taking personal responsibility for the Serbian decision to withdraw from Kosovo). Athissari declined Milošević's invitation to speak to the Yugoslav legislature, and also an invitation that he and Chernomyrdin dine with Milošević. The legislators dutifully approved what Milošević's henchman Milan Milutinović described to them as a Serbian "victory." Only Vojislav Šešelj, head of the ultra-nationalist Serbian Radical Party, denounced the agreement as a sell out. The next day the emissaries met with Milošević. Ahtissari opened the conversation by bluntly asking: "What next?" Milošević replied: "We accept your terms." It took close to another week to work out all the technical details and obtain a UN resolution authorizing the agreement, but the war had essentially ended.

Milošević's decision to accept the agreement hammered out by the Kosovo troika caught NATO leaders by surprise. In Washington there was a sigh of relief. Indeed, only a day before Milošević agreed to accept the terms for peace, Sandy Berger had been drafting a memorandum advising President Clinton to prepare for a massive ground invasion of Yugoslavia using 175,000 NATO troops, including about 100,000 from the United States.[100] Berger presented the President with three options: first, "to arm the Kosovars, but that would cause a chain of events that would produce a war that would last for years; second, wait until spring [2000], but that would require NATO to supply and protect thousands of refugees inside Kosovo through the winter; third, launch a ground invasion." Clinton had never favored the use of ground troops and the likelihood of taking significant casualties, but in view of Milošević's intransigence, the American president had decided to authorize plans for the early fall invasion of Kosovo. However, the peace deal in Belgrade made the ground invasion plan moot. Strobe Talbott, the president's close friend and a major adviser on foreign relations, later commented on Milošević's decision: "What would have happened if he had not accepted the terms? We would have kept bombing. And the strains in NATO–Russia relations would have become more difficult over time to manage. I think there would have been increasing difficulty within the Alliance in preserving the solidarity and resolve of the alliance. I don't think it was a matter of days by any means, but I think it was a good thing that the conflict ended when it did and on the terms that it did."[101]

So why did Milošević capitulate? Clearly the bombing campaign had started to take a heavy toll on the Yugoslav military and civilian infrastructure, not to mention psychologically impacting the soldiers and civilians in the country. Moreover, should the heavy bombing campaign in Kosovo continue, Milošević had to contemplate that the low morale in the Yugoslav front-line military ranks might foster mass desertions, and begin an overall process of socio-political collapse. But in the short term, the war had also galvanized national unity in Serbia—if not behind Milošević at least behind the nation—and political opposition and dissidence while growing, had still not become a serious threat. The Yugoslav president could not count on how long such a situation would prevail, however, and was well aware that allied bombers had targeted him personally. Still, the pressure of the air campaign alone was not likely to break his will to resist. Indeed, in certain quarters he had even accrued credit for standing up to a powerful nineteen-country coalition. Moreover, opposition to the war in NATO countries was also growing.

But if Milošević might have been willing to endure more bombing, he also weighed a number of additional factors that probably convinced him to end hostilities. Four such factors seem particularly significant. First, acceptance of the proposed peace agreement would enable him to extract his military and security forces from Kosovo more or less intact. Second, acquiescence to the troika's plan presented in Belgrade by Ahtissari and Chernomyrdin would enable Milošević to short-circuit NATO planning for a ground invasion of Kosovo, which in all likelihood, combined with NATO's continued air campaign, would have severely depleted his military and security assets.[102] Indeed, ground action could have eventually led to the invasion of Serbia itself, and thereby constituted a direct threat to his power. Third, Milošević's persistence had not been able to break the unity of the NATO coalition, and though the Alliance was torn by major tensions and divisions, its basic cohesion on the need to triumph in the Balkans did not seem likely to crumble in the immediate future. Fourth, Milošević could not expect any significant help from external actors. Russia, although sympathetic to Serbia's plight, was not likely to interfere to stop the bombing campaign. Indeed, once the Russians had reached agreement with the American side and the EU on how the war should be ended—the troika discussions—Moscow probably exerted considerable behind-the-scenes pressure on Milošević to concur with the plan being offered. Serbia's dependency on Russian gas and oil supplies for the coming winter gave the Russians considerable leverage in making their case to Milošević about the urgent need to reach peace terms with NATO. Moreover, there was some hope that the Russians might assist Serbia in creating a Russian-monitored northeastern zone in Kosovo that would effectively bifurcate or partition Kosovo into a Russian-protected Serbian sector on the one side and a KFOR-protected Albanian (or UCK) sector on the other. Although loosing any part of Kosovo was unsatisfactory to many Serbs, such an arrangement was very appealing to

Milošević, and he likely calculated that it could allow him to claim a considerable level of success in the war.

Indeed, some observers believe that the subsequent Russian gambit of transferring troops from their Bosnian peace-keeping contingent into Kosovo was part of a secret plan worked out between Milošević and Chernomyrdin that was the crucial reason Milošević capitulated.[103] Such a Russian caper to acquire more influence in Kosovo's future actually began just a week after Milošević's capitulation in Belgrade, that is, at a time when talks between Serbian and NATO officers—held in a tent at Kumanovo, Macedonia—to implement the peace settlement and coordinate Serb withdrawal from Kosovo, had broken down. On June 10 and 11, 1999, at the moment when KFOR troops were entering the province from the south, the Yeltsin regime decided, without consulting NATO, to transfer a small contingent of its peace-keeping forces from Bosnia into Kosovo, as an attempt to establish a Russian-controlled sector in the province. After passing through Serbia, Russian troops managed to reach Priština airport before British General Mike Jackson, in overall command of KFOR, could take control of the facility for his planned headquarters. The Russian dash to Kosovo exhilarated the Serb minority in the province, not to mention official Moscow and the Milošević regime (which very well may have connived in the scheme). NATO General Wesley Clark, incensed and embarrassed by the Russian maneuver, ordered his subordinate, NATO's southern commander U.S. Admiral James Ellis, to land helicopters on the runway so that the Russians could not send in further reinforcements. Clark also demanded that General Jackson take immediate steps to prevent the Russians from consolidating their control. But both the American and British officers reportedly refused to carry out Clark's orders. According to the Chairman of the U.S. Joint Chiefs of Staff, General Shelton, who later reviewed the matter, General Jackson told General Clark: "No, I'm not going to do that. It's not worth starting World War III."[104] Ultimately, Russia's effort to expand and set the terms of its presence in Kosovo failed when, at U.S. urging, the Hungarian and Bulgarian governments refused the Russians access to their airspace, thereby making it impossible for Moscow to reinforce the small contingent of its troops that had already reached Priština. In diplomatic discussions with U.S. and NATO officials, the Kremlin persisted with efforts to obtain a separate Russian sector in Kosovo. But on June 18, Moscow was finally compelled to allow its troops to be dispersed within three of the five NATO-controlled zones established by KFOR. If Milošević had, in large part, decided to capitulate because of a far-fetched hope that a joint Russo–Serbian maneuver—which may or may not have been officially sanctioned in Moscow—would salvage Yugoslav control over part of Kosovo's territory, then he had badly miscalculated.

The prospect of Russian assistance in Kosovo may have been significant in Milošević's early June decision to make a deal with NATO, but some other important, albeit less decisive factors, may have also helped sway the Yugoslav president. For example, by the end of May, the military strength of the UCK was undergoing a resurgence thanks to NATO assistance. Should Serb military forces be compelled to fight back against the Albanians, they would become increasingly exposed to NATO bombing. Additionally, the strong economic and political sanctions against Serbia (including financial measures and travel restrictions), had placed the ruling establishment in Serbia under considerable pressure. Milošević could not help but worry that the loyalty and political reliability of the Serbian elite was becoming more doubtful. He was also personally in a more difficult situation owing to his indictment in May as a war criminal.[105] Although it is impossible to know exactly what led to Milošević's capitulation, and particularly, how various factors ranked in his estimation, it is reasonable to assume that all the foregoing considerations played a role in prompting Milošević to end the military struggle with NATO. Once he had done so, Milošević could turn his full attention to preserving, and possibly reconstituting, his political power base within Serbia.

Milošević's agreement for the withdrawal of Yugoslav troops from Kosovo was an occurrence that was far less emotional to the power-driven Yugoslav leader than it was to many of his countrymen. Indeed, Milošević could convince himself, and also many of Yugoslavia's citizens, that he had not surrendered. Thus, the agreement, as fleshed out in a UN Security Council resolution (June 10), was in large measure the "artful dodge" that he had been offered at Rambouillet. As Richard Holbrooke later put it: "Resolution 1244 states in a very artful and creative piece of opaqueness, which was necessary for the bombing to stop, that—Kosovo will remain part of Yugoslavia, pending a final settlement. . . . For the Russians and Chinese, it is the phrase up to the comma [before the word pending] that counts. For the United States, it is clearly implied that there has to be a final settlement [and] . . . that settlement cannot take place as long as Milošević is president of Yugoslavia."[106] Moreover, the final settlement included or omitted various features that Milošević's delegation had been unable to obtain at Rambouillet. Most significant for Belgrade was the fact that the UN, not NATO, would have overall authority in Kosovo. And Appendix B to the Rambouillet agreement, allowing NATO troops to transit through not only Kosovo, but also Yugoslavia, had been dropped. These changes were enough for the Serbian regime to declare "victory" in the NATO–Kosovo war, and to withdraw from the province.

Following the Kosovo conflict, the U.S. Department of Defense's final "lessons-learned" report also would claim that the NATO air campaign against Yugoslavia "was extraordinarily successful." But the report also suggested that no one, apart from Milošević, actually knew precisely why Belgrade capitulated. Indeed, the Pentagon's post-conflict evaluation suggests that military action may not have been the complete solution at the time the bombing began. "Planning focussed," the report maintains, "on air strikes and diplomacy as primary tools to achieve U.S. and NATO objectives. As it became clear that Milošević intended to outlast the Alliance more attention was paid to other ways of bringing pressure to bear including economic sanctions. While ultimately these instruments were put to use to good effect, more advanced planning might have made them more effective at an earlier date." The report also implies that better inter-agency planning might have resulted in an entirely different approach to the Kosovo conflict and the war. "Our experience in Operation Allied Force has shown that Presidential Directive 56 (PDP–56) Managing Complex Contingency Operations has not yet been fully utilized throughout the inter-agency planning process. As a result of this experience the inter-agency has applied the lessons learned to further institutionalizing PDP–56, routine participation of senior officials in rehearsals, exercises and simulations [and] the broad range of available policy tools."[107] Presidential Directive 56—an unclassified white paper that calls for a variety of nonmilitary multidimensional operations "to deal with regional territorial disputes, armed ethnic conflicts and civil wars—states "that many aspects of complex emergencies may not be best addressed through military measures."[108] It is remarkable that seven months after it conducted an eleven-week high-technology military campaign—that wrought tremendous damage in Southeastern Europe—designed in part to address the consequences of purported ethnic cleansing, to obtain implementation of an agreement creating a self-governing authority within a province of another state, and also hopefully to remove the leader of that state (who was deemed to be a war criminal), the U.S. Department of Defense should conclude that nonmilitary methods recommended in a 1997 Presidential Directive may not have received adequate attention as a mode of conflict resolution prior to the outbreak of the NATO–Yugoslav hostilities over Kosovo. Considering the distractions faced by President Clinton and his administration on the eve of the Kosovo conflict, it seems fair to ask whether the after-action Pentagon report might have been more properly titled "Who Was Minding the Store?"

NOTES

1. *Reporter* (Banja Luka), October 25, 1998, pp. 14–15, October 29, 1998 in *BBC-SWB*: Part 2, Central Europe, the Balkans, Federal Republic of Yugoslavia; Serbia, EE/D3370/A, October 29, 1998.
2. Reported in *VND*, November 7, 1998, pp. 12–14.
3. *Danas*, December 15, 1999.

4. *BETA*, November 5, 1998.
5. Zagorka Golubović in *Republika*, September 22, 1998.
6. *New York Times*, November 20, 1998, p. 1.
7. *Večernje Novosti*, November 28, 1998.
8. *Blic*, July 22, 1999.
9. See the remarks of Ognjen Pribičević on the role of the police in the Serbian party system. *Naša Borba*, February 17, 1998, p. 5.
10. *Federal News Service*, State Department Briefing, December 1, 1998.
11. Dušan Pavlović traces the beginning of serious international concern about Milošević's role as a factor in Balkan peace efforts to the protests in Serbia during 1996 and 1997. "Kriza od 17. novembra," in *Srpska političke misao*, Vol. 2 (1997), pp. 149–162.
12. Fehim Rexhepi, "Rejecting Hill's Plan While Waiting for Spring," *AIM*, December 11, 1998.
13. *Moral Combat: NATO at War*, BBC Two Special, March 12, 2000. A Canadian captain working with the KVM later remarked that "Ambassador Walker was not just working for the OSCE. He was part of the American diplomatic policy that was occurring which had vilified Slobodan Milošević, demonized the Serbian administration, and generally was providing diplomatic support to the UCK or the KLA leadership." Ibid.
14. *Observer*, July 18, 1999.
15. Ibid.
16. *Frontline: War in Europe*, February 22, 2000.
17. *Blic*, July 2, 1999.
18. *Federal News Service*, June 8, 2000.
19. *FDCH Transcripts*, November 3, 1999.
20. *Washington Post*, April 18, 1999, Section A, p. 1.
21. *Le Soir*, February 25, 1999, p. 6 in *FBIS-EEU–1999–0225*, February 25, 1999.
22. *FDCH Transcripts*, August 31, 1999.
23. *United Press International*, April 30, 1999.
24. *VND*, June 26, 1999, pp. 6–7.
25. *Le Soir*, February 25, 1999, p. 6 in *FBIS-EEU–1999–0225*, February 25, 1999. For an interesting Serbian perspective on the politics leading up to the conference, see Predrag Simić, *Put u Rambuje: Kosovska kriza, 1995–2000* (Belgrade: Nea, 2000).
26. *Dani*, March 15, 1999, p. 36.
27. *Moral Combat: NATO at War*, BBC Two Special, March 12, 2000.
28. Prepared statement of Thomas Pickering, Under-Secretary of State for Political Affairs, before the Senate Armed Services Committee, "U.S. Policy on Kosovo," February 25, 1999, Federal Information Systems Corporation.
29. *Moral Combat*, BBC Two Special, March 12, 2000.
30. BBC, February 26, 1999.
31. *Moral Combat*, BBC Two Special, March 12, 2000.
32. *National Public Radio*, February 24, 1999.
33. *Dani*, March 15, 1999, p. 36.

34. *Newsweek*, July 26, 1999.

35. Warren Bass, "Cold War: The Albright–Holbrooke Feud," *The New Republic*, Vol. 221, No. 24 (December 13, 1999), pp. 16–18. James Traub, who interviewed Holbrooke extensively, also suggests that "he felt that a more deft negotiator—himself perhaps—could have avoided a war in Kosovo." "Holbrooke's Campaign, *New York Times Magazine*, March 20, 2000, p. 66. Holbrooke rejects the notion that the Kosovo issue exploded at the end of the 1990s because he had not adequately dealt with the issue at Dayton: "At Dayton there was no way to settle Kosovo. But before, during, and after Dayton we discussed it with Milošević. We were able to keep things under control for a while. But then they exploded, not because they weren't dealt with at Dayton. That in my view is reconstructive history. They exploded because Milošević played directly into the hands of the most extreme elements within Kosovo . . . [as] the KLA's greatest recruiting poster." *Federal News Service*, November 2, 1999.

36. *Daily Telegraph*, February 19, 2000, p. 14.

37. *Boston Globe*, March 20, 1999.

38. *The Independent*, March 20, 1999.

39. *Federal News Service*, October 14, 1999. Hearing of the Senate Armed Services Committee: Lessons Learned from Military Operations and Relief Efforts in Kosovo.

40. *United Press International*, October 14, 1999.

41. British General Sir Charles Guthrie would later comment that psychiatrists hired by NATO failed to fathom Milošević's mind, and that the British Ministry of Defense had been surprised that the Yugoslav president would be willing to withstand extensive bombing of his military and civilian infrastructure before capitulating. After all, Guthrie observed: "We didn't have to bomb Belgrade [in 1995] to achieve Dayton." *The Times*, March 16, 2000.

42. *Los Angeles Times*, July 25, 1999, p. 3.

43. BBC, March 21, 1999. Jamie Rubin claims that Belgrade was given "every reasonable opportunity to resolve the crisis diplomatically" on the basis of the fact that in the "crucial weeks" prior to the NATO bombing, Mrs. Albright telephoned Milošević suggesting a meeting in Geneva to discuss changes in the Rambouillet accords. But Rubin's account of the conference reveals the strong pro-Albanian tilt of U.S. policy, including the fact that four UCK members of the Albanian delegation were allowed to leave the conference site and receive a special briefing on NATO bombing plans from General Wesley Clark. *Financial Times*, September 29, 2000 and October 3, 2000.

44. *International Herald Tribune*, July 3, 1999, p. 5.

45. *Federal News Service*, June 24, 1999. Hearings of the Senate Foreign Relations Committee: Nomination of Richard Holbrooke as U.S. Ambassador to the United Nations.

46. U.S. Newswire Inc., June 25, 1999. Transcript of Press Conference of June 25, 1999 by President Clinton.

47. Belgrade, RTB Television, June 17, 1992 in FBIS-EEU–92–118, June 18, 1992, p. 26.

48. Rubin's views are presented in Timothy Garton Ash, "Kosovo: Was it Worth It?" *New York Review of Books*, September 21, 2000.

49. *Federal Document Clearing House Inc.*, FDCH Political Transcripts, July 1, 1999, U.S. Senate Armed Services Committee: The Situation in Kosovo.

50. *United Press International*, April 30, 1999.

51. *Washington Post*, April 18, 1999, p. A01.

52. *Federal News Service*, March 24, 1999. President Clinton's Address to the Nation Regarding NATO Bomb Strikes Against Serbia.

53. *International Herald Tribune*, March 27, 2000, p. 1.

54. *FDCH Transcripts*, November 3, 1999.

55. *The Observer*, July 18, 1999, p. 13.

56. *Kosovo: An Account of the Crisis* (London: Ministry of Defense, 1999), p. 9.

57. *International Herald Tribune*, July 29, 1999, p. 1.

58. Transcript of *Frontline: War in Europe, Part I*, February 22, 2000. In June 2002, retired German general Klaus Naumann claimed that at a meeting with Milošević in October 1998, the Serbian leader had threatened to solve Kosovo's problems by shooting Albanians. Naumann quoted Milošević as saying, "We'll do the same we did in [the Kosovo region] Drenica in 1945/1946. We got them together and we shot them." *Agence France-Presse*, June 13, 2002.

59. Jamie Shea, "The Kosovo Crisis in the Media: Reflections of a NATO Spokesman," *Address to the Summer Forum on Kosovo organized by the Atlantic Council of the United Kingdom and the Trade Union Committee for European and Trans-Atlantic Understanding* (London: Reform Club, July 1999), pp. 3, 10.

60. *Dani*, No. 100 (April 26, 1999).

61. UN Special Envoy for Human Rights in the Former Yugoslavia, Jiri Dienstbier, claims that ethnic cleansing of Yugoslavia's Albanians only erupted after NATO launched its air strikes. "Before [the] bombing Albanians were not driven away on the basis of ethnic principle. In the summer and autumn of 1998 many were victims of the brutal war between the Yugoslav army and the Kosovo Liberation Army. *Prague CTK*, April 20, 2000. The Human Rights Watch Report, *Under Orders: War Crimes in Kosovo (2001)* employs comprehensive interviews and advanced statistical methods to conclude that it was planned violence by the Serbian authorities that resulted in the extensive killing of ethnic Albanians and also the related massive exodus of Albanian civilians from Kosovo during the war. The report also documents that NATO violations intensified Yugoslav civilian deaths, and also KLA violations resulting in the murder of both Serbs and non-Serb Kosovo minorities, as well as the massive post-conflict murders and flight of those groups from the province.

62. *FDCH Transcripts*, July 26, 1999. Remarks on Kosovo at the National Press Club, Washington, D.C.

63. Milošević may have used last-minute negotiations in Belgrade to seek a partition of Kosovo, retaining the mineral rich northern areas for Serbia. Although many commentators view such a partition proposal as legitimizing "ethnic cleansing," a contrary view suggests that redrawing borders along national lines can sometimes minimize violence, and even assist democratization. Steven Ratner, for example, argues that "in certain instances account may have to be taken of the need to avoid leaving peoples in new states where they do not wish to be or that will not treat them with dignity."

"Drawing a Better Line: *Uti Possidetis* and the Borders of New States, *American Journal of International Law*, Vol. 90 (1996), p. 617.

64. See, for example, Ivo Daalder and Michael O'Hanlan, *Winning Ugly: NATO's War to Save Kosovo* (Washington, D.C.: Brookings Institution Press, 2000), and Janusz Bugajski, "Breakup Yugoslavia, Independent Kosovo Would Reduce Tensions," *Washington Times*, August 1, 2000, p. A21. Michael Ignatieff offers a more nuanced argument in favor of the NATO intervention in order to force a Serb withdrawal from Kosovo, although he believes that the bombing campaign did not and could not achieve its humanitarian goals. *Virtual War: Kosovo and Beyond* (New York: Holt, 2000). For Ignatieff, military interventions such as in Kosovo are justified only if, among other things, all diplomatic alternatives are exhausted, although he does not present a convincing case that such a situation prevailed at Rambouillet.

65. *BETA*, January 12, 2000.

66. *Inter Press Service*, June 27, 2000.

67. *Danas*, January 24, 2000. In September 2000, Yugoslav officials would stage an trial in absentia of 14 leading Western politicians and NATO officials for war crimes against the Yugoslav civilian population and other criminal acts. The indictment claimed that between March 24 and June 10, 1999, air attacks on the Federal Republic of Yugoslavia had been responsible for the deaths of 890 people: 503 civilians, 240 members of the Yugoslav Army and 147 policemen.

68. *Los Angeles Times*, June 10, 2000, Part A, p. 8.

69. *Federal News Service*, October 21, 1999.

70. *Times*, January 27, 2000.

71. *Washington Post*, July 20, 1999, p. A14.

72. Ibid.

73. NATO Headquarters Transcript, May 4, 1999.

74. Colin L. Powell, *My American Journey* (New York: Random House, 1995), p. 576. Powell observed that he was so incensed by Albright's comment that he thought he would have an aneurysm. After General Powell criticized the conduct of the war in Kosovo, Albright bristled in her remarks to Congress, suggesting that Congressional members should wait and read her autobiography regarding the use of force in Bosnia and Kosovo before arriving at any final conclusions. "Let me also say that it is very hard for a mere mortal to argue with General Powell, but I have tried and I believe that if we had followed his advice we would not have had the Bosnia settlement and would not have stopped that . . . and the successful bombing of Bosnia came just as his book was published. . . . So wait to read me." April 21, 1999.

75. Michael Dobbs, *Madeleine Albright: A Twentieth Century Odyssey* (New York: Henry Holt, 1999), pp. 358–364.

76. *Washington Post*, September 21, 1999.

77. *ABC Nightline*, August 30, 1999, Transcript #99083001–j07.

78. *Washington Post*, September 21, 1999, p. A01.

79. *New York Times*, March 31, 1999.

80. Mrs. Albright together with Robin Cook at a BBC interview with David Frost, April 24, 1999.

81. See William Shawcross, *Deliver Us from Evil: Warlords and Peacekeepers in a World of Conflict* (London: Bloomsbury, 2000), p. 374.

82. *Danas*, January 5, 2000.

83. Ljiljana Smajlović, "Don't Shoot the Messenger," *Transitions On Line*, October 7, 1999.

84. Vera Matić, "These Bombs Don't Help," *New York Times*, April 1, 1999, Section A, p. 27.

85. *Lisbon Publico*, May 4, 1999 in *FBIS*–West Europe, East Europe, May 4, 1999. A survey of 1,000 citizens in Yugoslavia, conducted in the spring of 1998 by the organization Argument and the Institute for Advanced Studies in Vienna, revealed that the majority of Serbs "look towards the West," and that the population was highly polarized about Milošević, with young, educated, urban dwellers most opposed to the regime. Clair Wallace in Christian Haerpfer, "Who is Against Milošević," (unpublished paper, 1999).

86. *Washington Post*, April 26, 1999, p. A01.

87. *Inter Press Service*, April 28, 1999.

88. Milošević's attempt to portray himself as a heroic leader under global assault and working to shore up public morale was not made easier when, only a few days after the onset of the NATO bombing campaign, his son Marko announced a multi-million dollar deal to build a Disneyland-style amusement park called "Bambiland" in the family's hometown of Požarevac.

89. *U.S. News and World Report*, May 17, 1999.

90. The United States maintains that the embassy bombing was the result of a tragic accident that arose as a result of a mistaken identification by the CIA of the building as the Yugoslav Federal Directorate of Supply and Procurement, and that there was a failure of U.S. and NATO officials to check the target adequately. Although the CIA dismissed one officer and punished six others for their roles in the matter, and the United States agreed to pay the Chinese compensation, the government of China and most Chinese citizens did not accept Washington's interpretation, but rather viewed the bombing as deliberate. There has also been some speculation that the Chinese were sharing satellite information with the Yugoslavs through embassy channels, or allowing the Yugoslavs to use Chinese equipment at the embassy.

91. *Times*, May 23, 1999, and *Sunday Telegraph*, June 6, 1999.

92. *Canberra Times*, September 20, 1999, Part A, p. 9.

93. *Federal News Service*, September 16, 1999.

94. *Federal News Service*, July 26, 1999.

95. Radomir Marković, Chief of the Secret Police; General Dragoljub Ojdanić, Chief of the General Staff; Col. General Nebojša Pavković, Commander of the Third Army; Nikola Šainović, Deputy Prime Minister of Yugoslavia; Major General Vladimir Lazarević, Commander of the 3rd Army's 52nd Corps; and Vlajko Stojiljković, the Interior Minister.

96. *Berlin die Tageszeitung* in *FBIS-EEU–1999–0504*.

97. *Los Angeles Times*, June 10, 2000, Part 8, p. 8.

98. *Corriere della Sera*, July 21, 1999, p. 1 in *FBIS-WEU–1999–0721*.

99. *Sunday Telegraph*, June 6, 1999. Ahtissari has described his negotiations in *Misija u Beogradu* (Belgrade: Filip Višnjić), 2001.

100. *Los Angeles Times*, June 11, 2000.

101. *ABC Nightline*, August 30, 1999, Transcript #99083001–j07. See also Strobe Talbott, *The Russia Hand: A Memoir of Presidential Diplomacy* (New York: Random House, 2002), p. 329.

102. General Sir Charles Guthrie, Chief of the British Defense staff, later observed that Tony Blair had been "within a month" of mobilizing reserve troops for a forced entry into Kosovo when Milošević capitulated in June. *The Times*, March 16, 2000. According to a senior Yugoslav official, the fear of a NATO ground invasion, combined with the offer Milošević received from Ahtissari and Chernomydrin was the primary factor motivating him to withdraw from Kosovo. *Balkans Security: Current and Projected Factors Affecting Regional Stability* (Washington, D.C.: U.S. General Accounting Office, April 2000), p. 59. See also Stephan T. Hosmer, *The Conflict Over Kosovo: Why Milosevic Decided to Settle When He Did* (Santa Monica, Calif.: RAND/Project Air Force Report, 2001).

103. Zbigniew Brzezinski, "Why Milošević Capitulated in Kosovo," *The New Leader*, September 20–October 4, 1999, pp. 9–10.

104. *Federal News Service*, September 9, 1999. See also Wesley Clark, *Waging Modern War* (New York: PublicAffairs, 2001), pp. 389–403. On the Russian intra-elite conflict that led to this crisis, see Strobe Talbott, *The Russia Hand*, op. cit., Chapter 13.

105. General Henry Shelton and William Cohen, "Joint Statement on the Kosovo War: After Action Review," (U.S. Department of State), October 14, 1999.

106. Holbrooke, November 3, 1999. Senate Hearings. The actual wording of Resolution 1244 is as follows: "the people of Yugoslavia can enjoy substantial autonomy within the Federal Republic of Yugoslavia, . . . pending a final settlement of substantial autonomy and self-government in Kosovo."

107. Report to Congress. *Kosovo/Operation Allied Force. After-Action Report* (Washington, D.C.: Department of Defense, January 31, 2000), pp. 15–16, 126.

108. PDD/NSC 56, *Managing Complex Contingency Operations* (Washington, D.C.: Presidential Decision Directive, May 1997).

CHAPTER 7

Postwar Politics in Yugoslavia: Kosovo and Serbia–Montenegro

We have never been able to develop into democrats, because we went straight from the Ottoman Empire to Serbian rule. We have to make the transformation from an Ottoman province to a modern European nation. On top of that we have an undigested communist past. We have to evolve from an apartheid nation into a country where equal rights and obligations apply to all population groups.

—Veton Surroi, Kosovo Albanian journalist and political figure (June 26, 1999)

The truth is that, as Serbian politicians we have problem with direction. Since the beginning of the century part of our political life has been sick, demented, radical, full of messianism and a sense of mission, very easy to manipulate. The Balkan problem cannot be solved without a change of values and our mistake was to think that we would resolve everything by replacing Milošević with the people who share his values.

—Zoran Djindjić, President of the Democratic Party (May 27, 1999)

"Nobody's Country": Kosovo's Protectorate-Induced "Democratization"

The First Stage

In mid-June 1999, as NATO's air campaign wound down, and Yugoslav military and police forces completed their departure from Kosovo, the international community scrambled to establish security and civil administration in the war-torn province. UN Security Council Resolution No. 1244 stipulated that "there would be no change of Kosovo's constitutional status." But for the immediate future Kosovo would exist as a UN-administered entity, with

351

a NATO-led multinational force—KFOR—providing an "international security presence." During the second week in June, 14,000 KFOR troops, under the command of British General Mike Jackson, entered Kosovo. Within a month, KFOR had grown to 33,500 troops, headquartered under a unified command and control structure in Priština with five subordinate multinational brigade headquarters under the control of military contingents from the major NATO states (a predominantly American sector in the east, British in the center, French in the north, Germans in the south, and Italians in the west). By the end of 1999, KFOR troop strength in the province had reached over 40,000.

Civilian officials from the UN Interim Administration Mission in Kosovo (UNMIK) and other international agencies initially numbered only in the dozens. Though the international community had almost four years of experience governing Bosnia and Herzegovina as a *de facto* protectorate, this first stage of establishing international civilian control in Kosovo proved to be highly chaotic. For one thing, the UN—which was largely sidelined both during the pre-war diplomatic negotiations and also the ensuing war—had not adequately prepared to take over civilian management of Kosovo. Moreover, unlike in Bosnia, where the return of refugees and displaced persons was much more protracted than hoped for by the international community, the opposite problem pertained in Kosovo, namely, the rapid return of thousands of Albanians to their homes from neighboring countries and other parts of the province. The catastrophic humanitarian/refugee crisis, and the infrastructure damage throughout the province, was compounded by the bitter revanchist attitudes of the Albanian population towards Kosovo's remaining Serb minority. Thus, most Albanians believed their Serbian neighbors shared responsibility for the atrocities committed against Albanians by various members of Serb paramilitary organizations and security personnel.[1] Such sentiments, shaped by recent events, were reinforced by the accumulated grievances that the Kosovars nursed against heavy-handed Serb political/police control during the previous decade and earlier (see Chapter 1), and also the "culture of vengeance" that was an integral historical feature of Albanian socio-political culture. Indeed, by the end of the 1999 war in Kosovo, most Albanians considered that it would be preferable if the remaining Serbian minority quit the province altogether.

As the dominant organizational force advancing Kosovar political aspirations, the UCK had, by the end of the war, become a *de facto* "ally" of NATO. The UCK's top military commander, Agim Ceku, boasted, for example, that while his organization could not claim all the credit for forcing the Serbian withdrawal from Kosovo, it shared in the "victory" over Milošević because "after all the UCK brought NATO to Kosovo."[2] Although the UCK's dominance was contested by other Albanian political groups, the UCK's political directorate, under the leadership of the 29-year-old former political science student Hashim Thaci—who had been selected as prime minister of a Kosova transitional government by most members of the Kosovar delegation at the pre-war Rambouillet peace conference—overshadowed other political forces in the province. For example, Ibrahim Rugova and his LDK party continued to challenge the political ascendancy of Thaci and the UCK. Thaci and the UCK also had to contend with a claim to political authority from Bujar Bukoshi, who had technically headed a Kosovo Albanian government in exile since 1992, and had returned to the province following the war. Emerging from the war as the strongest Albanian military force, the UCK enjoyed widespread legitimacy and support among Kosovo Albanians. It soon became apparent that beyond the ongoing intra-Albanian political struggle, which was far from settled, Kosovo was also experiencing the first stage of a political tug-of-war between the UCK and the international community over who would control Kosovo. During the 1990s, the Albanians had established a parallel state to challenge the Serbian regime's control from Belgrade. In the postwar (1999–2000) period, the political dualism in the province was between KFOR/UNMIK on the one side, and the UCK on the other.

The initial difficulty faced by the international community in Kosovo was the security vacuum left by the war. KFOR troops provided a strong deterrent to the return of Yugoslav military forces, and also overshadowed the strength of UCK forces (which had supposedly grown to over 26,000 by the end of the conflict).[3] But as the number of refugees returning to the province mounted, and the discovery of atrocities committed against Albanians during the war unfolded, the defenseless Serb minority became the target of ethnic violence, including intimidation, kidnapping, looting, arson, and assassination by hard-line Albanians, some directly or closely associated with the UCK. KFOR and UNMIK officials quickly found that their limited resources and personnel were incapable of providing the security necessary to preserve the "multi-ethnic Kosovo" that had been a prime goal of international intervention. Prizren, Orahovac, and Priština, and their surrounding areas, were among some of the worst areas of anti-Serb hostilities, all regions of earlier anti-Albanian crimes by Serb forces. Approximately 150,000 Serbs and Montenegrins fled the province during June and July 1999 (roughly a third of whom left even before NATO troops arrived); a period when approximately 685,000 embittered Albanian refugees returned from neighboring countries. Thousands of Gypsies, who had become targets of Albanian intimidation and brutality, were also forced to flee from Kosovo, as well as ethnic Croats, Muslim Slavs, and members of other minority groups. By the late fall, the UN estimated that approximately 100,000 Serbs still remained in the province. For example, in October, roughly 400 to 600 Serbs remained in Priština out of a pre-war population of approximately 27,000. Throughout the summer and fall of 1999, and into 2000, a vicious cycle of ethnic vengeance and violence unfolded in Kosovo. It was cold comfort to innocent Serbs forced to flee the province under such circumstances that international commentators described their exodus as a disaster unprovoked by any formal state authority, while noting the earlier expulsion of Albanians had occurred as a result of Milošević's state-sponsored policy. One departing Serb official expressed the view of many of his ethnic brethren when he described the Albanian revanchism as an act of fate, not unlike many earlier stages of Kosovo history: "We chased them, but we lost the war; it is their turn to chase us."[4] In addition to the problem of violence against Serbs and other minorities, there was also a striking increase of general crime by organized gangs, many associated with criminal networks in neighboring Albania.

Perhaps the major difficulty impeding a smooth transition process in the province was the delay in establishing a robust international police force for Kosovo. Training a professional, impartial and trusted Kosovo-based domestic police force also occurred at an excruciatingly slow pace. Less than 175 foreign police officers had arrived in Kosovo by mid-July, with that number only rising to 700 by the last part of August. By this time, the number of KFOR troops had increased to over 40,000, but military personnel were not trained to maintain public order, and could not ensure adequate protection for the harassed and anxious minority communities. The cold-blooded massacre of 14 Serb farmers in the village of Gračko, while they were gathering their harvest, hastened the exodus of Serbs from multiethnic rural areas, and general Serb out-migration from Kosovo.

The international community was overwhelmed by the turbulence and ethnic violence in Kosovo during the summer of 1999. But UNMIK unquestionably had admirable goals, and also an energetic new leader in the person of Bernard Kouchner, Special Representative of the UN Secretary-General, who took over as the top international official in Kosovo during July. "I intend to build a multi-ethnic Kosovo," Kouchner ambitiously exclaimed in mid-August 1999, "which will not ignore history, but neither will it be a slave to its own past. . . . The name 'Balkans' is synonymous with explosions, atrocities. If I succeed, we all succeed. The Balkans should be synonymous with freedom, open society, and brotherhood." But in the face of the Serb exodus from Kosovo, the only significant aspects of multi-ethnic cooperation in the province were the structure and operation of KFOR, and the internal operation of the fledgling but rapidly growing UNMIK bureaucracy.

Following the advent of UNMIK/KFOR control over Kosovo, Serb political influence in the province dropped off sharply. Although both the Belgrade regime and Serbia's democratic opposition did not chose to abandon the idea

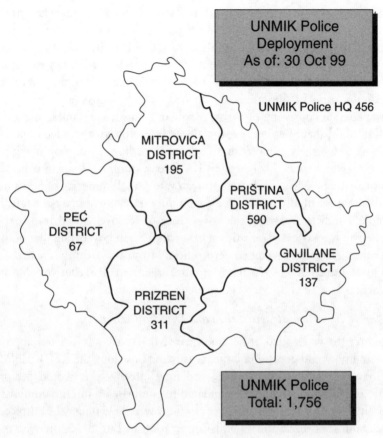

UNMIK Police
Deployment
As of: 30 Oct 99

UNMIK Police HQ 456

MITROVICA
DISTRICT
195

PRIŠTINA
DISTRICT
590

PEĆ
DISTRICT
67

GNJILANE
DISTRICT
137

PRIZREN
DISTRICT
311

UNMIK Police
Total: 1,756

Map 7.1 UNMIK Police Deployment in Kosovo, October 30, 1999

that Kosovo should remain part of Yugoslavia—and utilized the "occupation" of the province in different ways as a political mobilizing tool—there was very little real prospect of Kosovo's future reintegration into Yugoslavia. Direct Serbian political representation in Kosovo shrunk to the two members (Bishop Artemije, a liberal cleric in the Serbian Orthodox church, and Momčilo Trajković, the head of the Kosovo Serb Resistance Movement) initially serving on the twelve-person Kosovo Transitional Council, an "interim consultative body" set up by Special Representative Kouchner. Near the end of August, Transitional Council member Trajković proposed establishing designated Serb cantons in Kosovo as a means of protecting the remaining Serb minority. Faced with strong Albanian opposition to the plan, the idea was quickly rejected by Kouchner, who remarked that the concept reminded him of "a lot of bad things."[5] UCK leader Thaci, also a Council member, observed that anyone who wanted to discuss cantonization further "should go to 7 Francuska Street in Belgrade;" an allusion to the role of the Serbian Writers' Association in promoting Serb nationalism in the 1980s and 1990s.[6] UNMIK continued to hope that multi-ethnic solutions could be reached in specific areas. For example, a new police training academy was opened in which 6 percent of the first recruits were Serbs. And in the ethnically divided city of Kosovska Mitrovica, an interim council consisting of Serbs, Albanians, Turks, Romanies, and Bosniaks was established. But in the early fall of 1999, Kosovo appeared on its way to becoming a largely mono-ethnic unit; a nearly ethnically homogeneous protectorate, which was likely to evolve into a future Albanian-controlled "national state." Meanwhile, the protectorate's small minority of Serbs hunkered down, essentially becoming a community statelet within a parastate. For example, conflicts regarding the governance of Kosovo would lead Serbian members of the Kosovo Transitional Council to begin boycotting that body in September. And by November, Serb officials from the recently created Serb National Council of Kosovo and Metohija, organized an executive committee to function as a *de facto* Serb "government" in Kosovo.

Problems of Transition: Reconstruction and Deradicalization

Soon after the war ended, it became clear that Kosovo's future development and stability would depend in large measure on how long the KFOR/UNMIK governance system would endure, and how effectively it would perform. KFOR and UNMIK were only mandated to comprise an interim administrative framework for Kosovo until free elections were held under the auspices of the Organization for Security and Cooperation in Europe. Moreover, most international leaders hoped that, at some point in time, the province's coexistence within a democratic Yugoslavia would also become possible. But in view of the daunting challenges facing political and economic transition, both in the province, and in Milošević-governed Yugoslavia, some form of the existing transitional structure in Kosovo appeared likely to have a long lifespan. Progress in the economic reconstruction of Kosovo began gradually during the second half of 1999. And, though they proved unable to preserve the multi-ethnic fabric of Kosovo, international officials did expand the ambit of their control in areas such as postal services, utilities, and telecommunications. A so-called bubble econom" was also spawned by the arrival of tens of thousands of assistance workers from abroad, along with NATO troops. However, the task of building a strong and viable indigenous economy, which would be linked to regional and European markets, was certainly a long-term challenge. The Albanians of Kosovo proved resourceful at beginning the process of reconstruction, but the impact of foreign assistance projects, not to mention humanitarian endeavors, proceeded at a very slow rate. Squabbles between Serbs and

Albanians about the ownership and management of important enterprises, and also internal conflicts in UNMIK concerning foreign involvement in the province, also complicated the initial phase of economic reconstruction. Indeed, early on UN Secretary-General Kofi Annan suggested that the economic reconstruction of the province alone would take over a decade.

In addition to the crucial area of economic development, Kosovo's overall transition was also linked to the evolution of the UCK and Albanian political development. During the summer of 1999, the UCK, much like its pre-war and wartime postures, showed little sign of genuine enthusiasm for ethnic tolerance and power sharing. Aspiring to establish its own governmental institutions in the province, and in no hurry to completely disarm, the UCK used the early months of the postwar period to assume control of many local areas and sectors of activity. Although having no internationally recognized legal standing in Kosovo, the UCK established a network of ministries and local councils which collected taxes and customs payments. The UCK "government" also controlled the lucrative gray economy, collecting revenue from imports and trade in oil, cigarettes and alcohol. KFOR's first commander, General Mike Jackson, criticized the UCK for attempting to establish an underground police force.

Established in an authoritarian atmosphere as an armed movement engaging in a struggle with Serbian security forces—not to mention in a society with almost no liberal democratic experience—the UCK initially eschewed political pluralism as a "luxury," which would have to be postponed until a future independent Kosovo was created. The escalation of Serb–Albanian violence during 1998 and the first half of 1999 intensified this militant mindset, and strengthened hard-line elements in the movement (many of whom, because of their "Enverist roots," i.e., past sympathy for the Albanian communism of Enver Hoxha, or preference for statist Marxism, were already ill-disposed toward democratic dynamics). The UCK's power struggle with Ibrahim Rugova's more passive brand of independence seeking, as well as the revanchist syndrome among certain elements in Kosovo political life, also made it difficult for the UCK to de-radicalize and accept direction from its NATO "allies." The UCK did not, of course, constitute a monolithic movement. The moderate or pragmatic wing of the organization proved more willing to cooperate with the KFOR/UNMIK protectorate. By July 1999, UCK moderates organized a political party, "the Party of Democratic Progress" (PPDK, later changed to PDK), looking toward representation in the protectorate's new political process. For the moderates, it seemed prudent to play the game designed by the international community and patiently await the next opportunity to advance their goal of Kosovo independence. But the UCK's sudden change in tactics from guerilla war to pluralist politics did little to inspire interethnic coexistence. "During the war I shot every Serb I came across in the head," remarked a top UCK officer Seidi Veseli in July 1999, "but I do not hate the Serbs, now it is time for peace. . . . We have surrendered a large share of our weapons because the West has promised that it will represent our interests. But if it is necessary then we will take up arms again and go back into the mountains." Veseli also claimed that he had been preparing for an insurgent war in Kosovo since 1969 and had been reading Asian books about fighting guerilla wars and other material regarding military methods that he obtained from "friendly freedom armies from Asia, Africa, and Latin America."[7]

UCK hard-liners were less willing to accept imported notions of democracy and the policies advanced by the international community. Indeed, the hard-liners were most vociferous in their desire to ensure that former UCK cadre assume a high profile in Kosovo's reorganized defense and security structures. Such UCK hawks took pains to emphasize that "demilitarization does not mean disarmament." As UCK commander Ceku pointed out in early August 1999: "The UCK is undergoing two processes, demilitarization and transformation. . . . But demilitarization does not mean in any way that the people of Kosova are not going to have its proper defense structures." Ceku emphasized that the UCK should receive preferential treatment in the civilian police force, as specified in Paragraph No. 25 of an "Undertaking" the UCK had signed with KFOR on June 21, 1999. The UCK, the "youngest army in the world," wants to eventually be transformed, said Ceku in July 1999, "into something like the U.S. national guard. . . . The UCK will not disarm. Its arms will be placed in depots and will be guarded by troops under the supervision of KFOR."[8] In this view, some former members of the UCK will become involved in government, in "a life of politics." But for the most part, the UCK will become the "Army of Kosova." "We have a mission ahead of us," proclaimed Ceku, "and its successful completion will only be achieved with the existence of an army." The UCK was particularly distressed when KFOR reneged on a promise made in the June 1999 "Undertaking" (a section drafted at the last minute by Secretary of State Albright's public affairs assistant, James Rubin)[9] that would have given the rebel organization preferential treatment in the recruitment of the civil police. Thus, fewer than five persons in the first batch of 200 police trainees were former UCK members.[10]

In September, agreement was finally reached for the establishment of a Kosovo Protection Corps (TMK), which would begin operating in early 2000 (projected to grow to 3,000 active members and 2,000 reservists). The TMK was envisioned by the UN to be a civilian successor to the UCK, taking on tasks such as cleaning up the war-torn province. German General Klaus Reinhardt, who succeeded General Jackson as KFOR's commander, claimed that the UCK was being transformed "into a non-military, non-political, multi-ethnic civil defense organization."[11] But hard-line UCK leaders viewed the TMK as an Albanian national guard to be employed "if the integrity of Kosovo is threatened," or a force that, at some future time, would become the army of an independent Kosovar state.[12] On January 21, 2000, forty-three leaders of the TMK were sworn in, all of whom were former UCK members. Unofficially, international officials doubted that the creation of the TMK would actually deprive the UCK of arms; first because no one was really aware of how much military equipment the UCK had amassed, or had concealed, and secondly, because the Balkan environment was rife with a surfeit of arms available from the recent wars and civil strife. Meanwhile, Serbs in Kosovo were deeply anxious over the future role of the TMK, discontinued their cooperation with UNMIK's Transitional Council, and threatened to form a "Serb Protection Corps." Kosovo leaders Ceku and Thaci generally condemned incidents of violence against Serbs. But Albanian leaders also usually took pains to explain the basis of the anti-Serb activity, and to underscore that such activity did not represent typical Kosovar behavior.

After being chosen as "prime minister" of Kosovo's Albanians at the Rambouillet conference, Hashim Thaci attempted to straddle the fence between the hard-liners and the pragmatists in the UCK. "The UCK is in the process of transforming itself politically and militarily," he claimed in July. "We are interested in building a pluralistic society. . . . We fought for freedom not for power . . . for a state of our own, which we must now develop. Our goal is neither anarchy or dictatorship . . . the flight of the Serbs is not good, and is hurting the process of democratization. Those people [attacking the Serbs] are using the UCK's emblem to discredit the liberation army. We have distanced ourselves from these people."[13] But throughout 1999 and 2000 Thaci, who was trying with difficulty to make a transition from guerilla movement leader to peacetime politician, made clear what he hoped to ultimately achieve: "We are still a part of Yugoslavia during the three-year transition period [stipulated in the Rambouillet accord]. But afterwards, staying in Yugoslavia or Serbia after everything that has happened is incomprehensible for the Kosovars, and I think for the entire world as well." Thaci and the UCK were particularly upset by the fact that UNMIK had proposed allowing the laws of Yugoslavia, except for certain human rights provisions, to continue to apply in Kosovo. "Totalitarianism will prevail," Thaci cautioned, "if the Milošević laws are accepted."[14] Meanwhile, Thaci made no apologies for the dominant position held by the UCK in Kosovo Albanian political life immediately after the war: "The UCK is the state. No one must forget this."[15] Indeed, for some observers it appeared that Thaci was the state, after he appointed various friends and relatives to important posts in his "acting government."[16]

Not all Kosovar political leaders were pleased with the early postwar political climate in Kosovo, nor with the UCK and the means its leaders used to achieve their goals. Directly before and during the NATO bombing campaign the UCK's fundamentally militant perspectives had overshadowed Ibrahim Rugova's long-standing moderate perspectives. But during 2000, as international officials in the protectorate laid the groundwork for fall local elections, the differences between Rugova and the UCK's political heirs would become the most salient cleavage in Kosovo political life. For his part, Rugova saw the situation in Kosovo during the second half of 1999 and 2000 as a transitional period between Serb control from Belgrade and the eventual nonviolent achievement of the Kosovo independence he had always espoused. He also strongly condemned the surge of violence against the Serb minority in Kosovo. But Rugova had been sharply criticized by fellow Kosovars for his seemingly cooperative behavior with the Milošević regime both before and during the war, and was considerably marginalized during 1998 and 1999 due to the UCK's growing popularity as a liberation movement. Indeed, at the end of the war Rugova was considered "politically dead" by many Kosovars. Rugova continued, however, to enjoy a reservoir of respect and support in Kosovo Albanian society, especially among the older generation. His nonviolent approach also recommended him to many in the international community. I have learned a great deal about power and social relations," he told an interviewer in July 1999.

> There have always been people who wanted to take up arms more quickly . . . who believed in an armed struggle. . . . My aim was to save my people. Then came the exodus. I went crazy. It looked as though the Serbian plan would become reality: a Kosovo without Albanians, a Serbian zoo. Perhaps I was too cautious before . . . The people in the LDK [Rugova's party] were abroad. The UCK was here. It was logical that it should have occupied all kinds of posts. But now the LDK and myself are coming back. . . . The UCK can't hold on to power. Perhaps for one or two months but no longer.

Asked about Kosovo's future ties with Serbia, Rugova emotionally blurted out his new position: "No, not with Serbia, never again with Serbia."[17] Rugova also tried to explain why he appeared to be cooperating with Milošević during the early part of the war: "I took no pleasure in doing that. I am sorry. I was a prisoner. They could have killed me. There was a life at stake, the continued existence of Kosovo was at stake." But Rugova's chief political rival, Hashim Thaci, remained unforgiving toward the LDK leader, and ridiculed Rugova's delay in returning to Kosovo after the 1999 war: "I don't understand Rugova and his attitude. I can't understand the boycott he is conducting against his own people . . . its not good when a politician is afraid of his own people." And, Thaci cautioned: "Rugova must first ask the Kosovars for forgiveness, and then speak about the Serbs."[18] By August 1999, Rugova and Thaci were both taking part in sessions of Kouchner's Transitional Council, but their political rivalry continued. Rugova's resurgent political support and influence during the year following the NATO bombing was one of the most interesting trends in Kosovo's political development as an international protectorate. In part this was due to the considerable respect he enjoyed in earlier years as a figure working for Kosovo independence. But exasperation with the behavior of the UCK and its leaders also contributed to Rugova's comeback. This was particularly true among members of Kosovo's Albanian elite and middle class, who were disturbed by the influx of rural and less educated Albanians into Kosovo's cities during 1999 and 2000, and also the increasing violence in Kosovo society.[19]

The independent activist and journalist Veton Surroi, who also served on the Transitional Council, and at first seemed likely to become a leading contender along with Rugova and Thaci in future elections for the presidency of Kosovo, was quite outspoken regarding political trends in the protectorate. "The international community," Surroi emphasized in August 1999, "will probably not punish us [Albanians] for failing to defend multi-ethnicity in Kosovo. After all, even before the war the number of non-Albanians in Kosovo was akin to that of non-Slovenes in Slovenia, yet nobody talks about a multi-ethnic Slovenia.... [But] anybody that thinks that the violence will end once the last Serbs have been driven out is living an illusion. The violence will probably be directed against other Albanians. Is this really what we fought for?"[20] Surroi's colleague, the independent Albanian journalist Baton Xaxihu, also complained that members of his profession who try to be professionally impartial had found themselves for some time practicing "sandwich journalism," that is, caught between harassment and brutality by the Serb authorities (before June 10, 1999), and the one-sided views of "Albanian autocrats," who were "ready morally to destroy everybody.... Here [in Kosova] are not yet to be found the elements of democracy and of a civil society."[21] Surroi and Xaxihu echoed the feelings of a political minority of Kosovars who worried that the UCK had garnered too much power, and were also concerned with the growing crime wave and the appearance of Albania-based mafia-type elements in the province. In the event that a closer linkage developed between those mafia groups (heavily involved in smuggling and the trafficking of drugs) and local UCK political power brokers, progress toward the democratic institution-building goals of UNMIK and KFOR would be extremely difficult. At the end of the year, KFOR attempted to ensure security control over Kosovo's borders in order to crack down on the smuggling of weapons and cigarettes by illegal groups. How the former UCK movement would evolve in 2000 and 2001 remained one of the most significant open questions in Kosovo's future political development. Should the insurgent movement remain strong and politically radical, it could constitute a major challenge to the plans of the international community. However, the disintegration of the UCK— either because of internal factionalism or actions taken by UNMIK/ KFOR—also posed the danger of political violence, or noninstitutionalized rivalry between competing armed groups that could impede the creation of a law-governed state and the consolidation of pluralistic democracy. What appeared the most likely outcome was that the UCK's development would be uneven, with portions of the organization undergoing gradual deradicalization and transformation into peacefully competing political party organizations, and other sections opting for less peaceful and less democratic modes of political participation. The latter tendency seemed rooted in the still powerful and traditional aspects in Albanian political culture that place a low priority on pluralist practices.[22]

In mid-December 1999, UN and Kosovar officials established a non-governing body, the Provisional Administrative Council of Kosovo. Leaders from the three major Albanian political formations in the province took part in the creation of the new Council, which held its first meeting early in January 2000. Kosovo Serb officials boycotted the one seat reserved on the Council for their community. However, the operation of the Council, which was headed by UNMIK's Kouchner, went ahead without the Serbs, and it was subsequently decided that the new governing body would eventually be composed of 19 administrative departments: 15 headed by Albanians, three by Serbs, and one by a non-Albanian Muslim. The agreement establishing the Council provided that any self-proclaimed "governments" organized by Kosovo Albanians or other ethnic groups were to terminate their activities. However, in mid-January 2000, Hashim Thaci announced that Kosovo's new administrative council had already set up seven departments; four allegedly controlled by his Kosova Interim "Government" (QPK), and two by Ibrahim Rugova's party. According to Thaci, all the Albanian participants in the new council and departments were working and waiting for the independence of Kosovo. He also stated confidently that no Serb forces would ever return to the province, despite almost daily claims to the contrary by Yugoslav officials. "Serbia," Thaci emphasized, "is out of Kosova once and for all and is not going to come back no matter what changes it may undergo. . . . Neither the forces of Milošević, nor those of opposition leaders Drašković, nor Djindjić, or some other personality who may come to power in Serbia, will ever return to Kosova again."[23] Although Thaci was strongly committed to Kosovo's independence he appeared to be cooperating with the effort by UNMIK and KFOR to civilianize the UCK and stabilize Kosovo. A potentially more ominous development that began in the first part of 2000 was the appearance of a UCK-type Albanian insurgency in the southern parts of Serbia inhabited by large Albanian ethnic communities. The activities of the self-styled Albanian liberation army of Southern Serbia (UCPMB, or Liberation Army of Preševo, Medvedja, and Bujanovac) intensified Serb–Albanian tension in Yugoslavia as well as making the border area between Serbia and Kosovo a more combustible zone.

Throughout the first part of 2000, the security situation in Kosovo continued to be unstable. Early in the year, only some 1,800 partially equipped UN civilian police were operating in the protectorate, despite UNMIK's request for 6,000 police personnel (about 3,800 police had arrived by late May). Plans to recruit additional Kosovar police became bogged down when Thaci and Rugova could not agree on the role of their respective parties in the recruitment process. Lawlessness stemming from the cycle of revenge, inadequate policing, and competing centers of political control, however, was not the only cause of violence in the province. Thus, in the wake of the war, the traditional structure of Albanian society had undergone a severe shock. Faced with the destruction around them and material deprivations, thousands of returned Albanian refugees had migrated to locations away from their original homes. In Priština, an estimated 300,000 people had arrived from villages, many moving into apartments and houses previously owned and occupied by Serbs. Many of these people had been accustomed to living in a closely knit environment where nearly everyone knew everyone else, and "an unwritten moral code" had made it an embarrassment to stray from accepted community norms. These people were now thrust into an anonymous society without any established authority. As Shkelzen Maliqi has pointed out: "Pater familias who had controlled everything had become a poor refugee in a big city, and can't ensure daily existence. This is a psychological trauma for hundreds of people. Teenagers don't have any kind of control. Schools have collapsed, as well as the authority of the teachers. . . . Socialization doesn't exist and one can't control that. Things which were thought to be very firmly fixed have now broken down."[24]

Despite its ongoing difficulties, the UN made some gradual progress during 1999 and 2000 in establishing an administrative framework for Kosovo. For example, several hundred judges were appointed near the end of 1999. But dissatisfied with the ethnic composition of the judicial appointees, and the fact that the use of the Yugoslav criminal code was being ignored (an alleged violation of UN Resolution 1244), Serb leaders in Kosovo threatened to organize their own judicial bodies in the province. Regrettably, judicial decision-making in the province continued to be characterized more by ethnic considerations than the impartial rule-of-law. As one examination of the problem concluded in the spring of 2000, "the notion of a pluralist, tolerant, and multi-ethnic Kosovo remains a distant goal." The study found that Albanian jurists "regardless of their personal views . . . are fearful of being perceived as 'pro-Serb' in any way . . . many judges fear retaliation by extremists if they give stiff penalties to members of their own ethnic group, or light penalties to other ethnic groups. At times judges are under pressure to let off defendants with strong ties to the KLA [UCK], political leaders, or organized crime."[25] Meanwhile, from behind the scenes in Belgrade, Slobodan Milošević attempted to manipulate

Kosovo Serb activities in order to keep the issue of the province's future alive for his own political purposes, and to give the appearance that he had not totally abandoned Serbian hopes of re-establishing influence over Kosovo. Milošević's efforts were particularly focussed on maintaining the ethnic division of the city of Kosovska Mitrovica, where the province's remaining Serbs were heavily concentrated, and which he hoped could be the nucleus for the formation of a formally partitioned Serb enclave consisting of at least a portion of northern Kosovo. After Serb–Albanian conflict escalated in Mitrovica in March 2000, UNMIK and KFOR struggled to calm tensions, disarm extremists on both sides, and prevent any further deepening of the ethnic cleavage that had been accelerated by the events associated with the recent war and meddling from Belgrade. By mid-2000, the Serbs of Kosovo had become a beleaguered ethnic minority, significantly reduced in their size and influence compared to earlier years. Milošević had waged a policy effectively leading to the fiction that Kosovo was still within Serbia. But the province was now without most of the Kosovo Serbs who had helped him to come to power over a dozen years earlier. Ironically, despite their plight, most Kosovo Serbs, who expressed deep animus toward the international community, continued to trust Milošević[26] and the SPS far more than any other political force on the Serbian political landscape.

The institutional and security vacuum that characterized the first year of Kosovo's postwar transition, and contributed to the already serious climate of interethnic conflict in the province, did not auguer well for the protectorate-province's stability and democratization. Thus, various administrative bodies established by leading Albanian political organizations continued to compete for authority, as well as with international agencies and quasi-state bodies set up by the remaining Serb leaders. Indeed, there was not even consensus within the international community regarding sovereignty in Kosovo. For example, some foreign officials stressed the need for close adherence to UN Resolution 1244, and cooperation with the Federal Republic of Yugoslavia in shaping Kosovo's future. But others in the UNMIK/KFOR protectorate establishment took a more expansive view of their powers, and envisioned Kosovo as an entity that would and should no longer be linked to Yugoslavia. Moreover, though the international community provided a safe environment for the return of Albanian refugees to Kosovo, and was committed to the economic and political transformation of the province, its initial failure to provide adequate protection for Serbs and other non-Albanian minority communities in the province severely undermined any long-term chance of creating a "multi-ethnic democracy."[27] Indeed, this failure also served to deepen the already very wide chasm of distrust between Albanians and Serbs in the province. Short of money and personnel, particularly police, Special Representative Kouchner admitted that Albanians and Serbs "could agree on virtually nothing." And at the end of 1999, he also acknowledged, rather belatedly and naively, that "we found out, and it's a lesson, that one oppression could conceal another."[28] Six months later, he was hardly more optimistic. "I have not succeeded in human terms . . . they still hate one another deeply. Here I discovered hatred deeper than anywhere in the world, more than in Cambodia or Vietnam or Bosnia."[29] Kouchner's insights were painfully illustrated as the campaign began for internationally managed local elections scheduled to take place on October 28, 2000. By August, 34 political parties were registered to compete in the election. However, the electoral process was marred by intimidation, including open violence and murder, as extremists associated with the two spin-off parties from the Kosovo Liberation Army—the Democratic Party of Kosovo (PDK) and the Alliance for Kosovo's Future (AAK)—attacked leaders and members of one another's parties, and also members of Rugova's Democratic Alliance of Kosovo (LDK).[30] The under-staffed UN police made as little headway in stopping the intra-Albanian violence as they had in protecting the province's Serbian minority. The acting head of one of Rugova's branch units remarked that the current violence "is much more painful because from childhood we knew who the Serbs were and could never expect anything good from them. But we never expected we Albanians could do this to ourselves."[31]

In the fall of 2000, the future of Kosovo appeared likely to mime the experience of Bosnia, with alternating periods of progress and regress in political stabilization and interethnic reconciliation; a condition reflecting both the deep intergroup polarization in the protectorate and the international community's operational difficulties and errors regarding Balkan transformation. But in the longer run, no matter what policies would be adopted by the international community, the Albanians of Kosovo appeared determined to pursue their state-building dreams. As Hashim Thaci remarked at the end of January 2000: "We will not live under the UN guardianship forever. . . . We make no secret that we wish for a separate and independent Kosovo."[32] Even Ibrahim Rugova, whose political star had begun to rise again as many Kosovars became disenchanted with postwar extremism, and the slow pace of normalization in the province, spoke out for a rapid transition to independence. Survey research in mid-2000 also indicated that 95 percent of the Kosovo Albanians favored independence, although only 89 percent thought they would have such a status in another five years (Table 7.1). Serbs in Kosovo were just as adamant that the province remain part of Serbia, but rather less optimistic that it would be the case in five years. Interestingly, in the Albanian case, there was hardly any support for the idea of an international protectorate as the best outcome for Kosovo, or the expectation that protectorate status would last. But for the moment, the international community appeared only willing to grant the Kosovars a vague status of self-determination, or what Kouchner referred to

Table 7.1   Kosovo Albanians and Kosovo Serbs Concerning the Best Option for a Permanent Solution in the Province, April–July, 2000

	"Which of the following do you think . . ."			
	Would be the best permanent solution for Kosovo?		*Is the most likely to be Kosovo's status five years from now?*	
Answer	*Albanians (%)*	*Serbs (%)*	*Albanians (%)*	*Serbs (%)*
1. Kosovo remains part of Serbia[a]		89	—	62
2. . . . but gains increased autonomy in economic, cultural and administrative matters[a]	—	4	—	11
3. Kosovo gains republic status on par with Serbia and Montenegro	—	2	1	3
4. Partition of Kosovo into Serb and Albanian regions	—	5	—	9
5. International protectorate[b]	1	—	4	11
6. Independence	95	—	89	2
7. Union with Albania	4	—	6	1
8. None of the above	—	1	—	1

SOURCE: *Opinion Analysis,* Office of Research, U.S. Department of State, May 30 and July 20, M-61-00 and M-104-00.

Data: Face-to-face interviews with a nationally representative sample of 995 Albanian adults age 18 and older conducted in Kosovo between April 25 and May 14, 2000, and 465 ethnic Serb adults aged 18 and older in northern and central Kosovo between June 26 and July 4, 2000.

[a]Choice 1 and 2 offered as a single choice to Albanian respondents.

[b]Offered Albanians as survey choice in May 2000; recorded if volunteered in October 1999.

as "substantive autonomy." How soon the international community would tire of its protectorate responsibilities,[33] and how vociferous the Kosovo Albanians would pursue their goal of independence, remained open questions at the end of 2000.

The potential for Albanian–UN/NATO conflict and renewed Albanian–Serb violence over the province certainly could not be ruled out. (Near the end of August, KFOR troops arrested a commander and three other members of the Albanian guerilla group UCPMB, who had been crossing into Serbia to attack Serb security forces). But it seemed unlikely that Kosovo would again come under Belgrade's control in the foreseeable future, even when the Milošević regime ceased to control Serbia.

Prospects for a New Serbia: Power Struggle in a Pariah State

The Politics of "Victorious Capitulation"

At the conclusion of the NATO bombing campaign against Yugoslavia, Slobodan Milošević remained in power, and the basic pillars of his regime were still intact. But Yugoslavia's president now faced the most difficult political challenge of his twelve-year rule. The situational patriotic unity engendered by the war no longer could serve as a barrier to a burgeoning of political opposition activity. Indeed, cracks in the façade of national solidarity had already begun to appear near the end of the bombing campaign against Yugoslavia, and undoubtedly had been one of the major considerations motivating Milošević's acquiescence to NATO's terms for ending the struggle (see Chapter 6). In many respects both the wartime and immediate postwar anti-regime sentiment represented a continuation of a trend that had been very apparent during 1998–1999, and which had been interrupted by the NATO bombing campaign. Technically, Milošević was entitled to retain his office until July 2001, that is, up to the regular expiration of the four-year term that he had been elected to by the Yugoslav Assembly in July 1997. But under the prevailing circumstances—the loss of Kosovo and the country's overall isolation and deprivations engendered by his policies—Milošević could not help but notice that politically he was in mortal danger.

Quickly trying to regain political momentum and detract from his blighted record in the aftermath of NATO's military operation, Milošević's propaganda apparatus began to emphasize four major themes: (1) Yugoslavia's victory in the struggle with NATO; (2) the country's resolution to regain Kosovo as soon as possible; (3) the regime's commitment to rapid reconstruction; and (4) the importance of castigating "traitors," a group loosely and broadly defined as all those who had betrayed the country during the struggle with NATO, or were opposing the regime's postwar efforts to guide the country's future. Regime spokesmen took pains to emphasize that the country's resoluteness in standing up to the Rambouillet "diktat" had ultimately allowed the UN to supplant NATO as the principal organizational authority in Kosovo. In a speech to the citizens of Yugoslavia on June 10, 1999, announcing the end of the NATO attack, Milošević brazenly claimed that he had "again put the UN on the international scene, the UN which was not functioning for about eighty days before the start of the aggression . . . I believe this will be an enormous contribution to history."[34] Moreover, Belgrade could rightly claim that Yugoslavia was not subject to the offensive Appendix B to the Rambouillet accord—that would have allowed NATO troops to transit through the country—offered to the Serbian side in the last hours of negotiation in France. Thus, while forced to withdraw his army and police from Kosovo, Milošević could also claim that under UN Resolution 1244, Kosovo was still technically part of Yugoslavia. Initially, Milošević seemed to be making an argument that was convincing to a large number of his countrymen. For example, a poll taken by the Belgrade weekly *NIN*, and published only a week after the NATO bombing ended, revealed that 46 percent of the Serbian citizens who were surveyed thought that Yugoslavia had won the struggle, 21 percent that NATO had won, and 26 percent felt that the war was a draw. Moreover, two-thirds of those surveyed did not feel that the Serbs were responsible for the atrocities in Kosovo, 15 percent accepted partial responsibility, and only 15 percent blamed Serbs.[35]

Over the next months, the situation for the shrinking Serb population in Kosovo became far more difficult. But in his end of the year message for 1999, Milošević would still confidently claim that "Nobody can take Kosovo from us." He also threatened that the Yugoslav army would return some day to the province and restore order. But it was a hollow boast at most, as UN forces in Kosovo gradually grew to nearly 50,000 during the last six months of 1999. Milošević could claim, however, that he had stood up to a 19-member alliance, that his regime had survived, and that he had been able to withdraw most of his military and police security apparatus from Kosovo. Milošević also wasted no time in associating the regime with postwar reconstruction efforts, although it proved difficult for him to demonstrate achievements in this area, partly because of the extensive devastation of the country's infrastructure[36] but also because of the shortage of funds for development and the lack of access to international lending institutions. But despite the magnitude of infrastructure damage, Milošević seized every opportunity to associate himself with new projects, departing from his usual aloof manner and taking advantage of photo opportunities whenever incremental progress could be demonstrated (erecting pontoon bridges, visiting construction sites, etc.). The urgency and challenge of the reconstruction issue also was a good excuse for the regime to demand conformity and commitment from the population. As Milošević remarked on June 10, using his favorite imagery that harkened back to the late 1980s: "Our great imminent tasks shall require a great mobilization . . . we need unity and great mobilization to carry out reconstruction. In all of that, I wish all the citizens of Yugoslavia a lot of happiness and luck."[37]

While Milošević employed his media machinery in an attempt to salvage his image and spin a new message of victorious performance, reconstruction, and revanchism, as well as protecting the country against supposedly subversive elements, the Yugoslav opposition forces attempted to exploit the regime's vulnerable position and to challenge its power. Three broad phases of postwar opposition activity can be identified in the year following the NATO attack:

first, the period from June to September 1999, during which the opposition continued its characteristic highly personalized organizational wrangling over leadership and tactics; second, the period from the fall of 1999 to early 2000, during which anti-regime parties finally began cooperating more effectively to present a united front against the regime; and third, the period from the winter to the late summer of 2000, when the regime and a loosely united democratic opposition jousted in preparation for a coming face-off either at the ballot box in September, or in the streets.

During the first phase, the opposition exhibited many of the classical deficits that had allowed Milošević to maintain power since 1987 (see Chapter 3). Once again, the old phenomenon of *liderstvo*—the unbridled ambition and uncompromising nature of top leaders in each of Yugoslavia's many political parties—was apparent. This problem would seriously weaken anti-regime efforts to politically confront Milošević, and was vividly illustrated in the dispute between the heads of Yugoslavia's two main opposition parties: Vuk Drašković of the Serbian Renewal Movement, and Zoran Djindjić of the Democratic Party. The Drašković–Djindjić rivalry had destroyed the *Zajedno* coalition in 1997 (see Chapter 5), and in 1999–2000 threatened to prevent any strong and sustained opposition alliance to Milošević's regime.

Both Drašković and Djindjić also had political records that made it difficult for either one of them to assume leadership of a broad opposition front. Drašković was viewed by many as an erratic figure, who had moderated his very nationalist positions only after the full extent of the wars of the Yugoslav secession had become apparent, and also had compromised himself as an opposition figure through his participation in the Yugoslav government during early 1999. But having broken with Milošević during the war, Drašković managed to position himself as a contender to replace the Yugoslav president and the existing regime. Meanwhile, Djindjić had tried to maneuver between moderate liberalism and a credible nationalist posture during the early 1990s. But the Bosnian born Djindjić's support for the Bosnian Serb cause in the mid-1990s caused many Yugoslav liberals and foreign observers to view him as a consummate pragmatist who could not be relied upon to maintain the solidarity of the democratically oriented political forces. Many observers also blamed Djindjić for the break up of the *Zajedno* coalition in 1997, a charge he did not deny (see Chapter 5). Fearing that Milošević would use the war as a rationale for taking brutal measures to injure or eliminate all opposition figures, Djindjić had relocated to Montenegro early in the NATO bombing campaign. Under the protection of the Montenegrin reformer, Milo Djukanović, Djindjić had spoken out against the Belgrade regime, and had only returned to Belgrade in July.

For his part, in the period immediately following the hostilities with NATO,

Drašković concentrated on his old games, that is, outmaneuvering Djindjić and assuming leadership of the opposition forces. Near the end of the war, for example, Drašković remarked that in the future he would not "accept a piece of power without democratic changes. . . . I do not want to protect the present system; I want to change it peacefully and democratically, but rapidly."[38] But that kind of formulation gave Drašković plenty of political flexibility in dealing with both the regime and the opposition. In any case, for the moment, Drašković avoided calling for either elections or street rallies, perhaps hoping that Milošević would invite him to replace Šešelj and his SRS party in the Serbian government's ruling coalition. In the meantime, the struggle against Milošević could wait. "I am the king of the streets," Drašković bragged to an interviewer near the end of June 1999. "I know better than anyone else in the world what could be the best moment for demonstrations to bring down Milošević. This is not the time."[39] Djindjić, in contrast, blamed the authorities for the bombing of the country and for the loss of Kosovo, and called for peaceful protests to force the government to step down: "The people, one or two million of them, shall come out into the streets and all the towns. Milošević as always will wait until the last minute. He will say 'no,' but will end up by saying 'yes.'"[40]

Despite the serious divisions in their ranks during the early postwar period, most democratic opposition parties called upon Milošević to resign, or hoped that he could be replaced at coming elections. Independent centers of influence and nonparty activists such as the Serbian Orthodox Church, and various members of the Serbian Academy of Sciences and Arts, also pleaded with Milošević to step away from power. Notwithstanding their views that Milošević should depart from power, most opposition leaders roundly criticized NATO's bombing and, like the regime—although with different programmatic elements—endorsed the idea of Kosovo's formal constitutional status within Serbia, and the need for Serbs to regain their influence over Kosovo's future development. Established opposition leaders also hurried to ensure their patriotic credentials were in order during the imminent competition with Milošević. "I have to say," Zoran Djindjić remarked, for example, "that this war [with NATO] was not a real war, but a massacre with risk-free bombardments and many civilian victims. It has amounted to a punishment of Serbia, conducted cynically by the international community. A dirty war . . . I think we will be able to recover Kosovo."[41] And even Vesna Pešić, the former head of the Civic Alliance of Serbia, commented: "I believe Kosovo is part of our state. But the Rambouillet proposal did not let us keep this territory. I did not understand the West's position: Did it really want us to live together with the Albanians, [or] for us to separate? When you want to create a state within another state you separate people."[42] Bishop Atanasije, Vicar of the Patriarchy in Belgrade and a cleric close to Patriarch Pavle, also pointed out that the

Orthodox Church condemned Milošević's methods and sought his resignation, but still felt strongly that Kosovo belongs in Serbia: "We blame Milošević not for trying to defend the nation but for failing."[43]

One of the major obstacles facing the opposition at the end of the war was that the Serbian people seemed to have lost their trust in all politicians, whether in the ruling coalition or in the ranks of the opposition. The combination of the failed anti-regime protests of 1996–1997, the failed struggle of 1998–1999 to defeat the UCK and maintain *de facto* control over Kosovo, and the continued economic deterioration of the country, had left Serbia's citizens extremely disillusioned and angst-ridden. Most people focussed on day-to-day survival, and the mood of the population in Serbia, captured in public opinion surveys, was highly cynical and fearful regarding their future. Thus, while Milošević could no longer rely upon the surge of national solidarity that had helped to buoy his regime during the NATO bombing, few citizens in Serbia were as yet prepared to engage in active and sustained anti-state dissidence. Public opinion researcher Srbobran Branković has commented that citizen attitudes in Serbia at the conclusion of NATO's bombing campaign resembled those of citizens in a country devastated by an earthquake, who were attempting to sort out their future.[44] There was also a sharp drop in support for the ruling SPS compared to before the war (from 29 percent to 22 percent).[45] Drašković's SPO had the support of about 15 percent of the population, or about five times the level of Djindjić's Democratic Party. Moreover, 69 percent of those surveyed believed that the current authorities were either "very responsible" (23 percent) or "mostly responsible for the country's deteriorated situation. But 21 percent remained staunch supporters of the ruling party, which Branković has described as a "suicidally inclined section of the electorate."[46]

In addition to relying on his own SPS, Milošević also continued to enjoy the support of the other two parties in the ruling coalition: the JUL organization headed by his wife, and the far more popular Serbian Radical Party, headed by Vojislav Šešelj. "Milošević's resignation would lead to dangerous confusion and de-stabilization at the current time," Šešelj remarked not without some accuracy at the end of June 1999. "I favor early elections—so far it has been easier for us to find a common language with the Socialists than with the opposition parties. How am I to cooperate with Vuk Drašković? He is a madman and a drug addict . . . Djindjić and Obradović [the leader of the Social Democrats] are traitors." Šešelj, whose ultra-nationalist message continued to resonate with a fringe, but not inconsequential, segment of Serbia's voters (approximately 5–10 percent of the electorate), was particularly incensed about American political and financial support for the liberal opposition arranged not long before at a meeting in Montenegro. "The West simply does not understand," claimed Šešelj. "There is no better guarantee for Milošević to stay in power than to insist on overthrowing him. The West does not understand the Serbian soul."[47] But while Šešelj supported Milošević for the moment, the wily leader of the Radical Party was biding his time, hoping to pick up the mantle of power should Milošević falter. Bitter over Milošević's deal to end the struggle with NATO, Šešelj had resigned from his office as a deputy prime minister in the Serbian government. But his departure was never accepted, and he remained "Deputy PM in resignation."

Meanwhile, democratic opposition leaders counted on the fact that Milošević, although still enjoying considerable assets, could no longer provide sufficient patronage and perks to ensure the loyalty of his political elite. Thanks to EU sanctions, the ruling oligarchy was an isolated elite that could not travel to Western Europe. As the Chairman of the Civic Alliance, Goran Svilanović, observed: "Milošević cannot promise anything to anybody any more. He cannot offer a type of financial security to those around him as before, and I'm afraid he will not be able to guarantee their physical security either. I hope that those who contributed to his rise and power—and meanwhile have stolen a lot of money from the people—will ask themselves where they are leading their families to."[48] From the beginning of the postwar period, the liberal opposition had also been counting on the international community to assist them in bringing about Milošević's departure from power. The NATO countries who had carried out the war were willing to help—particularly since they had failed to topple Milošević—provided the opposition coalesced in a manner that suited the international community. Indeed, between the end of hostilities in mid-June and late August 1999, Serb opposition leaders met with international officials on three different occasions.

At the end of June the Alliance for Change (SZP) held its first rally in the central Serbian town of Čačak. The meeting attracted about 8,000 people. By the end of July, the SZP had held rallies in about twenty towns across Serbia, and also gathered some 550,000 signatures on a petition asking for Milošević's resignation. In mid-July 1999, Vuk Drašković's SPO began its own parallel anti-government rallies; with the first held at Kragujevac on July 17. But such divided efforts to tap into Serbia's substantial popular discontent made little headway. Most demonstrations were attended by crowds of less than 10,000, and only a few drew more than 20,000, a significant failure compared to the civic and student protest of 1996 and 1997. Passivity, fear, and a struggle for survival were the predominant emotions in the population. Much of the citizenry was cynical regarding the utility of political activism, or too fatigued and fearful of challenging the regime. This situation and Milošević's control of his technology of domination prevented the opposition from gaining any substantial momentum. Moreover the most successful expressions of anti-regime discontent were organized by forces not directly controlled by the established opposition parties (e.g., discontent among unpaid soldiers, activists in towns which had held protests during the war).

Recognizing their weaknesses, the Alliance for Change and the SPO both sought to coordinate their efforts with other opposition groups and even made tentative steps toward mutual cooperation (e.g., a so-called non-aggression pact was even entered into between the two parties in July 1999). Throughout the summer of 1999, the Alliance for Change opposed the idea of participating in any election that would be organized by the regime, and continued to rely on organized protest rallies as the main tactic to force Milošević's resignation. But by late summer it was clear that public participation at rallies was waning. Meanwhile, Drašković's SPO, although calling for Milošević's resignation, and organizing a few rallies in mid-summer, had generally adopted a cautious strategy distancing itself from the SZP and Djindjić, and waited to see where the best opportunities would present themselves. The SPO had the advantage of already controlling the Belgrade City Council and Yugoslavia's second largest television network (Studio B), and also holding 45 seats in Serbia's 250 seat Assembly. In contrast, the Alliance for Change was a substantially extra-parliamentary organization (the Democratic Party had two seats in the Federal Assembly) without complete control in any of the municipalities run by the opposition coalition.

On August 19, a major rally of opposition supporters took place in Belgrade. This event—held on the traditional religious holiday of the Transfiguration—drew an estimated 120,000–150,000 people, and was the largest demonstration since the 1996–1997 protests. Organized by economic experts and intellectuals from the G-17 group who had drawn up a so-called Serbian "stability pact," the demonstration also had the support of the Serbian Orthodox Church. Vuk Drašković made an unexpected appearance and put forward the idea of holding emergency early elections. Despite his reputation as a charismatic speaker, the crowd was not uniformly pleased by his unscheduled appearance, particularly when he counseled the demonstrators not to aggressively confront the authorities. Perhaps for the first time in his career Drašković became the target of angry mutterings and whistles from the crowd. He later blamed the whistling on Djindjić supporters.

The August 19 rally marked a clear parting of the ways between the Alliance for Change and the SPO with respect to the best methodology for opposing the regime. But when Drašković indicated that his SPO would take part in early local elections hinted at by the authorities, the Alliance was forced to clarify its position, realizing that a boycott of the electoral process by the bulk of the democratic opposition would only strengthen the Milošević regime. Thus, at a series of opposition round tables held in the weeks following the "Transfiguration rally" representatives of 21 opposition parties, including the

Alliance for Change and Drašković's SPO, met to discuss disagreements in the opposition ranks concerning the issue of staging early elections in accordance with international standards. An expert group on elections was also formed and a common agenda for developing legislation was accepted. However, the Alliance would only take part in elections, its spokesman indicated, if the regime met certain precise conditions that would ensure democratic competition. Thus most members of parties in the Alliance simply did not believe that free elections really could be held with Milošević in power.

Meanwhile, Vuk Drašković continued to push for early elections, although he was aware that the regime was unlikely to provide a fully democratic electoral framework and also aware of the difficulties that the Alliance and Djindjić faced regarding participation in regime-run elections. For the moment, Drašković, who had claimed he was "king of the streets," maintained that it was not possible to actually challenge the authorities by going to the streets. In fact, Drašković claimed that the focus by the SZP and Djindjić on street protests might draw the country into civil war, something the SPO leader cautioned he would never allow. Drašković instead called for the formation of an interim government followed by early elections. When asked by an interviewer if he would be willing to retire from politics in order to obtain Milošević's removal, Drašković responded negatively,[49] asserting that Milošević would eventually leave as a result of everything the SPO had done to oppose him since 1990. It was not surprising to observers of Drašković's record and ambition that his overwhelming concern was the issue of who would replace Milošević, and not the urgency or centrality of ousting the Yugoslav president. Thus, throughout September, Drašković refused serious discussions with other opposition forces concerning the formulation of a joint strategy against the regime.

In sharp contrast to Drašković, the leaders of the Alliance for Change continued to support the idea of mass protest—or what one of its leaders called a "peaceful, democratic rebellion"[50]—and that Milošević should be forced to resign before any elections would take place. In early September, Zoran Djindjić announced that planned rallies in the fall would have a new character, and that they would take the form of day-long political events rather than rallies at which leaders would give prepared speeches. Djindjić continued to reject participation in any elections organized along with the regime. On September 21, 1999, after a disappointingly small demonstration in Belgrade (about 20,000 people), the Alliance began holding daily protest marches demanding that Milošević leave office. By September the Alliance had been able to enlist Dragoslav Avramović, the respected former Governor of the National Bank, as the potential head of a transitional government that could be put in place should Milošević decide to resign.

As in earlier years, the conflict between the leading opposition forces over political tactics proved very useful to Milošević, who in any case was unprepared to resign in response to street protests, or even to proceed with early elections that might threaten his continued rule. Indeed by September, the regime intimated that it no longer supported the idea of early elections that had been floated earlier. Under more international and domestic pressure than ever before, Milošević pursued a course that he had begun directly after the 1996–1997 anti-regime street protest, namely, tightening the authoritarian facets of his control system, and abandoning practices that had been typical of his earlier "soft dictatorship." For example, rigid laws restricting universities and the media continued to be enforced, while the tone and atmosphere of regime repression that had accelerated during the NATO bombing campaign was stepped up. The rising number of assassinations of public officials who had been close to Milošević's inner circle, as well as criminals associated, to a greater or lesser degree, with the authorities in Belgrade, gave politics in Yugoslavia the character of a "thugocracy," that is, a state where arbitrary repression and uncertainty were the order of the day. At the same time Milošević and regime authorities continued their propaganda campaign, including public appearances at reconstructed factories and refineries, in order to demonstrate that they were the only force capable of rebuilding the country. For example, opening an oil refinery near the end of September 1999, Milošević claimed that "the reconstruction of our country is victorious, just as the defense of our country was heroic and victorious."[51] But as a result of his seriously depleted legitimacy Milošević was forced to abandon his typical aloofness and image of a statesman who simply dealt with matters of global importance. Thus, during the second part of 1999 he appeared frequently in public, attempting to reinforce the accusation in the state-run and pro-government media that the opposition forces were essentially a subversive arm of NATO, endeavoring to foment violence in Serbia, and to turn the country into a Western colony. For its part, the official media ignored opposition demands for democratic change, and the police prevented any anti-regime demonstrations from getting out of control. On September 29, for example, riot police intervened in Belgrade to break up demonstrations (an attempt by the Alliance leaders to lead a column of some 20,000 demonstrators to the elite suburb of Dedinje, where Milošević lived in his personal residence).

Meanwhile, recognizing that Milošević was in no mood to back down, the rounds of street protests begun on September 21 failed to swell to expected levels. And concerned that the Djindjić–Drašković rivalry was helping perpetuate the Belgrade regime, international officials pressed hard for a reconciliation between the two major opposition leaders, or at least some way around their seemingly irreconcilable conflict. Paradoxically, the crucial breakthrough in Serbia's intra-opposition conflict came about because of an unpredictable event. On October 3, at Lazarevac, 25 miles south of Belgrade, Vuk Drašković narrowly escaped death in an automobile crash that looked suspiciously like an assassination attempt on the SPO leader. Three of Drašković's bodyguards were killed in the crash, along with his brother-in-law. The truck that hit Drašković was abandoned at the site of the crash, had no license plates, and the truck's driver and owner mysteriously disappeared. The badly shaken Drašković blamed the Milošević regime which, he charged, at the funeral of his wife's brother, "produces only death each day in Serbia without letting life grow."[52] Drašković's advisers claimed he had escaped a similar accident on September 29. Rival opposition leader Zoran Djindjić also indicated that he shared Drašković's suspicions about who was responsible for the car accident. Djindjić and the Alliance for Change continued with their demonstrations, but by now they realized that without the participation of Drašković's SPO there seemed very little chance to force Milošević from power.

Interestingly, just a few days before the Drašković crash, 21 opposition parties and coalitions, including the SPO, had agreed at roundtable talks convened by the Democratic Center that they would continue discussions on October 3 regarding the formulation of minimally acceptable electoral procedures. It was also rumored that Drašković had been subjected to enormous pressure by members of the international community to improve his relations with Djindjić and the Democratic Party. Indeed, on a visit to the Czech Republic in late September 1999, after meeting with U.S Ambassador John Shattuck, Drašković characterized the Democratic Party as "an important party" that he could cooperate with to topple the regime in Yugoslavia.[53] He also told an interviewer in Prague that Milošević was "now far weaker than he was a year or two ago. But on the other hand Milošević was more dangerous, because he is completely isolated."[54]

Did Milošević order Drašković's assassination as a means to prevent a broad opposition coalition from forming, and did the coincidental timing of the accident or assassination provide an impetus to the reconciliation process? There are not yet any definitive answers to those questions. But in any case, the political consequences of the Lazarevac car crash would eventually prove extremely significant. Thus, the first sign of a tentative rapprochement between the Alliance for Change and Drašković's SPO was the October 10 adoption by the Belgrade City Assembly of a declaration calling for Milošević's resignation. In return for supporting the declaration, members of the Democratic Party in the Assembly agreed to join with the majority SPO members and condemn the alleged assassination attempt against Drašković (along with police intervention against the supporters of the Alliance during the Belgrade demonstrations). Mutual political necessity drove the SPO–SZP cooperation: the SPO was convinced that the regime had attempted to kill Drašković, and Milošević would not support its demand for early elections, while the Alliance had little hope of attracting additional popular support without Drašković. It is against this background of mutual need that representatives of the opposition parties, including both the SPO and Alliance for Change, signed an agreement on October 14 concerning acceptable electoral conditions.

Though the relationship between the two wings of the Serbian opposition was somewhat more conciliatory after the October 14 agreement, old antagonisms and rivalries impeded the formation of a solid anti-regime front during the last two months of 1999. Members of the Alliance for Change continued to talk about early elections, and SPO leaders suggested that it might become necessary to launch street demonstrations if the regime balked at holding such elections. But, despite stepped-up international pressure on the opposition forces to overcome their differences, real progress in achieving unity proved extremely difficult. Drašković continued to avoid any full embrace of the Alliance for Change, and also appeared unwilling to make a really radical break with the regime. Several reasons seemed to account for his position. For one thing, Drašković feared that his control of Belgrade—where he drew most of his revenue—and other towns in Serbia would be threatened should he begin aggressively attacking Milošević. Indeed, a new regime-sponsored Law on Self-Government, passed by the Serbian legislature in mid-November, made it easier for the regime to control the municipal level of authority. The SPO leader also feared that the regime might try another assassination attempt against him. Moreover, the possibility of launching street protests in cooperation with the Alliance for Change could result in a situation where his rivals would be able to attract more support for themselves.[55] Meanwhile, the Alliance for Change, and especially Zoran Djindjić—who was loosing support and whose street demonstrations were attracting increasingly smaller turnout—found it extremely difficult to cooperate with the SPO, or defer to Drašković's leadership. Drašković, Djindjić could point out, was a man who after all, had been directly associated with the Milošević regime for a time. But Djindjić was also painfully aware that, in the pursuit of a strong, cohesive Serbian opposition, international officials generally viewed him as a more dispensable political figure than Vuk Drašković. That is, the removal of Drašković as SPO leader was likely to intensify divisions in the already fractured anti-regime forces, while the Alliance for Change, and the opposition movement generally, would probably be able to survive Djindjić's departure from the leadership of the Democratic Party. Meanwhile, Drašković and his supporters felt that as the SPO was the largest single opposition party, it deserved to be the leading force in any democratic opposition alliance or in any decisions made on anti-regime tactics.

By December, partly as a result of international pressure, and partly due to self-realization of their weaknesses, most opposition leaders were becoming reconciled to granting Drašković the principal leadership role in the struggle against Milošević. Indeed, at the same time, Djindjić came under increasing pressure from some of his colleagues in the Democratic Party and in the Alliance to step down from leadership. In mid-December, acknowledging that their strategy of public protest had failed, the Alliance for Progress suspended the series of rallies begun on September 21, and which had continued for 89 days. Speaking to a crowd of some 300–400 demonstrators, Dragoslav Avramović announced that the rallies would not resume until January 2000, after a meeting of the so-called Trilateral Commission, composed of representatives of the EU, the U.S. and the Serbian opposition (the idea for the Commission was negotiated at a November OSCE summit meeting in Istanbul). A few days before Avramović's announcement, the Serbian legislature's Judiciary Committee had again postponed holding a session, thereby confirming the ruling coalition's non-responsiveness to SPO demands for early elections. After half a year of pressing for Milošević's removal through one strategy or another, the Serbian opposition remained substantially divided—albeit now having an enhanced network for communication and discussion—and lacking a common strategy or agreement on tactics or a single leadership core to carry their struggle forward.

But Vuk Drašković, who had promised to begin street protests if the regime did not schedule early elections, and who, as usual, hoped to assert his leadership over the anti-Milošević forces, now organized a meeting of opposition parties to finally launch a joint strategy. The first such meeting took place on December 11, 1999 in Belgrade. Drašković then sent out invitations to 19 parties for a meeting to be held on January 10, 2000. At the January 10 meeting (Djindjić from the Democratic Party and Goran Svilanović of the Civic Alliance were absent, but were represented by Vladan Batić, the coordinator of the Alliance for Change), appeared to be a step forward toward greater opposition unity in Serbia. At the meeting, opposition leaders from 17 parties more or less confirmed Drašković's leading position. After more than six hours of talks behind closed doors, agreement was also reached on two documents. One called for early general elections (before the end of April 2000), and the other announced new demonstrations to be convened at the beginning of March 2000. Other provisions demanded that the international community immediately end the oil embargo and air traffic ban against Yugoslavia, and also pledge to lift all sanctions if Milošević agreed to early general elections. In a separate statement on the same day, Zoran Djindjić announced that if he were to be re-elected president of the Democratic Party he would "retire into the background." For the first time, a rump group of opposition protesters who had continued anti-regime demonstrations in the center of Belgrade, even after the Alliance for Change discontinued such rallies in December, ceased shouting slogans against Vuk Drašković. A major impetus to the adoption of the January 10 agreement—along with continuous international pressure, and the spillover effects of Drašković's car "accident" in October—was the post-Tudjman victory of united opposition forces in the January 3, 2000 Croatian parliamentary election. But while political developments in Croatia after the death of Franjo Tudjman may have had a positive demonstration effect on opposition politics in Belgrade, in the case of Serbia the target of opposition concern and his incumbent regime remained very much alive.

As the SPO moved towards closer cooperation with other elements in the opposition, the regime and ruling party became more critical of Drašković and his colleagues. The state-run media, for example, now accused Drašković of "provoking riots." Speaking to a group of graduates from a police training course, Serbia's Internal Affairs Minister Vlajko Stojiljković called opposition leaders "drug and alcohol addicts, unaccomplished scientists, and failed artists."[56] In December, the state-controlled media showed footage of Drašković kissing what was described as the "blood-stained" hand of U.S. Secretary of State Madeleine Albright. Drašković was also accused of having contacts with the French intelligence service. The tone and dynamics of political life in Milošević's Serbia seemed to be losing the traditional flavor of an intrigue-filled contest between manipulative authorities running a soft dictatorship on one side, and a squabbling opposition on the other. Most significantly, the Milošević regime appeared desperate and ready to take any and all measures, including political violence, to forestall its meltdown and replacement. As political polarization intensified, the prospects for success by the democratic opposition parties were once again linked to their ability at maintaining solidarity.

The Montenegrin Challenge: Two Systems—One Country

The increasing cohesion of opposition forces in Serbia during the last months of 1999 and the early part of 2000 was not the only domestic threat to Milošević's political control over the Yugoslav regime. In Montenegro—the smaller of the two republics in the Yugoslav federation—resistance to Milošević by the moderate and reform-minded coalition government of Milo Djukanović had been growing stronger for nearly two years. For example, under the federal constitution, Montenegro was entitled to elect half the members of the upper house in the Federal Assembly (the Chamber of Deputies). Djukanović used this provision in May 1998 to place his supporters in the federal legislature. But when Montenegro amended its own electoral law to ensure that its move could not be challenged, the federal Constitutional Court—under the control of Milošević's ruling coalition—declared the Montenegrin amendment unconstitutional. In response, Montenegro's government announced that it no longer recognized the authority of the Federal Assembly. Djukanović was also further offended in May when his die-hard political rival for control in Montenegro, Momir Bulatović—who headed the Socialist People's Party—was, at Milošević's instigation, elected by the Chamber of Republics to serve as Prime Minister of the Yugoslav federation.

The roots of the conflict between Milošević and Djukanović evolved slowly and could be traced back to the mid-1990s. Djukanović—who back in the late 1980s had been one of the "golden boys" of Milošević's "anti-bureaucratic revolution," and was first elected as the Montenegrin prime minister in 1991, at the age of 29—first began to have serious reservations about the regime in Belgrade when Milošević removed Dobrica Ćosić and Milan Panić from office during 1993 (see Chapter 4).[57] But while Djukanović became increasingly critical of Milošević, Momir Bulatović, the president of Montenegro (like Djukanović a member of the ruling Democratic Party of Socialists, DPS), continued to support the Belgrade leadership. Matters appeared to worsen during 1995 when Djukanović, who had made some unflattering remarks about the Yugoslav left, was attacked in the media by Mira Marković following his suggestion that Montenegro should pursue its own course of economic reforms and model of privatization. Insinuating, not entirely without some foundation, that Djukanović was involved in shadowy activity in Montenegro's gray economy and sanction-busting, Milošević's wife described the Montenegrin prime minister as a "secret smuggler" employed as an "important politician."[58] The regime in Belgrade was particularly chagrined about 1994 amendments to Montenegro's 1992 Ownership Transformation Act, which banned social ownership, and established an Agency for Foreign Investment and Restructuring of the Economy. After nearly two years of polemical sparring through the media, the Milošević–Djukanović dispute reached a head during the 1996–1997 civic and student protests in Serbia, when Djukanović sided with the anti-regime demonstrators and decided to completely distance himself from the Belgrade authorities (see Chapter 5). Yugoslav public opinion surveys conducted in 1996 revealed that Djukanović's policies were attracting support in Montenegro, and that the small republic's political institutions were viewed with considerably more confidence by Montenegrins than equivalent political and governmental structures in Serbia were regarded by that republic's citizens (see Figure 7.1).

By February 1997, Djukanović was willing to bluntly suggest that "it would be completely wrong politically for Slobodan Milošević to remain in

Confidence in Institutions (by percent)

INSTITUTIONS

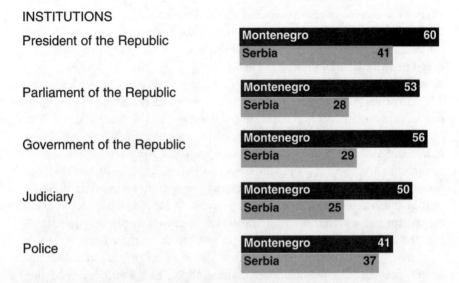

President of the Republic

Parliament of the Republic

Government of the Republic

Judiciary

Police

Institution	Montenegro	Serbia
President of the Republic	60	41
Parliament of the Republic	53	28
Government of the Republic	56	29
Judiciary	50	25
Police	41	37

Figure 7.1   Comparative Attitudes of Montenegrins and Serbs Towards Political Institutions in Their Respective Republics, 1996

SOURCE: Zoran Slavujević, "Kriza poverenja u institucije sistema," in S. Mihajlović (ed.), *Izmedju osporavanja i podrške: Javno mnenje u legitimitetu treće Jugoslavije* (Belgrade: Institut društvenih nauka, 1997), pp. 64–94.

any place in the political life of Yugoslavia . . . Mr. Milošević is a man of obsolete political ideas lacking the ability to form a strategic vision of the problems this country is facing, surrounded by unsuitable individuals who are following the time-tested method of many authoritarian regimes and for the sake of their own petty privileges."[59] In the several months between February and July 1997, a sharp schism occurred within the Montenegrin ruling party, the DPS, which had governed the republic for eight years. In mid-April, Djukanović faced down a challenge from Montenegrin supporters of Milošević led by the republic's president, Momir Bulatović. But by July, Djukanović had the upper hand, and forced Bulatović from his other post as leader of the DPS. Djukanović also blocked Milošević's attempt to change the federal constitution so that the federal president—an office now sought by Milošević—would become a directly elected and powerful post. But Milošević was ultimately able to find enough Serbian and Montenegrin votes in the federal assembly to win the post of president, albeit without the constitutional changes he had sought.

The October 1997 presidential elections in Montenegro became a bitter battle between the forces of Premier Djukanović and incumbent President Bulatović to acquire control of the republic's future development. The People's Party of Montenegro (NS) and the Liberal Alliance (LS), agreed to support Djukanović in return for his pledge to undertake democratic reforms.[60] Muslim and Albanian supporters of ethnically based parties in the republic also gravitated towards Djukanović. The outcome of the election was extremely close. In the first round on October 5, Bulatović received a slim majority, 147,615 votes (47.3 percent), while Djukanović garnered 145,348 (46.7 percent), and another six candidates shared the remaining votes. Bulatović won in two-thirds of the 21 municipalities of the republic, including the largest cities, Podgorica and Niksić. In the second round between the two front-runners on October 18, Djukanović—who had worked hard to bring out younger voters and members of the minority communities—received 50.8 percent of the votes, and Bulatović 49.2 percent. The close results in the presidential contest reflected the polarization of the republic's population regarding the question of reform and future relations with Serbia, and also heightened the atmosphere of distrust between the Djukanović forces and supporters of the Bulatović/Milošević orientation. For example, following Djukanović's narrow presidential victory, the SNP had tried to stir up civil strife in order to invalidate the election. But Milošević's effort to use the army in order to prevent Djukanović's inauguration proved unsuccessful (see Chapter 6). At the inauguration in mid-January 1998, 56 diplomats accredited to Yugoslavia attended the proceedings in Podgorica. Milošević, however, failed to show up at the event. In parliamentary elections held in May 1998, the Djukanović-led coalition "For a Better Life" (the DPS together with the People's Party of Montenegro and the Social Democratic Party of Montenegro) received 49.5 percent of the votes, and 42 seats out of 102, while the major rival party, the Socialist People's Party (SNP) newly founded by Bulatović, received 36.1 percent of the vote and 29 seats. During 1998 and 1999, relations between the two units in the federation significantly worsened, with Montenegro becoming *de facto* a semi-independent entity governed by Djukanović and his supporters. The 1997–1998 elections in Montenegro represented a small step forward in the republic's nascent democratization process, and resulted in a consolidation of power by a reformist political team. Although Djukanović was formerly an apparatchik in a one-party system (a background that resembles many new democratic politicians in Eastern Europe), who also relies on traditional family and clan influence in order to retain a tight grip on the strings of power in Montenegro, he appears committed to reform and democratic politics and is not excessively interested in amassing personal wealth. The Montenegrin polity remained polarized between supporters of the Djukanović line, and those backing close ties with

Serbia and the Milošević regime. But international support for Djukanović, his liberal policies, and Serbia's continued isolation, was gradually increasing the popularity of the "sovereigntist option" in Montenegro.

Belgrade's stepped-up military and police action against the UCK in Kosovo during 1998 and early 1999 only deepened the schism between Serbia and Montenegro. The Djukanović government, which endorsed a moderate policy towards Montenegro's minority communities, and had considerable support from the local Albanian population, had opposed the pre-war policies of the Belgrade regime in Kosovo. In consideration of Montenegro's position on Kosovo, NATO forces, although bombing a few Yugoslav military installations in Montenegro, rewarded the Djukanović government by refraining from any substantial bombing of the republic. Although the president of Montenegro was one of the members of the Supreme Defense Council of the federation, which constitutionally was entitled to play a role in wartime and in the peacetime control of the armed forces, Milošević excluded Djukanović from membership in the Council. Indeed the Council did not even function during the 1999 NATO bombing of Yugoslavia. During the war, federal army personnel stationed in Montenegro attempted to provoke the local authorities by establishing roadblocks in attempts to control the movement of traffic and goods, and laying charges against top Montenegrin officials for draft dodging. Federal troops would occasionally also provocatively stray into a UN-monitored demilitarized zone on the Prevlaka peninsula adjacent to Montenegro's border with Croatia.

Following the war in Kosovo, support in Montenegro for the republic's outright secession from the federal state structure increased substantially. But public opinion surveys indicated that Montenegrin citizens were divided over their republic's future affiliation with Yugoslavia. Three rather evenly differentiated viewpoints toward the federation were apparent: (1) those favoring independence for Montenegro; (2) those preferring some kind of loose confederal-type union between Serbia and Montenegro; and (3) those wanting to stay firmly tied to Serbia on the basis of the extant 1992 constitution (which had been supported by a referendum in Montenegro in 1992). The second or confederal option, approximated a proposal for a future confederation, "Platform on the New Relationship Between Montenegro and Serbia," advanced by the government of Montenegro on August 5, 1999. As far as party divisions on Montenegro's future, the government proposal was supported by parties belonging to President Djukanović's "For a Better Life" coalition (composed of the DPS, the People's Party and the Social Democratic Party) that controlled 42 out of 78 seats in the Montenegrin legislature. Support for outright independence from Serbia and Yugoslavia was strongest in the Liberal Union (five seats) and the parties representing the Albanian

384 Serpent in the Bosom

minority (two seats). Bulatović's pro-Milošević SNP, holding 29 seats in the Montenegrin assembly, was the only strong backer of the existing federal arrangements established in 1992. Not surprisingly, the Montenegrin proposal for a reconfiguration of the federation along confederal lines met with little enthusiasm on the part of the regime in Belgrade, or for that matter by most members of the Serbian opposition. Milošević stalled on Montenegro's request for a discussion of a confederation, and it was only in late October 1999 that he sent a member of Šešelj's nationalistic Serbian Radical Party to ostensibly negotiate the issue. Predictably, the talks quickly broke down, and no date was specified for resumption of the talks. Meanwhile, relations within the federation continued to deteriorate.

In September and October 1999, a trade war broke out between the two republics, which substantially amounted to a blockade of commerce enforced by Serbian border police. At the end of October, Montenegro ratified a new law on citizenship, which provided for Montenegrin citizenship distinct from Yugoslav or Serb citizenship. The law stipulated that those individuals applying for citizenship who were not ethnically Montenegrin or born in Montenegro, had to be able to prove residence in the republic for the previous ten years. The law banned any other Serbs living in Montenegro, as well as Kosovo refugees who had entered the republic, from Montenegrin citizenship. A further step toward self-determination by Montenegro occurred with the introduction in November 1999 of the German mark as legal tender. Montenegrin national consciousness was also reinforced by the regime in Podgorica through its encouragement for the reestablishment of a separate Montenegrin Orthodox Church (that ecclesiastical entity had originally been formed in 1786, but in 1920 had been incorporated into the Serbian Orthodox Church under the Kingdom of Serbs, Croats and Slovenes). In a revealing interview, the Metropolitan of the Montenegro Orthodox Church provided a personal and very interesting sociological analysis of recent Montenegrin nationalism:

> At this time Montenegro is literally divided. The northern regions, workers and retirees are on the side of the Serbian option, that is Momir Bulatović; the urban areas, businessmen and the youth are on the side of Milo Djukanović and independence. [Federal] army and [Montenegrin] police—each representing its option—have already unsheathed the bayonets. The outcome may be bloody . . . very bloody. . . . The mentality of our people is still very patriarchal: knife, revenge, and a tribal system such as exists nowhere else. The whole country is inter-connected, almost everyone knows everyone else. . . . Quarrels within a family are the worst, the pain the deepest.[61]

During 1999 and 2000, Montenegro became the international commu-

Serbian protestors hooting and whistling during 1996/1997 civic and student demonstrations. *Credit:* Balkan Historical Archive.

Opposition leaders, Drašković, Pesić and Djindjić (left to right), leading protests against the regime and symbolically indicating their opinion of Milošević. *Credit:* Boris Subašić.

Vojislav Šešelj, President of the Serbian Radical Party (SRS), with the Party's nationalist logo in the background. *Credit:* Balkan Historical Archive.

Šešelj carrying arms in Kinin, center of the Serb Krajina Republic, wearing trademark Chetnik fur hat (*šubara*) during the war in Croatia (1991/1992). *Credit:* Balkan Historical Archive

Ibrahim Rugova, President of the Democratic Alliance of Kosovo (LDK) (on left), meeting with NATO Secretary-General, Javier Solana in Brussels (June 24, 1998). *Credit:* NATO Office of Information and Press.

General Momčilo Perišić, Chief-of-Staff, Army of Yugoslavia. *Credit:* Balkan Historical Archive.

Serb police in Kosovo, ecorting the body of one of their fallen comrades to burial site. *Credit:* Balkan Historical Archive.

Serb delegation at Rambouillet peace conference (February 1999). *Credit:* William Dudley.

Albanian delegation at Rambouillet peace conference (February 1999). On extreme left is U.S. Ambassador, Christopher Hill seated next to U. S. Secretary of State, Madeleine Albright. *Credit:* William Dudley.

Secretary of State Albright meeting with the heads of the Albanian and Serbian delegations in Rambouillet. On the extreme right is UCK leader, Hashim Thaci, who is seated next to Ibrahim Rugova. *Credit:* William Dudley.

Column of Albanian refugees fleeing Kosovo on mountain roads, a group not atypical of hundreds of thousands of other Kosovars fleeing their homes during the hostilities between NATO and Yugoslavia. *Credit:* Balkan Historical Archive.

U.S. President William Clinon, surrounded by other NATO leaders at the Alliance's 50th anniversary summit meeting in Washington, D.C. (April 23–25, 1999). This meeting would provide an important opportunity for tactical and strategic discussions on the course of hostilities with Yugoslavia. *Credit:* NATO Office of Information and Press.

President Clinton (on left) at NATO headquarters during the bombing of Kosovo and Yugoslavia (May 5, 1999) with NATO Secretary-General, Javier Solana. In center behind them is U.S. Secretary of Defense, William Cohen. *Credit:* NATO Office of Information and Press.

General Wesley Clark, Supreme Commander of NATO forces in Europe, in battle dress. *Credit:* NATO Office of Information and Press.

Yugoslav automobile factory at Kragujevac, Serbia destroyed by NATO bombing. *Cedit:* Boris Subašić.

UCK troops in the field bearing dead comrade. *Credit:* Balkan Historical Archive.

Yugoslav armored unit leaving Kosovo (June 1999). *Cedit:* Boris Subašić.

Yugoslav troops leaving Kosovo (June 1999), flashing the three-fingered Serbian national salute. *Cedit:* Boris Subašić.

Albanian leader, Ibrahim Rugova (on far left) shaking hands with new NATO Secretary-General, Lord Roberston (center). Bernard Kouchner, the UN Secretary-General's Special Representative for Kosovo, looks on (far right). General Wesley Clark, wearing army fatigues, stands in background between Rugova and Robertson. *Credit:* NATO Office of Information and Press.

KFOR amored column entering Kosovo (June 1999). *Cedit:* Boris Subašić.

KFOR troops entering Kosovo (June 1999) stop to assist disoriented elderly Albanian man seated on the road. *Cedit:* Boris Subašić.

Serbian family fleeing Kosovo (June 1999). *Cedit:* Boris Subašić.

Fearful and emotional Serbs meeting with the Patriarch of the Serbian Orthodox Church in Kosovo (June 1999). *Cedit:* Boris Subašić.

Montenegrin political leaders, Momir Bulatović (on left holding child) and Milo Djukanović in happier days. *Credit:* Balkan Historical Archive.

Opposition leader, Vuk Drašković. *Credit:* Balkan Historical Archive.

Vojislav Koštunica, President of the Democratic Party of Serbia (DSS).

The winning candidate of the Democratic Opposition of Serbia (DOS) in the September 24, 2000 presidential election.

Milošević and his generals in Belgrade (1999). *Credit:* Balkan Historical Archive.

Demonstrators storming the Federal Assembly to demand Miloshevica's resignation, October 5, 2000. *Credit:* Balkan Historical Archive.

The ruling couple in 2000, anxious but determined to survive. *Credit:* Balkan Historical Archive.

Poster of the Serbian resistance organization, Otpor. Below the clenched fist is the slogan: "He is finished." Above the date fo the September election is the assertion: "It won't take much to see the last of him!" *Credit:* Narodni pokret OTPOR.

nity's back door through which to influence developments in Milošević's Yugoslavia. Operating what in effect was a quasi-independent state, Montenegro maintained an open-door policy for visitors. For example, most foreigners entering Montenegro were not required to obtain visas. Taking advantage of this relatively liberal political climate, foreign officials flocked to Montenegro to offer Djukanović support, and also to use the republic's seaside as a site to convene meetings and workshops with members of Serbia's political opposition. Djukanović's past activities as a member of Milošević's political team, the involvement of Montenegrin leaders in quasi-legal economic operations, and the tight hold still exercised by the DPS over Montenegrin political and economic life, as well as the media, were overlooked by international officials in view of the republic's relative political progress and Djukanović's political break with Milošević. The Montenegrin regime had now embraced "European standards" and the international community, and the international community welcomed that development by responding in kind. During the NATO bombing of Kosovo, Djukanović allowed Serbian opposition leaders such as Zoran Djindjić to seek safe haven from Milošević's police, and to plan with Montenegrin government officials the best way to move towards a post-Milošević Yugoslav regime. As a result of his activities in this regard, Djukanović was invited to various international postwar meetings to encourage stability in Southeast Europe. Indeed publicly, it appeared that Djukanović would soon take Montenegro out of the Yugoslav federation. As he told an audience at a November 1999 meeting in Thessolaniki held to consider Southeastern Europe's reconstruction: "Milošević's authoritarian regime persists in desiring power, quasi-patriotism, manipulation and the destructive tactic of creating new crisis points . . . no one can behave like the master of the house forever and treat the little brother like a tenant. This must end. . . . Already two years ago we learned that we have to gather our strength and jump off the train that is heading for the abyss."[62]

But fearful of provoking yet another secessionist military confrontation along the lines of the UCK–Serbian conflict, or of encouraging Kosovars— along with other Albanians in the Balkans—to form an independent ethnic Albanian state entity, international officials advised Djukanović to proceed cautiously. They also encouraged the Montenegrin leader to postpone a unilateral declaration of independence, or the achievement of greater autonomy and federal rights for Montenegro, until Milošević had departed from power. Thus, while Western officials warned Milošević not to use force or meddle in Montenegro, they also refrained from backing the republic's threat to seek independence should Milošević not immediately accommodate their proposals to develop a confederal arrangement between Serbia and Montenegro. Moreover, should Montenegro become formally separated from Serbia, it would no longer be as easy to use the republic as a conduit and meeting site to influence events in Serbia. Sensitive to such advice, and realizing Milošević's capacity to use force, Djukanović proceeded cautiously. However, he continued to be cross-pressured between some of his coalition partners who wanted him to be more assertive in breaking with Belgrade, and Western leaders who advised a more prudent approach.[63]

In his New Year's statement (delivered at the end of 1999), Milošević's suggestion that Montenegro could freely choose whether it wanted to stay or leave the Federal Republic of Yugoslavia, did little to alleviate political concerns in Podgorica regarding future actions by the Belgrade regime: "The best solution," Milošević remarked, "is the one suitable for the Montenegrin people. If the Montenegrin people are of the opinion that life outside of Yugoslavia would be better, then they have the right to chose such a life. And vice versa . . . in that case they should respect the rules set up for life in a joint state. That is above all, the constitution, that they adopted together. . . . Joint life is nice and easy for those people that want to live together, and difficult and ugly for those who are forced to live together." Possibly alluding to Kosovo and his preference to partition that province-turned-protectorate, Milošević added, "in places where people are forced to be together, not only is life not nice and easy, but it has no prospects."[64]

Commenting on Milošević's interview, Miodrag Vuković, a colleague of Djukanović, wondered why Montenegro was being asked to respect the federal constitution, when it was the Yugoslav president who had, in essence, kicked Montenegro out of the federation, suspended federal institutions, and ignored Montenegrin deputies in the federal assembly. What mattered, Vuković observed, is not the "democratic potential" in Milošević's words, but what he does. "And it remains to be seen how his [Milošević's] people in Montenegro will understand his New Year's statement."[65] Faced with a tense situation in Montenegro, and the potential that events might unfold rapidly in Serbia during the spring and summer of 2000, Djukanović bided his time. In February 2000, he observed: "We cannot be over-hasty in holding an independence referendum, as every uncertain step could cost us our internal stability . . . to call an independence referendum would also contravene the Balkan politics of the international community."[66] But Djukanović was gambling that public opinion in Montenegro would slowly become less polarized, and also that if a move toward independence became necessary, Milošević would be in an even weaker position. As he told a Zagreb newspaper in April 2000:

Today Montenegro is closer to independence than it has been in the last 80 years. . . . [But] we want to avoid the negative experiences of Croatia, Bosnia—

Hercegovina and others who had to squeeze through the window of war. At that, nevertheless, we do not want to sit on our hands, but want to conduct state politics so that we can take over more and more authority from the federal level. . . . The reason we are so cautious is our awareness of the man with whom we live . . . a man who initiated four wars in the Balkans . . . who is a pyromaniac . . . and he wants to start the fifth.[67]

Djukanović, nevertheless, prepared for the worst. Thus, by the early fall of 1999, the small republic was already quietly taking measures to strengthen its internal security forces, and even setting up the framework of a separate Montenegrin army.

As the Djukanović regime took tentative steps towards more political autonomy, Bulatović and his SNP, working closely with Milošević, made an effort to subvert Montenegro's self-determination. One Bulatović tactic—especially in the pro-Yugoslav and pro-Serb northern parts of the public—was to organize so-called tribal assemblies based on Montenegro's clan structure. Such tribal assemblies constituted an archaic form of social organization, which played an important role during the nineteenth and early twentieth century in gathering male members of clans together for community decision-making and military service. At the end of the nineteenth century there were some 36 tribes in Montenegro, a total of roughly 120,000 inhabitants, but not a single substantial town. Tribal sentiments later assumed the features of political parties. By the beginning of the twentieth century, two predominant political options were also apparent in Montenegro: the Greens (*Zelenaši*), advocating continued Montenegrin independence, and the Whites (*Bijelaši*), favoring union with Serbia. Attempting to re-traditionalize Montenegro's customary clans and cleavages in the service of current politics, the Milošević–Bulatović forces attempted to manipulate revived tribal assemblies in pro-Serb areas, hoping to eventually topple the authority of President Djukanović and the legitimately elected Montenegrin authorities.[68] In response, Djukanović supporters accused Bulatović of promoting the tribal assemblies, or what they labeled a pre-civic formation and type of Serbian nationalism, in order to subvert the democratic process. For the Bulatović forces, the tribal assemblies were a customary nongovernmental association that served their political interests and—under the guise of obstructing separatism, and combating an attempt to weaken intra-Serb ties and the Orthodox faith—and could be used to restore their political power. No longer able to rely on the spontaneous Serb populism of the late 1980s and early 1990s, Milošević and his allies appeared to be falling back on the mobilization of tribal populism in Montenegro. Such efforts seemed unlikely to have much impact on the reformist Djukanović regime. But the overall Milošević–Bulatović tactics threatened to unleash turbulence and violence in Montenegro which, together with other possible Milošević maneuvers, had the potential to seriously destabilize the small republic.

NOTES

1. By the end of August 1999, the UN War Crimes Tribunal had identified more than 400 "crime scenes" in Kosovo where bodies had been found, some of which were in mass graves, or graves.

2. *BBCSWB*: Part 2, Central Europe, The Balkans; Federal Republic of Yugoslavia: Kosovo Albanians, EE/D3603A, August 3, 1999.

3. *FDCH Political Transcripts*, June 8, 2000. Committee for European Affairs, Sub-Committee of the Senate Foreign Relations Committee.

4. *Le Monde Diplomatique*, March 1, 2000.

5. *Agence France-Presse*, August 25, 1999.

6. *BBCSWB*: Part 2, Central Europe, Federal Republic of Yugoslavia: Serbs, EE/D3624/A, August 27, 1999.

7. *De Volkskrant*, July 14, 1999, p. 4 in *FBIS-WEU–1999–0714*, July 14, 1999.

8. *Kosovapress News Agency*, July 31, 1999.

9. Rubin, who claimed that Thaci was his close "friend," played a substantial operational role promoting the UCK's case abroad, and typically dismissed criticism of Washington's Kosovo policy as simply "U.S. bashing."

10. *Washington Times*, August 20, 1999, p. A1.

11. *Agence France-Presse*, December 2, 1999.

12. *Agence France-Presse*, December 4, 1999.

13. *FBIS–1990721*, July 21, 1999.

14. *FBIS*, August 12, 1999.

15. *FBIS*, August 8, 1999.

16. *FBIS-EEU*, August 2, 1999.

17. *Corriere della Sera*, July 29, 1999, p. 4.

18. *FBIS-WEU–1999–0811*, August 8, 1999.

19. *Paris Agence Free Press*, July 9, 1999. By mid–2000, Rugova had re-emerged as the most trusted and favorably viewed Kosovo politician. *Opinion Analysis*, Office of Research, Department of State, June 2, 2000, M–66–00.

20. *Washington Times*, November 23, 1999, p. A15.

21. *Radio Free Europe*, November 9, 1999.

22. Reports by the International Crisis Group and other analysts in the spring of 2000 indicated that the UCK remained an important and powerful element in all spheres of activity in Kosovo. See Granit Gurri, "What Has Become of KLA?" *AIM*, Priština, March 23, 2000.

23. *BBCSWB*, Former Yugoslavia: Kosovo, EE/D3738/C, January 12, 2000.

24. *Danas*, January 22–23, 2000.

25. Kosovo Judicial Assessment Mission Report (Washington, D.C.: United States Department of State, April 2000), pp. 19–20.

26. "Kosovo Serbs Loyal to Milošević and SPS Don't Plan to Vote in Local Elec-

tions," *Opinion Analysis*, Office of Research, U.S. State Department, July 20, 2000, M–114–00.

27. The UN Secretary-General's special representative in Bosnia, U.S. General Jacques Klein, observed that Bosnia is the only Yugoslav successor state where the building of a multi-ethnic democracy by the international community is possible. "Croatia is mono-ethnic. Slovenia is mono-ethnic. Kosovo will shortly be mono-ethnic. Bosnia–Herzegovina is the last place." ABC News *Nightline*, November 29, 1999.

28. *Agence France-Presse*, January 1, 2000. In the spring of 2000, after much prodding, Kouchner was able to secure the participation of some Serbian representatives on Kosovo's Provisional Administrative Council.

29. *New York Times*, July 17, 2000, Section A, p. 4. Shortly earlier, Kouchner observed "the hatred between the two peoples has come into existence not just since the NATO bombing, but has existed for centuries." *Der Spiegel*, May 22, 2000, pp. 190–194 in *FBIS*-WEU–2000–0522, May 22, 2000.

30. *BETA*, August 9, 2000.

31. *Los Angeles Times*, August 19, 2000, Part A, p. 1.

32. *FBIS*, January 28, 2000.

33. In August 2000, U.S. presidential candidate George W. Bush said that if elected he would review "open-ended deployments" such as Bosnia and Kosovo, and also pledged an "orderly and timely" pullout from such missions. *Daily News*, August 22, 2000, p. 20.

34. *Belgrade Radio*, June 10, 1999.

35. *NIN*, No. 2529 (June 17, 1999).

36. The scope of the devastation that the NATO air campaign inflicted on the country's military and civilian infrastructure is quite daunting. For the Belgrade regime's tally see "Economic, Humanitarian and Ecological Consequences of NATO Aggression Against Yugoslavia—Basic Facts and Appraisals," *Yugoslav Survey*, No. 1–2 (1999), pp. 9–20; and *NATO Crimes in Yugoslavia, Documentary Evidence* (Belgrade: Federal Ministry of Foreign Affairs (May and July 1999), Vol. I (March 24–April 24, 1999) and Vol. II (April 25–June 10, 1999).

37. *Review of International Affairs*, Vol. L, No. 1085–86 (October–November 1999), p. I.

38. Vuk Drašković, "What Did Milošević Know?" *New Perspective Quarterly*, Vol. 16, No. 4 (Summer 1999), p. 15.

39. *International Herald Tribune*, June 28, 1999, p. 1.

40. *Agence France-Presse*, July 7, 1999.

41. *Le Monde*, June 12, 1999.

42. *Le Monde*, June 17, 1999.

43. *International Herald Tribune*, July 5, 1999, p. 4.

44. *VND*, June 29, 1999, pp. 2–3.

45. *BETA*, June 21, 1999.

46. Ibid.

47. *Der Spiegel*, June 28, 1999, p. 143.

48. *Budapest Duna TV*, June 30, 1999.

49. *Blic*, September 19, 1999, p. 7.

50. *Blic*, August 30, 1999.

51. *BBCSWB*, December 9, 1999.

52. *Agence France-Presse*, October 6, 1999.

53. *BETA*, September 29, 1999.

54. *Lidovny Noviny*, September 28, 1999, p. 2.

55. *BETA*, November 24, 1999.

56. *BETA*, December 16, 1999.

57. Djukanović rejects the idea that he underwent "belated political maturation," and asserts that he has followed the reformist political orientation since 1990–1991. *HRT-TV Zagreb*, June 16, 2000 in *BBCSWB*, June 20, 2000, Former Yugoslavia, Federal Republic of Yugoslavia, EE/D3871/C.

58. *Inter Press Service*, September 29, 1995.

59. *BBCSWB*: Part 2, Eastern Europe, February 27, 1997, EE/D2854A.

60. *Presidential Elections in Montenegro* (Washington: Commission on Security and Cooperation in Europe, February 1998).

61. *Delo*, January 15, 2000, p. 36.

62. *Delo*, November 10, 1999, p. 8.

63. Some Montenegrin nationalists wanted to assert independence because of a concern that a destabilized post-Milošević Serbia would mean even greater problems for Montenegro. See Milorad Popović, *Mali narod i nacionalizam* (Cetinje: Crnogorski i kulturni krug, 1997), pp. 132–133.

64. *Politika*, December 31, 1999.

65. *BETA*, January 4, 2000.

66. *Agence France-Presse*, February 10, 2000.

67. *Vjesnik*, April 19, 2000, p. 3.

68. *BETA*, September 1, 1999.

PART IV

POLITICAL TRANSITION IN A DECOMPOSING DICTATORSHIP

The "Velvet Revolution" and Concluding Reflections

CHAPTER 8

Drifting Towards Demise: "Hard Dictatorship" and a Fresh Opposition Challenge

Long ago the right question ceased to be "Where are we going?" Instead there is a much more explicit and compelling question: "How long will we be falling?" The role of celestial mechanics stopped applying here long ago . . . the Red Queen calls for heads to roll on television. Croquet is played with human heads. . . . Is there an end? If gravitation exists then the end exists too. But if it does not exist, then falling can easily turn into endless floating.

—*Velimir Curgis Kazimir (June 1999)*

Milošević has no ideology, and his only goal is to rule unchecked for as long as possible. . . . This is a man who is ready to defend his power at any cost, to the last drop of his blood. . . . Milošević is in a phase where he has equated his biological survival with his survival in power . . . he no longer trusts anyone. His choice is Serbia, however it might be—with Kosovo, without Kosovo, in the future maybe without some other parts.

—*Milo Djukanović (June 2000)*

Two crucial questions preoccupied observers of Serbian politics during the first year of the new millennium: How long would the Milošević regime survive in power, and would Serbia's citizens be able to replace that regime with a sustainable democratic political order? Almost all observers agreed that until those questions were resolved, political development in Serbia-Montenegro, and indeed throughout the Balkan region, would remain highly troubled and turbulent. During the first nine months of 2000, three different scenarios seemed most pertinent when Serbia's future political development was considered: (1) a continuation of Milošević's rule; (2) a peaceful transition to democratic rule led by some segments of the political opposition; or (3) a violent or armed confrontation between the forces of stasis and change. Factors facilitating and impeding the realization of each of those scenarios could be found throughout the various periods of Serbia's political evolution in 2000. But a clearer notion of which direction Serbia was headed would have to await the important elections scheduled to be held near the end of September 2000.

Dictatorship Under Assault: Milošević Stands His Ground

Ruling by Virtual Legitimacy

Milošević attempted to launch the new millennium with a sense of optimism and confidence, including the notion that his country did not stand alone in the world: "The West wants to conquer the whole world," he remarked in his New Year's statement on December 31, 1999. "Let us hope that the developed part of the world will come around and see the danger that they themselves are posing to the world. But we should also expect that the other part of the world will find the strength to unite and stand firm." Milošević singled out China for special praise, as a country with views "very close to Yugoslavia."[1] But China, he added, "is also incredibly close to all other nations and countries that are potential victims of aggression and humiliation." The Balkan region, he claimed, was a clear example of the effort by the "New World Order" to strategically control the "East, both Near and Far."

Milošević's New Year's interview also included some rare comments on his personal life, perhaps as part of a new effort to humanize himself and his family by conveying a new image as "Grandpa Milošević." "The birth of our grandson Marko on January 14 this year [1999] made this difficult year more pleasant than it would have been had not this very happy event not occurred in our family. Of course little Marko has changed our lives. . . . Our little grandson is a pretty, loving boy, and takes a lot after our own children Marija and Marko when they were his age. . . . He is growing up with a lot of love from his mother's and father's families, and I hope this will affect the development of his personality."[2] It is intriguing to speculate on whether Milošević's last comment was prompted by his own youth in a broken family, and the later suicide of his mother and father.

But Milošević's upbeat rhetoric, and comments on the joys of family life, could not mask the increasingly seamy and brutal side of his dictatorship. Indeed, during the first several months of 2000, anxious over the growing threat of Montenegrin secessionism, the increasing unity of opposition forces,

Serbia's continued international isolation, and internal economic decay, the Milošević regime became increasingly capricious and authoritarian. Throughout most of his rule, the Serbian polity manifested the characteristics of a soft dictatorship: an intrigue-filled contest between manipulative authorities employing a panoply of techniques for domination on the one side, and a squabbling opposition occupying the various niches within the structure of limited pluralism permitted by the regime on the other side. But in the wake of the Kosovo conflict, the regime in Belgrade acquired the harsher features of a desperate, hard-boiled dictatorship run by an isolated elite, which was willing to employ any and all measures, including violence, to forestall its replacement by internationally backed reformist forces. High-profile political assassinations, such as the murder of the criminal figure and one-time Milošević ally Arkan and the federal government's minister of defense, Pavle Bulatović, could not be fully explained or necessarily linked to the regime, but they added to the generally bleak prospects of an insecure dictatorship that feared it might be experiencing its death throes. Indeed, some observers believe that even before the NATO intervention in Kosovo, as popular support for the Belgrade regime eroded, Milošević had completely given up the pretense of rule on the basis of democratic legitimacy. As Nebojša Popov remarked, the Milošević regime changed in 1998–1999 from a system based on the "power of authority" to one employing the "authority of power."

The changing political climate in Serbia, and the impediments to democratic political change in the republic, came into sharp focus when Milošević's Socialist Party of Serbia held its Fourth Congress in mid-February 2000. It was the party's tenth anniversary as a reconfigured organization, which had been fashioned in 1990 from the former League of Serbian Communists and the Serbian branch of the mass socio-political organization the Socialist Alliance of Working People of Yugoslavia. Over 2,300 party delegates attended, and also 86 delegations from 57 countries. In view of Serbia's isolated and pariah status in the international community, most foreign delegations came from SPS "partner parties" that had maintained relations with the Milošević regime, including parties in China, Russia, Cuba, Libya, Iraq, Angola, Belarus, Ukraine, and Vietnam. Touted as the "Congress of Reconstruction, Development, Reforms," Milošević and his party stressed the same themes they had been advancing since mid-June 1999 when the NATO bombing had ended: The ruling party had won the struggle for "survival, freedom and independence" against overwhelming odds; the country would never yield its claim to reassert control over Kosovo; only the SPS could direct the process of "heroic reconstruction"; and the opposition was betraying the Serb national cause.

Gorica Gajević, the general secretary of the party, maintained that "reconstruction," the main theme of the Congress, "is another word for patriotism.

396 *Serpent in the Bosom*

Reconstruction is the same as unity. Reconstruction is as important as knighthood and heroism on the battlefield." The SPS claimed to have over 600,000 members, and that close to 167,000 were new members who had joined since the last Congress in March 1996. More than 5,000 SPS supporters were bused into the city to welcome Milošević to the Congress, where he took his seat at the Sava Center beside his wife, Mira Marković, the head of the neo-communist Yugoslav Left, and close to his now-and-again political crony Vojislav Šešelj, leader of the ultra-nationalist Serbian Radical Party. Running as the only candidate for the post, Slobodan Milošević was reelected president of the SPS by 2,308 out of 2,314 delegates. Five delegates did not vote, and one vote (perhaps a courageous dissenter) was declared invalid.

In his major address to the Congress, Milošević was unrepentant about his regime's record of accomplishment. He unashamedly gave the SPS credit for having preserved Yugoslavia by avoiding participation in the civil wars that had devastated other parts of the former Yugoslavia, and indeed for having also preserved the "Yugoslav idea" that had led to the formation of Yugoslavia in 1918. Milošević had absolutely no qualms in claiming that the SPS and Serbia had made war "easier and shorter" for the Serbs in Croatia and Bosnia. But whether those Serbs outside Serbia had acted properly with the assistance they had received, Milošević asked, remained an open topic for contemporary Serbian history and ethics. As for Kosovo, Milošević claimed that the alleged Serbian genocide against the Albanians was really only a pretext for genocide against the Serbs: "Had we accepted at the many talks from Belgrade to Rambouillet during 1998–1999 the proposals from the so-called international community concerning relations between the Serbs and Albanians of Kosovo, it would have been the same as if at the end of the 1930s and beginning of the '40s the Jews in Germany had agreed they had committed genocide against the Germans in Germany. [applause] So this led to three months of daily bombing of Serbia."

For Milošević, "little Serbia" was a leading force in the resistance to the "New World Order," or what he also called the "New Fascism." And stressing a classical theme in Serbian political culture that "only unity can save Serbia," he equated the Serbian democratic opposition with those Serbs who had willingly or forcibly collaborated with the Ottoman Turks from the fourteenth to the twentieth century. He charged that the opposition represented "modern day janissaries" who have become representatives of the "colonizing superpowers who have tried to dominate Balkan affairs." He continued: "We have a group of bribed weaklings and blackmailed profiteers and thieves, who, exploiting the harsh times . . . and utilizing sizeable finances pouring in from abroad, manipulate the sentiments of a certain number of people, often very young ones."

To a certain extent, Milošević's pugnacious and proud speech was consistent with his reputation for unflappability under pressure. But the tone and sarcasm of his address also betrayed a certain directness and engagement in routine political conflict that he had generally avoided in his rare public commentaries. Indeed, one Belgrade psychologist has suggested that Milošević's sharp and sarcastic attack on the opposition could damage his "cult of the great leader." By departing from his usual aloof and arrogant style, Milošević "jeopardized his aura of the man who is above daily politics and who does not like to get involved in party bickering."[3]

Notwithstanding his bravado at the SPS Congress, Milošević recognized that his political position within Serbia was becoming more desperate and that it was not a time to avoid the political fray. He was also fully aware that many members of his own party were deeply dissatisfied with his failure to improve Serbia's position over the previous decade, and to adequately protect Serbian nationalist interests. Many SPS members were also disenchanted with the party's personnel policy, which seemed to be controlled by Milošević's wife and the Yugoslav leftists. For example, the former SPS leader, Radovan Raka Radović, observed that the socialists had fallen into the Yugoslav left's "dangerous embrace" and that "one marriage and the state of that marriage had begun to be the condition on which the fate not only of the spouses, their immediate and possibly extended family, but also a huge number of people, the members of both parties, and almost the whole nation depended."[4] Other SPS members were uncomfortable about their party's coalition with Šešelj's extremist Radicals. Under these circumstances, Milošević could hardly afford to look weak or make any concessions that internal party factions might utilize as an invitation to broader criticism of the SPS record. After all, many such discontented SPS members still remembered Milošević's 1990 speech at the founding Congress, when he had declared that "the main goal of our party is a rich society . . . in which all of us can live in peace."[5]

In 1992, at the Second SPS Congress, Milošević had also, among other things, committed himself to "break the isolation, maintain peace, avoid poverty, triumph over hatred and chauvinism, provide a peaceful life and successful work to the citizens." And in March 1996, at the Third Congress of the SPS, "Serbia 2000—A Step into the New Country," Milošević, following up on the post-Dayton euphoria in the region, had boasted that painful sanctions "were a thing of the past, the refugees from Croatia and Bosnia would start returning home, and Serbia could now economically recover." In 1999 and 2000, however, there seemed little way out of the poverty, isolation, and unemployment caused by years of international sanctions and the complications of the recent military struggle with NATO.

But if SPS activists remembered his broken promises, and chafed because of Western restrictions currently isolating Belgrade's ruling elite from normal travel and the benefits of trade with Europe, they also realized the considerable difficulties they would personally face in a post-Milošević setting. It was not accidental when, at the end of his address at the Fourth Congress, Milošević reminded his comrades of that uncertain and potentially troubled future: "To the new SPS leadership of the Socialist Party of Serbia I wish that in the time until the next Congress it does everything in its power to make the party even bigger and stronger, mostly for the sake of our own country but also for its own sake." Nebojša Čović, who had defected from the SPS and become leader of the opposition Democratic Alternative Party, aptly remarked that only 10 percent of Milošević's main address at the Fourth Congress was devoted to the results of the regime's policy, "because there are really no results at all. Well there are, but they are negative for the people and the state. The second segment was aimed against the international community and took up 40 percent of his speech. The third segment, which took up half of his speech, was aimed at something that he said did not exist—the opposition: That segment shows Milošević's considerable degree of fear, and it shows that he knows there is no more unlimited power for him and that there is no more unlimited trust in him on the part of the citizens of this country."[6] For over a decade, Milošević's soft dictatorship had permitted a kind of authoritarian pluralism to function in Serbia. But as both internal and external pressure mounted, the Serbian leader was compelled to move towards a more repressive mode of authoritarian governance.

Clearly indicating that he had no intention of leaving power without a struggle, Milošević took strong measures to solidify his control over Serbia. For example, he employed a variety of methods, including fines, closures, and personal threats, to increasingly curtail and intimidate the independent media, which was attracting three times more readers and listeners than Yugoslavia's state-run media services. The most ominous invective against the press was put forward by Šešelj, who accused local opposition journalists of being traitors, and threatened that such behavior could engender "the worst possible consequences." "Nothing," Šešelj ominously cautioned, "will be done with gloves on now. Whoever is working for the Americans will have to bear the consequences."[7]

The regime initiated legal proceedings pursuant to the Public Information Act, adopted in 1998, against opposition publications that were suspected of "damaging the reputation of the Federal Republic of Yugoslavia." Thus, by early 2000 the courts had dealt with as many as 60 cases involving alleged media violations. The Belgrade private and independent media were the first and hardest hit by the crackdown. High fines were levied on the publishers, directors, and journalists involved in such violations. For example, in early

December, the Belgrade-based dailies *Blic* and *Danas* and the City Television Studio B were fined nearly 54,000 deutsche marks because they carried a statement accusing the Yugoslav Left and the Serbian Radicals of "state terrorism."[8] At the same time, the regime justified its actions by claiming that "media terrorism" was an integral part of external pressure against Yugoslavia.

Towards a Hard Dictatorship

Milošević's selective intimidation of the nonstate media typically endeavored to curb, but not to totally silence, organized anti-regime criticism in Serbia. As the irreverent and highly popular Serbian political cartoonist Predrag Koraksić ("Corax") once remarked: "The free press is like Milošević's personal flower arrangement. In an information desert, he shows only a few small flowers as proof there is a free press. And even then, he keeps changing them."[9] During the NATO bombing campaign, Corax was not allowed to publish his brilliantly satiric images belittling the regime and the ruling couple. But his cartoons quickly appeared after hostilities ended. Other outlets for the popular expression of anti-regime sentiment also were permitted to function, such as Belgrade theatre groups, staging plays that lampooned the ruling couple. But by late 1999, Milošević was becoming more thin-skinned with respect to the nongovernmental media. Politically challenged as never before, the safety valve function of the independent media, which had been tolerable in a soft dictatorship, was now regarded by Milošević as threatening the regime's survival. Like many times in the past, Milošević used Šešelj to present the coarsest and most belligerent side of the regime: "Do you think you'll survive our liquidation?" he asked a reporter in February 2000. "You from B-92 [the radio outlet operating within Studio B] and other treacherous media . . . [do you think that] we will allow you to pick us off one by one, like rabbits?"[10]

Šešelj's threats against the nongovernment journalists led the majority of the independent media to boycott the activities of his Serbian Radical Party. Though Šešelj's allies in the ruling coalition, the SPS and JUL, tried to portray themselves as more liberal than the SRS, the independent media were still barred from attending parliamentary sessions and subjected to other forms of pressure, such as higher broadcasting fees, fines, and the denial of supplies and newsprint. In mid-March, the regime also closed more than 250 unlicensed stations, most of which had been affiliated with the Association of Independent Electronic Media (ANEM) and the Association for Developing Private Broadcasting (SPEKTRA). In mid-May the Serbian government took over the Studio B radio and television stations run by Belgrade city authorities, thereby ending the control of Vuk Drašković's SPO over that media outlet. The seizure also resulted in the closure of the influential radio station B-92 (which continued to broadcast via satellite and the Internet).

Radio Index was also temporarily shut down, and when it resumed broadcasting it was periodically jammed.

By the summer of 2000, the regime had stepped up warnings to institute security measures against "media aggression," and had begun legal proceedings against one journalist on charges of espionage and spreading lies. The government also increased the number of local stations under its direct control and strengthened the signals of others in order to counter the influence of the democratic opposition in various areas of Serbia. Localities where the ruling SPS–JUL–SRS coalition was in power had almost no independent electronic or print media. However, citizens and towns controlled by the opposition parties still enjoyed a choice between progovernment and nongovernment media outlets. For example, inhabitants of Niš could tune in to seven local television stations and about ten radio stations. Five television stations operated in Kragujevac, and the town's widely viewed private station, "KANAL 9," presented the views of both the SPS and the opposition.[11] Thus, the media landscape in Serbia was not uniform, and remained more characteristic of an authoritarian polity than a totalitarian state. But in a context of increasing assassinations and arbitrary violence, and with members of the ruling coalition issuing threats against regime critics, the political climate had chilled considerably, as had the risks of nonconformism.

The increasing repressiveness of the Milošević regime in mid-2000 was also reflected in the preparation of draconian anti-terrorism legislation. For example, the draft bill envisioned long-term prison sentences for those convicted of publishing information deemed a threat to the state. The underlying purpose of the anti-terrorism legislation went well beyond control of the media; the regime was particularly interested in stifling the activity of the student resistance organization, "Otpor," which had been a thorn in Milošević's side since 1998. The political radicalization of student activity was, in part, a reaction to the regime's stringent use of the University Law adopted in late May 1998. Otpor had been formed five months later as a "cell" of resistance to the regime's crackdown on self-governing autonomy and free expression at the university. One Otpor leader, Ivan Marović, claimed that, from March 1999 to March 2000, 190 activists from the movement had been detained by the police, and that around 50 had been beaten and had sustained slight injuries.[12] The police also were used to prevent Otpor demonstrations in a number of cities. In response to police harassment, Otpor formed "rapid reaction teams." Composed of lawyers and NGO members, these teams were organized to react as soon as police action against an Otpor member took place, in order that there was maximum opportunity for publicity about the movement's activity and a chance for a legal defense. Another Otpor leader, Vukašin Petrović, claimed that the movement had been highly successful in disseminating propaganda material and offering a challenge to the regime. "In the last three or four months," Petrović claimed in early March 2000, "Otpor provided the only real work against the regime and which confronted the regime. The opposition still hasn't taken concrete action, and their entire activity focuses on interparty agreements, which are good, but are not action."[13]

Recognizing that Otpor represented an important new mode of political dissent, Milošević moved swiftly to employ harsh measures designed to stamp out the organization. The threat to his regime from the traditional opposition parties had never been taken lightly by Milošević, but the simultaneous appearance of unconventional forms of dissidence by the student radicals now made matters far more serious. For the beleaguered regime, all oppositionists, and those outside the country who aided or encouraged the opposition in Serbia, constituted a "terrorist bloc." The unexplained murder of the state airline's chief executive in late April (Žika Petrović, who had been a friend of Milošević's from their teenage years in Požarevac) and the assassination on May 13 of a high SPS official from Vojvodina (Boško Perošević)—two incidents in a string of similar acts of violence in Serbia over the preceding year— were quickly identified by the regime as terrorist acts that were likely engineered by Otpor. Between May 13 and late June, the police maintained open files on some 640 activists from Otpor.[14] Most members of Otpor, which was banned as a terrorist organization, were held for only a short time, but other members of the movement were beaten by the police for handing out anti-government posters or simply drawing graffiti or wearing T-shirts with the Otpor symbol—a clenched fist. One attorney for an arrested Otpor activist claimed that to his knowledge it was "the first time drawing a fist on the wall has been qualified as a criminal act. Criminal charges for drawing a fist have so far usually boiled down to damage to property."[15]

Although the stepped-up campaign against Otpor and the independent media coincided with discussion of the anti-terrorist law, the bill itself was withdrawn from legislative consideration possibly because of demands by the Radicals that Šešelj be given the job of public prosecutor, and that the Radicals receive more profits from state companies, patronage positions, and assurances that the new law would never be used against them.[16] Although never officially proclaimed, the bill served its major goal of intimidating free expression in the country. Police and judicial action against the student resistors and other reputed "terrorists" proceeded under existing rules of the game in Serbia. The regime may have also been involved in a second attempted assassination against Drašković on June 15, in which he was only wounded in an attack that occurred in his home in Budva, Montenegro. The SPO leader claimed the act was another example of state-sponsored terrorism by Milošević to weaken the opposition's momentum and potential unity. Some commentators, however, suggested that Drašković and the Montenegrin authorities staged the incident for their own purposes. Drašković, who was already quarrelling with other opposition parties over potential electoral tactics—the SPO opposing participation in imminent local and federal elections because of mounting state repression—quickly attacked them for not reacting more firmly and sympathetically to the assassination attempt.

The Year 2000 "Constitutional Coup"

After having adopted a series of measures in the spring of 2000 that effectively transformed his regime into a more repressive subspecies of authoritarian rule, Milošević proceeded in July to enact new constitutional and legal measures as a means to institutionally anchor and perpetuate his new style of personal rule. In early July, surprising most of the opposition and the international community, Milošević was able to have the federal legislature adopt new constitutional provisions that provided for the direct election of Yugoslavia's president (instead of by the legislature), and also that deputies in the Federal Assembly's upper chamber, the House of Republics, be elected by direct vote instead of by the assemblies of Serbia and Montenegro. These changes were especially designed to weaken the position of Montenegro in the two-republic federation. With only some 650,000 inhabitants, compared to over nine million in Serbia, Montenegro would now have little influence over the choice of the country's president. Moreover, Montenegro's reformist governing authorities, led by President Djukanović, would no longer be able to exercise control over the twenty seats in the upper house of the federal assembly set aside for their republic (Serbia controls the other twenty). Milošević was able to obtain the required two-thirds legislative support for the constitutional changes owing to his control over a sufficient number of deputies in the lower chamber, the House of Citizens of the federal legislature, and also his ability to control dissident Montenegrin deputies in the upper chamber. The final vote in favor of the provisions in the federal legislature was 96 to 9 in the House of Citizens and 27 to 13—passing by one vote—in the House of Republics. Milošević obtained the 27 supporting votes in the House of Republics by flying one deputy from Montenegro to Belgrade in the presidential plane.[17] In vintage Milošević style, the entire process of promulgating the constitutional changes was pushed through in roughly 24 hours.

In effect, by unilaterally altering the federal balance of power in a kind of "constitutional coup" that humiliated Montenegro, Milošević made it politically impossible for the Djukanović government to take part in the political process. Thus, by means of his constitutional provocation, Milošević effectively pushed Montenegro out of the upcoming federal electoral process, thereby making it harder for opposition forces to win control of the federal presidency and the federal legislature. At the same time, because most of Serbia's opposition parties had counted on the electoral support of Montenegro's anti-Milošević forces, Milošević was able to strike a strong blow against anti-regime elements in his own republic. Technically, the new constitutional provisions, which changed the federal political structures from a parliamentary to a presidential system of authority, would also allow Milošević, whose term expired in July 2001, to run for two more terms (not one term as previously stipulated), which potentially could extend his rule until 2009! The new arrangements for the Yugoslav president to be elected by direct vote would also permit Milošević to avoid any dependence for his position on party politics and remaining Montenegrin representatives in the federal legislature, and to claim that the new rules enhance the democratic legitimation of the country's top office. The post of federal prime minister is also weakened under the new provisions, with the appointment and removal of ministers now requiring parliamentary approval.

One observer who was not surprised by Milošević's constitutional maneuver was Montenegro's Milo Djukanović. Over two weeks before the new measures were promulgated he had remarked that Milošević needed a new constitution "to turn the existing state into a unitary state where he can rule a long time as dictator. . . . What is certain is that Montenegro, the way it is now, with a majority oriented toward reform and democracy, will not accept any amendments to the constitution, which would be to our detriment."[18] But while Djukanović vigorously rejected the new constitutional framework designed in Belgrade, two factors motivated his continued caution about unilaterally moving towards independence: first, the fact that Montenegro public opinion was still very divided over the issue of what kind of ties to maintain with Serbia and the Milošević regime;[19] and second, the continued presence in Montenegro of federal military and police forces controlled by Milošević.

In the wake of Milošević's coup, the Serbian opposition parties and Montenegrin reformist officials held several meetings to try to find some common ground that would allow Montenegro to take part in the scheduled federal elections. However, opposition parties working under the umbrella of the Alliance for Change, coordinated by Zoran Djindjić, and those forces working with Drašković's SPO, arranged to meet separately with the Montenegrins. But while the non-Drašković opposition forces implored the Montenegrins to become involved in the coming election, Djukanović's reformist bloc had little interest in validating Milošević's new constitutional rules. In fact, in a session held on July 7, 2000, the Montenegrin legislature passed a resolution declaring as void all the acts of federal bodies made without Montenegro's "legitimate" representatives, that is, those deputies in the upper house of the federal assembly selected by the Montenegrin legislature. Montenegrin prime minister

Filip Vujanović claimed that Milošević's constitutional revisions had "practically aimed at turning the Federal Republic of Yugoslavia into a Greater Serbia . . . a unitary state with one president, one assembly, and one government . . . destroying the concept of the federal state as a community of equal republics."[20] Meanwhile Drašković, who had been supporting a boycott of future elections, expressed sympathy with the position of the Montenegrin authorities and ruling parties. Indeed, he used Montenegro's boycott to help justify his own nonparticipation, a perspective that had been sharply attacked in opposition circles, and also by a faction of his own party. Thus, Milošević's political maneuver not only provided a useful institutional base to help him preserve dictatorial power, but had also inserted a new wedge in the classically divided opposition ranks.

Milošević's new constitutional framework made it extremely difficult to remove him from office. The president could only be relieved from duty if the federal-level Constitutional Court establishes that he has violated the constitution, and a procedure for removal is initiated by half the deputies in both chambers of the federal legislature. Two-thirds of the deputies must then adopt the proposal to remove the president. Although already in full control of the court system and legislature at the federal level, Milošević lost no time in extending his hold on the entire judiciary and electoral process. For example, in mid-July, the Serbian assembly removed eighteen judges in the republic's constitutional, supreme, and district courts, who were accused of engaging in opposition political activities. Among those removed were three judges from Milošević's home town of Požarevac, who had disapproved of the handling of a May 2 fight between two Otpor members and the employees of the Madonna night club, owned by President Milošević's son, Marko. "The state pays the judges," Serbian justice minister Dragoljub Janković remarked, "they cannot work against the state."[21] The July 2000 actions were part of a major purge of the judiciary that had begun in 1997–1998, which had resulted in the replacement of some 900 out of 2,000 judges for one reason or another. In December 1999, for instance, three prominent judges were removed from office because they were active in the Independent Association of Judges of Serbia. In a court system where the salary of judges is extremely low, the authorities have also been able to exercise influence over the judiciary by granting some judges apartments and higher salaries.

Near the end of July, less than three weeks after constitutionally customizing his regime for political longevity, Milošević prepared for elections by having the federal assembly adopt a new package of electoral legislation. According to the law on presidential elections, a candidate could now win an election by taking 50 percent of the votes cast in the first round, or the most votes in the second-round contest between the two leading candidates. However, the law omitted an earlier requirement that a valid election must include at least 50 percent of the registered voters. This omission essentially prevented the opposition from voiding an election by means of a boycott strategy, and in theory at least would allow Milošević to win the presidency if he was the only person voting, and he chose to cast his vote for himself. The planned boycott of the election by Montenegro and Drašković supporters, and any other non-participants, thereby became a largely symbolic act, which might undermine Milošević's claim to democratic legitimation, but could not prevent his preservation of formal authority.

The number of electoral units for federal legislative elections was also reduced from 29 to 26, with two former units in Montenegro combined into one, and a transfer of Kosovo's previous two units to the southern Serbian unit of Prokuplje and Vranje. The fact that the latter two districts, two small towns and their environs—containing a large number of displaced non-Albanians— would now elect 18 percent of the federal parliamentary deputies opened the door to electoral manipulation by the regime[22] (similar to the pattern previously practiced in elections due to the pattern of Albanian electoral boycotts in Kosovo). The likelihood that Milošević would employ the army to set up polling stations in Montenegro in order to provide a place for the republic's pro-Milošević voters to cast their ballots also would undoubtedly assist in avoiding the symbolic sting of the official Montenegrin boycott. Thus, Milošević's supporters in Montenegro could win all 50 of the republic's seats in the federal legislature even while the Djukanović authorities and the majority of Montenegrins boycotted the elections. Having thus rigged the rules to test his strength against the again divided opposition forces, Milošević called for local, legislative, and presidential elections for September 24, 2000.

Breakthrough by the Opposition? Democratic
Nationalism as an Alternative

Although the opposition parties had managed to hammer out a unified position and a commitment to cooperation in January 2000, the unity of the anti-regime forces remained very fragile. The opposition threatened to launch substantial demonstrations against the regime should no promise of elections be forthcoming by the spring of 2000. But that deadline came and went. Clearly, the crucial linkage between the anti-regime parties and the public that is necessary for democratic change was still absent. Though the building blocks of a democratic electoral victory, or some sort of peaceful "democratic revolution," were present in Serbia, they had still not coalesced to the necessary degree to threaten dictatorial rule. As Ghia Nodia has argued: "A revolution in the modern sense cannot take place unless both 'push' and 'pull' factors are present. In practice the 'pull' factor of ideology is usually represented by enlightened elites while the 'push' factor is embodied by disgruntled masses. The former are powerless without the latter; without the former the latter have no sense of direction. . . . Revolutions are unlikely when factors opposed to the 'push' and 'pull' factors prevail."[23]

What Nodia calls the "stay factors" preserving the incumbent regime were still readily apparent in Serbia in mid-2000. And while the prospects for opposition "pull" connecting with mass "push" were considerably better than at any time since 1996–1997, they seemed insufficient to precipitate a radical breakthrough against the ruling coalition. For a short period in the first half of the year, the old Djindjić–Drašković rivalry seemed to diminish. But that latent cleavage, and Milošević's ability to divide and conquer his rivals, remained a major impediment to democratic change.

The growing radicalization of anti-regime youth, particularly in the Otpor resistance student organization, suggested that the "push" factor was present in Serbia but could not easily be exploited by the established opposition parties and leaders. Indeed, opposition leaders quickly began to associate themselves with Otpor. For example, at a rally on May 15, many party leaders, including Zoran Djindjić, wore Otpor T-shirts. And the same month, the venerable nationalist intellectual and nonconformist political figure Dobrica Ćosić met with a student leader of Otpor, and then joined the organization. Activists in Otpor claimed that their movement had become a real force and that the authorities feared a student rebellion more than anything else.[24] As early as the fall of 1999, the emboldened leaders of Otpor characterized Milošević as a "falling star," and claimed that what was necessary was "a more open rebellion. The emperor is naked, and there will be no more games. There is just us and them in the street, and one of us has to go."[25] But fully aware that he was facing a new mode of political opposition, it was not surprising when Milošević took harsh action to obstruct Otpor's activity.

Meanwhile, many in Serbia's established opposition, unable or disinclined to generate massive street protests or a "civil" upsurge in the early months of 2000, pinned their hopes on finding some kind of "pact model" of political change, that is, a negotiated transfer of power between the opposition and the regime. One frequently mentioned variant of that model was a "coalition pact" whereby the ruling and opposition parties would constitute a coalition government of "national unity." A series of roundtable negotiations between the opposition and the authorities leading to agreement on fair electoral conditions was another hypothetical variant of this pact model. For example, in early 2000, Dragoslav Avramović, of the Alliance for Change, suggested that Milošević should be engaged in a "serious discussion about the conditions for his withdrawal and the withdrawal of his closest aides, in order to make a decision that would suit his own and the national interest." If the opposition groups could agree, Avramović felt, then consultations should begin with representatives of the international community, and the opposition should "consider possibilities that would make Slobodan Milošević's future easier and that would yield a solution regarding the Hague Tribunal war crimes indictment."[26] Most Serbian opposition observers believed that the May 1999 indictment against Milošević for war crimes, while perhaps warranted on evidentiary grounds, had severely and unnecessarily complicated any chance for his negotiated exit from power, or a scenario that could ensure peaceful change in Serbia. The Democratic Party's Zoran Djindjić indicated, for example, that he would favor some deal whereby Milošević could leave power peacefully, and cautioned against any revanchism against regime stalwarts following such a scenario. But Djindjić did not think it was very realistic to expect that the opposition and the authorities could really sit down and reach an agreement: "People are getting killed every day and officials are hunted down like rabbits."[27]

In early 2000, it remained an open question whether the democratic opposition parties, even functioning in a more coordinated manner as they superficially agreed to do in January, and associating themselves with Otpor's new momentum, would be able to spark broad enough public support for their goals either in the streets or at the ballot box. The opposition's prospects hinged in part upon the political outlook and behavior of the citizens of Serbia, that is, the crucial "push" factor in any democratic revolution. During the last part of 1999, the public mood as indicated in various opposition surveys did not suggest the basis for such mass support. For example, the first major survey following the war in Kosovo, conducted in early September 1999, revealed a population that was extremely fearful that the deteriorated standard of living—a situation already making Yugoslavia the poorest country in Europe, with about one-half of the population at the level of bare survival, and 20 percent living in extreme poverty—would continue to slide downward. Feelings of disappointment, anxiety, hopelessness, fear, confusion, and also rage were widespread in the fall 1999 findings of a study of 1,588 Serbian citizens conducted by a team of experts led by Srećko Mihajlović from Belgrade's Institute of Social Sciences. Over 60 percent of those surveyed said they had no trust in the present institutions of the political regime and the state-controlled media. But half of those polled also did not trust the opposition, and only a quarter of the respondents expressed a high interest in politics. Over two-thirds of the surveyed citizens could be considered politically passive, did not believe that political activity could change much, and were disinclined to take risks to bring about change. But while the survey indicated that most Serbian citizens were personally risk averse, the findings also demonstrated that the respondents overwhelmingly wanted change, and nearly one-fifth believed that a revolt or a spontaneous and unpredictable rebellion of the people would force major changes in the regime. Indeed, though reform was regarded as a preferred mode of change, and risk-taking was shunned by an extremely angst-ridden population, a large number of people (35 percent) nevertheless favored "quick and deep changes by force if need be."[28]

Broad dissatisfaction with the status quo was also revealed in a December 1999 study of 2,039 citizens by the Center for Political Research and Public Opinion of the Institute of Social Sciences. Even supporters of the parties in the ruling coalition were dissatisfied with Yugoslavia's international standing (57 percent of the SPS followers and 85 percent from the SRS); the dissatisfaction of those citizens who supported the various opposition parties ranged from 96 to 100 percent. The survey revealed that, over the previous two years (1997–1999), there had been a steady decrease in popular support for President Milošević, as well as for the three parties in the current ruling coalition (SPS, JUL, and SRS). Indeed, near the end of 1999, Avramović, the new Alliance for Change leader, emerged as the most popular politician in the country, and the moderate democratic nationalist Vojislav Koštunica, heading the Democratic Party of Serbia, was the second most popular. But although Milošević had suffered a drop in his popularity, and his party's rating had waned considerably, he was still viewed as the leader most likely to win a future election in comparison with any other party or leader taken separately. Thus, set against a divided opposition, the Milošević family's party duo, SPS/JUL, still prevailed in terms of relative standing.

Another important finding, not necessarily favorable to the regime, also emerged in the December survey. Namely, approximately two-fifths of the electorate were undecided about which party they would vote for in the election, and roughly the same proportion of respondents did not extend their support to any major politician. This indicated the existence of a very substantial free-floating group of voters—a group far outnumbering the supporters of and sympathizers for any single individual or party on the political landscape—who were likely to decide the outcome of a free election in Serbia. As a rule, Milošević had been able to use his control of the state to influence the undecided vote (e.g., by increasing wages, expediting pension payments, and reducing the price of electricity), particularly before elections. The nightmare scenario for Milošević was that one day those voters would no longer give their support to parties in the ruling coalition and, even more seriously, that the individual leaders and parties in the opposition would coalesce in a united coalition behind a single team of leaders. The challenge for the opposition was that most voters who were undecided might potentially abstain from voting, or vote for the ruling coalition because they did not believe that the established opposition parties could successfully unify and go on to emerge victorious in an election.

Faced with this cynicism about their role, and also a record of political fragmentation, the parties in Serbia's democratic opposition struggled in the first half of 2000 to formulate a joint political strategy and obtain early and internationally supervised general elections. In an effort to show they were seriously committed to change, the leading opposition parties announced their intention to launch demonstrations in the spring of 2000 should the regime refuse to hold elections. However, at the beginning of March 2000, opposition leaders remained undecided about when to launch such rallies. For example, Vuk Drašković's SPO favored holding a rally on March 9, the ninth anniversary of violent demonstrations against the regime, which had helped to forge Drašković's reputation as "king of the streets" (or "king of Serbia's squares"). In a sign that old inter-opposition rivalries remained, his major rival, Zoran Djindjić, felt that a rally on March 9 might be identified solely with the SPO. Agreement with all opposition parties was finally reached regarding a joint opposition manifesto. The chairman of the Democratic Center Party, Dragoljub Mićunović, who chaired the meeting that drafted the agreement, expressed the opposition's most deeply felt point of consensus: "We do not want guns, but democratic elections at all levels."[29]

After continued disagreements among the opposition leaders, a major rally to be held in Belgrade was finally scheduled for April 14. The two-hour rally, which attracted more than 100,000 people, was the largest public demonstration against the regime since August 1999. The regime made an effort to cut down attendance by showing pirated popular films on state TV, including *American Beauty*, throughout the day of the rally. In a show of at least symbolic unity, the rally began with Drašković and Djindjić shaking hands. Speakers from the various opposition parties then proceeded to call for an end to repression, the resignation of Slobodan Milošević, and the holding of early elections. The spokesman for the student movement, Otpor, lectured opposition party leaders: "You must remain united . . . not squabble among each other. Ten thousand students will demonstrate under the window of any opposition leader . . . who betrays that unity."[30]

Djindjić told the crowd that the people of Serbia must be determined and united to bring about change: "At that moment you will hear a sound in Serbia which Europe has never heard. You will hear the sound of people who want freedom, the sound which will topple dictatorship like a house of cards."[31] Djindjić also issued a call for members of the ruling SPS to join the "force which will liberate Serbia," although he implored Mirjana Marković's "[political] left from Dedinje" to "stay away." Drašković claimed that the country was currently in the hands of a "gang of murderers" and "national traitors." "We want to be human, we want to have free lives, to have free media, free speech, free university," he told the crowd. And he warned the ruling elite (revealing a less conciliatory tone than Djindjić) that those demonstrating would "find, catch and bring to justice all the murderers." The language at the April 14 rally was stirring, and the show of solidarity rather impressive in view of earlier opposition difficulty at cooperation. But this show of solidarity was maintained mainly for the crowds and opposition supporters abroad. In reality, agreement among opposition leaders on substantive issues was still lacking. Thus, while the opposition leaders and those in the international community who encouraged them spoke a good deal about the unity of the opposition, each party continued to push its own "line." As Nebojša Popov remarked:

> They announce that they seek the support of the people, but one still doesn't know exactly for what, or how, or when nor how they will acquire the confidence of the people and build up the forces of society. Of course, it's good that the opposition meets and agrees; it would even be better if the government would discuss matters normally with the them. But, how can one decisively set matters in motion about which there hasn't been serious discussion, still less agreement. And at [protest] meetings and demonstrations there can't be a real dialogue. Conversations and agreements, of course, but they can only take place among actors who take responsibility for future events, as well as for the present situation, but especially for their mistakes.[32]

Yet the new Milošević-engineered constitutional and electoral provisions adopted in the summer of 2000 left Serbia's democratic opposition in disarray. The boycott strategy of Drašković and the Montenegrins had little potential to unseat Milošević, and when the nonparticipation of those major actors was added to the widespread apathy and fear of the general population in Serbia, it appeared highly unlikely that Serbia's dictator could be overthrown at the ballot box. Polls taken in June and July 2000 indicated that more than one-third of those surveyed did not trust any Yugoslav politician.[33] And, although most citizens in Serbia opposed the idea of an opposition boycott of the election (43 percent) as against those who favored the idea (22 percent),[34] a study also revealed that as many as 60 percent of the voters would boycott the election if the major opposition parties ran individually rather than as a united bloc.[35] Overall, survey research in the summer of 2000 indicated that more voters in Serbia favored the opposition parties than the ruling parties, but that the majority could only prevail if the anti-regime or anti-Milošević forces acted in solidarity.

Faced with a divided opposition, Milošević once again emerged as the strongest personality on the Serbian political landscape, and the SPS as the strongest party organization. As one very thorough analysis by the U.S. State Department's Office of Research put it: "While the opposition leads in potential support, Milošević's support is limited, but solid and stable." Trend data also revealed, for example, that Milošević remained the most trusted leader in Serbia. His ratings had declined from results obtained before the NATO bombing campaign against Yugoslavia, and even from November 1999, but trust in almost all other leaders had also declined, leaving Milošević well ahead of all other political actors.[36] Keeping in mind that one-third of the voters trusted no one, or could not make a choice, Milošević—who had now made sure that abstentions would have very little impact on the election—was in a relatively favorable position. Indeed, at the outset of the electoral campaign, SPS officials, who claimed at their party's tenth anniversary celebration in mid-July that their organization had grown from 200,000 members in 1990 to 700,000 in 2000, seemed confident of victory in September.

A crucial question for the Alliance for Change and other sectors of the opposition participating in the September 2000 election was whom to select as the presidential candidate to run against Milošević. Drašković's initial decision to boycott the process, not to mention his erratic behavior, had eliminated his candidacy, and Djindjić's hopes to run for president were undermined by his very low standing in both public opinion and opposition circles. The choice of those opposition parties in the Alliance for Change soon fell on the one middle-aged opposition leader who still enjoyed some popular support, namely, Vojislav Koštunica, a 46-year-old former law professor who headed the Democratic Party of Serbia (DSS). Viewed by most Serbs as uncorrupted, albeit noncharismatic, the choice of Koštunica offered Serb voters a moderate or democratic nationalist who was also perceived as being independent of foreign ties, and thus difficult for the regime to demonize as a traitor or foreign collaborator. Koštunica was a veteran oppositionist who helped Djindjić and others establish the Democratic Party in 1990, but in 1992 he had moved towards a more nationally oriented view, and established the DSS. One of Koštunica's major assets was that he never had become acquainted with, or negotiated with, Slobodan Milošević, in sharp contrast to both Drašković and Djindjić. Koštunica also claimed to have the only party that combines adherence to democratic principles with the defense of Serb national interests.

In the opinion of most members of the democratic opposition, this background provided Koštunica with the potential to steal Milošević's monopoly on nationalism, but also to guide the country in a democratic direction. Although he has been attacked for advocating a "Serbia first, democracy later" policy during the early 1990s, Koštunica has supported a democratically organized

Table 8.1   Serbian Leaders by Level of Public Trust, 1998–2000 (in percent)

	Time of Survey					
Leader	*March 1998 (%)*	*October 1998 (%)*	*January 1999 (%)*	*August 1999 (%)*	*November 1999 (%)*	*June 2000 (%)*
Milošević	22	25	21	22	29	16
Drašković	7	6	5	13	10	8
Avramović	14	13	20	20	9	8
Koštunica	6	3	4	4	6	9
Šešelj	18	11	8	6	5	6
Djindjić	4	2	2	4	3	4
None	18	31	21	n/a	15	25
Don't know	6	6	8	9	5	8

SOURCE: *Opinion Analysis,* Office of Research, U.S. Department of State, June 27, 2000, M-91-00.

federation of all Serb state units, including Serbia (which for him includes Kosovo, Montenegro, and the Republika Srpska in Bosnia). For Koštunica such a Serbian federation would ideally be a national state for the Serb people, but with strong protections for minorities.

By June 2000, polls suggested that among Serbian citizens Koštunica was the second most trusted leader after Milošević (Table 8.1), and that his relative standing compared to other leaders was on the upswing. A poll taken in mid-July revealed that if Koštunica was backed by a united opposition, he could defeat Milošević in the presidential race (42 percent to 28 percent).[37] Koštunica appeared to be most popular with voters under 50, and he shared equal support with Milošević in appealing to those 50 to 59 years of age. The research also suggested that Koštunica's democratic nationalism would enable him to attract some 19 percent of the voters that regularly gave their support to Šešelj.

In early August, Koštunica was selected as the presidential candidate of the joint opposition, now configured as the Democratic Opposition of Serbia (DOS). DOS consists of the parties comprising the Alliance for Change (SZP), along with the DSS, the Alliance of Democratic Parties (a group of parties mainly from Vojvodina), the DAN coalition (Democratic Alternative, Democratic Center, and New Democracy), the Vojvodina Coalition, Social Democracy, and the Movement for a Democratic Serbia. While indicating his support for Koštunica, Djindjić pointed out that he also considered Dragoslav Avramović as an alternative, but many people viewed him to be too old. "We do not need somebody to replace Milošević," Djindjić remarked. "We do not need a Genghis Khan, but a Mahatma Gandhi, somebody who will reconcile."[38]

For his part, Drašković continued to maintain that his idea of a boycott was the only way to eliminate Milošević, and that "even if all registered parties, over 180 of them, were to run against [Milošević], his victory in the federal elections would already be certain. These are not democratic elections." When asked why he condemned Djindjić's support for an electoral boycott in the 1997 presidential election, but now advocated a similar boycott, Drašković responded that Djindjić had only taken this measure because he had wanted to stop him (Drašković) from becoming president.[39]

In early August, Drašković, in his usual mercurial manner, finally decided that his SPO would boycott only the parliamentary elections, but would take part in the presidential and local elections. However, the SPO refused to endorse Koštunica and instead nominated Belgrade mayor Vojislav Mihajlović, the grandson of World War II Chetnik leader Dragoljub (Draža) Mihajlović, as a candidate for the post of president of Yugoslavia. The SPO also demanded that, as the traditionally largest single opposition party, 60 percent of the seats be reserved for the SPO if it were to take part in a joint opposition ticket in local elections. Drašković's break with the rest of the opposition infuriated a good portion of democratically oriented public opinion in Serbia, and seriously threatened Koštunica's chance of defeating Milošević. Not surprisingly, Koštunica began referring to the SPO as "an alleged opposition party." Mladen Dinkić, the executive director of the organization G-17 Plus went even further: "The SPO leadership is working in direct collaboration with the regime on the destruction of the opposition."[40] Angered over Drašković's tactics, the DOS-affiliated parties decided not to run with SPO candidates in local elections.

No one factor seemed to offer a satisfactory explanation of why Vuk Drašković perversely refused to cooperate with other democratic forces to construct an opposition front capable of defeating Milošević. But several factors undoubtedly played a role in the SPO leader's decision: personal and political jealousy of the other opposition leaders, unbounded ambition to control the opposition and become Milošević's replacement, fear of assassination or bodily injury after several attempts on his life and earlier physical attacks on him by the police, ideological divergence from the other parties, and also the possibility that Milošević possessed material that could seriously compromise Drašković. Perhaps most important was his fear that Milošević would slowly eliminate the SPO's control over Belgrade, and therefore completely shut off his party's, and his own, lucrative economic underpinning. Whatever the most salient factor, or factors, motivating Drašković's political behavior, his refusal to forge a link with the other democratic opposition parties in 2000 provided Slobodan Milošević with an enormous political gift.

Meanwhile, despite the application of strong international pressure on the Montenegrin authorities to participate in the election, Djukanović's DPS and the other parties in the ruling Montenegrin coalition decided to boycott the September 2000 vote. Djukanović realized that he was undermining the Serbian opposition's chances of unseating Milošević or of capturing a sizeable portion of seats in the federal assembly—all of Montenegro's 15 mandates in that 178-seat body would probably go to pro-Milošević forces—but he also knew that Montenegro would continue to enjoy Western support, potential military protection, and even an eventual bid for independence should Milošević be re-elected. For Djukanović, the election seemed to be a win–win situation, no matter what the ultimate outcome. However, in view of Milošević's record of provoking crises, the Montenegrin leader continued to proceed cautiously.

Although delighted by the divisions and boycotting forces in the opposition ranks, Milošević by no means took electoral victory for granted. For one thing, Šešelj's SRS, though still part of the ruling coalition, decided to run its own candidate for president, the deputy president of the party, Tomislav Nikolić. While Nikolić's candidacy might be regarded as a regime-inspired maneuver to soak up some of the nationalist votes that would otherwise go to Koštunica, it also provided the SRS with a more independent position in the Serbian political arena. Šešelj would undoubtedly want to stay in power if Milošević won the election (in fact he indicated he might become prime minister), but Nikolić's candidacy could also drain votes away from Milošević, and together with votes going to the SPO candidate, this would probably force a second round between Milošević and Koštunica. Indeed, Koštunica expected a second-round face-off, which would make the September presidential election a referendum on Milošević. Anxious to whip up pro-regime patriotism by demonstrating to ordinary citizens of Yugoslavia that foreign agencies were plotting with "internal enemies" against the country, Milošević's police began making an example of any foreigners they could detain on charges of espionage or "terrorism." The arrest and trial of four Dutch nationals for having plotted to assassinate Milošević, which was followed by the detention of two Britons and two Canadians who had been working in Kosovo, and who then traveled to Montenegro on holiday, were part of the official campaign to stamp out alleged subversion.

By late August 2000, the election campaign was in full swing. Milošević had the clear lead and many advantages, a major one being the opposition's disunity. But it was impossible to forecast the outcome of the presidential race, particularly in view of Koštunica's candidacy. Should Serbia's voters, despite their apathy, cynicism, fear, and fatigue after so many years of dictatorship and opposition disarray, decide that Koštunica's middle-of-the-road policies were worth endorsing, Milošević could face an electoral surprise he had not counted upon. The conventional wisdom is that Milošević would only have called elections if he was 100 percent sure that he would win them. But even in a hardening dictatorship, frustrated voters can often surprise their rulers. Counting on that possibility, the United States decided to open a special office in Budapest, Hungary (headed by the former U.S. ambassador to Croatia William Montgomery), where assistance to the democratic forces in Serbia could be more directly coordinated. It was unclear, however, whether such support would prove beneficial, or would be seen by Serbian voters as untoward meddling in their country's political life, and thereby actually assist Milošević.[41]

Meanwhile Koštunica, a long-time foe of U.S. interference in Serbia, who was also very mindful of not appearing as a foreign puppet, strongly condemned the Budapest operation: "You need to have a huge dose of arrogance, but hypocrisy as well in order to claim that a long-term U.S. goal is the improvement of democracy in Serbia. Democracy in Serbia is exclusively a Serbian goal and nobody else can claim it. The real U.S. aim is the destruction of FRY [the Federal Republic of Yugoslavia] and Serbia." For Koštunica, the opening of the Budapest office was a "kiss of death for all truly democratic and patriotic forces" in Serbia.[42] But Koštunica aimed his major criticism at Milošević, whom he blamed for the "10-year-long ruination of the state and people," as well as for the "capitulation in Kosovo."

Violence as a Potential Mode of Transition: Civil Strife and Armed Conflict

In the fall of 2000, the Yugoslav opposition's failure at fashioning a united coalition seemed to dim the chances for a peaceful transition of power in Serbia. Milošević appeared likely to win the September 2000 election, but should the increasingly dictatorial regime lose the election and then refuse to accept an electoral defeat there could very well be an eruption of citizen political discontent and opposition rallies on the order of those held during 1996–1997. The chances for peaceful regime change would then be greatly reduced. Under such circumstances—an anxious and brutal regime confronting civil disobedience by an angry, although still loosely coordinated opposition—the likelihood of a smooth transition process, and a relatively peaceful post-Milošević future, would appear rather dismal. For Milošević, retaining power was critical. But avoiding arrest and trial by the UN International Tribunal for Former Yugoslavia (ICTY) in connection with the indictment against him for war crimes had also become a growing concern, and if he lost the election he would have no place to hide.

In mid-June 2000, there were reports that as a means of obtaining regional

416 Serpent in the Bosom

stability and fostering political transition in Serbia, the United States and Russia had discussed cutting a deal with Milošević whereby he would leave office and be allowed to retain the bulk of his financial assets. But reports of such negotiations, even if true, or a trial balloon, were quickly denied in Washington, Moscow, and Belgrade. Milošević's former adviser, Zvonimir Trajković, observed that the Yugoslav president would only seek guarantees of safety in Yugoslavia "from his citizens and his opposition, and only then, he will be sure that he will not be handed over to the ICTY." Milošević would leave his post, Trajković remarked, only when "he finds an adequate replacement . . . when he finds his Putin."[43] But unlike the Russian case, where President Yeltsin felt safe in turning over power to Vladimir Putin, there was currently no strong figure or domestic political organization in Serbian politics that could guarantee Milošević's future safety and well-being. Koštunica had said that sending Milošević to The Hague would not be a priority of his post-Milošević government, but that was hardly a formulation that would satisfy the concerns of Milošević and his family. The Cypriot government's decision to close down the Yugoslav regime's offshore banking operation, which had been conducted for years through Beogradska Banka on Cyprus, under pressure from the United States, the EU, and ICTY, had also narrowed Milošević's options in finding a safe and comfortable haven outside Yugoslavia (and may have also accounted for the assassination of some top Yugoslav officials, who Milošević may have felt knew too much about his financial operations).

Both Milošević's possible unwillingness to leave power by means of a negotiated settlement and also the likelihood that the regime would take repressive measures to retain power in the event of an electoral defeat, or at least ruthlessly quash serious popular demonstrations, seemed to increase the prospects that any political transition in Serbia might be preceded by massive violence or armed conflict. And even if Milošević won the September 2000 election, there was little likelihood that he could again revert to the "softer" dictatorial style he had maintained when he enjoyed a modicum of genuine democratic legitimacy. In 1992, student protesters had used posters quoting Diderot's letter to Louis XIV: "You are sitting on a volcano, there is no way to avoid the eruption!"

In the period after the NATO bombing of Yugoslavia, Serbia's *de facto* loss of Kosovo, and the introduction of a more repressive regime, Milošević's oligarchy appeared to be in the same posture as the French court. In fact, prior to the mid-2000 decision to hold fall elections, some opposition leaders argued that the regime was actually provoking civil strife by radicalizing the political situation and creating a civil war atmosphere. Momčilo Perišić, the former Yugoslav army chief of staff who Milošević had sacked in 1997 (see Chapter 6) and who resided in Montenegro, where he had formed an opposition party

(Movement for a Democratic Serbia), was rather pessimistic about the ability of Yugoslavia and Serbia to resolve the issue of political transition in a peaceful manner:

> Knowing Milošević, the current state leadership, Mira Marković and Šešelj, they are not going to hand over power, even if they lose the elections. The international community made a big contribution here by not leaving them a way out. They publicly proclaimed Milošević and four others war criminals. If there are changes here they will have to face the music. The prospects of this frightens them. They want to stay in power at any price. . . . The situation is even worse when you consider that the army and police chiefs who head the armed institutions have also been changed. Obviously the opposition doesn't have weapons. If the regime finds itself in danger it could cause conflicts. This could create wider disturbances and end up in a civil war . . . a real civil war among a single people.[44]

The electoral campaign in the autumn of 2000 seemed to lessen the possibility of an explosive outcome in the short term, but only because a large segment of the opposition decided to play by the rules of the game, such as they were, after Milošević's constitutional coup and elaboration of a new electoral framework. But in the long run, the threat of civil strife remained a serious possibility. The routine violence that had taken the lives of scores of underworld and political figures in recent years continued. The disappearance of Ivan Stambolić, Milošević's one-time political mentor (see Chapter 2), while jogging in Belgrade on August 24, 2000, may have added a new name to the list of famous and infamous individuals who have been the subject of violence. It also raised the question once again of whether such murders were ordered by a dictator intent on removing individuals who knew too much or who might even become alternative candidates for high office. Moreover, all of the political machinations and brutality in Serbian politics were occurring within the context of a deteriorating economy, which itself was a major source of potential instability and violence. With an isolated economy, steadily falling gross domestic product, industry in ruins, and for the first time fear that the country may face a food crisis (in the winter of 2000) owing to drought and drastically lower yields of agricultural products, the possibility of socio-political unrest had seriously increased. Although the failure of the 1996–1997 civic and student protests, the chronic exhaustion of the population, and the country's economic depression had resulted in widespread political cynicism and apathy, this situation could rapidly change. Thus, the psychological state of a depressed and traumatized population can be fertile ground for manipulation by a dictatorial regime, but it also can be highly combustible should the population be subjected to additional shocks, such as famine or heightened internal strife.

The growing tension between the Djukanović regime in Podgorica and the Belgrade authorities also raised the specter of a civil war between Serbia and Montenegro, or between Milošević and anti-Milošević forces within one or both of those republics. By April 2000, several ominous developments had already occurred in relations between Serbia and Montenegro. For example, Belgrade had instituted a complete embargo on trade between the two republics, established TV broadcasting facilities to transmit Milošević's propaganda to the Montenegro population, and kept up military and police pressure against the Djukanović regime. A potentially dangerous provocation engineered by Milošević had occurred in December 1999, when armed federal troops took control of Montenegro's main airport in Podgorica to prevent a Montenegrin takeover of the commercial and military facility. The Montenegrin authorities continued, however, to appreciate the need to proceed cautiously. As the small republic's prime minister told a Zagreb newspaper: "Secession might entail either an internal conflict or the risk, albeit a much smaller risk, of violent external aggression on Montenegro, with an aim of establishing a military dictatorship and jeopardizing the civilian authorities in Montenegro."[45] The climate for potential violence was particularly combustible in northern Montenegro, an area torn between supporters of the pro-Milošević Socialist Nationalist Party of Momir Bulatović (which includes many Serbs in the region) and Djukanović loyalists. The high level of Muslim and Albanian support for Djukanović in the northern region—groups that according to some reports have received weapons from the Djukanović police—also created an ethnic divide for Milošević and the federal military to potentially exploit.

Tension between the federal army and Montenegrin authorities steadily increased during the first half of 2000, as Milošević continued to subject the Djukanović regime to pressure and harassment. But Milošević held back from declaring a state of emergency in the country, possibly because he did not fully trust the military establishment to support the regime. Though he had regularly relied on the police apparatus to support his regime, Milošević endeavored to win the allegiance of the army's top leadership by promoting loyal officers and showering a small number of generals with honors, privileges, and perks. For example, in February, not long after the assassination of Defense Minister Bulatović, Milošević awarded Bulatović's post to army general Dragoljub Ojdanić, who had, as army chief of staff, loyally conducted Yugoslav military operations in Kosovo during NATO's bombing operation. Ojdanić's post went to Col. General Nebojša Pavković, also a Milošević loyalist, who had advanced the regime's official line during and after the Kosovo war. Meanwhile, Pavković's faithful subordinate in the Kosovo war, General Vladimir Lazerević, was made both commander and chief of staff of the important Third Army.

Nonetheless, Milošević, who was generally distrustful of the military elite's political reliability, also began building up selective elements within the military police that were directly responsible to his control rather than to that of the army high command. For example, the Seventh Battalion of military police in Montenegro, which was outside the control of the Yugoslav Second Army stationed in that republic, was reinforced. In view of his depleted legitimacy, Milošević's reliance on dependable armed bureaucrats and supporters—the army's highest echelon, the military police, the Serbian police, and police irregulars—had become increasingly crucial to the maintenance of the regime. By the fall of 2000, having already presided over Serbia's direct or indirect involvement in over four wars over a period of ten years—including the 1999 Kosovo conflict when the Belgrade regime was already in serious political difficulty—there seemed every reason to assume that Milošević would, if necessary, use force to maintain his political power.

Milošević's success at recruiting a loyal and dependent top echelon in the VJ during the 1990s also helps explain how he was able to avert the threat of a military coup against his regime. In essence, the top military elite in Yugoslavia had little motivation to bite the hand that had fed it so well. At the same time, the reportedly less reliable middle echelon of the VJ was subjected to extensive monitoring and control by loyal regime operatives within the security apparatus of both the police and the military. Indeed, although the regime adhered to the notion that the military should be depoliticized, even a member of the ruling coalition such as Vojislav Šešelj had drawn attention to the fact that the regime and high command impart a distinct notion of what is ideologically correct behavior for members of the VJ.[46] For their part, Montenegrin authorities had been particularly sensitive about statements by the highest-ranking officers in the VJ that although the army does not "interfere in politics," the VJ would "prevent a civil war at any price," and also preserve the constitutional order as presently designed by the "Supreme Commander" of the military forces, Slobodan Milošević.[47] As Army Chief of Staff General Pavković put it: "Attacks on the President [of Yugoslavia] and his function in commanding the army were attacks on the VJ."[48] For many Montenegrins, it is the Yugoslav Supreme Defense Council (which includes the presidents of both republics in the federation) that has constitutional authority over the military, and therefore the Montenegrin president is equally legitimate as Supreme Commander as Milošević.[49] But Milošević's loyalists in the military high command made no apologies for their subordination to the "Supreme Commander embodied in the President of the state." Moreover, Chief of Staff Pavković pointed out in August 2000 that the VJ's primary functions were to deter a potential aggressor against the country, and also "combating terrorism or rebellion in cooperation with the police."[50]

On the Cusp of the Democratic Revolution:
Leadership Trends and Neo-nationalism

By the early fall of 2000 there seemed little likelihood that Milošević's domination of Serbian politics would be quickly ended on the basis of his own volition through some kind of negotiated arrangement, by peaceful free elections, or through anti-regime violence. But even if one of those scenarios of transition, or some other mode of regime change would eventually take place (e.g., assassination, illness, or accident), there seemed a strong probability that the subsequent phase of Serbian and Yugoslav political development would be turbulent, and very likely include episodic violence. For one thing, there was a high possibility that some of the extremists and criminal actors who had recently played a major role in Serbian political life would still be present, and would not likely remain passive in any power struggle that would accompany Milošević's departure. For example, Šešelj's Radical Party, although weakened in 2000 in comparison with its position in 1997, still remained a force to be reckoned with. Indeed, even if the more immoderate and nationalistic wing of the SPO, together with remnants of Milošević's SPS and Marković's JUL, may have had difficulty working with Šešelj, he continued to be a magnet attracting many segments of the ultra-nationalist and illiberal wing of Serbia's political spectrum.

Furthermore, the rampant corruption that had afflicted Yugoslavia over the previous decade, and that was closely tied to political dynamics in the country, would likely transcend the life of the Milošević regime and be extremely difficult to root out (as the international community's experiences in Bosnia and Kosovo had amply demonstrated).[51] And though the moderate forces in the democratic opposition, at least those supporting Koštunica's candidacy for president in the September 2000 elections, had begun to cooperate, it seemed doubtful whether such unity could be sustained. It was also unclear whether Koštunica could quickly evolve into a popular political leader who both moderate nationalists and democratic forces could rally around after Milošević's departure. With the absence of a strong and broadly supported post-Milošević political leader, Serbian politics would likely become highly anarchic. Most importantly, all the political forces in the country would have to face the difficult challenge of acclimating themselves to an entirely new political order. Indeed, the challenge of fundamentally transforming the illiberal and collectivist authoritarian features of Serbian political culture—political attitudes that had been reinforced by a dozen years of negative experience under the dictatorial Milošević regime—could not be underestimated. Thus, it seemed naive to assume that the climate of violence, coercion, and deceit so prevalent throughout the 1990s would quickly give way to the routine give-and-take of democratic politics, compromise, and peaceful negotiation in the likely climate of continued economic deprivation and rampant corruption.

The possibility that the various opposition political forces would eschew a policy of moderation and reconciliation in dealing with their former foes in the Milošević regime, and decide that justice must be obtained through a harsh settling of accounts, also seemed likely to provoke strife following Milošević's expected exit from power. Some anti-regime leaders, such as Veran Matić of Radio B-92, recommended the eventual establishment of a Truth and Reconciliation Commission along the lines of South Africa's, but such a solution would prove exceedingly difficult in Serbia. How the eventual post-Milošević party leaders would deal with such dynamics, which have bedeviled all postcommunist transitional regimes to some extent, would prove to be a crucial determinant in shaping Serbia's political future (see Introduction). Indeed, it could be surmised that peaceful democratic transition in Serbia—even after Milošević's departure—would not occur until after the emergence of a new generation of Serbian leaders who are not afflicted by the habits and experience of the last several decades of dictatorship and debilitating intra-opposition rivalry.

Comments by opposition leader Zoran Djindjić, which were made during the Democratic Party's internal leadership race in April 2000, revealed how one of Serbia's ostensibly most "liberal" leaders perceived the nature of the political game in Yugoslavia. Djindjić made his remarks on the eve of his victory over a rival candidate for the leadership of the party, after deciding not to go through with his promise to step away from that post: "To lead a party, a man has to possess certain personal qualities, a firm and strong character, and authority. He has to be able to be curt, to hurt feelings, to say no, and to accept being hated since that is in the nature of politics. Someone who is involved in winning sympathy, in cajoling, and avoiding conflicts still has a lot to learn to be able to lead a serious party." Djindjić said that he changed his mind about withdrawing from politics after he failed to obtain support for a new leader who was his hand-picked choice. "Ambitions" started burgeoning. "There was a danger that the party would split into factions if I resigned without a true successor."[52] Although to some, such a preference for strong leaders (who are entitled, among other things, to select their successors) was an understandable response to the absence of opposition unity in Serbia, and also a reflection of the kind of rule favored in traditional Serbian and Balkan political culture, such views may well impede the process of democratic consolidation by the Serbian elite. Thus, future Serbian politicians might have to develop new characteristics and styles of leadership in order to facilitate a process of democratization in their country. Indeed, it was not difficult to make a comparison between some of the traits Djindjić admired and certain features of the incumbent president of Yugoslavia, whom he had long sought to replace.[53] But there were indicators that matters might slowly be changing. In July 2000, temporarily giving up his own presidential ambitions, Djindjić praised opposition candidate Koštunica for his Gandhi-like capacity for reconciliation.

Boris Tadić, a psychologist, an official of the Democratic Party, and director for Belgrade's Center of Development of Democracy, has also emphasized the need for Serbia to develop a new political elite, with a fresh style of leadership:

> I think our politics is anachronistic and our preference for charismatic leaders is the best evidence of that anachronism. A leader today in the world isn't a person who governs because of being better than everybody, but is an expression of a team outlook . . . an exponent of some new policy, or new interests. We don't have that in Serbia because parties don't take account of their reform and their need for team work. We must establish a process of discovery, building, and forming new political personalities who are not leaders in the classical sense of the word, whose charisma would not, as up until now, contribute to the abuse of [public] trust, but would represent a model for establishing new societal values, a model which young people could identify with.[54]

Another important factor that might possibly undermine a peaceful transition in post-Milošević Serbia, and inhibit the development of strong democratic institutions, was the Serbian population's relative unfamiliarity with a civic conception of national identity. Thus, support for a collectivist notion of nationalism remained an important dimension of Serbian political culture. Citizen dissatisfaction with the nationalist and ultra-nationalist policies of the Milošević regime had steadily increased during the 1990s and into 2000. However, it did not automatically follow that Serbian citizens, including the younger generation, were no longer deeply committed to their country's national interest. The "retraditionalization" of societal values and increased religiosity of the population that took place during the 1990s have had a deep impact on Serbian society. That process of retraditionalization also involved the resuscitation of authoritarian political views and patriarchal sentiments that were present even before the Titoist regime, and that were reinforced by the illiberal values and practices associated with the one-party communist system. The intensification of interethnic conflict and ethnic distance associated with Yugoslavia's disintegration tended to reinforce such values. Indeed, despite Milošević's failures—indeed because of them—and the strong military response his policies engendered from the international community (especially the 1999 bombing campaign associated with the Kosovo conflict), the climate of ethnocentrism, xenophobia, and authoritarianism, it seemed, might consti-tute a substantial impediment to democratization within Serbia.

But research on Serbia also indicated that the "ethnification of conscious-ness" encouraged by the Milošević regime, especially in its initial stages, while contributing to a high level of generalized mistrust and ethnic distance on the part of Serbs towards other ethnic groups, has not manifested itself in a strong and immutable "exclusivist nationalism" among Serbs. For example, not only did the extent of xenophobia as measured in surveys decrease significantly when the war in Bosnia came to an end (although still at higher levels than before 1992), but support for an "ethnically clean state" was quite low among Serbian citizens, and preference for a civic state governed by the rule of law and providing rights and freedoms to all citizens received more support than Milošević's formula of "unity of all Serbs in one state." Survey data available for Serbia during the 1995–1997 period suggested that although both latent and manifest xenophobia, and also authoritarianism, are quite strong, those attitudes must be balanced against a roughly equal proportion of the popula-tion who support interethnic coexistence and a democratic state. The educated and more urban population is represented less prominently in the survey results, but by no means exclusively, among the nonxenophobic, nonauthori-tarian segment of the population. As one study concluded, the "reactive eth-nocentrism" and intolerance expressed in a kind of hyper-nationalism, which has burgeoned in Serbian society during the 1990s among all groups, depends a good deal on citizen perceptions of the changing situation faced by Serbia.[55]

Indeed, it could be argued that the end of Serbia's hegemony over Kosovo, and the negative consequences of the wars in Slovenia, Croatia, and Bosnia during the 1990s, might actually prove beneficial to the demise of ethnic nationalism in Serbia. But should the internal political and economic situation within Serbia not quickly improve in the aftermath of the Milošević regime, and should Serbia remain isolated from the international community, the prospects for the political mobilization of nationalism and revanchist goals could still become a problem seriously impeding democratic transformation. Indeed, even if Milošević remained in power for a considerable period—a pos-sibility that could not be ruled out in view of the summer 2000 constitutional changes and electoral prospects for September 2000—situational factors could lead to another upsurge of nationalism (mobilized by Milošević or his foes). Moreover, further outbreaks of ethnic separatism—for example, among the Muslims of the Sandžak region, the Hungarians of Vojvodina, or the Albani-ans of southern Serbia—could trigger a new wave of Serbian reactive ethnic nationalist fervor that could undermine peaceful and democratic political evo-lution. There was also always the possibility that the issue of Kosovo would itself engender a new wave of Serbian revanchism and become the basis for a new Balkan war in the early years of the twenty-first century. Whether or not such a conflict would occur depended on many factors, including the tenure of the current UN–NATO protectorate in Kosovo and its ability to successfully dampen Serb–Albanian violence in the province (as well as Kosovar-inspired provocations among the Albanians in southern Serbia).

There was, however, some reason for optimism that the eventual departure of Milošević and the current ruling coalition from power might provide an opportunity for the peaceful coexistence of Serbs and Albanians, if not necessarily reconciliation. Indeed, survey results indicated that only one-sixth of Serbia's citizens favored the redeployment of state security personnel to Kosovo. A return to Serbia's pre-war policy in Kosovo was mostly preferred by supporters of Šešelj's Radical Party (46 percent) and Milošević's SPS (31 percent), as well as among persons older than sixty years of age (21 percent) and younger than twenty-nine (19 percent). The largest proportion of respondents (34 percent) favored granting Kosovo a high degree of autonomy within Serbia, while 24 percent favored partition of the province into Serbian and Albanian parts, and 7 percent preferred granting Kosovo a confederal or federal status within Yugoslavia.[56]

Another hopeful sign of future opposition to the politics of intolerance, expansionism, and violence was survey results indicating that 56 percent of the citizens in Serbia desired a connection with European states, and that a majority (48 percent) favored Yugoslavia's entry into the European Union. Those most opposed to the EU option were the old, the least educated, housewives, pensioners, and agricultural workers.[57] The same research team found that almost half of those surveyed in early July 2000 claimed that Serbia should be a civic state based on the equal rights of all citizens, regardless of their ethnic affiliation. Another 40 percent believed that Serbia should be a state of the Serb people, but in which the rights of ethnic minorities would be protected. The conclusion reached on the basis of such findings was that nationalism was no longer the dominating perspective in Serbia.[58]

In the first months of 2000, Yugoslavia's short-term political development following the demise of the Milošević regime seemed unlikely to occur without serious difficulty or episodic violence. However, in the longer term, the building blocks for a more peaceful and more democratic state certainly existed. But Serbian pride and a penchant for political independence made it highly unlikely that the international community would be able to play the same intrusive role in Yugoslavia's political evolution that it recently had elsewhere in the Balkan archipelago of protectorates and semi-protectorates. Like so much of the Serbian past, the political destiny of the Serbs following Milošević's departure from power seemed likely to be arduous, and would depend largely on their own efforts and resources. But after their most recent and traumatic experience with politicized ethnicity and dictatorship, it appeared highly doubtful that the Serbs would blithely offer their support en masse to the sirens of collectivist nationalism and extremism: the serpent in the bosom of the Serbian people that had been uncoiled and nourished by Slobodan Milošević.

NOTES

1. *Politika*, December 31, 1999, in *BBCSWB*, January 5, 2000, EE/D3729/C.
2. Ibid.
3. *BETA*, February 19, 2000.
4. *BETA*, January 13, 2000.
5. *United Press International*, July 17, 1990.
6. *Glas javnosti*, February 20, 2000.
7. *Los Angeles Times*, February 19, 2000, p. 11.
8. *BETA*, December 16, 1999.
9. *Los Angeles Times*, July 22, 1999, Part A, p. 18.
10. *Deutsche Presse-Agentur*, February 25, 2000.
11. *BETA*, July 25, 2000.
12. *BETA*, March 3, 2000.
13. *Danas*, March 2, 2000.
14. *BETA*, June 27, 2000.
15. *BETA*, June 23, 2000.
16. *BETA*, July 5, 2000.
17. The constitutional changes were facilitated by the fact that SPO members in the legislature were boycotting the body. Under a law passed in April, the seats of the boycotting parties are split among the parties of the ruling coalition.
18. TV Zagreb, June 16, 2000, in *BBCSWB*, Former Yugoslavia; Federal Republic of Yugoslavia; Montenegro; EE/D3871/C.
19. In June, Djukanović's ruling coalition scored an electoral victory in elections for the Podgorica municipal council (taking 28 out of 54 seats and 49.6 percent of the vote). But the rival coalition, "For Yugoslavia," led by Momir Bulatović, won an absolute majority in the local election held at the coastal town of Herceg Novi.
20. *BETA*, July 8, 2000.
21. Inter Press Service, July 17, 2000.
22. *Deutsche Presse-Agentur*, July 21, 2000.
23. "The End of Revolution," *Journal of Democracy*, Vol. 1, Issue 1 (2000), p. 165.
24. *BETA*, February 17, 2000.
25. *BETA*, October 16, 1999.
26. *BETA*, February 17, 2000.
27. *BETA*, February 10, 2000.
28. Vesna Bjekić, "What the Citizens of Serbia Fear," *AIM*, October 12, 1999.
29. Radio B-92, March 2, 2000, as reported in *BBCSWB*: Part 2, Eastern Europe; The Balkans: Former Yugoslavia; Serbia; EE/D3780C, March 4, 2000. Opposition

figure Vesna Pešić remained cynical about the prospects for opposition unity. In an interview on March 21, she observed that "Vuk Drašković is scared, but he may be corrupt too. He lives virtually under house arrest. Very few have seen him over the past few months. If he wanted to speak at any of the rallies he would have to deploy hundreds of bodyguards on roofs of nearby buildings. . . . The Serbian opposition simply does not match the current situation." *Delo*, March 21, 2000, p. 8.

30. *Deutsche Presse-Agentur*, April 14, 2000.

31. Radio B-92, April 14, 2000.

32. "Snaga društva i sila vlasti," *Republika*, No. 230–231.

33. *Agence France-Presse*, July 18, 2000.

34. *BETA*, July 26, 2000.

35. *BETA*, July 25, 2000.

36. "Serbs Believe Peaceful Transition Is Possible," *Opinion Analysis*, Office of Research, Department of State, June 27, 2000, M–91–00, p. 3.

37. *BETA*, July 26, 2000.

38. *BETA*, August 4, 2000.

39. *Der Spiegel*, August 7, 2000, in FBIS-EEU–2000–0805, August 7, 2000. In April 2000, the Serbian justice minister claimed that 195 parties were registered with his ministry. Tanjug, April 20, 2000.

40. *BETA*, August 8, 2000.

41. By September, sources suggested that the U.S. had given the Serbian opposition somewhere around one million dollars for training, computers, etc., although far larger sums of money were often discussed as being available for the democratization process.

42. Radio B-92, August 16, 2000.

43. *Agence France-Presse*, June 22, 2000.

44. *El Pais*, November 13, 1999.

45. *Vjesnik*, February 20, 2000, p. 7.

46. *Vijesti*, July 25, 2000.

47. Tanjug, July 13, 2000, and *BETA*, July 18, 2000.

48. *Glas javnosti*, May 30, 2000.

49. TV Crna Gora, July 19, 2000.

50. Tanjug, August 21, 2000.

51. In a September 2000 ranking of 90 countries according to their degree of corruption, Yugoslavia ranked 89th, the second from the bottom and the most corrupt country in Eastern Europe. Yugoslavia's rank placed it just above last place Nigeria and directly below Angola, Indonesia, Azerbaijan, and Ukraine. *Agence France-Presse*, September 13, 2000.

52. Djindjić was clearly less concerned with the personal defects of current political leaders—including his own and others in the opposition—than he was with the urgency of defeating Milošević. "There are always unhealthy ambitions—from Milošević and his coalition to the farthest village and local community. . . . The question is how long this country can wait to cool all unhealthy ambitions. If right now, the present opposition of the year 2000 does not achieve its goals I don't think 2001 will prove to be politically dramatic, and Milošević will routinely achieve victory, and the other political par-

ties will not recover from their eventual defeat. They [the regime] will beat us, but that doesn't mean they will overcome reality. . . . It will depend on who is more stubborn— Milošević or the opposition. The weaknesses 'of the system' are certain, and the collapse of the system will come about without a political structure to dispose of problems. This is the major question of the opposition, but it is also the question of Serbia. If this opposition indicates that it does not know how to assume its responsibility, Serbia remains without an opposition, and this means that standing opposite to Milošević is a hungry and dissatisfied people, which is the worst [potential] variant [of development]." *Danas*, March 4–5, 2000.

53. After defeating Slobodan Vuksanović in the leadership to head the Democratic Party, Djindjić took measures to purge the party of his rival's main supporters. Vuksanović commented that Djindjić's staying on as party leader "contributes to the sense of a frozen political system, and the frozen political system is what Milošević wants." *New York Times*, April 14, 2000, p. 14.

54. "Da li su lideri Srpske opozijije potrošeni?" Radio-Most, February 13, 2000.

55. Bora Kuzmanović, "Stepen i činioci autoritarnosti," and Mirjana Vasović, "Karakteristike grupnih identifikacija i odnos prema drugim etnickim grupama," in S. Mihailović (ed.), *Izmedju osporavanja i podrške* (Belgrade: Institut društvenih nauka, 1997), pp. 229–277.

56. *BETA*, December 28, 1999.

57. Srećko Mihailović *et al.*, *Javno mnjenje Srbije-Izmedju razočaranje i nade* (Belgrade: Institut društvenih nauka, 2000).

58. *BETA*, July 25, 2000.

CHAPTER 9

Dictatorship Defeated: The Koštunica Phenomenon and the Meltdown of the Milošević Regime

With regard to our nation, I believe that it will be able to find the right answer, now just as it did in the past, to all evils that befell it. . . . The difference is between its own and foreign interests . . . between what must be done and what must not be done.

—*Slobodan Milošević*
(September 13, 2000)

On September 24, 2000, there will be a repeat of the uprising against the Dahis [early-nineteenth-century Serbian revolt against four robber baron families freelancing alongside Ottoman rule]. That day we will turn a new leaf in history and start to turn to Europe. We will re-create Serbia as she was at the beginning of the 20th century.

—*Vojislav Koštunica*
(September 18, 2000)

The Opposition Finally Unites: The Rise of a "New" Political Star

In late July 2000, when Slobodan Milošević called for elections in Yugoslavia—for the federal presidency and legislature, municipalities, and the province of Vojvodina—his political position, though weakened compared to in earlier years, was still quite secure. The major levers of power that had sustained his regime for some thirteen years were still under his control, and the perennially fragmented opposition appeared to be living up to its reputation and record of disarray. It was this situation, and the continued rift between Zoran Djindjić and Vuk Drašković, that emboldened Milošević to call for early elections on September 24, 2000.

But in the year since the end of the NATO hostilities against Yugoslavia,

429

opposition leaders had begun to earnestly explore the question of how to form a united front against the Belgrade regime. Indeed, they had received a good deal of Western encouragement and resources in support of that goal. What Milošević had not counted on in his calculation to call early elections was the ability of the opposition to unite behind a new leader and presidential candidate who could tap into the large reservoir of voters—Serbia's "silent majority"—who routinely indicated in polls that they trusted none of the established political leaders, within or outside the regime. For example, an opinion poll published in August 2000 by Belgrade's Institute of Social Sciences claimed that 42 percent of Yugoslavs between 18 and 29 years old had still not made up their minds about how they would vote, and that 13 percent did not know whether they would turn out to vote at all.[1] Sensing that a new leader might successfully challenge Milošević, opposition leaders working together in the newly formed Democratic Opposition of Serbia (DOS)—a coalition of eighteen parties—decided to circumvent the two top opposition figures and choose Vojislav Koštunica to oppose the incumbent in the race for the Yugoslav presidency. Few people, however, expected the surge of public support that his candidacy attracted.

Koštunica, who had helped found the Democratic Party in 1989 and then established and headed the Democratic Party of Serbia (DSS) in 1992, was regarded as a rather uncharismatic and bookish opposition figure heading a relatively marginal political party. But by early September, Koštunica had managed to take a 20 percent lead over Milošević in public opinion polls, and threatened to swamp the regime in the coming election. The Koštunica phenomenon, and particularly his success at politically mobilizing the latent dissatisfaction and anti-Milošević sentiments in Serbia, was largely attributable to his record as an uncorrupted, democratically oriented nationalist. Born in Belgrade in 1944 to a family from Serbia's heartland region of Šumadija, Koštunica is the only son of a prominent Supreme Court judge, who was removed from office by the communists after World War II. Not only was Koštunica a modest man, who drove a battered-up Yugo and lived in an unassuming Belgrade apartment, but he had a reputation for preferring principle to private profit. Moreover, Koštunica had managed to stay clear of any association with the Milošević regime, and was perceived as being genuinely committed to Serbian national interests.

In 1974, he had lost his job as an instructor at the Law Faculty at Belgrade for opposing elements of a new Titoist constitution, which ultimately gave more autonomy to the provinces of Kosovo and Vojvodina. Fifteen years later, when Milošević tried to co-opt members of the Serb intelligentsia by offering to rehire those fired earlier, Koštunica declined the offer. During the wars of the Yugoslav succession, he had consistently supported close ties between Serbia proper and the Serb communities in Bosnia and Croatia. Koštunica was not a proponent of aggressive expansionism or ethnic hegemony—ideas associated with ultra-nationalism and the goal of a "Greater Serbia." Rather he hoped that through political negotiation all branches of the Serb nation in the Balkans could become closely associated in a single state. Such a state of affiliated Serb communities could, in his view, be organized on a regional basis to allow substantial sectional autonomy and democracy. As he told an interviewer for a Bosnian Serb magazine in June 1999: "The major part of what I have been doing over the past ten years boils down to an effort to change things in Serbia and at the same time preserve our national interest—the interests of Serbs wherever they may be—and preserve the state."[2] Koštunica was opposed to any effort that would diminish the territorial borders of the post-Tito Yugoslav state (Serbia–Montenegro). But he seemed more flexible than Milošević at being able to deal with sovereigntist-oriented forces in Montenegro. As he remarked in one interview, the Montenegrin authorities "do not display all the attributes of a democracy," but "are more democratic than the Serbian authorities."[3]

Koštunica also resented the unyielding foreign pressure on Serbia during the 1990s, such as the debilitating Western economic sanctions and efforts by The Hague Tribunal to extradite Serb war criminals, such as Bosnia's Radovan Karadžić and Serbia's Slobodan Milošević. Regarded as an independent political figure, Koštunica was not beholden to any domestic or foreign political forces. He was particularly offended by superpower meddling in Balkan affairs, and his desire to break Yugoslavia's isolation and rejoin the international community had a decidedly pro-European and pro-Russian tone. When asked by an interviewer if he was a nationalist, Koštunica answered: "U.S. nationalism is more extreme than mine, because it is being spread all over the world. I am exclusively concerned about the situation of my people—without arrogance to other peoples."[4] From Koštunica's perspective, international efforts to aggressively engineer democratic change often proved counterproductive. As he said during the civic protests of 1996–1997, when many opposition figures were desperate to receive more external assistance: "For people who have not experienced democracy it is important that democracy grow in this country. If it was somehow imported, it would not give people the right idea."[5] But while highly critical of American foreign policy, and also of Washington's efforts to export state-building and nation-building in the Balkans and elsewhere, Koštunica was not anti-American. Indeed, he was an admirer of American democratic development and political culture, and had even translated the *Federalist Papers* into Serbian.

As for Kosovo, Koštunica blamed Milošević for mismanaging the entire problem of Serb–Albanian relations. But he also regarded the province as an integral part of Serbia, which had been the object of manipulation and unwarranted attention by the international community. For example, speaking at a

symposium a year before the province would become a UN protectorate, Koštunica pointed out that, in contrast to claims by Madeleine Albright and
Richard Holbrooke, what concerned the Kosovo Albanians "was neither the
'deprivation' of human rights, nor the 'revocation' of Kosovo autonomy, but
the independence of Kosovo. The question of human rights only represents a
means by which the Kosovo Albanians are striving to acquire an independent
Kosovo, with a final aim of becoming a component part of Greater Albania."
Koštunica advocated that Serbia–Montenegro, including Kosovo, should be
organized on a regional basis before the Albanians of Kosovo demanded the
status of "a constituent nation" in Yugoslavia, which would have the same
level of countrywide political influence as the majority Serb population. Should
the Albanians obtain that goal, he warned, the existing country "would
become a bi-national state or state of 'ethnic duality' susceptible to processes"
that, in his opinion, "also endangered the stability of democratic states in the
West, such as, for example, Canada."[6]

Koštunica, who supported a tough policy against the Kosovo Liberation
Army during 1998 and early 1999, was outraged by NATO's threat to use force
against Yugoslavia in 1999 as a way to force acceptance of the Rambouillet
agreement, and also by the subsequent bombing of Yugoslavia for ostensibly
humanitarian reasons. "The Serbs must never forget," he emphasized in one
interview, "[the NATO] bombardments during the night, or they will stop being
Serb. In my soul the attacks will always remain an open wound . . . the NATO
intervention in Kosovo was a great fiasco."[7] "It is absurd," he also remarked,
to condemn Milošević "for his refusal to accept the plan that was suggested in
Rambouillet. . . . It turns out that Milošević was condemned for the only correct move he made. And it was only then that it was recalled that he is authoritarian and undemocratic."[8] Koštunica also sharply criticized the establishment
of an international protectorate in Kosovo, and the inability of NATO and the
UN to prevent the tragic fate of the local Serb community at the hands of Albanian revanchists. But though he denounced recent foreign intervention in the
Balkans, Koštunica also recognized the need to overcome his country's isolation. As he remarked about the NATO air campaign: "Serbia must not forget
it otherwise it will stop being Serbia. But we have to survive in the world."[9]

In view of his background as an independent and uncorrupted figure with
solid credentials as an "enlightened nationalist" who, as Milošević himself had
to concede, invited few "useable negatives," it was very difficult for the regime
to smear Koštunica as a traitor or NATO sycophant who was serving the
"colonial" interests of the United States and its allies. It was also difficult to
impugn Koštunica's personal integrity (regime loyalists lamely resorted to
accusations that he was childless and had several cats) and political record.
Accordingly, Milošević concentrated his electoral message on the regime's

record of reconstructing the country following the NATO air campaign, and on broadly characterizing the opposition as a tool of foreign powers. Milošević's electoral appeal failed for two major reasons. First, by the fall of 2000, Serbian voters were deeply bitter and cynical regarding Milošević's earlier record of broken promises and were not prepared to renew his mandate. Second, Yugoslav citizens had finally been presented with a viable alternative leader who they perceived could not only begin to reverse the damage that Milošević had inflicted on Yugoslavia and end their country's isolation, but also—and this was extremely important to Serbia's citizens—could defend their national interest. After years of Milošević's inconsistent, opportunistic, and ultimately unsuccessful nationalist populism, and also his shopworn appeals for sacrifice and "mobilization," Serbian voters were simply fed up and disgusted. Koštunica offered a fresh approach: honesty, a nonflamboyant style, and a nonaggressive brand of nationalism.

In the early stages of his career, Milošević had won a good deal of respect for allegedly being an assertive but modest (*skroman*) individual, who presented a novel and patriotic approach compared to the old and obsolete ideas of the stale communist oligarchy. In somewhat similar fashion, Koštunica's modesty mixed with self-confidence was extremely appealing to Serb voters in 2000. But, in contrast to the reclusive and aloof Milošević, whose public appearances were carefully choreographed, and whose character often led Serbs to reverentially or disparagingly refer to him as a "strange man" *(čudan čovek)*, Koštunica, although uncharismatic, presented a down-to-earth and comfortable image as he campaigned among his fellow citizens with relatively little security. Over thirteen years after his legendary meeting with ordinary Serbs at Kosovo Polje, Milošević had become a distant and despotic figure to most of his countrymen. Koštunica, though the head of a small opposition party—sometimes called a "van party" because supposedly all of its supporters could fit into a single minivan—seemed to be an ordinary man (*običan čovek*) who had not betrayed his people. As his campaign posters stressed: "Who Can Look You Straight in the Eyes?—Koštunica." "He is a quiet man not a politician in the typical Serbian way," observed Vesna Pešić.[10] Moreover, whereas Milošević had presided over an authoritarian model of rule and a predominantly state-run economy, Koštunica was an anti-communist who had always advocated the rule of law, democracy, and a free market. Indeed, as a young legal analyst, he had completed his master's thesis (1970) on the theory and practice of Yugoslavia's constitutional courts, a doctorate (1974) on the role of the opposition in capitalist democracies, and later (1983) a co-authored monograph on how the communists had eliminated the multi-party system in early post–World War II Yugoslavia.

During the 1980s, he gained renown as a lawyer and human rights activist, working with the Committee for the Defense of Thought and Freedom of

Speech. His clients included Vojislav Šešelj, but also Bosnian Muslim leader Alija Izetbegović and former Croatian president Franjo Tudjman. Because of his strong convictions on Serbian national interests, Koštunica was sometimes labeled "Šešelj in a tuxedo," a "Milošević with gloves," or a "Serbian nationalist" who is not a "national democrat." Such assessments, while accurately alluding to Koštunica's support for traditional Serbian concerns, usually overlooked his equally sincere dedication to democratic principles. At the onset of his campaign, Koštunica vowed: "I'll try to change [Yugoslavia] in accordance with the laws of God and man, and I will not allow power to change me."[11] Indeed, his position on the moderate right of the political spectrum also aligned him closely with the dominant political views supported by Serbia's younger generation. For example, survey research on the student participants in the 1996–1997 protests against the regime revealed that the majority of demonstrators exhibited a strong national identification, a patriotism that rejected expansionist policies, the political centralization of Serbia, and the so-called kitsch-patriotism of the 1990s, but promised parliamentarism, a civil society, and free initiative.[12] Koštunica's message resonated with the young, but also with most other segments of Serbian society. For example, Dobrica Ćosić referred to Koštunica as a "tested patriot and convincing democrat . . . smart and honest, a man worthy of the people's trust."[13] Nikola Barović, a noted Belgrade human rights lawyer, agreed: "He is a very good lawyer and has a high regard for fair play. Because he is very strict and correct I think he will do all he can to keep things peaceful."[14] "He appeals to all," observed Belgrade analyst Aleksandar Tijanić, "disillusioned nationalists, traditionalists, monarchists, urbanites, farmers, refugees, and the young."[15] In Koštunica's opinion, one could be both a nationalist and a democrat. "Presently," he remarked during the 2000 campaign, "I'm getting support from Hungarians and Muslims in Serbia . . . one can be a nationalist without harming other races."[16]

At his final electoral rally in front of the Yugoslav Federal Assembly on September 20, Koštunica told a crowd of some 200,000 people: "I am an ordinary man like most of you, and don't want to change the world. My intention is to change the country with you. I know that you want to live in an ordinary, normal, democratic European country." And expressing the widespread fatigue with dictatorial rule, Koštunica explained to the rally: "Slobodan Milošević does not want to step down. He is the Sun King, the King who said: 'après moi le déluge.' Today our state is being destroyed and flooded and is sinking under him. . . . We wish to live in a state in which the authorities will fear the people, and the people will not fear the authorities." When the sound system failed during the entertainment portion of the rally, the crowd raised their hands in the clenched fist symbol of the popular student movement, Otpor, and chanted: "Save Serbia from this madhouse, Koštunica!"

Though emotions ran high throughout September, Koštunica ran a calm and dignified campaign, sticking to his independent and nationally oriented course. He sought to remove Milošević from office, but the extradition of Milošević to The Hague war crimes tribunal in the Netherlands was not, in his opinion, the responsibility of Yugoslavia's president, nor would extradition be a high priority for a newly elected post-Milošević regime. In a September interview with Bosnian Serb radio, Koštunica even characterized the influence of the former Bosnian Serb leader Radovan Karadžić as "great in the moral and national sense." Koštunica praised Karadžić for stepping away from power, and for refusing to hold his entire nation hostage, unlike Slobodan Milošević.[17] When asked by another interviewer about war crimes in the former Yugoslavia, Koštunica observed that "crimes were committed on all sides," adding that the issue cannot be solved by "one-sided and premature apologies" (an allusion to the apology that Montenegro's Milo Djukanović made to Croatia regarding the war in 1991 and 1992).[18] Koštunica also strongly attacked the establishment of the U.S. State Department office in Budapest assigned to coordinate efforts at unseating Milošević. He acknowledged that Yugoslavia would have to cooperate with the international community, but without tolerating any interference with the country's national interest.

By mid-September, public opinion polls indicated that Koštunica was poised to win the presidential election in the first round, or even in a second round, and that Milošević, who had clearly miscalculated in calling the election, was now in serious political trouble. In view of Milošević's long-time penchant to maintain power at any cost, and particularly the fact that losing power would significantly increase his vulnerability to extradition by The Hague Tribunal as an indicted war criminal, speculation turned to how Milošević would endeavor to "fix" the election in his favor. Electoral chicanery had always played a part in his technology of domination, especially during the second half of the 1990s, but Koštunica's apparent lead in September 2000 would require the regime to engage in fraud on a very large scale. The constitutional coup carried out by Milošević in the summer of 2000, and new electoral legislation, had already set the stage for such violations. For example, by stripping Montenegro of its previous equality in the federation, Milošević had provoked the government and ruling parties in Podgorica to boycott the election. This not only ensured that pro-Milošević voters and parties would have the field to themselves in polls organized by federal officials in Montenegro, but that the opportunity was also clear to fraudulently inflate the pro-Milošević vote.

A similar situation prevailed in two electoral constituencies in southern Serbia, where most of the republic's (non-Kosovo) Albanian population lived, and which was also designated as the place for Serbian refugees from Kosovo to vote. Milošević also hoped to manipulate the voting returns of the Serbs in

Kosovo who were to be allowed by the international protectorate to cast ballots for the Yugoslav elections. The polling in Kosovo opened the possibility for Milošević to claim that ethnic Albanians in the province had voted for the SPS. The difficulty for him was that by the eve of the election, Koštunica's lead was so strong that Milošević could only claim victory through the kind of massive and highly transparent electoral fraud that would effectively delegitimate his regime, and likely provoke massive protests by the opposition. Preparing for such an eventuality, Milošević refused the entry of independent electoral observers into Yugoslavia. Some foreign observers were invited, but only from countries and agencies deemed friendly to the regime.

In laying his plans to steal the elections of 2000, and also control and manage any potential mass resistance, Milošević's calculations depended heavily on maintaining the loyalty and reliability of the police and army. Not long before the end of the campaign, Yugoslav army chief of staff Nebojša Pavković sounded an ominous note when he referred to election day as "D-day." It was unclear whether this was a veiled threat to use force against the reformist and independent-oriented Montenegrin government, or an intention to quash electoral results that were unfavorable to Milošević. In clarifying his controversial remarks, Pavković explained that he was only referring to the military's commitment to fight against armed foreign interference with the electoral process, and that the army would accept whatever electoral outcome that would emerge. Opposition leaders remained highly skeptical regarding Pavković's clarification, but were also confident that ordinary soldiers and policemen would not be willing to use force against demonstrators who might have to protest a blatant reversal of an opposition victory at the ballot box. In fact, no one could accurately predict just how the police and military would behave. The police, and especially anti-terrorist units and special formations of the MUP (Ministry of Interior) forces, had been a privileged sector, specifically strengthened by Milošević to deal with internal dissent.

But by the autumn of 2000, the regime's position had eroded considerably compared to earlier years, and the police—as well as paramilitary units loyal to Milošević—would have to confront a much more confident and determined populace and opposition that had coalesced behind Koštunica's leadership. Moreover, except for specific elements of the top command echelon, Milošević could not trust the military to actively take his side in a domestic political conflict. Indeed, many military officers blamed Milošević for the army's failure to emerge victorious in the four successive armed struggles since the disintegration of Yugoslavia in 1991, not to mention the VJ's generally deteriorated status and material position compared to the police. Milošević was also painfully aware that the Serbian military's twentieth-century heritage included intervention in political affairs when the survival of the state appeared to be at stake or when political leadership was perceived as fundamentally incapable of carrying out its responsibilities. The Serbian military ethos had always been devoted to patriotic defense of the state and nation. But Milošević was no longer regarded as a Serb patriot, much less a genuine nationalist by most of the army or people.

However, as the election campaign wound to a conclusion, Milošević, who had been compelled to become more aggressively involved in campaigning than he would have preferred, continued to inform voters that only patriotic efforts and even future armed struggle led by his regime would allow Yugoslavia to achieve a glorious future. Yugoslavia, he told a final electoral rally that was approximately ten times smaller than Koštunica's, had the chance of living in freedom or sharing the destiny of the colonized nations. As a colony, claimed Milošević, Yugoslavia would never rid itself of sanctions "which cannot be lifted with negotiations and resolutions but only with arms. As a colony we will have fake peace, peace in a dungeon where the only chance for salvation would be a liberation war." The opposition, he continued, consisted of "dissatisfied, unsuccessful, blackmailed or bribed people who are representative of the interests of certain Western governments and the great military alliance which waged war against our country."[19] For a population seeking normality and prosperity on a scale at least comparable to their neighboring Balkan post-communist states, after years of conflict, deprivation, and international isolation, Milošević's patriotic and pejorative campaign rhetoric fell largely on deaf ears. The wide lead in the electoral campaign enjoyed by Koštunica in the first part of September appeared to diminish somewhat as a result of Milošević's direct engagement in the election (in mid-September, for the first time in three and a half years, he even made a quick visit to Montenegro under tight security), although Koštunica remained seven to ten points ahead in the polls. But most polls underestimated Koštunica's appeal; Serbia's silent majority, the uncommitted, were yet to make their choice publicly known.

On the eve of the election, Yugoslavia's citizens exhibited signs of palpable tension and anxiety, expectation and hope. The country was clearly approaching a political crossroads. The opposition seemed to have the numbers on its side, but no one could predict how events would unfold. Perhaps the most nervous segment of Serbian society—beyond the ruling couple—was the network of officials who had managed the regime with Milošević. Hundreds of these functionaries, Milošević's fellow travelers, were already blacklisted by the international community, and a number of top leaders, like Milošević, had been indicted for war crimes. A major question that would determine the future of the regime, along with the issue of the reliability of the police and army, was how long Milošević's inner sanctum and top administrative apparatus would remain loyal to him. For over a dozen years, Milošević's patron–client network had labored successfully to support a decomposing dictatorship, but the leader's

Table 9.1   Results of the September 24, 2000, Presidential Election in Serbia (in percent)

Candidate	Party	Federal Electoral Commission Official Results	Opposition (DOS) Results
Slobodan Milošević	SPS	38.62	35.01
Vojislav Koštunica	DOS	48.96	52.54
Vojislav Mihajlović	SPO	2.90	2.99
Tomislav Nikolić	SRS	5.79	6.0
Miroljub Vidojković	AFS	0.92	0.93
Invalid votes		2.68	2.35
Total votes		100.0	100.0

privileged clients were now well aware that if Milošević refused to recognize electoral defeat, the popular volcano might finally erupt.

On September 24, Koštunica's message of Serbian renewal through democratization and a new style of defending the national interest won the day. Regrettably for Slobodan Milošević, the opposition had finally chosen as its presidential candidate the right man at the right time with the right message and attributes. The magnitude of Koštunica's victory was initially reported on September 25 by the opposition parties based on their observation of the vote count at polling stations throughout the country, and was later confirmed on the basis of more complete data.[20] By September 27, opposition calculations showed that 52.54 percent of those voting had chosen Koštunica for president, and 35.01 percent had voted for Milošević. The remaining vote was shared by candidates from three other parties (see Table 9.1). Koštunica's first-round victory was quickly challenged by the Socialist Party of Serbia, who claimed that Milošević was ahead. After several days of vacillation, the Federal Election Commission (SIK), dominated by Milošević appointees, officially conceded that Milošević was in fact trailing Koštunica. However, SIK claimed that because Koštunica had won less than 50 percent of the vote cast, a runoff between the two leading candidates would be necessary on October 8. Final figures from SIK were provided on September 28, allegedly based on a count of 96 percent of the ballots, with a turnout of 64 percent (DOS's estimate of the turnout was approximately 10 percent higher). According to SIK, Koštunica had received 48.96 percent of the presidential vote to Milošević's 38.62. DOS described the SIK results as blatant fraud—the votes of some 600,000 counted by DOS seemed to have been overlooked by SIK—and initially refused to participate in a second round. DOS also claimed that SIK had awarded an extra 400,000 votes to Milošević and deducted 200,000 from Koštunica.

The electoral victory by DOS was not limited to the presidential race. In Serbia, the opposition coalition won 58 seats in the federal assembly's Chamber of Citizens to 44 for the SPS–JUL team, 5 for SRS, and 1 for the Alliance of Vojvodina Hungarians. Half of the 20 seats from Serbia in the Chamber of Republics also went to DOS, while the SPS-JUL coalition took 7 seats, 2 went to Šešelj's Radicals, and 1 to Drašković's SPO (see Map 9.1). However, despite DOS's impressive victory in the legislative elections in Serbia, the boycott of the electoral process in Montenegro would still allow Milošević to control the federal assembly. Thus, the pro-Milošević Montenegrin opposition organization, the Socialist People's Party (SNP), headed by Milošević's crony, federal prime minister Bulatović, won 19 of Montenegro's 20 seats in the Chamber of Republics, and 28 seats in the 138-member Chamber of Citizens. Together, the SPS–JUL–SNP bloc would potentially be able to control the two chambers of the Federal Assembly.[21] This would apparently enable Milošević to appoint the next prime minister of Yugoslavia, or even, in a bizarre gambit to retain power, to assume that position himself (conceding the presidency to Koštunica). Milošević also claimed to have taken 91.5 percent of the federal presidential vote in Montenegro. On the local level, however, Milošević's SPS and JUL suffered an ignominious defeat, as DOS swept to power in about 90 cities. In Belgrade, for example, DOS took 96 of the 110 seats in the city assembly.

Before the election, informed observers had been confident that Milošević would make every effort to rig the vote count. Belgrade journalist Aleksandar Tijanić observed that "the system of pumping in between 500,000 and 700,000 ballots has been created and tested, and works at a satisfying level. Milošević has no intention of admitting to the real electoral result or stepping down. The election result should only show how many people have been cured of 'Sloboism,' and that is after all more than one-half of the Serbs."[22] Tijanić's pre-election prediction had been quite accurate. But on September 24, Koštunica and DOS had racked up such an impressive victory that even Milošević's well-oiled mechanism for changing "the people's electoral will" proved incapable of stealing the first round. It was rumored that some high officials had balked at "pumping in" the requisite number of fake votes. It was also highly probable that potential reservoirs of votes usually garnered by the ruling party, such as the ballots of soldiers and policemen, did not materialize. Indeed, opposition leaders claimed that some 80 percent of the military vote went to Koštunica. Koštunica had predicted that the election would constitute a "new Serbian democratic uprising," and he had been proved correct.

The Regime's Final Days: A Managed Insurrection

In the election on September 24, 2000, Slobodan Milošević effectively lost the basis for exercising state power in a democratic polity, namely, the consent of the

Electoral Units in Serbia (including Kosovo and Vojvodina)

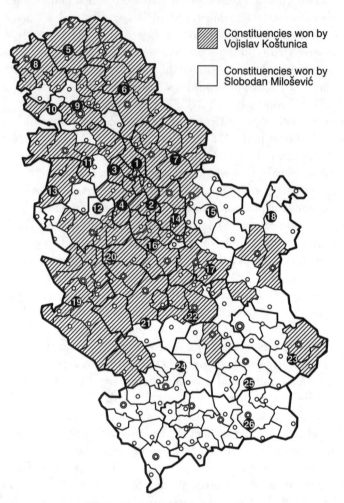

Map 9.1   Election for President of Yugoslavia, September 24, 2000

governed. But though the democratic underpinning of his authority had evapo-
rated, he refused to acknowledge his defeat by means of a peaceful and orderly
transfer of power. Disappearing from public view, he remained secluded at his
home in Požarevac (where he had also lost the vote to DOS) and, together with
his wife and a few close advisers, licked his wounds and plotted his next move.

As the unofficial election results emerged from the opposition parties,
there was a widespread international call for Milošević's resignation and the
installation of Vojislav Koštunica as president. For example, Britain's Tony

Blair told Milošević bluntly: "You lost. Go." U.S. President Bill Clinton also urged Milošević to leave, and promised that the United States and its allies would lift economic sanctions against Yugoslavia when that occurred. But some Serbian opposition leaders worried that Milošević could still make capital out of such foreign interference in Serbian affairs. As one opposition figure, former army chief of staff Momčilo Perišić, put it: "If they want Milošević to leave they should keep quiet. They should stay out of this. Elections are our business."[23] Perišić was expressing a view that was similar to what Koštunica and many DOS members were saying, namely, the often maligned Serbian opposition and public had done the job of voting Milošević out much on its own, and also had chosen a new leader who was no pawn of the foreign community. Indeed, on the important domestic front, the election defeat had made Milošević vulnerable to increasing pressure from a variety of new forces. For example, the Serbian Orthodox Church, which had always had an uneasy love–hate relationship with Milošević, quickly recognized Koštunica as the "president-elect" and called for a peaceful transfer of power. Even more politically threatening for Milošević, Vojislav Šešelj, whose SRS had run its own candidate for president, but had previously been part of the ruling coalition, recognized Koštunica as the first-round victor in the September 24 poll. "For us the elections are over," observed Šešelj. "According to our data Koštunica has won in the first round and thus we will not take part in the run-off." But Šešelj rejected the idea of having his supporters take part in street protests regarding the latest theft of votes from the opposition. "After all," he observed, "they [the other opposition parties] didn't take to the streets when my presidential office was taken away from me" [in Serbia, in 1997].[24]

Šešelj's SRS also began negotiating with Drašković's SPO regarding a possible coalition in the Serbian legislature, where together the two parties constituted a majority and could potentially form a new government. Drašković, who remained in Montenegro, had been completely marginalized in the electoral campaign, and publicly admitted he was wrong to have argued for the opposition to boycott the September 24 contest. Although Šešelj and Drašković had been bitter enemies for years, they had originally entered politics as allies in 1990, had close family ties, and now both had a common interest in politically surviving Milošević's eventual departure from power. Drašković and his SPO supporters may also have been impressed with the potential political payoff of mixing moderate nationalism with a democratic appeal, a formula very effectively used by Koštunica.

As a result of the election, Milošević had become a discredited and delegitimated leader without any real legal authority. But as Koštunica and the democratic opposition struggled to obtain recognition and actually grasp control of formal power, Milošević could still entertain a number of options to avoid total political defeat, or worse. The voting habits of Serbia's citizens may have changed, and Yugoslav politics would never be quite the same, but Milošević remained his old self. For example, under a loophole in the constitution, Milošević could try to fill out his former presidential term until mid-2001, that is, even after his September 2000 defeat at the polls. But since he had called the September election, this course of action would be very controversial. He could also try to use his allies in the Federal Assembly to become prime minister of Yugoslavia, and endeavor to undermine Koštunica's presidency from that power base. Alternatively, he could become the president of Serbia, a venue he had used earlier to rule Yugoslavia. This could be accomplished by filling out the term of the current incumbent, who would graciously resign, or Milošević could run for the Serbian post in 2001. However, should the SRS and SPO form an independent coalition in the Serbian legislature that scenario would become more difficult. Initially it appeared that Milošević would wait to see what the October 8 runoff would bring. If DOS and Koštunica decided not to contest the runoff, Milošević could claim a victory even if only a small percentage of the eligible voters turned out to cast their ballots.

Meanwhile, Koštunica and his collaborators hoped that Milošević would come to see the wisdom of making a peaceful and dignified exit to a foreign destination, such as Belarus, Russia, or China, if some guarantee could be worked out to prevent his extradition to The Hague. However, in order to intensify the pressure on Milošević, DOS decided to call for massive street demonstrations, a public strike, and civil disobedience beginning on October 2. Such tactics, they hoped, would paralyze the country and force Milošević's departure. But at the onset of October, it remained to be seen whether such tactics—really amounting to a peaceful democratic revolution—would prove successful and ultimately force a change in government, or would provoke Milošević into declaring a state of emergency and perhaps even call off the election's disputed second round. DOS also called upon the army, police, and justice system to support the victory by the opposition parties, and asked for a meeting with military officials. Initially the army ruled out contact with Serbia's opposition leaders, and a VJ spokesman claimed the army "would not change its position towards the office of the Yugoslav president as its commander-in-chief."[25] But according to the VJ's chief of staff, General Pavković, Slobodan Milošević would "never order the army to intervene against the people."[26]

Speculation swirled about which scenario of succession, if any, would prevail in the wake of the September 24 election. It was clear, however, that Milošević could no longer recover the patina of legitimacy that had previously buoyed his authoritarian regime. Thus, though he could prolong or postpone his demise, there was no going back. His regime had "fallen" in terms of legitimate power. Indeed, anti-regime demonstrators at the end of September had begun wearing badges bearing a single autumn leaf with the slogan: "*Pao je*" ("He's fallen").

Milošević's defeat in the September presidential election should have represented the final act in the drama of his authoritarian dictatorship. Unfortunately, the old cast of political actors refused to leave the stage, and it initially appeared that an odd situation might develop, namely, "Milošević after Milošević." Thus, it was unclear how Milošević could be compelled to transfer authority to the legitimate winners of the election. For example, if DOS and Koštunica stuck to their decision not to participate in the second round of the presidential election, called by the Federal Election Commission for October 8, it was entirely possible that Milošević might run unchallenged in the next round, proceed to claim victory, and then simply begin a new presidential term. Indeed, despite some advice to the contrary, Koštunica had no intention of entering a runoff (he did call for a fair recount of the September 24 vote), accurately perceiving that he had won the election fairly, and that Milošević should not be allowed to further manipulate the electoral process. But the possibility that Milošević might try to interpret a technical win in a second round as a new mandate for ruling Yugoslavia presented Serbia with a profound and potentially dangerous historical choice: whether the majority of those who had voted Milošević out of office would accept, or would not accept, a continuation of the old regime. An equally important issue was whether the pillars of Milošević's authoritarian regime, and especially the army and police, would maintain solidarity with him or abandon the regime to its fate. "We came to power amid bloodshed and only by bloodshed shall we leave," Mira Marković had told a Yugoslav rally several years earlier, referring to the World War II communist regime. Many within and outside Serbia feared that her words might be an omen of Serbia's future. Indeed some Serbian analysts believed that if bloodshed or a "Romanian" scenario occurred it would be largely owing to Mira's influence. As Dušan Mitević pointed out: "She draws into herself, becomes passive, but harbors great aggression."[27]

Slobodan Milošević, on the other hand, typically preferred to camouflage his machinations with some pretense of constitutional or legal formality if possible. "Milošević was never a proper dictator who launched states of emergency so easily," Belgrade analyst Bratislav Grubačić pointed out. "He was more a 'semi-dictator' always trying to have a semi-legal basis for what he was doing."[28] However, the time for legal niceties appeared to be over. Milošević was more or less cornered. Meanwhile, Serbia at the beginning of October 2000 was rife with rumors: Milošević's family had arrived in Moscow, where his brother served as ambassador; a plane was ready to take him to Kazakhstan; Mirjana had suffered a nervous breakdown, and so on.

Although the national campaign of civil disobedience initiated by DOS on

October 2 began slowly with selected strikes, protests, and roadblocks throughout Serbia, it quickly gathered momentum, and remarkably, in less than a week, forced Milošević to concede political defeat. A major blow undermining the regime was the massive strike by coal miners at Kolubara, 40 kilometers south of Belgrade, which began on September 29. The Kolubara complex of mines had a daily production of some 70,000 tons of coal, produced two-thirds of all Serbian coal, and provided the raw material that fueled roughly half of Serbia's total electricity needs. Thus, an interruption of coal production at Kolubara would have an immediate impact on Yugoslavia's already weakened energy infrastructure and create episodic power cuts for thousands of Serbia's citizens.

The strikes at Kolubara, and similar protests and demonstrations around Serbia, suggested to Koštunica that a new post-election element had emerged in Yugoslavia's gathering democratic "uprising." As he prepared to visit various locations around Serbia, including Kolubara, he observed "that there are sometimes historic situations in which parties and political leaders do not lead the people, but the people to a large extent lead them. This is one such situation."[29] When Koštunica visited Kolubara on Monday, October 2, he was greeted with shouts of "Long live the President!" Like the authorities, he realized that with the onset of cold weather the need for fuel from Kolubara was perhaps even more important than the size of street demonstrations, particularly in view of Milošević's earlier record of disregarding manifestations of popular dissent.

Despite being subjected to tremendous pressure by cordons of police, as well as by their own managers (who began to send miners duty notices), local gangs, and the military (who sent some miners military maneuver notices), the miners of the Kolubara Basin remained firm in their defiance. On October 3, Yugoslav army chief of staff Pavković traveled to Kolubara and told the striking miners that if they did not return to work, they would be forced to do so. But the complex's 13,000 striking workers refused to back down. The next day police broke in to the Tamnava surface pit of the Kolubara complex in an effort to convince the miners to return to work. As news of the standoff spread, thousands of civilians from all over Serbia arrived at Kolubara over the next several hours to express their solidarity with the miners. When a small group of demonstrators on a tractor headed for a police cordon set up at the mine, the police gave way with little resistance and let the civilians pass. On the evening of October 4, Koštunica returned to Kolubara and urged the miners to remain steadfast. Meanwhile, efforts by the regime to bring in other miners—for example, from the Trepča pits in Kosovo—proved unsuccessful. The fact that the regime had concluded that use of the army or police was either too risky or unwise as a method to break the strike at Kolubara sent an important signal to the opposition and society at large that the authorities could no longer defend themselves from the will of the people.

At the same time that the drama at Kolubara was unfolding, Milošević appeared on state television on October 2 and gave a bizarre speech claiming that he had no personal stake in how the current crisis ended, but warning that if the opposition took power, the country would fall under the control of foreign powers and would also disintegrate. The NATO countries were not, he said, "attacking Serbia because of Milošević, but are attacking Milošević because of Serbia."[30] In a feeble effort to split the opposition, he maintained that DOS's real chief was not Koštunica but rather Zoran Djindjić, who was NATO's puppet. If the opposition was allowed to win, Milošević cautioned, Kosovo would never be reintegrated into Serbia, and Montenegro would "be handed over to the Mafia." Moreover, Milošević warned, the Sandžak and Vojvodina would be allowed extensive autonomy, or what would be the precursor to separatism from Yugoslavia. The speech was a desperate address by a desperate man. Yet he could no longer rely on whipping up patriotism and nationalism to deflect attention from his mistakes, or to gain support for new ventures. The serpent of Serbian nationalism had finally been defanged at the ballot box through the courage and determination of the Serbian people themselves.

October 4 brought another key moment in the regime's quickening collapse. After days of indecision and obfuscation, the Milošević-dominated Federal Election Commission (SIK) announced that the presidential election of September 24 was annulled. There would be no runoff as previously announced by SIK on the basis of its earlier manipulation of ballots. A new presidential election would be held sometime before the conclusion of Milošević's current term was due to end in July 2001. SIK's decision to prolong the Milošević regime and make a complete farce of the electoral process outraged the opposition forces and all those throughout the country who had voted for DOS. It was the proverbial straw that broke the camel's back.

Although Milošević had governed an authoritarian regime—a "semi-dictatorship" that throughout most of its existence had functioned as what has been called in this study a "soft dictatorship"—it had also been a "semi-democracy" that had conducted elections (albeit not fully democratic in every respect) and had permitted political parties, some independent media, political satire, and other facets of what may be termed "authoritarian pluralism." Indeed, utilizing the limited but still real political space within the existing system—the pluralist interstices of an authoritarian regime—and also experience garnered from earlier political confrontations between the opposition and the regime (e.g., the 1991 and 1992 demonstrations, the 1996–1997 protests), the structure of Serbian civil society had gradually burgeoned in the 1990s (e.g., the growth of nongovernmental organizations, the dissident orientations of the younger generation, and the autonomy of the Serbian Orthodox Church). Milošević had ruled dictatorially and had tried to harden his control in 1999 and 2000, but the basis and disposition for democratic participation had also flourished within the confines of his repressive rule. By using SIK to invalidate a presidential election that had clearly resulted in his electoral defeat, Milošević had crossed a tacit line that the majority of the Serbian people—however apathetic, cynical, and fearful they might be—simply would not tolerate. In part, Milošević had repeated what he had done in 1996, when he had abrogated opposition victories in local elections. That step had resulted in months of civic and student protests, but had failed to bring down the Milošević regime. However, those protests, it should be noted, had forced him to restore the opposition's electoral victories. This time around, however, Milošević could satisfy the popular will only by vacating his own political office, an outcome he was determined to avoid unless faced with another overwhelming demonstration of the popular will. He did not have long to wait.

On October 5, the critical mass necessary to topple the regime finally coalesced in Belgrade as hundreds of thousands of people (estimated at eventually over 600,000) gathered to protest Milošević's refusal to transfer power to DOS, and to escalate the general strike that had begun three days earlier. People arrived in Belgrade from all over the country, many of whom had been following the regime's gradual collapse for several days on those local radio stations that had dropped the regime's official propaganda line and had begun to openly expose the regime's manipulation of the electoral process, as well as to report what was occurring throughout the country. The final phase of the Milošević regime began when protesters at the center of the demonstrations, in front of the Federal Assembly, tried to storm that building. Initially a lone man in a track suit rushed the police line. He was followed by dozens and soon hundreds of other protesters. When a confused and half-hearted effort by riot police to prevent entry into the Assembly by use of tear gas, stun grenades, and clubs failed, the protesters surged into the legislature (led, among others, by Čedomir Jovanović, an opposition leader who had first emerged in the 1996–1997 demonstrations) and began setting fires and looting offices. Other police within and outside the building fled. The crucial decision by the police in refusing to obey Milošević's orders to crush the demonstration resulted from secret negotiations the night before between Zoran Djindjić and Milorad Ulemek (generally known as Legija), the Serbian secret police commander in charge of the Special Operations units (JSO). Ulemek had told Djindjić: "I'm not a politician, I'm a professional. I see that Milošević lost the election." Ulemek's promise to Djindjić that the JSO would not intervene to obstruct the October 5 demonstration was a major signal that emboldened the anti-regime activists in DOS and helped to end Milošević's rule. As demonstrators poured into the federal parliament building on October 5, Ulemek called Djindjić on his cell phone and said: "It is all over."[31]

Demonstrators also stormed the headquarters of Radio-Television Serbia, where special anti-terrorist units of the army deployed earlier had fled through the rear exit. Over the next several hours, protesters took control of the official news agency, Tanjug, the B-92 radio station, the daily newspaper *Politika*, the Studio B television studio, and the City Assembly, and also ransacked the Belgrade headquarters of Milošević's SPS.[32] Meanwhile, hundreds of thousands of citizens from all over the country demonstrated throughout Belgrade, and rapturously celebrated the fall of the old regime. As revolutions go, the collapse of the ruling authorities was relatively bloodless. It was reported that two people were killed and 65 injured in the "people's revolution" of October 5. During the demonstrations, representatives from the opposition, including former general Momčilo Perišić, met with senior military leaders to ensure the neutrality of the armed forces. That evening, Vojislav Koštunica made an appearance before the crowd. Using a handheld loudspeaker, he announced to the jubilant demonstrators that they were living through "the last twitches of Milošević's regime." Koštunica also observed that history was being made by the Serbian people themselves. "We do not need Moscow or Washington," he exclaimed. "Serbia is capable of fighting for its freedom by itself, and your presence here in such great numbers is proof of this."

On Friday, October 6, Koštunica met for an hour with Milošević (who apparently had been "persuaded" by senior military officers that the meeting was imperative). Koštunica also met with army chief of staff Nebojša Pavković. The meeting with Milošević was reportedly very difficult. Milošević claimed that he would remain as president until his mandate expired in July 2001. Koštunica replied: "I don't think so, sir. Not according to my knowledge of the law."[33] But Koštunica reported that both Milošević and Pavković congratulated him on his electoral victory. Meanwhile, the constitutional court reversed its two-day-old annulment of the election and proclaimed Koštunica the winner in the first round.

The same day, in a prerecorded public message, Slobodan Milošević conceded defeat in the presidential election that had occurred almost two weeks earlier. His son and family would quickly leave by plane for Russia. But to everyone's surprise, Milošević and Mirjana Marković decided to remain in Yugoslavia. Indeed, he declared his intention to continue playing a role in political life. In vintage style, Milošević expressed a sense of relief that he could finally divest himself of the "great burden" of his office. He announced that, after taking a "short break," he would work to strengthen his party so it could become a "strong opposition," and, he added, he would also purge the organization of those who "out of greed, had entered the party while it was only a ruling party."[34] Apparently the ruling couple had calculated that they would be more vulnerable if they left Yugoslavia than if they remained in the country, and also decided they might as well hold onto whatever shreds of influence they still retained.[35] It was reported that on the night of October 6, Milošević supporters had attempted to organize a counter-takeover of the state television studio and other institutions, but that the plan failed after it was leaked, and also did not receive sufficient support from the police and military. The next day, on Saturday, October 7, Vojislav Koštunica was finally sworn into office as president of Yugoslavia in front of a hastily convened meeting of the Federal Assembly.

As the end of 2000 approached, Serbia had only just begun the very difficult, possibly still turbulent, and certainly prolonged post-Milošević political and economic transformation. The major challenge for Milošević's successor undoubtedly would be to jettison the old regime's legacy of governance and find a way to combine Serbia's rich national and cultural traditions with democratic practice. Along with reconciling the sharply divided segments of the Yugoslav body politic, a new Serbian leader and regime would also need to find a basis to restore normal cooperation with the international community and with regional neighbors. Indeed, even Koštunica's relatively moderate nationalism engendered a certain degree of discomfort in reformist Montenegro (although President Djukanović hailed the "victory of democracy in Serbia"), not to mention foreign capitals and Kosovo (where some Albanians regard him as Milošević incarnate). During the electoral campaign, Koštunica had reassured his audiences that Milošević had betrayed them and that they personally were not responsible for all of the problems that had befallen Serbia. As he told Serbs in Kosovo on September 14, 2000: "Let [Milošević] come and look the people in the eyes. You raised a hand against a section of the people. He made you do it. . . . The Lord will forgive you, but not him."[36]

In the late 1980s, Milošević had reassured Serbs that they need not be ashamed for chauvinistic sentiments, and indeed should be prepared to struggle against their putative ethnic enemies. Koštunica now exonerated the Serbs for following a false prophet, and preached a more benign defense of national interests. Whether or not such a leader-guided reorientation of Serbian sentiments would prove sufficient to set Serbia on a new course and encourage a more pacific mode of Serbian nationalism, or whether Serbian society would have to undergo a deeper and more comprehensive form of catharsis and self-examination, was still an open question. The Serbian people remained immensely proud of their cherished traditions and their resilient record under external pressure. But their experience with Milošević had, temporarily at least, diminished their enthusiasm for heroic and unaccountable leaders. As a consequence of such a changed mood, a hard nationalist had been replaced by a soft nationalist. But what was perhaps even more important, a dictator disdainful of real political pluralism had been defeated by a genuinely democratic leader.

To some extent, the international community will be able to assist with the daunting tasks that lie ahead for Serbia. However—even more than in most other transition states—the process of political, socio-economic, and value transformation in Yugoslavia will ultimately depend upon its own citizens. Vojislav Koštunica will face enormous obstacles in stimulating Yugoslavia's recovery; this task will be even more difficult should Slobodan Milošević continue to linger in the shadows. Indeed, near the end of 2000, it was still not clear whether Koštunica would be a transitional figure or would have an extended opportunity to help shape his country's future. There may also be considerable tension and some violence ahead as members of the old regime are forced to step down, and as people try to settle old accounts without resort to the rule of law. Yugoslav political life would not be a simple replica of political developments elsewhere in Eastern Europe, although the Serbian people had decidedly signaled their commitment to a post-Milošević and democratic future. As Koštunica aptly remarked on September 25, 2000, to his fellow citizens: "Dawn is coming to Serbia."

NOTES

1. *Agence France-Presse*, September 15, 2000.

2. *Washington Post*, September 28, 2000, p. A1.

3. *BETA*, September 12, 2000.

4. *Der Spiegel*, September 18, 2000, pp. 202–204.

5. *USA Today*, January 14, 1997, p. 1A.

6. "Postoji li ustavno rešenje za Kosovo," in Pavle Nikolić (ed.), *Ustavno-pravni status Kosova i Metohije* (Belgrade: Jugoslovensko Udruženje za Ustavno Pravo, 1998), pp. 129–131.

7. *Der Spiegel*, September 18, 2000, pp. 202–204.

8. *Kommersant Daily*, p. 1, Russica Information Inc., October 4, 2000.

9. *BETA*, September 20, 2000.

10. *International Herald Tribune*, September 29, 2000, p. 5.

11. September 8, 2000.

12. Andjelka Milić and Ljiljana Čičkarić, *Generacija u protestu: Sociološki portret učesnika studentskog protesta 96/97 na Beogradskom univerzitetu* (Belgrade: Institut za sociološka istraživanja, 1998), pp. 179–186.

13. *Agence France-Presse*, September 10, 2000.

14. *London Times*, September 27, 2000.

15. *Toronto Star*, September 19, 2000.

16. *Vienna Die Presse*, September 4, 2000, p. 3.

17. *BETA*, September 18, 2000.

18. *ONASA*, September 10, 2000.

19. Radio Belgrade, September 20, 2000. Milošević's failure to recognize profound change in the political mood of the Serbian people by the summer of 2000 was probably in large part due to the influence of his wife and hard-line advisers at the summit of the SPS–JUL coalition.

20. Systematic vote counts based on observation were made by the DOS coalition,

the Serbian Radical Party, the Serbian Party of Renewal, and the independent Center for Free Elections and Democracy.

21. A split in the SNP, with one faction leaning to DOS and away from Milošević, soon made the "bloc" less likely.

22. *BETA*, September 13, 2000.

23. *The Independent*, September 27, 2000, p. 12.

24. *BETA*, September 28, 2000.

25. *Deutche Presse-Agentur*, September 29, 2000.

26. Radio B-92, September 27, 2000.

27. BBC, September 27, 2000.

28. *Los Angeles Times*, September 27, 2000, p. 1.

29. FoNet, October 2, 2000.

30. RTS Sat TV, October 2, 2000.

31. CNN, "People vs. Slobodan Milošević," February 9, 2002, transcript #020900CN.V79, and Dragan Bujošević, *5. Oktobar, Dvadeset četeri sata prevrata* (Belgrade: Medija centar, 2001), pp. 47–48. Ulemek would continue in his police post until February 2001.

32. Advance preparation by various opposition elements to seize power in Belgrade on October 5 constituted a significant factor contributing to the collapse of the Milošević regime. For example, the mayor of Čačak, Velimir Ilić, headed a group of opposition activists—including anti-regime policemen and military personnel—who were determined to break through the police cordons around the Federal Assembly, and also seize control of the state TV. "I was aware," Ilić later claimed, "that something had to be done to finish the job properly. Otherwise we would have marched for another 100 days." The convoy of oppositionists that arrived in Belgrade from Čačak was joined by a bulldozer and operator, who subsequently played an important role in removing police barricades. Other opposition leaders had prepared some small armed detachments to assist their cause, gathered intelligence from contacts in the security forces, and worked to win over, and politically neutralize, elements of the police and army. Such planning, albeit without a detailed blueprint for insurrection, would later prompt Milošević regime loyalists to describe the DOS takeover as a "coup d'état." The growing radicalization of anti-regime youth in Serbia during 1999–2000—and particularly the growing association between the organization Otpor (Resistance) and the established opposition parties—also must be recognized as a major factor assisting in the ouster of the old regime.

33. *Los Angeles Times*, October 8, 2000, Part A, p. 1.

34. BBC, October 7, 2000.

35. Many observers believed that in the end Milošević would take his own life. But Slavoljub Djukić observed that such an option was out of the question. "He is a man who wants lasting life and lasting rule. The tragedy of his parents made no impact on him. He is ruthless on that matter. He never mentions it. . . . The problem with Milošević is that he makes moves that no one expects." *Washington Post*, October 4, 2000, Section A, p. 25.

36. FoNet, September 24, 2000.

CHAPTER 10

Unraveling the Balkan Conundrum:
The History–Policy Nexus

Cultures are both tenacious and volatile. It is neither true that they are virtually immutable . . . nor is it the case they are ever reinvented, even spurious in their pretense of continuity. Both things happen, and if there are any laws concerning which predominates, we do not know them.

—*Ernest Gellner (1997)*

I think memory . . . is a shield against hatred, except in those places, [like] in Bosnia and in Kosovo [where] memory fed hatred.

—*Elie Weisel (1999)*

Paradigms and Political Imperatives

During the 1990s, Western elite perceptions of the Balkan region underwent significant change. At the outset of the decade most observers, including political leaders in the "Euro-Atlantic" democracies, viewed the Balkan peninsula in much the same way as it had been seen throughout most of modern history, that is, as a turbulent area of deep-seated ethnic enmities, endemic violence, political fragmentation, lawlessness, and corruption. The twentieth-century history of Southeastern Europe reinforced the prevailing image of the region: the two Balkan Wars (1912–1913), the factors provoking the outbreak and devastation of World War I, the descent of the area's interwar regimes into authoritarian dictatorships, the savage civil and interethnic wars in the region during World War II, and—after Tito's defiance of Stalin gave Yugoslavia's maverick communist one-party state and worker's self-management system a temporary luster abroad—the resurgence of politicized ethnicity during the 1970s and 1980s.

The disintegration of socialist Yugoslavia at the onset of the 1990s, followed by the wars in Slovenia, Croatia, and especially Bosnia, further con-

451

tributed to the stereotype of the Balkans as a zone of persistent instability, eth-noreligious divisions, and blood-letting. As Maria Todorova observed in 1997, summarizing her comprehensive examination of historical and contemporary discourse on the Balkans, over time the image of the region was transformed from a geographical expression "into one of the most powerful pejorative designations in history, international relations, political science, and nowadays general intellectual discourse."[1] Such negative perceptions of the Balkans, a "frozen image" that persisted into the early post–Cold War period, influenced how policy was shaped towards the region on the part of the sole remaining superpower. Thus, seeking to justify limited American involvement in the war in Bosnia for fear of diverting resources away from other priorities, U.S. President Clinton initially embraced the notion that the Balkan region was an area of primordial or perennial hatreds that was largely impervious to change sponsored by external intervention.

By the mid-1990s, however, a paradigmatic shift had occurred in Western policy-making assumptions regarding the Balkans. This reorientation was traceable in large measure to the persistence and escalation of violence in Bosnia, to the threat that the regional conflict would spread throughout Southeastern Europe, and also to the growing frustration and sense of outrage in Western public opinion concerning human rights violations and "ethnic cleansing." Indeed, during the summer of 1995, the U.S. representative to the United Nations, Madeleine Albright (one year before she would become Secretary of State), cautioned President Clinton that his reelection prospects depended on resolution of the war in Bosnia. With United Nations forces bogged down in the area, and successive diplomatic efforts proving futile, Clinton turned to NATO as an organization that might more effectively assist in exercising military pressure on the obstreperous Bosnian Serbs, thereby combining force with diplomacy behind an American-led initiative to resolve the war, and also provide the military muscle to monitor a potential peace agreement. In the fall of 1995, this U.S. policy shift, which also built upon an American-inspired alliance between the previously warring Bosnian Muslims and Croats, resulted in the Dayton peace accords, and the entry of a NATO-led military peace-keeping force into Bosnia. Determined to follow a more assertive posture in Bosnia—to fill a vacuum created by what was perceived as European dithering on the issue—the Clinton administration needed a new policy rationale to justify and explain Balkan intervention.

The intellectual underpinning elaborated by Clinton administration policy-makers to account for the change in U.S. Balkan policy partially drew upon traditional American foreign policy perspectives—sometimes called "Wilsonian idealism"—supporting robust intervention in world affairs as a means of accomplishing worthy goals. This proactive perspective was supported by an emerging academic and journalistic literature that encouraged international intervention in the Bosnian struggle, as well as other troubled areas of the globe, in order to thwart massive violations of human rights, build liberal democratic institutions, and create law-governed states. Commentaries that had warned against military intervention, or stressed the intractable nature of Balkan ethnic conflicts, were now subject to harsh criticism, and even held responsible for the continuation of the carnage in Bosnia. As the pendulum shifted in U.S. foreign policy from caution and limited engagement to active involvement and management of Balkan peace-making, the possibilities of transforming Southeastern Europe and bringing the Balkans up to European standards of democratization and human rights observance became the new mantra employed to justify a significant commitment of Western resources, and to re-conceptualize NATO's mission in the new post–Cold War world. For example, unlike during the U.S.–Soviet nuclear standoff, when Tito's Yugoslavia was regarded as a "gray area" and the Balkans was considered "out of area" for NATO, the Yugoslav successor states now became a central focus of NATO's newly conceived role in the management of violent interethnic squabbles and low-intensity (nonnuclear) conflicts that threatened Europe's stability.

As negotiations were under way at Dayton in late 1995 to reach a Bosnian peace accord that would involve the deployment of U.S. troops in the Balkans, Deputy Secretary of State Strobe Talbott offered the first systematic rationale for more robust American involvement in Bosnia. It was a view that other members of the administration, such as Madeleine Albright and Richard Holbrooke, had been privately advancing for some time, and that President Clinton, driven by the exigencies of resolving the Bosnian crisis before the 1996 presidential election, had gradually come to embrace. Talbott stressed a need for American leadership in order to confront "aggressive nationalism" and "greaterism" (ethnic expansionism) in the Balkans, which, he argued, were symptoms of the general "postcommunist disorder" in the world. He took issue with those skeptics and cynics who questioned whether European and American notions of multiculturalism could take root in the former Yugoslavia, and who viewed the region as a "quagmire," a word Talbott rejected owing to its "cautionary echoes of Vietnam."

Listen carefully, you sometimes will hear in the current debate a hint that there is something in the air or water of the Balkans that doom those wretched people to slaughter each other. That's often, I think, the subliminal message in the cliché about ancient hatreds. . . . [H]aving lived in Yugoslavia for two years of my career as a journalist, and having seen how the South Slavs could live harmoniously with each other, I find this view . . . to be wrong-headed in the extreme.

There was nothing predestined about the horror that has been raging in the Balkans for the past four years. It was foolish, demagogic, local politics, along with short-sighted international diplomacy that helped trigger, in the late 1980s and early 1990s, the third Balkan war of this century.[2]

Talbott's answer to "wrong-headed thinking" was "far-sighted diplomacy, including plenty of American statesmanship and leadership," unencumbered by the "excess baggage of historical, not to mention ethnic determinism." Moreover, in his view, the mass deportations and other human rights violations in Bosnia threatened the peace of Europe, the viability of NATO, and U.S. relations with its allies and Russia. As a result, Talbott pointed out, the Balkans was now an issue of both "moral politik" and "real politik." Talbott's remarks signaled the demise in the Clinton administration of what might be considered the primordial hatreds school of thought, which had stressed the significance of atavistic impulses in the Balkans, and its replacement by what may be termed the paradise lost/loathsome leaders perspective.

This latter view focuses on the long period of Balkan history during which groups with different languages, religions, and other facets of cultural identity had managed to peacefully coexist. This second perspective also downplays the influence of divisive forces in Balkan history, as well as the role of authoritarian regimes in providing the socio-political cohesion during periods of historical political stability. Instead, the paradise lost school of thought attributes late-twentieth-century violence in the Balkans to self-aggrandizing nationalist leaders who have whipped up ethnic antagonisms in order to suit their political agendas. In many respects, the dichotomy between the primordial approach and the loathsome leaders perspective reflects the contending primordialist versus instrumentalist debate between students of nationalism. Thus, adherents to the primordial hatred approach tend to view Balkan violence as traceable to the area's long history of interethnic conflicts and antagonisms. In contrast, advocates of the paradise lost approach see Balkan ethnic divisions and hatreds as instrumentally constructed or imagined by ambitious and unscrupulous political leaders.[3]

For example, looking back in 1998 at the war in Bosnia and the Dayton process, Richard Holbrooke emphasized his long-held belief in the inapplicability of the primordial or ancient hatreds approach. Holbrooke conceded that Bosnia was an area of strong ethnic animosities, but the problem as he saw it was that policy-makers (including President Clinton), seeking to "excuse their own reluctance or inability to deal with problems in the region," had been reading "bad history," some written by "pro-Serb" writers. Balkan history, Holbrooke argued, had been incorrectly viewed as "too complicated (or trivial) for outsiders to master." Indeed, he observed, Yugoslavia's dissolution was not "foreordained." What had to be clearly understood, according to Holbrooke, was that Bosnia was an area of "considerable inter-marriage" and interethnic coexistence. Thus, the problems that had befallen Bosnia, and Yugoslavia more generally, resulted from "criminal" political leaders who had fanned ethnic divisions, especially through the state-controlled media, for their personal gain.

Holbrooke acknowledged that Balkan problems could be difficult to resolve. But, he suggested, the United States could make real progress in the region if it improved its policy-making process and concentrated on taming bad leaders (or removing them if indicted for war crimes), as he had done with considerable success at Dayton, and also avoided the dangerous inertia resulting from reading "bad history." President Clinton, according to Holbrooke, had been misled by reading and depending too heavily on the "ancient hatred" thesis advanced in Robert Kaplan's 1993 book *Balkan Ghosts*, which, Holbrooke emphasized, relies excessively on the "pro-Serb" views of Rebecca West's 1941 classic *Black Lamb and Grey Falcon*. For Holbrooke, a more convincing account, which he enthusiastically recommended, was presented in Noel Malcolm's 1994 treatise *Bosnia: A Short History*.[4] Malcolm wasted no time in returning the compliment in a November 1998 review of Holbrooke's book, which recounts the involvement of the American diplomat in the Bosnian peace process. Thus, David Owen, the British diplomat who tried to fashion a settlement to end the Bosnian war, is described by Malcolm as a man "eaten up by egomania" and a "bully" trying to "enhance his own status and reputation." But Holbrooke—who Malcolm claims has been wrongly accused of having similar traits—had written a book revealing himself as "a much more human and thoughtful figure," and a man who "struggled mightily against Americans and Europeans opposing intervention in Balkan affairs."[5]

Endeavoring to ground American policy in "better" history—which he has borrowed from selectively depending on how it suited his view of Washington's objectives in Southeastern Europe—Holbrooke identified what he considered to be the most positive and negative features in both the Balkan past and the record of American interventionism. Thus, in the case of multiethnic Bosnia, intervention by the international community and his role in fashioning the future of the Balkans represented a worthy effort that, for a time, had been impeded by policy-making and commentaries that failed to understand that the recent ethnic violence had resulted from a few corrupt nationalist political leaders who had destroyed Yugoslavia. Interestingly, for Holbrooke earlier American internationalism that had created multi-ethnic Yugoslavia had been a bad idea, presumably because of deep-seated historical problems among the South Slavs (whom Strobe Talbott, in contrast, had described as being able to live together "harmoniously"). As Holbrooke told

a Senate subcommittee in October 1996, it was his view "that the original decision at Versailles to create a Kingdom of the South Slavs [sic] was a mistake . . .
something that Woodrow Wilson, in the name of self-determination, did,
which really wasn't self-determination. To put Slovenes, Croats, Montenegrins, Bosnians, and Serbs into a single country may have made some sense 80
years ago. But it doesn't strike me as the correct solution. There should have
been some other approach."[6] Holbrooke proudly rejected the suggestion that
he was an "expert" on the Balkans, or what he labeled a Bosnia "wonk." But
his assessment exemplifies how different interpretations of Balkan history by
"experts" have been selectively employed by government officials to justify
changing policy preferences.

The decision by the Clinton administration to become more actively
involved in Bosnia during 1995, and to adopt interpretations of Balkan history
that seemed to support that policy, had profound implications for the Balkan
region and the NATO alliance during the second part of the 1990s. The implementation of the Dayton peace accords in Bosnia assigned NATO a new mission. The alliance was now on the front line of peace-making and guarding a
massive project in civilian reconstruction and societal transformation. A new
set of assumptions implicitly guided the Dayton implementation process: The
failure of the international community to act forcibly after Yugoslavia's violent
disintegration that dated back to 1991 and 1992 should not be repeated; international action in the Balkans would not result in countries becoming bogged
down in a quagmire; zones of Balkan instability, such as Bosnia, required the
kind of *de facto* international protectorate outlined in the Dayton process, or
perhaps an even more hands-on internationally controlled regime; historical
animosities in the Balkans could be minimized and eventually erased by determined international action; NATO could be used to contain, dampen, and
eventually eradicate "aggressive nationalism"; Balkan political leaders (even if
democratically elected) who were considered "anti-Dayton" might have to be
removed by civilian administrators backed by NATO forces, and media outlets supporting such views closed down; and the credibility of the NATO
alliance, and its potential to effectively serve existing and new member states
in the post–Cold War world, depended on seeing the Bosnian project through,
no matter how long that effort would take.

Initially during 1995 and 1996, the new policy assumptions guiding Washington and the NATO alliance, and the paradigmatic shift that they entailed,
that is, from knee-jerk historicism (the extreme primordialist view) to an ahis-
torical overoptimism (from a paradise lost in Bosnia owing to self-serving
nationalists to a NATO-restored state of reconciled ethnic groups living in two
entities), led to unrealistic expectations and a detectable triumphalism on the
part of international officials. Thus the divisions between Bosnia's three eth-

noreligious groups, which only shortly before had been viewed as intractable facets of a hellish "quagmire," were almost overnight considered amenable to rapid reconciliation through international action. Bosnia and Herzegovina was once an "oasis of harmony," Washington was reassured by Bosnian Muslim leader Alija Izetbegović. The region had simply been torn asunder in recent years by loathsome (for Izetbegović, Serbian and Croatian) nationalist leaders. Indeed, the Clinton administration suggested at an early point in its planning that a substantial portion of the multilateral military force guarding the civilian implementation personnel would be able to leave Bosnia after only one year. That prognosis, which underscored the danger of overselling policy and exaggerating expectations based upon political expediency, was eventually scrapped. It was decided instead that there should be no calendar for goal attainment and implementation, as to do so would only encourage "anti-Dayton" politicians to bide their time, not to mention making NATO political leaders vulnerable to criticism for not meeting timetables. Leading international administrators in Bosnia in fact were eventually forced to concede that the Dayton process would be very slow going and would probably last for decades. There was also, not surprisingly, a gradual recognition that it would also take longer than first expected to reverse the impact of history and the deeds of "criminal leaders," and to restore the positive facets of the Bosnian legacy.

But though policy-makers in Washington were willing to concede some early mistakes in the Dayton implementation process, and also to fine-tune the calendar and methodology of their efforts of transforming that ethnically segmented country, they remained steadfastly committed to the fundamental premises of their new policy assumptions for the Balkans. For example, in the fall of 1997, Sandy Berger, President Clinton's adviser for national security affairs, reiterated the Clinton administration's current theoretical paradigm for approaching Balkan matters: "We knew that the Bosnian people needed help to repair and rebuild not just their houses and factories but their tolerance and confidence. We believed this was possible because this century, for all its bloodshed, has shown that hatred is not transmitted inexorably from one generation to another through iron laws of genetics or culture. Hatreds can be aroused by cynical leaders, as they were in Bosnia. But people can lift themselves out of hatred with a hope of a better future."[7]

The impact of the international community's experience in Bosnia came into vivid focus during the Kosovo crisis of 1998–1999. Confronted with another serious Balkan challenge, the obvious preference was to utilize NATO military power—this time more rapidly than in Bosnia, but again justified by moral imperatives and national interests—to support an exercise in containing the consequences of interethnic strife, and eventually to establish a Dayton-like international protectorate. Indeed by the time the Kosovo crisis erupted, President Clinton had become wholly converted to the notion that ethnic hatred in the Balkans was traceable primarily to nationalist leaders and media manipulation, and that the deleterious influence and morally repugnant policies of such leaders could and should trigger a forceful international response. In a speech at the National Defense University on May 13, 1999, Clinton publicly confessed the errors of his earlier primordialist thinking, and explained his new view of the Balkans. The speech came some seven weeks into NATO's air war against Slobodan Milošević's Yugoslavia, an operation that was initially launched to force the Yugoslav president's acceptance of a Kosovo peace plan, and also to stop a humanitarian crisis that Milošević had accelerated following NATO's attack on Yugoslavia (see Chapter 6).

> There are those that say . . . that the ethnic conflicts . . . are the inevitable result—those conflicts, according to some—of centuries old animosities which were unleashed by the end of the Cold War restraints in Yugoslavia and elsewhere. I myself have been guilty of saying that on an occasion or two, and I regret it more than I can say, for I have spent a great deal of time in these last six years reading the real history of the Balkans. . . . The truth is that for centuries these people have lived together in the Balkans in Southeastern Europe, with greater or lesser degrees of tensions, but often without anything approaching the intolerable conditions and conflict that exist today. . . . We've got to get straight about this, this is something leaders do. And if people make decisions to do these kind of things, other people can make decisions to stop them; and if the resources are properly arrayed, it can be done.[8]

Clinton's revised views on the "real" Kosovo were reportedly influenced by his reading of Noel Malcolm's controversial historical studies on Bosnia and Kosovo,[9] which had come so highly recommended by Holbrooke, and which attributed the escalation of ethnic strife in both areas during the 1990s primarily to Serbian nationalist politicians, and particularly Slobodan Milošević. Malcolm correctly emphasizes that the 1990s can be considered a period when Serbian myths "have been harped on so constantly in the service of modern political hatred." His observation that contemporary Balkan politicians have worked hard to "create active hatred" is also accurate. But Malcolm offers evidence for harmonious interethnic coexistence in Balkan history in much the same obsessive and preconceived manner as many of those in the primordialist school have provided evidence of intractable ancient hatreds, or what Malcolm has described as "the gory bits"[10] (a "few bloody episodes" and some "gruesome practices"). For Malcolm, recent Balkan conflicts arose when "low level prejudices" were quickly transformed into "red hot hatreds" by Serb nationalist politicians. In fact, he maintains, "the wounds of war [from the 1940s] that had genuinely healed were violently reopened"; a "truth" that is only known, he claims, to those who had traveled in areas such as Bosnia long before the 1990s.[11] Studies of recent Balkan history that allude to "preexisting tensions and animosities" are characterized by Malcolm as a "sort of pseudo-historical flimflam." Moreover, research, such as the work of Misha Glenny—who, while rejecting the essentialist notion that Balkan ethnic conflict is characterized by a "mysterious congenital bloodthirstiness," convincingly argues that Great Power intervention in Southeastern Europe is responsible for much of the region's violent history[12]—is criticized by Malcolm as being excessively concerned with "murder and mayhem."[13]

In the case of Kosovo, Malcolm not only downplays ethnic animosity between Albanians and Serbs, but discredits many Serb historical claims, including their hallowed belief that the 1389 Battle of Kosovo Polje had marked the collapse of the Serbian Empire (a nineteenth-century doctrine manufactured, he suggests, by Serb ideologists for modern nation-building purposes)[14] and the story of the "Great Migration" of Serbs from Kosovo to the Hapsburg empire in the late seventeenth century.[15] Some Albanian myths are also critically examined by Malcolm and, in some cases, found lacking in historical accuracy. His intention, Malcolm claims, is not to be "anti-Serb, but anti-myth."[16] But when comparing the Serbian view that the Serbs liberated Kosovo in 1912 with the Albanian argument that the Albanians were subsequently colonially dominated by the Serbs, Malcolm maintains that the "truth experienced by the Albanians could be described as the more important of the two truths."[17] Moreover, for Malcolm, Serbian myths have been more of an impediment than Albanian myths, because (before June 1999 and the end of the war in Kosovo) the Serbs have had "for the time being at least the power to make change or to block it."[18] Presumably, according to such logic, the Albanians' "blinkered view of the history of Kosovo" would become more egregious and dangerous if such views became power-backed myths (as in the case of Kosovo after June 1999).

In any case, when it comes to current history, Malcolm clearly sides with Albanian interpretations of events, as well as with Kosovar aspirations. Indeed, Malcolm has been highly critical of the international community's reluctance to allow the Kosovars to completely sever their relationship with Serbia and Yugoslavia. In fact, even before the 1999 NATO–Yugoslav war, at a time when the international community was attempting to secure Serb-Albanian rapprochement in Kosovo by means of a plan for the province's self-government, Malcolm advocated an independent state of Kosovo.[19] But more interesting than Malcolm's inventory and assessment of Balkan myths, and his personal political preferences regarding Kosovo, is the often simplistic use of his arguments by Western policy-makers and pundits. Thus, regrettably, Malcolm's exaggerated view of Kosovo's history as a saga of interethnic coexistence—not "a wonderland of tolerance" as he admits, but marred simply by "low level prejudices," and inflamed only recently by the actions of evil leaders, modern media, and negative foreign influences (reopening wounds that he claims had "genuinely healed")[20]—has been selectively employed by policy-makers and others seeking a scholarly or conceptual rationale for their decisions.

The view that Balkan ethnic conflicts are fundamentally driven by evil elites who have sought to disrupt "healed" societies that are far in fact less ethnically divided than stereotypes of the Balkans would have us believe, and that intervention by the international community can relatively quickly reverse the damage done by local nationalist leaders in the region, naturally has a strong appeal to foreign actors endeavoring to comprehensively transform Southeastern Europe. Such well-meaning officials or aid workers generally have little time or patience to consider and address the deeply held fears underlying the strong latent intercultural hatreds that have long existed throughout the region. For example, it is fair to argue that historical Serbian "folk traditions" about the battle of Kosovo do not constitute "ancient ethnic hatreds," and also that nineteenth- and twentieth-century Serbian politicians have used and abused the Kosovo myth for their own ideological-political purposes.[21] But the negative depiction of one religious group by another in centuries of old folk poetry, and other forms of communication, can also serve as the basis for the development of deep interethnic animosities and anxieties. Moreover, according to Edith Durham—whom Noel Malcolm claims "knows the region well," and whom he selectively cites—the ethnic division between Serbs and Albanians, and also a propensity for violence in Kosovo at the beginning of the twentieth century and earlier, was far from "low level prejudices." Indeed prior to 1912, when Albanian predominance in Kosovo was well established, Durham observed that an "elemental struggle for existence and survival of the strongest" underlay the prevailing intergroup behavioral axiom: "'There is not place for you both. You must kill—or be killed.' Inerraticably fixed in the breast of the Albanian—of the primitive man of the mountain and of the plain is the belief that the land has been his rightly for all time. The Serb conquered him, held him for a few passing centuries, was swept out and shall never return again. He has done to the Serb as he was done by."[22]

As the war in Kosovo drew to a close in mid-1999, President Clinton frequently advanced his newly embraced historical perspective—confirmed by his alleged reading of Malcolm—that if Milošević could be stopped, and Serbian repression in Kosovo could be ended, multi-ethnic harmony in the province could be restored. Clinton also acknowledged that his foreign policy team viewed the Kosovo crisis "through the lens of Bosnia"[23] (see Chapter 6). Ironically, Clinton's hardy embrace of the anti-primordialist perspective concerning the Balkans, and his confession that his earlier views accepting the "ancient hatreds" perspective had been in error—as Richard Holbrooke had already politely pointed out in his own book on the Dayton peace accords—came during a period when Holbrooke himself was taking pains to differentiate the situation in Kosovo from that in Bosnia. As Holbrooke told the Senate Foreign Relations Committee on June 24, 1999: "the animosity in Kosovo, the ethnic hatred is real, not like Bosnia, where it was manufactured by demagogues and racists, and mafioso crook. . . . Albanians and Serbs are really different people, and there's very little interaction and intermarriage, and the hatred is much deeper."[24] Obviously the president and the administration's foreign policy heavyweights did not share a monolithic perspective on the matter,[25] and though enthusiastically hoping to ground their policy in the appropriate scholarly literature, did not always advance consistent arguments.

Despite their full embrace of the paradise lost/loathsome leaders perspective regarding the Balkans, President Clinton and the members of his administration rarely drew attention to the fact that, despite being fully aware of Milošević's role in the wars in Croatia and Bosnia during the early 1990s, they had worked closely with the Serbian leader for many years in trying to achieve Balkan "stability." Indeed, Holbrooke had often touted Milošević's positive record in this regard. Holbrooke, as an envoy for Clinton, was naturally required to negotiate directly with Milošević in order to carry out his assigned task, and could legitimately emphasize Yitzhak Rabin's adage that "you don't make peace with your friends." Perhaps this also accounts for Holbrooke's tendency to attribute nationalist problems in the former Yugoslavia to second- and third-echelon "criminals" and "crooks," whom he preferred not to shake hands with (e.g., Radovan Karadžić and Ratko Mladić), while generally stressing the charming and pragmatic side of Milošević.

Meanwhile President Clinton, whose evolving views, like those of most Western policy-makers, were shaped by a variety of changing imperatives and influences, found it necessary to explain his increasingly jaundiced view of Milošević. For example, speaking in Sarajevo only two months following NATO's military campaign to free Kosovo from Serbia's control, President Clinton illustrated his personal need for policy self-justification, his ambivalence and difficulties in coming to grips with Milošević, and the now conventional wisdom at the White House that current problems and fears in Southeastern Europe are basically elite-manufactured difficulties that are largely attributable to the Serbian leader's "dark and terrible ideas."

I think that President Milošević is a very intelligent man. I think that he can be very charming but I also think that there are two problems that have proved to

be fatal. First he built his political power on the idea of religious and ethnic superiority of the Serbs and their inherent right not only to be part of, but to completely dominate what he decides to be Greater Serbia. . . . [B]asically he created
that fear and paranoia in the Serb people, which he lit like a fire, with the bodies and lives of others. As you know, there have been other excesses in the region.
The others do not have clean hands either but he provoked the conflict, first in
Bosnia and then in Kosovo. . . . The second thing I noticed watching him—perhaps because of the tragedy in his life . . . is that I think he does not feel things
like normal people when he takes decisions. . . . You see I was aware when I
ordered the planes to fly over Serbia, I knew that innocent people would be killed.
And I hated it. And the only reason I did that was because . . . I would save more
of them than would get killed.

Well, those are my two problems with Mr. Milošević . . . I think that it is a
tragedy, because he is an intelligent man and he could have been a very interesting man. I talked to him in Paris [in 1995] and I thought we had understood each
other. . . . And I think it is really a tragedy because he has a lot of potential.[26]

Not every political leader of a NATO country found it necessary to offer
an evaluation of Balkan history and Milošević's character in order to justify
military intervention in the Kosovo crisis. For example, among Washington's
NATO allies during the war in Kosovo, the most vocal and hawkish advocate of the Clinton administration's robust interventionism came from
Britain's prime minister, Tony Blair. In a speech in Chicago on April 22, 1999,
just prior to the fiftieth-anniversary NATO summit meeting in Washington,
Blair provided a conceptual framework to explain his own policy position.
Blair shared the view that current problems in the Balkans were due to the
"ruthless and dangerous" Milošević, whose deeds required a vigorous and
forceful response from the international community. The prime minister also
observed that Milošević, after coming to power in an "ethnically diverse
state," had waged a "vicious campaign" against a section of his own community. But Blair avoided making any other judgments about the nature of
Balkan history, or ethnic relations in the various regions of the former
Yugoslavia. NATO action in Kosovo was imperative, he argued, because of
the humanitarian crisis. Historical inhibitions regarding the Balkans, in
Blair's view, no longer applied: "Bismarck famously said that the Balkans
were not worth the bones of one Pomeranian Grenadier. . . . Bismarck was
wrong."[27]

For the British leader, the war was not really intended to establish a modern Balkan regime by drawing upon the region's alleged record of interethnic
coexistence, but rather to build a future society that was linked to the increasingly stronger integrational forces in a globalized world. Globalization, for

Blair, is "not just economic, but also a political and security phenomenon." Perhaps drawing partially on the "missionary" and military/colonial facets of Britain's own tradition (and myths), Blair argued passionately against isolationism, and for what he would soon term a "new internationalism." "We are also internationalists now, whether we like it or not," claimed Blair. "We can not turn our backs on conflicts and the violation of human rights within our countries." The British prime minister shared the view of the Clinton foreign policy team that internationalism must be anchored in both morality and the national interest, "a subtle blend of mutual self-interest and moral purpose." He conceded that "war was an imperfect instrument for righting humanitarian distress," but should nevertheless be used against dictators, if the alliance is "sure" of its case; has exhausted all other options; can "sensibly and prudently" launch military operations; is prepared to stay committed "once the fight is over"; and has national interests at stake. In his opinion, reversing the expulsion of ethnic Albanians from Kosovo, that is, "in such a combustible part of Europe," met all of those tests.

Blair's views fit in well with Clinton's notion regarding the role of the international community and the purpose of NATO in the post–Cold War world. A notable difference between the views of the American president and the British leader, however, was that the latter's perspective constituted an essentially post-modern formulation. Thus, Clinton claimed he was trying to build the present on a harmonious past record that had been disturbed by evil leaders. In contrast, Blair, more or less, was relying on global economic and political forces to erase past enmities—whether primordial or recent, strong or "low level"—and the role played by the dictator, Slobodan Milošević. By acting decisively in Kosovo, Blair hoped that "the next decade and the next century will not be as difficult as the past."[28] By July 1999, after Yugoslavia had been forced to relinquish *de facto* control of Kosovo, Blair felt he could confidently state: "This will be the last Balkans conflict—and after all they have been there dogging the whole of Europe for over a hundred years."[29] In a flourish sounding very similar to Francis Fukuyama's thesis on the "End of History," and the prognosis of a post-1989 world based on Western democratic values, Blair decided that NATO bombing had set the stage for a Balkan future devoid of conflict.

A key element in the kind of globalization process favored by Blair and Clinton is the idea that there are "universal values," connected with a "cosmopolitan democracy," worth dying for. In this perspective, the "humanitarian bombing" of dictators and societies that abuse global norms is not viewed as negative interventionism. But the question naturally arises concerning whether the brutal measures ordered by Milošević in Kosovo before the NATO bombing in 1999, and indeed the broader actions he planned that eventually resulted in terrible atrocities for the civilian population, could not have been stopped more effectively and without enticement to even more ethnic violence had more sophisticated and even-handed diplomacy been employed. Moreover, although it is true that the NATO bombing—once the initial "heroic" solidarity exhibited by the Serbs had waned—further weakened political support for Milošević in Yugoslavia, the bombing did nothing to contribute to the more difficult tasks of building a culture of democracy, a stronger civil society, and enhanced interethnic civility.[30]

Following the conclusion of the Kosovo conflict, and the establishment of an international protectorate to govern the province, NATO policy-makers had more reason than ever to advance their thesis that Balkan ethnic conflicts could be eradicated by removing political decision-makers who had blatantly exploited nationalism for their own political ends. For example, speaking two and a half months after NATO troops entered Kosovo, Deputy Secretary of State Strobe Talbott—who nearly four years earlier had mapped out the Clinton administration's rationale for intervention in the Balkans—snapped that "there's no such thing" as "ancient ethnic hatreds." The strife and ethnic violence suffered by Balkan citizens rather was the result of "bad luck in the governments they've had."[31]

Talbott also explained that the South Slav state set up at Versailles after World War I had a certain "inclusiveness" and multi-ethnicity that "might" have been more promising than a proliferation of mono-ethnic states (here he differs from Holbrooke's negative appraisal of Yugoslavia). He also observed that he didn't think that Titoist Yugoslavia had functioned all that badly up to the 1980s. In the late 1980s, Talbott observed, Balkan "party hacks who were good at mouthing the international slogans about the solidarity of the working class morphed, almost overnight, into hate-mongering jingoists. Serbia, while by no means the only offender in this regard, was the best armed, the most offensive."[32] But, in Talbott's analysis, unlike in the 1930s, the international community "stepped in" and in the case of Kosovo had ended the "fourth Balkan war." As a result, Kosovo had become a "ward of the international community," although its ultimate status is a "question for the future." With the end of that war, the international community, "to put the point in Wilsonian terms," he added, has made "the entire continent safe for democracy, thereby creating an environment in which self-determination can flourish without requiring the proliferation of ethnically based micro-states." The international community successfully ended the "fourth Balkan war. Now we're deep into the no less difficult task of imposing a Balkan peace." The world was unfolding as it should, Talbott concluded, and the U.S. intervention would help the Balkans to join in "the experiment underway in the laboratory of European politics."[33]

Beyond the Old Debate: Culturally Based
Sentiments and Political Pragmatism

The analysis presented in this book suggests that both the primordial hatred interpretation of Balkan politics and the paradise lost/loathsome leaders perspective, and for that matter the post-modern globalization thesis presented by Prime Minister Blair, when cast in their starkest forms by scholars and journalists and then employed by political decision-makers to justify and guide Balkan policy, have tended to miss the mark.[34] Indeed both polar positions—the view of primordialists that politicized ethnicity flows inexorably from underlying cultural cleavages, and the perspectives of instrumentalists who regard ostensible ethnic politics as totally manipulated by interest-maximizing elites—reflect a reductionism that obscures a good deal of political life in ethnically divided societies. The tendency to succumb to such reductionism is particularly apparent during the flare-up of ethnic violence in world crisis zones, that is, a time when journalists rush to meet deadlines in order to explain ethnic conflict, and politicians scramble for a rationale that will justify either their inertia or militant interventionism.

Karl Kraus, the Austrian journalist and playwright, once observed (as Thomas Friedman recently reminded us)[35] that European wars have begun because diplomats lie to journalists, and then believe what they read in the newspapers. Kraus might have added that the brightest diplomats and politicians also seek to support their views by reference to expert opinion. Experts of course are typically divided in their analysis of situations. But some of the most thoughtful students of ethnicity and nationalist politics have expressed considerable reservations about the ability of either primordialists or instrumentalists to fully explain ethnic violence. For example, as Anthony Smith has pointed out:

> To see nations as composed largely of "invented traditions" designed to organize and channel the energies of the newly politicized masses, places too much weight on artifice and assigns too large a role to the fabricators. The passion that the nation could evoke, especially in time of danger, the sacrifices it could command from the "poor and unlettered" as well as the middle classes, cannot be convincingly explained by the propaganda of politicians and intellectuals or the ritual and pageantry of mass ceremonies—unless, that is, the problem was already attuned to both propaganda and [the] ceremonial. . . . [T]he "inventions" of modern nationalists must resonate with large numbers of the designated "co-nationals" otherwise the project will fail. If they are not perceived as "authentic" in the sense of having meaning and resonance with "the people"

to whom they are addressed, they will fail to mobilize them for political action.[36]

Nationalist leaders may be unscrupulous and brutal, but the passions they exploit in order to support their policy may be quite genuinely felt. As Smith cautions: "[We] should not dismiss the evidence provided by the intense nationalist concern with the 'heroic legends' of antiquity, and with the 'poetic spaces' of the homelands."[37]

Ernest Gellner, through his long career as a student of nationalism, subscribed to a "modernist" and instrumental notion of ethnicity—including the idea that "the attribution of immemorial antiquity to nations is an illusion." He concluded, in his final words on the subject, that "cultures are both tenacious and volatile. It is neither true that they are virtually immutable . . . nor is it the case that they are ever re-invented, ever capricious in their pretence of continuity. Both things happen, and if there are any laws concerning which predominates, we do not know them . . . abstract argument can and does provide us with plausible, sometimes pervasive models, but it cannot on its own clinch the matter." Indeed Gellner suggests that there are some cases, such as the Balkans, where religiously based ethnic passions have quite "ancient" roots, and which exhibit the "extreme virulence of nationalism on certain occasions," for example, in societies that inculcated "in their numbers an ethos of honor, vengeance, and the need for self-enforced legality. Societies in which men prove their manhood not by success and a career, but by quickness on the draw, may and do retain these values even when the unit on behalf of which offence is taken is no longer, or not exclusively, the local lineage, but the cultural category [i.e., 'the nation']. This condition seems to apply in large parts of the Balkans and no doubt helps explain the ferocity of ethnic conflict in this area, whether around 1912 or in the 1990s or during the Second World War."[38] In Gellner's opinion "the political sex appeal of cultures," that is, the ability of cultures to inspire political action and "loyalty in the past," varies from one nation to another. As a modernist he believes that the political power of cultures is "exceptional" and "occasional." The Balkans, the Caucasus, and a few other areas stand out as locations where historically shaped attributes are reflected in "the intensity of the ethnic intrusion in politics." "Some nations," Gellner quips, "possess genuine ancient navels, some have navels invented for them by their own nationalist propaganda, and some are altogether navelless."[39]

Of course, the selective and self-serving use of historical scholarship and fashionable concepts by policy-makers endeavoring to explain and rationalize their decisions (e.g., Clinton embracing the work of Kaplan, and then apologetically turning to studies by Malcolm) is hardly surprising or, for that matter, inappropriate. Grounding policy in sober and careful reflections on the historical record and current trends can provide a sensible basis for decision making and action. Policy-making is also a learning process in which decision makers are expected to make and benefit from certain mistakes. Efforts by policy-makers are also often well meaning as they endeavor to quickly grapple with serious crises in complex regional settings. But even when policy-making is not a hurried and reactive process, decisions, especially on major issues, are made in a politically charged context and later inevitably justified by leaders and "spinmeisters" to satisfy public opinion. Unfortunately, the uncritical replacement of one historical perspective and conceptual paradigm by another under the pressures of political expediency can lead to serious mistakes, unrealistic expectations, and unintended consequences in policy implementation. Overreliance on one or the other of these perspectives, often crudely and triumphally utilized without due consideration to the case at hand, has proved detrimental as a guide to international engagement in the Balkans.

Many of these difficulties arose in Bosnia after 1995 and, as discussed in this book, were repeated, with tragic results, by the international community in Kosovo. For example, antagonisms between and among ethnic communities is not a primordially conditioned facet of Balkan societies, but violence in the pursuit of politicized ethnic goals has been characteristic of the Balkan region throughout at least the nineteenth and twentieth centuries, and is not simply the product of the political ambitions and pathological behavior of particular leaders in recent years. In their rush to transform Eastern Europe in accordance with "global norms," the leaders of the international community often lose sight of such nonancient but tenacious historical legacies. In fact, "experts" on the Balkans—often the product of a quick junket to the region or a cursory reading of the latest well-regarded account of recent events—seeking to justify international action are especially prone to viewing Southeastern Europe as amenable to rapid engineering by external actors.

It is just as much a trivialization and oversimplification to regard Balkan history, and especially the recent conflagrations in Bosnia and Kosovo, as entirely the product of criminal leaders manipulating modern media technology, as it is to glibly assume that Balkan history is wholly and immutably violent, and that when it comes to violence-prone regions, the international community should stand idly by in the face of massive human rights violations. Intervention can offer opportunities for change, but can also have pitfalls if conducted in a manner that employs coercion as a substitute for carefully crafted diplomacy, and that relies more on tutelary democracy and neocolonial-type external management of Southeastern Europe than on a sophisticated nurturing of value change that allows local populations and leaders to find their own way forward. Bad governments and bad leaders are often the product of their societies, and external efforts to refashion a society's values often backfire. Taking one side in an interethnic quarrel, and attempting to weaken the ostensible "aggressor," may sometimes be necessary for humanitarian imperatives. But if adequate preparations are not made for the safety of all the ethnic communities involved once external intervention gets under way, such action may prove highly injurious to the innocent members of the ethnic group targeted as the aggressor, and may also even have the unintended consequence of deepening ethnic divisions and intractable problems.

Foreign assistance and guidance can prove crucially advantageous to Balkan development. But externally induced transformation of the Balkans in a manner that ignores the historical and cultural peculiarities of the region, and simply endeavors to replicate or impose the institutions and political cultures of NATO countries on the Balkans, will delay democratization and short-circuit the indigenous development of sustainable civil societies. The installation of a chain of semi-permanent NATO-run protectorates, which assume that ideal societies can be externally engineered in the image of Western democracies, is as inaccurate and potentially injurious to Balkan self-determination and the future stability of Southeastern Europe as the primordialist pessimism that assumes that Balkan political cultures and patterns of violence are completely unique and forever constant. NATO can assist in ameliorating the problems in the Balkans, and even nurture the takeoff stage of interethnic reconciliation and democratization, but the international community should be under no illusion that sustainable democratic change can be induced by external diktat, or that it is somehow restoring political dynamics and a societal fabric that closely resembles the historical experience of the "Euro-Atlantic community," which was simply interrupted by a gang of bad political leaders, or by a particular Balkan ethnic group.

In a 1927 preface to Bagehot's *The English Constitution*, Lord Balfour sounded an important warning against copying or exporting specific democratic political institutions without due regard for the setting into which they are transferred: "If it should transpire that the borrowed constitution and the indigenous temperament are not suited to each other, then serious consequences might arise from the misshapen product."[40] The international political architects of the new Bosnia and the new Kosovo might pause to ponder Balfour's observation before demanding the literal implementation of political rules that are designed in Washington, New York, and Brussels. The Balkans may be able to break out of the "shackles of history," just as other societies with a violent past have done, but that development is not likely to occur according to a recipe designed and spoon-fed by foreign officials. Prince Metternich, Austria's chancellor at the beginning of the nineteenth century, once declared that "Serbia must either be Turkish or Austrian." Today's theory, manufactured in the West, is that Serbia must queue up for EU and NATO membership—meeting norms mandated by those organizations—or remain an isolated sanctioned state. Moreover, the international sanctions that punished the Serbian people more than their leaders, and employed economic deprivation to combat collectivist nationalism, did little to stimulate the substantial pro-European impulses that already existed in Serbia.

Not all efforts at value transformation in the Yugoslav successor states have, of course, been conducted by overly zealous government officials who have wrapped their policy preferences and agenda in the latest academic garb. Thus, nongovernmental associations who assist in the process of ethnic reconciliation and encourage political tolerance in the Balkans have provided invaluable assistance to the region. Far less useful, however, are some crusading members of NGOs who have staked out their sphere of authority in the region—often bureaucratically competing with each other—and proceeded to condescendingly inform local populations that their long-held memories and traditions are unacceptable, and to stipulate which values they should now espouse. NGOs can certainly assist Balkan citizens in understanding ways to improve their societies, and how to avoid repeating past mistakes, but that must be done in a manner that gives the population pride in its society. Similarly, international intervention in Kosovo proved able to assist the Kosovars against the Serbian regime, but the external application of a carrot-and-stick policy by UN and NATO officials does not ensure the adoption of democratic values by Albanians, and certainly did not inoculate Kosovo society against the travesty of reverse ethnic cleansing.[41] Building "new" Balkan societies that are substantially "dependency cultures" in which local elites simply parrot a lexicon of politically correct protectorate-sanctioned rhetoric in order to partake in the resources available from international agencies will not create viable and stable "democracies," or allow the international community to eventually terminate its present control over most of the region. As Robert Barry, the U.S. ambassador to Bosnia and Herzegovina, admitted in January 2000, international officials—after nearly five years of activity in Bosnia under the Dayton agreement—were still awaiting new elections that might "produce a generation of leaders that are more committed to resolving the economic crisis themselves and are far less focussed on waiting on donations from the international community."[42]

The fact that many Serbs and Albanians in Kosovo, or different ethnic groups in Bosnia, have peacefully coexisted for long periods, mainly under tightly controlled authoritarian regimes, does not necessarily provide a sound pretext for externally modeled programs of institution-building in the 1990s and beyond. Thus, fear that members of a different ethnoreligious group will take advantage or commit violence against one's own group during periods of political disorder is also an important facet of Balkan "coexistence." Such fear and beliefs, rooted in myth and experience, constitute a "tenacious" reality in the Balkans, a region truly afflicted by "memory fed hatred."[43] Recognition of the existence of such deeply held beliefs and myths does not constitute an alibi to exonerate Balkan politicians, such as Slobodan Milošević, who have exploited interethnic fears and helped precipitate violent conflagration in their region. Historians and social scientists may also be able to elucidate the inaccuracies and ambiguities in those myths and cultural beliefs. But the historical record is always contentious, and in Balkan popular imagination myths generally crystallize into facts that are not easily discarded or dislodged. Moreover, it would be a mistake to rely upon glib and ethnocentric psychological analogies between individuals and entire ethnic groups or political units by writers who, for example, have suggested that Serbia is a society entirely "locked in the past," exhibiting "excessive behavior that is a sure sign of deep and pervasive unresolved problems at a mass psychological level."[44] Such a perspective, Traian Stoianovich has correctly warned, is "too simplistic a view of the problems."[45] The "myths of collectivities" in themselves, Stoianovich aptly points out, may help justify ethnic violence, but they do not cause the violence. "Conflicts arise not because people have different collective myths, but because one people belittles, disrespects and disparages the myths of another."

For Stoianovich, the European and American media have been particularly "insensitive to mythmoteurs of the Balkan and Southeastern European cultures, and especially to the Serbian mythmoteur." This is because, he observes, "an ostensibly anachronistic myth of self-sacrifice and honor like the myth of Kosovo can have little appeal for the consumer cultures of transnational corporate capitalism." Nor are the Serbs the only Balkan group to have constructed powerful and often dangerous myths. The Croatian writer Ivan Zanić, for example, has pointed out that the "national mystification" and mentality that fostered the "phantasm of greater Serbia is by no means exclusive to the Serbs." He adds that the benefits that will follow from the disintegration of the Serbs' Kosovo myth and the possible defeat of Milošević's Serbia "will be reduced by the same extent such mythic mentalities remain vital among Serbia's neighbors in the Balkans."[46]

President Clinton was on solid ground when, near the end of the war in Kosovo, he railed against vulgar primordialism, and asserted that the people of the Balkan region are not "genetically predisposed" to ethnic and religious strife. He was also justified in arguing that the world has a "moral responsibility to oppose crimes against humanity and mass ethnic and religious killing and cleansing where we can."[47] But the repugnant nature of Milošević's policies and Serbian brutality in Kosovo does not imply that Serbian fears about their potential treatment by Kosovar Albanian insurgents, or by Albanians in a future independent Kosovo (or "Greater Albania" including Kosovo), are completely unwarranted or manufactured. Unfortunately, much of the positive work done by American and other foreign officials to provide a reasonable framework for both Serbs and Albanians to live together in Kosovo (see Chapter 6) was undermined not only by Milošević—whose self-serving resistance to certain facets of the Rambouillet peace plan he was offered could have been foreseen—but also by Washington's take-it-or-leave-it-and-be-bombed type of diplomacy, and an adamantine commitment to the existence of a NATO-led operation in Kosovo modeled on Bosnia. "Kosovo," Strobe Talbott observed in October 1999, "is a classic case of having to establish the strategic wisdom of an action we have taken—that is, its long-term beneficial consequence, by the way in which we implement the peace we have imposed. We're off to a solid start." In fact, the imposed peace yielded a rather uncertain and chaotic start. Operation Joint Guardian against Yugoslavia in 1999 illustrated that NATO can conduct a complex bombing operation and undertake an ambitious multi-country peace enforcement project. But the circumstances associated with the launching and implementation of that operation have undermined efforts to forge the establishment of a viable multi-ethnic democracy in the province, and are unlikely to assist in improving Serb–Albanian relations in the region (even following Milošević's departure from power).

The international community can begin the process of building a civil society in Yugoslavia, but protectorate-induced democracy, especially after coercive diplomacy has been directed at one side in an ethnic conflict, cannot easily engender cooperation and civility between citizens from different and deeply divided ethnic groups.[48] NATO has consolidated a new "strategic order" in Southeastern Europe, consisting of protectorates, semi-protectorates, countries newly admitted to NATO, and other countries hopeful of joining the alliance as soon as possible. But while the "strategic wisdom" of that accomplishment may be considerable in terms of achieving regional stability, that achievement is a long way from political success at building democratic states and multi-ethnic democracies in the Balkan region.[49] For example, Slovenia, Croatia, and Kosovo are substantially mono-ethnic societies with small minorities, while democratic multi-ethnic political institutions remain fragile in segmented Bosnia and troubled Macedonia.[50] The claim by President Clinton in August 2000 that the "only vestige of the Balkans' undemocratic past is Serbia"[51] can only be regarded as hyperbole or wishful thinking.

In the case of Kosovo, for example, it did not take long for the international community to realize that even "imposing a Balkan peace," leave alone democratic pluralism, was a far more difficult task than it had expected. Although geographically close to the previously established protectorate in

Bosnia, Kosovo has its own unique features. The virulence of ethnic hostility between Serbs and Albanians is greater than the ethnoreligious tensions in Bosnia, and the province has had a far less extensive history of interethnic mixture, trust, and cooperation, which could serve as the foundation for a stable multi-ethnic society. When that background is combined with the impact and mistakes associated with the NATO bombing campaign, and the early stage of peace-keeping in the province (see Chapter 7), the basis for protectorate-induced peace, democratization, and intergroup harmony becomes even more tenuous.[52] By the spring of 2000, for example, American officials were already toning down their earlier rhetorical idealism about multi-ethnic democracy, and also the assumption that all Kosovo's difficulties could be attributed to evil leaders. "The depth of estrangement between factions in Kosovo is profound," observed Secretary of State Albright, still taking care to suggest that Kosovo's ethnic conflicts should not be viewed as deeply embedded or irreconcilable. But she also added, with far more caution and modesty than U.S. policymakers had approached Southeastern Europe over the previous half decade: "A sense of interethnic community may or may not develop; but pragmatic coexistence is clearly possible."[53]

Pragmatic coexistence now appeared to Washington as the best way to cope with the fact that both deeply embedded antagonisms and malevolent leaders are at the root of Balkan violence. Indeed, the need for Washington to maintain its own pragmatic coexistence with the Russian federation and the new administration of Vladimir Putin prompted the United States to adopt a far less robust posture to the suffering of the Chechens than to the plight of the Kosovars, and contributed to the more prudent tone of post-Kosovo rhetoric coming from the Clinton administration's foreign policy elite. The balancing of morality and pragmatism in the pursuit of national interests is hardly surprising, but the result was inconsistency with regard to "humanitarian intervention" by the international community.

The notion that the phenomenon of "aggressive nationalism" in states is almost entirely the result of political leaders and state-manipulated media obscures the complex relationship between deeply held values in political cultures and elite strategies of political mobilization. In societies where collectivist nationalism has historically excited the popular imagination, and is rooted in the mythic lore passed from one generation to another—however inaccurate the contents of those myths may be—almost all political leaders tend to instrumentally appeal to the national interest and to offer various types of nationalist messages to garner political support. Treating every concern advanced by nationalist leaders as inappropriate or unacceptable in diplomatic negotiations ignores the fact that while leaders are exploiting nationalism for their own ends, they may also be reflecting deeply held and genuine attitudes in their society. Transforming the "patterns of history" to reduce bloodshed and ethnic strife is a worthy goal. The checkered past should not be allowed to dictate the present in the Balkans, and those political leaders who manipulate the past for their own purposes should be exposed. But the way in which the international community addresses the task of societal transformation must carefully take into account the cultural sensitivities and mythic beliefs of the society in question. While historically shaped fears held by members of a particular ethnic community can never be used to justify genocidal actions, or to establish "moral equivalency,"[54] such fears may constitute a real facet of an ethnic conflict and become a crucial factor influencing any effort to manage and resolve interethnic antagonisms. No group can rely on the "immortality of entitlement to revenge." But any attempt to ignore or erase memory by international officials who have fast-tracked a policy of building a better world can seriously complicate well-intentioned efforts at political change.[55]

Reducing the hold of historically grounded nationalism will certainly require more than just the elimination of one leader or a specific incumbent political party or elite group. Leadership change can be enormously important in stimulating democratization and combating expansive nationalism—as events in Croatia following the death of Franjo Tudjman have illustrated. But sustainable value change and institution-building are a protracted process. Moreover, overconcentration on hastening the exit of malevolent and manipulative leaders without recognition of the legitimate claims and concerns of those leaders' constituents can prove highly counter-productive in achieving the long-term goals sought by the international community. For example, there is a natural frustration when military action fails to secure the removal of a nationalist leader such as Slobodan Milošević, or to fulfill the implied goals of the conceptual premises used to rationalize a particular policy. But the temptation to punitively isolate the state governed by that leader, and to deny its citizens any economic assistance and integration into the international community until they see the wisdom of removing the leader in question, can prove counter-productive in the long run. Thus, even if such a policy may ultimately prove successful in ousting the targeted leader, it can also have the dangerous potential of stimulating the very xenophobic and illiberal attitudes that traditionally have been responsible for the political ascendancy of nationalist leadership.[56]

An even more counter-productive and dangerous policy is the notion that maintains that the international community should quickly use military force to intervene in countries—and more or less reprogram the population—where state-sponsored outrages have frequently occurred against minority groups.[57] Serbian political development in the 1980s and 1990s, as this study has tried to illustrate, is the by-product of both socio-cultural and situational patterns in Serbia and the Balkans, and also the policies and personality of Slobodan

Milošević. The particular interdependence between Serbia's "collective political personality" or political culture and Milošević's personality is a kind of closed circle of interaction that has had a profound and very negative influence on Balkan history at the end of the twentieth century. But the end of Milošević's rule, however desirable that may be, will not by itself mean the elimination of the deeper socio-cultural values and national sentiments that are embodied in Milošević's political persona—and, for that matter, in that of most other Serbian politicians—and that he all too often misrepresented and manipulated. Indeed, the Serbian political actors most likely to replace Milošević, and hopefully take Serbia in a more democratic and productive direction, are also likely to be deeply committed to national interests, and committed to forging political linkages among Serbian communities throughout the Balkans. As Vojislav Koštunica, the major opposition candidate in the September 2000 presidential election, observed: "Genuine Serbian nationalism should be pro-European and defensive, like that of General de Gaulle's French nationalism in the 1960s. . . . Milošević is a great manipulator . . . [but] the issue now is the survival of the nation."[58] In any case, external efforts to nurture new socio-political values and cultural patterns in Serbia should be carefully crafted to both relate to, and respect, the many positive attributes of the traditional Serbian cultural fabric.

Recognition of the subtle linkage between the past and the present, and respect for historical tradition, must provide the basis for successful international engagement. Extricating societies, especially old cultures, from the often harmful grip of history and manufactured mythic mindsets does not require a complete assault on the factual basis of an ethnic group's entire legacy, or assertion of the superiority of one's own "truth" regarding the past. Balkan history and contemporary development are complex, and recognition of that fact does not imply that the region cannot be understood through a balanced appraisal, or that the course of Balkan political evolution cannot take a turn for the better without heavy-handed and imperatorial external direction.

At the UN's Millennium Summit in September 2000, President Clinton proudly affirmed that the international community had faced and met a major test "when Milošević tried to close the last century with the final chapter of ethnic cleansing and slaughter." But international decision-making about the proper response to the "scourge" of conflicts that are ethnically and religiously based should carefully weigh the ability of militant and anti-pluralist secessionist movements to provoke brutal responses from their stronger adversaries, and thereby ratchet up the level of violence in ethnic and civil wars in order to invite external attention and engagement. And evaluations of the consequences of intervention must also carefully consider methods to prevent "collateral" violence, particularly owing to the fact, as Bernard Kouchner has observed, that "one oppression could conceal another." As President Clinton has aptly remarked: "conflicts and disputes are not so clear-cut. Legitimate grievances and aspirations pile high on both sides."[59]

Efforts to comprehend the Balkan conundrum must proceed from an open-minded and critical approach to contending scholarly perspectives, as well as towards the various policy formulations and punditry that usually simplistically rely on such views for justification, and that tend to become rather skewed and inaccurate during the heated propaganda battles and partisanship typically exhibited in wartime. All research is influenced to some extent by the values of the scholar conducting the inquiry, but it is necessary to avoid reaching conclusions designed solely to serve "pragmatic considerations," or simply to satisfy "what the mind dwells on with peculiar satisfaction."[60]

NOTES

1. Mariia Nikolaeva Todorova, *Imagining the Balkans* (New York: Oxford University Press, 1997), p. 7.

2. Federal Document Clearinghouse, November 9, 1995.

3. The distinction between the paradigms as used here and in the general literature on nationalism is a general dichotomy into "ideal types." In the real world, scholars and policy-makers who write and speak on the Balkans or other ethnically diverse areas rarely can be fitted neatly into one paradigm or the other. For the most comprehensive discussion of the two paradigms in the rich and highly diversified literature on the development of nations and nationalism, see Anthony D. Smith, *Nationalism and Modernism: A Critical Survey of Recent Theories of Nations and Nationalism* (London: Routledge, 1998).

4. Richard Holbrooke, *To End a War* (New York: Random House, 1998), pp. 22–24. The influence of Kaplan's book on Clinton's reservations about bolder involvement in the Balkans is supported by Elizabeth Drew, *On the Edge: The Clinton Presidency* (New York: Simon and Schuster, 1994), p. 157, and Richard Reeves, *Running in Place: How Bill Clinton Disappointed America* (Kansas City: Andrews and McMeel, 1996), pp. 91–92. David Halberstam claims it was Colin Powell (not Hillary Clinton as reported by others) who gave Kaplan's book to Clinton. *War in a Time of Peace.* (New York: Scribner, 2001), p. 228. Robert Kaplan condemns Serbian war crimes, as Holbrooke takes note. Holbrooke has also observed that his negative comments about Kaplan have made the latter feel "abused," and that Kaplan claims he did not intend to provide a justification for the actions of others. Indeed, Holbrooke admits that historically in Bosnia there were hostilities among Serbs, Croats, and Muslims, but he compares those conflicts to the April 1992 death rate in Los Angeles. "But," Holbrooke remarks, "the authorities in LA got the situation under control again. And people were replaced, and new rules were put into order" National Press Club Luncheon, June 18, 1998. Writing before Holbrooke, Warren Zimmerman criticized those who argue that ancient Balkan hostilities account for the area's violence, and he instead blames Milošević and Croatia's Franjo Tudjman for "the manufacture of ethnic hatred." *Origins of a Catastrophe: Yugoslavia and Its Destroyers* (New York: Times Books, 1996, 1999), p. 120. Susan C.

Woodward's *Balkan Tragedy* (Washington, D.C.: Brookings Institution, 1995), pp. 7–8, 426, note 6, also takes issue with Kaplan's "history as destiny" school of thought.

5. *Los Angeles Times*, November 15, 1998, p. 11.

6. *Federal News Service*, October 1, 1996. "Holding the six republics of Yugoslavia together was an impossibility," Holbrooke has remarked elsewhere. "They had been stitched together rather arbitrarily in my view at Versailles. . . . I don't think they either exemplified the self-determination which President Wilson said he supported, or that combination made much sense to begin with. It was held together by force and history, by the power of men like Tito, power that combined cunning and a police state." National Press Club Luncheon, June 18, 1998.

7. *Federal News Service*, September 23, 1997.

8. *Federal News Service*, May 13, 1999.

9. *New York Times*, July 31, 1999, and David Remnick, *New Yorker*, June 14, 1997, p. 14.

10. "Seeing Ghosts," *The National Interest*, No. 32 (Summer 1993), p. 85. See also the debate between Aleksa Djilas, Malcolm, and others. "Imaging Kosovo," *Foreign Affairs*, Vol. 77, No. 5 (October 1998), pp. 124–131, and "Is Kosovo Real? The Battle Over Kosovo Continues," *Foreign Affairs*, Vol. 78, No. 1 (January/February 1999), pp. 130–139.

11. *New York Times*, October 19, 1998, p. 6. Malcolm maintained that contrary to Robert Kaplan's argument in *Balkan Ghosts* "the Bosnia war was not caused by ancient hatreds, it was caused by modern politicians, mostly Mr. Milošević and Dr. Karadžić with the help of Radio-Television Belgrade." Those actors worked to "create active hatred where it did not exist before," according to Malcolm. Malcolm reassuringly informs us that during World War II, only "18,000 Muslims joined the SS, out of a population of nearly one million." As for early-twentieth-century Bosnia, Malcolm cites approvingly a study by the American journalist W. E. Curtis, who in 1903 maintained that "life is as safe in Bosnia as in Illinois." "Seeing Ghosts," *The National Interest*, No. 32 (Summer 1993), pp. 84 and 87.

12. Misha Glenny, *The Balkans 1804–1999: Nationalism, War and the Great Powers* (London: Granta Books, 1999), pp. xxiv and 661. Glenny is no fan of the "ancient hatreds" approach to the Balkans, but rather believes that the "impetus for violence in the region is both a modern phenomenon and one for which the Great Powers or Russia and the West bear a decisive responsibility. . . . Scurrilous rumor has it that Balkan peoples are different; less sensitive to human life than others. The Balkans is a twilight world which has absorbed Asiatic values and so on. . . . I would argue however, that notwithstanding these chronic misrepresentations, modern Balkan nationalism and the violence associated with it has been fashioned and encouraged much more by the post-enlightenment Western world than a pre-enlightenment Orient." Misha Glenny, "The Road to Bosnia and Kosovo: The Role of the Great Powers in the Balkans," *EES News*, September-October 2000, p. 7.

13. *Sunday Telegraph*, November 21, 1999. A critique of Glenny's work even less sympathetic than Malcolm's is Atila Hoare, "Misha Glenny and the Balkan Mind," *A Bosnia Report* (March-May 1998), New Series No. 3.

14. Branomir Anzulović points out that the myth of the Kosovo battle appeared in Serbia soon after the actual event. *Heavenly Serbia: From Myth to Genocide* (New York: New York University Press, 1999), p. 11. Malcolm acknowledges that early strands of the Kosovo myth appeared in the fourteenth century, but rejects the idea of the Serbian historian Dušan Bataković that there is a "permanent connective tissue" between these strands and the Serbs' historical-national self-consciousness." Malcolm, *Kosovo: A Short History* (New York: New York University Press, 1998), pp. 63, 77–80, and Dušan Bataković, *The Kosovo Chronicles* (Belgrade: Plato, 1992), p. 35. Bataković's view is supported by Thomas Emmert in a review of Malcolm's book on Kosovo. "Challenging Myth in a Short History of Kosovo," *Hapsburg* (on-line), May 1999.

15. Malcolm, *Kosovo: A Short History*, pp. 139–162.

16. Preface, 1999, reprinting of *Kosovo: A Short History*.

17. Malcolm, *Kosovo: A Short History*, p. xxxi.

18. Ibid., p. 356.

19. During the war, he restated his support for Kosova independence. "Western Policy and Kosova's Future," *Bosnia Report* (April-June 1999), New Series, No. 9/10, which reports his June 9, 1999, article in the *New York Times*.

20. *New York Times*, October 19, 1998, Section E, p. 6.

21. Malcolm supports the view that Serbian folk traditions influence Serb–Albanian relations, but only because political leaders later incorporated them into Serbian national ideology. *Sunday Telegraph*, April 25, 1999, p. 13. For the response by a number of Serbian historians to the study by Malcolm see Slavko Terzić (ed.), *Response to Noel Malcolm's Book, Kosovo: A Short History* (Belgrade: Institute of History of the Serbian Academy of Sciences and Arts, 2000).

22. Edith Durham, *High Albania* (Boston: Beacon Press, 1985; Edward Arnold, 1909), p. 294.

23. *Federal News Service*, June 25, 1999.

24. *Federal News Service*, June 24, 1999.

25. At the time Holbrooke was waiting for his confirmation as U.S. representative to the United Nations.

26. *Public Papers of the Presidents*, July 30, 1999, Doc. 1529. Remarks in a Roundtable Discussion with Regional Independent Media in Sarajevo, Bosnia–Herzegovina.

27. *The Guardian*, April 23, 1999, p. 1.

28. "Doctrine of the International Community," *10 Downing Street Internet Site*, (www.number=10.gov.uk) April 23, 1999.

29. BBC Interview, Sarajevo, July 30, 1999, and *The Guardian*, July 31, 1999, p. 14.

30. *Sunday Herald*, May 2, 1999, p. 11.

31. *Washington Times*, August 29, 1999, p. B1.

32. U.S. Department of State, Department of State Digest, *Address at the Aspen Institute*, Aspen, Colorado, August and September 1999.

33. "The Balkan Question and the European Answer," *Address at the Aspen Institute*, Aspen, Colorado, August 24, 1999.

34. For two useful and interesting discussions that illustrate the complexity of Balkan politics and how aspects of both the paradigms discussed in this chapter can

inform analysis of this subject, see Steven Majstorević, "Ancient Hatreds or Elite Manipulation: Memory and Politics in the Former Yugoslavia," *World Affairs*, Vol. 159, No. 4 (Spring 1997), pp. 170–182, and Ivan Zanić, "War and Peace in Herzegovina," *Budapest Review of Books*, Vol. 8, No. 3–4 (1998), pp. 125–135.

35. *New York Times*, March 17, 2000, p. 21.

36. Anthony D. Smith, *Nationalism and Modernism: A Critical Survey of Recent Theories of Nations and Nationalism* (London/New York: Routledge, 1998), p. 130.

37. Ibid., p. 198.

38. Ernest Gellner, *Nationalism* (London: Weidenfield and Nicolson, 1997), p. 94.

39. Ibid., pp. 58–61, 90–101. Katherine Verdery draws attention to nationalism as a kind of ancestor worship, and points out that politicians such as Milošević have exploited the strong emotions of their fellow countrymen regarding ancestors and kinship in order to mobilize political passions, or what she calls "dead-body politics." And while she is careful to avoid treating Yugoslavia as a "'tribal' or primitive place," she emphasizes that state-building in the Balkans "continually shored-up the existence of supra-nuclear family groupings . . . to supplement an emphasis on lineal ancestry with that of blood brotherhood, as a metaphor for nationhood." She also aptly comments that "for Serbs 'living memory' seems to mean as much as 600 years." *The Political Lives of Dead Bodies: Reburial and Postsocialist Change* (New York: Columbia University Press, 1999), pp. 104–105, 160.

40. Cited in Ernst Fraenkel, "Historical Obstacles to Parliamentary Government in Germany," *The Path to Dictatorship 1918–1933* (New York: Anchor Books, 1966), p. 21.

41. In late June 2000, after a year of rather ineffective activity by the UN and NATO to stop Albanian revenge killings and brutality against Serbs and other minorities, international officials in Kosovo prepared to establish a new court in the protectorate to try both wartime crimes and "ethnic crimes."

42. Remarks at OSCE Meeting in Washington, cited in *CER*, Vol. 12, No. 24 (June 19, 2000).

43. *Los Angeles Times*, June 10, 1999, Part A, p. 6.

44. See, for example, Sabrina Ramet, *Nationalism and Federalism in Yugoslavia 1962–1991* (Bloomington: Indiana University Press, 1992), p. 254.

45. Traian Stoianovich, *Balkan Worlds: The First and Last Europe* (Armonk, N.Y.: M. E. Sharpe, 1994), pp. 305–306.

46. "Kosovo: Nationalism and Myths," *Index on Censorship*, No. 4 (1999), pp. 159–165.

47. *Federal News Service*, June 2, 1999. *Remarks by President William Clinton at the U.S. Air Force Academy Commencement*, Colorado Springs, Colorado.

48. Three months after the NATO intervention in Kosovo began, Secretary of State Albright was warning Kosovar leaders that "some in the international community" had concluded that they could not build a peaceful multi-ethnic democracy: "You have heard the stories. You have been described as prisoners of Balkan history, interested only in doing to the Serbs what they have already done to you. I can't tell you how to feel. No one can. But I hope and believe that you will aim higher and achieve more than

the cynics and bigots expect." *FDCH Transcripts*, September 14, 1999. In March 2000, Albright spokesman Jamie Rubin observed: "We are deeply disappointed by the failure of Kosovo Albanian leaders in all aspects of Kosovar Albanian life." Rubin claimed that with every attack on Serbs or other non-Albanians, "our determination to help Kosovo weakens." *Houston Chronicle*, March 13, 2000, p. 15.

49. As Strobe Talbott remarked in June 2000: "We've got into a 50-year habit of waging the Cold War ... now that the Cold War has ended the international community including the United States, has to develop a mindset ... that part of what we do is to make sure we're keeping these different threats dampened down and under control."

50. U.S. Balkan envoy General Jacques Klein has commented that: "Croatia is mono-ethnic, Slovenia is mono-ethnic, Kosovo shortly will be mono-ethnic. Bosnia–Herzegovina is the last place [where multi-ethnicity] has a chance." ABC News *Nightline*, November 29, 1999.

51. Remarks by the president to the National Democratic Institute, August 16, 2000.

52. The tendency of international officials to attempt to "homogenize" values and dictate policies in an area such as Kosovo not only can exacerbate difficulties between and among different ethnic communities but can actually backfire with respect to the previously victimized or aggrieved community that the foreign intervention was originally designed to assist. As one student of Albanian politics has remarked regarding UN officials in Kosovo: Just "as they arrogantly administered Africa since the end of European colonialism [they] have perpetuated collective alienation, a relational tension that only strengthens fear and resentment. The world community has proven to have little patience for nuances inherent in the country—rather than adopting an approach that respects local [methods] towards resolving local issues. Kosovo is still colonized, this time by a cadre of over-paid bureaucrats. ... Instead of learning from past mistakes and attempting to move away from central control, the UN is enhancing efforts to dominate local life. The social inequalities created in Kosovo over the last 70 years have been reassigned to new leaders, while the vast majority of people find themselves politically marginal. Their marginality has meant that almost all Kosovars have become pawns to 'representatives' who have climbed over many human corpses to find a place at the Interim Council Bernard Kouchner has set up in Priština." Isa Blumi, "Forging a New Kosovo," *Central European Review*, Vol. 2, No. 26 (July 3, 2000).

53. *New York Times*, March 28, 2000, p. A27.

54. Some authors, who have been disturbed by efforts to equate Serbian and non-Serbian responsibility for violence in the Balkans, often adopt a highly skewed interpretation of their group's historical record of rectitude and civilized behavior. For example, angered over the media's alleged demonization of Croatia and the Bosnian Muslims for historical crimes, the sociologist Stjepan Mestrović downplays Serbian anxieties and concerns in his cultural interpretation of differences among Balkan ethnic communities. *Genocide After Emotion: The Postemotional Balkan War* (New York: Routledge, 1996). In an earlier study, Mestrović and fellow authors maintain that "Croatia and Serbia exist at different levels of cultural development. ... Serbia is more of an expansionist 'civilization' compared with the still Gothic Croatia. ... Croatia has never shown expansionist tendencies ... the history of Serbian culture is based on the prin-

ciple of Balkan particularism—the myth and cult of Serbian uniqueness and superiority. For example, Serbia insisted on maintaining the Cyrillic alphabet among its minority in Croatia, even though Serbia is the only European nation to use this outmoded alphabet." Stjepan Mestrović, Slaven Letić, and Miroslav Goreta, *Habits of the Balkan Heart* (College Station: Texas A&M University Press, 1993), pp. 127, 142. For another Croato-centric view criticizing the diverse works of various experts and reporters who allegedly provide "elaborated rationalizations for Serbian aggression and genocide" see James Sadkovich, *The U.S. Media and Yugoslavia 1991–1995* (Westport, Conn.: Praeger, 1998).

55. Louise Arbour, the former chief prosecutor of the United Nations War Crimes Tribunals for Rwanda and the Balkans, points approvingly to a Kosovo Serb who has grown frustrated with Milošević and now exclaims "we have learned that you cannot live from history. Americans have no history and they live wonderfully well." "The Inevitable Deficits of Memory," *Toronto Star*, November 20, 1999. Actually, despite its relative youth, American society is replete with examples of myths and political behavior shaped by history (not to mention Canadian and Quebec political history, which is better known to Arbour). Arbour neglects the need for sensitivity and patience when dealing with southeastern Europe's complex past, especially when gratuitously offering external counsel regarding the region's future history.

56. Having failed to topple Milošević in 1999, some members of the international community, such as the EU, sought a constructive change of strategy towards the Balkans. A March 2000 report by the EU's Javier Solana, senior CFSP (Common Foreign and Security Policy) representative, and Foreign Relations Commissioner Patton suggested that "Serbia's isolation could become a major obstacle to political change." The report advocates "Open Serbia" strategy, which entails dialogue with the democratic opposition, the churches, the NGOs, the independent media, and other organizations. *Le Monde*, March 23, 2000, p. 2.

57. Daniel Jonah Goldhagen, "A New Serbia," *The New Republic*, Vol. 220, No. 20 (May 17, 1999), pp. 16–18.

58. *Focus*, August 21, 2000, pp. 224–225 in *BBCSWB*, August 25, 2000, EE/D3928/C.

59. *New York Times*, September 7, 2000, Section 8, p. 16.

60. Reinhardt Bendix and Guenther Roth, *Scholarship and Partisanship: Essays on Max Weber* (Berkeley: University of California Press, 1971), p. 70.

INDEX